Practical Guide to Environmental Management

10th Edition

Practical Guide to Environmental Management

10th Edition

Frank B. Friedman

ENVIRONMENTAL LAW INSTITUTE
WASHINGTON, D.C.

ELI publishes books that contribute to education of the profession and disseminate diverse points of view and opinion to stimulate a robust and creative exchange of ideas. These publications, which express opinions of the authors and not necessarily those of the Institute, its Board of Directors, or funding organizations, exemplify ELI's commitment to dialogue with all sectors. ELI welcomes suggestions for book topics and encourages the submission of draft manuscripts and book proposals.

Copyright © 1988, 1990, 1991, 1993, 1995, 1997, 2000, 2003, 2005, 2006
Environmental Law Institute
1616 P Street NW, Washington DC 20036

Published 1988. Tenth edition January 2006.

Printed in the United States of America.
ISBN 1-58576-097-8

To my wife, Esta, and to my daughters, Amy and Emily.

Acknowledgements

Any truly "practical guide" rests on the experiments and experiences of others. The dedication, experience, and effort required to develop, test, and manage a successful environmental program for a major corporation cannot come from only one individual. The ideas set forth in this book come from a great many teachers and colleagues who have applied their knowledge to a wide variety of specific situations.

Professionals in the environmental area generally do not hold ideas for improvement of policies and programs close to their vests. This is a group willing to share ideas and solutions. It includes environmental managers, governmental employees, citizen advocates, lawyers, consultants, and other specialists.

Few people get the opportunity more than once—if at all—to develop state-of-the-art programs and to work with respected and enlightened executives. I was one of the fortunate few.

Successful programs depend on competent, professional staff. My staff at Elf Atochem impressed me with their dedication and creativity. I am also grateful to my former staff at Occidental Petroleum Corporation, particularly the late Jerry Wilkenfeld, whose creative ability in initiating and implementing many programs played a major role in the success of our department.

I also want to thank my clients, who continue to force me to continue to be creative and productive.

Finally, I want to thank Linda Johnson, Caroline Hermann, and the Environmental Law Institute publishing staff for their assistance and many helpful comments.

—F.B.F.

Contents

Foreword

Frank Friedman's *Practical Guide to Environmental Management (PGEM)* has earned its place among the classic texts on environmental management. *PGEM* provides readers with the firm grounding in history necessary to put environmental issues in context and a practical survey of the management systems and tools to produce good environmental performance.

PGEM now enters its 10th edition with new material on social responsibility, the Sarbanes-Oxley Act, criminal sentencing guidelines, and several other areas. This edition of *PGEM* retains its focus on the practical, while also surveying the developing trends in environmental management. As Friedman notes, environmental management systems (EMS) and corporate behavior, particularly in developing countries, increasingly serve as the de facto system of environmental governance and are key to ensuring environmental protection goals are met. In this new edition, Mr. Friedman does a superb job of orienting the environmental manager in this new era.

As a former environmental executive in federal and state government as well as two corporations, I would stress that Frank Friedman's book has much to offer to both public and private sector environmental lawyers and managers. Professionals in both sectors contend with the day-to-day demands of promoting compliance with laws and encouraging foresight to head off new problems. In the end, they can succeed only by building environmental awareness, responsibility, and competence in the other disciplines and operations in their organizations. That is true whether they work in a corporation, a municipal water treatment agency, or a big department of state or federal government. Friedman's book contains good advice on what and how to communicate about environmental objectives inside organizations to achieve broader support and stronger performance by business and government.

Mr. Friedman's long history in the environmental management arena has served only to inform, not date, *PGEM* as he has kept it current with this quickly developing field. After graduating from Columbia Law School in the mid-1960s, he joined what was then the Lands Division (now known as the Environment and Natural Resources Division) of the U.S. Department of Justice. He moved to Atlantic Richfield Corporation in 1970 when major companies began responding to the cleanup challenges presented by the new federal pollution control laws. Friedman also served as Vice President of Occidental Petroleum Corporation and later as Senior Vice President at Elf Atochem North America, Inc. He also served as a partner with the law firm of McClintock, Weston, Benshoof, Rochefort, Rubalcava & MacCuish. He now heads a successful consulting business.

Few people could have written *PGEM* with Friedman's depth of understanding and clarity. Frank is an exemplar for the modern environmental manager, with his focus set firmly on the goal of achieving common-sense environmental protection without being swept away by the politics and controversies of the day. In that way, he typifies the goals and aspirations of the Environmental Law Institute (ELI). This is no coincidence; ELI turned to Friedman to write *PGEM* in 1988 because of these qualities. While the opinions and content of *PGEM* are Friedman's alone, ELI has a long history of promoting environmental law, policy, and management in its various forms by:

- drafting environmental law, regulation, and policy;
- assessing and improving implementation of environmental law;
- encouraging adoption of EMS;
- training regulators, judges, advocates, lawyers, and managers; and
- identifying and pioneering new trends in environmental governance.

ELI has long recognized that corporations play a central role in ensuring environmental protection and is proud to have some of the foremost domestic and international corporations as members. In expanding its focus on the role of corporations in achieving environmental protection, ELI recently created the Center for Business Environmental Strategy to bring together both businesses and their stakeholders to identify and spread best practices and new ideas to advance environmental, social, and business goals.

We are enormously grateful to Frank for his many contributions to the field of environmental protection as a lawyer, manager, author, colleague, ELI board member, and friend. We are proud to publish this 10th edition of *PGEM*, and hope you will find it a useful guide and reference.

—Leslie Carothers, President
Environmental Law Institute

Chapter 1:
Introduction

This book was written to help managers deal with the complex problems of environmental protection. Although the environmental protection field arising from federal environmental law is only 35 years old, it is quite complicated. I have been privileged to work in this field almost from its beginning, first as a lawyer and then as a manager-lawyer. My work has taught me many lessons, sometimes at considerable cost. In the hope that these lessons can benefit other managers, I have included in this book a wide variety of practical hints based on the experiences of myself and others in finding creative solutions to complex environmental problems. The book also tries to sort out industry concerns as to what types of regulations make sense, examine environmental programs that improve productivity and ensure environmental compliance, look at the interaction of business with the community and government, and perhaps dispel some of the myths surrounding industry and its attitudes and motivations toward the environment.

Much of the book is based on my experiences at Elf Atochem North America, Inc. (Ato, now Arkema) and my prior experiences at the Occidental Petroleum Corporation (OPC), although filled in substantially by further experience as a consultant to a broad variety of industries. The book emphasizes program aspects that are generally applicable, rather than those unique to Ato or Occidental. I have used these experiences to make the book more specific, concrete, and—I hope—helpful. Therefore, my frequent references to Ato's and Occidental's programs should not be taken as puffery, but as illustrations of how companies use the principles of environmental management. These principles apply to many different industries with varied cultures.

Gus Speth, past president of the World Resources Institute, noted:

> Important as pressure from environmentalists and governmental direction are to stimulating change, in the end only the corporate community can efficiently provide the necessary organization,

technology, and financial resources needed to design and implement change on the scale required. Companies that are trying to
be leaders on a new path to a sustainable future merit our encouragement and support, just as the inevitable backsliders deserve a
vigorous shove onto the trail.[1]

I would add that to encourage businesses to lead the way to a sustainable future, the government must regulate intelligently. Too many regulations deliver little significant environmental protection while imposing enormous
costs. Even the most responsible businesses have legitimate concerns when
a company or company official can be convicted criminally for violations of
environmental laws without proof of criminal intent and when recordkeeping offenses can make an executive eligible for as many years in prison
as a Medellin drug dealer, without many of the legal protections available to
the drug dealer.

The impact of industry on the environment today needs to be placed in
perspective. There is little question that U.S. industry in the past has been
guilty of serious environmental depredations, some of them quite dramatic.
But most of us, whether in industry, citizen organizations, or government,
are wiser today than we were in the past. We have had our consciousness
raised. Many of us now working for business in the environmental area
came out of the environmental movement or government. Many executives
today grew up with an environmental ethic or have adopted the values such
an ethic implies. Economic concerns and stakeholder and customer demands require that businesses give environmental issues a high priority.
Along with expanding and tightening environmental controls, the impact of
civil and criminal liabilities has made environmental irresponsibility too
costly for any competent businessperson to consider.

Responsible businesses recognize that regulation is a cost of doing business. As long as regulations address real environmental problems, are understandable, avoid micromanaging a business or generating unnecessary reports, and if the "punishment fits the crime," regulation is not only acceptable, it may be necessary to provide a level playing field for companies with
managements that want to do the right thing. The most sophisticated businesses integrate environmental concerns into all aspects of operations and
planning—and environmentally aware business planning can create markets
or competitive advantages that result in net gains. Indeed, environmental regulations have in many cases improved efficiency and product quality. They
have encouraged innovative approaches to package design, raw material accountability, and selection of customers. Increased management oversight of
the environmental impacts of operations has, in many cases, led to process
improvements that enhance operating reliability and reduce hazards.

Early regulation forced a recognition in many cases that pollution was actually "product" going up the smoke stacks, into the rivers, or on waste piles, and that capturing this product was often cost effective. For example, so-called floating roof storage tanks, designed to minimize hydrocarbon evaporation, often paid for themselves in product that could be sold rather than lost as emissions. Much of pollution prevention is today economically, not environmentally, driven. As smaller and smaller increments are captured, however, costs may outweigh the benefits.

This book has one overriding theme: good environmental management techniques benefit everyone. They help protect the environment. They make managers' jobs easier. They even save companies money, although some of these savings may not appear in the short term. Most importantly, environmental management, like employee-relations management, is not optional. A company that does not make the effort to manage well its environmental affairs will manage them badly. If you are responsible for environmental management at your company, it is in everyone's interest for you to do as good a job as possible. I hope that the suggestions in this book will help you do that job.

In later editions of the book, I have particularly tried to include references and comments that can be helpful to the smaller company. A smaller company, for example, needs assistance in finding a laboratory that will provide accurate data. I have now included a reference to a detailed analysis of this issue.[2] Although they face essentially the same civil and criminal liabilities as major corporations, smaller companies simply cannot have the resources in house to digest the extensive and constantly changing laws and regulations discussed in this book. Responsible officers and employees of smaller companies can, however, do enough reading to stay abreast of major developments and identify areas in which they must exercise special care or seek outside advice.[3] Many local and industry-specific trade associations and chambers of commerce publish newsletters dealing with state and local matters and legislation and regulations. The agencies themselves often have specific booklets and publications to help small businesses deal with specific compliance issues. The Internet can also provide access to valuable information. For example, the U.S. Environmental Protection Agency (EPA) offers "Envirofacts" at http://www.epa.gov/enviro/. However, its accuracy in the early days was sometimes questionable, e.g., an Ashland Chemical Company plant was listed as a "chocolate manufacturing facility".[4] The criminal liability section of this book is particularly important reading because many criminal prosecutions are against smaller companies and officers of smaller companies.

I have expanded the book to add material on developing corporate objectives and strategies, total quality management, downsizing, analytical techniques for environmental management, job descriptions, international standards, sustainable development, and government efforts to reform regulations and encourage good management practices. While many companies (and I discuss this concept in detail) use and advocate progressive concepts such as "sustainable development," they sometimes have not maintained the basics needed for process control and compliance. It is important to focus on what they should do—not necessarily on what they say. The book now also contains a variety of appendices, including EPA and DOJ policies.

If you are new to environmental management, the difficulties you will face depend partly on your background. If you were a general manager, merely learning the jargon of environmental management may seem an overwhelming task. If you have had environmental experience as a manager or lawyer, you may find the problems of organizing an effective program within the context of your corporate structure and its specific culture equally overwhelming. This book should be helpful regardless of your background. It introduces some of the jargon that you will need to know and includes a list of the key acronyms (Appendix A). It also outlines an approach to developing an environmental program within your corporate culture.

I hope that both new and experienced environmental managers enjoy the field as much as I do. I can think of few areas that present greater challenges; few areas demand creative solutions to such complex technical and legal problems in the context of complex social policies. In addition, one of the most pleasant aspects of this field is that those who have been in it for a long time generally know one another and, whether we represent industry, government, or citizen groups, we all talk to one another. Although there are now more environmental professionals than I thought possible 35 years ago, just as there are more laws and regulations than I would have dreamed of, I hope you will be fortunate enough to experience the professional interactions and creative challenges that make this field so exciting.[5] I think I can safely predict that the complexities, at least, will be with us for quite some time.

Notes to Chapter 1

1. B. SMART, BEYOND COMPLIANCE — A NEW INDUSTRY VIEW OF THE ENVIRON-
MENT ix-x (1992).

2. *See* James A. Ploscyca, *Choosing an Environmental Laboratory*, HAZMAT
WORLD, Oct. 1992, at 59.

3. A basic library for this purpose might include the following references. The Environmental Law Institute (ELI) publishes deskbooks on subjects such as the
Toxic Substances Control Act, European Community environmental law, environmental crimes, and wetlands law. The deskbooks provide an excellent basis
for understanding the intricacies of federal law and include copies of key background materials. ELI also publishes *ELR®—The Environmental Law Reporter®*,
a print and Internet service with daily updates, the monthly *News & Analysis*, and
ELR UPDATE, a newsletter published electronically each weekday and available
to subscribers via e-mail or at www.eli.org. Each provides information about the
latest developments in environmental law. A description of and prices for these
and other publications are listed in ELI's publications catalog or at www.eli.org.
The catalog and ELI publications can be obtained from ELI, 2000 L St., NW,
Suite 620, Washington DC 20036, or by contacting ELI by telephone at (800)
433-5120 or (202) 939-3844, by fax at (202) 939-3817, by e-mail at or-
ders@eli.org, or by visiting ELI's website at www.eli.org.

Members of the ELI Associates Program receive *The Environmental Forum*, an
excellent bimonthly magazine. Annual dues for individual membership in the Associates Program are $95 ($60/year for public interest, $60/year for government
and academic memberships, and $25/year for law students). There are institutional
memberships available to corporations and law firms. ELI Associates benefit from
discounts on ELI publications and information about various management and legal education programs. For more information, contact ELI at (202) 939-3800 or
visit www.eli.org.

Examples of other basic publications include *Inside EPA* and *Inside EPA's Environmental Policy Alert*. In addition, *Environment, Health & Safety Management*
may be of particular interest to environmental managers.

4. Personal Interview with Glenn Hammer, Vice President, Environment, Health,
and Safety, Ashland Chemical Company (1997).

5. For an amusing look at environmental jargon, see Michael Allan Wolf, *Environmental Law Slogans for the New Millennium*, 30 ELR 10283 (Apr. 2000).

Chapter 2:
Historical Perspectives on
Environmental Management

I t may appear to be the prejudice of a legally trained manager to begin a book on environmental management with a discussion of the historical development of the laws and regulations that drive the field. Regardless of whether a manager's training is technical or legal, however, basic environmental management requires an understanding of the development of these laws and regulations, together with a perspective on the phenomena driving that development.[1] Indeed, I hope that this historical perspective will help relieve the frustration of the technically trained manager who would like to be free of some of the legal and regulatory constraints to developing technical solutions to problems. These constraints grow out of yesterday's legal and technical compromises. I may be the bearer of bad tidings by focusing on the legal basis for constraints on managers, but these constraints are reality.

Few corporate activities have been influenced by law as much as those in the environmental, health, and safety area, although they should be driven by management concerns as to productivity, quality, and integration. As managers, we try to avoid legal issues by finding technical solutions to problems. We focus on eliminating an effluent or hazardous waste, for example, to avoid the requirement of obtaining a permit. We cannot, however, ignore that it is the legal issues that drive corporate programs in this area, although they should be driven by management concerns as to productivity, quality, and integration. And, as discussed below, environmental law is essentially social legislation. Social issues as opposed to legal issues, exemplified by growing "environmental justice" and "sustainable development" concerns, may increasingly influence corporate decisions.

The Development of Environmental Law

Until the early 1970s, there was virtually no significant role for lawyers in environmental management. Most state and local laws imposed limited environmental, health, and safety requirements, such as mandatory air and water sampling and permitting, which technicians could handle. For the most part, these issues did not require senior management attention. They were considered very limited parts of operating activities, and responsibility for them was usually lodged at lower management levels. Moreover, confrontation between industry and regulatory agencies was not the rule. Because laws and regulations frequently were not specific, differences were settled primarily by technical negotiation. Although industry sometimes developed environmental protection mechanisms that went beyond legal requirements, these steps, such as odor control, were largely influenced by concern for local public relations.

While the period of the 1960s was a time of long, stable economic growth, it was also a time of anger and frustration. College graduates saw a questionable future, including the possibility of serving in a war in Vietnam that did not seem understandable. The "system" was not responding to their concerns, and, for many, the only answer was taking to the streets in protest. Hopes for a decent future seemed equally bleak in the area of environmental pollution, which slowly began to be recognized as a social problem.

Public awareness of pollution, along with general dissatisfaction with government and the quality of life, greatly increased social consciousness. Interest in pollution control grew as the public recognized that pollution might endanger public health, as well as fish and wildlife. For years, conservationists had cared about wildlife and natural preservation, but often seemed to care more for trees than people. The activist of the 1960s—the new environmentalist—was in many respects of a different breed. Concern over visible industrial pollution and the issues raised in Rachel Carson's *Silent Spring* and John Kenneth Galbraith's *The Affluent Society* culminated in Earth Day in 1970 with a call for new initiatives to resolve environmental problems.

This concern also resulted in the federal environmental revolution of the early 1970s, which produced a vast outpouring of federal legislation.[2] There was a general belief that government could manage the economy and solve the country's social problems by concentrating on redistribution of wealth and improving the quality of life. This belief increased what had once been only a limited emphasis on the law as a tool for social change. Moreover, the relative emphasis on the role of the federal government increased. The new environmental laws were based on the assumption—which has not changed much over the years—that the states needed federal prodding to ensure that pollution would be controlled uniformly.[3] The theory was that there should be no "pollution havens." The preference for federal control was not limited to environmental legislation; the expanded federal role in what President Lyndon Johnson called the "Great Society" addressed a wide variety of social ills, including race discrimination and poverty.

Although there had previously been some limited federal presence in the environmental area, federal enforcement powers had been weak.[4] For example, before enactment of the Clean Air Act (CAA) Amendments of 1970,[5] the federal government's air pollution enforcement activities consisted of the monumental effort of cleaning up one chicken rendering plant and one small phosphate rock defluorinating plant.[6]

Federal environmental legislation of the early 1970s presented new challenges for industry in that these statutes, like many of the new regulatory laws in other fields, expanded the enforcement powers of both the federal government and the public. Although there had been very little environmental litigation before their passage, the new statutes generated considerable work for environmental lawyers by allowing private individuals and citizen groups to enforce permit requirements and other regulatory standards. Some of these statutes, such as the air and water laws, not only encouraged citizen suits in both rulemaking and direct enforcement when the federal government failed to act, but also specifically provided for recoverability of attorneys fees from the federal government.[7] This was "part of a broadly based effort to open up the regulatory process to others than regulated industries."[8] Even statutes that did not provide for attorneys fees against the federal government were interpreted to allow such fees against private parties when a citizen group won even a partial victory.[9] The attorneys fees provisions thus encouraged lawsuits.

Offensive projects could also be blocked under the National Environmental Policy Act (NEPA) with proof that possible (and, in some cases, improbable) impacts had not been adequately considered in environmental impact statements (EISs), which NEPA requires for all "major Federal actions significantly affecting the quality of the human environment."[10]

That private parties could influence governmental and corporate decisions gained grudging acceptance as a fact of life. This recognition came only after some initial efforts by government and industry to argue that some citizen groups did not have "standing" to bring a case. The doctrine of standing requires plaintiffs in lawsuits to prove they have suffered injury—or are threatened with injury—to legally protected interests. In the context of environmental litigation, however, courts define "injury" very broadly, and injuries to only aesthetic or recreational interests generally suffice. Some environmental groups discovered that the standing doctrine does have limits and lost cases in which they failed to include as plaintiffs members of their organizations who might be injured by the actions challenged.[11]

The wave of federal environmental legislation built on the foundation of social consciousness laid in the 1960s also helped dictate the employment choices of young graduates with broadly based social and environmental concerns. Their options included the Department of Justice (DOJ), other government organizations, and new public interest groups. Creation of EPA in 1970 also provided employment opportunities. The enforcement theory of these new regulators was that the "mule," namely industry, needed to be hit over the head with a large two-by-four (regulation or enforcement) to get its attention.

The new federal statutes were heavily regulatory. In many instances, they did not simply provide general guidelines, but were the virtual equivalent of regulations,[12] establishing detailed standards without the benefit of peer review or even practical experience. Congress wrote highly specialized legislation for the same reason it promoted private civil lawsuits: it distrusted not only states and industry, but federal agencies as well. The political nature of hearings before passage of legislation, plus the confrontational atmosphere between the lobbyists for industry and those for citizen groups, precluded peer review of technical issues.

In addition to establishing regulatory standards, the new environmental legislation engendered significant rulemaking. While the rulemaking did not require formal hearings, it was subject to the notice-and-comment requirements of the Administrative Procedure Act.[13] Environmental organizations began to see the value of formal comments on proposed regulations, and soon felt that they had as much power to influence the process as industry—indeed more, considering the environmental orientation of the new regulators. In any event, EPA soon learned that failure to document the basis for its regulatory decisions could lead to reversal by the courts. The relationship between the regulators and the regulated community grew strained as the regulators saw themselves less as technical experts and more as mediators between warring factions. As regulations became more specific, regulated industries found themselves in a more adversarial position, with little room for resolving issues by negotiation.

Recognition of the dual presence of the government and citizen groups did not mean that industry would accept every regulation or lawsuit without a fight. Corporate managers, accustomed to dealing with engineering and science, understood "scientific truth" but not "regulatory truth," which, although purportedly based on science, is strongly influenced by political factors. For example, it is a scientific truth that public health specialists rarely have enough information to specify a threshold below which exposure to carcinogens is entirely risk-free. Regulators responded to this scientific truth by creating a simplified, regulatory truth that any exposure to a carcinogen, no matter how trivial, results in a quantifiable risk that should be minimized or eliminated. Confrontations arose because "regulatory truths," which were administered by people who did not necessarily understand or were hostile to corporate managers' businesses, began to bite financially. This classic clash of two cultures generated an ideal climate for litigation.

Industry challenges to regulations were not usually motivated by attempts to gain competitive advantage. Companies' comments on regulations tended to raise basically the same issues as did trade associations' consensus-based, lowest-common-denominator comments. The exception was when one company was already meeting higher standards and was anxious for the rest of its industry to catch up. Many industries, such as the steel industry, however, saw the new regulations as a threat to their very existence. No one knew the actual economic impact of the new laws, and all factions were extremely skeptical about the others' estimates of that impact. Industry's credibility was not enhanced by overstatements of economic impact, which were common. Conversely, EPA's credibility was not strengthened by gross understatements of that impact, which were equally common.

Lawsuits challenging regulations often named 10 or more trade associations as parties.[14] While trade associations took the lead in broadly challenging the new statutory provisions, they were joined by individual company members participating as separate parties, if for no other reason than to avoid attacks on standing analogous to those made when environmental organizations failed to name individual members as parties in their lawsuits.[15]

With some justification, industry perceived the regulators as attempting to stretch the new statutes' broad language as far as the courts would let them. As a result, industry felt it had no choice but to attack virtually all regulations as they were promulgated. On the other side, citizen groups uniformly attacked regulations on the grounds that they were not tough enough. These were not just blind attacks by both sides, but attempts to obtain clear regulatory interpretations that were not forthcoming from the regulators. Sometimes, early interpretations were unobtainable, even after rulemaking and appeals. For example, under the CAA, a company may be in the dubious position of either complying with the law or challenging a specific enforcement action, at its peril, while it seeks court review of the underlying regulations.[16]

It was particularly difficult to challenge a scientific interpretation by EPA. The burden of proof was on the plaintiff, and no matter how strong the plaintiff's case, EPA could probably win as long as the record provided some basis for its interpretation.[17] Courts give great deference to an agency's interpretation of a statute, particularly in its area of expertise.[18] While principles of administrative law placed a difficult burden on industrial plaintiffs, who argued that EPA regulation had gone too far, activist courts—notably the U.S. Court of Appeals for the D.C. Circuit—often placed a less-stringent burden on environmental groups who argued that EPA decisions were not sufficiently pro-environment. The U.S. Supreme Court soon reminded these courts that the rule of deference to agency expertise cuts both ways, and that the courts could not substitute their judgment for EPA's if EPA had a rational basis for its decision on a technical issue, or if its interpretation of a statute in its area of expertise was rational.[19]

The Challenge for the Corporate Attorney

Appropriate responses to the legal issues raised by the government and citizen groups required industry to adopt new approaches. These were not always forthcoming. In counseling their clients, many traditional company lawyers failed to understand that environmental legislation was social legislation and would be broadly interpreted. As vague statutory provisions and the regulations implementing them became subject to definitive rulings by the courts, however, different company policies emerged. Many companies began to realize that there was a new regime and that old ways of doing business had changed. These companies began to look for individuals who understood these changes so they could develop environmental, legal, and technical policies that responded to the changes, but that still allowed cost-effective management.

Enlightened attitudes were not widespread at first. I was asked to give a speech to a group of oil company attorneys on the CAA Amendments of 1970, shortly after their enactment. The title chosen for me was "Ecology in Gasoline Marketing." The impacts of the new legislation and resulting regulation on gasoline marketing and petroleum refining were obvious: costs were going to increase significantly and the industry would have to change its air pollution control strategies radically. About one-half of my audience took these messages back to management and began to prepare their companies for the coming changes. The other one-half could only be described as incredibly hostile, arguing that as an industry newcomer with a governmental bias, I had to be wrong in predicting extensive and expensive regulatory changes.

Efforts to convince some of my own management were also not entirely successful. There was, for example, considerable resistance to making many necessary changes in the operations of Atlantic Richfield Corporation's (ARCO's) Philadelphia refinery. I raised the appropriate legal issues, but many of the old-line managers still perceived that conditions really were not that bad. Some felt that the odors emanating from the refinery "smelled like money." Finally, out of frustration (overriding good judgment), I wrote a memo quoting my then three-year-old daughter: "I don't like Daddy's refinery. It doesn't smell too good." That the need for change was obvious to a young child finally helped get local management attention and helped senior management change the culture.

As attitudes gradually changed, corporate attention began to focus on the dollars being spent and possible means of reducing expenses. Many corporate executives were frustrated because these issues generally could not be resolved using standard rational engineering and financial procedures. As discussed above, the statutes did not give agencies broad discretion to fill in the blanks, but rather were written as regulations, unaided by the practical operating experience and scientific input of the regulatory and regulated communities. Moreover, even when they had discretion, most agency staffs had little understanding of, or concern about, economic impacts. Traditional problem-solving tools such as engineering and financial analysis were less effective in this tight regulatory situation.

Management continued to struggle with the real differences between "regulatory truth" and "scientific truth." This struggle was particularly frustrating for many well-meaning corporate executives who did not understand the regulatory and political concerns that overwhelmed their economic and scientific perspectives. Perhaps those who gave advice as attorneys, rather than as scientists, had some advantage, for lawyers more easily swallowed the difference between "technical truth" and "regulatory truth" than scientists.

During this pressurized and confusing period, major corporations used their new technical and legal staffs to give sophisticated advice to management and to resolve environmental issues. These people became the core of today's environmental profession. Corporations also upgraded the importance of these professionals in terms of compensation and internal reporting structure. The professionals' increased significance to the corporations required shorter lines of communication and reporting to high levels of management.

The first "pioneers" to move from the public to the private sector were both suspicious of the industry regime of which they had become a part and ill at ease with colleagues who had remained in the public sector. As a DOJ attorney in the 1960s, about the last place where I expected to consider working was an oil company. That would have been the ultimate "sellout." I was approached, however, by the then-general counsel of ARCO, an experienced Washington lawyer who was specifically looking to recruit government attorneys to work on environmental and civil rights issues. His attitudes surprised me. He strongly appreciated and supported the social developments that had radically changed the country.[20] That the atmosphere at the DOJ had changed under Attorney General John Mitchell, who was indirectly an excellent recruiting agent for private industry, also influenced my decision to take a chance on working for the "enemy." Moreover, the role of an advocate for environmental concern in a corporation during those early years was clearly defensible. In 1971, having crossed this line from the public to the private sector, I described the philosophy of this new breed.

> Basically, [the corporate attorney's] position is that of educating the corporation to the vast changes that have taken place in recent years in terms of new laws, regulations, and public attitude. Corporate insensitivity and lack of familiarity with these changes can be expensive. Yet, too many corporations either lack the required knowledge or attack these changes with the standard blanket condemnation (perhaps with a little more subtlety than in the past) which has characterized industry's response over the years to new pollution laws and regulations. Indeed, this "cry of wolf" is largely responsible for many of industry's difficulties. If the claim is continually made that new laws or regulations are unworkable when, in fact, industry is able to comply with these laws and regulations, clearly no regulatory official is going to accept industry's argument when a problem does arise. The war on pollution has its own credibility gap; which, I submit, can be closed by a more realistic response. I suggest that the best means of improving industry's reputation for veracity is compliance with these new laws and regulations. If nothing else, economic self-interest should dictate this conclusion, since today all industries are regulated industries in the environmental area.[21]

At that time it was also necessary to argue that compliance was needed and that credibility was invaluable.

> Credibility is the most important asset for this new breed of corporate lawyer. Government agencies and environmental groups are sophisticated enough to understand the difference between form and substance, and the attorney who is not suggesting reasonable positions will not be believed. If the attorney cannot establish credibility, his [or her] value is lost and [the attorney] would be considered simply a company spy.[22]

Most corporate environmental work at that time was in the fire-fighting mode. Permits were delayed, litigation was threatened, and environmental organizations assumed the worst from companies. The skills of the new breed of environmental professional were put to the test, and opportunities to plan for the future and ensure cost effectiveness were extremely limited. Gradually, as they gained more experience, corporations became able to manage environmental issues rather than fight them.

Senior management was not interested in environmental problems per se, but rather in their impacts on operational planning and costs and, more importantly, in the action plans for resolving them. This focus required environmental managers to use all their abilities to develop solutions to problems that at first seemed unsolvable. For those who understood the concerns of regulatory agencies and environmental groups, the task was easier. But it still was difficult to explain control plans to senior managers who were unaccustomed to the type of problem resolution required. It was often particularly difficult to describe adequately the political and social implications of recommended actions.

The "public to private" pioneers, together with forward-thinking realists already in the private sector, focused corporate interests on the new trends, helping to avoid costly siting decisions and other pitfalls. For example, energy projects that might otherwise make economic or technical sense, might not make sense if stalled for several years by litigation over EISs. To many traditional corporate executives, these judgments looked astounding, but the environmental professionals were simply realistically examining the signs of the times. The increasing influence of this new group affected not only individual business decisions, but the overall corporate approach to broad environmental issues. For example, companies began to realize that the "Petroleum Club" syndrome of talking only to each other in the industrial sector did not provide the necessary grasp of the political and social situations in Washington, D.C., and the states.

Throughout the era of modern environmental law, legislation and regulation have reflected public perceptions of a variety of events. Well-known environmental episodes had profound impacts on environmental legislation, regulation, and policy. Interest groups used these events to press for legislation, arguing that new laws were needed to prevent similar incidents and to force slow-moving industry to respond. Thus, the discharge of kepone into Virginia's James River was a major impetus for the passage of the Resource Conservation and Recovery Act (RCRA) of 1976,[23] which regulates hazardous waste management. Alleged health impacts on residents of Love Canal, a toxic waste disposal site near Niagara Falls, New York, were the catalyst for the 1980 Superfund law (the Comprehensive Environmental Response, Compensation, and Liability Act (CERCLA)),[24] which requires remediation of waste sites and embodies the concept that the "polluter pays," regardless of fault. The death of thousands of people in Bhopal, India, from the accidental release of an acutely toxic chemical, methyl isocyanate, resulted in increased focus on safety and general concern about chemicals. It also led to the 1986 passage of the Emergency Planning and Community Right-To-Know Act (EPCRA),[25] which requires disclosure of information about potentially dangerous chemicals and development of local response plans. The strong public response to the *Exxon Valdez* incident, which released some 11 million gallons of oil into Alaska's Prince William Sound in March 1989, was a major factor behind Congress' enactment of the Oil Pollution Act of 1990.[26]

The major federal environmental statutes, as largely enacted in the 1970s, seldom, if ever, carried with them appropriations sufficient to reach their goals and sometimes only a small fraction of the necessary funding was allocated. They were often undermined by continuing resources development programs such as below-cost timber sales, and often catered to either environmental, recreational, industrial, or resource user groups rather than to the broad interests of the public. Additionally, the laws transferred to the bureaucracy virtually all of the dirty work—the unpleasant, unpopular, or impossible tasks. The laws forced the agencies to set the real priorities in policy and leave them with no choice but to cast aside many of the goals they were legally obligated to achieve. Thus, the laws enabled congressional members to make symbolic statements of support for a trendy cause and set unrealistic deadlines, without appropriating sufficient funds or imposing the sacrifice that would be required actually to attain the environmental goals.[27]

Have matters improved? As one commentator notes, it can be argued that U.S. environmental programs still largely address only the "low-hanging fruit":

> Over the past three decades, the knowledge problem in environmental policy has only gotten worse. The first wave of environmental regulations addressed large, obvious environmental problems that impacted most parts of the country, such as lead in gasoline and raw sewage in rivers and streams. Addressing such low-hanging fruit did not require particularly efficient regulation, nor did it require much knowledge about local ecological conditions.[28]

Still, Congress has strengthened many of the statutes, through reauthorizations of the major environmental laws that "all exhibit the same trend. Each eliminated substantial EPA discretion, imposed more deadlines, and included more prescription. . . . The fundamental purpose of all these reauthorizations was 'to minimize the possibility of bureaucratic neglect and compromises and of agency capture by regulated industry.'"[29] Moreover, "the [EPA] is now the federal government's largest regulatory agency, with 18,000 employees and a budget of $7.8 billion for fiscal year (FY) 2001. . . . Compliance costs induced by environmental regulations in the United States are estimated to have cost the regulated community $180 billion in 1999." The number of employees at EPA is still approximately the same as in 2000, about 18,000.[30] "The [EPA] alone accounts for nearly 10% of all of the federal government regulatory activity."[31] In "October 2000, there were 4,699 entries in the *Unified Agenda of Federal Regulations*. Of these, 449 were for EPA."[32] The number of employees is still approximately the same in 2005 as it was in 2001. Moreover, "the complexity and arbitrariness of many environmental rules makes compliance immensely difficult. Once a new federal regulation is promulgated, its application often remains unsettled until after years of wrangling and litigation. Guidance documents, interpretative rules, and the like further shift the sands of regulatory requirements."[33]

The incredible growth and complexity of environmental law and regulations was in some cases exacerbated by a cultural gulf that still is not entirely resolved. As Prof. James Lofton of Cambridge notes in contrasting the American and British environmental legal systems: "Civil servants in the United States, including officials of regulatory agencies, were never able to acquire either the power or the prestige of their counterparts across the Atlantic. Far from viewing them as social equals, American business executives regard regulators as their social and intellectual inferiors."[34]

The history of environmental law is one of expanding liabilities, sometimes from old laws used in new ways. The latest wrinkle is the use of the False Claims Act (FCA),[35] a Civil War-era statute, to assert environmental claims against federal government contractors.[36] Plaintiffs' attorneys are now alleging under the FCA that defendants have failed to comply with environmental compliance provisions contained in government contracts and made false claims for payment by implicitly and explicitly representing that they have so complied. These suits, known as *qui tam* actions, are filed by private parties on behalf of the government.[37] Under the Alien Tort Statute[38] "the district courts shall have original jurisdiction of any civil action by an alien for a tort only, committed in violation of the Law of Nations or Treaty of the United States." In one case decided by the U.S. Court of Appeals for the Fifth Circuit, the court rejected plaintiffs' alleged violations of "the aspirational goals of individual rights to life, to culture and to a healthy environment as embodied in various statutes and treaties."[39] The Court has recently ruled that courts should use great caution in adopting the law of nations to private rights in a case holding that a doctor abducted from Mexico to stand trial in the United States could not bring a lawsuit for false arrest under the Alien Tort Statute.[40] So long as there are creative attorneys, environmental law will continue to challenge environmental managers and corporations.

Criminal Liability—A Key Concern for the Environmental Manager

The use of criminal law to protect the environment has also expanded over the past 35 years.[41] As former Attorney General Richard Thornburgh stated: "Criminal enforcement is one of the most radically expanding areas of environmental law, with the use of criminal sanctions becoming one of the most effective means of deterring deliberate non-compliance."[42] It is important for today's environmental manager to recognize that you no longer have to be a bad person to be prosecuted, and in terms of intent, "deliberate" can also mean purposely attempting to avoid knowledge or willful ignorance. Criminal liability may have serious personal consequences for environmental managers and corporate officials, as well as major financial consequences for companies.[43]

The federal government has prosecuted a substantial number of environmental crimes. From October 1, 1983, to December 13, 1995, the DOJ sought and obtained environmental criminal indictments against 1,674 corporate and individual defendants, and 1,176 guilty pleas and convictions. Of the 1,674 defendants indicted, 495 were corporations or organizations, and the remaining 1,179 were individuals. Of the 1,176 convictions, 365 were against organizations, and the remaining 811 were against individuals.[44]

In 1993 and 1994, there was a dramatic increase in the number of criminal prosecutions. In FY 1993 (ending September 30, 1993), EPA figures indicate that environmental criminals were sentenced to total prison time of nearly 80 years.[45] Criminal charges were brought against 161 defendants in 140 criminal cases, and 135 defendants were convicted. EPA obtained an estimated $133.5 million in criminal fines and civil penalties.[46] FY 1994 was a "banner year" for EPA enforcement. EPA brought a record number of 2,246 enforcement actions, including 220 criminal prosecutions, 1,596 administrative penalty actions, and 430 new civil referrals.[47] Since then, new reforms have been established. Table 2-1 shows the amounts of criminal fines and civil penalties obtained by EPA from 2000 through 2004, as well as the number of criminal and civil cases referred to the DOJ during that time.

Table 2-1
Criminal Fines and Civil Penalties Obtained by EPA and
Number of Criminal and Civil Cases Referred by EPA to the DOJ[48]

Fiscal Year	Criminal Fines (in millions)	Criminal Cases Referred to DOJ	Civil & Judicial Penalties (in millions)	Civil Cases Referred to DOJ
2001	$ 95	256	126	238
2002	12	251	90	252
2003	71	249	96	268
2004	47	188	149	265

The foregoing detail will give you an idea that the civil and criminal enforcement machine is alive and well and still living on numbers. The George W. Bush Administration is able to show a substantial increase in civil penalties, and although the number of referrals to the DOJ for civil actions are down, referrals to the DOJ on the criminal side are up 10%. Kevin Gaynor observes that despite rumors to the contrary, the data suggests that EPA has not defaulted on its enforcement responsibility:

> Any suggestion that [EPA's] enforcement activity is less than vigorous is incorrect. Instead, EPA is pushing enforcement on all fronts. Its cases are also increasingly innovative. EPA referrals of criminal cases to the [DOJ] steadily and dramatically increased from 20 in fiscal 1982 to 107 in 1992 to a record 278 in fiscal 1997 and declined slightly in fiscal 2000 to 236. Criminal fines, which in fiscal 1997 reached a record $169.3 million, declined in fiscal 1999 to $61.5 million but doubled in fiscal 2000 to $122 million. Federal courts imposed jail time of 146 years in fiscal 2000. At the close of fiscal 2000, the total of all criminal fines assessed under the criminal enforcement program neared $720 million.
>
> Overall, EPA brought a record total of 6027 civil judicial, criminal and administrative enforcement actions in fiscal 2000, an increase of nearly 65% from fiscal 1999. EPA referred 368 civil cases to DOJ, a slight reduction from fiscal 1999 and a 30% increase over fiscal 1996. EPA also issued a record 1,763 administrative complaints, up nearly 8% from fiscal 1999. Additionally, EPA forced defendants to spend $2.6 billion to correct violations and take additional steps to promote environmental protection. Civil penalties dropped slightly in fiscal year 2000 to $102.6 million from the record $166.7 million in civil penalties assessed in fiscal 1999, which included the largest [CAA] and [RCRA] penalties in EPA's history.[49]

The 2004 EPA numbers have been challenged, "particularly from the Environmental Integrity Project (ELP), a nonprofit watchdog organization headed by former EPA regulatory enforcement director Eric Schaeffer."[50] ELP claims that the present Administration is "claiming credit for settlement and fines resulting from suits filed during the previous administration, while not reporting the 75% decline in lawsuits filed (from 152 in three years of the Clinton Administration to thirty-six in three years of the Bush II Administration."[51] As noted by Robert Collings: "The time required for resolution of suits undoubtedly gives each current administration credit for some of the initiatives of its predecessor. Precise annualized accounting is difficult and the reality of enforcement as a lengthy process creates many opportunities for dispute over the current system of reports of annual accomplishments. Nevertheless, there appears to be a downward trend in enforcement overall."[52]

Note that in 2004, EPA determined not to publicly publish the criminal cases referred to the DOJ (188) for the first time. However, the basis for not publishing these number should also be considered, particularly as the enforcement program matures:

> That decision reflected the fact that a criminal referral can differ in fundamental ways from a civil enforcement referral. While a civil referral is generally a formal request for DOJ to file a complaint, a criminal referral can be a request for prosecutorial assistance at any stage of the criminal enforcement process (e.g., a request for a grand jury subpoena or assistance in securing a search warrant). Such requests for prosecutorial assistance can come fairly early in the investigative stage and does not necessarily result in a formal request for DOJ to file a criminal indictment. Given these differences between civil and criminal referrals, the criminal enforcement program felt that a criminal referral was not an important indicator of the program's prosecutorial caseload that needed to continue to be publicly reported annually.[53]

While the numbers are down (and some of this may be a result of EPA personnel pulled away to work on homeland security issues), the issue of enforcement "risk" should be looked at in a longer term context than whether or not in a specific year or during a specific administration, the numbers are down. Files are large, memories are long and so are statutes of limitation, particularly since many violations are considered "continuing" violations which toll any statute of limitation. Bad publicity about a company or an industry can trigger specific actions regardless of trends.

A continued long-term emphasis on criminal prosecution is still likely. EPA and the DOJ have sought to improve their enforcement efforts overall. EPA urged its regional offices to increase enforcement in 1997,[54] and they did. The DOJ has also pressed EPA to expedite the processing of enforcement cases.[55] And the federal government has increased staff to do it. EPA had over 200 criminal investigators on staff by the end of FY 1997 (ending September 30, 1997).[56] Its success was measured in a referral of 426 criminal cases to the DOJ during that FY.[57] Perhaps more significantly, the Federal Bureau of Investigation has designated environmental crime as a priority and has shifted agents from cold war activities to the environmental area.[58] The DOJ's Environmental Crimes Section has grown as well.

The sheer size of the federal bureaucracy engaged in criminal prosecutions of environmental crimes has led to several concerns. On December 20, 2003, Larry Thompson, then-Deputy Attorney General, issued a revised policy memorandum on criminal prosecution of corporations.[59] That memorandum states:[60]

> One factor the prosecutor may weigh in assessing the adequacy of a corporation's cooperation is the completeness of its disclosure including, *if necessary*, a waiver of the attorney-client and work product protection, both with respect to its internal investigation and with respect to communications between specific officers, directors and employees and counsel. . . . [T]hey are often critical in enabling the government to evaluate the completeness of a corporation's voluntary disclosure and cooperation.[61]

The exception, "if necessary," appears to have been ignored in many cases. It has become increasingly important for the DOJ to have some form of centralized oversight of prosecutions by U.S. attorneys around the country, many of whom lack expertise in environmental law and are unfamiliar with established civil and administrative options for environmental violations. Indeed, whether a violation is treated criminally, civilly, or administratively can be more a function of what type of investigator first learns of the infraction and in which judicial district it occurs rather than its environmental severity.[62]

There is also a tendency to look for "bad guys" by expanding the scope of criminal liability to cover actions formerly subject to civil penalties. There is strong pressure for prosecutors to give in to what attorney Dan Riesel—drawing from a popular Tom Wolfe novel—calls "the *Bonfire of the Vanities* syndrome": go after a high-profile, white-collar defendant on what amounts to almost strict liability under statutes such as RCRA or the CAA. This certainly beats trying to prosecute a nickel bag heroin dealer.

Some also fear that increased criminal enforcement may be sought to support the expanding federal bureaucracy. As indicated by Jud Starr, a former chief of the DOJ's Environmental Crimes Section: "[T]here is now a machine and the machine must be fed."[63] Roger Marzulla, a former DOJ Assistant Attorney General, Environment and Natural Resources Division, stated that

> EPA and the Justice Department measure the success of the environmental enforcement program not on the basis of environmental improvements made, but rather on the number of convictions and the size of penalties obtained. These statistics are, in turn,

used to justify annually increasing environmental enforcement budgets. The Justice Department now has 31 full-time environmental prosecutors, a four-fold increase since 1986. In turn, these "new hires" must create still more prosecutions, feeding the vicious cycle that leads to next year's enforcement report and budget request.[64]

David Buente, a former Chief of the Environmental Enforcement Section, Environment and Natural Resources Division, DOJ, notes that the late 1990s witnessed a blurring of the line between civil and criminal liability almost to the point of extinction under many federal environmental statutes. Federal prosecutors, assisted by the courts, are largely responsible for this sea of change, spurred on by aggressive enforcement agendas and an increasingly vocal citizenry. Over the past decade, the mens rea requirement has all but disappeared as an element of proof from many statutes; EPA's and the DOJ's enforcement priorities and polices have shifted dramatically; and have become much harsher and more substantial. As a consequence of all these factors, it is far more challenging today to counsel corporations and their employees as to how they should conduct themselves so as to avoid criminal investigation or prosecution and to defend clients once a criminal investigation has commenced.[65]

The focus on environmental prosecutions, coupled with the federal "body count" mentality that relies on statistics to justify the continued existence or expansion of programs, to me seems inappropriate. Such statistics create "a false metric for evaluating the success or failure of an environmental enforcement program."[66] Moreover, it would be hoped that as the regulated community improves compliance through self-policing that the trend toward increased federal criminal enforcement would diminish rather than increase.

Note that the Corporate Counsel Association has protested to the Attorney General's office the tactic of encouraging prosecutors to force corporate suspects to waive attorney-client privilege to cooperate with the government and to avoid prosecution. This has been a particular problem in the environmental crimes area.[67] At the same time the federal government is pushing criminal prosecutions, state and local governments are also bringing criminal enforcement actions pursuant to an extensive list of laws, ordinances, and regulations. Ambitious state and local district attorneys are also looking for cases. Aside from the various federal antipollution statutes,[68] many state statutes dealing with environmental issues have criminal penalty provisions, some of which are very broad. For example, various transportation, storage, and disposal activities are now punishable as felonies under the California Health and Safety Code.[69] In addition, any violation of California hazardous waste laws and regulations, or any related "permit, rule, standard or requirement" is punishable as a misdemeanor.[70] The Pennsylvania Solid Waste Management Act imposes liability regardless of fault for criminal misdemeanor violations.[71] New Jersey has used a statute adapted from a European law designed primarily to protect against fires and avalanches to impose potential criminal liability on any "person, who purposely or knowingly, unlawfully causes an explosion, flood, avalanche, collapse of a building, release or abandonment of poison gas, radioactive material or any other harmful or destructive substance. . . ."[72] The New Jersey Criminal Code imposes second-degree criminal liability on anyone who purposely or knowingly unlawfully causes a hazardous discharge, a release, or abandonment of a hazardous waste or toxic pollutant.[73]

Thus, whether you are concerned with federal or state law, it is vital to recognize that "in today's enforcement climate, no one, not even those remotely responsible for environmental compliance, is immune from criminal prosecution."[74]

Knowledge Requirements

It is important for individuals and corporations to understand the kind of behavior that tends to give rise to criminal liability and what degree of knowledge is required to hold someone accountable.

> As a general rule, environmental statutes do not require the government to prove that a defendant purposefully violated the law. Rather they establish crimes of *general intent* where the government's burden is limited to demonstrating that an *act* took place with the knowledge of the defendant. Generally, the government need not prove knowledge by the defendant that the act was prohibited by law. The familiar refrain—ignorance of the law is no excuse—controls.[75]

Some case law supports a trend toward relaxing the traditional requirements of *mens rea* and willfulness. "One does not have to *be* bad to *do* bad when it comes to environmental crimes. The 'black heart' requirement commonly associated with other criminal activity is not necessary to sustain a conviction."[76] The government's position on what is "knowing" and "willful" is suggested in one commentator's analysis of a case involving a prosecution under RCRA.

> In the context of *public welfare* offenses, courts have repeatedly held that "knowingly" requires only that one act voluntarily, with knowledge of one's actions. It does not require knowledge of the law or a specific intent to break the law. . . . Willfully is

viewed similarly, as not requiring or denoting specific intent or evil purpose.[77]

In the context of RCRA and the Clean Water Act (CWA),[78] at least six U.S. appellate courts[79] have upheld the concept that environmental statutes are "public welfare" statutes—laws that address such issues as food and drug safety and are cited to support the imposition of strict criminal liability.[80] As noted by the Fifth Circuit and quoted with approval by the U.S. Court of Appeals for the Eleventh Circuit, RCRA "is undeniably a public welfare statute, involving a heavily regulated area, with great ramifications for the public health and safety."[81] The Fifth Circuit and U.S. Court of Appeals for the Sixth Circuit have also indicated that "knowing" for purposes of RCRA does not require specific knowledge of a regulation:

> "Knowingly" means no more than that the defendant knows factually what he is doing—storing, what is being stored, and that what is being stored factually has the potential for harm to others or the environment, and that he has no permit—and it is not required that he know that there is a regulation which says what he is storing is hazardous under the RCRA.[82]

The U.S. Court of Appeals for the Second and Ninth Circuits have taken similar positions with respect to the CWA.[83] The Ninth Circuit held that ordinary negligence was sufficient to uphold a conviction under the CWA.[84] However, in *United States v. Ahmad*,[85] the Fifth Circuit expressly found that the CWA is not a public welfare statute as "serious felonies" are potentially involved and therefore appropriate knowledge or *mens rea* is required.

The concept of broad criminal liability is carried further in the CAA Amendments of 1990. For purposes of criminal liability under the CAA Amendments, the term "operator" includes any person who is in senior management or who is a corporate officer.[86] The CAA Amendments significantly limit the actual operator's liability and focus on managers, including officers and directors.[87] The person actually responsible for the operation of the equipment can only be subject to criminal liability if the violation was "knowing and willful"—still a relatively low threshold of knowledge under public welfare statutes. Under the "knowing endangerment" provision, actual knowledge is required that through a release, an individual placed another person in imminent danger of death or serious bodily harm. Circumstantial evidence may be sufficient, including evidence that a defendant took affirmative steps to be shielded from knowledge of a release.[88]

Barry Hartman, a former Assistant Attorney General in charge of the DOJ's Environment and Natural Resources Division, "says one of the best guides to appropriate behavior is common sense. 'What I tell general counsel is: 'Never give your waste to a guy named Bubba driving a pick up truck.' Remember that the standard of knowledge is very, very relaxed. There is not specific knowledge of the law or of the facts required for conviction."[89] Another criminal lawyer, Nancy Luque, a former federal prosecutor, provides the following advice: "Never talk to investigators without help, even when questions are routine. . . . I don't buy the argument that anything is routine."[90]

Reporting Requirements

In addition to the broad definition of knowledge, managers should also consider the reporting requirements specified in several environmental statutes. The CWA, RCRA, the Toxic Substances Control Act (TSCA), and particularly the CAA Amendments of 1990, have a vast array of self-reporting requirements. Failure to report can result in civil or criminal liability. "The environmental laws are about as close as you can get in a criminal context to strict liability,"[91] and knowing failure to meet a reporting requirement is particularly dangerous from the standpoint of potential criminal exposure.

Responsible Corporate Officers

The government has also taken the position that "corporate management can, in certain circumstances, be held criminally liable as individuals for environmental violations even where those managers did not personally participate in, or direct, each of the actions which gave rise to criminal liability."[92] DOJ policy "has been, and will continue to be . . . to conduct environmental criminal investigations with an eye to identifying, prosecuting, and convicting the highest ranking truly responsible corporate officials."[93] In the context of RCRA enforcement, the government "attempts to hold corporate officers and chief executive officers . . . criminally accountable for the actions of their employees and subordinates, even when those top executives did not have *actual* knowledge of their employees' illegal conduct."[94] This is known as the "responsible corporate officer" doctrine.[95]

According to one commentator, in *United States v. Dee*,[96] the U.S. Court of Appeals for the Fourth Circuit "summarily approved a remarkable set of instructions permitting the jury to infer willful blindness and, therefore, the requisite degree of knowledge on the part of corporate officials based on their respective positions of responsibility in an organization."[97] In an Ohio prosecution, the facility manager of a hazardous waste site was held to have constructive knowledge of RCRA guidance documents, which collectively amount to a pile literally several feet high.[98]

The executive can, however, receive some comfort from case law arguably indicating that "the government must prove *actual* knowledge (and effective consent) of the prohibited conduct, even for 'responsible corporate officers.'"[99] Note that the concept of a "responsible corporate officer" has been further expanded by one recent case. In *United States v. Hong,* [100] convicting an individual as a "corporate officer" even though he did not have a specific title: "The gravamen of liability as a responsible corporate officer is not one's corporate title or lack thereof; rather, the pertinent question is whether the defendant bore such a relationship to the corporation that it is appropriate to hold him criminally liable for *failing to prevent* the charged violations" of the CWA.[101] It remains to be seen whether these cases, which seem to distinguish environmental law issues from public welfare cases, will be generally followed.

Corporate entities themselves must be wary of criminal liability, because although

> [m]any states sanction corporations criminally only for the acts of management . . . , federal courts have adopted a broadly defined doctrine of imputed liability that permits the criminal conviction of a corporation for acts of its low-level employees or outside agents. A corporation can be convicted of federal crimes even if its employees and agents act without management's knowledge or approval and even if management has specifically prohibited the offensive conduct and taken reasonable steps to prevent it.[102]

Sentencing Guidelines (Guidelines) and Revisions

The *U.S. Sentencing Commission Guidelines Manual* includes a specific "environmental offenses" category.[103] "In what used to be a highly subjective process, the rules remove nearly all discretion that judges have traditionally enjoyed at the sentencing stage. Now sentencing is more a matter of making mathematical computations."[104]

Summary of Sentencing Guidelines Revisions[105]

The Guidelines determine the sanctions that will be imposed in federal criminal cases whether or not they are environmentally based. However, it is widely known that the Guidelines serve a much broader function in the area of corporate compliance programs. Since 1991, the Guidelines have provided a concrete financial benefit to companies that implement compliance programs by allowing judges to show leniency to such companies at sentencing. The leniency is based on whether or not the company's compliance plan passed muster with the Guidelines' criteria for an "effective program to prevent and detect violations of law."

The Guidelines' criteria for sentencing quickly became the criteria to determine which cases were selected for enforcement, and how seriously a particular violation may be viewed. Simply put, companies with compliance plans that did not meet the basic Guidelines requirements in the view of government personnel were almost automatically viewed as outliers seeking to avoid the legal responsibilities imposed by government regulations.

Now, for the first time since 1991, the Guidelines that address the requirements for an effective compliance plan have been revised. The changes to the Organizational Guidelines were partly in response to the new requirements imposed by Sarbanes-Oxley.[106] The U.S. Sentencing Commission, the quasi-legislative body that drafts the Guidelines, revised Chapter Eight of the Guidelines, the "Organizational Guidelines," which govern the sentencing of companies.

The new provisions will require new efforts in order for the government to consider that a corporate compliance plan is "effective" in preventing and detecting violations of law. The amendments will require corporate directors and executives to undertake a far greater responsibility and oversight role in the design and implementation of compliance plans and will for the first time require that companies show they have taken steps to promote an "organizational culture" that encourages a commitment to compliance. While the Court recently ruled that federal judges may now only consider the Guidelines to be "advisory" in nature,[107] it is not likely to diminish the importance of the Guidelines to organizations, particularly in the area of compliance.. "[I]n exercising discretion when sentencing, courts will almost certainly be asked to consider whether organizations have met these criteria as a good faith part of their compliance programs."[108]

The new Guidelines do the following:

- For the first time require the organization to "promote an organizational culture that encourages ethical conduct and a commitment to compliance with the law";

- More specifically define the term "standards and procedures" as "standards of conduct and internal controls that are reasonably capable of reducing the likelihood of criminal conduct";

- Replace the general requirement that high-level individuals be assigned overall responsibilities with more specific requirements that clarify the roles and reporting responsibilities of an organization's compliance authorities;

- Require more aggressive efforts by an organization to determine when an employee with substantial authority over a compliance area has a history of engaging in illegal activities or other conduct inconsistent with an effective compliance and ethics program;

- For the first time require training for and the dissemination of training materials to all levels of an organization's employees and agents, including upper level management;

- Mandate the use of auditing and monitoring systems designed to detect criminal conduct;

- Require a periodic evaluation of the compliance program;

- Require that organizations provide a means, which may include the use of anonymous or confidential reporting, to enable employees and agents "to seek guidance regarding the potential or actual criminal conduct without fear of retaliation"; and

- Enforce compliance standards through "appropriate incentives," in addition to disciplinary actions.

The EMS and those charged with its implementation should consider these changes and determine whether or not the existing program satisfies these requirements. Simply put, even a fairly well-functioning EMS will be considered suspect in the event of a violation if it does not address each of the new Guidelines provisions.

Criminal law is critical in the context of environmental assessments or audits. As noted by George Van Cleve, former Deputy Assistant Attorney General for the DOJ's Environment and Natural Resources Division:

> The United States has used audit results to good effect in criminal prosecutions to prove that corporate management was aware of the existence of environmental violations and did not act to correct them when it could have done so. The United States has consistently refused to limit access to audit results for criminal enforcement purposes.[109]

Van Cleve also notes that "[i]n deciding whether to voluntarily adopt an audit program, a company will likely take a series of factors into account. Among them certainly should be whether the liability resulting from uncorrected violations is likely to be manageable."[110] While he notes that there may be a benefit in performing an audit rather than running "the risk of prosecution without knowing in any detail what the risk actually looks like,"[111] he cautions that the DOJ will look closely at claims of attorney-client privilege. Of course, the threat of criminal prosecution, which has to be made indirectly and artfully, also can be used as leverage to "facilitate" civil settlements. With the increasing realities of potential civil and criminal penalties, there is a tendency up and down the line—particularly if there is a perception that management does not care or will not back the employee—to document alleged problems so that the next person up the line will also have liability exposure, and to limit the exposure of the person lower down. Management programs that do not have the safety valve of a corporate commitment to dealing with significant issues will find many of these memoranda in their files when there is a civil or criminal prosecution.

EPA and the DOJ recognize the value of environmental audits, but ordinarily reserve the right to obtain such material.[112] Indeed, the agencies desire to encourage these programs by holding out the carrot of possible—though not assured—limits on criminal prosecution, if the audit and entire management program are sufficiently comprehensive. DOJ policy limits the use of information developed in environmental audits for criminal prosecutions under environmental statutes. The excerpt in Figure 2-1 indicates, however, that the audit and compliance program must be very comprehensive to secure any form of consideration. (For a more detailed analysis of environmental auditing, as well as its implications for enforcement, see Chapter 6.)

Figure 2-1
Excerpt from *Factors in Decisions on Criminal Prosecutions for Environmental Violations in the Context of Significant Voluntary Compliance or Disclosure Efforts by the Violator*

The attorney for the Department should consider the existence and scope of any regularized, intensive, and comprehensive environmental compliance program; such a program may include an environmental compliance or management audit. Particular consideration should be given to whether the compliance or audit program includes sufficient measures to identify and prevent future noncompliance, and whether the program was adopted in good faith in a timely manner.[113]

Figure 2-2
Questions to Ask When Evaluating Compliance Programs

• Was there a strong institutional policy to comply with all environmental requirements?

• Had safeguards beyond those required by existing law been developed and implemented to prevent noncompliance?

• Were there regular procedures, including internal or external compliance and management audits, to evaluate, detect, prevent, and remedy circumstances like those that led to the noncompliance?

• Were there procedures and safeguards to ensure the integrity of any audit conducted?

• Did the audit evaluate all sources of pollution (i.e., all media), including the possibility of cross-media transfers of pollutants?

• Were the auditor's recommendations implemented in a timely fashion?

• Were adequate resources committed to the auditing program and to implementing its recommendations?

• Was environmental compliance a standard by which employee and corporate departmental performance was judged?

While a January 20, 2003 DOJ policy[114] describes compliance programs in general and their significance in criminal prosecutions, it doesn't deal specifically with environmental issues (commonly known as the Thompson memorandum). However, it is a standard reference to prosecutors in environmental matters and contains some relevant language. That policy does state, among other matters, that

> the existence of a compliance program is not sufficient, in and of itself, to justify not charging a corporation for criminal conduct undertaken by its officers, directors, employees or agents. Indeed, the commission of such crimes in the face of a compliance program may suggest that the corporate management is not adequately enforcing its program.[115]

The policy also notes that prosecutors should

> attempt to determine whether a corporation's compliance program is merely a "paper program" or whether it was designed and implemented in an effective manner. In addition, prosecutors should determine whether the corporation has provided for a staff sufficient to audit, document, analyze and utilize the results of the corporation's compliance efforts. In addition, prosecutors should determine whether the corporation's employees are adequately informed about the compliance program and are convinced of the corporation's commitment to it.[116]

Social Concerns: Environmental Justice and the Redevelopment of Industrial Areas

Over time, individuals, community groups, government, and industry have become increasingly aware that environmental problems may unfairly affect certain socioeconomic groups. It is argued that industry and governmental efforts to avoid environmental costs have led to decisions to locate a disproportionate number of industrial sites and undesirable government projects, such as incinerators and prisons, in minority or low-income communities with limited political clout. This awareness has led to an effort to seek greater "environmental justice."[117]

Environmental justice "is concerned with the benefits and burdens of all past, present and future environmental decisions. It is likely that most urban areas have exceeded the carrying capacity of their land base."[118] The carrying capacity of land "is of direct importance to environmental justice concerns, because when the land exceeds its carry capacity waste increases, industrial byproducts may begin to bioaccumulate in vulnerable parts of the community, and public health becomes threatened."[119]

Robert Collin and Robin Morris Collin point out that

> the test of the maturity of the environmental movement as we enter the 21st Century will be whether it can include communities of color in meaningful and authoritative ways. If sustainability is the ecological goal of environmental public policy, then history shows us that dialogues must include all stakeholders. Today, the emerging values that unite both traditional environmentalists and urban environmentalists are based in the recognition that the values and environmental consequences of industrial capitalism were and continue to be instrumental in contributing to the exploitation of people and natural resources. Both constituencies now recognize that the common concern that must unite

the post-industrial world of environmentalists and urban dwellers is sustainable use of resources and equitable treatment of people.[120]

A tough question is the extent to which the siting and pollution control decisions of concern result from racism or economic decisions. Nelson Smith has addressed this topic.[121] The use of code terms such as "environmental justice" or "environmental racism"

> suggests that one either believes that the location of a disproportionate number of landfills and toxic waste sites in minority communities is a deliberate act, or simply an unfortunate result of more complex societal factors. The term "justice" connotes "fairness." In many instances, unfairness isn't necessarily caused by racism. It could be the result of educational or economic disparities. "Racism" on the other hand, is generally intentional, also resulting in unfairness to those who are oppressed.
>
> Racism advances unfairness; however, unfairness does not necessarily establish racism.[122]

Unfortunately, racism has led to environmental injustice.[123] For example, the government built public housing projects for minorities near railroad tracks and highways. They were located deliberately to divide the minority community so that the police and other law enforcement officials would have quick access to the community to suppress any "uprisings."[124] The result was location of minority neighborhoods in places where the people would have greater exposure to chemical pollutants and noise.

There are other, more complex reasons for disproportionate environmental impacts. Many of the

> environmental problems now affecting minority and other low-income communities result from their location near industries, such as chemical factories, steel mills, refineries, incinerators, and the like. A careful study of how so many of these industries ended up in such communities reveals that many of the housing projects were built *after* the industrial plants arrived. In fact, many of these communities grew when people came to the factories looking for jobs.[125]

In addition, because property values were lower in these locations, housing was more affordable for those with lower incomes. Zoning plus cost factors made such areas more attractive for additional industrial and infrastructure development, compounding the impacts on nearby neighborhoods.[126]

Whatever the causes of the problem, environmental managers must be very aware of the issue. Charges of injustice may result in lawsuits, bad press, and bad relations with the community, all of which are time-consuming and difficult for company management and employees. Smith notes:

> Because [a] lawsuit [under Title VI of the Civil Rights Act] itself or the accompanying press release brands a company or a local government as a "racist," companies feel compelled to fight the allegation, spending their time trying to convince the minority community that the company is not racist. Meanwhile, the accusers attempt to convince the community that the company is racist. Scientific principles and environmental remedies are ignored. When all is said and done, the environmentalist who equates the company with environmental racism goes home to the suburbs, where he or she is not exposed to such an alleged "problem," as does the corporate officer. Those who remain living in the minority community have become the political football in the battle between the two groups. Many times, the pitched battles have little or nothing to do with the minority community at all. Instead, the battles are fought based, at least in part, on the dislike of one group by the other, or on some other ulterior motives.[127]

To minimize or avoid such situations, corporations and public entities need to be willing to sit down with members of a community, determine what their concerns are, and develop a scheme that not only reduces their concerns, but provides the community with a meaningful solution.[128] Such solutions might include providing for job training programs or educational opportunities. It has been suggested that programs to address community concerns be made a part of the permit conditions for construction or expansion of facilities.[129]

Indeed, in February 1998, EPA issued interim guidance under Title VI of the Civil Rights Act to deal with administrative complaints alleging discrimination in the environmental permitting context. EPA bases its guidance on an executive order issued by President William J. Clinton on February 11, 1994, entitled "Federal Actions to Address Environmental Justice in Minority Populations and Low-Income Populations."[130] States were not consulted when the guidance was issued.

This guidance followed EPA's action on September 10, 1993, utilizing Executive Order No. 12898, which rejected a Louisiana air permit for the construction of a $700 million chemical plant by Shintech Inc. in the predominantly African-American community of St. Jones Parish, Louisiana, an area of the state sometimes referred to as "Cancer Alley."[131]

Students participating in Tulane Law School's Environmental Law Clinic and attorneys from Greenpeace represented the citizen groups. Despite active support for the Shintech project by the local National Association for the Advancement of Colored People (NAACP), based on the economic benefits to the region, EPA Administrator Carol Browner notified the state "that minority and low-income communities must not be subjected disproportionately to environmental hazards and that the State must consider environmental justice concerns in the permitting process."[132]

In June 2001, EPA's Office of Civil Rights issued its Interim Draft Guidance for Investigating Title VI Administrative Complaints Challenging permits.[133] As expected, the guidance failed to satisfy anyone.[134] As noted by Robert Shinn, New Jersey's Commissioner, Department of Environmental Protection, EPA has "clearly recognized that states need flexibility to design their environmental justice programs" but "no matter what a state recipient does in implementing a Title VI program, EPA reserves the right to a de novo investigation to determine if the state effort is sufficient."[135]

> EPA's statement that *no* single definition of adverse disparate impact is possible due to the differing nature of impacts and the various environmental media may doom the environmental justice effort. Without a consistent definition of disparate impact, how can anyone determine if discrimination has occurred? Can each stakeholder have a different definition?[136]

The difficulty of a successful filing was noted by the fact that "not one environmental justice challenge, either reported in the eight recent [environmental appeals board (EAB)] decisions or the decision under EPA's Interim Guidelines, has been successful.[137]

In a report prepared for the Congressional Black Caucus, the National Environmental Policy Commission noted that "[f]undamentally, [environmental justice] is a civil rights issue. However, it differs from conventional civil rights issues in that it concerns communities, not individuals, and focuses on environmental impacts rather than lost job opportunities."[138] The report also noted that

> [a]lthough the EPA, within its relatively narrow regulatory mission, has come up with a working definition of environmental justice, in our view, the concept of environmental justice can be much broader in scope, encompassing a wide range of domestic and international concerns, including labor, worker safety, transportation and international trade issues.[139]

However, all of this discussion may be academic. The Court, in *Alexander v. Sandoval*,[140] held that there was no private cause of action under Title VI for violation of agency regulations issued under §602. "The Court, assumed, but did not address, the issue of whether agencies had the authority under Section 602 to promulgate Title VI regulations that prohibit conduct based on discriminatory 'impact' as opposed to 'intent.'"[141] The litigant then attempted to rely on 42 U.S.C. §1983, which prohibits states "under color of law" from depriving citizens of rights secured by the "Constitution or laws." But the U.S. Court of Appeals for the Third Circuit held that because Title VI proscribes only intentional discrimination, residents of a predominately minority community do not have a right to enforce through §1983 EPA's Title VI §602 disparate discrimination regulations against a state agency that issued an air permit to a cement plant.[142] This decision barred citizens from using federal civil rights statutes to halt state action subjecting minority citizens to excessive pollution. An issue left open by that decision is "when if ever, are these [EPA] disparate impact rules enforceable and by whom and under what circumstances"[143] and whether the EPA regulations themselves may be unconstitutional based on this decision. Interestingly, states may develop their own regulations to avoid the lack of federal remedies. New Jersey is in the process of promulgating its own regulations.[144]

Environmental justice issues appear to conflict with efforts on other regulatory fronts; for example, the effort to increase air emission trading:

> Civil rights attorneys and organizations have become increasingly concerned with the [Bush] administration's stated desire to shift much of the agency's work away from traditional, command and control rules to a more liberal, market-based philosophy. A lack of strict rules and strong enforcement mechanisms are of particular concern to environmental justice activists, who argue minority and low-income communities have never been provided equal protection by EPA and states, and do not therefore have a baseline of adequate protection that could act as a backstop to the use of market mechanisms.[145]

Of course, this is exacerbated, from the advocates' standpoint, by the apparent inability now to gain relief through EPA regulations unless discrimination has been intentional.

Sometimes novel approaches are necessary in a disadvantaged community. For example, to overcome a challenge to a permit for a petrochemical complex, Formosa Plastics provided an ambient air monitoring program for the city of Point Comfort, Texas, and health tests for a sampling of residents.[146] The Calhoun County Health Department selected 15 non-Formosa employees from among the residents of Point Comfort to undergo full physicals, including liver and kidney function, blood screening, urine analysis, pulmonary function, electrocardiograms, chest X-rays, audiograms, and optional drug screening. The physicals were designed to provide a baseline to assess future health impacts on the community from the facility expansion. Physical examinations over the last four years have not revealed any health impacts related to the plant.[147]

In addition, a major effort is underway, with the support of both EPA and state agencies, to redevelop contaminated sites in urban or industrial areas.[148] This effort stems from the multiple goals of addressing environmental justice issues, providing appropriate uses for contaminated sites, giving a new life to decayed areas, and conserving undeveloped lands for other uses. The effort is often called "brownfield" redevelopment, in contrast to "greenfield" development in areas that are now undeveloped. As a practical matter, redevelopment is generally restricted to "light brown" areas.

The federal government is pursuing both tax and regulatory strategies to promote brownfields redevelopment. On August 5, 1997, President Clinton signed the Taxpayer Relief Act,[149] which included a $1.5 billion tax incentive to spur the cleanup and redevelopment of brownfields in distressed and urban areas. The theory is that approximately 14,000 brownfields can be returned to productive use and generate $6 billion in private investment.[150]

EPA has a "Brownfields Action Agenda" that seeks to facilitate brownfields redevelopment. One key obstacle to redevelopment is concern about liability for past waste disposal practices. To overcome this obstacle, EPA has developed a new Prospective Purchaser Agreement to increase flexibility in the "covenants not to sue" to protect new owners from liability for past disposal practices.[151] There is also increased flexibility in the criteria for entry into such an agreement if there is substantial indirect benefit to the community. EPA will sign agreements, however, only if the following criteria in Figure 2-3 are met.

Figure 2-3
Circumstances Required for EPA to Sign
Prospective Purchaser Agreements

- An EPA action at the facility has been taken, is ongoing, or is anticipated by EPA.

- The continued operation of the facility or new site development, with the exercise of due care, will not aggravate or contribute to the existing contamination at the property or interfere with EPA's response action. Here, EPA will review the situation on a case-by-case basis.

- The continued operation of new development of the site will not pose health risks to the community and those persons likely to be present at the site.

- The prospective purchaser is financially viable.

Virtually all state governments also have brownfields programs in place.[152] One such program is the Massachusetts Clean Sites Initiative. Some argue that this initiative does not go far enough, particularly in the area of potential liability concerns, but it does provide protection "when contamination is found later even though the contamination was not found during the initial site assessment, provided the appropriate standard of care was followed in performing the initial assessment."[153]

Late in December 2001, Congress passed the Small Business Liability Relief and Brownfields Revitalization Act.[154] The bill provides for relief from liability for small businesses and "demicromis" contributors of waste to Superfund sites, as well as additional funding for the assessment and remediation of brownfield sites. Liability protection for certain property owners and prospective purchasers is provided, and there is a bar on federal enforcement at a site at which a response action is conducted in compliance with a state program.[155] In order to obtain liability protection, owners must take reasonable steps to stop and prevent future continuing releases, cooperate with the performance of response actions by others, and comply with applicable use restrictions. In addition, the contiguous property owner must not have caused, contributed, or consented to the contamination. Prospective purchasers must acquire the property post-disposal and conduct an appropriate inquiry prior to acquisition. However, the prospective purchaser need not show that they did not know or have reason to know of contamination at the time of acquisition, thus eliminating the need for a prospective purchaser agreement. EPA is to adopt regulations as to what is "appropriate inquiry." While EPA is barred from issuing administrative orders and seeking cost recoveries at sites being addressed in accordance with a state program, EPA may still bring enforcement when a state so requests, if contamination reaches across a state line, if imminent and substantial endangerment exists, or if additional information is discovered indicating the need for further remediation.

EPA has completed a negotiated rulemaking and comments closed on November 30, 2004. The final rule has not yet been promulgated.[156] Note that this regulation may become the new standard for environmental due diligence.

> For many years the standard for environmental due diligence has been the one established by the American Society for Testing and Materials (ASTM) with virtually no direct government involvement and no government commentary on the subject. The ASTM standard was developed to qualify for the "innocent landowner" defense to Superfund liability. Currently, lenders almost universally require that an environmental site assessment (commonly called a "Phase 1"), meeting the ASTM standard, be performed prior to extending financing for property acquisition. It is likely that this standard will soon be replaced with a standard established by EPA, which lenders and others almost certainly will require in the same manner as they required use of the ASTM standard in the past.[157]

"The EPA would define an 'environmental professional,' as one who may conduct or supervise the appropriate inquiry, more precisely than does the ASTM. This may result in creating new state licensing requirements for conducting these audits."[158]

Despite these initiatives, significant concerns about brownfields redevelopment remain. Few contaminated sites would be eligible as housing sites because of the cost to clean or stabilize to that level of use. If these sites are not rehabilitated to a residential use level, citizens may be concerned about the impacts of new industrial development on their neighborhoods and their health. The community may raise the specter of environmental justice. Consequently, the community may wind up with a site that no one is willing to purchase and that contributes to vandalism and other symptoms of industrial blight. Moreover, the jobs, which would probably have had a positive impact on health of the workers and the community, would be lost.

Nevertheless, if the liability concerns and the stigma of being a contaminated site can be overcome, some of these sites are useful for industrial development. To proceed with redevelopment, there must be a strong commitment to public involvement. Yet this comes at a cost. The public nature of the process, the risk of bad publicity (allegedly taking advantage of the local community), and, above all, the potential for delay may make projects in brownfields areas very costly. Companies may well find it easier to locate in a greenfield that has the appropriate zoning and is not subject to the same environmental justice issues. I am by no means suggesting that it is not advisable under any circumstances to site in a brownfield, but I am advising that the practical problems (including *fully* understanding the politics of local activist organizations), is necessary.[159] A full discussion of these issues is beyond the scope of this book, but there is much literature on both the opportunities and pitfalls of brownfield redevelopment.[160] Note, that today there are a variety of insurance products that are available to minimize the exposure. Certain construction and engineering firms are offering "guaranteed" costs of remediation, backed up by a "stop loss" insurance policy. The guaranteed fixed price contractor would fully indemnify the clients, both as to remediation costs and regulatory closure, which indemnity would be backed by a top-rated insurance program, up to policy limits. Other stakeholders (regulators, successor owners, etc.) can be included as additional insureds. The advantage of the finite or stop loss policy is that the insurance company gets the policy money up-front and its role is only to pay out against invoices as opposed to a traditional policy where there are many unknowns as to payout.

It should be recognized that industry cannot shoulder the total blame—or responsibility—for the social ills that beset industrial areas and surrounding neighborhoods. Part of the problem is lack of sufficient resources for our social needs and the misallocation of resources devoted to environmental issues. Poverty is more of a health problem than all of the other environmental issues combined. Is someone in an urban ghetto or a rural slum entitled to clean air and water? Of course, but are we losing our perspective by focusing on smaller and smaller increments of pollution while we lose new generations to the health and related problems of lack of jobs, health care, and basic self-respect? We in environmental management must do our part to seek cost-effective means to manage our companies so that we can provide both jobs and a clean environment.

Conclusion

An article by Bradley Bobertz, while at the Environmental Law Institute, called *Transferring the Blame* helps put the development of environmental law into perspective. His theory is that environmental law in the United

States is designed to "deal harshly with culturally accepted *symbols* of environmental problems."[161] Dealing with the *symbol*, however, "makes it less likely that we will deal with the problems—and their causes—themselves."[162] Bobertz also describes a "scapegoating phenomenon," which

> deflects inquiry away from an environmental problem in its full context to mere signifiers of it, effectively blocking productive reform and stifling on-going debate by making the problem appear to vanish from public view with the enactment of apparently responsive legislation. Finally, as the simplistic assumptions of scapegoating laws meet with the hard facts of implementation and enforcement, the law itself grows in length and complexity in order to preserve its initial, but distorted, suppositions.[163]

Even so, technically trained managers may take some solace in the possibility that some day a book about environmental management will not have to start with an extensive description of legal and social developments. Although compliance with the law will always be necessary, the search for solutions to environmental problems may move from the realm of law to technology. To some extent, this movement has already begun. As the early federal environmental statutes—NEPA, the CAA, and the CWA—were promulgated, there was an initial flurry of primarily legal work. Although these statutes still provide considerable work for lawyers, the emphasis has now shifted to technical analysis. We are beginning to solve these problems less as lawyers and more as managers. Implementation of the more recent hazardous waste statutes has been intensely focused on legal actions; in time, I hope this emphasis will also shift to technical solutions that protect health, the environment, and communities.

Notes to Chapter 2

1. *See generally* Frank Friedman, *Corporate Environmental Programs and Litigation: The Role of Lawyer-Managers in Environmental Management*, 45 PUB. ADMIN. REV. 766 (1985). A portion of this chapter is adapted from this article with permission from *Public Administration Review,* © 1985 by The American Society for Public Administration, 1120 G St., NW, Ste. 500, Washington DC 20005. All rights reserved.

2. *See generally* ROBERT A. KAGAN & EUGENE BARDACH, GOING BY THE BOOK: THE PROBLEM OF REGULATORY UNREASONABLENESS (1982). For a compilation of what EPA has viewed as the top environmental stories during the 35 years of EPA existence, see *A Retrospective: Three Decades of Top Environmental Stories*, ABA Section on Environment, Energy, and Resources, Corporate Counsel Committee Newsletter, June 2001, at 10-13.

3. Bud Ward, *Reflections*, ENVTL. F., Nov. 1984, at 2. *See also* R. SHEP MELNICK, REGULATION AND THE COURTS: THE CASE OF THE CLEAN AIR ACT 5-13 (1983). Although they relied on the federal government to control states and corporations, environmentalists distrusted various elements of the federal government as well. R. Shep Melnick notes that the specificity of many of the early regulations resulted from the bureaucrats' suspicions about the Nixon Administration's commitment to environmental issues and was an attempt to "protect their initiatives from executive branch sabotage." *See* MELNICK, at 8.

4. JOHN QUARLES, CLEANING UP AMERICA: AN INSIDER'S VIEW OF THE ENVIRONMENTAL PROTECTION AGENCY (1976).

5. Pub. L. No. 91-604, 84 Stat. 1676.

6. Bishop Processing Co. v. Gardner, 275 F. Supp. 780 (D. Md. 1967) (chicken processing plant); United States v. Bishop, 287 F. Supp. 624 (D. Md. 1968), *aff'd*, 423 F.2d 469 (4th Cir. 1970), *cert. denied*, 398 U.S. 904 (1970) (chicken processing plant); Dutton v. Rocky Mountain Phosphate, Inc., 438 P.2d 674 (Mont. 1968) (damages upheld against phosphate rock defluorinating plant, remanded on injunction), 450 P.2d 672 (Mont. 1969) (injunction against excessive phosphate emissions upheld).

7. *See, e.g.,* 33 U.S.C. §1365(d), ELR STAT. FWPCA §505(d); 42 U.S.C. §7607(f), ELR STAT. CAA §307(f). For a discussion of the availability of attorneys fees and the statutes specifically allowing such fees at the time, see Alyeska Pipeline Serv. Co. v. Wilderness Soc'y, 421 U.S. 240, 5 ELR 20286 (1975).

8. MELNICK, *supra* note 3, at 9.

9. The U.S. Supreme Court has ruled that a party must be victorious on at least one substantive claim on the merits to obtain attorneys fees. Ruckelshaus v. Sierra Club, 463 U.S. 680, 682, 13 ELR 20664, 20665 (1983) (reversing attorneys fees award under CAA §307(f)).

10. 42 U.S.C. §4332(2)(C), ELR STAT. NEPA §102(2)(C).

11. To obtain standing, "a party must demonstrate that the challenged action has caused him [or her] 'injury in fact' and that the injury was to an interest within the zone of interests protected by the applicable law." Richard E. Schwartz & David P. Hackett, *Citizen Suits Against Private Industry Under the Clean Water Act*, 17 NAT. RESOURCES LAW. 327, 332 (1984) (citing Sierra Club v. Morton, 405 U.S. 727, 733-34, 2 ELR 20192 (1972)). "In short, a plaintiff may not rely on an interest, no matter how strongly felt, to attain standing unless he [or she] can demonstrate a specific interest that has been injured by the defendant's action." Id. at 333.

12. MELNICK, *supra* note 3, at 9.

13. 5 U.S.C. §553, *available in* ELR STAT. ADMIN. PROC.

14. See, for example, the litigation concerning EPA regulation of prevention of significant deterioration under the CAA, Alabama Power Co. v. Costle, 606 F.2d 1068, 9 ELR 20400 (D.C. Cir. 1979). Along with the Sierra Club and Environmental Defense Fund, plaintiffs included the American Petroleum Institute, the National Coal Association, the Mining and Reclamation Council of America, the American Iron and Steel Institute, the American Paper Institute, the National Forest Products Association, the Manufacturing Chemists Association, the American Mining Congress, and the Montana Coal Council, as well as more than 30 power, chemical pipeline, mineral, and coal companies.

15. *See Morton*, 405 U.S. at 727; Ruckelshaus v. Sierra Club, 463 U.S. 680, 13 ELR 20664 (1983).

16. *See* Union Electric Co. v. EPA, 427 U.S. 246, 6 ELR 20570 (1976).

17. *See* Paul Leventhal, *Environmental Decisionmaking and the Role of the Courts,* 122 U. PA. L. REV. 509 (1974).

18. Udall v. Tallman, 380 U.S. 1 (1969); Chevron, U.S.A., Inc. v. Natural Resources Defense Council, 467 U.S. 837, 14 ELR 20507 (1984).

19. Vermont Yankee Nuclear Power Corp. v. Natural Resources Defense Council, 439 U.S. 519, 8 ELR 20288 (1978). In 1985, the *Washington Post* reported that the Burger Court overturned more D.C. Circuit cases in one year than the Warren Court did in a decade. Al Kamen, *U.S. Court's Liberal Era Ending: Reagan Nominees Seen Giving Conservatives a Majority*, WASH. POST, Jan. 27, 1985, at A1.

20. Other corporate executives exhibit this kind of social conscience. The man who was my boss for many years at Occidental, for example, was a former attorney in the DOJ's Civil Rights Division and the author of a moving account of his representation of those who suffered in the tragic failure of a mine slurry dam. See GERALD STERN, THE BUFFALO CREEK DISASTER (1976).

21. Frank Friedman, *Corporate Responsibility and the Environment,* 1 NEW PRIORITIES 37 (1971).

22. *Id.*

23. Pub. L. No. 94-580, 90 Stat. 2795 (1976) (codified as amended at 42 U.S.C. §§6901-6992k), ELR STAT. RCRA §§1001-11011.

24. Pub. L. No. 96-510, 94 Stat. 2767 (1980) (codified as amended at 42 U.S.C. §§9601-9675), ELR STAT. CERCLA §§101-405.

25. Pub. L. No. 99-499, 100 Stat. 1729 (1986) (codified as amended at 42 U.S.C. §§11001-11050), ELR STAT. EPCRA §§301-330.

26. Pub. L. No. 101-380, 104 Stat. 484 (1990) (codified as amended at 33 U.S.C. §§2701-2761), ELR STAT. OPA §§1001-7001.

27. Michael Lyons, *Congressional Self-Interest, Bureaucratic Self-Interest, and U.S. Environment Policy Implementation*, 30 ELR 10786, 10788 (Sept. 2000).

28. Jonathan H. Adler, *Let 50 Flowers Bloom: Transforming the States Into Laboratories of Environmental Policy*, 31 ELR 11284, 11286 (Nov. 2001).

29. Jonathan Z. Cannon, *EPA and Congress (1994-2000): Who's Been Yanking Whose Chain?*, 31 ELR 10942, 10943 (Aug. 2001) (quoting Prof. Richard Lazarus). Jonathan Cannon notes that

> [e]nvironmental politics at the national level continues to be defined by the dominant constituencies and ideologies of the two major political parties. However, it is important not to underestimate the influence of EPA as an actor separate from the political overseers on the Hill and in the White House. The Agency has its own interest, which are to some degree independent of party, and as we have seen can engage in actions effectively to further those interests. In the new configuration, the interaction among Agency interests, public preferences and expectations, and party politics will continue to determine, as it has in the past, the relationship between EPA and Congress.

Id. at 10956.

30. James A. Lofton, *Environment and Enforcement: The Impact of Cultural Values and Attitudes on Social Regulation*, 31 ELR 10906 (Aug. 2001). *See* http://www. epa.gov.

31. Adler, *supra* note 28, at 11284.

32. *Id.* n.5.

33. *Id.* at 11300.

34. Lofton, *supra* note 30, at 10910.

35. 31 U.S.C. §3730 (b).

36. In Pickens v. Kanawha River Towing, 916 F. Supp. 702 (S.D. Ohio 1996), the court recognized the federal FCA as a basis for claims either by citizens or the federal government against companies that: (1) contract directly or indirectly with the federal government; (2) violate an environmental statute; and (3) do not fully report a violation. This case involved a federal contract to build a lock and dam. An employee of two subcontractors on the project—both tugboat companies—claimed that the tugboats had illegally dumped bilge into the Ohio River. The employee filed a fraud action against his employers under the FCA. When the federal govern-

ment declined to participate, the employee proceeded alone. In denying the subcontractors' motions to dismiss, the court made the following rulings.

(1) The Federal Water Pollution Control Act (FWPCA) does not preempt the [FCA] because they address different conduct. The FWPCA provides a remedy for water pollution, the [FCA] for defrauding the government.

(2) A [FCA] claim may be maintained if subcontractors submitted bills for payment without acknowledging they had violated the FWPCA and the government had required, and all contracts specified, that work on the project be conducted in compliance with the FWPCA.

(3) An action for false recordkeeping and reporting under the [FCA] may be maintained where a tugboat kept a log even though it was not required to do so, but did not record the discharge of bilge. If the government relies on or reviews such logs as part of its regulatory role, the log in question would constitute a false record.

SIDLEY & AUSTIN, ENVIRONMENTAL ADVISORY 1-2 (Aug. 1996). The court also denied motions to dismiss related FWPCA claims. *Id.*

37. *See, e.g.*, United States ex rel. Fallon v. Accudyne Corp., No. 93 C-801-S, 1995 U.S. Dist. LEXIS 11931 (W.D. Wis. June 19, 1995). For a detailed analysis, see Ridgway M. Hall Jr., *False Claims Act Litigation Based on Alleged Environmental Noncompliance*, 28th Annual Conference on Environmental Law, A.B.A. Sec. Nat. Resources, Energy & Envtl. L., Keystone, Colo., Mar. 11-14, 1999.

38. 2 U.S.C. §1350. "Created as part of the Judiciary Act of 1789, the history of the statute and congressional intent remain unclear." John C. Reynolds, *The Alien Tort Statute: The Expansion of International Environmental Law in U.S. Courts*, TRENDS, July/Aug. 2001, at 13.

39. Reynolds, *supra* note 38, at 13.

40. Sosa v. Alvarez-Machain, 124 S. Ct. 2739 (2004). *See* discussion in Theodore Garrett, *In Brief,* TRENDS, Nov./Dec. 2004, at 6.

41. For a detailed analysis of criminal enforcement of environmental law, see JOHN F. COONEY ET AL., ENVIRONMENTAL CRIMES DESKBOOK (1995); DONALD A. CARR ET AL., ENVIRONMENTAL CRIMINAL LIABILITY: AVOIDING AND DEFENDING ENFORCEMENT ACTIONS (1996); and Daniel Riesel, *Criminal Prosecution and the Regulation of the Environment*, 1991 A.L.I./A.B.A. COURSE OF STUDY—ENVTL. L. 375, 379, 421-23.

42. Sandy Moretz, *The Rising Cost of Environmental Crime*, OCCUPATIONAL HAZARDS, Mar. 1990, at 38.

43. In 1997, a record of 278 criminal cases were referred for prosecution, and $169.3 million was charged in fines. FY 1997 ACCOMPLISHMENTS, *infra* note 47. In 1998, the number decreased to 266 cases and $92.8 million in fines. FY 98 ACCOMPLISHMENTS, *infra* note 48.

The following analysis of the *Exxon Valdez* case, previously published in

Environment, Health & Safety Management, illustrates the zeal of the government in prosecuting corporations for environmental crimes and the potential costs involved.

The *Exxon Valdez* prosecution was settled [in 1993] for $250 million, the largest criminal fine in American history, in addition to nearly $1 billion in civil penalties.

Even with $125 million forgiven because of Exxon's earlier cleanup efforts, no other criminal fine has been greater. But it could have been much worse. The *Exxon Valdez* case provides some insight into the [DOJ's] current aggressive approach, even though it was settled before the government's theories were tested by the court.

The government reached deep into its arsenal of weapons, bringing charges under not only the Clean Water Act, but also under the Refuse Act and Migratory Bird Treaty Act.

The latter two statutes do not govern oil spills directly, but do provide a means of holding a defendant liable for criminal violations of environmental statutes without regard to intent or fault.

Under the Refuse Act, it is a criminal misdemeanor to discharge any refuse from any vessel into the navigable waters of the United States. The Migratory Bird Treaty Act makes it a criminal misdemeanor to kill "by any means" any migratory bird protected by certain international conventions.

Onto this strict criminal liability theory, the government grafted an agency theory, under which Exxon was to be held liable for the acts of its wholly owned subsidiary. By alleging that Exxon itself was liable for the acts of its separately incorporated subsidiary, the government sought to "pierce the corporate veil" and make Exxon's treasury answerable for the liability assessed in the case, in addition to the treasury of its shipping subsidiary.

The ramifications of this approach are disturbing. It attacks the limited liability protection of the traditional parent-subsidiary corporate structure, and by doing so, adds an entirely separate defendant to the case. This doubles the maximum amount of fines that can be assessed: Exxon Corporation and Exxon Shipping Company each could have been fined independently.

The government added a *coup de grace* to its prosecution by invoking the Criminal Fines Improvements Act. Under this federal law, a court can assess a fine of the greater of two amounts—either the amount that the defendant gained from the crime, or the amount that a third party lost because of the crime.

In the *Exxon Valdez* case, the potential liability was staggering. Based on Exxon's payments in excess of $350 million to settle civil damage claims from the oil spill, it could have faced an additional $700 million in fines under the Criminal Fines Improvements Act.

Moreover, because the Exxon Corporation and its shipping subsidiary could have been assessed separately, the total fine could have amounted to $1.4 billion.

It's no wonder that Exxon settled with the federal government. When contrasted with a potential $1.4 billion criminal fine, the $125 million settlement appears to be favorable indeed. In this context, the country's largest criminal fine ever looks like a good deal for the company.

Because the *Exxon Valdez* case was settled before trial, we don't know whether the government's legal theories and tactics would have withstood judicial scrutiny.

Certainly, they were an effective weapon in forcing Exxon to the bargaining table at a substantial disadvantage. And the message to the regulated community at large is clear: Growing public concern about the environment has caught the [DOJ's] attention, and the [DOJ] is willing to take Draconian steps to enforce the law.

Klingon, *Justice Department Pulls Out All the Stops*, ENV'T, HEALTH & SAFETY MGMT., Aug. 31, 1992, at 1, 3 (reprinted with permission).

44. Ruth Ann Ridel et al., *1995 Report of Environmental Crimes and Enforcement Committee*, 1995 A.B.A. SEC. NAT. RESOURCES, ENERGY & ENVTL. L. 171.

45. ENVTL. POL'Y ALERT, Dec. 22, 1993, at 36.

46. *Id.*

47. *EPA Has "Banner Year" for Enforcement Settlements*, INSIDE EPA CLEAN AIR REP., Dec. 15, 1994, at 31; U.S. EPA, FY 1994 ENFORCEMENT AND COMPLIANCE ASSURANCE ACCOMPLISHMENTS REPORT (1995) http://www.epa.gov/oeca/94accomp.pdf [hereinafter FY 1994 ACCOMPLISHMENTS].

48. Numbers in this chart were obtained from the following reports: U.S. EPA, EPA Releases FY 2000 Enforcement and Compliance Assurance Data (Jan. 19, 2001) (press release); U.S. EPA, EPA Sets Enforcement Records in 1999 (Jan. 19, 2000) (press release); U.S. EPA, ENFORCEMENT AND COMPLIANCE ASSURANCE FY 98 ACCOMPLISHMENTS REPORT (1999) http://www.epa.gov/oeca/fy98accomp.pdf [hereinafter FY 1998 ACCOMPLISHMENTS]; U.S. EPA, ENFORCEMENT AND COMPLIANCE ASSURANCE ACCOMPLISHMENTS REPORT FY 1997 (1998) http://www.epa.gov/oeca/97accomp.pdf [hereinafter FY 1997 ACCOMPLISHMENTS]; U.S. EPA, FY 1996 ENFORCEMENT AND COMPLIANCE ASSURANCE ACCOMPLISHMENTS REPORT (1997) http://www.epa.gov/oeca/96accomp/96accomp.pdf; U.S. EPA, FY 1995 ENFORCEMENT AND COMPLIANCE ASSURANCE ACCOMPLISHMENTS REPORT (1996) http://www.epa.gov/oeca/95accomp.pdf; and FY 1994 ACCOMPLISHMENTS, *supra* note 47. The number of EPA civil referrals, compliance orders, and civil penalty orders fell sharply in 1995 and the first half of 1996. There were 600 civil actions in the first half of the FY, compared with 1,400 in the previous comparable period. EPA blamed much of this drop on the government slowdown, but penalty order complaints dropped 25 percent from FY 1994 to FY 1995, before the government hiatus. AIR DAILY, July 24, 1996, at 3. EPA conducted un-

der 2,000 inspections by March 1996, compared with 7,309 inspections by the same period in 1995. There were only 161 penalty order complaints during the first half of FY 1996, compared with 1,105 in all of FY 1995. *Record Shows Traditional Enforcement Actions Against Industry Have Wilted*, ENV'T, HEALTH & SAFETY MGMT., Aug. 12, 1996, at 1.

For detailed analysis, see FY 1994 ACCOMPLISHMENTS, *supra* note 47.

49. Kevin A. Gaynor & Benjamin S. Lippard, *Environmental Enforcement: Industry Should Not Be Complacent*, 32 ELR 10488, 10488 (Apr. 2002).

50. *EPA Regions Urged to Step Up Traditional Enforcement in FY 1997*, ENVTL. POL'Y ALERT, Sept. 25, 1996, at 33.

51. Robert L. Collings, *Environmental Enforcement and Crimes 2004 Annual Report*, in THE YEAR IN REVIEW 2004, ABA SEC. OF ENV'T, ENERGY & RESOURCES L. (2005).

52. *Id.*

53. *Id.*

54. Comments from a spokesman for the EPA criminal enforcement program to author (May 15, 2005).

55. *DOJ Presses EPA to Speed Enforcement as Fiscal Year Nears End*, ENVTL. POL'Y ALERT, Sept. 25, 1996, at 33.

56. *EPA to Add 21 Criminal Investigators by End of Fiscal Year 1996, Official Says*, Daily Env't Rep. (BNA), July 8, 1996, at A-8. The Pollution Prosecution Act of 1991 authorized an increase in the number of criminal investigators to 200 by FY 1995. 42 U.S.C. §4321 notes (1994).

57. FY 1997 ACCOMPLISHMENTS, *supra* note 48.

58. Charles A. DeMonaco, Assistant Chief, Environmental Crimes Section, Environment and Natural Resources Division, DOJ, Remarks at the A.L.I./A.B.A. Conference (Feb. 14, 1992), *quoted in Criminal Enforcement Action No Longer Limited to "Midnight Dumpers,"* Lawyer Tells Conference, 22 Env't Rep. (BNA) 2406 (Feb. 21, 1992) [hereinafter *Criminal Enforcement Action No Longer Limited*].

59. Kevin A. Gaynor & Thomas R. Bartman, *Frontier Justice*, ENVTL. F., Mar./Apr. 1991, at 23, 24. The DOJ amended the environmental crimes provisions of the U.S. Attorney's Manual making it clear that the Environmental Crimes Section must approve virtually all environmental criminal prosecutions made by U.S. Attorneys. The amended provisions specifically define environmental crimes that may be prosecuted only after approval by DOJ headquarters. *Amended Environmental Crime Procedures for U.S. Attorneys Manual Released by DOJ*, 23 Env't Rep. (BNA) 2488 (Jan. 22, 1993).

Vicki O'Meara, the DOJ's Acting Assistant Attorney General for Environment and Natural Resources, was quoted as noting "that courts had made conflicting decisions and DOJ needed to consider prosecutions on a national level. 'We are sending people to jail here. We are talking about people's lives,' she added." *Id.*

60. Memorandum from Larry D. Thompson, Deputy Attorney General, *Principles of Federal Prosecution of Business Organizations* (Jan. 20, 2003), *available at* www.usdoj.gov/dag/cftf/corporate_guidelines.htm (last visited Aug. 22, 2005).

61. *Id.* at 5.

62. *Id.* (Emphasis supplied.) *See also* Richard M. Cooper, *Privilege Under Fire*, NAT'L L.J., Mar. 14, 2005, at 12.

63. Judson W. Starr, Address at the A.B.A. Section of Natural Resources, Energy, and Environmental Law 19th Annual Conference (Mar. 15-18, 1990).

64. Roger J. Marzulla, Testimony Before the Judiciary Committee of the House of Representatives Subcommittee on Commercial and Administrative Law 19 (May 2, 1996).

65. David T. Buente & Kathryn B. Thomson, *The Changing Face of Federal Environmental Criminal Trends and Developments—1999-2001*, 31 ELR 11340 (Nov. 2001).

66. Judson W. Starr et al., *Prosecuting Pollution*, LEGAL TIMES, May 31, 1993.

67. *See* Andrea Foster, *GCs Protest Prosecutor Tactics*, 22 NAT'L L.J., May 29, 2000, at B1.

68. *See* NICHOLSON, CRIMINAL PROVISIONS IN FEDERAL ENVIRONMENTAL STATUTES, A COMPILATION (Cong. Res. Serv. 1989).

69. CAL. HEALTH & SAFETY CODE §§25189.5-25192 (Deering 1988 & Supp. 1994). Note also the California Corporate Criminal Act of 1989, which provides criminal liability for a corporation or business manager who (1) has actual knowledge of a serious concealed danger subject to regulatory authority and associated with a product or business practice and (2) knowingly fails to provide notice thereof to the California Occupational Safety and Health Administration and affected employees in writing, unless the corporation or manager knows that such notices already have been given. The notices must be given immediately if there is an imminent risk, otherwise within 15 days, unless the condition is abated within those time frames. CAL. PENAL CODE §387 (West 1990) (§387 was added by A.B. No. 2249 §2, 1990 Cal. Adv. Legis. Serv. 166 (Deering)).

70. CAL. HEALTH & SAFETY CODE §25190 (Deering 1988 & Supp. 1994).

71. 35 PA. CONS. STAT. ANN. §6018.606(i) (West 1990).

72. N.J. STAT. ANN. §2C:17-2(a)(1) (West 1995). Thanks to Gerald Krovatin of the law firm of Lowenstein, Sandler, Kohl, Fisher & Boylan in Roseland, New Jersey, who supplied the material in notes 72-73.

73. *See* N.J. STAT. ANN. §2C:17-2(a)(2). A person who has been convicted of a second-degree offense in New Jersey faces a presumption in favor of incarceration for a term of 7 years, which can be lowered to a minimum of 5 years or raised to a

maximum of 10 years, depending on the court's evaluation of aggravating and mitigating factors. *Id.* §2C:44-1(d). The presumption in favor of incarceration applies unless the sentencing court "is of the opinion that the [defendant's] imprisonment would be a serious injustice which overrides the need to deter such conduct by others." *Id.* The New Jersey Supreme Court has indicated that this language must be given very limited reading. *See, e.g.,* State v. Roth, 471 A.2d 370 (N.J. 1984).

74. Judson W. Starr & Thomas J. Kelly Jr., *Environmental Crimes and the Sentencing Guidelines: The Time Has Come and It Is Hard Time,* 20 ELR 10096, 10104 (Mar. 1990).

75. A.B.A. Sec. Nat. Resources, Energy & Envtl. L., 1990 The Year in Review 213-14 (1991) [hereinafter The Year in Review].

76. Starr & Kelly, *supra* note 74, at 10104.

77. Stephen R. McAllister, *Trial of the Criminal Environmental Case: Defense Point of View, in* Criminal Enforcement of Environmental Laws 252 (A.L.I./A.B.A. 1990) (citing United States v. Protex Indus., Inc., No. 87-CR-115 (D. Colo. Mar. 4, 1988), *aff'd,* 874 F.2d 740, 19 ELR 21061 (10th Cir. 1989)). *See generally* M. Diane Barber, *Fair Warning: The Deterioration of Scienter Under Environmental Criminal Statutes,* 26 Loy. L.A. L. Rev. 105 (1992); G. Nelson Smith III, *No Longer Just a Cost of Doing Business: Criminal Liability of Corporate Officials for Violations of the Clean Water Act and the Resource Conservation and Recovery Act,* 53 La. L. Rev. 119 (1992).

78. 33 U.S.C. §§1251-1387, ELR Stat. FWPCA §§101-607 (Federal Water Pollution Control Act).

79. United States v. Kelley Tech. Coatings, Inc., 157 F.3d 432, 29 ELR 20022 (6th Cir. 1998); United States v. Hopkins, 53 F.3d 533, 25 ELR 21178 (2d Cir. 1995), *cert. denied,* 116 S. Ct. 773 (1996); United States v. Weitzenhoff, 35 F.3d 1275, 24 ELR 21504 (9th Cir. 1994), *cert. denied,* 115 S. Ct. 939 (1995); United States v. Baytank (Houston), Inc., 934 F.2d 599, 613, 21 ELR 21101 (5th Cir. 1991); United States v. Brittain, 931 F.2d 1413, 1419, 21 ELR 21092 (10th Cir. 1991); United States v. Hayes Int'l Corp., 786 F.2d 1499, 1503, 16 ELR 20717 (11th Cir. 1986).

The government has also filed several motions in limine since these cases to exclude evidence of a defendant's reasonable belief that conduct was permissible and of a lack of any actual harm. For example, on October 11, 1994, the United States filed such a motion in United States v. Mooney, CR No.-S-93-302 FL (D. Cal.). In a case pending in the Supreme Court of California, People v. General Motors Corp., No. S0 53729 (Cal. July 24, 1996), many industrial organizations and companies submitted a letter on June 5, 1996, noting that

> [t]he court of appeal ruled that a discharge of wastewater in January 1993 from the 'chiller plant' at a GM automobile assembly facility in Van Nuys was a criminal violation of the California Fish & Game Code. The court of appeal[s] reached that conclusion even though the discharge was fully authorized by GM's state-issued (Regional Water Quality Control Board) National Pollutant Discharge Elimination Sys-

tem (NPDES) permit, and despite careful evaluation and approval of
GM's permit application by numerous instrumentalities of the State of
California, including the Fish & Game Department and several agen-
cies of the City and County of Los Angeles.

80. *See* United States v. Park, 421 U.S. 658 (1975); United States v. Dotterweich,
320 U.S. 277 (1943), *cited in* George Van Cleve, *The Changing Intersection of Environmental Auditing, Environmental Law and Enforcement Policy*, 12 CARDOZO
L. REV. 1215, 1227 n.36 (1991). *See also* David D. Aufhauser, *Crime and Punishment*, SONREEL NEWS (A.B.A. Sec. Nat. Resources, Energy & Envtl. L., Chi-
cago, Ill.), Jan./Feb. 1992. For a detailed discussion of the entire public welfare issue and criminal law issues generally, see Riesel, *supra* note 41; Barber, *supra* note
77; and Smith, *supra* note 77.

81. *Hayes*, 786 F.2d at 1503. *See* United States v. Hansen, 262 F. 3d 1217 (11th Cir.
2001) in which the Eleventh Circuit interpreted the "knowing endangerment" provision as applying if the defendant had knowledge of the "general hazardous character" of the chemical and knew that the chemical had the "potential to be harmful"
to others. See discussion in Environmental Crimes and Enforcement, *2001 Annual
Report, in* A.B.A. SECTION OF ENVIRONMENT, ENERGY & RESOURCES LAW, 2001
THE YEAR IN REVIEW 239 (2001).

82. *Baytank*, 934 F.2d at 613. *Baytank* specifically distinguishes United States v.
Johnson & Towers, Inc., 741 F.2d 662, 14 ELR 20634 (3d Cir. 1984), which does
appear to require specific knowledge of a regulation and appears to reject the public
welfare concept. *Id.* at 669 (specific knowledge of statute required, rejects public
welfare concept); 934 F.2d at 613 (distinguishing *Johnson & Towers*). In United
States v. Hoflin, 880 F.2d 1033, 1037-38, 19 ELR 21140 (9th Cir. 1989), the Ninth
Circuit also declined to follow standard set forth in *Johnson & Towers. But see
Weitzenhoff*, 35 F.3d at 1275, *cert. denied*, 115 S. Ct. at 939 (government need only
prove that defendants knowingly discharged a pollutant, not that defendants knew
that their acts violated their discharge permit or the FWPCA).

In United States v. Dean, 969 F.2d 796, 22 ELR 21296 (6th Cir. 1992), the Sixth
Circuit affirmed the conviction of the manager of a Tennessee metal-plating plant
for four RCRA violations and conspiracy to violate RCRA. The court said it could
see no basis on the face of the Act to require knowledge of the permit requirement as
an element of the crime. The court also observed that the force of RCRA's statutory
scheme would be significantly weakened if anyone who claimed ignorance of the
permit requirement was exempt from prosecution. *Id.*

Note that in the context of the CWA, "knowing endangerment" refers to endangerment of U.S. waters. Although certain conduct "was utterly reprehensible" in
endangering employees, according to the court, the conduct did not meet the specific statutory requirement of endangering U.S. waters. United States v. Borowski,
977 F.2d 27, 32, 33 ELR 20102, 20104 (1st Cir. 1992).

83. *Hopkins*, 53 F.3d at 533; *Weitzenhoff*, 35 F.3d at 1275.

84. United States v. Hanousek, 176 F.3d 1116, 29 ELR 21049 (9th Cir. 1999). The Court rejected Hanousek's petition for certiorari in January 2000. Hanousek v. United States, No. 99-323 (U.S. Jan. 10, 2000).

85. 101 F.3d 386, 390-91 (5th Cir. 1996).

86. 42 U.S.C. §7413(h), ELR STAT. CAA §113(h). Section 113(c)(6) of the CAA also provides that for enforcement purposes, the definition of "person" specifically includes "any responsible corporate officer." *Id.* §7413(c)(6), ELR STAT. CAA §113(c)(6).

87. *Id.* §7413(h), ELR STAT. CAA §113(h).

88. *See, e.g.,* 42 U.S.C. §7413(c)(5)(B), ELR STAT. CAA §113(c)(5)(B); Frank Friedman, *Environmental Management for the Future: Environmental Auditing Is Not Enough*, 12 CARDOZO L. REV. 1314, 1324-25 (1991); *see also* United States v. Lanza, 790 F.2d 1015, 1021-22 (2d Cir.), *cert. denied*, 479 U.S. 861 (1986) (upholding charge of conscious avoidance of knowledge in fraud case, even though underlying substantive offense was not charged); United States v. Rothrock, 806 F.2d 318, 323 (1st Cir. 1986) ("The purpose of the willful blindness theory is to impose criminal liability on people who, recognizing the likelihood of wrongdoing, nonetheless consciously refuse to take basic investigatory steps."); Illinois EPA v. Citizens Utils. Co., No. 79-142 (Ill. Pollution Control Bd. Jan. 12, 1984) (holding that knowledge element is fulfilled when major equipment and operational failures are due to operator's ignorance of plant design and failure to investigate).

89. Margaret Graham Tebo, *Guilty by Reason of Title*, ABA J., May 2000, at 44-45.

90. *Id.* at 47.

91. Ridgway M. Hall Jr., Remarks at the A.L.I./A.B.A. Conference (Feb. 14, 1992), *quoted in Criminal Enforcement Action No Longer Limited, supra* note 58, at 2406. *See* Moore et al., *Why Risk Criminal Charges by Performing Environmental Audits?*, 6 Toxics L. Rep. (BNA) 503 (Sept. 18, 1991).

92. Van Cleve, *supra* note 80, at 1226-27 (referencing United States v. Dotterweich, 320 U.S. 277 (1943); United States v. International Minerals & Chem. Corp., 402 U.S. 558 (1971); United States v. Johnson & Towers, Inc., 741 F.2d 662, 14 ELR 20634 (3d Cir. 1984)).

93. F. Henry Habicht II, *The Federal Perspective on Environmental Criminal Enforcement*, 17 ELR 10478, 10480 (Dec. 1987).

94. Keith A. Onsdorff & James M. Mesnard, *The Responsible Corporate Officer Doctrine in RCRA Criminal Enforcement: What You Don't Know Can Hurt You*, 22 ELR 10099, 10100 (Feb. 1992).

95. Starr & Kelly, *supra* note 74, at 10101-04.

96. 912 F.2d 741, 21 ELR 20051 (4th Cir. 1990).

97. THE YEAR IN REVIEW, *supra* note 75, at 215; United States v. Dee, 912 F.2d at 745-46, 21 ELR at 20053.

98. State v. Stirnkorb, No. 85-CR-5240B (C.P. Clermont County May 15, 1989), *aff'd*, 580 N.E.2d 69 (Ohio Ct. App. 1990), *motion for leave to appeal denied*, 568 N.E.2d 690 (Ohio 1991).

99. Aufhauser, *supra* note 80, at 2 (citing United States v. MacDonald & Watson Waste Oil Co., 933 F.2d 35, 21 ELR 21449 (1st Cir. 1991); United States v. White, 766 F. Supp. 873, 22 ELR 20050 (E.D. Wash. 1991) (government precluded from arguing that a responsible corporate officer is liable for acts that he "should have known of" in a RCRA prosecution)). *See also* Onsdorff & Mesnard, *supra* note 94, at 10104. Charles A. DeMonaco, Assistant Chief of the Environmental Crimes Section of the DOJ's Environment and Natural Resources Division, has stated that the DOJ intends to follow the approach of the First Circuit in *McDonald & Watson*. This approach requires that before an individual can be found guilty, there must be proof that he or she had actual knowledge of the criminal wrongdoing. However, he said, "managers cannot defend their inaction by saying that they did not know about the non-compliance." *Criminal Enforcement Action No Longer Limited*, *supra* note 58, at 2407.

100. 242 F.3d 528, 31 ELR 20509 (4th Cir. 2001).

101. *Id.* at 531 (emphasis added).

102. Giuffra, *Sentencing Corporations*, Am. Enterprise, May/June 1990, at 85.

103. U.S. Sentencing Commission, Federal Sentencing Guidelines ch. 2, pt. Q, *reprinted in* 18 U.S.C.A. (West 1996) [hereinafter Guidelines].

104. Starr & Kelly, *supra* note 74, at 10096. For a discussion of the use of the guidelines in a specific case involving individual sentencing for "six counts of knowingly dredging a canal and discharging fill materials into wetlands in violation of the Clean Water Act," see McGregor, *Sentencing Program Permits Flexibility*, Hazmat, Nov. 1992, at 61.

105. *See* Steven Solow, *Environmental Management Systems: Not Just for Environmental Compliance Anymore*, Executive Couns., Oct. 2004, at 39. The following on the Sentencing Guidelines revisions are primarily excerpted from that article with permission of the author.

106. *See infra* discussion in Chapter 6.

107. *See* United States v. Booker, No. 04-104, 2005 WL 50108 (U.S. Jan. 12, 2005), and United States v. Fanfan, No. 04-105, 2005 WL 50108 (Jan. 12, 2005).

108. *U.S. Supreme Court Holds Sentencing Guidelines Advisory, Not Mandatory*, Hunton & Williams Client Alert (Jan. 2005), *available at* http:// www.hunton.com (last visited Aug. 22, 2005).

109. Van Cleve, *supra* note 80, at 1227 (citations omitted).

110. *Id.* at 1228.

111. *Id.*

112. *See* Environmental Auditing Policy Statement, 51 Fed. Reg. 25004 (July 9, 1986) (reproduced as Appendix B of this book), which is reaffirmed in a revised policy, 65 Fed. Reg. 19617 (Apr. 11, 2000) (reproduced as Appendix H of this book). EPA's auditing policies are more fully discussed in Chapter 6.

113. U.S. DOJ, FACTORS IN DECISIONS ON CRIMINAL PROSECUTIONS FOR ENVIRONMENTAL VIOLATIONS IN THE CONTEXT OF SIGNIFICANT VOLUNTARY COMPLIANCE OR DISCLOSURE EFFORTS BY THE VIOLATOR (July 1, 1991) (reproduced as Appendix C of this book).

114. *See* Memorandum from Larry D. Thompson, Deputy Attorney General, DOJ, to Heads of Department Components, United States Attorneys (Jan. 20, 2003) (available at http://www.usdoj.gov/dag/cftf/business_organizations.pdf).

115. *Id.*

116. *See Brownfields Cleanup and Redevelopment, at* http://www.epa.gov. *See also* Craig A. Werle, *All Appropriate Inquiry Standards Modify Environmental Due Diligence Procedurrees,* 15 ENVTL. L. IN N.Y. (Dec. 2004, at 245).

117. For an extensive discussion of the history of this issue and citations to various studies, see A.B.A., REPORT OF THE STANDING COMMITTEE ON ENVIRONMENTAL LAW (Aug. 1993) (supporting an Aug. 11, 1993, A.B.A. Resolution on Environmental Justice). *See also* Maryanne Lavelle & Marcia Coyle, *Unequal Protection: The Racial Divide in Environmental Law,* NAT'L L.J., Sept. 21, 1992, at S1. For a detailed analysis of environmental justice (broken down into distributive procedural corrective and social justice), see Robert R. Kuehn, *A Taxonomy of Environmental Justice,* 30 ELR 10681 (Sept. 2000); Dennis Binder et al., *A Survey of Federal Agency Response to President Clinton's Executive Order No. 12898 on Environmental Justice,* 31 ELR 11133 (Oct. 2001).

118. Robert W. Collin & Robin Morris Collin, *Sustainability and Environmental Justice: Is the Future Clean and Black?*, 31 ELR 10968, 10979 (Aug. 2001).

119. *Id.* at 10979.

120. *Id.* at 10977. In an effort to assist in determining if there is an issue that raises environmental justice concerns, the Environmental Law Institute has published a workbook entitled COMMUNITY ENVIRONMENTAL HEALTH ASSESSMENT WORKBOOK: A GUIDE TO EVALUATING YOUR COMMUNITY'S HEALTH AND FINDING WAYS TO IMPROVE IT (2001). In addition, the Institute has released a report which illustrates how citizens can use existing authorities within federal pollution laws to help ensure that communities of color and low-income communities do not bear a disproportionate share of pollution. The handbook is designed to introduce citizens to some of the ways in which environmental protection laws can be used to secure environmental justice. A CITIZEN'S GUIDE TO USING FEDERAL ENVIRONMENTAL LAWS TO SECURE ENVIRONMENTAL JUSTICE (Environmental Law Inst. 2002).

121. A portion of the following discussion on environmental justice is adapted from G. Nelson Smith III, *The Use of Title VI of the Civil Rights Act to Defend Corporations in Environmental Justice Actions: A Potential Wrong Searching for a Remedy,*

A.B.A. Sec. Nat. Resources, Energy & Envtl. L., San Francisco, Cal., May 1995. Copyright ©1995 by The American Bar Association. All rights reserved. Reprinted by permission.

122. *Id.* at 1.

123. Lavelle & Coyle, *supra* note 117.

124. Smith, *supra* note 121, at 1-2.

125. *Id.* at 2.

126. For a detailed discussion of environmental justice and land use regulation, see Craig Anthony (Tony) Arnold, *Land Use Regulation and Environmental Justice*, 30 ELR 10393 (June 2000). See also the discussion of nonconforming uses in Collin & Collin, *supra* note 118, at 10981.

127. *Id.* at 3-4.

128. See Chapter 10 for further information on dealing with citizen groups and the public. Efforts are underway to develop more real data. The U.S. General Accounting Office (GAO) has a study underway to provide data on whether industrial development in minority communities has in fact provided those areas with a substantial economic benefit. *GAO Expands Equity Study to Provide Key Data on Economic Debate*, ENVTL. POL'Y ALERT, Jan. 23, 2002, at 43. The Commission on Civil Rights is also involved in an investigation of potential environmental inequities in minority communities. *Civil Rights Panel Launches Environmental Equity Inquiry*, ENVTL. POL'Y ALERT, Jan. 23, 2002, at 42.

129. Smith, *supra* note 121, at 8-9.

130. Exec. Order No. 12898, ELR ADMIN. MAT. 45075.

131. J. Samantha Carson, *Emerging Trends in Environmental Justice*, Ballard, Spahr, Andrews & Ingorsoll, Environmental Issues Memorandum, 1-4 (Dec. 1997). *See also* Luke W. Cole, *"Wrong on the Facts, Wrong on the Law": Civil Rights Advocates Excoriate EPA's Most Recent Title VI Misstep*, 29 ELR 10775 (1999).

132. Carson, *supra* note 131, at 2. For discussion of some of the practical problems in brownfields development, see Christopher J. Daggett, *Brownfields: An Entrepreneur's Perspective*, 9 ENVTL. L. IN N.Y. 33 (1998).

133. U.S. EPA, Draft Revised Guidelines for Investigating Title VI Administrative Complaints, 65 Fed. Reg. 39649 (June 27, 2000). *See* Eileen Gauna, *EPA at 30: Fairness in Environmental Protection*, 31 ELR 10528 (May 2001); Bradford C. Mank, *The Draft Title VI Recipient and Revised Investigative Guidances: Too Much Discretion for EPA and a More Difficult Standard for Complainants?*, 30 ELR 11144 (Dec. 2000).

134. *EPA's New Civil Rights Guidance—The Controversy Continues*, ENVTL. F., Sept./Oct. 2000, at 46.

135. Robert Shinn, *Draft Creates Guessing Game for the States*, ENVTL. F., Sept./Oct. 2000, at 54.

136. *Id.* at 54.

137. *See* Sheila R. Foster, *Meeting the Environmental Justice Challenge: Evolving Norms in Environmental Decsionmaking*, 30 ELR 10992, 10993 (Nov. 2000).

138. NATIONAL ENVIRONMENTAL POLICY COMMISSION, REPORT TO THE CONGRESSIONAL BLACK CAUCUS & CONGRESSIONAL BLACK CAUCUS FOUNDATION ENVIRONMENTAL JUSTICE BRAINTRUST 12 (2001).

139. *Id.* at 13.

140. 121 S. Ct. 1511 (2001).

141. Jeffrey M. Gaba, South Camden *and Environmental Justice: Substance, Procedure, and Politics*, 31 ELR 11073, 11075 (Sept. 2001); Bradford C. Mank, South Camden Citizens in Action v. New Jersey Department of Environmental Protection: *Will Section 1983 Save Title VI Disparate Impact Suits?*, 32 ELR 10454 (Apr. 2002).

142. South Camden Citizens in Action v. New Jersey Dep't of Envtl. Protection, 274 F.3d 771 (3d Cir. 2001).

143. Marcia Coyle, *N.J. Group Loses Appeal, Turns Eye to High Court*, NAT'L L.J., Jan. 28, 2002, at A8.

144. *Court Paves Way for New Jersey's First-Time Equity Rule*, ENVTL. POL'Y ALERT, Jan. 23, 2002, at 42. On February 18, 2004, the state issued Executive Order No. 96, Statewide Environmental Justice Policy which "serves as a call to action for all government agencies to consider urban-environmental and public-health concerns and to increase public participation in the environmental decision-making process. Under the Executive Order, the Environmental Justice Task Force provides the collaborative mechanism necessary to effectively address environmental justice concerns." *See State of New Jersey Environmental Justice Task Force, at* http://www.nj.gov/ejtaskforce/ (last visited Aug. 22, 2005).

145. *Whitman Faces Clash Between Equity, Market Approach in 2002*, ENVTL. POL'Y ALERT, Jan. 9, 2002, at 30, 31.

146. Ken Mounger, *Permitting a Major Grassroots Petrochemical Plant Which Includes an IEM Chlor-Alkali Plant, in* ANNUAL CHLORINE INSTITUTE SEMINAR, Mar. 1995, at 6.

147. *Id.*

148. *See* E. Lynn Grayson & Stephen A.K. Palmer, *The Brownfield Phenomenon: An Analysis of Environmental Economic and Community Concerns*, 7 ELR 10337 (July 1995).

149. Pub. L. No. 105-34, 111 Stat. 788 (codified as amended in scattered sections of 26 U.S.C.).

150. Sven-Erik Kaiser & Elizabeth Bennett, *The Federal Role in Financing Brownfield Revitalization, in* Financing Brownfield Reuset 53, 55 (Northeast-Midwest Institute Working Paper No. 10, 1999). For a detailed analysis, see Adam

Gropper, *Getting the Green Back: Remediating Brownfields Under Internal Revenue Code §198*, 5 ENVTL. LAW. 281 (Sept. 1998)

151. 60 Fed. Reg. 34793 (July 3, 1995).

152. ENVTL. LAW INST., AN ANALYSIS OF STATE SUPERFUND PROGRAMS: 50-STATE STUDY, 1997 UPDATE (1998).

153. These are described in detail in Ned Abelson & Maura McCaffery, *Brownfields: Recent Massachusetts and Federal Developments*, 26 Env't Rep. (BNA) 2152, 2153 (Mar. 15, 1996).

154. Pub. L. No. 107-118.

155. *See* Brownfields Cleanup and Redevelopment, at http://www.epa.gov. *See* Craig A. Werle, *All Appropriate Inquiry Standards Modify Environmental Due Diligence Procedures*, 15 ENVTL. L. IN N.Y. 245 (2004).

156. *EPA Proposal Likely to Become New Standard For Environmental Due Diligence*, WolfBlock Environmental & Land Use Alert, Winter 2004-2005, at 1. *See also* Heather P. Behnke et al, *Environmental Transactions and Brownfields 2004 Annual Report, in* THE YEAR IN REVIEW 2004, ABA SEC. OF ENV'T, ENERGY & RESOURCES L. (2005).

157. Behnke, *supra* at 65.

158. Dale A. Guariglia, *The Small Business Liability Relief and Brownfields Revitalization Act: Real Relief or Prolonged Pain?*, 32 ELR 10505 (Apr. 2002).

159. For example, a staff member with the Natural Resources Defense Council, Inc. pushed construction of a paper recycling plant as a redevelopment project in the South Bronx. The plant will bring 2,200 construction jobs and 600 permanent jobs to the area. Yet, a local activist almost torpedoed the project rather than let another group get credit for it. *If You Can Make It Here*, ENV'T, HEALTH & SAFETY MGMT., Aug. 26, 1996, at 6.

160. *See* ENVTL. LAW INST., A GUIDEBOOK FOR BROWNFIELD PROPERTY OWNERS (1999). *See also* Ann S. Andrew, *Brownfield Redevelopment: A State Led Reform of Superfund Liability*, 10 NAT. RESOURCES & ENV'T 27 (1996); R. Timothy Weston, *Contaminated and Industrial Properties—Challenges and Opportunities in Structuring Business Transactions* & Nancy J. Marcel, *EPA Efforts to Facilitate the Transfer and Reuse of Contaminated Property*, 25th Annual Conference, A.B.A. Sec. Nat. Resources, Energy & Envtl. L., Keystone, Colo., Mar. 21-24, 1996. For an excellent discussion of legislation relating to brownfields and deed restrictions, see Elizabeth G. Geltman, *Recycling Land: Encouraging the Redevelopment of Contaminated Property*, 10 NAT. RESOURCES & ENV'T 3 (1996). *See also* Paul C. Nightingale, *Negotiating Contracts for the Purchase and Sale of Contaminated Property*, 10 NAT. RESOURCES & ENV'T 11 (1996); Karen M. Wardzinski, *Prospective Purchaser Agreements Under EPA's New Guidance*, 10 NAT. RESOURCES & ENV'T 24 (1996).

161. Bradley C. Bobertz, *Transferring the Blame*, ENVTL. F., Jan./Feb. 1996, at 22, 24 (emphasis in original).

162. *Id.*

163. *Id.* at 23.

Chapter 3:
Environmental Management in the 21st Century

Throughout the 1980s and 1990s, corporate management became generally more aware that environmental issues and potential regulatory constraints required a new approach. Businesses recognized that environmental laws are largely the product of ideas and social forces whose time had come. Sophisticated businesspeople learned that enforcement of these laws is important both as a matter of public policy and to prevent competitive advantage for those who ignore the law. They also recognized that the public and the environment cannot be asked to bear all the risks associated with scientific uncertainty and that industry sometimes must accept controls before all of the scientific evidence is conclusive. The public is their customer, and they have to satisfy their customer even when they think the customer is wrong.

Acceptance of the reality of environmental costs, liabilities, and risks led to the development and increasing importance of the field of environmental management. Until 1988, there were no environmental management courses in business schools. Now many business schools incorporate "environmental business" courses into their curricula, as well as consider other social impact issues.[1] There is much work in this area as schools, organizations, and businesses in the United States and abroad seek ways to develop and implement strong environmental management programs.

Today companies are working to address environmental issues cost effectively and in a way that makes sense. The costs of environmental programs are enormous; it is essential that government agencies and companies work together to make sure that the money is well spent. There are also a variety of management techniques that companies can use to improve their environmental performance and control costs. These include synthesis of environmental and business goals; Total Quality Management; careful, well-planned downsizing or reengineering; and use of analytical techniques such as life-cycle analysis, sustainable manufacturing, and full cost accounting to improve environmental performance. Sophistication in environmental management has grown at the international level, and various international entities have developed programs and initiatives to assist environmental managers and businesses in making changes and identifying opportunities to further improve environmental performance.

This chapter discusses the key issues of concern for environmental managers and suggests a variety of techniques that managers and companies can use to address them.

The Cost of Environmental Protection

The cost of complying with our current tangle of federal, state, and local environmental laws is staggering. Much of the capital necessary to make technological changes mandated by environmental standards throughout the 1970s has been or soon will be expended. Issues surrounding compliance with existing environmental regulations, including those relating to previous hazardous waste disposal, by now should be identified, and action plans should be underway. Even so, the 1990 CAA Amendments, the next round of FWPCA permitting, and resolution of other issues will still require substantial effort as we seek to address even more difficult areas of environmental protection.[2]

Although cost estimates must be read with caution,[3] total annual pollution control costs in the United States were expected in 1992 to reach $250 billion by the year 2000.[4] EPA estimated that total annual environmental expenditures in the United States rose from $74 billion in 1988 to $114 billion in 1992.[5] From 1985 to 1987, total capital investment for environmental benefits was between $25 to $35 billion per year, and rose to between $43 and $46 billion per year between 1988 and 1992.[6] EPA's estimate of the cost of complying with environmental regulations in 1997 was $200 billion.[7] Some companies[8] and industries[9] are hit particularly hard by environmental requirements. Preliminary figures from an American Petroleum Institute survey shows that in 1997 the industry spent about $8.1 billion in the United States, about the same as in 1996. This is about one-fourth the net income of the top 200 oil and gas companies at that time.[10] And according to Forbes magazine, every American pays, on average, about $450 more annually in taxes and higher prices as a result of pollution controls.[11] For additional discussion of costs, see Chapter 2.

In 1972, roughly 61 percent of total U.S. expenditure on the environment was borne by the private sector. EPA posits that the figure increased to about 63 percent in 1992. Many people outside EPA believe these estimates are very low, particularly considering the projected costs of the CAA Amendments of 1990. For example, some estimate that the cost of the Act's operating permit regulations alone will be in excess of $3 billion per year when fully implemented, far higher than government estimates. This number, like any other number related to this Act, is difficult to verify and the numbers on general costs depend on who is making the claim. Some try to argue that the benefit is greater than the costs.[12] In any event, as a practical matter, compliance with the Clean Air Act is usually a major function for a facility EHS staff person and also entails significant work at corporate headquarters.

In large part, the increased costs of pollution control can be traced to regulations designed to reduce the last increments of pollution. Many of the most cost-effective steps to control pollution have already been taken. As efforts continue to control smaller and smaller amounts of air and water pollution, costs generally increase. It is always easier and cheaper to control the first 90 percent than the last 10 percent.

Costs are also increasing as tightened environmental laws eliminate important "safety valves" that served to mitigate the economic damage caused by environmental controls. Expansion of RCRA's programs and definitions, addition of new FWPCA[13] requirements, and changes in the CAA regulatory system may significantly reduce flexibility and increase environmental costs.

For example, the 1990 CAA Amendments tightened the regulation of hazardous air pollutants both by increasing the number of regulated chemicals and by setting a low threshold for what is a "major source." Amendments to the Act's nonattainment program, which applies in areas of the country that have missed deadlines for meeting national standards for concentrations of certain pollutants in ambient air, expanded the geographic scope of the nonattainment controls. The amendments also made the nonattainment program more stringent by requiring that more emission reductions from existing sources offset the emission increases that invariably result from new or expanded economic activity. In the past, a plant that had to make changes quickly could do so either because its emissions were not federally regulated (as was the case with many air toxics) or because it could avoid delay by "netting," i.e., making reductions that kept its net emissions increase to less than the regulatory threshold. The 1990 law provides far fewer opportunities for facilities to find ways to stay in compliance even if they can neither tolerate delay nor accommodate new controls triggered by changes.

Because of the high costs of environmental controls, it is essential that we set priorities and ensure that the costs do not exceed the benefits received. Many environmental laws today employ a sort of averaging; that is, to ensure that excess risks (however defined in the particular statute) are eliminated, the law accepts overregulation in some cases. For example, RCRA imposes similar regulatory standards on entire categories of facilities and chemicals, although individual facilities vary dramatically in the relative degrees of risk they pose. The CAA applies "maximum available control technology" to all major sources, even if it can be shown that the risk posed by a particular source is negligible. Thus, the process we see today inevitably will make "mistakes" in particular cases. For those cases, the result is economic damage unaccompanied by benefit.

In some instances, distorted priorities result in high expenditures in low-risk situations while lower cost steps could result in even greater net benefits. The Harvard Group on Risk Management Reform commented on this phenomenon in the excerpt reproduced in Figure 3-1.

Figure 3-1
Excerpt from *Special Report, Reform of Risk Regulation:*
Achieving More Protection at Less Cost and Other Comments on Risk

More regulatory attention is given to the hazards of eating tiny amounts of pesticide residues on fruits and vegetables than to the health of farmworkers and pesticide applicators, who incur larger exposures to pesticides. More generally, low levels of exposure to animal carcinogens in the environment receive greater regulatory priority than much higher levels of exposure to carcinogens in the workplace. Government devotes more effort regulating outdoor air than indoor air, even though people spend more time indoors and concentrations of pollutants are greater indoors. The remote possibility of children ingesting lead in soil at outdoor industrial waste sites is a major concern in EPA's Superfund program while the lead in house dust now being ingested by millions of children is only beginning to be addressed. The recent health concerns about the presence of asbestos in school buildings, a relatively minor and speculative hazard to children, have received a disproportionate share of governmental attention compared to more serious dangers in schools such as the risk of contracting AIDS from intravenous drug use, unprotected sexual behavior and traumatic injury from accidents and violence. Some type of counterargument can be made about each of these examples but these are indications that regulatory priorities can be improved.

If priorities were better set, risk regulation could be made more protective, without increasing the overall cost of regulation. David L. Mulliken, Jennifer D. Zambone, and Christine G. Rolph have recently noted the implications to world public health of the bans and restrictions on DDT.[14]

A recent study examined 200 programs designed to advance human health in the United States. Some highly cost-effective programs were not fully implemented (e.g., childhood immunization against mumps, measles and rubella) while other highly cost-ineffective programs were widely implemented (e.g., control of low-level exposures to chemicals emitted into the air from factories). The study estimated that a reallocation of resources to more cost-effective programs could save an additional 60,000 lives per year at no increased cost to taxpayers or the private sector. Alternatively, the country could save the same number of lives we are currently saving but do so at a $31 billion annual saving to taxpayers and the private sector.[15]

Weighing risks and setting priorities is a formidable task. Many scientific and regulatory uncertainties and disagreements remain, particularly in areas such as carcinogenic risk assessment.[16] New areas of concern arise,[17] and many older disputes, such as the global-climate-change controversy, are still hotly debated and political.[18] A study by Resources For The Future recognizes these uncertainties.

We conclude that the pollution control regulatory system has deep and fundamental flaws. There is a massive dearth of scientific knowledge and data. The system's priorities are wrong, it is ineffective in dealing with many current problems, and is inefficient and excessively intrusive. Most of the participants are aware of those defects.[19]

There are many proposals to promote regulatory reform, including greater use of risk assessment and cost-benefit analysis in EPA decisionmaking.[20] Such assessments and analyses are needed to avoid making matters even worse. Professor Jonathan Weiner of Duke Law School makes the following observation.

From a safety or risk perspective, the presumption in favor of preserving nature untainted may even be counterproductive. It may have led our food safety laws to expose us to greater cancer risks from natural substances than from synthetic ones and to discourage consumption of natural foods that provide great health benefits in order to avoid much smaller risks from chemical contaminants. It may also have led our water safety laws to expose us to greater infection hazards than the hazards posed by chemicals added to kill the infectious microbes.[21]

Professor Weiner notes that Peru's decision to stop chlorinating drinking water because of the perceived carcinogenic risk of chlorinating compounds may have been a factor in helping to unleash a cholera epidemic that killed thousands.[22] Ruth Greenspan Bell and James Wilson further observe that

> [m]ore importantly, the information derived from risk assessment can be illusory without explicit incorporation of the institutional realities within which the decisionmakers work. For example in the early 1990s, the Peruvian government received warnings about the possible cancer hazard posed by chlorinated drinking water. The government stopped chlorinating the water and a cholera epidemic ensued. Given the existing infrastructure in that country, it was a huge mistake to have tinkered with what was clearly working.[23]

Trying to obtain meaningful figures on the value and cost of environmental regulations is difficult, unless you know the assumptions. It makes a major difference, for example, if the benefits are discounted to present value, a standard economic concept. "Discounting attempts to translate the future effects of investments, such as environmental protection efforts, to present terms."[24] Some commentators are strongly opposed to the use of discounting.[25] There is now much interest in improving the flexibility and cost effectiveness of U.S. environmental controls. The President's Council on Sustainable Development, a group that represented a spectrum of interests and was intended to create a broad vision of the future, reported that "certain goals, approaches, and strategies . . . could result in more environmental protection, less economic cost, and . . . greater opportunity for the poor and disadvantaged."[26] The Council recommended that "federal and state environmental regulatory agencies . . . accelerate efforts to identify and act on opportunities to reduce the economic cost of current environmental regulatory standards. . . ."[27] It also recommended development of more cost-effective environmental management systems based on performance, flexibility, and accountability, noting that "[r]egulation . . . has frequently focused attention on cleanup and control remedies rather than on product or process redesign to prevent pollution."[28]

An initiative called "The Enterprise for the Environment," was described as "a broad based effort assembled to develop a comprehensive set of recommendations for the systematic reform of EPA's statutory authority."[29] The National Academy of Public Administration joined with William D. Ruckelshaus, then-Chairman of Browning Ferris Industries and former EPA Administrator, to seek "to provide EPA with a coherent, well-defined statutory mission and flexibility to carry it out," leading to a cleaner environment at a reasonable cost.[30] The Enterprise noted that "[w]hat we have now is a regulatory system that is perceived as rigid and inefficient, insensitive to the needs of local communities, and that fails to take advantage of new tools which maximize environmental benefits while reducing costs."[31] While the Enterprise failed to reach a consensus on reform, its approach has helped spur a growing "second generation" movement that seems to be supported by the Bush Administration.

Some advocate radical changes in environmental controls. One alternative to the present system would be for each company to negotiate a 10-year plan, setting ambitious performance goals that exceed current environmental standards.[32] In return, companies would be freed from the requirement to use particular methods and movement of the "goal posts" for 10 years.[33] The proponents of this alternative recognize that independent auditors might be required and community involvement would be essential. They recommend that EPA and the participating states set up a management advisory board to keep the "program sharply focused, to ensure its integrity and to recruit new industries and players."[34] (For a further discussion of regulatory reform initiatives, see this chapter under The Challenge of Regulatory Reform.)

A new statute, the Small Business Regulatory Enforcement Fairness Act, may have a significant impact, particularly Subtitle D amending the Regulatory Flexibility Act. Although nominally applied to small business, it requires that rules, including executive orders and statements of policy, be submitted to Congress before promulgation and requires that the General Accounting Office write a report on any major rule with an impact of over $100 million.

Unless steps are taken to ensure that environmental benefits outweigh the costs of controls, the coming years may seriously undermine environmental improvement. As we (meaning all of us whose job is regulation of the environment) tighten the laws, we increase society's ability to achieve the environmental goals it has set. The price of meeting these goals is that there will be a certain amount of economic damage. The issue is whether or not the damage will occur against a backdrop of regulatory behavior that is seen as prudent as well as effective. A regulatory system that produces seemingly arbitrary economic pain could be very harmful to any consensus we now have in favor of environmental controls. Accordingly, both the regulated community and EPA should seek and preserve opportunities to expand EPA and state discretion to accept solutions that address the practical needs of specific situations. The most fruitful area is not discretion that allows EPA or a state to relax substantive control requirements, but rather discretion that allows them to relax implementation elements that force delays or unnecessary complexity that is not clearly mandated by law.

Environmental Management Terms and Jargon

There is considerable confusion as to the meaning of "sustainable development." The standard definition assumes that present development must not compromise "the ability of future generations to meet their own needs."[35] A wide variety of management terms and concepts are discussed in this book. A detailed discussion of each one is beyond the scope of this volume. However, a short description of the key concepts and terms is useful at this point to provide a general understanding and also as a basis for understanding the scope of some definitions of sustainable development.

A recent discussion by William L. Thomas,[36] published by the Environmental Law Institute in an extensive volume which examines the issue of how the United States has promoted sustainable development since the Rio Summit of 1992, is the most comprehensive discussion of sustainable development as it relates to business. It is also extremely valuable for its analysis of the definition of recent business concepts (or jargon), including the following:

Voluntary Codes of Conduct

Codes of conduct formalize and unify a company's commitment to short-term and long-term environmental and sustainability goals. They can also be used as a model for a corporation's own policies. Some codes or standards include a comprehensive implementation and follow-up process while the guidelines serve as terms of reference and are most effective as a supplemental tool to inform and enhance current policies. Usually, these tools are issue-oriented and can apply to different industries and sectors.

Environmental Impact Minimization

□ *Life Cycle Assessment.* Life cycle assessment or analysis (LCA) is a technique used to evaluate the environmental impacts of products from extraction of raw materials to disposal.[37] The ISO 14000 series of environmental standards, e.g., ISO 14040, 14041, 14042, and 14043, divides an LCA into four main elements: (i) definition of goals and scope; (ii) an inventory quantifying the use of resources as well as the amount of waste and emissions created by the product over its entire life cycle; (iii) a life cycle impact assessment to evaluate the product's environmental impact; and (iv) an interpretive step, during which the results of the impact assessment are interpreted in light of the goals of the assessment.

Reducing Waste Through Product and Process Redesign

□ *Cleaner Production.* Cleaner production involves the continuous application of an integrated preventive environmental strategy to processes, products, and services to increase efficiency and reduce risks to humans and the environment. It includes the conservation of raw materials and energy, reduction of toxic raw materials, and reduction of the quantity and toxicity of all emissions and wastes.

☐ *Design for Environment.* Design for the environment (DfE), or "eco-design," is a technique organizations can use to incorporate environmental considerations into the design of processes, products, and services. By assessing environmental impacts over the whole life cycle at the developmental stage, firms can practice DfE to reduce material and energy intensity as well as emissions and waste. DfE also provides a framework through which to undertake eco-efficiency, pollution prevention, cleaner production, and other management efforts.

☐ *Eco-Efficiency.* The World Business Council for Sustainable Development (WBCSD) coined the term "eco-efficiency" to describe the delivery of competitively priced goods and services that satisfy human needs and bring quality of life, while progressively reducing ecological impacts and resource intensity throughout the life cycle, to a level at least in line with the earth's estimated carrying capacity. As even the WBCSD takes pains to point out, however, "eco-efficiency is not sufficient by itself because it integrates only two of sustainability's three elements, economics and ecology." Companies, and society, must take other steps to ensure the third pillar of sustainability, social progress, is addressed.

☐ *Factor 4/Factor 10.* In their 1997 book *Factor Four: Doubling Wealth, Halving Resource Use*, Ernst Ulrich von Weizsäcker, Amory Lovins, and Hunter Lovins argued for a radical increase in resource and energy efficiency, contending that humanity could live twice as well while at the same time consuming only half the resources consumed today. In their view, an increase in eco-efficiency by a factor of four should be made a global goal. The notion underlying Factor Four is that resource productivity can and should grow fourfold. Factor Ten is the idea that per capita material flows caused by OECD countries should be reduced by a factor of 10, rather than a factor of 4. Globally, proponents of Fact Ten proclaim, material turnover should be reduced by 50 percent, but because OECD countries are responsible for material flows five times as high as developing countries, and world population is inevitably increasing, the OECD should set more aggressive long-term targets.

☐ *Pollution Prevention.* Like the term "cleaner production" used commonly in other parts of the world, the term "pollution prevention" is often applied in the United States to describe the strategy of continuously reducing pollution and environmental impact through source reduction, i.e., eliminating waste within the process rather than at the end-of-pipe. EPA defines "pollution prevention" in terms of source reduction, i.e., preventing or reducing waste where it originates, at the source, including practices that conserve natural resources by reducing or eliminating pollutants through increased efficiency in the use of raw materials, energy, water and land.

Reducing Waste Through Operations and Purchasing

☐ *Extended Product, and Producer, Responsibility.* The principle of extended product responsibility states that actors along the product chain share responsibility for the life-cycle environmental impacts of the entire product system, including the upstream impacts inherent in selecting product materials, impacts from the manufacturers' production, and downstream impacts from the use and disposal of the products. As Gary Davis and Catherine Wilt explain, the concept is "to identify opportunities to prevent pollution and reduce resource and energy use in each stage of the product life cycle (or product chain) through changes in product design and process technology." Extended producer responsibility is a narrower concept that places responsibility on producers and focuses primarily on post-consumer waste disposal.

☐ *Industrial Ecology.* Industrial ecology is a field of science that examines local, regional, and global flows of materials and energy in products, processes, industrial sectors, and economies. As Reid Lifset observed upon the launch of the *Journal of Industrial Ecology* in 1997, industrial ecology "focuses on the role of industry in reducing environmental burdens throughout the product life cycle from the extraction of raw materials, to the production of goods, to the use of those goods, and to the management of the resulting wastes." The focus is on achieving closed loop systems in which wastes from one part of the industrial system are reused or become raw materials for other parts.

☐ *Product Stewardship.* Product stewardship is a principle that directs all actors in the life cycle of a product to minimize the impacts of that product on the environment. Under product stewardship, all participants in the product life cycle designers, suppliers, manufacturers, distributors, retailers, consumers, recyclers, and disposers share responsibility for the environmental effects of products.

☐ *Supply Chain Environmental Management.* The term "supply chain environmental management" encompasses a range of activities, such as screening suppliers for environmental performance, working collaboratively with suppliers on green design initiatives, and providing training or mentoring to build suppliers' environmental management capacity. It involves working with suppliers upstream in the supply chain as well as downstream distributors and consumers. This concept is also being applied to promote sustainability.

Systems for Identifying, Organizing, and Managing Environmental Impacts

☐ *Environmental Management Systems.* An environmental management system (EMS) is the part of a businesses' overall management system that includes organizational structure, planning activities, responsibilities, practices, procedures, processes, and resources for developing, implementing, achieving, reviewing, and maintaining an environmental policy.

☐ *The ISO 14001 EMS.* The International Organization for Standardization (ISO) developed *ISO 14001: 1996 Environmental Management Systems Specification With Guidance for Use* as a means to provide organizations of all sizes and types with the elements of an effective EMS. The core themes of ISO 14001, one of ISO's 14000 series of international environmental standards, are: (i) environmental policy; (ii) planning; (iii) implementation and operation; (iv) checking and corrective action; and (v) management review. The requirements of ISO 14001 may be objectively audited for certification and/or self-declaration purposes. There are now more than 80,000 registrations worldwide, of which 8,000 occurred in the United States, 800 in Canada, and 250 in Mexico.

☐ *Sustainability Management System.* As Andrea Spencer-Cooke pointed out, "environmental management systems (EMS) are limited in what they can achieve. If every company in the world adopted . . . ISO 14001 tomorrow, we might have a cleaner environment but we would still not be sustainable." The quest for sustainability will involve other tools, including management systems that encompass organizational structure, planning activities, responsibilities, practices, procedures, processes, and resources for developing, implementing, achieving, reviewing, and maintaining the company's sustainable development or sustainability policy.

☐ *Total Quality Environmental Management.* Total Quality Management is a systematic approach to constantly improving the quality of products, processes, and services of the organization. Its key elements are: a high level of senior management commitment; a strong customer and stakeholder focus, employee involvement, teamwork, and empowerment; data-driven decisionmaking; prevention; continuous improvement; a systematic approach; and a long-term focus. The Global Environmental Management Initiative (GEMI) coined the term Total Quality Environmental Management (TQEM) to describe the application of Total Quality Management practices to corporate environmental strategies. According to GEMI's *TQEM Primer*, four basic elements of TQEM provide guidelines for planning in business: (i) identify your customers: environmental quality is determined by customer preferences; (ii) continuous improvement: systematic, progressive improvement of environmental performance is necessary and desirable; (iii) do the job right the first time: recognize and eliminate environmental problems before they occur; and (iv) look at each part of environmental management as a system.

☐ *The Natural Step*. Founded by Swedish oncologist Karl-Henrik Robèrt in 1989, The Natural Step (TNS) is a nonprofit international organization that uses a scientifically based framework to help organizations and communities understand and move toward sustainability. The TNS framework is based on four "systems conditions" that describe the scientific underpinnings of all environmental problems and their solutions.

☐ *Environmental Accounting*. The term "environmental accounting" is susceptible to various definitions. It is used in connection with national income accounting, financial accounting, and internal business management accounting. The tool can be used to measure costs that directly impact a company's bottom line, as well as costs to individuals, society, and the environment resulting from a company's activities. There are three main types of environmental accounting: (i) national income accounting, which is a macro-economic calculation of national environmental costs for an external audience; (ii) financial accounting, which enables companies to estimate and report on environmental liabilities and financially material environmental costs to investors, lenders, and other external stakeholders; and (iii) management accounting, which is the process of identifying, collecting, and analyzing information principally for internal purposes, e.g., to integrate environmental costs into cost allocation, capital budgeting, and process/product design.

☐ *Auditing Systems*. An audit is a systematic, documented verification process of objectively obtaining and evaluating verifiable information, records or statements of fact to determine whether specified activities, events, conditions, management systems, or information about these matters conform with policies, practices or requirements, and communicating the results of this process to the client. Auditing techniques can be applied to environmental, and broader sustainable development, concerns.

☐ *Corporate Communication and Reporting Systems*. A corporate report is a tool that can be used to communicate the company's environmental, economic, and social performance. It can also be used to describe the organization's sustainability management system, corporate responsibility, and the implementation of voluntary initiatives and codes of conduct. In addition to satisfying stakeholders' demands, such reports can be used by the company as a vehicle for tracking progress and identifying internal strengths and weaknesses.

☐ *Global Reporting Initiative.* Convened in 1997 by the Coalition for Environmentally Responsible Economies in partnership with the United Nations Environment Programme, the Global Reporting Initiative (GRI) is an international, multi-stakeholder effort to create a common framework for economic, environmental, and social reporting that will elevate sustainability reporting practices worldwide to a level equivalent to financial reporting. More than 50 companies worldwide have volunteered to apply the *Sustainability Reporting Guidelines,* released by GRI in June 2000.

☐ *Triple Bottom Line Reporting.* John Elkington created the concept of the "triple bottom line" to describe the integrative measurement of a company's economic, environmental, and social performance. Triple bottom line reporting provides information to enable others to assess an organization's contributions to sustainable development. Indicators to increase accountability in these fields are gradually taking form.

Performance Evaluation Systems

☐ *Benchmarking.* Benchmarking is the process of comparing and measuring an organization's business process and performance against a given standard, e.g., "best-in-class," with the objective of promoting process or product improvement. Any process or business activity can be a candidate for benchmarking.

☐ *Environmental Performance Evaluation.* Environmental performance evaluation (EPE) is a process to facilitate management decisions regarding environmental performance by selecting environmental indicators, collecting and analyzing the data, and assessing the information against environmental performance criteria established by the organization's management. These techniques are being expanded to encompass broader questions of business sustainability.[38]

Sustainable Development

The following is an explanation of the derivation of the term "sustainable development," how it has developed, and what it has come to mean today.

The sustainable development model began its development in 1972, with the first major global conference on the environment, the United Nations Conference on the Human Environment, commonly known as the Stockholm Conference. The Conference led to the adoption and implementation of environmental laws in many countries and to a rapid increase in the number and variety of treaties concerning protection of the environment. It did not, however, suggest a way to reconcile development and environment.

The Stockholm Conference produced a declaration of 26 principles, known as the Stockholm Declaration, "to inspire and guide the peoples of the world in the preservation and enhancement of the human environment."[39] It also recognized the relationship between development and environment by stating among other things that "[e]conomic and social development is essential for insuring a favorable living and working environment for man" and that the "environmental policies of all States should enhance and not adversely affect the present or future development potential of developing nations."[40] During the 1980s, it became increasingly clear that development was imposing substantial economic and human costs. The United Nations (U.N.) General Assembly formed the World Commission on Environment and Development to inquire as to the relationship between development and the environment. The Commission was headed by the Norwegian Prime Minister, Gro Harlem Brundtland and the report which was issued in 1987, *Our Common Future*, is commonly known as the Brundtland Report. The Brundtland Commission found that the four basic components of development—peace and security, economic development, social development, and proper governance—require environmental protection.

Our Common Future raised concerns that, among other things, the "use of fossil fuels such as coal and oil for energy is adding greenhouse gases to the environment; threatening to raise sea levels and inundate coastal areas; and also threatening to affect agriculture, forests and ecosystems in significant but unknown ways."[41] Unsustainable agricultural practices and destruction of tropical rainforests are also condemned.[42] As John Dernbach notes, "developing countries' economies tend to depend on exports of agricultural products, timber, minerals and other natural resources. Such exportation contributes to environmental degradation as well as displacement of local people who have traditionally used those resources to meet their own needs."[43]

The sustainable development model is tied to both developing and developed nations. It is important to understand this assumption, as will be discussed subsequently, because of the ties to sustainable development of social policies affecting both developed and developing nations that are much broader and encompass a wider scope than what are traditionally considered environmental issues. Bill Blackburn, in an upcoming book to be published by the Environmental Law Institute, notes that the concept of "sustainable development" is "aimed at producing long-term global well being through the wise use and management of economic and natural resources, and through respect for people and other living things."[44] That book will have a variety of "explanations, practical strategies, checklists, forms, tips and reference information appendices" relating to sustainable development, "provides background information on the topic and its importance to business," and "proposes an approach for managing companies in an efficient, holistic way that takes into account important sustainability trends shaping our world of tomorrow."[45] Those issues, as identified by the Brundtland Commission, included peace and security, economic development, social development, and proper governance. As summarized by Professor Dernbach:

> The future of developed and developing countries are inseparable. Developed countries have tended to be primarily interested in global environmental problems, recognizing that their high level of economic development is responsible for most of these stresses. Developing countries have tended to be primarily interested in development because they see it as a way of escaping poverty. Yet conventional development uses additional raw material and energy, and creates pollution. It thus puts greater pressure on ecosystems and natural resources, the integrity of which humans require for survival. To the extent that ecological carrying capacity imposes barriers on development, developing countries appear to have only two choices, and both are unattractive. They can develop and thereby threaten ecosystems on which development depends, or they can refrain from developing and thus accept poverty. Sustainable development is intended to provide a third choice—for both developed and developing countries—that blends environmental protection and equity.[46]

Besides the definition of "sustainable development" previously cited, the Brundtland Commission also added that the concept contains within it two key precepts. These are "the concept of 'needs,' in particular the essential needs of the world's poor, to which overriding priority should be given; and the idea of limitations imposed by the state of technology and social organization on the environment's ability to meet present and future needs."[47]

The U.N. Conference on Environment and Development was held in 1992 in response to *Our Common Future*. This Conference, commonly known as the Rio Conference, represented a concerted effort to synthesize and integrate environment and development issues. "For the first time the international community endorsed sustainable development. Sustainable development changes the prior approach to development, which calls for peace and security, economic development, human rights and supportive national governance, by adding a fifth element, protection of the environment."[48] The delegates to that Conference approved what is known as the Rio Declaration on Environment and Development, a statement of 27 principles for sustainable development. In turn, out of the Rio Declaration, came Agenda 21, which is "a comprehensive international 'plan of action' or blueprint for sustainable development. It represents a broad and detailed commitment by nations around the world to take actions to further sustainable development."[49]

Agenda 21 is very comprehensive, with 40 chapters dealing with social and economic issues, conservation and management of natural resources, poverty, production and consumption patterns, combating deforestation and the role of nongovernmental organizations, among other subjects. "Agenda 21's comprehensiveness provides a way of determining whether a particular government is doing all it can to foster sustainable development."[50] Specific indicators of performance should be utilized to measure national progress in implementing Agenda 21.

Chapter 30 is, from a business standpoint, the key chapter in Agenda 21. As William Thomas notes:

> Although several other chapters of Agenda 21 bear on the conduct of business, we need not review them here. It should suffice to point out the plan, when read in its entirety, charts a course of action in five main areas: (i) global corporate environmental management; (ii) environmentally sound production and consumption patterns; (iii) risk and hazard mitigation; (iv) full cost accounting; and (v) international environmental support activities.[51]

There have been a variety of U.N. international conferences to examine progress on Agenda 21 issues. In 2002, a major U.N. conference (Rio + 10) was held in Johannesburg, South Africa, which was designed to look closely at progress. Many countries had a long wish-list of items to be added to the list of sustainable issues already addressed in Agenda 21. There is controversy whether there was much substantive progress toward either inclusion of new priorities or achievement of Agenda 21 objectives.

Much of the focus was on "targets and timetables" and commitments to achieve specific targets by specific dates. The Plan of Implementation is 54 pages long and focuses on poverty eradication. However, in many cases specific timetables, such as reduction in subsidies, were incapable of being negotiated.

The United States developed its own position and stuck with it at Johannesburg. Allan Hecht of the Council on Environmental Quality noted that sustainability is a variety of processes and the critical concern is getting the right institutions in place. He defines those processes as stewardship—the ability to help each other; innovations—everything within regulation and technology; science-based decisionmaking; federalism—government involvement at appropriate levels; and compliance—more flexibility to allow sustainability. On the international level, the U.S. government is promoting good governance. In other words, countries such as India and Mexico need to take responsibility for their own destiny.[52]

Jonathan Margolis from the State Department has emphasized that most countries do not view the environmental aspects of sustainability as the primary concern. Rather, the primary emphasis is upon poverty eradication. Money is the issue. This is particularly important for the G77, which views "poverty eradication" as sustainable development and which was the emphasis of the Plan of Implementation.

As can be seen from the above history, sustainable development encompasses far more than traditional environmental issues, reaching out to the entire panoply of social issues. This is the basis for the change in the emphasis on traditional environmental issues to a much broader value base as well as the genesis for such efforts as the Global Reporting Initiative (GRI), which is discussed below. " [S]ustainable development is based on an understanding that a nation's wealth is the sum of its economic, social and environmental assets."[53] Thus, the scope of Agenda 21 is extremely broad:

> Agenda 21 emphasizes the desirability of direct participation in governance by identifying important roles for women, youth, indigenous people and their communities, nongovernmental organizations and local authorities, workers and their trade unions, business and industry, the scientific and technological community and farmers.[54]

Among the most important principles articulated in the Rio Declaration and in Agenda 21 are "integrated decisionmaking, the polluter-pays principle, sustainable consumption and population levels, the precautionary principle, intergenerational equity, citizen participating, and common but differentiated responsibilities for developed and developing countries."[55]

John Dernbach's conclusion is that

> sustainable development is not going to be achieved in the United States and other developing countries with only the same kind of laws that currently exist. As important and necessary as these laws are, they do not reflect the range or depth of actions necessary for protection of the environment and natural resources, nor are they necessarily the most economically efficient

means of achieving the protection. The basic reality is that we have little, if any, present or historical experience with technologically advanced societies that are ecologically sustainable.[56]

Industry and Organizational Responses

Alan Horowitz of AstraZeneca suggests "potentially fruitful and meaningful roles for U.S. law, regulation, and policy in the pursuit of sustainable development" include:

- Risk-based regulations and enforcement;

- Performance-based alliances as pilots for "sustainability profile";

- Disclosure requirements.;

- Programs that simplify and promote risk-based cleanup and re-use of contaminated land; and

- "Sustainable" public leadership e.g., land use policies hat discourage sprawl, etc.[57]

Industry response to the increasing emphasis upon sustainable development has included life cycle analysis and sustainable manufacturing. The International Chamber of Commerce created a "charter for sustainable development" in 1990 as a guideline for the environmental management of world business. The many U.S. companies that are part of the Global Environmental Management Initiative, including a variety of oil and power companies such as Ashland, Duke Energy, Dupont, Elf Atochem North America (now Arkema), Koch Industries, Occidental Petroleum, Phillips Petroleum and Southern Company, have endorsed this charter. The Charter states that signatories should recognize environmental management as among the highest corporate priorities and should establish policies, programs, and practices for conducting operations in an environmentally sound manner.

In 1999, the World Economic Forum launched an initiative to develop an Environmental Sustainability Index (ESI). The ESI, released in 2001[58] reflects five broad components of environmental sustainability—environmental systems, environmental stresses and risks, human vulnerability to environmental impacts, social and institutional capacity to response to environmental challenges and contributions to global stewardship.[59] "The ESI project seeks to gauge the ability of countries across the world to meet the environmental needs of their people and to achieve environmentally sustainable development. The EIS assesses environmental circumstances, results, and capacities across 222 core 'indicators' based on 67 underlying variable, each supported by an independent database."[60] The utilization of broad indicators shows the United States at a high level of sustainability.[61] This approach deals with the "lack of analytic rigor [that] has made the environmental field seem 'soft' and has allowed critics to dismiss the seriousness of pollution control and natural resource management issues."[62] A "strong factual foundation, underpinned by carefully constructed indicators and systematic analysis, should help to clarify the challenges, focus attention and set priorities. More specifically, indicator-based policymaking will facilitate the identification of programs that are succeeding (and those that are failing), thus giving policymakers a capacity for more decisive policy judgments and course corrections."[63]

Companies can subscribe to the philosophy of sustainable development without being perfect. The WBCSD, "a coalition of 140 companies united by a shared commitment to sustainable development," has a program looking toward a sustainable cement industry.[64] I included the Brundtland language in the Elf Atochem Health, Environment, and Safety policy, stating that the company would "endeavor to conduct our activities in a manner which protects the well-being of our employees, the public, and the environment and promotes environmentally sustainable manufacturing which meets the needs of the present without compromising the ability of future generations to meet their own needs (sustainable development)." This is the most common definition but "[o]ne researcher found over 60 definitions of the term [used] by various government and non-governmental organizations."[65] Reading some of the "green" reports issued by various businesses, it would be easy to believe that sustainable development is becoming institutionalized. But as Richard MacLean, an environmental consultant, notes, "[d]o not confuse all the talk and anecdotal case studies as evidence of companies with a comprehensive and fully integrated action plan. Sustainability as a business issue is still largely in play."[66]

> The buzzwords abound: sustainable development, natural capitalism, triple bottom line, pollution prevention, life cycle assessment, and so on. When you cut through all the jargon, it boils down to this: *responsible resource strategies.* Visionary business executives are just beginning to see the implication of the transition form managing emissions to the broader question of who gets to use what slice of the earth's (pie) crust and when.[67]

In the past, "resources" were viewed by EHS professionals in the very narrow context of raw materials and wastes within the plant property lines. Today, this concept includes the entire supply chain, from basic raw material up to an including finished products *and* their eventual recycling back as raw material for the next cycle of products. Traditional safety and health programs were limited to employee accident prevention, exposure monitoring, and heath management. Not so today. The idea of corporate social responsibility also draws in from the concept of the care and development of human resources, both internal to the company and involving external stakeholders.

The parent company of Elf Atochem, Elf Aquitaine of France (obviously heavily involved in fossil fuel and power production) did an excellent job at looking at the practical aspects of sustainable development in its *Annual Environmental Report*, using language that is a good practical summation of the issue:

> We have always preferred results rather than just talk about the environment. This is all the more important since the vocabulary is evolving all the time, making it hard to keep one's bearings. Sustainable development has long been a central feature of our vocabulary. New concepts . . . have entered the vocabulary. In fact these somewhat complex terms all refer to the same idea, more or less, namely "doing more with fewer raw materials." All play a part in the drive to boost productivity and improve product performance, analyze materials flows, cut waste and so forth. This is hardly new in industry, whose lifeblood is profitability. The only difference is that we used to be driven by economic considerations alone; today our motivation is both economical and ecological. The mechanisms remain the same, however.[68]

Beyond Existing Regulations

Compliance Only Approach

Business is driven by costs, and environmental costs are in large part driven by environmental regulations. These costs cannot simply be ignored. Government and industry must look for ways to achieve environmental goals efficiently and in a way that makes sense. Some refer to this approach as "beyond compliance." Frankly, I do not like that term because it connotes a regulatory rather than a management approach to environment, health, and safety. The goal is that these functions are fully integrated into the business. I normally use the term "regulations only" or "compliance only" to describe a more narrow perspective.

Progressive companies recognize that they need to move beyond compliance. Former DuPont Chairman and Chief Executive Officer, Edgar Woolard, who was also DuPont's Chief Environmental Officer, called for an ethic of "corporate environmentalism." Woolard did not "hesitate to describe what he sees as the shortcomings of industry's historic approach to environmental issues" and indicated "that improved performance was the only way that industry could hope to earn and keep public good will on environmental matters."[69] Former Chevron Chairman George Kellogg noted in 1987:

> At Chevron, we're very proud of a corporate environmental policy that says we comply fully with the letter and spirit of all laws affecting our operations. But as long as our environmental philosophy is framed by the concept of compliance, we won't get much credit for our positive actions. Compliance means that the moral initiative lies elsewhere outside of industry.[70]

The time had come, he added, for the industry to move beyond regulations.[71] This chapter deals with methods such as life-cycle analysis and sustainable manufacturing. These are industry's responses to sustainable development, which assumes that present development must not compromise "the ability of future generations to meet their own needs."[72] As previously discussed, Prof. John Dernbach's article, *Sustainable Development as a Framework for National Governance*,[73] does an excellent job of explaining the history of sustainable development and proposes a wide variety of legal changes to allow better integration of sustainable development principles into the U.S. and international legal systems.

There are many examples of companies moving beyond compliance, such as ARCO's innovations in producing less polluting fuels; widespread reductions in reported releases under the Toxics Release Inventory (TRI); waste-reduction programs of Dow, 3M, and Chevron; plastics labeling and recycling; massive energy-conservation efforts that reduce emissions related to power generation; and development of lower impact forestry practices. The Global Environment Management Institute (GEMI) has published a booklet, *Environment: Value to Business*, which details how many companies have identified value creating opportunities.[74]

Braden R. Allenby's book, *Industrial Ecology: Policy Framework and Implementation*,[75] which argues for an industrial ecology approach that focuses on materials, products, sources, and operations over life cycle rather than traditional remediation and emissions controls that focuses on industrial sites, media, or substances, is also worth reading. (Important industrywide and international efforts to protect the environment are discussed later in this chapter.) However, talk about sustainable development and other good management practices may be met with skepticism within EPA, particularly on the enforcement side. Eric Schaeffer, formerly Director of Regulatory Enforcement at EPA, stated that "EPA's docket is full of cases involving prominent companies that have sophisticated management systems and terrific codes of behavior written into their corporate policies and posted on their walls."[76]

Social Responsibility Reporting and Corporate Values

Social responsibility reporting, discussed subsequently, is part of the broader issues of corporate values. Booze Allen Hamilton and The Aspen Institute recently conducted a major global study of corporate values.[77] That study included a survey that sought to "1) understand how companies define corporate values, 2) expand on research about the relationship of values to business performance, and 3) identify best practices for managing corporate values."[78]

The survey produced the following "fundamental" findings:

- Ethical behavior is part of a company's license to operate.
- Most companies believe values influence relationships and reputations, but do not see a direct link to growth.
- Most companies are not measuring their return on values.
- Financial leaders are taking a more comprehensive approach to values.
- Values practices vary significantly by region.
- Most companies rely on explicit CEO support to reinforce values.[79]

"The survey results show that 89% of respondents have written values statements, and nearly 75% believe that executives and employees are under significant pressure to demonstrate strong corporate values. Ethical behavior and integrity are emphasized in 90% of values statements,"[80] but surprisingly "environmental responsibility and diversity are articulated by fewer than 50%.[81] Environmental responsibility ranked higher in Europe and Asia than in North America.[82] Note also that "financial leaders", "defined as public companies who categorized themselves as leaders in their industry, and whose financial results in the past three years were at least 10% ahead of industry competitors"[83] approach values more comprehensively emphasizing values such as commitment to employees, drive to succeed and adaptability. Moreover, these financial leaders also believed that social and environmental responsibility have a positive financial impact (49% vs. 34% of other public companies).[84]

Transparency seems to be the new buzzword for corporate conduct. Perhaps the best-known effort encouraging such transparency is the Sustainability Reporting Guidelines developed by the GRI for the UNEP.[85] As noted in a recent publication from GEMI: "Properly implemented, transparency may drive improvement in corporate governance, stakeholder relations and performance reporting, all of which can deliver business value by enhancing the credibility and trustworthiness of an organization. Defining a strategic approach and establishing clear goals for transparency can help ensure that this value is delivered at the same time as associated risks are managed."[86] In some organizations, the environmental function is now part of a broader "social responsibility" effort.

The Guidelines include generally applicable indicators in the three categories that are part of sustainability—economic (e.g., wages, community development, etc.), environmental (e.g., waste generation, energy consumption, etc.) and social (e.g., workplace issues, human rights, etc.). The environmental guidelines have been through a year of "rigorous testing." The social and economic indicators are "experimental, very controversial. The next version is expected to be published in 2006."[87] Note that the environmental reporting provisions were much less controversial that the broader based social and employment issues. But those issues are clearly subsumed under "sustainable development"—meeting the needs of the present without compromising the ability of future generations to meet their own needs.

GRI released its own sustainability report in November 2004.[88] Note the International Organization for Standardization (ISO) has decided to develop a guidance document on social responsibility "that will not be intended for use in certification."[89] It is anticipated that this guidance will be issued in early 2008.[90] GRI now has a web-based research tool[91] which "clarifies the intersections between different sustainable development and corporate social responsibility tools and initiatives,"[92] including the results of several separate linkage pagers that GRI has produced. "The GRI hopes that this tool will help users see where the four large initiatives connect, the different roles they play, and where they reinforce one another."[93] It also plans to develop a standard format in which to present technical protocols. And draft protocol template components have been developed.[94]

The concept of the GRI is to have a uniform and consistent approach to reporting this variety of issues of concern to the public. However, there are also the Sullivan Principles, named after the late Rev. Leon Sullivan, not to mention the Dow Jones Sustainability Index, among other indicators of performance. More than 300 firms have signed up for the Global Compact. Participating firms are to post their techniques for dealing with the many labor, human rights an environmental challenges spawned by globalization.[95] The Association of British Insurers also has reporting guidelines.[96]

At least 2,000 companies around the world voluntarily report on their economic, environmental, or social policies, practices, and performance. Thirty-one companies from 10 countries will participate in a structured program to share these GRI guidelines. These include eight companies from the United States—Agilent, Baxter International, Ford, General Motors,

Halliburton, Nike, Procter & Gamble, and Texaco. API and IPIECA have developed an Oil and Gas Industry Guidance on Voluntary Sustainability Reporting for voluntary use by companies in reporting their environmental, health and safety, social and economic performance. A Joint API/IPIECA Corporate Reporting Task Force developed the guidance, which is aimed at improving the quality, consistency and credibility of performance reporting and is sufficiently flexible to meet individual company needs. The Guidance was officially released during an April 7 Reporting Workshop held in Buenos Aires during the IPIECA Annual General Meeting; a Reporting Workshop for API members and other interested North American oil and gas companies is scheduled for June 16, 2005 in Houston, Texas.[97]

Frankly, I am not sure, even assuming that the GRI guidelines are generally accepted, what this reporting will achieve for companies. Perhaps my view is somewhat colored after participating in a conference recently with a variety of activist groups during which some of the companies agreeing to participate were savaged because they did not report certain items the way the groups wanted, or for what the data showed. If a group is opposed to your business or industry or a specific operation, this will truly be an instance of "no good deed goes unpunished." The Internet allows instant communication of every rumor, misdeed and an occasional fact to be spread instantaneously throughout the world. As for the regulators, as noted previously, I have also seen very little interest in how strong your environmental program is or how good your social policies are if there is an easy "bean" to be found from the enforcement side.

Conversely, the reporting of Toxic Release Inventory (TRI) data has probably done more to reduce these emissions that all the rest of the pertinent regulations. Many companies had no idea of the scope of these emissions and when they were reported moved rapidly to reduce the gross numbers. These numbers have in many instances been taken out of context in a regulatory or permit challenge situation, but overall the reporting has been valuable, both for the companies who have chosen to respond and for the environment.

Transparency is being particularly pushed in Europe, where there is not a Freedom of Information Act safety valve available and where regulatory requirements that allow for broad circulation of data are only now being developed. The implications in the United States, where there is already broad reporting, for companies who choose to voluntarily report information that is not required to be disclosed may be different.[98]

The companies that are examining the GRI reporting data are generally multi-nationals, who will be inspected under a microscope everywhere they go. In may be in their business interest to have such reporting. Their decisions to participate may also be based on assumptions of increased value that may not be justified. Note that, in any event, if one signs up for any of these initiatives and then decides to withdraw, the political and economic consequences might be severe.

In short, there will be a continuing trend to require more transparency in corporate reporting. Agencies, the general public, and financial organizations will continue to demand more data and measure companies on what they perceive to be their social responsibility. Some of this concern as to social responsibility and its impact on the company are already reflected in stock valuations. If increased voluntary reporting improves corporate environmental, social and economic policies, the activity will have positive outcomes. But if voluntary reporting becomes primarily a basis to provide additional data for use in attacking corporations, it will not be worth the effort. Companies should proceed cautiously before embracing these efforts. However, it is important to understand the implications of reporting or not reporting. Companies should:

(1) Do a search of the public data, particularly the websites of activist groups, or other stakeholders whose influence may be important and review the data on the company, both positive and negative.

(2) Closely examine the proposed indicators of performance and determine the extent to which the corporation would be viewed positively and where it would be viewed negatively. As in the case of the TRI, there may be surprises in the corporate profile that can be fixed easily and/or should be fixed.

(3) Be realistic in what will be achieved. If the company is involved in products that are viewed favorably, there may be competitive value in showing that you stand out favorably in terms of social values among your competitors. If your product is not necessarily viewed favorably, participation in this kind of reporting will not necessarily gain you acclaim among your critics. One critic, Prof. Carol Adams, a professor at the University of Glasgow, noted "corporations that follow various guidelines even after a number of years are still publishing incomplete environmental reports, which omit material issues affecting stakeholder groups."[99] She claimed, with respect to ICI, a large British chemical company, that there was a very different portrayal by ICI and the media and that a number of issues important to stakeholders were missing from ICI reports.[100] She noted that "[i]t is very easy to comply with GRI, for example, and report on the indicators and issues or Responsible Care. It is much harder to set up processes linked to governance structures, which are

designed to take in a wide range of views that will often be critical of the company, and respond to those views and issues."[101]

(4) Even if your product is not necessarily viewed favorably or if you are involved in extractive industries, it may still valuable to perform this exercise. It may not be that difficult to make appropriate changes. If nothing else, it will highlight your vulnerabilities and allow you to improve your short- and long-term responses to environmental challenges.

International Trade and the Environment

The protests in Seattle and later on in other parts of the world as the World Trade Organization (WTO) has tried to hold meetings underscore the global issues of trade and the environment. Some would argue that these protestors are modern day King Canutes, trying to turn back the wave of globalization, or neo-Luddites, trying to protect jobs in local industries that will be lost as a matter of simple economics. As noted by Frank Arnold,

> trying to use trade policy to achieve other objectives, such as overthrowing dictators and getting other countries to step up their environmental protection efforts, often doesn't work. In the case of electing not to import certain goods from some country whose environmental practices do not meet our standards, this often simply results in a reconfiguration of world trade in the relevant goods without producing and environmental improvement. In addition, many recent trade disputes have been about clearly protectionist policies thinly disguised as environmental concerns.[102]

Ironically, environmental groups "want to limit the power of the WTO."[103] Their interest is usually in expanding a governmental interest. Conversely, "labor unions want to expand the power and scope of the WTO. They want to include enforceable labor standards in trade agreements (and in the WTO's body of law) and thus use the power of trade as a lever to improve labor practices in other countries."[104] They believe that "loose labor standards overseas will result in job losses in the United States."[105] It is "this marriage of convenience between two opposites that has derailed progress in free trade, culminating in the breakdown in Seattle."[106]

Gregory Shaffer, writing in *The Environmental Law Reporter*, observed that

> [t]he U.S. public is relatively government-adverse and foreigner-wary. It is thus far less likely to support financing of domestic and international programs that directly address environ-

mental concerns than to support trade restrictions against foreign imports. . . . WTO critics employ the rhetoric of fighting
"multinational corporations," but the sanctions that they advocate can harm developing country workers, and these workers
are rarely consulted about them. . . . Yet whatever political party
is in control, domestic political processes prefer to shift costs
through trade restrictions onto foreigners who, in a world of
asymmetric power, tend to come from poorer, smaller countries.
The result is North-South, trade-environment policy controversies brought before the WTO on account of U.S. imposition of
unilateral trade restrictions against developing country imports,
as opposed to negotiated package agreements involving financial and technical assistance.[107]

The view of the developing countries is, according to Professor Shaffer, that
"the cause is *not* just if no financial assistance is provided to them and that
self-interested producers are always in league with well-meaning environmental activists when it comes to bans on the importation of developing
countries' competitive products."[108]

"Polluting industries have not, in fact, shifted operations to the developing world to any significant extent. Rather, liberalized trade appears to have
helped leverage up standards, not ratchet them down, through informal
means."[109] The irony is that the WTO, which was only founded in 1995,
states in its opening paragraphs of its charter that parties to the Organization
should "allow for the optimal use of the world's resources in accordance
with the objective of sustainable development, seeking to both protect and
preserve the environment."[110] Similarly, the WTO allows countries to impose trade restrictions specifically to achieve environmental objectives
"necessary to protect human, animal or plant life or health" or "relating to
the conservation of natural resources."[111] The issue, from the environmentalists' standpoint, is the difference between the product and how it is produced. Under the WTO rules, "it is illegal to treat products produced overseas differently from those produced domestically, once the foreign goods
have entered the domestic market."[112] Jenny Bates and Debra Knopman of
the Progressive Policy Institute argue that the method for addressing these
issues is a "third way," through more multilateral environmental agreements and economic assistance, both domestically and foreign. They contend that imposing tariffs and other trade sanctions on countries that are
contributing to environmental degradation is an indirect, ineffective, and
inefficient way of tackling the problem, and involves significant economic
side-effects and distortions. Imposing trade sanctions on goods from poor
countries with lax environmental standards lowers economic growth there

and does nothing to counter the poverty that may well be contributing to the environmental problem.[113]

Prof. Sandy Gaines has written an excellent piece entitled *Triangulating Sustainable Development, International Trade, Environmental Protection, and Development*,[114] which places all of these issues in perspective in the trade debate. While noting that international trade policy has come "an enormous distance since Rio in its consideration of the effects of trade and investment flows on the environment and on the sustainability of patterns of development,"[115] and that "[e]nvironmental policy has come an equal distance in thinking about how international trade and the rules governing it play into the implementation of the full range of environmental objectives,"[116] and that "trade policy has begun to account for its contribution to sustainable development through a more sophisticated and self-observant integration of policy going well beyond the pre-Rio mantra that international trade and environmental protection are mutually supportive,"[117] he nonetheless feels that these achievements "ultimately disappoint."[118] However, he notes: "[t]he fault, though, does not lie exclusively, or even primarily, with trade officials and trade policy."[119] "More generally, though, trade policy reform by itself cannot move economic systems and patterns of trade onto the sustainable development path. What goods are produced where and what services are provided where are influenced not by trade policy but by the economic, social, and geographical conditions of each country and the economic and social policies of national governments."[120]

Professor Gaines notes that there is a need to look at the third side of the policy triangle He believes that a "major factor in the failure" of the so-called "Rio bargain," which tied sustainable development to economic development and trade, has been the "insistence by the North that trade should replace aid as the main vehicle for transferring economic resources to the South, without attending in a timely or adequate manner to the other conditions, such as debt repayments, deteriorating environmental conditions in the developing countries, that must also be adjusted if the resource flows of trade are to promote development on a sustainable basis."[121]

Thus, "the more that northern reformers insist on the right to apply trade-based or trade-affecting environmental measures like eco-labels oriented to developed country concerns, packaging requirements that discourage low-cost materials like jute, and at the extreme the right to ban products from the richest market if they are made in an allegedly environment-harming manner, the deeper the suspicion among governments and peoples of the South that their developmental aspirations, which cannot be realized without the effective opportunity to trade with the North, will be frustrated in the name of environmental protection."[122]

The Challenge of Compliance

While most of us from the environmental management community, would like to talk about sustainable development, the triple bottom line, sustainable manufacturing, etc., like it or not, we still must spend a substantial amount of time on compliance issues. This includes many companies, which talk about the future but in essence are still managing in the past. (See Chapter 12, Green Arthritis.)

The incredible increase in technically complex regulations impedes efforts to move beyond compliance and focus business planning on long-term issues. Today's environmental manager, while being able to take advantage of the ready availability of extensive material on the Internet, is still frustrated by the need to read the equivalent of hundreds of pages in the *Federal Register*—including references to computer disks containing even more material—and equally complex regulations on the state level.[123] Appendix A contains many pages of acronyms—the abbreviations that environmental managers may need to know to do their jobs; Linda Clark, Manager of Product Regulatory Affairs in the Environmental Services Department of FMC Corporation in Philadelphia, developed a 100-page list of acronyms. Businesses require more professionals and technicians to monitor compliance and to manage the flow of burdensome, legally required paperwork (despite the use of increasingly sophisticated computer programs) that limits the ability to focus on anything but day-to-day operations.

The amount of required paperwork is mind-boggling. A study by the Chemical Manufacturers Association reports that, in 1994, American businesses spent 54.6 million hours and nearly $3 billion filling out paperwork required by the eight major statutes that EPA enforces.[124] While computerization may have reduced the amount, it has also increased the demands for data. In commenting on EPA's CAA permitting regulations, the California South Coast Air Quality Management District indicated that in a best-case scenario, permit applications alone would fill about one-half mile of shelf space. This does not include monitoring and other reports that regulated companies would also have to file.[125] Occidental has estimated that establishment and implementation of a system for monitoring approximately 150,000 potential emission points at five petrochemical plants as required by new fugitive emission regulations will require from 1.4 to 7 million data entries. The costs of paperwork for compliance may well in some instances dwarf the actual pollution control costs.[126]

Moreover, it is difficult to go beyond compliance when defining compliance, let alone maintaining compliance, may be extremely challenging. In a 1993 survey of corporate legal officers, 70 percent said that they did not believe that full compliance with the matrix of federal and state environmental requirements was possible, and a 2002 survey indicates even less confidence in full compliance. It is doubtful that if the confidence level has increased since that time.[127] Since that time, laws and regulations have become even more complex. Because of the vague requirements in some laws and regulations, companies cannot even be confident that they have achieved compliance before attempting to go beyond it. Moreover, with the passage of time, we can detect pollutants in increasingly smaller amounts and concentrations. When the original FWPCA in 1972 set a goal of zero pollution, pollutants could be detected at the parts-per-million level. Today, we can, in some instances, detect pollutants at parts per *quadrillion*. Many regulators are privately sorry that these new, sophisticated instruments of detection are available because the instruments create regulatory problems. The public often does not recognize the difference between detectable quantities and harmful quantities. Because the mere presence of a carcinogen or hazardous pollutant is sufficient to cause concern, many people will accept only zero or at least background levels. The so-called precautionary principle is invoked which assumes that action should be taken before "all" (depending on the ideology ranging from conjecture to very limited data) the data is in. For this reason, many environmental managers feel that Shakespeare's advice to "kill all the lawyers" should also apply to analytical chemists. And as Prof. Christopher Stone notes, with respect to the "precautionary principle," "when we seek global guidance, we are confronted with national and cultural variance not only in rankings of harm, but also in tolerance and tastes for risks. One person's 'unacceptable consequence' is another's 'regrettable necessity.'"[128]

The following anecdote, which was supplied to me by Prof. Richard Stewart of the University of Wisconsin at Superior, illustrates the difficulty in dealing with science and regulation. A freshman at Eagle Rock Junior High won first prize at the Greater Idaho Falls Science Fair on April 26, 2001. He was attempting to show how conditioned we have become to the alarmists practicing junk science and spreading fear of everything in our environment. In his project, he urged people to sign a petition demanding strict control or total elimination of the chemical "dihydrogen monoxide." And for plenty of good reasons, since it can:

1. Cause excessive sweating and vomiting.
2. It is a major component in acid rain.
3. It can cause severe burns in its gaseous state.
4. Accidental inhalation can kill you.
5. It contributes to erosion.
6. It decreases effectiveness of automobile brakes.
7. It has been found in tumors of terminal cancer patients.

He asked 50 people if they supported a ban of the chemical.. Forty-three said yes, six were undecided, and only one knew that the chemical was—water! The title of his prize-winning project was: "How Gullible Are We?"

Scientific advances have made compliance both difficult and expensive.

> Environmental regulatory compliance under both federal and state statutes is commonly determined by detecting the presence or measuring the quantity of particular pollutants present at or near regulated facilities. Because such regulatory schemes set numerical standards for determining compliance, serious civil or criminal liability may arise whenever compliance standards are set too near the detection limits of the test method used. This generic problem arises from the variability inherent in all testing methods when they are used to determine the presence or the quantity of extremely low levels of pollutants. While this area is highly complex, the basic idea is that as the level of detection gets lower and lower, the chances of error increase to the point that the range of error is larger than the measurement itself. Yet, surprisingly, some federal and state environmental agencies continue to propose permit limits or cleanup levels for toxic pollutants at levels near the detection level, where total compliance may be impossible or may require the expenditure of significant costs to remedy false indications of the presence or excess of certain pollutants.[129]

The regulatory truth that almost any detectable level of pollution must be analyzed and regulated makes it difficult for today's environmental manager to reduce risks. The scientifically trained manager is frustrated by the lack of time and resources to deal effectively with more significant issues in reducing risk. These problems will continue as scientists find means of measuring concentrations of pollutants at increasingly lower levels. An article in *Science* magazine noted:

> Advances in low-level risk detection threaten to engulf us with information. Regulators typically respond to each newly highlighted risk, whether painstakingly uncovered through scientific investigation or divulged with fanfare by the media, on an *ad hoc* basis. This response makes it hard to relate disparate risks to the overall risk level and impedes intelligent risk reduction, which must consider the costs and benefits involved. Efficient risk management requires decisions not only about what to regulate and how stringently, but also about the appropriate division of labor among the agents influencing risks. These agents in-

clude individuals, whose potential contributions too often are
overlooked, corporations, and government.[130]

There is no such thing as pure science in the regulatory area.

Environmental policy is always based on science—up to a point.
But defining that point is often a matter of fierce dispute and political combat. Then the quality of the science involved becomes
an issue . . . . The debates burn hottest where scientific uncertainty is the greatest and economic stakes are the highest.[131]

We all have to live with this reality, and it does not make the job any easier.
Yet as corporations more closely review costs, emphasis will also be on reducing operating costs. These goals can be complementary: if toxics and
wastes can be eliminated, operating costs can be reduced. While the watch-
word in management today is "cost effective," American industry needs to
seek not only cost effective but *more* effective ways of managing environmental programs.

A recent piece of legislation does provide an opportunity to deal with
"questionable scientific evidence and/or unjustified technical/regulatory
assumptions."[132] That legislation is the Data Quality Act enacted as part of
the Treasury and General Appropriations Act of 2001.[133] As noted by Dan
Steinway of Baker & Botts:

Congress obviously wanted the OMB and other federal agencies
to adopt a refined set of standards for ensuring that agency decision-making is based on accurate and reliable scientific and/or
technical information. Second, Congress also intended to provide private parties with the means to enforce these guidelines in
order to ensure that specific agencies did indeed comply with
their guidelines in rulemakings and other actions.[134]

However, the use of this statue may be limited. EPA in developing its own
guidelines, noted that its "guidelines do *not* apply to information filed or prepared by EPA specifically for use in an administrative adjudication or judicial
case, including information developed in the course of a civil or criminal action or administrative enforcement action, investigation or audit."[135] "EPA
guidelines suggest that the Agency will apply this higher quality standard to
'influential scientific, financial or statistical information... [when] the
Agency can reasonably determine that dissemination of the information will
have or does have a clear and substantial impact (i.e., potential change or effect) on important public policies or private sector decisions."[136] The guidelines also specify that the petitioner must show "that the information at issue

did not comply with EPA's guidelines and/or otherwise did not constitute 'sound science'" and "any request for the correction of scientific or technical information should fully explain how the information at issue does not comply with the EPA or OMB guidelines and provide a recommended course for correcting thee inaccurate information."[137] Note also that if the issue is part of a rulemaking, it is treated as a comment to that rulemaking not as a separate proceeding. There have been very few proceedings so far since the EPA guidelines are only two years old, but its probable advantage is that its existence acts as a quality control on agency actions.

The immense complexity of the regulatory system creates broader problems. These problems are not simply the costs of regulation that flow directly from the control or reduction of pollutant releases and exposures, nor the paperwork burdens that are simply costly and wasteful. The requirements that create the greatest risks of driving industry offshore are those that make it impossible to operate certain types of businesses, or to operate in certain areas, no matter how willing a company may be to comply. Perhaps the best analogy is the Grimms' fairy tale of Cinderella. Her wicked stepsisters told Cinderella that she could go to the ball if she performed a variety of impossible tasks. After performing all these tasks, however, she still did not receive permission. Industry often feels it is in the same position as Cinderella. The situation may be "grim" but it is no fairy tale!

Even where substantive compliance is possible, uncertainties in the regulatory system relating to permit issuance and compliance is of paramount concern. Uncertainty is a major problem even for those with good intentions, sophisticated planning, quality management programs, and extensive familiarity with the regulatory process. Unpredictability, coupled with the criminalization of environmental law, poses personal legal risks that could drive talented managers from the field.

Many of the industries with the best promise for stability and future growth in the manufacturing sector depend on an ability to respond to technological change at a pace dictated by competition, not by regulatory processes. These growth industries include electronics, advanced materials, aerospace, custom and specialty chemicals (including pharmaceuticals), and automotive manufacturing. Many of these are prime targets of foreign competition. They cannot wait for regulatory processes that take years when their products can go through an entire life cycle in 18 months. Certainty is the key word. If companies cannot obtain required permits in an expeditious manner, or at least know approximately how long it will take if they perform the appropriate studies and provide the appropriate data, they will not be able to operate efficiently or economically. If the time frame for obtaining a permit is too far in the future, a company has little choice but to seek alternatives elsewhere, no matter how good its planners are. This is neither a proenvironmental nor an antienvironmental decision, but simply a business decision taking into account the leveraging impact of time and uncertainty. Thus, uncertainty must be addressed if this country is to remain competitive and keep manufacturing jobs in the United States.

Agencies are also extremely slow to approve new, innovative technology. Expensive and unnecessary testing requirements, which make the Japanese testing requirements for imports look simple, are common.[138] It is usually easier to go with existing and in many cases less-efficient technology than to try to have new technology approved.

The Challenge of Regulatory Reform

In the early 1990s, EPA began to recognize that the value of "command and control" as the regulatory option of choice needed to be reconsidered. Its high costs have increased political pressures from all sides. Vice President Gore's Reinventing Government initiative began to look at unnecessary regulations, but progressed very slowly and received minimal publicity. The 1994 "Republican Revolution" accelerated the pressures to find alternatives, but the political rhetoric on all sides (such as "gutting environmental laws and regulations" and "removing the dead hand of the liberal government from the economy") made it hard to proceed. It has proven difficult to overcome the history of environmental law, where if somehow, some way, somebody could beat the system, the system had to be tightened. Moreover, the "numbers" mentality of EPA, the DOJ, and Congress discussed in Chapter 2 (i.e., the higher the number of enforcement cases, the better the protection of the environment) made change difficult. (If you are a hammer, everything looks like a nail.)

Ernie Rosenberg of the Soap and Detergent Association noted at an American Association of Law Schools meeting that "measuring the number of cases being brought is just useless." In Rosenberg's view such data says nothing about the "overall universe of performance" within jurisdictions. In counting cases and penalties, he urged "we're measuring failure, we are not measuring success."[139] I agree with Ernie Rosenberg's view, but the author of the article does not. A study by Prof. John Scholz of "OSHA enforcement suggests that the level of cooperation employed by enforcing agencies increases the effectiveness of their enforcement efforts, as measured by lower injury rates among workers."[140] In 1996, OSHA reported that in the prior three years, participation in the program had doubled, and that injury rates at participating companies were 45% below the industry average. As discussed subsequently (see Chapter 6, Environmental Auditing and Environmental Management, EPA and OSHA Environmental and Safety Audits), OSHA's voluntary safety programs are popular with industry because of the perception that they encourage improved safety performance while not increasing the odds of enforcement. Industry is still concerned, however, about the enforcement implications of EPA programs and, unsure whether there is sufficient improvement in performance to justify the additional work involved.

EPA is looking toward a more integrated approach to enforcement, which includes compliance assistance, incentives and pollution prevention.[141] However, there still seems to be a disconnect between these programs and EPA's performance measurements outcome, despite the Agency's efforts to "shift in focus toward more outcome-based measures of program performance, including the performance of integrated activities."[142] Regional staffs "still perceive that traditional enforcement activity measures such as inspections" and referrals to the DOJ are what is really "measured."[143] Yet "[i]ntegrated initiatives are disadvantaged if regional staff fear that headquarters will judge them based on performance measures that do not reward resources invested in integrated approaches, or do not capture the compliance outcomes of such efforts."[144] Unfortunately, "many state personnel have the perception that EPA is not supportive of *any* innovative state activity in the area."[145]

This issue is exacerbated by EPA Inspector General reports that allege problems in enforcement whenever the numbers go down. At a House Commerce Subcommittee on Oversight and Investigations hearing on the findings of a GAO Report, a state commissioner testified about his state's problems with EPA.

> David Struhs, commissioner of the Massachusetts Department of the Environment, told the subcommittee his state encountered a problem in 1997 with EPA's inconsistency when the state's air inspection program was targeted for an audit by the EPA Inspector General "because our statistics for traditional air permit inspections dropped below historic levels."
> The call for the audit, Struhs said, came after the state, in trying to revamp its inspection program, created a multimedia effort to look at all aspects of a facility's compliance rather than just its compliance with Clean Air Act requirements. To facilitate this process, Massachusetts received EPA permission to reduce the number of required inspections at the same few sources every year to expand the use of state resources to look at more facilities, some of which have never been inspected.
> "EPA actually gave us grants to help pay for our new comprehensive inspections of previously ignored facilities," Struhs said.
> However, the audit called into question whether the state wasted its resources in trying to improve its enforcement pro-

gram and demoralized the DEP, Struhs said.

"It's even more troubling when the efforts that led to that situation were not just sanctioned but encouraged by the same agency that is conducting the audit," he said.[146]

At that same hearing,

Nikki Tinsley, EPA's acting inspector general, told the subcommittee that EPA audited the air enforcement programs in six states, including Massachusetts, in 1997 and part of 1998. Even though the audit focused on the air programs, she said, the agency believes the results are indicative of the broader environmental programs.

What the agency found were significant enforcement lapses.

States, Tinsley said, are required to identify and report significant violators of the Clean Air Act to EPA.

"Despite performing more than 3,300 inspections during the years we reviewed, the six states, we audited reported only 18 significant violators to EPA," she said. "In contrast, while reviewing 430 of the 3,300 inspections, we identified an additional 103 significant violators the states did not report."

The reasons for the underreporting varied, she said. Some said when EPA officials were aware of the violations, they meddled in state activities, which delayed resolution. Other states did not agree with EPA's definition of significant violator. In other cases, inspectors did not document inspections adequately to determine if there had been a violation, she said.[147]

This issue of numbers was addressed by Robbie Roberts, then-Executive Director of the Environmental Council of the States (ECOS), who characterized the focus on numbers by stating "that drawing conclusions about the state of the environment from the numbers of enforcement actions was like estimating how many high school students understood Shakespeare by counting the number that had been expelled from English class."[148]

Many of the states believe that they, rather than EPA, are the hotbed of innovation. Peder Larsen, Commissioner of the Minnesota Pollution Control Agency, believes that "[r]einventing environmental protection is as much about managing our agencies for change as it is about realigning our policies. States that have adopted a philosophy of innovation are already ensuring better environmental protection for their citizens." He believes EPA can, and must, do the same.[149]

EPA must substantially restructure its approach to regulation if the regulated community is to meet the challenges of complying with the requirements that Congress and EPA have imposed and will impose in the future. Over the past few years, EPA has taken a number of steps to address industry concerns. It has been a struggle for many reasons, most importantly the rigid command-and-control mentality and the statutory framework now in place. As detailed over the next several pages, EPA's initiatives have had limited success.

EPA is "trying to improve the agency's use of the burgeoning number of voluntary programs that are intended to encourage pollution cuts, EPA sources say, as the agency is facing long-term budget shortfalls that could make it more reliant on such programs in future years." "The number of voluntary programs has skyrocketed to 75 at EPA headquarters and regional offices since President Bush took office, according to the last agency survey on the issue that was conducted in December 2003, nearly twice as many than the Clinton EPA Administration." "EPA's Office of Policy, Economics & Innovation is also developing internal guidelines that will be issued sometime this year [2005] laying out how EPA should measure the effectiveness of voluntary programs and guidelines to band and rank the efficacy of the programs."[150]

Industry has undertaken a dialogue with EPA and state and local agencies to address some carefully chosen existing rules that may require scrutiny, not necessarily because they were developed in error, but because new laws and rules may have rendered them obsolete.[151] A review of the regulatory process that EPA is now undertaking shows program overlaps or pollution controls that no longer make sense. While such reviews will not necessarily lead to a retreat from any deadline or currently mandated level of control, EPA's own analysis[152] and its emphasis on risk-based regulatory priorities imply that some substantive rules should be changed. The dialogue is also beginning to address the effect of various rules on corporate environmental management and the allocation of corporate and agency resources.

EPA and state agencies should also consider a process that asks questions of program officers instead of imposing answers on them. The new process would ask for an analysis of each layer of implementation machinery, such as setting the standard (with the potential for stiff enforcement), requiring state permit review, requiring EPA review of state decisions (with the concomitant lack of flexibility that results from federal citizen suit authority, inflexible comment periods, and mandatory delays), and requiring EPA review of state actions between permit reviews for generic classes of changes, even if no new control requirement is triggered. Furthermore, someone needs to ask how much additional benefit is achieved by each increment of these measures. In some programs it would also be helpful to establish a review of how changes to one part of the program (e.g., factors that determine which substances are controlled) will affect the costs, flexibility, and value of other program elements (e.g., facility standards or permitting requirements).

In addition, EPA needs to focus its efforts on pollution prevention that goes beyond mere compliance. EPA's and industry's pollution prevention efforts are undermined by restrictions that tend to penalize companies that make reductions too soon. EPA has shown little interest in using its discretion under the law to ensure that companies that make early reductions are not disadvantaged relative to those that fail to reduce—or that even increase—pollution.[153] Rather, EPA's provision of credits for such reductions has been rather grudging, apparently based on a fear that someone might get credit for a reduction they would have made anyway. EPA has given no indication that it would oppose legislation that would impose percentage reductions in release or generation of waste without giving adequate consideration to those who have gone beyond mere compliance. Because EPA staff have shown little understanding of what it means to set baselines for determining credits in the future, it is difficult for companies to justify making reductions before a baseline is determined. If managers in corporate environmental departments urge their operations to make reductions, as they have, and the companies are punished for it, the managers will not long retain credibility and effectiveness within their organizations. Thus, when efforts to reduce emissions or waste result in increased permitting difficulties, under the theory that "no good deed goes unpunished," such desirable programs will suffer major setbacks.[154]

EPA's response to these allegations would be in reference to its Project XL initiative, which is looking at incentives for early reductions. As discussed later in this section, however, that program also has major implementation problems.

EPA should also incorporate more efficient market mechanisms into its environment regulations. Although EPA has made such attempts,[155] under the current statutory framework, such mechanisms only address the thin, uppermost layers of a massive and rigid structure. That structure, much of which is imposed directly by statute, relies heavily on command-and-control regulation—an attempt to control pollution by bureaucratic fiat rather than by providing incentives for development of creative solutions. Indeed, aspects of the 1990 CAA Amendments reduced the availability of market mechanisms and added to the command-and-control nature of air pollution control. The amendments really only embraced new, more efficient market approaches in the provisions designed to control acid rain. Thus, despite EPA's good intention, it may be difficult to achieve broader use of market approaches.[156]

EPA to its credit has undertaken a number of initiatives seeking to address the problems that environmental regulations pose for industry. EPA has recognized the need to change and is struggling to find ways both to protect the environment and address the concerns of industry and citizens. For example, in 1994, EPA promulgated a rule intended to reduce toxic air emissions from approximately 400 large chemical plants. The rule included an innovative provision with a compliance option that relied on "emission averaging." This provision was "intended to ease compliance burdens by allowing facilities to forgo controlling emissions in one part of a plant, if other control measures could offset the resulting emission increase."[157] EPA was proud of its innovation, but the provision was not used. Under the rule, companies had to submit detailed plans by the end of 1995 if they intended to use the innovative provision. This date passed without a single facility signing up.[158] Industry sources said that the averaging provision was "too complicated to implement."[159] People also "lament[ed] that the averaging provision in EPA's original proposal appeared to offer significant benefits, but critical elements were removed in the final rule due to objections from state officials and environmentalists."[160]

EPA has developed a variety of other initiatives, including the Environmental Leadership Program, Project XL, and a policy on environmental auditing discussed in Chapter 6. For the reasons discussed below and in Chapter 6, these programs have met with only limited success.

Environmental Leadership Program

EPA's Environmental Leadership Program (ELP) was designed to promote development of innovative compliance management systems within the framework of existing regulations. It has a facility-based program overseen by EPA's Office of Enforcement and Compliance Assurance. EPA's 1993 notice of intent requesting comment on the initiative[161] indicated that participating companies would sign a "Statement of Environmental Principles"[162] and individual facilities within the company could become part of a Model Facility Program. Participation in the program would potentially bring recognition to the facility as being a "green" facility and corresponding value in marketing a company's products. Under this initiative, a company could be eligible for fewer inspections, expedited permitting, reduced reporting and monitoring, and public recognition for participation.[163]

Ten companies and two federal facilities completed a one-year pilot program to test various components of the ELP.[164] As a "carrot" for participating in the project, facilities participating in the pilot program did not undergo routine (as opposed to mandatory) enforcement inspections. Each participant focused on one of five elements intended to be part of the final ELP.[165] The five elements were:

- creating incentives for program participation;

• defining the elements of and implementing environmental management and compliance systems;

• evaluating opportunities for ELP facilities to serve as mentors for other companies;

• with employee and community involvement, developing ways to measure a facility's environmental accountability; and

• verifying that a facility's environmental management or compliance system is working.[166]

For example, EPA Region X and WMX Technologies, using WMX's computerized environmental management system that monitors environmental factors in landfills, looked at self-auditing procedures for monitoring compliance with RCRA. The theory is that EPA could reduce the number of inspections, if the management system fosters compliance with existing regulations.[167]

EPA has planned to press ahead with implementation of the full ELP[168] and is encouraging regions and state agencies to develop their own ELPs.[169] For example, the EPA-New England ELP, also called the "StarTrack" initiative is a related project looking at third-party certification.[170] Companies participating in this initiative would be expected to develop environmental management systems appropriate to their operations, modeled largely after the developing international environmental management standards, the International Standards Organization's (ISO's) ISO 14000 standards, discussed in Chapter 6. "The companies agree to assess environmental management and compliance performance and submit to an independent third-party audit. In return, they can carry on their business with minimal EPA involvement."[171] Minimizing EPA involvement would certainly be a goal of one industry lawyer, who characterized working with EPA as fulfillment of the Yiddish curse: "May you have partners."[172]

Industry had been hesitant to embrace the ELP. Key concerns are what will be the criteria for selection and the criteria for removal from participation.[173]

According to the draft framework, each participant will likely need to meet certain criteria prior to participating in the ELP. First, the facility must have had in place an Environmental Management System (EMS) for at least two years prior to applying. The EMS must include an internal environmental auditing procedure. In addition, the facility must show a willingness and ability to participate in community outreach programs.

Other pre-application requirements include: submission to "pre-selection visits," by the EPA to verify that the application accurately represents the facility's current compliance status; a demonstration that the facility is not subject to any ongoing enforcement actions, and is not a chronic violator; a willingness to participate in the ELP for six (6) years; an agreement to submit to full EMS internal audit by certified independent auditor in years two and five of the program[;] and submission of and preparation of an Annual Environmental Report containing environmental performance data and audit information which will include all instances of non-compliance during the year.[174]

"Currently, the program is on hold pending the outcome of a study on the role of incentives in reinvention."[175] Senior corporate officers, who are proud of their programs and who see marketing/public relations value in being considered outstanding corporate citizens, should consider the operation of such programs in practice. If there is marketing/public relations value in signing on to the program, the downside of backing out or being removed from the program could be far worse.

Some also question whether the ELP will encourage improved performance, particularly if a company has a good program in place. EPA's concept of encouraging good environmental management practices is admirable, but the proposed ELP relied heavily on practices that are primarily still in the conceptual stage, such as life-cycle analysis, sustainable manufacturing, and full cost accounting discussed later in this chapter. Although these concepts hold promise, many issues need to be resolved. Industry fears that ELP participation may make environmental management even more difficult, particularly for those with good programs already in place.

The area of most concern is how ELP participation, or participation in other EPA programs, would play out as a potential enforcement mechanism. EPA is looking at compliance-verification systems, such as third-party audits and self-certification. (Problems posed by third-party audits and verification are discussed in Chapter 6.) Industry is also concerned that entry into the program would actually invite more enforcement difficulty. A routine enforcement action could become a high-profile issue if the company or facility were involved in the program. The threat of losing membership in the program could also affect a company's ability to negotiate with enforcers, if EPA or state enforcement officials found threatening a company's status in the program to be an irresistible bargaining tool. This concern is further exacerbated by EPA's Sector Facility Indexing Project, designed to provide better public understanding of the compliance status and environmental responsibility of various industry sectors. The data for this project was severely criticized, as has the project design and implementation.[176] Indeed, all you have to do is look at EPA's website and the data on your own company to see the many inaccuracies in EPA's data (see Chapter 1, Introduction). This has considerably improved. Currently, the ELP is on hold pending the outcome of a study on the role of incentives to reinvention.[177]

A broader concern with the adoption of any leadership program is the tendency for voluntary programs to become mandatory. Congress and agencies tend to believe that anything that is a good idea if voluntary can be even better if made mandatory. All of us in this field should encourage good environmental management programs, but it remains to be seen if the bells and whistles in any "voluntary" program that EPA establishes are worth the limited rewards, especially considering the potentially significant restraints and liabilities they place on management. For example, industry is concerned that independent environmental audits and mandatory source reduction (e.g., toxics use reduction) would quickly move from being simple evidence of excellence to minimum elements of acceptable environmental behavior.

An additional concern is the interplay between ELP participation and the ISO 14000 series discussed in Chapter 6. EPA insists that it will not require ISO certification for participation in the ELP or Project XL, discussed below.[178] As detailed in Chapter 6, industry has substantial concerns with many aspects of ISO 14000 and fears that these standards will become a de facto expectation, if not a requirement, for ELP participation. EPA may in fact go beyond these standards.[179] There are many similar elements and the proposed ELP already contains certain elements not now part of ISO 14000, such as community outreach. If EPA requires ISO compliance or moves beyond it, EPA's carrots for participation in the final program will need to be very significant to justify the costs and efforts in participation.

In summary, if the final ELP imposes excessive disincentives for entry into the ranks of leadership, which would divert attention from pollution reductions to ancillary activities (such as planning and disclosure of releases not covered by current reporting requirements), it could create competitive disadvantages for participants, increase costs without commensurate reductions in releases, disrupt management structures and approaches that are working, and expose companies to added enforcement jeopardy. I hope that EPA will sufficiently evaluate the program's components to address potential participants' concerns and avoid discouraging participation.

Project XL

Project XL, EPA's "EXcellence" and "Leadership" initiative, is a second regulatory reform effort. In contrast with the ELP, which addresses compliance with existing regulations, Project XL is looking for creative ways that differ from prescribed regulatory methods for companies to meet and exceed regulatory standards. EPA hopes to stimulate regulatory flexibility on a facility-by-facility basis.[180]

EPA has targeted for 50 XL projects. Each participating facility would develop its own environmental strategy and site-specific performance standards in collaboration with "interested stakeholders." The theory of Project XL is that

> [o]nce the program is in place, individual companies will create pilot projects from the bottom up that will be based on performance standards rather than the more stifling "one size fits all" technology-based controls. These projects are anticipated to foster technological innovation and reduced compliance costs while resulting in greater pollution prevention. Participating facilities will be able to use multimedia approaches and market-based controls in realizing the performance-based standards.[181]

Some of the program participants have not yet signed agreements with EPA and involved state agencies. There are several key issues that impede progress. First, the ability to implement some proposals is hampered by statutory restrictions. Legislation may well be needed for facilities to use technology or standards other than those required by law or regulation. Companies that veer from these requirements may face EPA enforcement; there may be different philosophies within EPA itself on how to handle enforcement and compliance issues.[182] Even with federal and state exercise of enforcement discretion, there is no immunity from citizen suits. Legislation is needed to avoid third-party lawsuits, which could sink projects before they get started. This is an important concern; some citizen groups have characterized the Project XL as Project "EXtra Leniency."[183] A similar attitude cratered a potential agreement between EPA and state environmental commissioners. EPA did not consider different approaches providing the same level of environmental control that would result in significant cost savings to be an "environmental benefit." EPA and the states seem to be continuing negotiations.[184]

Even without enforcement or litigation, the process of negotiating performance standards may well be difficult—and slow. As noted by Ginsberg and Cummis:

> [T]he initial requirement for acceptance into the XL program is that the proposal will "guarantee better" environmental results. Obviously, judging what constitutes "better" is a highly subjective task susceptible to political mischief. Given that other consensus-based initiatives for administrative improvements have encountered difficulties, EPA would be wise to circumscribe the public participation, or "stakeholder," process as well as the process by which final agreement is negotiated to prevent a stale-

mate from occurring between affected industries and environmentalists over this issue.[185]

The "guarantee" aspect sank several projects as Lucent, 3M, and
Anheuser-Busch pulled out of the XL program.[186]

Overall, this program probably requires more trust by all parties than is
possible given the history of regulatory development and the long-term enforcement mentality. As the projects appear to be the equivalent of individu-
alized rulemaking, citizen groups wonder if it is worth spending their time
on projects that may not be duplicatable and enforcers see minimal value.
Industry nonparticipants often feel that legislative changes (which do not
appear to be politically possible) are the only way the program can provide
any real value. They find that the program provides too few carrots, given
the number of sticks.

In addition, in a report issued in July 1999 called *Aiming for Excellence:
Actions to Encourage Stewardship and Accelerate Environmental Progress*, EPA set itself the goal of "develop[ing] a 'performance track' that rewards environmental leaders."[187] Many critics have problems with the program. As Elliott P. Laws, then-Executive Director of Outlook Policy Forum, notes: "[O]ur current regulatory system, which is based on our traditional 'ethic' of environmental protection, is not designed to promote or
support a performance track system. It is questionable whether the system
can even allow it."[188]

Performance Track

On June 26, 2001, the Agency released its new national "performance
track" program. EPA proposed two main areas of flexibility for participating facilities—reduced monitoring, recordkeeping and reporting requirements under its Maximum Achievable Control Technology (MACT) program and some additional flexibility under the Agency's new source review
(NSR) program. Industry is still skeptical of the advantages, and not sure
whether the time and effort involved to get these incentives is worthwhile or
whether these incentives can be granted through existing regulations, although some see the program it as a way companies can maintain good relationships with EPA and with other businesses. As of December 2001, "Performance Track has about 250 participating facilities around the country of
all types and sizes, and more than 1,000 'commitments' on how these facilities plan to achieve improved performance."[189] "Performance track companies have existing EMS or develop EMS. EPA recognizes Performance
track companies as good performers because of their EMS and compliance
history. As an incentive, EPA performs routine inspections at a lower frequency at performance track companies."[190]

Some companies "have stated that the primary reason for participating in Performance Track is public recognition. Participants also listed 'public relations' as a top reason, as well as having access to EPA and EPA management to discuss regulatory issues face to face."[191] Environmental NGOs remain skeptical. And industry sometimes leaps before looking. Jack Stein of Anheuser Busch has observed that "[o]ccasionally, the law is perverse. . . . Often what we find when we go in for a new project [is that] we start getting things tacked on that are technically inappropriate for what we're trying to do and take enormous resources."[192] As discussed subsequently, the program has been substantially improved.

EPA's National Environmental Performance Track program is "designed to recognize and encourage top environmental performers—those that go beyond compliance with regulatory requirements to attain levels of environmental performance and management that benefit people, communities and the environment." "Performance Track is designed to recognize facilities that consistently meet their legal requirements and have implemented high-quality management systems. Performance Track encourages facilities to continuously improve their environmental performance and to work closely with their community and employees.[193] Frankly, as I have discussed with EPA, I am not sure if this program accomplishes this goal, but it does have some public creditability. I believe and have suggested to EPA, the use of the risk management approach as a better indicator.[194] The management system requirement is equivalent to ISO 14001 and if a facility is already certified to ISO 14001, the assumption is that the management system is in place. The Responsible Care (RC) ISO 14001 certification would also qualify. There are currently more than 340 members, although this includes multiple facilities of several companies such as Johnson & Johnson.

To qualify for Performance Track, a facility will demonstrate[195] that it:

- Has adopted and implemented an environmental management system (EMS) that includes the following elements:

  - Is able to demonstrate specific environmental achievements and commit to continued environmental improvement;
  - Commits to public outreach and performance reporting; and
  - Has a record of sustained compliance with environmental requirements.

The EMS must include a policy that includes commitments to:

- Compliance with both legal requirements and voluntary commitments;

- Pollution prevention;
- Continuous improvement in environmental performance, including areas not subject to regulations; and
- Sharing about environmental performance and the operation of the EMS with the community.

Planning is required which includes:

- Identification of significant environment aspects and legal requirements, including procedures for integrating anticipated changes in the facility's requirements or commitments in the EMS.

- Measuring objectives and targets to meet policy commitments and legal requirements, reduce the facility's significant environmental impact and to meet the performance commitments made as part of participation in the program.

- Active documented programs to achieve the objectives, targets and commitments in the EMS.

Implementation and Operation include:

- Establishing roles and responsibilities for meeting objectives and targets of the overall EMS and compliance with legal requirements, including top management representative with authority and responsibility for the EMS;

- Defined procedures for achieving and maintaining compliance and meeting performance objectives, communicating relevant information regarding the EMS, including the facility's environmental performance, throughout the organization;

- Providing appropriate incentives for personnel to meet the EMS requirements, and document control including where documents related to the EMS are to be located and who will maintain them;

- Training;

- Documentation of key EMS elements; and

- Operation and maintenance programs for equipment and for other operations that are related to legal compliance and other significant environmental aspects.

Note that the operation and maintenance programs would require some form of risk management program.

Checking and Corrective Action include:

- An active program for assessing performance and preventing and detecting non-conformance with legal and other requirements of the EMS, including an EMS audit program; and

- Active corrective action program.

Management Review includes:

- Documented management review of performance against the established objectives and targets and the effectiveness of the EMS in meeting policy commitments.

- Facility will retain EMS documentation and provide a summary of performance, including performance against objectives and targets and a summary of result in its Annual Performance Report.

Note that with respect to Public Outreach and Performance Reporting:[196]

EPA expects that applicants will already have established a public outreach program. For example, participants in the Responsible Care program or endorsers of the CERES (Coalition for Environmentally Responsible Economies) principals typically have outreach programs that may include a community advisory panel, newsletters, performance reporting, sponsorship of community activities, and other outreach activities. Many small facilities have adopted lower-cost but effective outreach programs.

In completing a Performance Track application, an applicant must complete a comprehensive review of all activities conducted at the facility that could impact the environment. This is known as an "aspect analysis." An aspect analysis includes both regulated and unregulated activities and products and their associated impacts, Note that after such a review (but not part of Performance Track) a company may decide, based on its review of impacts, to "detoxify" a product.[197] "The framework for reporting on performance is based on the Global Reporting Initiative (GRI) which EPA also has used in Region I's StarTrack Program." "EPA's approach to reporting is consistent not only with the GRI but with generally accepted EMS practice."[198]

Following such a review, these aspects must be classified based on their potential harm to the environment, or community concerns and /or other objective factors. The EMS must include a consistent method for determining which of the aspects are significant. In addition to environmental risk, "this method may consider other factors such as regulatory requirements, community concerns, or opportunities for pollution prevention."

The applicant must make future commitments for at least four environmental aspects and must choose those aspects for a detailed environmental performance table.

Past achievement must be shown by selecting a minimum of two environmental aspects from any of the categories in this table. Note that "EPA encourages each facility to use the results of its participation in EPA, state, and other partnership programs to documents its progress in improving performance."[199]

The facility must have had its program in place for one year after an independent assessment prior to application. A third-party audit is required within a three-year period prior to the date of application. It can include a corporate audit team where the team leader is Registrar Accreditation Board (RAB) or Board of Environmental, Health & Safety Auditor Certification (BEAC) certified as long as the Team Leader did not play a substantive role in developing the EMS for the facility. A trade association-based audit is also acceptable as long as the Team Leader is qualified such as the above (which also includes, as an alternative, certain training courses and performance of Performance Track Audits). This would include, for example, RC ISO 14001 audits.

The applicant must make future commitments for at least four environmental aspects and must choose those aspects from a detailed environmental performance table. Past achievement must be shown by selecting a minimum of two environmental aspects from any of the categories in a detailed table.

In order to qualify for Performance Track, a facility must:

> 1. Adopt and implement an EMS that includes very specific and detailed elements including the aspect analysis discussed above.

> 2. Be able to demonstrate specific environmental achievements and commit to continued environmental improvement

> 3. Commit to public outreach and performance reporting.

> 4. Have a record of sustained compliance with environmental requirements.

With respect to compliance, Performance Track bars a facility from participation if there has been:

Criminal Activity:

• Corporate criminal conviction or pleas for environmentally-related violations of criminal laws involving the corporation or a corporate officer within the past five years.

• Criminal conviction or pleas of an employee at the same facility for environmentally related violations of criminal laws within the past 5 years.

• Ongoing criminal investigation/prosecution of a corporation, corporate officer, or employee at the same facility for violations of environmental law.[200]

Civil Activity:

• There cannot be:

• Three or more significant civil violations at the facility in the past 3 years.

• Unresolved, unaddressed significant non-compliance or significant violations.

• Planned but not yet filed judicial or administrative action at the facility.

• Ongoing EPA or state-initiated litigation at the facility.

• Situation where a facility is not in compliance with the schedule and terms of an order or decree. EPA may also consider "whether there are significant problems or a pattern of non-compliance in an applicant's overall civil or criminal compliance history."[201]

On April 14, 2004, EPA signed the first Performance Track Rule, which grants member facilities increased procedural flexibility and reduced administrative burdens.[202] "The Rule reduces the frequency of reports required under the Maximum Achievable Control Technology (MACT) provisions of the Clean Air Act, streamlined reporting requirements for Performance Track facilities that achieve MACT or better emission levels." In addition, the Rule extends the site storage times for hazardous wastes in certain units under RCRA. "Specifically large quantity hazardous waste generators are given up to 180 days (and 270 days if the waste is transported 200 miles or more) to accumulate hazardous waste without a RCRA permit or interim status, providing the generator meets certain conditions."[203]

Recently, Performance Track is now encouraging corporate certification. "EPA will enhance the current Performance Track program by adding a corporate membership component for companies that participate substantially in the facility program and who performance, practices, and policies at a corporate level meet criteria associated with environmental excellence."[204]

The GEMI Self Assessment Program

The GEMI Self Assessment Program[205] assumes four levels of development of management systems and is a good test for management integration and ability to meet program requirements such as Performance Track. It contains a variety of questions and assumptions as to level of development depending on the answers to specific questions with respect to a specific aspect.[206] "They focus on environmental management systems and the extent to which they have been *integrated* into general business processes in the company."[207]

Level 1 is Compliance, a "policy of regulatory compliance."

Level 2 is Systems Development and Implementation. This assumes a "formal environmental management system" which "provides compliance management methods and also facilitates the company's efforts to reach environmental performance extending beyond regulatory compliance to meet more comprehensive corporate policies."

Level 3, Integration Into General Business Functions, assumes that environmental management is integrated into management functions and general business conduct on a regular basis.

Level 4 is "Total Quality Approach," which assumes an integrated system applied globally and continuously evaluated for improvement opportunities.

The 16 Principles in the Assessment are:

1. Corporate Priority

2. Integrated Management ("To integrate these policies, programs and practices fully into each business as an essential element of management in all its functions.")

3. Process of Improvement

4. Employee Education

5. Prior Assessment ("To assess environmental impacts before starting a new activity or project and before decommissioning a facility or leaving a site.")

6. Products and Services ("To develop and provide products or services that have no undue environmental impact and are safe in their intended use, that are efficient in their consumption of energy and natural resources, and that can be recycled, reused or disposed of safely.")

7. Customer Advice

8. Facilities and Operations ("To develop and operate facilities and conduct activities taking into consideration the efficient use of energy and materials, the sustainable use of renewable resources, the minimization of adverse environmental impact and waste generation, and the safe and responsible disposal of residual waste.") Note that this principle also has elements for employee health and safety and risk evaluation.

9. Research

10. Precautionary Approach ("To modify the manufacture, marketing or use of products or services or the conduct of activities, consistent with scientific and technical understanding, to prevent serious or irreversible environmental degradation.")

11. Contractors and Suppliers

12. Emergency Preparedness

13. Transfer of Technology ("To contribute to the transfer of environmentally sound technology and management methods through the industrial and public sectors.")

14. Contributing to the Common Effort ("To contribute to the development of public policy and to business, governmental and intergovernmental programs and educational initiatives that will enhance environmental awareness and protection.")

15. Openness to Concerns

16. Compliance and Reporting

Making the System Work

We in industry want the system, including programs such as Performance Tracking, the ELP, and Project XL, to work. Government and citizen groups want the system to work. The core premise to examine now and in the future is that some approaches to environmental (and health and safety) regulation encourage good environmental management and others either discourage it or divert government and industry resources away from activities that have greater potential to benefit the environment. Agencies tend to overlook the normal and predictable behavior of corporations and their employees, failing to recognize that it is usually not in the best interests of an individual or a company to risk serious civil or criminal liability for improper actions. Agencies sometimes insist on prior review of industry actions even when it would not be in the corporations' best interests to take the chance of trying to game the system, as games are not viewed favorably in permit renewal or enforcement proceedings. EPA's enforcement would be far more effective if the Agency focused its power on making it costly for those who do try to avoid clearly applicable controls and making it more likely that such parties will be caught.[208]

In looking at the future of the interrelationship between compliance and enforcement, George Hawkins, then an EPA attorney working on Vice President Gore's national performance review, noted the importance of support for

> EPA's ongoing efforts to devise performance-based measures to replace traditional beans [enforcement goals]. Debate about the effectiveness of different types of actions is hampered by the difficulty in measuring the consequences of such actions in environmental terms. Until these measures are understood, it will be too easy to judge EPA by counting enforcement actions taken and harder to justify other problem-solving actions that are designed to eliminate the causes of environmental harms.[209]

The numbers issue is very difficult one for EPA. For example, the Agency was criticized by the U.S. General Accounting Office (GAO) for disparities between regional offices in their actions to enforce environmental laws.[210] EPA replied, quite properly, that "some variation in management approaches is desirable and appropriate" questioning the GAO report's assumption that variation is somehow inappropriate or a widespread problem. However, GAO contends that EPA is lacking "accurate and complete enforcement data to determine whether core requirements are being met and whether significant variations among regions should be corrected," also noting a 1999 EPA report citing "significant gaps in enforcement-related databases."[211]

The Environmental Council of the States (ECOS) issued a statement on

August 14, 2001, that the Environmental Working Group (EWG) had used misleading and inaccurate data in its reports criticizing state-level inspections. The EWG had used a federal compliance database called the Integrated Data for Enforcement Analysis (IDEA), which the ECOS report says is difficult to use and frequently outdated. EPA is trying to develop a single Internet source called the Central Data Exchange, but this is still far away. ECOS argues that the EWG should have obtained data from each state, which EWG argues is impractical. The obvious point is that without good data bases, transparency is simply not there, and it is difficult to get good data on state and federal efforts.

There are some fundamental issues that make regulatory reform difficult, if not impossible, despite some equally unambiguous weaknesses in the system. For example, "[a]lthough regulations are usually effective in reducing emissions from large and obvious point sources, they do not allow EPA and state regulators the flexibility to reduce pollution among numerous small sources that account for most environmental degradation."[212] "The Wisconsin Department of Natural Resources points out that the current regulatory system in the United States applies to only about 20% of the sources of environmental problems, and that addressing the remaining 80% will require means that go beyond regulatory controls."[213] These weaknesses occur despite the enormous regulatory system that governs environmental issues. "The number of federal, state, and local environmental rules and regulations in the United States exploded from about 2,000 in the 1970s to more than 100,00 at the end of the 1990's. Environmental regulations are now listed in over 789 part of the *Code of Federal Regulations*."[214] Between 1970 and the mid-1990s, EPA issued more than 11,000 pages of environmental regulations. Yet "one EPA official argues that relying on command-and-control approaches to environmental management is analogous to using emergency rooms as the primary instrument of health care."[215] Such a system "neither encourages preventive measures nor provides incentives for maintaining good health."[216]

Because Congress passes environmental legislation piecemeal, consolidates diverse environmental regulations under EPA's control, and adds new environmental rules and regulations without reviewing the scope and impacts of previous laws, the Agency lacks a coherent mission and a clear direction. More than 40 committees and subcommittees of Congress have some type of oversight responsibilities for or jurisdiction over EPA. More than a dozen statutes govern EPA's mandate to control pollution and require the Agency to organize into numerous offices with different environmental management philosophies, control strategies and "legal cultures."[217]

Moreover, EPA does not have the means to effectively address difficult cross-media problems, given that it is largely divided among different media programs.

Performance Measures

There may be some logical ways of measuring performance. John Pendergrass of the Environmental Law Institute reasons that

> [t]he primary standard ought to be, how did the environment, or at least those aspects of it for which an agency chief (or governor) had responsibility fare during that person's term? Did air and water quality improve? Was there less pollution released to the air, water, land, and groundwater? Other similar questions can be posed regarding contaminated land, people who health was affected by chemicals in drinking water or by air pollution, regions that meet air quality standards, and water bodies that meet water quality standards.[218]

EPA now has an action plan for promoting the use of EMS.[219] EPA notes that it has made a commitment to "encourage organizations to use EMSs that improve compliance, pollution prevention, and other measures of environmental performance."[220] However, "EPA does not prefer one EMS model over the other, but rather supports the use of any EMS model . . . that focuses on improved environmental performance and compliance as well as source reduction (pollution prevention) and system performance."[221] John Voorhees, writing in *The Environmental Law Reporter*, has extensively examined EPA's approach.[222] Despite the movement toward management systems throughout corporate America, "the complex, costly, and inflexible command-and-control regulatory system that dominates environmental policy in the United States neither encourages nor rewards corporate EMS that exceed compliance requirements."[223]

The government is suspicious of even third-party certification. Sylvia Lowrance, then-Deputy Assistant Administrator in EPA's Office of Enforcement and Compliance Assurance, claims that "the concept of third-party certification 'needs more work'" and cites numerous instance of widespread "fraud" on the compliance side.[224] By contrast at the same panel in which Lowrance was quoted, Susan Moore, Vice President of Environment, Health, and Safety for Georgia Pacific and a former federal official, stated that "self certification leads to changed behaviors and attitudes and a 'real world wake-up call for facility managers.'" She also felt that ISO 14001 is "highly overrated as a behavior modification tool,"[225] a view that I share.

The National Environmental Performance Partnership System (NEPPS) between EPA and various states is designed to restructure the relationship with states to focus on results. However, EPA and the states are largely concentrating their focus on the traditional elements of permits, emissions, inspections, and enforcement actions. NAPA has "concluded that the viability of NEPPS is in doubt because of weak leadership at EPA, explicit opposition by many program managers within both state agencies and EPA, and uneven or half-hearted implementation by EPA and many states."[226] The result has been characterized as "every state gets to participate in agreements that officially grant them greater autonomy, while EPA regional offices remain free to micro-manage unofficially."[227]

There is still a culture class between government and industry:

> Eliminating rather than controlling pollutants through prevention and eco-efficiency will be essential in supplementing regulations in the future. Implementing a collaborative policy of environmental management focused on pollution prevention and eco-efficiency will require a better understanding by EPA and state environmental protection agencies of trends in the private sector to adopt beyond-compliance EMS and the motivations for doing so.[228]

But as discussed throughout this book, "beyond compliance" is itself a misnomer. An effective EMS is not designed for compliance but to manage functions. If you are managing only for compliance, you have a poor management system. Compliance follows if you are managing effectively.

We should be able to work cooperatively together to achieve environmental goals. When the system cannot operate as it is nominally intended to, unpredictable holes appear that provide opportunities to those who take their environmental responsibilities less seriously, while those who want to do the right thing are undercut. EPA and industry need to eliminate obstacles to compliance and redirect resources so that more environmental regulators will know that they are contributing to environmental quality and not just pushing paper—and taking an unnecessary ration of abuse at that. To get the best performance, and in particular to foster innovation, those in industry who are assigned to environmental matters also need to know that they are involved in a process that makes a difference.

EPA and Data Management

While computerization may eventually make the job easier, there are many roadblocks. "In the era of the Internet, the U.S. system of environmental protection by and large still relies on regulatory tools forged in the era of the punchcard."[229] Notwithstanding efforts by both the federal and state governments, the changes are agonizingly slow. Federal and state systems are not integrated and probably won't be for many years. The focus has been on hardware and software, but the fundamental problem is the need to slog through the enormous number of conflicting and duplicative information requirements, with estimates of between 900-1,100 plus areas of duplication.

As Mark Cohen of Vanderbilt University has so aptly noted,

> [d]espite many successes, environmental information mechanisms in the United States were not forced as part of a well-designed system of integrated programs. Instead, they have largely evolved in isolation of traditional environmental regulatory policy and developments in the law. Furthermore, the audiences and potential uses of the data provided by environmental information disclosure programs are not well defined. Thus, before new information programs are designed, it is important to first ask why we are collecting the information, for whom the information is being collected, and for what purposes and in what contexts it is necessary to collect the information.[230]

EPA has been making some progress.[231] It now has a limited website (http://www.epa.gov/guidance) containing policy and guidance documents, which it calls its "Interpretive Documents Collection." It is intended to provide a "central point of access to non-binding general policy, guidance and interpretive documents that describe how the Agency intends to exercise its discretionary authority and explain what a statue or regulations means," but it only includes guidance documents issued since January 1, 1999. EPA has also now developed an "Integrated Error Correction Process," described at http://www.epa.gov/enviro, to be used to correct errors in EPA databases. Still, the largest repository of EPA documents resides (and will likely continue to reside) with the Environmental Law Institute, with its *ELR—Environmental Law Reporter* Guidance and Policy service at http://www.eli.org. Its database is far larger than EPA's (and easier to use).

The most difficult job is to get the state and federal agencies to agree on common definitions and data needs. Enforcement personnel seem virtually paranoid that electronic reporting will make it more difficult to make cases. There is concern as to electronic signatures and the legal implications as to whether someone can deny actually "signing" a document. Electronic reporting may occur on a limited basis if all of these issues can be resolved and will likely be implemented at some state level first if the states can secure the necessary federal clearances. There is a strong reluctance of the federal government to give up any oversight. The funding to allow such changes and the interest in the government is limited. A General Services Administration (GSA) study noted that EPA's ability to assess risk and establish risk-based priorities has been hampered by data quality problems, including critical data gaps, databases that do not operate compatibly with one another, and persistent concerns about the accuracy of the data in many of EPA's data systems.[232]

For those of you who are new to the area of environmental regulation, but experienced in data management, you will find significant frustration. Environmental policy is controversial and data available to deal with these controversies is often insufficient and conflicting. NAPA has stated quite properly that the nation needs authoritative information about environmental condition and about where agency efforts have helped improve these conditions. EPA has recognized this concern and now has a new OEI that is designed to promote the use of information as a "strategic resource." But as noted by NAPA, that office "is too weak, too narrowly focused, too focused on access to data instead of on the existence and quality of data."[233] EPA should instead "galvanize its weak [OEI] by giving it independence and authority to build far better information about environmental conditions and results."[234] Those have been some improvements, but the quality of data still varies and budetary restriction reduce the opportunities for improvement.

"[N]either Congress, nor EPA has given this new office the mandate, authority, funding, staff or other tools to establish multimedia monitoring systems to develop the information needed for performance based management of all agency programs."[235] Notwithstanding major efforts by the federal and state government, it is unlikely that there will be significant short-term change. Political pressures will still demand bean counting. (See Chapter 3, The Challenge of Regulatory Reform.) The process of change is agonizingly slow. The bureaucracy is not about to give up "just in case" reporting. Turf problems between the "silos," i.e., the EPA program offices, are intense, let alone those involving the states. Who will have ownership of the data? What are the incentives to change? It may be good public policy, but not if you have been doing the same thing and with strong statutory backing for over 30 years. Who will fund the necessary changes? The money is not there, and if requirements to make changes are imposed on the states, is it another "unfunded mandate"? Of course there is no incentive for software manufacturers to develop software that integrates both state and federal permitting requirements. Think how complex this would be and the difficulty in integrating changes. In essence, the requirements are simply too varied to make such programs economically viable.

The issue of collection and dissemination of environmental information is a very broad-based concern. A letter was written to the then Administrator Whitman by a group that included organizations as diverse as the Natural Resources Defense Council, Environmental Defense, the American Chemistry Council and the American Petroleum Institute stated that the groups urged making reform of environmental information policy, management and systems a top priority.[236] The group also united behind an effort to revise a pending EPA rule on electronic reporting and record keeping with the mouthful name of Cross Media Electronic Reporting & Recordkeeping Rule (CROMERRR). That rule, "which is supposed to reduce burden, requires elaborate audit trails that are not achievable through off-the-shelf software, meaning industries large and small would have to develop software and make it compatible with their systems."[237] The proposal would also require electronic data to be accessible to new computer systems over time. The rule was subsequently withdrawn.[238]

Management Techniques to Control Costs and Improve Environmental Performance

Even with the best of efforts to establish and maintain a rational, cost-effective regulatory system, the costs of environmental protection will continue to be high. No effectively managed company can ignore them. Today, environmental issues are rapidly being integrated into business decisionmaking. They are considered as important to business as finance, tax, employee relations, and other functions that are traditionally part of the management process.

Over the past 25 years, a number of management techniques have been developed or refined in a way that may be useful for environmental managers. These include synthesizing environmental and business goals, Total Quality Management, careful downsizing or reengineering, and analytical methods to improve decisionmaking. Each technique offers a means to help support the underpinnings of environmental management programs discussed later in this book.

At the same time, care must be taken to avoid the latest fads. For example, the zeal to avoid overcentralization has lead to overdecentralization and downsizing for the sake of downsizing has led to loss of institutional memory and an inability to manage outside providers that may not necessarily reduce long-term costs. Many of us cynically believe that new labels are frequently put on old means of management to sell consulting services. Michael Hammer, an internationally respected management consultant, quipped that "[m]ost management books should not be tossed aside lightly; they should be hurled against the wall with great force."[239]

At present, various management techniques are voluntary, but regulatory agencies and international entities are showing increasing interest in the adoption of management techniques that improve environmental accountability. For example, New Jersey's Pollution Prevention Act requires companies to perform, as part of a required pollution prevention plan, "a comprehensive financial analysis of the costs or savings realized by investments in pollution prevention options compared to the costs of using hazardous substances, generating hazardous substances as nonproduct output, and releasing hazardous substances."[240] The intent is to require that project financial evaluations take into account the full range of costs and savings: direct and indirect, tangible and intangible. This requires a systematic analysis of conventional capital and operating costs plus those items often omitted from conventional project financial evaluation. It is not clear how rigorous these requirements will be in practice.

Synthesis of Environmental and Business Goals

Both the challenge of competition in domestic and international markets and legal requirements necessitate the development of corporate environmental strategies. The strength of an environmental strategy may well affect the strength and profitability of an entire company.

Companies typically follow one of three alternative environmental strategies. The first is grudging compliance with regulatory requirements while seeking to turn a profit. The second is "pushing beyond standards, codes, and regulations and devising new products and materials that create market demand while addressing environmental concerns."[241] Many companies are now pursuing this strategy.[242] A third alternative is a mixture of these two, blending ready compliance with environmental laws with innovation and responsiveness to market forces.[243]

As noted previously, Elf's philosophy was stated as follows:

> We have always preferred results rather than just talk about the environment. This is all the more important since the vocabulary is evolving all the time, making it hard to keep one's bearings. Sustainable development has long been a central feature of our vocabulary. Now concepts such as "eco-efficiency," or "factor 4" and even "factor 10," or "eco-restructuring," "eco-purchasing," and "dematerialization," have entered the vocabulary. In fact these somewhat complex terms all refer to the same idea, more or less, namely "doing more with fewer raw materials." All play a part in the drive to boost productivity and improve product performance, analyze materials flows, cut waste, and so forth. This is hardly new in industry, whose lifeblood is profitability. The only difference is that we used to be driven by economic considerations alone; today our motivation is both economic and ecological. The mechanisms remain the same, however.[244]

The most successful companies synthesize their business strategy and their environmental strategy. This approach, sometimes termed "strategic environmental management," may be defined as the pursuit of competitive advantage through environmental management strategies. Potential sources of competitive advantage that can be enhanced through environmental strategies are listed in Figure 3-2.

Figure 3-2
Competitive Benefits of Strategic Environmental Management

> **Margin improvement**—seeking cost savings at every stage of the product life cycle through more efficient use of labor, energy, and material resources;
> **Rapid cycle time**—reducing time to market by considering environmental issues as part of the "concurrent engineering" process during the early stages of design;
> **Market access**—developing global products that are environmentally "preferable" and meet international eco-labeling standards in Europe, Japan, and other regions; and
> **Product differentiation**—introducing distinctive environmental benefits such as energy efficiency or ease of disassembly that may sway a purchase decision.[245]

We as environmental managers are uniquely positioned to influence and enhance these strategies.

To do so, however, environmental managers may need to change their focus. Many of us come from regulatory backgrounds, either technical or legal. Because many still view their role in this way, it is no wonder that they are ignored by their employers. An Arthur D. Little survey of 185 environment, health, and safety (EHS) officers at 185 corporations in the United States and Canada found that these managers bemoan "their own failure to convince management that environment is an important business issue."[246] The managers surveyed said they thought colleagues viewed them as having no real value to their companies, and 70 percent said counterparts from other departments did not accept the need for EHS programs.[247] The author noted that the "good news is that, over the past 10 or even 20 years, we've come to the point where the environmental professionals are seen as part of the organization," but they are not seen as equal partners by other business functions.[248]

Today, the focus of environmental managers should be neither technical nor legal, but *management*.[249] No longer is expertise in regulatory and technical matters the primary criterion for advancement in the EHS area. We must still understand the technical and legal issues, but must approach their resolution in a management context. We must be able to speak "managementese" as well as "regulatoryese," particularly in this era of downsizing and cost control.

Tearing down the "green wall" provides an opportunity for environmental managers to have a more meaningful role in the business. As Robert Shelton, then with A.D. Little noted, for "an interactive environmental strategy" we must use "innovative, tailored approaches that focus on developing a sustainable program within the corporate structure, including the management of technology, human resources, and financial resources. This requires a highly interactive climate where the environmental concerns are intimately entwined in the appropriate business functions."[250] An analogous phenomenon is breaking down the "'blue wall' between data processing staff and the mainstream of the organization."[251] In this case,

> [t]he bottom-line impact of the [personal computer] offered a positive return on investment in the form of improved sales, customer service, flexibility and responsiveness. In the same manner, after the EHS revolution, the organization will recognize environmental opportunities as well as risks and value justify both vis-a-vis the bottom line. As the green wall crumbles, each functional "silo," from legal to finance to operations, will build EHS considerations into its processes and measure the value of the pursuit in dollar terms.[252]

Environmental managers could and should do more to be a part of their corporations, as indicated in Figure 3-3. Bob Garton, senior EHS manager at Apple Computer, stated that "we come out of two different worlds, the environmental people and the business people," and environmental managers need to do more self-promotion.[253] As he quite correctly noted, "many of us got into this field because we were concerned about the moral issues, it is a bottom-line issue."[254] "If we keep our people healthy, we keep them at work. If we prevent an environmental problem like a spill or not getting an application for a permit filed on time, we avoid a business interruption."[255]

Figure 3-3
Responsibilities of Environmental Managers in Business

- Make environmental management a business issue that complements the overall business strategy,
- Change environmental communication within the company to use traditional business terms that reflect business logic and priorities,
- Adopt metrics to measure the real costs and business benefits of the environmental management programs,
- Embed environmental management into operations, similar to the successful Design-for-Environment models, and
- Radically change the job descriptions and compensation of environmental managers—and line managers—to reflect the realities of doing business.[256]

Total Quality Management

Total quality management (TQM) is an increasingly popular management concept based on common sense: constantly attempting to improve performance and seeking to measure the improvement.[257] TQM focuses on the customer, defined broadly. Indeed, "[m]eeting customers' needs is the driving force behind the entire quality revolution in the United States."[258]

In the environmental context, we can look at "the corporation as the supplier of environmental behavior and the community and the general public as the customers."[259] Perhaps the term "corporate constituencies" better captures the idea. Many companies, whether or not they use the term TQM, are beginning to apply the concept to environmental management in the same way as they apply it to production quality control and other more traditional aspects of general management. It is assumed that

> when businesses apply total quality to environmental management they reap three basic benefits:
>
> - an alignment with business strategy,
> - continuous improvement with measurable results, and
> - a customer and supplier alignment.[260]

This book makes a variety of suggestions to achieve TQM goals, but I have not necessarily phrased them in TQM terms. If a term is necessary to identify good business practices that improve quality and responsiveness to customers, the public, and regulatory agencies, then TQM is a good vehicle.

As discussed throughout this book, it is important for environmental management to be accepted as an integral part of all levels of management. TQM assumes that by integrating environmental aspects of business into this effort throughout that business, environmental management can become part of a company's strategy on how to conduct its business. The very same tools and strategy that apply to production, sales, and distribution can be applied to specific environmental programs. Environmental management then speaks the same language as the rest of the business and jumps the hurdle of being viewed as an outsider to basic business strategy.[261] "In today's corporate world the discussion is not about which management system to embrace, but rather how many management systems can be meaningfully combined into a single, viable management structure."[262] Such integration facilitates the continuous improvement model. "The use of the latest technology to integrate a range of systems (financial, human resources, monitoring, production and maintenance schedules, training, monitoring databases, etc.) combined with increasing web browser functionality is providing management with the IT tools to effectively implement integrated management systems."[263]

Continuous improvement, another TQM tenet, is a concept we all can agree with. "Success in TQM is measured by continuing quality improvement. Achieving continuing quality improvement depends on good organization, management and environmental policy, and good acceptance of that policy throughout the corporation."[264] But placing numerical assumptions on matters other than those that easily lend themselves to statistics—such as waste reduction, violations, and citations—can be difficult[265] and counterproductive. For example, failure to recognize that soft dollar savings can be just as important as hard dollar losses could be detrimental.

Continuous, measurable improvement in environmental performance is increasingly recognized as a core element of corporate management and governance. There is, however, a potential problem with excessive reliance on quantifiable measures of environmental performance. In such a system, what is not quantified—or quantifiable—is often treated as something that does not exist. Some risks may not be quantified because of the inherent weaknesses in quantification methods relative to unanticipated releases. The value of such quantification should be compared on a case-by-case basis to the liability that it might create. Such liability may be far out of proportion to the actual expectation of the likelihood and magnitude of potential incidents. (Note that this may sound like the kind of risk that insurers are only now becoming aware of, and do not yet fully insure.) Moreover, quantifying a particular risk at a particular facility is far different from quantifying a category of risks for a category of facilities.

It is also difficult to quantify performance in preparing for future requirements or liabilities. Beyond measurable parameters, a corporate program needs to have appropriate incentives and disincentives, so that the program can encourage good long-term planning. Effective preparation will, in turn, reduce long-term costs, refine product design and development, and revitalize marketing activities. A system of incentives and disincentives will work to maintain the corporation's influence over rules and laws that might have a dramatic impact on its economic health.

TQM has its critics. One excellent analysis identifies mistakes that companies make in implementing TQM. These mistakes are listed in Figure 3-4.

Figure 3-4
Mistakes Frequently Made in Implementing
Total Quality Management

• Focus on Changing Culture vs. Changing Behavior.
• Failing to Fully and Accurately Define Performance Requirements.
• Failing to Perform a Gap Analysis and Develop a Strategic Quality Plan Prior to Implementing TQM.
• Failure to Establish a Functioning Executive Quality Council.
• Failure to Establish Key Quality Measures and Goals for Every Level of the Organization, Linked to Organization-Wide Requirements for Market Leadership.
• Failure to Change Compensation Systems to Hold Senior Executives and Middle Managers Responsible for Quality Leadership and Achieving Quality Results.
• Failing to Restructure to Place Managers, Supervisors and Employees Physically and Emotionally Close to the Customers They Serve.
• Relying Upon Training and/or Quality Improvement Techniques as THE Way to Implement TQM.
• Failing to Do "Just-in-Time Training" and to Provide Follow-Up Coaching to Ensure That Skills Taught in the Training Are Immediately Applied on the Job.
• Seeking Short-Term Breakthroughs vs. Long-Term Continuous Improvement.[266]

The authors of this critique also note that the promise and reality of TQM is "continuous improvements; not sudden breakthroughs; and retention of profits and market share rather than significant gains."[267] If your company has major problems and

you need to get $20 million out of your operating costs in six months, TQM isn't the answer. Instead you are probably going to have to close plants, lay off workers, shut down product lines, and do all of the other traditional things you might do to get those $20 million worth of savings. Once you have made and executed those tough decisions, then turn to TQM for the future.[268]

In summary, a commitment to quality, however phrased, is critical to good management, including environmental management. As discussed throughout this book, "the major barriers to quality superiority are not technical, they are behavioral. The root cause why we have not moved further faster is the intractability of many organizations in the face of change."[269]

Environmental Management and Downsizing

In this era of cost control, the environmental budget is no longer sacrosanct. Environmental management productivity, like productivity in other areas of management, must continually improve. This is forcing environmental managers to manage as business people, rather than as compliance managers. In essence, successful EHS management requires "redesigning EHS management processes to streamline work activities and eliminate low-value-added steps; pushing down responsibility and accountability for some EHS work into the line organization; and leveraging the effectiveness of remaining EHS staff by extending their reach and improving their use of technology."[270]

Management will often look at EHS staffing as they would any other staff group and demand justification data. The assumption, often applied, is that this is a "commodity" and there should be some form of standard ratio or that benchmarking with other companies in the industry would be helpful. Yet "benchmarking staffing levels are useful only when: (1) the activity is well defined; (2) operations and structures are standardized across the survey base; and (3) data is adjusted to take into account the structures and process (a nearly impossible feat). It depends might be the operative expression for determining the best and most cost effective staff."[271] Richard MacLean has identified several alternative criteria that can serve as a useful basis for determining appropriate staffing.[272] They include nature of the business/risk of operations (e.g., industry group, environmental "footprint," proximity to sensitive areas; legal/regulatory requirements (e.g., different states or countries, chemicals and processes); company goals; company culture (e.g., degree of integration of environment into line management, tolerance for risk); number of separate sites/employees, communication obstacles (e.g., language barriers, distance between sites); company regulatory compliance history; profitability and production rate of facility; competency of the staff; experience level of the individuals; morale and work ethic of the group; maturity of the existing programs; organizational structure; departmental processes (e.g., use of information management systems); program mix and priorities given; cost of staff; willingness to share information and resources.

A research project by the Center for Environmental Innovation, in which I am participating, is attempting to get real data. The Center is currently conducting research on current approaches to sizing and organizing EHS departments within small and medium and large companies. It is not a theoretical look, but a real time assessment of actual practices, including the specific issues of outsourcing, shared services, transnational staff groups and major business restructurings such a mergers and divestments.

In a recent article describing that study[273] it was noted:

> There are, however, no standardized methods and procedures for assessing the performance of EHS organizations. Among the difficulties impeding such standardized approaches are issues relating to data quantification and validity, as well as information collection and "mining."

"The challenge for this study is that no single rating or scoring system can provide an absolute measure of the 'best' EHS organization. Indeed there is not even common agreement over the definition of 'Superior EHS performance.'"

The key objects of this phase of the benchmarking research are to:

- Develop an evaluation matrix for the assessment of corporate EHS performance;

- Identify the top companies with superior EHS performance (i.e., those that are more likely to have superior EHS organizations and staffing practices); and

- Serve as a preliminary explanation of the organizational factors that contribute to EHS success.

The article mentions a variety of matrixes.[274] Five categories[275] are subdivided into 19 outcome indicators:

- Awards [six indicators];

- Peer recognition [two indicators];

- Classical performance measures [three indicators];

- Financial results [two indicators]; and

- Published composite EHS outcome indices [six indicators].

Phase II looks at "input variable, measuring management support and the characteristics of the industry sector" and "intervening variable," measuring sophisticated organization processes, participation in progressive or cutting edge trade associations or activities and specific cutting edge programs. "The rational for considering these factors is that a company that cultivates effective EHS leadership is more likely to focus its employees on environmental, health, and safety goals while also fostering EHS programs that maximize the potential of all employees."[276] It is also assumed that companies that support progressive trade associations and involvement with cutting-edge EHS programs "are more likely to be well organized and staffed, since they have resources focused in issues beyond day-to day compliance and 'firefighting.'"[277] Additional research indicates that "companies with a higher level of potential liabilities and larger levels of pollution over unit of output are more likely to have a higher-quality environmental management system."[278]

While I reviewed the matrixes as part of this effort, I am not convinced that there is a sufficient data base or even empirical data to fully support the final matrix. However,[279] "when senior EHS professionals were surveyed their evaluation matrix identified as among the top 25 companies were 100% accurate in identifying top EHS performers, i.e. those companies that the evaluation matrix identified as among the top 25. Even the relative ranking within the top four closely approximate the top positions in our study." Exxon-Mobil was in the top 25 for strong programs despite their perceived combative attitude on social policy issues.

At the outset, we in environmental management must take a careful look at our own value. A Novartis executive suggested that we need to perceive our jobs as outsourced and therefore ask the questions listed in Figure 3-5.

Figure 3-5
Self-Assessing the Value of the Environmental Manager

- What do my customers want?
- What is the added value of my activities?
- Are they useful for my customers?
- What economic value do I create for the company?
- Am I networking properly?
- Am I an indispensable link in my own network?
- Am I correctly communicating within the company?
- Are we doing our work at an acceptable cost?

We must also assess the value of the activities themselves. An "activity value analysis" is designed to determine what activities in a functional area are recognized by the organization being evaluated, what is the relative value of that activity to the organization, what is the priority ranking of the activity as determined by that organization, what tasks are associated with each activity, and who in the organization currently performs the tasks associated with each activity. Also part of this evaluation is the organization's estimate of the time committed and relative cost (if available or known) of conducting each task. The evaluation process is conducted in an interview format and is designed to be both objective and, where appropriate, subjective. In some respects, it challenges the individuals being interviewed to justify their routine and periodic activities, the tasks they associate with each activity, and the time dedicated to each activity or task. Ato is pursuing this effort with plant-led teams, at the working level, closest to the work.

Grover Vos, former Director of Health, Environment and Safety (HES) Policy and Programs at Ato, developed the list of questions in Figure 3-6 for an activity value analysis.

Figure 3-6
List of Questions for Activity Value Analysis

- Where in the organization are there resources capable of addressing the pertinent issues, activities, or tasks?
- Who is responsible for conducting each activity or task?
- Who performs each activity or task?
- How much time is spent on each activity or task?
- What is the cost of addressing each activity or task?
- Is there a value associated with the issue, activity, or task not included in the cost of addressing that issue, activity, or task? If so, what is it?
- What EHS issues are of concern to this plant? List by all major categories and subcategories.
- For each issue, delineate the activities and associated tasks performed on a routine, periodic, or occasional basis.
- Why are these issues, activities, or tasks important?
- How important is each issue, activity, or task?
- How would you rank these issues, activities, or tasks in order of priority?
- What resources are needed to address each issue, activity, or task?

Often, management will try to "benchmark" against other companies as to staff sizing. This invariably is the apples and oranges issue and the data is of limited value, even if the study is "exclusive." As noted by Richard MacLean:

The exclusivity of these studies may give the impression of value. But, for the most part, it is extremely difficult to interpret the results accurately. Much about an organization's design is related to subjective issues such as the influence of company culture, business objectives, productivity, and even personality and legacy issues. These rarely are captured in a "fill in the blanks" questionnaire.[280]

As was noted in a recent study of DuPont[281]:

First, EHS staff size can be minimized when there is greater "ownership" of EHS concerns, and more personal responsibility. Fewer individuals are needed to watch over compliance and governance issues. Second, a shared service organization is more likely to succeed (if staffed with competent professionals) or fail if it does not live up to the quality demands of the customers. Even if the internal organization's services cost more than those of external providers, if its quality proposition is desirable, an internal organization will prosper. Third, cooperation and communication are improved when employees really are working on a shared value, and not just an issue that executives have little interest in (other when things go wrong).

These forms of analysis may lead to organizational changes and increased efficiencies. Raymond Hill of A.T. Kearney advocates "activity based costing" (which was undertaken at Ato as "activity value analysis") to focus on "what people do rather than where they report in the organization."[282] This allows the EHS function to be more integrated into the business and may result in more work being performed by people outside of the EHS unit. Such analysis has also identified opportunities, such as:

• Reducing reporting efforts by 30-50% through elimination of unnecessary reports, and streamlining the data collection and consolidation through information technology;

• Reducing issue management costs by 40% through clear accountability in tracking and "owning" issues;

• Reducing permit cycle time from 6 months to 6 weeks through use of multi-disciplinary teams;

- Outsourcing non value-added activities to more cost effective suppliers, saving from 10-30% of costs; and

- Reducing environmental purchasing costs by 10-30% through consolidation and greater use of unit cost contracts.[283]

This form of reengineering does not necessarily lead to downsizing, but at least gives a basis for understanding the scope of work and how it is managed. Downsizing per se is not evil. It continually forces management to shift resources and in so doing forces management to reevaluate its priorities regularly. It can be and has been a positive force by helping ensure that issues posing the greatest degree of risk are identified and managed first. This in turn helps prioritize the allocation of limited resources. The danger of downsizing is when risks are not prioritized and cuts are made on the theory that "everyone gives blood," regardless of the short-term or long-term consequences.

If downsizing is necessary, it should proceed simultaneously with process reengineering. David Sweet of Loral Corporation adds to the old definition of an optimist and a pessimist: An optimist looks at a glass as half full, a pessimist as half empty, and a reengineering specialist looks at a glass and sees twice as much glass as necessary.[284] Just how you eliminate the "unnecessary" glass is the key question.

There are diverse views on how to accomplish downsizing. George Carpenter of Procter & Gamble notes that "[a] company that cuts staff first and then begins to look for process improvements runs a significant risk of failure,"[285] and that "cuts in technical staff headcount can often be accompanied by a loss of mastery far out of proportion to the reductions themselves."[286] Dennis Macauley, then of Union Carbide, has stated that "[o]ne reason for the company's success is that it did not follow the advice of its consultants to decentralize. It recognized that blind decentralization was merely swinging the pendulum back to the '60's when EHS staffs were totally decentralized and small."[287] On the other hand, I was told by a chief operating officer of a major company that he recognizes that in making major personnel cuts throughout a company, the cuts go too deep in some instances. However, his view is that it is easier to fix the resulting problems later and mandate the cultural changes now of doing more with less through deep personnel cuts.

Overall, to "achieve the best results from reengineering and downsizing of EHS operations, companies must align their EHS goals with the company's business vision and objectives."[288] If the critical programs are not in place and there are still significant capital expenses, you need to engineer first before you reengineer. Nevertheless, the business pressures will require that the processes be parallel and there is still the opportunity, as discussed subsequently, to improve how the job is done while getting the programs and facility in shape.

Analytical Techniques for Environmental Management

Companies seeking to improve their financial performance seek techniques to assist them in analyzing the short- and long-term costs and benefits associated with alternative environmental strategies. Life-cycle analysis (LCA) is a relatively new technique that can be used for policy analysis or industrial self-improvement. An LCA is a detailed balance sheet of the energy and material inputs and outputs of a carefully defined system, such as a product, activity, or set of processes. LCA is usually described in terms of "product LCA," which encompasses everything from raw material production to end-of-life alternatives such as incineration. There are other, more discrete types of LCAs, which can be of equal or greater value.

Attempts have been made to define the LCA-related concepts of "life-cycle inventory," "life-cycle impact analysis," and "life-cycle improvement analysis."[289] The appeal of this analysis may be to better understand the full environmental cost of production[290] and to provide useful data for internal and external purposes.

Europe, unlike the United States, has begun to incorporate the concept into regulation. For example, the British Standards Institute's environmental management specifications (BS77520) indicate that companies should address effects "arising at all stages of the life cycle,"[291] and the ISO has proposed an LCA standard as part of its ISO 14000 series (see discussion in Chapter 6, The ISO 14000 Series). Other efforts to codify the use of LCA include Denmark's Environmental Protection Act[292]; the European Union's eco-label award, which is intended to "promote the design, production, marketing and use of products which have a reduced environmental impact during the entire life cycle"[293]; and the European Union's directive on packaging and packaging waste, which "sets high sorting and recycling targets for all materials in the waste stream, which can only be modified if scientific research, or any other evaluation technique . . . proves that other recovery processes show greater environmental advantages."[294] Several incentives have fostered public- and private-sector application of formal LCA methods in the European Union. These include tax incentives, the ability to market a product with an "eco-label" indicating relative environmental benefit, and word-of-mouth information about economic performance improvements stemming from LCA research.

It has been argued that the environmental performance of a product can be improved if the guidelines in Figure 3-7 are observed throughout the design process.

Figure 3-7
Guidelines for Improving the Environmental Performance
of Products

- Does the design minimize environmental impact by the product?
- Is it energy efficient?
- Are hazardous materials controlled in a closed loop?
- Are wastes minimized throughout the life cycle?
- Does the design minimize use of nonrenewable resources?
- What happens at the end of the product's life? Are the constituent components and materials reusable, recyclable, or recoverable?
- Does the product design help achieve sustainable development?[295]

Ladd Greeno, then of Arthur D. Little, divides uses for LCA into internal and external categories.[296] Internal uses include shifts to more environmentally sound raw materials; improvements to product design, processes, and product use instructions; and improvements in product-distribution profiles, which analyze the different impacts associated with selling to certain market segments.[297] External uses include positioning products; supporting marketing claims and labels; launching counterattacks on products of competitors; demonstrating a proactive environmental stance; and communicating environmental progress.[298]

An example of an external use of LCA comes from the controversy over cloth versus disposable diapers.[299] One analysis asserts that when one compares the greater use of water and detergents required for cloth diapers with the use of paper and other products in, and disposal costs of, disposable diapers, disposable diapers are of less concern to the environment.[300] Although some environmental groups take issue with its methodology, that analysis apparently has been very helpful to Procter & Gamble, which has included the study in its packages of disposable diapers.[301] Similarly, external use of LCA suggests that polystyrene containers threaten less overall impact to the environment than paper packaging, although the political pressure on fast-food companies such as McDonald's to change to paper has been overwhelming (see discussion of the McDonald's/Environmental Defense Fund study in Chapter 8, Waste Minimization).

Because LCA is complex and leaves ample room for debate about its methodologies and underlying assumptions, such studies do not eliminate controversy. The above cases demonstrate that LCA that is responsive to a political challenge takes place in a context that is not neutral. It must be rigorous enough to overcome a presumption of environmental insult. Indeed, the danger of using LCA is that it will provide a vehicle for assuring the political correctness of a product and, in turn, result in greater governmental intervention in the production and marketing of products. The concept of LCA makes sense, but the devil is in the details.

For example, the Society of Environmental Toxicology and Chemistry's Life Cycle Analysis Advisory Group argues that LCA "is too premature to apply, at least not outside the secure confines of a company's own R&D department."[302] Moreover,

> [r]igorous LCA analysis suffers from several shortcomings. It can induce paralysis by analysis, because there is a desire to include everything and it creates the false impression that it does include everything. It is data- and resource-intensive and is methodologically and analytically complex. It takes a limited input/output (chemical engineering) approach. It neglects qualitative or unquantifiable factors and it uses inadequate "surrogates" for environmental impacts. Despite these shortcomings, companies seeking to incorporate environmental considerations in product design are developing design tools that translate complex environmental data into simple forms that designers find useful.[303]

Other analytical techniques that fill some of the gaps in LCA are now evolving.[304] Sustainable manufacturing "applies the sustainable development concept to manufacturing operations"[305] and addresses materials selection,[306] production,[307] "Market and After-Market,"[308] and full cost accounting.[309] Such analysis may be useful in development and refinement of environmental strategies. Ato incorporated the concept of sustainable manufacturing into its health, environment, and safety policy, which states as a "guiding principle" that Ato "promotes environmentally sustainable manufacturing which meets the needs of the present without compromising the ability of future generations to meet their own needs (sustainable development)."[310]

Environmental Management in the International Context

Most major corporations now have overseas facilities or markets and are therefore undertaking increased scrutiny of their international operations. There was a growing recognition before the Bhopal tragedy that safety and environmental issues associated with international operations could subject a corporation to potential liability. Bhopal brought this recognition to the forefront for senior management. Many major companies have extended their domestic health, safety, and environmental assessment programs to their international operations. Many have also found that in completing these assessments, it does not pay to make significant distinctions between the standards demanded for domestic facilities and those required for international facilities. Companies with chemical or manufacturing operations susceptible to potential catastrophes developed this consciousness rather quickly in the wake of Bhopal. Other companies, however, have only recently begun to recognize the potentially significant environmental issues in their overseas operations.

Communicating in a Multinational Corporation and a Multinational World

Corporations have grown immensely in the last 30 years, along with the breath and scope of their businesses. Communication is instantaneous with a premium on up-to-date information on a worldwide basis. The Internet and company Intranets are further accelerating this trend. Companies have different cultures, but multinational companies, whether they are based in the United States, Europe, or Asia, talk the same language—business. I have worked for both U.S.-based and foreign-based multinational corporations. On a day-to-day basis, there is very little difference.

Expatriates are all over the world. Your "parent" company may be based in Europe or Asia, but your "local" operations in the United States would be a Fortune 500 company on a stand-alone basis. Similarly, a U.S. multinational may have equally large "local" operations outside of the United States. Large local operations are accustomed to substantial autonomy. These operations rebel against what they perceive as micromanagement from the parent corporation. They take the same view toward EHS issues, claiming cultural local knowledge. This is also the same view if you are a local U.S. subsidiary of a foreign parent. It is rare that the foreign parent has people in the EHS function who understand U.S. laws, regulations, and culture.

Similarly, particularly for a U.S. parent, there is always the concern that too much involvement in local operations may trigger "piercing the corporate veil" in situations where substantial liability could be involved. The best analogy may be the issue of whether a parent company can be held liable as "operator" of a subsidiary's contaminated facility.[311] There are also a variety of disclosure problems that may occur as a result of audits, etc.[312]

Brian Israel of Arnold & Porter, while raising the concerns with respect to piercing the corporate veil,[313] notes that "[n]otwithstanding the risks identified above, there are clear benefits to high-level corporate involvement in environmental and safety management systems. Most important, such involvement ensures that all levels of the organization understand the seriousness and depth of the company's commitment to environmental performance and workplace safety,"[314] as well as the fact that "corporate staff members possess expertise and experience that will aid in the achievement of environmental and safety goals."[315] He argues that there are several methods that "obtain the benefits of high-level involvement while not simultaneously assuming unnecessary liability or inadvertently making performance worse than better."[316] They are:

- Distinguishing general monitoring from audits and inspections.

- Distinguishing recommendations from requirements

- Distinguishing specific from overall responsibility.

However, there may be times when a balance may be necessary and a risk will be taken of corporate liability exposure simply because the exposure in not getting more involved may be greater than the exposure of being involved.

Professor Kurt Strassner[317] takes Israel's article one step further and raises a variety of policy issues with respect to direct and indirect liability of corporations. The article notes:

> To the extent that those [environmental] management systems seek to comply with existing environmental law, then the policies of those laws would determine parent company liability. Yet EMSs seek to go further, using the best of modern management tools to reach "beyond compliance" and pursue even better environmental performance than is required by current regulation. If we want to encourage companies to aim "beyond compliance," then an enlightened environmental policy would not make such a reach the source of additional liability.[318]

Strassner argues that

> a sophisticated idea of an entity's liability for environmental law would have to consider relieving parent companies of liability for their EMSs to pursue the greater environmental performance that such systems can offer. To encourage parent companies to aim "beyond compliance," an enlightened environmental law policy will not make a management system's effort toward this end the basis for parent company liability and enterprise liability should be informed by this enlightened environmental law.[319]

Environmental, health, and safety management is rapidly coalescing as a worldwide approach. As a personal example, this book in its seventh edition, was translated into Mandarin. Political sophistication and understanding of other legal systems has also increased dramatically, but there still can be issues, not so much in language translations, but in how different cultures react to issues. Integration of different cultures in a multinational company is critical. Elf Aquitaine, like many other companies, brought executives together from all over the world to attempt to instill common values. Similarly, it periodically held seminars with environmental; health and safety managers to network, trade information and help create a common culture.

Certain industries have published suggested worldwide industrial environmental management standards, which help develop common cultures. These are viewed as less legalistic (and therefore more acceptable in many cultures) than, for example, the functional equivalent of U.S. or European Community standards (discussed later in this chapter).

Sometimes the changes aren't as apparent. I have given talks in Europe to environmental managers of European companies on the coalescing of legal systems and requirements. Some members of the audience claimed that the last thing they needed was American lawyers bringing their systems to Europe (e.g., shooting the messenger!). Others recognized the trends, particularly to more proscriptive standards and greater involvement by NGOs. I recall similar experiences 30 years ago when explaining to U.S. lawyers and executives the impact of the new federal air pollution control legislation; some members of the audience recognized the impacts, while others attacked me as a new lawyer in industry, fresh out of government, with governmental biases. Conversely, I have seen many American executives and lawyers not being as aware as they should be of European trends, particularly efforts to ban certain chemicals and/or eliminate them from products, as well as proposals to require product "take back." It's an increasingly small world, and getting smaller, particularly from the perspective of companies that seek cost-effective uniformity in product design and manufacture. Producers of products in the United States who sell goods in Europe need to be aware of, and prepare for, European developments, as they will directly influence (if not dictate) decisions involving American consumers and users.

Reaching into each other's cultures can break the barriers to communication. Many years ago, I was involved in an acquisition of a chemical plant in Thailand. The joint venture partner was a self-made overseas Chinese capitalist. However, he agreed to maintain the same standards for that plant as in the company's other operations. I used the language from an American oil filter commercial: "pay me now or, pay me later," to illustrate the point. The partner was very bottom line-oriented and understood this point, rather than my trying to discuss environmental concepts.

Similarly, a few years ago I was dealing with a complicated air pollution issue and needed to explain these issues to a senior executive in France from our chemical operations. It would have been extremely difficult to explain this to a U.S. executive, let alone an executive (in this case, a very bright and well-educated man) from a different legal culture. French regulators are more technically oriented than in the United States and are not dominated by the lawyers and enforcement personnel, which is an integral part of U.S. regulations. Disputes are normally worked out by communication between technical personnel from the agencies and industry. I commented to that executive that in the United States, our regulations can be the equivalent of his Code Napoleon. The executive was taken aback, but that analogy helped him understand the difficulty of obtaining change.[320]

It is important for multinational companies to be aware of changes throughout the world. U.S. law and regulations have a leveraging impact elsewhere. Conversely, today, some of the most advanced programs are coming from Europe. However, it is also important to understand the differences in enforcement strategies on a country-by-country basis in order to understand their implications. Language alone does not always explain differences. This is true in commercial culture. Businesses understand the differences in a commercial setting and they are moving rapidly to bridge gaps of understanding in the environmental, health, and safety areas. Program reviews (discussed in Chapter 6) are one way of bridging the gap. Since these reviews are "management" reviews tied to management and system improvements, they transcend the cultures and avoid local issues as to enforcement, etc. They also avoid misunderstandings as to what are meant by terms such as "audits" and "assessments" in different cultures.

EHS management is challenging in the international context. However, knowledge of different customs and cultures and respect for those differences is critical. All knowledge is not found in the United States if you are an American, in the EC if you are European, or in Japan if you are Japanese. Examining these issues in the context of EMS, as you would in other areas of management, will allow for appropriate worldwide programs that meet corporate governance standards and assure legal compliance.

Internal Programs

If you have had long experience in dealing with environmental issues in the domestic industry context, discussions with your international management, local representatives, and local governments may, in the words of Yogi Berra, seem like "déjà vu all over again." Certain environmental groups are getting active in a country, inciting local people, and causing concern from the government. The government does not want to deal with these people, and under the local law it does not have to. Moreover, it views these people as unwanted activists and outside agitators. The local representatives cannot understand how these people could have political influence. How could some underfunded, local group aided by outside agitators (now connected through the internet) stall a development plan or interfere with a concession or other agreement involving a multinational giant?

Environmental issues now affect areas that could not have been foreseen 30 years ago. International and local managements, as well as local governments, may be finding it difficult to understand how environmental issues may affect them. Their operations may be influenced by outside constituencies that are not part of the traditional permitting and operational context. They may also find it difficult to anticipate the economic and political implications of changes in operation.

Many of you are now having such discussions, which virtually mirror discussions that occurred when I first joined industry more than 30 years ago. In the United States, we have spent more than 30 years learning to work with stringent environmental laws that affect business decisions and governmental and nongovernmental bodies that may have an even greater impact. Yet we are asking our own people (local management and expatriates on site) and local government officials to absorb and be comfortable with, in a very short period, major changes that affect how they operate.

Although we understand and sympathize with this almost instantaneous cultural change, if we are to continue to be successful, we must be certain that our own people and our host governments can adjust to these changes. Indeed, the pressure may be greater in other countries and changes will certainly take place in a more compressed time period than they have in the United States. The political and economic history of some of the host countries and their perception of the history of industry and manufacturing is helpful in understanding the significance of this concern.

The United States has had a history of due process of law from its inception. Unfortunately, very few other countries can make similar claims. For many, due process is only a recent phenomenon and for too many it is still a limited reality. We have assumed (whether in reality or as a national myth, depending on your political views) that we are a classless society, or at least that we have the opportunity to change our class. If nothing else, we have a long history of a large middle class. In many other countries, there have traditionally been only two classes—peasants and aristocrats. Only now is a middle class beginning to emerge, and in many cases there is still limited opportunity, if any, for a peasant to move into relative prosperity. The more than 30-year history of federal environmental regulation in the United States has been long enough for a whole generation to accept the reality of strict regulation of the environment. These laws have also provided the safety valve of citizen suits: the right of the individual to challenge actions that might be viewed as environmentally unacceptable. Before the importance of environmental protection was recognized in the United States, many industries performed in a manner that today's observers would characterize as environmentally unacceptable.

Outside the United States, the history of industry recognition of environmental concerns and compliance with environmental regulations is far worse. In many countries, the issue of compliance with environmental regulations is moot, because such regulations do not exist, or are not enforced. For anyone who has spent time in eastern Europe or the former Soviet Union, it is easy to understand why many of these citizens are still very suspicious about claims of "clean" industry. Operating practices in many cases have not been, and in many instances still are not, what we would consider prudent operations by any stretch of the imagination. With the history of pollution (and particularly with some industries, real dangers of illness and disease as a result of virtually unregulated operations), it is easy to see why industry may not be met with open arms. When the perception of uncontrolled pollution is added to the assumption that it will not benefit an individual's lifestyle sufficiently to consider additional pollution from a cost-benefit standpoint, opposition will grow. If such development, for example, is near areas such as rain forests, which support an incredibly diverse variety of plant, animal, and insect species and which may have already been exploited by locals, or as in the former Soviet Union or eastern Europe, where there can be an almost mystic attachment to the land, opposition becomes a real possibility.

It is also hard for those not involved to understand the growing green movements throughout the world. Politicians of all types have recognized that the environment is a good issue, particularly when, unlike in many instances in the United States, the concerns are real. The issues that made nonpolitical people in the United States environmentalists in the 1960s and 1970s are even more of a concern in many of the countries where you operate or may plan to operate.

In this context, international environmental groups such as the Natural Resources Defense Council, Defenders of Wildlife, and Greenpeace are rapidly becoming involved and allying themselves with local groups, nationalist movements, and opposition parties. The environmental groups are very effective in raising issues that have appeal in local politics. In many instances they do not have to try hard to find issues.

Some environmental organizations are becoming more sophisticated in distinguishing between the black hats and the white hats. Robert F. Kennedy Jr., then with the Natural Resources Defense Council, raised significant concerns over what he viewed as dubious environmentalist success in forcing Conoco to withdraw from oil development in Ecuador and Scott Paper to withdraw from a project in Indonesia, only to be replaced by what he viewed as less responsible developers.[321] He noted that

> [t]here are many times, of course, when companies deserve bashing. But platitudes will not save the world's remaining rain forests. We need a more sophisticated approach, one that will allow us to negotiate with those corporations willing to commit themselves to the highest environmental standards. The problem, after all, is not caused by U.S. corporations, but by government decisions driven by a complex cycle of debt, poverty and growing populations.[322]

Similar concerns were raised by Peruvian Indian leaders after Royal Dutch Shell and Mobil withdrew from a large project after obtaining "unprecedented" environmental promises. "After hearing of Shell's decision, we fear for the future of the region and our communities since we do not know how the new companies are going to receive our demands."[323]

The World Bank now looks actively at a country's environmental policies and specifically requires an environmental impact study before it will give any development grants. The World Bank has indicated that it will aggressively assess the environmental impacts of many of its development projects and add environmental components to existing and new projects when appropriate, although it has been criticized as not enforcing its own rules.[324] On September 24, 1999, Robert Watson, Director of the World Bank's Environmental Department, in an essay entitled "New Strategies, Strengthened Partnerships"[325] outlined the evolution of the Bank's environmental agenda and reviewed various political and economic trends driving that agenda.[326] "According to Watson, the Bank must turn from 'preventing harm to incorporating environmental and social values into the everyday operations of the major sectors in which the Bank invests.'"[327] Three main principles will guide the development of the environmental strategy. "It must (i) build on the Bank's mission to fight poverty and support development; (ii) target outcomes; and (iii) be selective and build partnerships."[328] When completed, "the bank will define long-term goals and short-term and medium-term performance benchmarks focusing on impacts and outcomes and provide at transparent basis to evaluate the Bank's environmental performance."[329] It now requires that prospective borrowers consult affected groups and make the results of the assessments available to them. This policy in turn increases pressures on governments to be more open with respect to internal development or industrial projects and their potential environmental impacts.[330] The World Bank is also involved in a special environmental program to support projects in developing countries that benefit the global environment and that developing countries could not fund on their own. The program, called the Global Environment Facility (GEF), is a joint venture among national governments, the World Bank, the United Nations Development Programme, and the United Nations Environment Programme. The GEF is funded with $1.5 billion, earmarked for projects to reduce and limit greenhouse gas emissions, preserve biological diversity and maintain natural habitats, control pollution of international waters, and protect the ozone layer from further depletion.[331]

The then-president of the World Bank, James Wolfensohn, stressed his own commitment to environmental issues. Mr. Wolfensohn stated that "10 years ago, we had one project directed specifically to the environment. I am happy to tell you that there are over 100 projects today, and that in every one of our projects, we are greening our portfolio."[332] The World Bank now has 49 industry-specific sector guidelines such as thermal power plants, general manufacturing, petrochemical manufacturing, and the export-import bank has set forth both generically applicable requirements and 8 industry sectors.[333] He also stated that "[w]hat I am finding is a growing awareness on the part of all at the World Bank that the environment is not an optional extra, but an essential element in everything that we do."[334]

The U.S. Agency for International Development has a department that focuses on environmental issues, with local representatives in many countries of interest. The United Nations Centre on Transnational Corporations is looking at means for ensuring sustainable development and has been examining corporate environmental programs, looking toward international codes of conduct. It has now published a paper that indicates the role of corporations that was envisioned in the Rio Declaration on Environment and Development and Agenda 21, the principles of action.[335]

Thus, the impact of your international operations has to be considered from an environmental standpoint in an entirely different political context. Changing government attitudes, required operational responses, active and informed opposition, and culture clashes complicate the industrial equation throughout the world.

Functional Equivalency

Many companies now believe that as the primary means of minimizing impacts in host countries, they must adopt standards of operation that are equivalent to those in their home operations. This protestation is usually greeted, at best, by a polite yawn from environmental organizations, because such a policy, unless it is clearly explained and implemented, is meaningless. The critical path is to document the basis for the standards, including specific numerical standards and operating practices. At Occidental we used the term "functional equivalent" to make clear that what we were talking about was the standard of protection for health and the environment equivalent to that which the company maintains at its U.S. locations. Today, the rapid changes in local laws and attitudes make such a policy an imperative. At Ato, we used a specific protocol for international assessments that deals with legal requirements for specific countries. This protocol is now being used by many companies.

"Functional equivalency" is usually understood as a concept for managing internationally. Companies assure that their business operations in jurisdictions where environmental regulatory standards or enforcement mechanisms are lacking or inadequate shall strive to achieve a level of environmental management and performance functionally equivalent to that of similar operations in jurisdictions where such standards or mechanisms are more fully developed. Similarly, they also strive to have the same compliance assurance with laws and regulations, company policies and standards worldwide. I have utilized a "functional equivalency" guide for some of my clients to be used worldwide which includes many of the items identified in most forward-looking EHS policies to which the company strives to achieve. These include such items as environmental footprint, management systems, compliance, planning, and communication.

The functional equivalency guide not only can be useful in areas where laws or enforcement may be inadequate, but both domestically and internationally as a transparent and easily understood guide for employees, stakeholders, and government agencies to what the company believes is required to implement its philosophies in the environmental area. It can be applied to advise diverse businesses in different business sectors, with different needs and concerns, what a company expects as to management systems, compliance, environmental footprint, planning, communication, etc, regardless of the nature of these businesses.

In a growing number of instances there are few, if any, differences between domestic and foreign laws and regulations. The European Union has adopted strict air and water quality standards, and most European countries heavily regulate hazardous waste disposal. In many South American and Asian countries, laws and regulations are rapidly changing to approximate U.S. standards. Enforcement has not yet caught up with these laws, but when the laws are enforced, they will usually be enforced against foreign-owned facilities.

In many instances, facilities are not completely aware of existing laws and regulations because of the lack of enforcement. The first step in implementing a "functional equivalency" policy is to complete research on the local requirements. When these requirements are placed in tabular form next to the requirements for a representative facility in the United States or

Europe, the differences are usually minimal. It is hard for a facility to argue that it should not at least meet the requirements of the host country.

Above all, and regardless of the legal requirements, a corporation should be guided by the simplistic principle established in a popular commercial for an oil filter: "Pay me now or pay me later." If laws or regulations will eventually require retrofitting, it is usually appropriate to make the necessary changes *now* rather than to spend much more later on.

Therefore, a means of avoiding problems is to establish an international policy with a standard of protection for health and the environment equivalent to that which the company maintains at its home locations.[336] Such a policy does not require slavish copying of all U.S. or European Union laws and regulations. There is ample evidence that equivalent means will protect health and the environment just as adequately as some of these laws and regulations, particularly those that are technology-based. Where existing or proposed control requirements or procedures would be inconsistent with those followed in the United States or the European Union, it is critical that a responsible expert, either in-house or outside, documents in the corporation's permanent records the basis for the conclusion that these requirements or procedures afford equivalent protection compatible with the policy's intent. In most instances, this documentation requirement will produce an interesting phenomenon: the number of requests for exceptions to the policy will be minimal.

The adoption of worldwide published industrial environmental management standards is an alternative approach, which (as noted in a previous paragraph) may be viewed as less legalistic (and therefore more acceptable in many cultures). It should provide for the same level of protections. Clearly, compliance with local laws is still required, but it is also less difficult for local entities to argue against acceptance of standards that have been adopted by the leaders in a worldwide industry. This approach is particularly useful in international oil and gas production where there are a multitude of joint ventures. This also makes for transparency, not only inside the industry, but also with the host countries and local NGOs.

The Oil Industry International Exploration and Production Forum (The E+P Forum) and the UN organization, the UNEP Industry and Environment Office, jointly published a technical publication entitled *Environmental Management in Oil and Gas Exploration and Production*.[337] As stated in the forward to this publication

> These guidelines on environmental management in oil and gas exploration and production are based on the collective experience gained by UNEP and the oil industry. They should help meet the challenge of fully integrating protection of the environment in the

regulatory and business processes that control the exploration and production of oil and gas. They can serve as a basis for preparing or improving regulations, policies and programs to minimize the impact on the environment of these activities.[338]

The forward also notes that the

document provides an overview of the environmental issues and the technical and management approaches to achieving high environmental performance in the activities necessary for oil and gas exploration and production in the world. Management systems and practices, technologies and practices are described that prevent and minimize impact. The continual sharing of host practices, and the application of comprehensive management systems by oil companies and their suppliers are essential.[339]

Finally, the forward also recognizes that "[t]he role of government in settling and enforcing regulations is also key to minimizing the potential environmental impact" but that "performance-based regulations" "has the potential to stimulate more innovative and effective environmental management in all areas of the world."[340] Elf Aquitaine followed these guidelines in its worldwide oil and gas explorations and also performed periodic environmental audits.

Most environmental controls do not require large and expensive equipment installations, but rather consist of tighter practices and procedures. Even where equipment is involved, environmental controls may result in sufficient savings in reduced loss of product, raw material, etc., that are good business in simple economic terms. In other instances, equipment and installation actually cost substantially less than in the United States, although the amount saved is difficult to quantify. This is not because the actual hardware costs less, but because extensive administrative costs (including costs of technical consultants, lawyers, and prolonged paperwork with regulatory agencies) that are endemic in the United States are much less prevalent in other countries. For example, an incinerator that would not be cost effective in the United States may be cost effective overseas because its cost in the United States is greatly increased by the cost and delay of obtaining permits. In addition, the normal design of most U.S. plants includes basic pollution control, and in many instances it is easier to use off-the-shelf design than to redesign purposely to eliminate pollution control devices. On the other hand, some aspects of good environmental management may be more difficult overseas.[341] For example, many parts of the world lack hazardous waste disposal areas that environmental professionals deem acceptable in the long term.

The international environmental program needs to include a system for prompt follow up and action on any identified issues. This system will usually be part of the regular environmental assessment process described in Chapter 6. The program must also include a reporting procedure and timetable for its implementation.

In developing its international environmental program, Occidental followed a procedure developed by its chemical subsidiary, OxyChem. This procedure establishes the milestone steps listed in Figure 3-8.

Figure 3-8
One Company's Milestone Steps in Developing an
International Environmental Program

☐ *List local standards for discharges to all media.* In many cases, no numerical local standards exist, and you must establish standards on a site-by-site basis through interpretation and discussion with local officials.

☐ *Determine typical U.S. standards for discharges to all media.* In many cases, no single typical U.S. standard exists. Standards for water are normally based on the capabilities of technology. Air emission standards are usually based on ambient air quality.

☐ *Formulate equivalent standards using professional expertise.* Use the local and typical U.S. standards to develop equivalent standards. If local standards are more demanding, they will govern. If typical U.S. standards are more demanding and are scientifically sound, they will govern. It is vital to document the logic you use in setting equivalents. In this regard, it is helpful to identify the intent of the U.S. Standards.

☐ *Establish equivalent standards with the plant, considering site-specific conditions.* Once equivalent standards are formulated, the plants must review and agree to the numbers, just as a U.S. plant does in negotiating a permit with a U.S. agency. In most instances there is little room for negotiation, but the plant

---

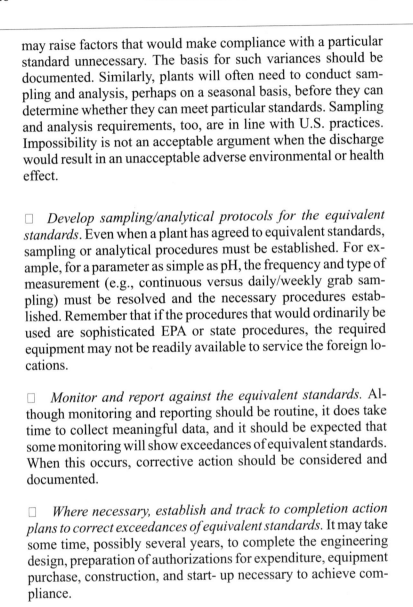

may raise factors that would make compliance with a particular standard unnecessary. The basis for such variances should be documented. Similarly, plants will often need to conduct sampling and analysis, perhaps on a seasonal basis, before they can determine whether they can meet particular standards. Sampling and analysis requirements, too, are in line with U.S. practices. Impossibility is not an acceptable argument when the discharge would result in an unacceptable adverse environmental or health effect.

☐ *Develop sampling/analytical protocols for the equivalent standards.* Even when a plant has agreed to equivalent standards, sampling or analytical procedures must be established. For example, for a parameter as simple as pH, the frequency and type of measurement (e.g., continuous versus daily/weekly grab sampling) must be resolved and the necessary procedures established. Remember that if the procedures that would ordinarily be used are sophisticated EPA or state procedures, the required equipment may not be readily available to service the foreign locations.

☐ *Monitor and report against the equivalent standards.* Although monitoring and reporting should be routine, it does take time to collect meaningful data, and it should be expected that some monitoring will show exceedances of equivalent standards. When this occurs, corrective action should be considered and documented.

☐ *Where necessary, establish and track to completion action plans to correct exceedances of equivalent standards.* It may take some time, possibly several years, to complete the engineering design, preparation of authorizations for expenditure, equipment purchase, construction, and start- up necessary to achieve compliance.

Notwithstanding such commitments, companies attempting to invest in eastern Europe and the former Soviet Union may be faced with extensive difficulties in building new facilities. Pollution from existing operations is severe, and there is a history of extensive pressure by the greens (including direct involvement of U.S. environmental organizations) to prevent new operations until existing operations are better controlled. In some cases, they have successfully prevented new construction. Many would argue that this strategy is counterproductive, because the new operations will bring in the newest technologies and funds as well as operational ethics that will be necessary in the long run to improve environmental controls. The greens, however, believe that U.S. companies are exporting pollution. This perception is extremely difficult to overcome because these people have never seen how a well-controlled industrial operation can function. They only know what they have seen, and in many instances what they have seen is not acceptable. A "functional equivalent" policy may help to overcome their skepticism, but this will be a long-term process.

If there is active environmental involvement in a country, it is also quite likely that the appropriate ministries are receiving offers from these governmental and nongovernmental entities to assist in the drafting of national and local environmental regulations. If you do not get involved, rest assured that you may see the worst command-and-control regulations in place. However, if you have a clearly articulated functional-equivalence policy, you are in a good position to offer credible assistance to the ministry with sound, technically based requirements that protect the environment. If you do nothing, you have no basis to complain.

Finally, the confusion of the local representative is shared by the governmental ministries and the local national company, which may be a partner. In many countries, environmental regulations are handled by an industrial ministry, but there are growing trends to create local environmental protection agencies to control the bulk of environmental permitting. This is analogous to the sharing of regulatory authority between the U.S. EPA and state governments (national and local regulation) and the U.S. Department of the Interior and EPA (resources and permitting). The industrial ministry will still control basic industrial rules, but the local EPA will control air and water permitting, etc. Such an agency has a constituency that is different from that of an industrial ministry. It may not prevent operations, but there can be extensive delays in permitting as the new agency raises concerns, enforces or tries to enforce new regulations, and deals with the local environmental community that now believes it has a specific governmental voice.

The local national company is also in a quandary over these changes. Its mission is development, and it sometimes does not fully understand and appreciate these new trends. Although local environmental organizations are suspicious of international companies, they usually reserve their particular wrath for the national company. Many of these national companies are now hiring environmental professionals who are gradually educating their managements about the importance of environmental issues. National companies and the government ministries, although deeply suspicious about environmental issues and their impact on development and cost, also recognize the importance of defending one's position to the public and the press. For them, like many corporations' international operations, it is difficult to adjust to major changes in operation in such a short period of time.

An international program that is as protective as a domestic program cannot be developed and implemented overnight (an issue often ignored in the world trade debates as to mandating strict environmental and safety standards in developing countries). It is usually easier to maintain high standards in the safety area than in the environmental area, although constant vigilance is necessary in areas where, for example, local customs do not normally include wearing hard hats, safety glasses, respiratory masks, safety shoes, and other safety equipment. In addition, local customs or religions sometimes include fatalistic or macho attitudes that must be overcome in improving safety awareness. Finally, while people in the United States are commonly familiar with mechanical equipment and vehicles, a country moving from a simple agrarian economy to one involving sophisticated machinery faces major problems of training and awareness. U.S. companies should set the highest standards for personnel safety. Industrial hygiene sometimes suffers due to lack of suitable testing equipment and of local personnel capable of completing appropriate monitoring. In most instances, however, this is not a major problem.

In summary, dealing with environmental issues in today's political climate is not easy, but if we do not recognize worldwide concern for the environment as an idea whose time has come, opportunities for continued investment and growth in industry will soon diminish. The basic and overriding objective in international operations is that no operation, activity, or product, when properly conducted or handled, should cause a significant or permanent adverse effect on health or the environment. Where adverse effects are foreseen or occur, ameliorative action must be taken to avoid or correct them. This is "sustainable development" in action.

Joint Ventures

Implementing the principles discussed above regarding environmental, health, and safety policies is difficult in itself and is much more difficult when your company is not the sole owner and operator of the facility. There are no easy ways to implement such policies in joint ventures, particularly when the partner is a host state or state-controlled quasicorporation and has a significant minority or even a controlling interest.

There are arguments against entering joint ventures where there could be substantial liability if your company cannot adequately control potential harmful exposure of workers and the surrounding public. This is not a common leveraging factor in business decisions, but it should not be ignored. The usual situation requires convincing either a governmental or private joint venture partner that a company's domestic environmental, health, and safety policies or worldwide guidelines, such as those adopted by major oil and gas producers (see previous discussion), should be implemented. The easiest way is to establish those policies as part of the basis for the joint venture. Tying actions to company policies protecting the environment, health, and safety, rather than to compliance with U.S. laws, avoids offending local sensibilities and national pride by avoiding perceived insults to local laws and regulations.

Local private investors who are sophisticated may be persuaded by the "pay me now or pay me later" concept, and, indeed, that specific language can be an effective sales tool to demonstrate the cost effectiveness of an environmental policy. This concept also helps mitigate the potential resentment of other corporations that are unwilling to adopt more stringent internal regulation. Introducing certain health and safety concepts gradually sometimes eases their acceptance.

Many countries provide criminal penalties for injuries and fatalities. In these countries, when the joint venture partner is a governmental entity, it is particularly important to document requests for improved safety practices and programs in the corporation's permanent records, in case the partner's refusal to approve implementation leads to an unfortunate accident.

Worldwide Management Initiatives to Promote Excellence

More than 20 years ago, approximately 15 U.S. companies with international interests, including Occidental, joined in an effort known as the Global Environmental Management Initiative or GEMI. GEMI, which is undertaken jointly with the International Chamber of Commerce and the United Nations Environmental Programme, is designed to develop guidelines for international business; to promote, assemble, and create worldwide critical thinking on environmental management techniques, systems, and results; and to share this thinking with the public.

A variety of needs resulted in GEMI's formation. It was felt that without industry leadership to establish expectations of responsible and effective corporate environmental behavior, groups such as consumers, governmental agencies, and others would set the standards for industry. As discussed throughout this book, changes and evolution in corporate behavior are most effectively driven internally.[342] Moreover, there have been few accepted or understood tools or measurement systems to gauge the effectiveness of environmental performance. Corporate goals and management systems to track health and safety performance need to be revised and, where appropriate, made applicable to the environmental area. Similarly, state-of-the-art codes of conduct, such as the chemical industry's updated Responsible Care®,[343] need to be shared with and adapted to the needs of multinational and multisector industries. All of these efforts need to be synergized for greater effect.

In this vacuum, particularly lacking guidance toward a global environmental ethic from a specific center for corporate leadership and thought on environmental management, GEMI was formed. This effort has had an impact on raising the level and effectiveness of environmental performance and management by businesses worldwide through the examples and leadership of successful corporations, as well as creating a comprehensive industrial ethic for environmentally sound development. Today GEMI has 42 members and has become primarily U.S. driven, but still composed of many multi-national companies who export "best in class" standards throughout the world, publishing various "tools" and publications and making them readily available.[344] In May 1990, the International Chamber of Commerce in Bergen, Norway, announced that world business will create a "charter for sustainable development" as a guideline for the environmental management of world business. This charter was unveiled at a conference in Rotterdam in April 1991.[345] GEMI was an active participant in this effort. Another organization, the World Business Council for Sustainable Development, composed of 175 companies, which is more international and EU driven, also grew out of this effort.[346] Some developments abroad also have trade implications. Various European Union directives require "take back" of packaging and in some instances, such as in motor vehicles, require almost complete recycling. "The End-of-Life Vehicles Directive passed into European law in October 2000 and was due to be transposed into national law in all Member States by 21 April 2002. This was delayed (as in most other Member States) and is now due to be transposed by the end of 2004."[347] As was noted when this legislation was developed: "European functionaries at the European Union and in Germany, Sweden and the Netherlands, to name but a few jurisdictions, are preparing measures under the fetching banner of 'producer responsibility' that would extend to automobiles and electronics the 'takeback' policy—for purposes of recycling—already developed for packaging."[348] This kind of statute affects not only the producers of a product but those who supply their materials and components. "As bureaucrats in Europe develop these proposals, their purpose is to impose environmental protection. It would be a sad irony if the principal result of their market meddling were protection of a less noble sort."[349]

Conclusion

Despite these concerns and challenges, we must recognize the good news that environmental law, by and large, is working. Gregg Easterbrook states that "[e]nvironmentalism has become a core American political value, close to unassailable even among conservatives."[350] He goes on to say:

> In both the United States and Europe, environmental trends are, for the most part, positive; and environmental regulations, far from being burdensome and expensive, have proved to be strikingly effective, have cost less than was anticipated, and have made the economies of the countries that have put them into effect stronger, not weaker.
>
> . . . .
>
> Nor are environmentalists the only people reluctant to acknowledge the good news; advocates at both ends of the political spectrum, each side for its own reasons, seem to have tacitly agreed to play it down. The left is afraid of the environmental good news because it undercuts stylish pessimism; the right is afraid of the good news because it shows that government regulations might occasionally amount to something other than wickedness incarnate, and actually produce benefits at an affordable cost.
>
> . . . .
>
> The ecological recovery in progress in the West has many heroes: pioneers such as Rachel Carson; environmental activists who carried on the fight; scientist and engineers who have increasingly made clean technology viable; even some business leaders who have become converts to conservation. Political liberalism, which provided the legislative muscle, deserves a large share of the credit, too. Yet liberalism resists the glad tidings of ecological rebound. When liberal intellectuals and Democratic politicians talk about nature in the vocabulary of fashionable defeatism, they sell themselves and their philosophy short.[351]

As managers implementing this core political value, we must focus on costs and management techniques to control costs. A major objective is to have senior management recognize two things. First, environmental management can be a profit center, as GEMI articulates and extensively documents.[352] It provides opportunities to reduce both present and future costs. Second, compliance is only a small portion of good environmental management. Resolution of compliance issues frees managers from spending time on environmental concerns, allowing them to focus on the business itself. On the other hand, reduced emphasis on compliance could lead financially oriented managers to curtail or reorient the environmental function. Thus, the challenge for the environmental manager is to keep staffing and costs lean and mean, while maintaining an organization fully capable of dealing with environmental management challenges.

Notes to Chapter 3

1. As of May 1995, up to 50 business schools and 100 other schools included "environmental business" courses in their curricula. ENV'T TODAY, May 1995, at 1. This book is used as a text in many of these courses. A 1998 survey of 67 leading U.S. graduate business schools revealed that 37 (of the 50 that responded) include some environmental management subject matter in their MBA programs. WORLD RESOURCES INST., GREY PINSTRIPES WITH GREEN TIES: MBA PROGRAMS WHERE THE ENVIRONMENT MATTERS (1998). As of 2002, the trend appears to be accelerating. A report has been issued by the World Resources Institute concerning the teaching of environment and social impact in business schools. The survey identified 8 of the top 50 business schools as having significant activities in the area of environmental studies and integration of environmental issues into the curriculum. *See Rankings Show Where to Recruit the Best Business Graduates*, 12 BUS. & THE ENV'T 9 (2001). The report is entitled BEYOND GREY PINSTRIPES (2001). *See* http://www.beyondgreypinstripes.org (last visited Apr. 20, 2002).

2. Prof. Dale Jorgensen of the Harvard Economics Department estimated in 1991 that the minimum total cost of the 1990 CAA provisions will be $24 billion (in 1990 dollars) by the year 2005, although regulatory agency interpretations of the law could push that number even higher. ENVTL. POL'Y ALERT, Sept. 18, 1991, at 42. A survey by Resources for the Future, an independent environmental and economic research group based in Washington, D.C., estimated in 1991 that the total (not just industry) yearly cost of compliance with hazardous waste regulations alone would be $32 billion by the year 2000. ENVTL. POL'Y ALERT, Nov. 13, 1991, at 15. It has been difficult to find real data to validate these estimates today, but the costs certainly appear to be very significant.

3. It is difficult to find and develop good environmental cost data. A study of eight U.S. telephone companies and "businesses with innovative programs in other sectors in North America" noted that "[t]o generate more comprehensive data would require major, costly and often unproductive changes to both the structure of BT's [the huge British telecommunication company that generated the study] accounting systems and the way in which the systems are used by staff at group, business, and operational level." *Comprehensive Green Accounting Is Costly and Complex, But Options Exist*, ENV'T, HEALTH & SAFETY MGMT., Apr. 22, 1996, at 6. Baxter International seems to have gone the farthest in developing detailed cost numbers, although in its case the detailed accounting was targeted to show environmental income, savings, and cost avoidance. *See Financial Accounting: Pushing the Envelope at Baxter International*, ENV'T, HEALTH & SAFETY MGMT., May 20, 1996, at 1-2.

A variety of models are used to account for uncertainties in evaluating environmental costs for remediation. *See* Gayle S. Koch et al., *Evaluating Environmental Costs: Accounting for Uncertainties*, 27 Chem. Waste Litig. Rep. 554 (Feb. 1994). It is worth noting, however, that some of the recently proposed environmental accounting techniques, such as total cost assessment, are oriented primarily toward project-level accounting. This reflects an opportunistic approach to cost-effective pollution prevention initiatives. These techniques do not provide the more fundamental perspective necessary for managerial accounting to encompass the true environmental costs and benefits traditionally allocated to overhead accounts. The traditional accounting community has begun to recognize this challenge and is beginning to incorporate environmental life-cycle thinking into the paradigm of activity-based accounting and management. JOSEPH FIKSEL, COMPETITIVE ADVANTAGE THROUGH ENVIRONMENTAL EXCELLENCE 4 (1996).

4. *See* Alan Carlin et al., *Environmental Investments: The Cost of Cleaning Up*, ENV'T, Mar. 1992, at 12, 17.

5. *Id.* For 1992, that cost was estimated at upwards of $130 billion dollars. *Id.* at 12. EPA has not broken down the capital expenditures, but it did look at different program areas such as mobile sources (bureaucratese for cars and trucks), radiation control, water pollution, Superfund remediation, and underground storage tanks.

6. *Id.* at 12, 17.

7. *Supra* note 4, at 2-3.

8. At Occidental, which is typical of other large chemical and natural resource companies, environmental costs in 1991 totaled $227 million, including $98 million in capital expenditures. Reserves for remediation (cleanup costs) totaled an additional $149 million. Occidental's profits for 1991 were $460 million. Thus, environmental costs were 82 percent of profits and environmental capital costs were 21 percent of profits. Union Carbide estimates that in 1990 its environmental capital expenses were $59 million, or 16 percent of total capital expenditures, up from $39 million and 9 percent, respectively, in 1989. Its environmental capital costs for 1990 were 31 percent of its $188 million total profits. Monsanto estimates that its 1990 environmental capital costs were $80 to $100 million, up from $60 million in 1989. Environmental capital costs were 18 percent of its total profits of $546 million. Monsanto's total environmental expenditures in 1990 were $376 million, equal to 69 percent of total profit. In 2003, Occidental spent $89 million on capital and $113 in operating expenses. The amounts are roughly comparable to 1990, although at that time the company had a different mix of properties. Oxy estimates that it will require $82 million for 2004 and $97 million in 2005 for capital expenses based on its latest EHS report (2003) on its website. *See* http://www.oxy.com.

9. Environmental costs for energy and chemical companies are particularly high. It has been estimated that the energy industry may spend up to 20 percent of new plant capital on environmental controls and technology. In 1994, the U.S. petroleum industry spent as much on environmental protection as it did seeking new domestic oil and gas supplies. AMERICAN PETROLEUM INST., PETROLEUM INDUSTRY ENVIRONMENTAL PERFORMANCE FOURTH ANNUAL REPORT 2 (1996). Finding later data is difficult. The numbers probably are about the same, although there have been substantial reductions in EHS personnel during the period 1995-2005.

The chemical industry also spends huge sums to meet environmental, health, and safety requirements. In 1994, DuPont spent over $1.4 billion (75 percent chemically related), Monsanto almost $300 million, and FMC slightly under $100 million in total environmental, capital, and remediation costs. Ato spent over $100 million for environment, health, and safety that year. The Chemical Manufacturers Association (now the American Chemistry Council) projected that the environmental costs for its member companies would be 6.1 percent of sales for 1994. CHEMICAL MANUFACTURERS ASS'N, CMA ECONOMIC SURVEY: OUTLOOK FOR 1994 AND BEYOND (Feb. 1994). Yet, Raymond Hill of A.T. Kearney estimates that the average Association member company spends in excess of 10 percent on such costs because now many EHS staff costs are considered part of other functions such as operations and maintenance. RAYMOND H. HILL, MANAGING HEALTH, SAFETY, AND ENVIRONMENTAL COSTS: AN EMERGING IMPERATIVE IN THE CHEMICAL INDUSTRY 1 (A.T. Kearney 1995).

10. American Petroleum Inst., *U.S. Environmental Expenditures*, Strategies for Today's Environmental Partnership Newsletter, March 1999, at 1.

11. Peter Brimelow & Leslie Spencer, *You Can't Get There From Here*, FORBES, July 6, 1992, at 59.

12. *See* for example, U.S. EPA, *The Benefits and Costs of the Clean Air Act, 1970 to 1990, available at* http://www.epa.gov (last visited Aug. 22, 2005).

13. 33 U.S.C. §§1251-1387, ELR STAT. FWPCA §§101-607.

14. See David L. Mulliken et al., *DDT: A Persistent Lifesaver*, 19 Nat. Resources & Env't, Spring 2005),at 3, for a history of the ban of DDT and its impact on world public health, particularly of the substantial increase in death and illnesses from malaria subsequent to its restriction.

15. Harvard Group on Risk Management Reform, *Special Report, Reform of Risk Regulation: Achieving More Protection at Less Cost*, 1 HUM. & ECOLOGICAL RISK ASSESSMENT 183, 187-88 (1995).

16. *See* Jonathan Tolman, *Rachel Was Wrong*, CEI Update, Mar. 1996, at 3 (citing NATIONAL ACADEMY OF SCIENCES, CARCINOGENS AND ANTI-CARCINOGENS IN THE HUMAN DIET (1996)).

17. One "concern" is increasing levels of endocrine disruptors in the environment. This topic, discussed in THEO COLBURN ET AL., OUR STOLEN FUTURE (1996), needs further study, but at the same time it should be recognized that there are a wide variety of foods (many types of vegetables, beans, and oils) that naturally contain endocrine disruptors. *See* Tolman, *supra* note 16, at 3.

Concern about endocrine disruptors has led EPA to propose an Estrogenicity Evaluation Program and prepare a report to Congress, following a final report of the National Academy of Sciences' Committee on Hormone Related Toxicants in the Environment. *See* U.S. EPA, *Crafting "Endocrine Disruptors" Testing Plan With Broad Input*, RISK POL'Y REP., May 17, 1996, at 3. The Safe Drinking Water Act Amendments specifically address testing for endocrine disruptors. *See* 42 U.S.C. §300j-7, ELR STAT. SDWA §1457.

18. There is substantial debate about whether or not global climate change is now occurring. For a very comprehensive review of the history of efforts to regulate global warming through December 2000, see Arnold W. Reitze Jr. *Global Warming*, 31 ELR 10253 (Mar. 2001). For a different view, see Robert C. Barnard

& Donald L. Morgan, *Global Warming: Significant Shortcomings of Computer Climate Models*, 31 ELR 10432 (Apr. 2001). Jonathan H. Adler, *Global Warming Controversy, Cool Climate*, 9 CEI UPDATE, July 1996, at 1. Nevertheless, there is intense political pressure to take action. The United States signed the 1992 Rio de Janeiro climate-change treaty, and the United Nations is now hoping for ratification of the Kyoto Protocol (adopted in December 1997), which arose from the Rio Convention. James M. Sheehan, *Global Warming Controversy, Hot Politics*, 9 CEI UPDATE, July 1996, at 1. The specific environmental controls that may arise from a climate-change treaty could have enormous practical and financial impacts on businesses. President George W. Bush, arguing that the costs outweighed the benefits and that the Kyoto Protocol did not require of developing countries such as India and China appropriate steps to reduce their contributions of greenhouse gases, announced that the United States would not implement the Kyoto Protocol. Although it can hardly be said that the Clinton Administration did much to support the Kyoto Protocol or seek its implementation (through, for example, ratification by Congress), Bush's announcement was met with considerable opposition from European environment ministers. Bush later announced an approach that relies on reducing the ratio of greenhouse gas emissions to economic output. *See* Donald A. Brown, *The U.S. Performance in Achieving Its 1992 Earth Summit Global Warming Commitments*, 32 ELR 10741 (July 2002). For the view that the Kyoto Protocol is flawed, see Richard N. Cooper, *The Kyoto Protocol: A Flawed Concept*, 31 ELR 11484 (Dec. 2001). One of the first acts of the Bush Administration was to state specifically that it would not ratify Kyoto, although it continued to participate in the negotiations. An agreement, excluding the United States in what is known as COP 6, Part II at Bonn, Germany, was reached in July 2001. *See* Miranda A. Schreurs, *Competing Agendas and the Climate Change Negotiations: The United States, the European Union, and Japan*, 31 ELR 11218 (Oct. 2001) for an analysis of the agreement through COP 6, Part II. The EU basically gave in to Japanese demands to include emission trading, joint implementation, and the clean development mechanism (CDM) as means for meeting emission reduction targets. (*Supra* at 11122.) Contrary to the wishes of the EU, there was no cap on credits for emission reductions from those sources, but they were to be supplemental to domestic reductions. The agreement also allows countries to meet their reduction targets through development and management of sinks. Nuclear development can be used to meet domestic targets but not by CDM. The United States as a non-party would be excluded from trading once 55 countries ratify the agreement. "The Russian federation ratified the Kyoto Protocol on November 18, 2004. With Russia's ratification added to that of other industrialized nations, the Protocol entered into force and became legally binding February 16, 2005." For the first time there are legally binding international limits on greenhouse gas emissions and legal systems for nonvoluntary trading. The Protocol does not directly apply to the United States and Australia, which are not participating in the Protocol. Nonetheless, in the United States, state actions, litigation, and voluntary efforts to address climate change intensified. SUSTAINABLE DEVELOPMENT, ECOSYSTEMS AND CLIMATE CHANGE, 2004 ANNUAL REPORT—THE YEAR IN REVIEW 2004, ABA SEC. OF ENV'T, ENERGY & RESOURCES L. 122 (2005). For further details as to how the Protocol will work see *id.* at 122-124.. See also detail as to voluntary actions, *id.* at 126-127. For discussion of what, if any SEC disclosure requirements are applicable to global warming issues see Assessing SEC Disclosure Requirements After Kyoto, Goodwin Procter Environmental Law Advisory, (Feb. 2005).

The underlying legal texts were essentially completed at a meeting in Marrakech, Morocco (The Marrakech Accords). *See* Donald Goldberg & Katherine Silverthorne, *The Marrakech Accords*, COMMITTEE ON CLIMATE CHANGE & SUSTAINABLE DEVELOPMENT, ABA SECTION OF ENV'T, ENERGY, AND RESOURCES (Jan. 2002) (www.abanet.org) for a detailed analysis of the specific issues addressed in these accords. Specific requirements were set on tradable emission units to limit the risk of overselling. The Russians in effect doubled the amount of forest management sinks that would qualify, as their price for ratification. The final compliance regime is still unclear.

Note that the Global Environmental Management Initiative (GEMI) has a website (www.businessandclimate.org) that allows a company to asses its potential exposure at either a facility or corporate level, as well as potentially take advantage of credits. The issue for multinational corporations is what if any trading they will be able to do with U.S. credits beyond the borders of the United States.

19. J. CLARENCE DAVIES & JAN MAZUREK, REGULATING POLLUTION: DOES THE U.S. SYSTEM WORK? 48 (1997). See also John C. Dernbach, *The Unfocused Regulation of Toxic and Hazardous Pollutants*, 21 HARV. ENVTL. L. REV. 1 (1997), which does an excellent job of reviewing the statutes in this area and argues for consolidation and prioritization.

20. The National Academy of Public Administration, the Harvard Group on Risk Management Reform, and many others recommend greater use of risk assessment and cost-benefit analysis. *See, e.g.,* NATIONAL ACADEMY OF PUBLIC ADMINISTRATION, SETTING PRIORITIES, GETTING RESULTS — A NEW DIRECTION FOR THE ENVIRONMENTAL PROTECTION AGENCY (1996).

The 104th Congress struggled with the concepts of risk assessment and cost-benefit analysis in its effort to promote regulatory reform. In February 1995, the House passed a bill that would require federal agencies to perform risk assessments and cost-benefit analyses for proposed major regulations, H.R. 1022, 104th Cong. (1995), *reprinted in* 141 CONG. REC. H2321 (daily ed. Feb. 28, 1995), but the effort died in the Senate.

21. Jonathan B. Weiner, *Law and the New Ecology: Evolution, Categories, and Consequences*, 22 ECOLOGY L.Q. 325 (1995).

22. *Id.* (citing Christopher Andersson, *Cholera Epidemic*, 354 NATURE 255, 346 n.109 (1991)).

23. Ruth Greenspan Bell & James Wilson, *How Much Is Too Much? Thoughts About the Use of Risk Assessment for Countries in Transition and the Developing World*, RESOURCES, Summer 2000, at 13. Professor Weiner reaches the same conclusion.

24. Frank S. Arnold, *Can't Do Cost Benefit Without It*, ENVTL. F., Nov./Dec. 2001, at 16.

25. Lisa Heinzerling, *The Temporal Dimension in Environmental Law*, 31 ELR 11055 (Sept. 2001); Profile, *Discount Stopper*, ENVTL. F., Nov./Dec. 2001, at 36 (discussing Heinzerling's approach).

26. ENVTL. POL'Y ALERT, Feb. 28, 1996, at 37.

27. *Id.*

28. *Id.*

29. Press Release, The Enterprise for the Environment (Mar. 1996). For a point-conterpoint discussion, see Karl Hausker, *Reinventing Environmental Regulation: The Only Path to a Sustainable Future*, 29 ELR 10148 (Mar. 1999) and Rena I. Steinzor, *Reinventing Environmental Regulation: Back to the Past by Way of the Future*, 28 ELR 10361 (July 1998).

30. *Id.*

31. *Id.*

32. Jonathan Lash & David T. Buzzelli, *Beyond Old Style Regulation*, J. COMMERCE, Feb. 28, 1995.

33. *Id.*

34. *Id.*

35. WORLD COMMISSION ON ENVIRONMENT & DEVELOPMENT, OUR COMMON FUTURE 43 (1987) [hereinafter OUR COMMON FUTURE].

36. William L. Thomas, *Business and Industry, in* STUMBLING TOWARD SUSTAINABILITY (Environmental Law Inst. 2002).

37. *Id.* at 552.

38. *Id.*

39. Declaration of the United Nations Conference on the Human Environment, June 16, 1972, 11 I.L.M. 1416.

40. *Id.*

41. OUR COMMON FUTURE, *supra* note 35, at 43.

42. *Id.* at 122-30.

43. John C. Dernbach, *Sustainable Development as a Framework for National Governance*, 49 CASE W. RES. L. REV. 1, 19-20 (1998).

44. *Supra* Introduction.

45. *Id.*

46. Dernbach, *supra* note 43, at 20.

47. *Id.* at 21 n.105.

48. *Id.* at 21.

49. *Id.* at 22.

50. *Id.*

51. Thomas, *supra* note 36.

52. Remarks of Allan Hecht at program on Sustainable Development and the Environmental Practitioner, jointly sponsored by the International Environmental Law, Climate Change & Sustainable Development and Second Generation Committees of the American Bar Association and the Environmental Law Institute, December 18, 2001.

53. Dernbach, *supra* note 43, at 29.

54. *Id.* at 41.

55. John C. Dernbach, *Sustainable Development: Now More Than Ever*, 32 ELR 10003, 10010 (Jan. 2002) [hereinfter Dernbach, *Sustainable Development*]. With regard to the precautionary principle, Dernbach argues that "[i]nstead of assuming that important natural systems are resilient or invulnerable, the precautionary principle presumes their vulnerability. By giving the benefit of the doubt to the environment when there is scientific uncertainty, the principle would shift the burden of proof from those supporting natural systems to those supporting development." *Id.* at 10013. As discussed subsequently, Professor Christopher Stone has a different take on the precautionary principle, arguing that the phrase is so vague, and applied in so many different contexts, as to be virtually meaningless. Christopher D. Stone, *Is There a Precautionary Principle?*, 31 ELR 10790 (July 2001).

56. *Id.* at 10017. For a view of sustainability as "intergenerational equity," see Duncan A. French, *International Environmental Law and the Achievement of Intergenerational Equity*, 31 ELR 10469 (May 2001).

57. Alan B. Horowitz et al., *Law Can Facilitate, Not Dictate*, ENVTL. F., July/Aug. 2003, at 48-49.

58. *See* http://www.yale.edu/envirocenter/esi/esi.html (last visited March.21, 2005); Daniel C. Esty, *Toward Data-Driven Environmentalism: The Environmental Sustainability Index*, 31 ELR 10603 (May 2001).

59. Esty, *supra* note 58, at 10603.

60. *Id.*

61. *Id.* at 10607.

62. *Id.*

63. *Id.* at 10611-12.

64. *See* http://www.wbcsd.org/sectoral/cement (last visited Apr. 20, 2002).

65. Richard MacLean, *Sustainable Development—Walking the Sustainable Development Talk to Achieve Business Value*, ENVTL. PROTECTION, Sept. 2001, at 21.

66. *Id.*

67. Richard MacLean, *Shifting Gears—Moving From Resource Management to Resource Strategy*, ENVTL. MGMT., Feb. 2002, at 14.

68. ELF AQUITAINE REPORT 3 (1998).

69. B. SMART, BEYOND COMPLIANCE–A NEW INDUSTRY VIEW OF THE ENVIRONMENT 188 (1992). Environmental improvement can also be recognized by industry. *See* Suzanne G. Harley, *The Greening of Eastman Kodak*, PRUDENTIAL SEC. RES. WKLY., Mar. 25, 1996, at 2-3.

70. *Id.* at 102.

71. *Id.*

72. WORLD COMM'N ON ENV'T AND DEV., OUR COMMON FUTURE 43 (1987). This report is commonly known as the Bruntland Report.

73. 49 CASE W. RES. L. REV. 1 (1998).

74. GLOBAL ENVIRONMENT MANAGEMENT INST., ENVIRONMENT: VALUE TO BUSINESS (1998) [hereinafter VALUE TO BUSINESS].

75. BRADEN R. ALLENBY, INDUSTRIAL ECOLOGY: POLICY FRAMEWORK AND IMPLEMENTATION 7 (1999).

76. Eric V. Schaeffer, *Enforcement in the Next Millennium—21st Century Approaches to Noncompliance*, A.B.A. SECTION OF ENVIRONMENT, ENERGY & RESOURCES, 29th Annual Conference, Mar. 9-12, 2000.

77. This study is discussed in detail in *Survey Links Financial Success and Focus on Corporate Values*, BUS. & ENV'T, Apr. 2005, at 1-4, *available at* http://www.aspeninst.org (last visited Aug. 22, 2005).

78. *Id.* at 1.

79. *Id.* at 1.

80. *Id.* at 2.

81. *Id.*

82. *Id.* at 3.

83. *Id.*

84. *Id.*

85. *See* http://www.globalreporting.org (last visited Apr. 20, 2002).

86. *Transparency: A Path to Public Trust*, GEMI (Sept. 2004), at iii, *available at* www.gemi.org (last visited Aug. 22, 2005).

87. EHS MGMT., July 17, 2000, at 4.

88. *See* Global Reporting Initiative *Sustainability Report* (Nov. 2004), *available at* www.globalreporting.org/GRISustainability Report/2004 (last visited Aug. 22, 2005).

89. BUS. & ENV'T, Sept. 2004, at 13.

90. *ISO Launches Development of Standard of Social Responsibility*, BUS. & ENV'T, Apr. 2005, at 13.

91. *See* Global Reporting Initiative, *at* www.globalreporting.org/MDG/intro.asp (last visited Aug. 22, 2005).

92. *GRI Tool Highlights Sustainable Developmenet Intersections*, BUS. & ENV'T, Mar. 2005, at 6.

93. *Id.*

94. *Id.; see also GRI to Update Technical Protocols,* BUS. & ENV'T, June 2005, at 6. A sample technical protocol is available at www.lgobalreporting. org/guide-lines/protocols/G3Protocols.asp.

95. *See More Than 300 Firms Sign Up for UN Global Compact*, PLANET ARK, July 27, 2001. *See http://*www.globalcompact.org (last visited Apr. 20, 2002).

96. *See http://*www.abi.org.uk/ResearchInfo/SocialResponsibility/Appendix1.pdf (last visited Apr. 20, 2002); *UK Insurers Issue Social Responsibility Reporting Guidelines*, BUS. & ENV'T, Dec. 2000, at 6.

97. API EHS Alert newsletter May 13, 2005. "The core and additional environmental performance indicators included: spills and ischarges; wastes and residue materials; emissions; resource use; and other environmental indicators" *See Oil and Gas Industry Issues Guidance on Sustainability Reporting,* BUS. & ENV'T, June 2005, at 7.

98. For a discussion of legal considerations in voluntary reporting, see David W. Case, *Legal Considerations in Voluntary Corporate Environmental Reporting*, 30 ELR 10375 (May 2000).

99. *See Reporting Guidelines Are Not Living Up to Expectations*, BUS. & THE ENV'T, July 2001, at 4 (citing Carol Adams, a professor at the University of Glasgow).

100. *Id.*

101. *Id.* at 5.

102. Frank S. Arnold, *Trade Rules Wrong Tool for Environment*, ENVTL. F., Jan./Feb. 2000, at 16.

103. Jenny Bates & Debra S. Knopman, *After Seattle*, ENVTL. F., Jan./Feb. 2000, at 30, 31.

104. *Id.*

105. *Id.*

106. *Id.*

107. Gregory Shaffer, *Symbolic Politics and Normative Spins: The Link Between U.S. Domestic Politics and Trade-Environment Protests, Negotiations, and Disputes*, 31 ELR 11174 (Oct. 2001).

108. *Id.* at 11176.

109. *Id.* at 11177.

110. Bates & Knopman, *supra* note 103, at 32-33.

111. *Id.* at 33.

112. *Id.* at 34.

113. *Id.* at 32.

114. Sanford E. Gaines, *Triangulating Sustainable Development: International Trade, Environmental Protection, and Development*, 32 ELR 10318 (Mar. 2002).

115. *Id.* at 10346.

116. *Id.*

117. *Id.*

118. *Id.*

119. *Id.*

120. *Id.*

121. *Id.*

122. *Id.*

123. Each month, EPA publishes in the *Federal Register* approximately 380 pages of air quality rules. Lash & Buzzelli, *supra* note 32.

124. CHEMICAL MANUFACTURERS ASS'N, ENVIRONMENTAL PAPERWORK (1996).

125. EPA's final operating permit regulations are at 40 C.F.R. pt. 70.

126. Dow estimated that "for one new rule, 80% of the company effort will go for documentation and 20% for the monitoring and maintenance of equipment." Lash & Buzzelli, *supra* note 32.

127. Marianne Lavelle, *Environmental Vise: Law, Compliance*, NAT'L L.J., Aug. 30, 1993, at S1, S2. I was quoted in that article as agreeing with that position. *See* J.B. Ruhl et al., *Environmental Compliance: Another Integrity Crisis or Too Many Rules*, NAT. RESOURCES & ENV'T, Summer 2002, at 24, describing a recent survey of environmental lawyers and their concerns about maintaining compliance with complex laws and regulations.

128. Stone, *supra* note 55, at 10799. *See also* Dernbach, *Sustainable Development*, *supra* note 56 at 10010.

129. Don G. Scroggin, *Detection Limits and Variability in Testing Methods for Environmental Pollutants May Produce Significant Liabilities*, 11 HAZ. WASTE & HAZ. MATS., Nov. 1, 1994, at 1.

130. Richard J. Zeckhauser & W. Kip Viscusi, *Risk Within Reason*, 248 SCIENCE 559 (1990). For a general discussion of developments in science, technology, and policy as they reflect on regulation and risk, see ENVTL. SCIENCE & TECH., Jan. 1996, at 27A.

131. James D. Wilson & J.W. Anderson, *What the Science Says: How We Use It*

and Abuse It to Make Health and Environmental Policy, RESOURCES, Summer 1997, at 5.

132. Daniel M. Steinway, *The Data Quality Act: An Emerging Approach For Reviewing EPA And Other Regulatory Decision-making*, 20 TOXICS L. REP. 700, July 28, 2005.

133. The Data Quality Act was enacted as part of the Treasury and General Appropriations Act of 2001, Pub L. No. 106-554, 515, 114 Stat. 2763A-153 (Sept. 30, 2001)]

134. Steinway, *supra* note 132, at 3.

135. *Id.* at 4 (emphasis in original).

136. *Id.* at 5.

137. *Id.* at 6.

138. *See* C. Foster Knight, *How Regulations Impact Innovative Environmental Technologies: A Recent Case Study*, TOTAL QUALITY ENVTL. MGMT., Spring 1995, at 119 (describing the barriers to getting a new software alternative to the conventional software). *See generally* Byron Swift, *Barriers to Environmental Technology Innovation and Use*, 28 ELR 10202 (Apr. 1998).

139. *See* Joel A. Mintz, *Scrutinizing Environmental Enforcement: A Comment on a Recent Discussion at the AALS*, 30 ELR 10639, 10644 (Aug. 2000). For a study on the value of enforcement, see Mark A. Cohen, *Empirical Research on the Deterrent Effect of Environmental Monitoring and Enforcement*, 30 ELR 10245 (Apr. 2000). *See also* Jon D. Silberman, *Does Environmental Deterrence Work? Evidence and Experience Say Yes but We Need to Understand How and Why*, 30 ELR 10523 (July 2000). As noted by the National Academy of Public Administration (NAPA): "The [EPA] Office of Enforcement and Compliance (OECA) is still a strong voice for strict adherence to regulatory requirement and it has become a powerful critic of flexibility." Dewitt John et al., *A Path to Peace*, ENVTL. F., May/June 2001, at 34, 40. "States feel that OECA is unwilling to credit or allow latitude for compliance assistance." Mark Stoughton & Jennifer Sullivan, *Mixed Results*, ENVTL. F., May/June 2001, at 44, 47. Meanwhile,

> [a]t one time it could perhaps be argued that states lacked the resources to address environmental problems, and an overarching federal presence was required. It is hard to make that case anymore, as states play the dominant role in implementing environmental policies, even if they are relegated to a marginal role in priority setting and the administration of environmental policy.

Jonathan H. Adler, *Let 50 Flowers Bloom: Transforming the States Into Laboratories of Environmental Policy*, 31 ELR 11284, 11289 (Nov. 2001). "Unleashing environmental innovation requires a formal mechanism that offers states the ability to experiment in and innovate in environmental policy, largely free of federal restraint." *Id.* at 11292. But in order for this to work politically, "it is necessary that states begin to demonstrate their ability to address environmental concerns before there will be widespread public support for the wholesale devolution of environmental programs." *Id.*

140. John T. Scholz, *Cooperative Regulatory Enforcement and the Politics of Administrative Effectiveness*, 85 AM. POL. SCI. REV. 115, 128 (1991) (cited in Clifford Rechtschaffen, *Competing Visions: EPA and the States Battle for the Future of Environmental Enforcement*, 30 ELR 10803 (Oct. 2000)).

141. *See* Mark Stoughton et al., *Toward Integrated Approaches to Compliance Assurance*, 31 ELR 11266 (Nov. 2001).

142. *Id.* at 11281.

143. *Id.*

144. *Id.*

145. *Id.* at 11282.

146. *GAO Reports EPA Inconsistency on Balance of State Enforcement, Compliance Activities*, Daily Env't Rep. (BNA) (June 24, 1998), at A-8, A-9.

147. *Id.*

148. Robert Roberts, Address at the 27th National Spring Conference on the Environment sponsored by the American Bar Association Standing Committee on Environmental Law, Potomac, Md. (June 13, 1998).

149. Peder Larson, *A Culture of Innovation*, ENVTL. F., Sept./Oct. 1998, at 20, 28.

150. U.S. EPA, *EPA Heightens Push to Embed Voluntary Programs Across Agency*, ENVIRONMENTAL POLICY ALERT (Mar. 2, 2005), at 21.

151. A group led by Bill Ruckelshaus, former Administrator of EPA, attempted to build a broad consensus for change. Unfortunately, nothing much has changed. *See* Karl Hausker, *Enterprise for the Environment Builds Broad Consensus for Evolutionary Change in the Nation's Environmental Protection System*, EM, Mar. 1998, at 30.

152. *See generally* U.S. EPA, UNFINISHED BUSINESS: A COMPARATIVE ASSESSMENT OF ENVIRONMENTAL PROBLEMS, OVERVIEW REPORT (1987) [hereinafter UNFINISHED BUSINESS].

153. *See* E. Lynn Grayson, *The Pollution Prevention Act of 1990: Emergence of a New Environmental Policy*, 22 ELR 10392 (June 1992).

154. *See id.* It remains to be seen whether state efforts will meet with better results. New Jersey's facilitywide permitting program is designed to provide some form of flexibility. The key in such programs is pollution prevention. *See* Steven Anderson & Jeanne Herb, *Building Pollution Prevention Into Facility-Wide Permitting*, 7 POLLUTION PREVENTION REV. 415 (1992).

155. An example of such an effort is EPA's "Policy Statement for Effluent Trading in Watersheds" that allows effluent trading within a watershed to meet water quality standards, provided that existing technology standards are met and "an equivalent or better water pollutant reduction would need to result from a trade." *See*

Memorandum from Robert Perciasepe, Assistant Administrator, Office of Water, EPA (Jan. 25, 1996). *See also* Karen M. Wardzinski, *Effluent Trading: Can It Provide Cost-Effective Option for Achieving Compliance With Water Quality Standards?*, Envtl. Reg. & Permitting, Aug. 1996, at 85.

156. *See* Frank Friedman & Ernie Rosenberg, *The Managers' Dilemma—Is There Any Good Advice in Preparing for Compliance With the Clean Air Act of 1990*, A.B.A. Sec. Nat. Resources, Energy & Envtl. L., 22d Annual Conference, Mar. 11-14, 1993, at tab 2; S. Rubalcava, *RECLAIM: South Coast Air Quality Management District Embarks on a New Direction in Air Quality Regulation*, A.B.A. Sec. Nat. Resources, Energy & Envtl. L., 22d Annual Conference, Mar. 11-14, 1993, at tab 18.

157. *Industry Rejects High-Profile Emissions Trading Program*, Envtl. Pol'y Alert, July 31, 1996, at 18, 19.

158. *Id.* at 19.

169. *Id.*

160. *Id.*

161. 58 Fed. Reg. 4802 (Jan. 15, 1993). *See also* Special Committee on Corporate Counsel, *1996 Annual Report, in* A.B.A. Section of Natural Resources, Energy & Environmental Law, 1996 The Year in Review 362 (1997) [hereinafter 1996 The Year in Review].

162. EPA did not define what would be included in the Statement of Environmental Principles, but was apparently looking for risk-reduction goals, means of measuring progress, public accountability, planning mechanisms, environmentally sound business practices, community and employee involvement, and compliance. We do know that EPA was looking at "life-cycle assessment" (i.e., life-cycle analysis) and "environmental cost accounting" (i.e., full cost accounting) as examples of good business practices. Pollution prevention would be measured primarily by EPCRA's TRI, but could include energy-efficiency goals and voluntary reduction of greenhouse gas emissions as part of setting national risk-reduction goals. Toxics use reduction and some form of verified environmental performance assessment are likely to be included in any program. This concept is still evolving.

Many environmental professionals are concerned by the oversimplification inherent in the TRI and how it affects their programs. Although toxics use reduction is recognized as a tool for limiting releases, the concept is not sufficiently developed to address basic problems, such as when one company's pollutant is another company's product, the questionable listing of some materials as toxic, the effects on international competitiveness, and whether there is a prospect for exposure, let alone harm. We tend to misplace our resources by taking too broad an approach to the issue of toxics without adequately considering whether there is really any significant risk.

163. See a discussion of this initiative in *Companies Might See Fewer Inspections, Faster Permitting Under EPA Initiative*, 26 Env't Rep. (BNA) 1289 (Dec. 1, 1995) [hereinafter *Companies Might See Fewer Inspections*], as outlined by Tai-ming

Chang, director of EPA's ELP. *See also* Memorandum from Tai-ming Chang to Interested Parties, Status of Environmental Leadership Program (Nov. 28, 1995).

164. *Innovative Initiative to Provide Facilities Relief Readied for Launch in 1997, Program Chief Says,* 27 Env't Rep. (BNA) 1347 (Oct. 11, 1996) [hereinafter *Innovative Initiative*]. EPA issued ELP Pilot Project Fact Sheets on each of the projects in September 1995.

165. *Companies Might See Fewer Inspections, supra* note 163, at 1289.

166. *Id.*

167. *RCRA Auditing Project Would Reduce Landfill Inspections,* Envtl. Pol'y Alert, Feb. 14, 1996, at 1.

168. *Innovative Initiative, supra* note 164, at 1347.

169. *Companies Might See Fewer Inspections, supra* note 163, at 1289.

170. For a detailed analysis of this program and other initiatives to improve efficiency in EPA Region I, see George S. Hawkins, *Compliance and Enforcement Changes in Congress and EPA,* 11 Nat. Resources & Env't 42 (1997).

171. *De Villars Seeks to Privatize Compliance With Star Track Initiative in New England,* 7 Env't, Health & Safety Mgmt., June 3, 1996, at 1, 2.

172. Robert A. Cohen, Commonwealth Edison, Oral Remarks at the A.B.A. Sec. Nat. Resources, Energy & Envtl. L. "Hot Topics" Program, Orlando, Fla., Aug. 5, 1996.

173. Under the program, a company's compliance status would be closely evaluated. EPA appears to be moving more toward a program like the Occupational Safety & Health Administration's (OSHA's) STAR Program, which recognizes safety excellence. *See* OSHA, Department of Labor, Voluntary Protection Programs, Draft *Federal Register* Notice, Apr. 22, 1992. In developing its STAR Program, OSHA asked industry's advice on what makes for strong programs and attempted to "base its program on the characteristics of the most comprehensive safety and health programs used by American industry." *Id.* at 7. In addition, sites accepted into the program "are not expected to be perfect, but they are expected to protect their workers effectively from the hazards of the workplace through their safety and health programs." *Id.* at 2.

174. 1996 The Year in Review, *supra* note 162, at 366 (citations omitted). For further information, see Draft EPA Proposed Framework for Full Scale Environmental Leadership Program, *reprinted in* Daily Env't Rep. (BNA), Oct. 16, 1996, at E1.

175. *See* www.vpppa.org/ GovAffairs/ EPA.cfm.

176. Letter from Donald R. Schregardus, Director, Ohio Environmental Protection Agency, to Carol M. Browner, Administrator, U.S. EPA 1 (Feb. 11, 1997).

177. *See* www.vpppa.org/ GovAffairs/ EPA.cfm.

178. *Innovative Initiative, supra* note 164, at 1347; 1996 The Year in Review, *su-*

pra note 161, at 365. Note that some companies may seek ISO certification. AT&T, one of the Project XL participants, is seeking to have its corporate program certified under ISO 14000.

179. *Id.* In a memo to EPA, the DOJ stated that ISO 14001 "does not appear to set or require compliance with any particular environmental performance standards" and "it is not yet clear whether ISO 14001 will have any utility for domestic regulatory or enforcement purposes." Memorandum from Lois Schiffer, Assistant Attorney General, Environment and Natural Resources Division, DOJ (Dec. 15, 1995). But see latest revisions to ISO 14001, effective November 2004, that now reference enforcement. See discussion in Chapter 6.

180. For the EPA view on Project XL, as well as a good history of the program, see Lisa C. Lund, *Project XL: Good for the Environment, Good for Business, Good for Communities*, 30 ELR 10140 (Feb. 2000). *See also* Benjamin Starbuck Wechsler, *Rethinking Reinvention: A Case Study of Project XL*, 5 ENVTL. LAW. 255 (1998).

181. Beth S. Ginsberg & Cynthia Cummis, *EPA's Project XL: A Paradigm for Promising Regulatory Reform*, 26 ELR 10059, 10060 (Feb. 1996).

182. The Office of Enforcement and Compliance Assurance issued a very detailed memorandum on enforcement and compliance issues. Memorandum from Steven A. Herman, OECA's Operating Principles for Project XL Participants (Oct. 2, 1995). Although EPA's Office of Policy, Planning and Evaluation acknowledges this position, it does state that "[d]ifferent implementation mechanisms may be appropriate for different XL projects. Part of the challenge of Project XL will be to explore *all* available mechanisms in the context of individual projects to determine which mechanism, or combination of mechanisms, is most appropriate." Memorandum from David Gardner, Principles for Development of Project XL Final Project Agreement, Dec. 1995, at 13 (emphasis added).

183. Cindy Skrzycki, *Critics See a Playground for Polluters in EPA's XL Plan*, WASH. POST, Jan. 24, 1997, at D1.

184. *EPA Offers New Draft Agreement on Regulatory Reinvention*, ENVTL. POL'Y ALERT, Mar. 26, 1997, at 31.

185. Ginsberg & Cummis, *supra* note 182, at 10062. A third EPA regulatory-reform effort, the Common Sense Initiative (CSI), illustrates the difficulty of circumscribing stakeholder involvement. The CSI is a regulatory reinvention effort to simplify the regulations affecting certain industries (automobile manufacturing, computer and electronics, iron and steel, metal finishing, petroleum refining, and printing). In contrast with the ELP and Project XL, the CSI seeks to approach regulations on an industrywide basis, rather than a facility-by-facility basis. For each of the selected industries, the initiative seeks to develop rules tailored to the needs of the that particular sector.

The CSI seeks to involve all interested parties in the process, yet involvement of groups with differing views has created difficulties. EPA efforts to dismiss certain environmental representatives from the CSI, allegedly because they were blocking consensus, has caused a threatened pullout by others. It has been reported that

[e]nvironmentalist and environmental justice groups have voiced concerns over the CSI process over the past year and have previously contemplated walking away from the negotiating table. For example, environmental justice groups say they are inadequately represented in CSI. Some environmentalists also say the "cleaner" component of the project has not been stressed enough, and that the rules for stakeholder involvement differ for CSI and Project XL, EPA's other major regulatory reform project. Several groups did leave the project.

EPA Regrets Groups' Withdrawal From Common Sense Initiative, PESTI-CIDE/CHEMICAL NEWS, Mar. 27, 1996, at 10; *see also EPA Dismissal of Environmentalist From CSI Prompts Outrage*, ENVTL. POL'Y ALERT, Feb. 14, 1996, at 36.

186. *See Minnesota Abandons Leading Regulatory Reform Project*, ENVTL. POL'Y ALERT, Sept. 11, 1996, at 33. *See generally* Rena I. Steinzor, *Regulatory Reinvention and Project XL: Does the Emperor Have Any Clothes?*, 26 ELR 10527 (Oct. 1996); Joel A. Mintz, *Rebuttal: EPA Enforcement and Challenge of Change*, 26 ELR 10538 (Oct. 1996). Both of these articles downplay the practical problems of the program. For a detailed review of Project XL and some case studies, see Carol Wiessner, *Regulatory Innovation: Lessons Learned From EPA's Project XL and Three Minnesota Project XL Pilots*, 32 ELR 10075 (Jan. 2001). For an EPA view on the value of Project XL, see Lisa C. Lund, *Project XL: Good for the Environment, Good for Business, Good for Communities*, 30 ELR 10140 (Feb. 2000). For an additional critique of Project XL, see Joel A. Mintz, *Whither Environmental Reform? Some Thoughts on a Recent AALS Debate*, 31 ELR 10719 (June 2001).

187. U.S. EPA, AIMING FOR EXCELLENCE: ACTIONS TO ENCOURAGE STEWARDSHIP AND ACCELERATE ENVIRONMENTAL PROGRESS 8 (1999).

188. Elliott P. Laws, *Need Statutory Authority for Reform*, ENVTL. F., Nov./Dec. 1999, at 51. *See also* Frank Friedman, *Is It Going to the Right Station?*, ENVTL. F., Nov./Dec. 1999, at 49.

189. *MSWG, Inc. to Become Incorporated*, INT'L ENVTL. MGMT. SYS. UPDATE, Dec. 2001, at 1.

190. Robert Repetto, *Are Companies Coming Clean?*, ENVTL. F., Sept./Oct. 2004, at 19. *See also* Van E. Housman, *Environmental Management Systems in Federal Enforcement Settlements*, 34 ELR 10451 (May 2004) suggesting that performance track can be "an effective means of encouraging companies to voluntarily act in an environmentally beneficial manner."

191. *Id.* at 18.

192. *Id.* at 19.

193. Criteria--EPA Performance Track *at* http://www.epa.gov/performancetrack/program/index.htm (last visited Nov. 9, 2005).

194. *See infra* p. 170. *See* Integration and Culture, the Linchpins for Success in a Scary World, AUDITING ROUNDTABLE, Sept. 2004.

195. Criteria--EPA Performance Track, *supra* note 193, at 3.

196. Criteria--EPA Performance Track, *supra* note 193, at 6.

197. *See* Richard A. Liroff, *Benchmarking Corporate Management of Safer Chemicals,* 12 CORP. ENVTL. STRATEGY, Jan./Feb. 2005, at 25.

198. Criteria--EPA Performance Track, *supra* note 193, at 4.

199. *Id.* at 5.

200. *Id.* at 7.

201. *Id.*

202. *See* http://www.epa.gov/performance_track/benefits/regadmin/ptrrule1.htm (last visited Aug. 22, 2005). M. Joel Bolstein, *Innovation Management Systems and Trading 2004 Annual Report,* THE YEAR IN REVIEW 2004, ABA SECRETARY OF ENV'T, ENERGY & RESOURCES L. (2005), at 362.

203. *Id.*

204. National Environmental Performance Track Program--Final Program Changes for 2004, *available at* http://www.epa.gov/performance track (last visited Aug. 22, 2005) ("The benefits may include linking the Performance Track website and recognition of their environmental efforts"), *see also* Bolstein, *supra* note 202.

205. *See* http://www.gemi.org (last visited Aug. 22, 2005).

206. *See id.* at 15.

207. *Id.* (Emphasis in original.)

208. Bob Sussman, a former EPA Deputy Administrator, advances the idea of an integrating statute to allow for more flexibility. Robert M. Sussman, *An Integrating Statute,* ENVTL. F., Mar./Apr. 1996, at 16.

209. Hawkins, *supra* note 170, at 47.

210. *EPA Regions Inconsistent in Enforcing Environmental Laws, GAO Report Says,* 31 ENV'T REP. (BNA) 1476 (July 14, 2000).

211. *Id.* at 1477.

212. Dennis A. Rodinelli, *A New Generation of Environmental Policy: Government-Business Collaboration in Environmental Management,* 31 ELR 10891, 10892 (Aug. 2001).

213. *Id.*

214. *Id.* at 10893.

215. *Id.*

216. *Id.*

217. *Id.* at 10894.

218. John Pendergrass, *Performance Still Not Primary Measure,* ENVTL. F., Nov./Dec. 2001, at 8.

219. U.S. EPA, ACTION PLAN FOR PROMOTING THE USE OF ENVIRONMENTAL MANAGEMENT SYSTEMS (2001), *available at* http://www.epa.gov/ems (last visited Apr. 20, 2002).

220. *Id.* at 4.

221. *Id.* at 4-5.

222. John Vorhees, *The Changing Environmental Management Scene: Federal Policy Impacts the Private and Public Sectors*, 31 ELR 10079, 10085 (Jan. 2001).

223. *Id.* at 10895.

224. Susan Bruninga, *Meaningful Incentives Needed to Spur Improved Facility Performance, Panelists Say*, 31 ENV'T REP. (BNA), 1225, 1226 (June 9, 2000).

225. *Id.*

226. Stoughton & Sullivan, *supra* note 139, at 39.

227. Rena I. Steinzor, *EPA and Its Sisters at 30: Devolution, Revolution, or Reform?*, 31 ELR 11086, 11089-90 (Sept. 2001). There is an important caution to adopting a performance-based system. "[N]o one can plausibly argue that a command-and-control system based on a catalogue of possibly irrelevant administrative statistics is preferable to comprehensive and reliable performance-based accountability. . . . However, adopting a performance-based system and adopting a performance-based system *that is enforced* are two very different propositions." *Id.* at 11094. As for a pollution prevention system,

> [c]orporations in some industries have been practicing pollution prevention for more than 30 years. But environmental protection policy based on pollution prevention and eco-efficiency has never been seriously tried in the United States because it requires flexibility and a multimedia approach that command-and-control regulations do not easily accommodate.

Id. at 10895. As noted previously, it is very unlikely that it ever will. As also noted previously in discussion of EPA reform efforts,

> EPA has not committed adequate financial resources to shift dramatically from a command-and-control regulatory approach to one that supplements regulation with a strong focus on collaboration with the private sector. Many of the initiatives were undermined by ham-handled implementation—the unwillingness of EPA's regulatory staff to grant flexibility in regulatory enforcement or by their perception that they have weak legislative authority to do so. *Id.* at 10896. The weakness of EPA's industry partnership programs arise primarily from the Agency's inability to refocus them from regulatory compliance to the business benefits for participating firms.

Id. at 10897.

229. *Id.* at 10905.

229. David Clarke, *EPA in the Information Age*, ENVTL. F., May/June 2001, at 22.

230. Mark A. Cohen, *Information as a Policy Instrument in Protecting the Environment: What Have We Learned*, 31 ELR 10425, 10431 (Apr. 2001). *See also* David W. Case, *The Law and Economics of Environmental Information as Regulation*, 31 ELR 10773 (July 2001).

231. Sherry Driber, *Creating An Integrated Data System Helped Integrate Our Work*, ENVTL. F., Mar./Apr. 2003, at 22, Suellen Keiner, *Finally Systems Are Lining to Support Performance Goals*, ENVTL. F., Mar./Apr. 2003, at 20.

232. U.S. GAO, ENVIRONMENTAL INFORMATION: EPA IS TAKING STEPS TO IMPROVE INFORMATION MANAGEMENT, BUT CHALLENGES REMAIN (1997).

233. Clarke, *supra* note 229, at 25.

234. John et al., *supra* note 139, at 41.

235. *Id.*

236. *Industry, Activists Unite to Push EPA Information Policy Reforms*, ENVTL. POL'Y ALERT, Dec. 26, 2001, at 38.

237. *Id.*

238. *See* http://www.epa.gov/cdx/ cromerr/propose/index.html.

239. Keith Ferrazzi, *Managing Management Fads*, HEMISPHERES, Dec. 1996, at 39.

240. N.J. ADMIN. CODE tit. 7, §1K-4.3(b)(6) (1993). Although the Part II cost analysis is referred to in the Act as a "full-cost accounting," the N.J. Department of Environmental Protection has decided to use the phrase "comprehensive financial analysis" for both Part I and Part II because it is a more descriptive phrase and is less easily confused with other concepts.

241. Bruce W. Piasecki & Kevin A. Fletcher, *The Changing Face of the Environmental Strategist*, 3 CORP. ENVTL. STRATEGY 25, 30 (1996).

242. Piasecki and Fletcher note that "AT&T's efforts to develop environmentally benign substitutes for [chlorofluorocarbons] and ARCO's creation of a cleaner gasoline characterize such as strategy." *Id.* They also stated that "[i]n our research of over 4000 firms, this has become a dominant and noteworthy development in corporate organizations represented by the example of the Global Environmental Management Initiative (GEMI)." *Id.*

243. *Id.*

244. ELF AQUITAINE, ENVIRONMENTAL REPORT 3 (1998).

245. FIKSEL, *supra* note 3.

246. *Companies Ignore Their Own Environmentalists*, BUCKS COUNTY COURIER TIMES, Jan. 3, 1966, at 10D. This was a widely covered Associated Press story. For details, see ROBERT SHELTON, HITTING THE GREEN WALL (Arthur D. Little ed., 1995).

247. *Id.*

248. *Id.*

249. *See generally* Susan J. Colby et al., *The Real Green Issue: Debunking the Myths of Environmental Management*, 2 McKinsey Q. 133 (1995).

250. Shelton, *supra* note 246.

251. Kenneth W. Ayers & Timothy T. Greene, *Breaking Down the Green Wall*, Responsible Transport, Mar./Apr. 1996, at 1.

252. *Id.* at 5-6.

253. Shelton, *supra* note 246.

254. *Id.*

255. *Id.*

256. *Id.*

257. GEMI, which is discussed later in this chapter, organized an extensive conference on TQM as it applies to environmental management. The numerous papers delivered at this conference were published in the volume Global Environmental Management Initiative, Proceedings—Corporate Quality/Environmental Management: The First Conference (Washington, D.C., Jan. 9-10, 1991) [hereinafter Proceedings]. It is beyond the scope of this book to deal with TQM in detail. Papers can be found in Proceedings on such subjects as organizing a TQM program, its use in engineering services and in federal agencies, environmental problem solving, competitive benchmarking, and tracking information. Proceedings also includes tools such as statistics and variation and fishbone cause and effect diagrams. Leskovian, *Use of Cause and Effect Diagrams and Pareto Charts for Environmental Quality Management, in* Proceedings, *id.* at 77.

258. Sands, *Developing Customer and Supplier Relationships at Dow, in* Proceedings, *supra* note 258, at 59.

259. Carpenter, *GEMI and the Total Quality Journey to Environmental Excellence, in* Proceedings, *supra* note 257, at 3.

260. *Id.*

261. *Id.*

262. David Hobler, *Integrated Quality, Environmental, Health and Safety Management Systems—Why Needed and How to Justify Them in the U.S. Industrial Environment*, EHS Mgmt., Aug. 14, 2000, at 7.

263. *Id.* at 80.

264. Bowers, *What Is Total Quality Management?, in* Proceedings, *supra* note 257, at 135.

265. Union Carbide claimed that it had an effective system for measuring compliance and the effectiveness of corporate systems. *See* Coulter, *Union Carbide's Audit Classification Program, in* Proceedings, *supra* note 257, at 177.

266. Boyett & Conn, *What's Wrong With Total Quality Management*, TAPPING NETWORK J., Spring 1992.

267. *Id.*

268. *Id.*

269. Heilpern & Limpert, *Building Organizations for Continuing Improvement*, in PROCEEDINGS, *supra* note 257, at 11.

270. John S. Wilson & J. Ladd Greeno, *Doing More With Less: Improving Environmental Management Productivity*, PRISM, 3d Quarter 1994, at 95, 97.

271. Richard MacLean, *Countdown to Zero—Environmental Staffs Are Becoming Smaller, but What Is the Ideal Size?*, ENVTL. PROTECTION, Oct. 2001, at 57-58.

272. *Id.* at 59.

273. Yihlun Yang and Richard MacLean, *A Template for Assessing Corporate Performance: Benchmarking EHS Organizations*, ENVTL. QUALITY MAG., Spring 2004, at 11.

274. *See id.* at 16-17.

275. *Id.* at 12.

276. *Id.* at 13.

277. *Id.* at 14.

278. *Id.*

279. *Id.* at 20.

280. Richard MacLean, *EHS Organizational Quality: A DuPont Case Study*, ENVTL. QUALITY MAG., Winter 2004, at 3.

281. *Id.* at 6.

282. HILL, *supra* note 9, at 2 (emphasis in original).

283. *Id.* at 3. See also the discussion of outsourcing in Chapter 4, Staffing and Turf Wars.

284. David Sweet, Remarks at the A.B.A. Section of Natural Resources, Energy, and Environmental Law 25th Annual Conference, A.B.A. Sec. Nat. Resources, Energy & Envtl. L., Keystone, Colo., Mar. 23, 1996.

285. Wilson & Greeno, *supra* note 270, at 99.

286. *Id.*

287. *For the EHS Manager Winning Means Mastering New Relationships*, 6 ENV'T, HEALTH & SAFETY MGMT., May 20, 1996, at 6-7.

288. J. Ladd Greeno et al., *Rethinking the Environment for Business Advantage*, PRISM, 1st Quarter 1996, at 5, 6.

289. These are as follows.

Life-Cycle Inventory - An objective, data-based process of quantifying energy and raw material requirements, air emissions, waterborne effluents, solid waste, and other environmental releases incurred throughout the lifecycle of a product, process or activity.

Life-Cycle Impact Analysis - A technical, quantitative, and/or qualitative process to characterize and assess the effects of the environmental loadings identified in the inventory component. The assessment should address both ecological and human health considerations, as well as other effects such as habitat modification and noise pollution.

Life-Cycle Improvement Analysis - A systematic evaluation of the needs and opportunities to reduce the environmental burden associated with energy and raw materials use and waste emissions throughout the whole life cycle of a product, process, or activity. This analysis may include both quantitative and qualitative measures of improvements, such as change in product design, raw materials use, industrial processing, consumer use and waste management.

Europe Leaping Ahead on Life Cycle Regulations, 3 ENV'T, HEALTH & SAFETY MGMT., Nov. 23, 1992, at 3 [hereinafter *Europe Leaping Ahead on Life Cycle Regulations*] (referencing paper on LCA applications prepared by James Fava of Roy F. Weston, Frank Consoli of Scott Paper Co., and Richard Denison of the Environmental Defense Fund, for a workshop held in Leiden, the Netherlands).

290. *See* Frank Popoff & David Buzzelli, *Full-Cost Accounting*, CHEM. & ENGINEERING NEWS, Jan. 11, 1993, at 8.

291. *Europe Leaping Ahead on Life Cycle Regulations*, *supra* note 289, at 1.

292. The Minister of the Environment is given "sweeping authority to issue bans, limits, or other restrictions on raw materials or substances in products in order to promote cleaner technology." *Id.* In deciding what measures are actually necessary, "the whole cycle of substances and materials must be considered 'with a view to minimizing wastage of resources.'" *Id.* at 3.

293. *Id.*

294. *Id.* The directive was finally approved on December 14, 1994, by the Council of Ministers and European Parliament. *EU Institutions Adopt Packaging Directive*, BUS. & ENV'T, Jan. 1995, at 13.

295. DEANA J. RICHARDS & ROBERT A. FRASER, CORPORATE ENVIRONMENTAL PRACTICES—CLIMBING THE LEARNING CURVE 13 (1994) (citation omitted). This short publication is the result of a workshop held in August 1993 and has considerable material of interest on life-cycle analysis, pollution prevention, and quality approaches.

296. J. Ladd Greeno & Arthur D. Little, *Product Life-Cycle Concepts: A Wider View of the Environment*, Conference Board Advisory Council on Environmental Affairs, Jan. 14, 1993 [hereinafter *Product Life-Cycle Concepts*].

297. *Id.*

298. *Id.*

299. *See* Popoff & Buzzelli, *supra* note 290, at 9.

300. *Product Life-Cycle Concepts, supra* note 296.

301. *Id.*

302. *Europe Leaping Ahead on Life Cycle Regulations, supra* note 289, at 1.

303. RICHARDS & FRASER, *supra* note 295, at 18-19.

304. *See* ENV'T, HEALTH & SAFETY MGMT., Jan. 1993, at 10.

305. *Id. See also Agenda 21, Adoption of Agreements on Environment and Development,* U.N. Conference on Environment and Development, at Parts I-IV, U.N. Doc. A/Cont.151/1; *see generally* NATIONAL WILDLIFE FEDERATION CORPORATE CONSERVATION COUNCIL, BUILDING THE SUSTAINABLE CORPORATION (1992) [hereinafter BUILDING THE SUSTAINABLE CORPORATION].

306. Materials can be selected to minimize use of virgin materials and maximize use of recycled materials, decrease waste, decrease the energy required to produce the product, and decrease the per-piece manufacturing time. The product can be designed so that finished dimensions are close to the incoming feed stock to reduce the need for excessive materials removal. Toxic materials can be avoided. BUILDING THE SUSTAINABLE CORPORATION, *id.*

307. Production:

• Optimize production using P2 [Pollution Prevention] and TUR [Toxics Use Reduction] strategies.

• Conserve energy. Many of the electric motors used to drive production machinery could be made 20 to 30 percent more efficient.

• Redesign processes to eliminate worker health and safety risks and the potential for operator error.

Id.

308. Market and After-Market:

• Reduce packaging, use recycled materials in packaging, use environmentally nondemanding printing inks, and use returnable/reusable packaging.

• Design products for repair and replacement of components, rather than disposal, and for easy disassembly for recycling.

• Reduce product persistence in the environment by design for recycling and reuse or for degradability of materials that cannot be recycled.

Id.

309. Cost Accounting:

- View wastes as materials that could be recovered for recycling or re-use and account for them as lost raw materials.

- Consider as potential revenue sources all costs associated with the treatment and disposal of process wastes, permit fees, and materials taxes.

- Consider as lost revenue costs associated with not recycling wastes and not conserving energy or materials.

- Include costs of training workers to safely handle toxic chemicals and of liabilities for spills and mishandling of toxic chemicals.

Id.

310. ELF ATOCHEM NORTH AMERICA, INC., HEALTH, ENVIRONMENT, AND SAFETY POLICY 1 (issued Jan. 11, 1995, revised Apr. 25, 1997). This policy is repro-duced in Appendix D of this book. The language is from the Bruntland Report, *su-pra* note 66.

311. In Best Foods v. Aerojet-General Corp., 173 F. Supp. 2d 729 (W.D. Mich 2001), on remand from the U.S, Supreme Court, United States v. Bestfoods, 524 U.S. 51, 28 ELR 21225 (1998), the court found that providing advice on environ-mental compliance, legal advice, sharing officers and directors, using the facility to develop and manufacture a product for the parent, and the parent's direction of certain operations of the subsidiary, did not constitute "operation" of the specific facility.

312. *See* Todd O. Maiden, *Disclosure Obligations and Confidentiality Issues in an International Context, in* DAVID D. NELSON, INTERNATIONAL ENVIRONMENTAL AUDITING 165 (1995).

313. Brian D. Israel, *Environmental and Safety Management Systems in Large Companies: Avoiding Pitfalls,* 36 TRENDS, Jan./Feb. 2005, at 1.

314. *Id.* at 4.

315. *Id.*

316. *Id.*

317. Kurt A. Strassner, *A Parent's Liability for its Subsidiary's Environmental Per-formance,* 36 TRENDS, Jan./Feb. 2005, at 1.

318. *Id.* at 14.

319. *Id.*

320. For a discussion of cultural differences in developing laws and interactions with NGOs, see Ruth Greenspan Bell, *Communications Breakdown,* ENVTL. F., Nov./Dec. 2001, at 20.

321. Robert F. Kennedy Jr., *Amazon Sabotage,* WASH. POST, Aug. 24, 1992, at A17.

322. *Id.*

323. *Peru's Amazon Indians Protest Shell Pullout to Fujimori*, ASSOCIATED PRESS WORLD NEWS, July 27, 1998.

324. *See* David Hunter & Lori Udall, *The World Bank's New Inspection Panel: Will It Increase the Bank's Accountability?*, Center for International Environmental Law (CIEL) Brief, Apr. 1994.

325. WORLD BANK, ENVIRONMENTAL MATTERS AT THE WORLD BANK 4 (1999).

326. *See* THE YEAR IN REVIEW 1999, at 292 (American Bar Ass'n, Section of Environment, Energy and Resources Law 2000).

327. *Id.* at 293.

328. *Id.*

329. *Id.*

330. *See* Dennis J. Scott, *Making a Bank Turn*, ENVTL. F., Mar./Apr. 1992, at 21-22.

331. *World Bank Strengthens Environmental Requirements for Major Project Funding*, POLLUTION PREVENTION NEWS, July 1991, at 5.

332. James Wolfensohn, *A New Sensitivity At the World Bank*, *in* WORLD RESOURCES INST., INTERNATIONAL PERSPECTIVES ON SUSTAINABILITY 3 (1996).

333. Andrew Giaccia & Erin Bradley, *World Bank's Standards: An Eco Authority*, NAT'L L.J., Dec. 22, 1997, at B7.

334. *Id.* For a critical look at "export credit agencies" as not being environmentally conscious, see Bruce Rich, *Exporting Destruction*, ENVTL. F., Sept./Oct. 2000, at 17.

335. For a detailed analysis, see Dernbach, *Sustainable Development, supra* note 55.

336. Note that your actions abroad may have implications in the United States. *See, e.g.*, Hartline, *Legal Consequences of Plant Failures—After the Smoke Clears*, Gulf Pub. Co. & Hydrocarbon Processing, First International Conference on Improving Refineries and Chemical and Natural Gas Plants, Nov. 10-12, 1992, at 18 (discussing the Texas Supreme Court's assertion of jurisdiction over corporate activities occurring entirely in Costa Rica).

337. OIL INDUSTRY EXPLORATION AND PRODUCTION FORUM AND UNITED NATIONS ENVIRONMENT PROGRAMME, ENVIRONMENTAL MANAGEMENT IN OIL AND GAS EXPLORATION AND PRODUCTION (1997), *available at* http://www. eandpforum.co.uk.

338. *Id.*

339. *Id.*

340. *Id. See also* OIL INDUSTRY EXPLORATION AND PRODUCTION FORUM AND INTERNATIONAL PETROLEUM INDUSTRY ENVIRONMENTAL CONSERVATION ASS'N, THE OIL INDUSTRY: OPERATING IN SENSITIVE ENVIRONMENTS (1997), *available at* http://www.eandpforum.co.uk and http://www.ipieca.org (describ-

ing a variety of case studies illustrating the petroleum industry's experiences in sensitive environments).

341. *See, e.g., Environment Is Reaching "Take-Off" Point in Europe*, ENVTL. MANAGER, June 1990, at 12.

342. *See* David R. Berz, *Keep Risk Reduction Decisions in the Board Room*, ENVTL. F., Mar./Apr. 1990, at 32. "The necessary corporate ethic to protect the environment must come from within, not from outside groups like [the Coalition for Economically Responsible Economies Project]." *Id.* at 34.

343. Responsible Care® is a voluntary chemical industry initiative designed to improve the management of chemicals. Begun in 1988, the program has expanded to include both chemical manufacturing member companies and numerous partner companies that transport, distribute, or otherwise handle chemicals. The partner programs encourage application of Codes of Management Practice to a variety of chemically related businesses and operations.

344. *See* www.gemi.org, *supra* note 205.

345. The following are the principles proposed by the International Chamber of Commerce and endorsed by GEMI:

(a) *Corporate priority*: To recognize environmental management as among the highest corporate priorities and as a key determinant to sustainable development; to establish policies, programmes, and practices for conducting operations in an environmentally sound manner.

(b) *Integrated management*: To integrate these policies, programmes, and practices fully into each business as an essential element of management in all its functions.

(c) *Process of improvement*: To continue to improve corporate policies, programmes, and environmental performance, taking into account technical developments, scientific understanding, consumer needs and community expectations, with legal regulations as a starting point; and to apply the same environmental criteria internationally.

(d) *Employee education*: To educate, train, and motivate employees to conduct their activities in an environmentally responsible manner.

(e) *Prior assessment*: To assess environmental impacts before starting a new activity or project and before decommissioning a facility or leaving a site.

(f) *Products and services*: To develop and provide products or services that have no undue environmental impact and are safe in their intended use, that are efficient in their consumption of energy and natural resources, and that can be recycled, reused, or disposed of safely.

(g) *Consumer advice*: To advise, and where relevant educate, customers, distributors, and the public in the safe use, transportation, storage, and disposal of products provided; and to apply similar considerations to the provision of services.

(h) *Facilities and operations*: To develop, design, and operate facilities and conduct activities in consideration of the efficient use of renewable resources, the minimization of adverse environmental impact and waste generation, and the safe and responsible disposal of residual wastes.

(i) *Research*: To conduct or support research on the environmental impacts of raw materials, products, processes, emissions, and wastes associated with the enterprise and on the means of minimizing such adverse impacts.

(j) *Precautionary approach*: To modify the manufacture, marketing, or use of products or services or the conduct of activities, consistent with scientific and technical understanding, to prevent serious or irreversible environmental degradation.

(k) *Contractors and suppliers*: To promote the adoption of these principles by contractors acting on behalf of the enterprise, encouraging and, where appropriate, requiring improvements in their practices to make them consistent with those of the enterprise; and to encourage the wider adoption of these principles by suppliers.

(l) *Emergency preparedness*: To develop and maintain, where significant hazards exist, emergency preparedness plans in conjunction with the emergency services, relevant authorities, and the local community, recognizing potential transboundary impacts.

(m) *Transfer of technology*: To contribute to the transfer of environmentally sound technology and management methods throughout the industrial and public sectors.

(n) *Contributing to the common effort*: To contribute to the development of public policy and to business, governmental, and intergovernmental programmes and educational initiatives that will enhance environmental awareness and protection.

(o) *Openness to concerns*: To foster openness and dialogue with employees and the public, anticipating and responding to their concerns about the potential hazards and impacts of operations, products, wastes, or services, including those of transboundary or global significance.

(p) *Compliance and reporting*: To measure environmental performance; to conduct regular environmental audits and assessments of compliance with company requirements, legal requirements, and these principles; and periodically to provide appropriate information to the Board of Directors, shareholders, employees, the authorities, and the public.

346. *See* http://www.wbcsd.org (last visited Aug. 22, 2005):

> The World Business Council for Sustainable Development (WBCSD) is a coalition of 175 international companies united by a shared commitment to sustainable development via the three pillars of economic growth, ecological balance and social progress. Our members are drawn from more than 35 countries and 20 major industrial sectors. We also benefit from a global network of 50 national and regional business councils and partner organizations involving some 1,000 business leaders globally. The WBCSD's activities reflect our belief that the pursuit of sustainable development is good for business and business is good for sustainable development.
>
> **Our mission**
> To provide business leadership as a catalyst for change toward sustainable development, and to promote the role of eco-efficiency, innovation and corporate social responsibility.

347. *See* website for the U.K. Department of Food, Environment and Agricultural Affairs, available on the Internet at http://www.defra.uk/environment/waste/topic/elvehicledir.htm (last visited Aug. 22, 2005).

348. Rod Hunter, *EU Recycle Laws Could Spark Trade War*, NAT'L L.J., Mar. 18, 1996, at A19.

349. *Id.* at A21.

350. Gregg Easterbrook, *Here Comes the Sun,* NEW YORKER, Apr. 10, 1995, at 38, 42.

351. *Id.* at 38, 41.

352. *See* VALUE TO BUSINESS, *supra* note 74.

Chapter 4:
Organization and Staffing for Environmental Management

People are the key to success of any environmental management program. A crisis—either within a company or in a similar company—may galvanize people to initiate or improve an environmental management program. Occidental, Ato, Allied Chemical Corporation, and Union Carbide Corporation each suffered traumatic experiences that raised awareness and inspired efforts to avoid future problems. Many others are rapidly changing and their management programs may also change to reflect their product mixes, philosophies, and management changes. The lessons learned, however, are still valid. Such crises catch management attention, increase understanding of potential problems, lead to development of strong programs, and increase support and funding for program implementation. A crisis also fosters greater cooperation, which may not always exist in corporations that have not had such experiences. Under any circumstances, however, management commitment, a good organizational structure, and appropriate staffing serve as the foundation of a strong environmental management program.

Environmental management (Occidental and Ato) programs develop in different ways. The discussions in this chapter draw heavily on examples from the companies where I have had responsibility for environmental management, as well as more recent experiences as a consultant. The experiences of these companies in developing broad-based programs to deal effectively with past problems, to avoid future problems, and to do both cost effectively with small staffs may be useful to others. I discuss them in detail to provide concrete examples of how the elements of an environmental management program can be implemented in specific situations. I also utilize my experiences as a consultant.

Since 1957, Occidental expanded primarily through domestic acquisitions in a wide variety of areas, together with rapid growth in the international oil and gas area and limited growth in domestic oil and gas operations. Its headquarters-level efforts to develop corporate-wide environmental programs began in September 1978 with the appointment of a director of health and environment. Divisional programs had in fact commenced long before. Between September 1978 and May 1981, significant progress occurred in developing and carrying out a range of environmental programs. These programs included informal assessments, reporting on significant issues and the status of permits, and limited identification of upcoming regulatory and legislative issues. Divisional staffing was upgraded to carry out corporate requirements. Progress accelerated with additional staff and resources. In May 1981, Occidental created a corporate environmental attorney position. Between June and October 1981, the company expanded the corporate staff to add a vice president, a records administrator, a manager of assessments, and a manager of external affairs (subsequently director of external affairs and compliance). Senior management's involvement continued and expanded. During 1980 and 1981, following a Securities and Exchange Commission (SEC) settlement and creation of the Board of Directors' Environmental Committee,[1] the Board and top management gave the corporate environmental department a mandate to develop and maintain systems that would independently determine the status of compliance and ensure that the company was properly addressing environmental concerns.

Today the Occidental staff is still small. In 1990, the Risk Engineering Department (then consisting of four professionals and now composed of two professionals with another professional in a divisional position) was added to the group in recognition of the close relationship between personnel safety and loss prevention. Occidental's environmental counsel was then based in Washington, D.C. (although he subsequently transferred to the chemical division in Dallas), along with two individuals handling legislation and regulation—one of whom doubled as the Director of Environmental Affairs. A manager of health, safety, and environmental programs was added in Los Angeles late in 1992. Although the Environmental Committee had always concerned itself with safety and health, in 1989 its name was changed to the Environmental, Health, and Safety (EHS) Committee to emphasize these concerns. In addition, a third outside director was added to the committee.

Ato was the U.S. chemical division of a large, but decentralized, French oil and gas, chemical, and health company, Elf Aquitaine. Elf Aquitaine was merged into another large French oil and gas, chemical, and health company, TotalFina, in the first quarter of 2000. The name of the chemical operation was then changed to Atofina. I refer generally to Ato rather than Atofina or Arkema, since my personal experience was with Ato, although the basic systems have not changed. Ato (now Arkema), which was the product of a 1990 merger of Pennwalt, M&T Chemicals, and a few chemical plants of the U.S. subsidiary of Elf Atochem, S.A., always had an EHS staff. Ato upgraded and expanded that staff in 1994 with the creation of my former position, Senior Vice President and Executive Committee member reporting directly to the President and Chief Executive Officer. As a member of both the Executive Committee and the Manufacturing Committee, I was involved in major management decisions, which helped ensure integration of our programs and sent a strong signal as to their importance. In addition, we significantly increased our staffing, particularly in environmental, health, safety, and auditing. (Appendix E contains a sample organization chart for a Vice President for Health, Environment, and Safety.) We also added two of my senior staff to the Management Group, the next level of management below the Executive Committee.

The following discussion outlines a variety of approaches to organization and staffing for environmental management that Occidental—and Ato—used to develop strong environmental management programs at minimal cost, together with the context in which these controls were—and are being—developed. These approaches have also been tested in my consulting practice in general manufacturing facilities, oil and gas exploration, power and utilities, manufacturing, and construction companies, among others. These approaches have several key characteristics, which are listed in Figure 4-1.

Figure 4-1
Key Characteristics of Strong Environmental
Management Programs

- Top corporate management is strongly committed to and involved in the company's environmental management programs.
- The organizational structure, whether centralized or decentralized, is designed for effective program implementation.
- The environmental function is integrated with the safety and risk engineering functions and integrated with the business.
- Turf problems among staff groups and divisions are minimized, primarily by maintaining a thinly staffed organization and focusing on the primary concern of getting a job accomplished. Decisionmaking is largely free from bureaucratic constraints.
- Both corporate and divisional staffs are committed to maintaining a high level of professional expertise encompassing a range of essential disciplines and backgrounds.

The policies, procedures, and controls implemented by Occidental's Health, Environment, and Safety Department are not unique. The combination of programs and the overall corporate philosophy, history, management support, and flexibility embodied in these programs, however, may well be unusual. Nevertheless, most of them are transferable to others in the environmental corporate community. Indeed, with support from senior management, we did so at Ato, and significantly expanded these programs.

You as an environmental manager will have to deal with organization and staffing in your own corporate culture. Your company may or may not have addressed these issues. This chapter can serve as the basis for a cross-check against your existing programs. It may also help bolster your case to senior management for making changes by explaining in detail the value of various program elements.

Management Commitment

A major element of an effective environmental program is management commitment throughout the corporation. Companies must have strong environmental policies and be structured and managed to implement their policies. (Environmental policies are discussed in detail in Chapter 5.) The policies should, at a minimum, require compliance with the law and establish a program to ensure that every employee will be able to report a violation of the policy confidentially and without fear of retribution.[2]

To send company personnel the strongest message, the chief executive officer should issue environmental policies. Years ago, relatively low-level corporate officials often issued environmental policies. Given increased corporate and public environmental awareness, they are now more appropriately issued at the highest level. When Dr. Armand Hammer, former Chairman of the Board and Chief Executive Officer, issued Occidental's environmental policy, his cover letter stated that he expected "full and complete adherence" to the policy. When Occidental issued its new environmental policy, the June 1991 cover letter of Dr. Ray R. Irani, Chairman of the Board and Chief Executive Officer, added, "we recognize the importance, at all stages of our businesses from strategic planning to the ultimate disposal of products, to consider the impact on the communities in which we operate and to use natural resources wisely to achieve a sustainable level of global development."

The commitment of top management must be carried throughout the corporation. The best way to emphasize this commitment is to state in the policy that line managers are charged with individual responsibility for the environmental performance of their activities. It may also be helpful for the policy to state, as does Occidental's, that "every employee is expected to carry out the spirit as well as the letter of this policy." Ato sends a strong, positive message by putting its policy and accompanying document entitled "Health, Environment, and Safety Policy" (see Appendix D) in TQM terms. The policy not only talks about principles, but mandates the development, implementation, and maintenance of management systems. It also provides that "[e]mployees will be held accountable if they fail to uphold" the program's "three guiding principles"—compliance, protection, and performance. In a cover letter dated January 24, 1995, Bernard Azoulay, Ato's Chief Executive Officer, and I stressed the importance of the new policy, but noted that it "is only *part* of Elf Atochem's HES management system." We included the following diagram and a statement of core values to emphasize how policies will be implemented.

Figure 4-2
Structure of Elf Atochem North America, Inc.'s Health,
Environmental, and Safety Management System

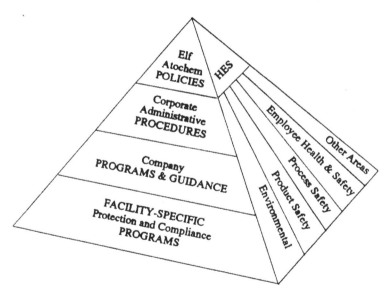

A second key step to help ensure commitment is establishing a mechanism to report EHS issues directly to the board of directors. At Ato, I served on the Executive Committee, Ato's equivalent of a board of directors, and EHS issues were a regular part of our agenda. The Occidental Board of Directors' establishment of an Environmental Committee (now the Environmental, Health, and Safety Committee) was a critical step in the development of the company's corporate support for environmental programs. The

Committee requires periodic review of and annual reports on environmental matters, including costs, the status of implementation of recommendations, identification of "unascertainable" matters,[3] and long-range plans to ensure that the Board is fully informed of significant environmental matters. Ato has been requiring similar actions, including quarterly status presentations to the Executive Committee by the group presidents. This concept was also helpful in building earlier programs at Allied-Signal and Union Carbide.

A system of reporting to and involvement by the board of directors gives tremendous clout to EHS programs. If nothing else, it is a symbol of management commitment. That members of the board of directors will be aware of significant issues is a major incentive for fixing what is wrong and avoiding impending problems. Many times, my simply indicating that I would like to advise Occidental's Environmental Committee or Ato's Executive Committee that something was being done to eliminate an issue ensured that action was in fact taken.

A third step to help ensure ongoing management commitment is designation of a senior-level manager as compliance officer. The compliance officer's principal responsibilities should be to provide a means, at the corporate level, to ensure compliance with company policy, laws, and regulations; maintain constant standards for policy enforcement; and, when necessary, report any policy violation directly to the corporation. This person should be backed up by counsel; it is advisable to appoint a compliance counsel to deal with the legal issues. In many cases, depending on the culture of the company, it is better to have the corporate compliance officer outside the normal chain of command in the environmental area. Otherwise, it might be argued that although the corporate environmental department needs to provide guidance and interpretation of the policy requirements and review all programs and reports for compliance, there is no outside check on the performance. In Ato's case, although I was the chief EHS compliance officer, I was part of a compliance committee of the most senior officers in the company, which provides a cross-check. This concept is even more significant with the adoption of the Sarbanes-Oxley legislation,[4] discussed subsequently.[5]

The primary responsibility for compliance should rest on the chief executive officer of each division, not the designated compliance officer. Those in charge of the actual operations are in the best position to ensure compliance. The compliance officer can help maintain consistency and provide another vehicle for understanding environmental issues at senior levels of management and for communicating their importance.

The day-to-day responsibility for program implementation must rest on the line managers. In any organization, the environmental staff can advise, cajole, and develop basic programs, but unless line management carries out those programs, they cannot be successful. Today's environmental manager must develop good relationships with the line people and must understand the significance of line operations. The environmental manager is in essence a salesperson, selling the advantage of his or her product in a nonthreatening manner to line and staff managers and, in turn, making the field more comfortable by supplying information. The successful manager, particularly in the early stages when he or she is developing credibility, must spend a substantial amount of time on the road with his or her counterparts in the divisions and in the field.

Only when people at all levels are committed will program implementation be fully successful.

Organizational Structure

The organizational structure for each company is different and evolves over time. An environmental manager must work within his or her own company with its unique history, organization, issues, and constraints. Obviously, environmental managers have to deal with the corporate culture as they find it. Nevertheless, there are certain issues that will be common to many companies. The approaches taken will depend in part on whether the company is centralized or decentralized and the allocation of responsibilities between the corporation and its divisions.

Centralized Versus Decentralized Structures

In general, most of the programs discussed in this book were designed primarily for a decentralized organization with a small corporate staff. I am not hiding my bias for that form of organization, where appropriate. The programs discussed, however, are equally beneficial to both centralized organizations and decentralized organizations with larger staffs. Indeed, as previously discussed, I applied them at Ato—a larger, more centralized organization that is essentially a combined corporate/divisional group that is part of a larger company. As discussed in Chapter 5, all organizations need strong policies, procedures, and programs; systems for reporting to senior management and the board of directors; information systems; planning efforts; systems for reviewing capital expenditures, acquisitions, and divestments; and legislative and regulatory programs. Implementation of these programs, however, may be somewhat different in centralized than in decentralized organizations.

In a centralized organization, virtually all specialized work is done at headquarters, with limited work in the field. One advantage of a centralized program is uniformity. This may be important in establishing plant parameters or specific policies for dealing with agencies. Centralization may also work well when facilities are too small to require full-time EHS staff and the limited services of centralized specialists are sufficient. An example of a strong centralized program is 3M. Ato's current practice of staffing a service organization for environment, health, and safety provides economies of scale.

Many organizations are decentralized in name, and to some extent in function, but still have large centralized staffs. These staffs may provide expertise, but they also spend substantial time collecting or, in some instances, prying information from the field, even in today's computerized environment. Such organizations do try to have more expertise available at the plant level than do centralized organizations. Large decentralized organizations may also have centralized groups that do nothing but training or program planning and have sizable budgets to deal with these issues. General Electric is a good example of such an organization. It has both a strong decentralized program and a sizable central staff performing broader functions. Ato was moving closer to the General Electric model because of the nature of its operations.

Centralization, which assumes that corporate staff, rather than field personnel, will do much of the more sophisticated environmental work, does not eliminate turf problems (see discussion later in this chapter) or the difficulty of obtaining information on significant issues. Nor does it necessarily ensure that corrective action is taken. Although centralized organizations normally are designed to handle most of the major permitting activities, and perhaps to coordinate contacts with government agencies, they often do not have timely access to critical data. Like decentralized organizations, they must develop their relationships with local plant managers to avoid long memo-writing exercises. As in the decentralized organization, the human factor cannot be overemphasized. Neither centralized nor decentralized management can be done from behind a desk.

In both centralized and decentralized organizations, primary environmental responsibility should rest with line managers. In centralized organizations, many field managers mistakenly assume that the corporate center bears this responsibility. The manager of the centralized organization must overcome this assumption. The centralized organization may provide uniform guidance and specialized expertise, but the best manual of policies and procedures is of no value unless it is read and followed. Lack of responsibility and sufficient expertise in the field can lead to major problems. For example, if field managers allow sloppy practices between corporate environmental audits, it is quite possible to have major problems with poor spill control and tank testing. Plant awareness is even more critical to strong programs in the safety area.

Some companies take the position that the centralized staff is providing services for which facilities should be charged. The experience of many managers in such organizations is that they spend considerable time fighting with the field over billing matters, which detracts from their primary management functions. More significantly, requiring divisions to pay for services creates a disincentive for them to seek advice when they may need it, which is counterproductive to a program. Frankly, I am convinced that in most instances, charging for these services is a paper exercise and does very little, if anything, to reduce costs. If an individual performs specific services for a division on a regular basis, this can be budgeted, but charging for services performed on an ad hoc basis discourages use of the staff specialist when needed. If the staff group also performs audit functions, it can be particularly galling for a division to pay for its own audit.

Definition and Allocation of Corporate and Divisional Responsibilities

In either a centralized or decentralized organization, corporate environmental protection staff must provide leadership to carry a strong environmental policy throughout the corporation. A corporate staff should be organized to step back and look toward longer range planning and implementation. Divisional staff, by their nature, must be more attuned to day-to-day problems as well as the specific mission of their division. With strong divisional staffs, broad procedures, and a strong database, the primary roles of a corporate group in a decentralized organization should be corporate governance, audit/assessment, longer range problem solving, and ensuring that the divisions have the necessary personnel and tools to do their jobs.

At Occidental, each divisional environmental department was required to define areas of responsibility for environmental matters, identify environmental programs and issues, and recommend corrective actions and strategies. The education, training, and experience of divisional staff must be commensurate with the types of environmental issues the organization faces. Ongoing programs must maintain or upgrade the technical expertise of professional and nonprofessional staffs. Those staffs must maintain active communication with other corporate environmental concerns, either directly or through the corporate HES Department.

The Occidental corporate group developed specific requirements for divisional environmental organizations throughout the corporation. These requirements, set forth in company policies, procedures, and guidelines and discussed in Chapter 5, defined the relationships among the corporate HES Department and its counterparts in the divisions. They provided for communication of corporate policies and procedures, review and comment on proposed divisional environmental organizations, and concurrence of the corporate Vice President for Health, Environment and Safety (or a designee) before appointment of a divisional chief HES administrator. Procedures also address organization of divisions, response to proposed and newly enacted environmental laws and regulations, monthly environmental reporting, implementation of environmental assessment programs, reporting of environmental matters on a timely basis, and employee awareness and training. Guidelines include requests for substantial expenditures and reporting of "substantial risk" under §8(e) of TSCA.[6]

Occidental found that this series of procedures and guidelines adequately covers its needs. None of these procedures was extensive. Other companies' procedures and guidelines generally cover the same subjects, but may differ in scope. The procedures developed for Ato were broader than Occidental's, but, as stated previously, Ato in the United States is more analogous to a decentralized division.

Integrating the Safety and Risk Engineering Functions With the Environmental Function

Introduction

A critical path toward integration of EHS as part of a "we just do it" culture is adopting a process safety or "risk-based" management approach. This is an important and in many cases the primary proposed strategy for implementing management improvement recommendations.

For example, many facilities and managers assume that "management of change" applies primarily to specific process change and applicable OSHA workplace safety regulations. However, "change" can have much broader and more significant implications and impact on the business. It can affect quality and general operations, not just process safety. Data management systems manage change, as do quality systems. Productivity is also impacted and means to improve productivity such as standardizing operating procedures, or establishing basic employee skill requirements such as computer literacy, can act as significant change agents.

In general, both as a matter of process safety and as a general manufacturing process, it is important that all the significant implications of "change," even a seemingly limited change in a manufacturing process, be identified, carefully evaluated, appropriately acted upon, and documented as part of a formalized Management of Change (MOC) process. This is not always the case. Specific and detailed procedures should be established for any change and that change must be clearly documented. For example, Piping and Instrumentation Drawings (P&Ids) in many facilities are very poor. Documentation of electrical work and engineering for new equipment may be better, but is often lacking in older equipment or older portions of a facility. This lack of documentation impacts production, process safety, and in some cases personnel safety and environmental compliance. Many environmental incidences and permit issues are a result of failure to adequately manage change.

Process Safety Management (PSM) is broader than the OSHA workplace regulations. While some company processes and facilities are directly subject to the OSHA regulations (although not to the PSM regulations), I define the concepts more broadly than regulatory compliance. The concept here is goal setting and performing "through" or beyond normal compliance requirements to establish a high performance culture that effectively "manages" overall EHS risk. Establishing such a process safety/risk management culture is vital to "best in class" management. An incident can hurt an individual, create environmental damage, and destroy valuable equipment, all of which negatively impact customers, the community, and the overall company. Thus, a process safety/risk management culture improves not only process safety, but also personnel safety and environmental controls. It avoids "stove piping"—looking only at environment or looking only at safety considerations, without examining the broader interrelationship of these functions, as well as their significance in operations. Preventive/predictive maintenance, data management, and incident investigation are part of PSM. This management concept ties the EHS functions together and in turn integrates them into general management as part of the culture, achieving "we just do it."

Development of such a "risk-based" culture will provide the sustainability necessary to assure that EHS is fully integrated into the company management culture. Most significantly, the institution of the risk-based culture will provide the base for any systematic approach to EHS management that will work best with the changing goals of the company, assure compliance, and allow a systematic approach to EHS to become the readily accepted way of doing business. In essence, this approach is an operations and overall business-inclusive approach to achieving the targeted EHS objectives.

Driving Culture

The responsibility to initiate integration of environment, health, and safety into business operations rests with management. Traditionally, environmental issues have been handled separately from safety and risk engineering. This no longer is advisable. Safety programs have been primarily concerned with various programs to reduce injury or illness without focusing on process reviews that could avoid major injuries or loss of life. Risk engineering has historically focused more on inspections than on broad-range process or risk analysis. Conversely, today many environmental departments are beginning to look closely at the problems of sudden and massive releases and the resultant threats to the environment. All of these areas need to come together to cope with, and hopefully prevent, events that create major environmental issues, affect personnel safety, and damage property. If you don't take the initiative, it will not happen.

The importance of integration has been brought home dramatically with the tragedies arising from terrorism on September 11, 2001. Some EHS departments have now been given the additional responsibility of security after management noticed that while the traditional security departments were good at investigation, they were not accustomed to the broad range of crisis management that is now part of many EHS operations. Of course, the September 11 tragedies also impacted nationally on EPA and on local regulations.[7] EPA is reviewing its authority to better respond to chemical and biological terrorist attacks. It has a new workgroup in coordination with the Homeland Security Office to "review EPA's structure, to determine how the agency could take on more responsibilities, including ensuring the security of the nation's water infrastructure and addressing chemical and biological attacks."[8] Security issues are being utilized to attempt to prevent regulatory changes. Congressman Waxman (D-Cal.) asked "the president's homeland security chief to investigate the national security implications of a GOP effort in Congress to consider terminating a number of environmental and other regulations under the Paperwork Reduction Act (PRA)."[9]

Regulatory agencies began to focus on the importance of integrating these functions because of a string of explosions involving chemical facilities. On October 23, 1989, a Phillips Petroleum polyethylene plant in Pasadena, Texas, exploded and burned, killing 23 people. In its review of the accident as a part of its Chemical Accident Prevention Program, EPA conducted a chemical safety audit of the Phillips complex. Other agencies participated in the audit.

> [T]he purpose of this audit was to assess the facility's chemical emergency preparedness and prevention procedures and to determine the potential for and consequences of releases that have a potential impact off site. Detailed information on the facility was collected from documents provided by Phillips and through discussions with company staff. This information included a description of the physical characteristics of the site, emergency preparedness and planning activities, community emergency response planning, public alert and notification procedures, safety and loss prevention activities and accidental release investigations. A list was compiled of the hazardous chemicals at the site and the procedures for handling and processing these chemicals were reviewed. Systems for monitoring the operation of the process and equipment and for mitigating the effects of process upsets were also reviewed. Recommendations were developed for emergency response planning, equipment for monitoring hazardous substance releases, reporting and notification procedures

for chemical releases, alarm equipment, and employee evacuation training.[10]

The Chemical Accident Prevention Program arises from EPCRA, the statute that requires disclosure of information about potentially dangerous chemicals and development of emergency response plans.[11] Under EPCRA, Congress directed EPA to conduct a review of emergency systems for preventing, detecting, and mitigating accidents, and alerting the public. This review has been the keystone of EPA's accident efforts. The resulting report, issued in 1988, stated that prevention of accidental releases requires a holistic approach: integrating technologies, procedures, and management practices at all stages in the life cycle of a facility. It also emphasized that site-, process-, and chemical-specific hazards dictate the choice of technology and techniques at specific facilities.[12] EPA is conducting audits "to identify both problematic and successful practices and technologies for preventing and mitigating releases."[13] Thus, EPA's traditional role has greatly extended into the safety area.

While EPA was calling for more process safety efforts, OSHA already required such reviews. As part of its review of the Phillips incident, OSHA made the following finding: "A process hazard analysis or other equivalent method had not been utilized in the Phillips polyethylene plants to identify process hazards and the potential for malfunctioning and human error and to reduce or eliminate such hazards."[14] Phillips was cited for willful violations under the general duty clause of the Occupational Safety and Health Act (OSH Act) for failure to complete such analysis.

On February 24, 1992, OSHA issued final process hazard management regulations.[15] The rule requires many facilities to conduct process hazard analyses. Employers are required to:

(1) compile process safety information and data on toxicity levels;

(2) maintain and communicate to employees safe procedures for process-related tasks;

(3) train workers so they understand the nature and causes of problems that might arise and increase their awareness of specific hazards;

(4) ensure that contractors on-site work safely and that contract employees are properly trained and informed;

(5) perform periodic inspections of equipment;

(6) issue "hot-work permits";

(7) establish and maintain written procedures prior to implementing changes in technology or equipment;

(8) use a team of experts to investigate potentially major incidents;

(9) develop emergency action plans; and

(10) conduct compliance safety audits at least every three years to assess the effectiveness of the process safety management program.[16]

EPA and OSHA have developed a close working relationship. As the press release announcing its report on the Phillips explosion stated, OSHA is committed to working "with [EPA] to develop a joint investigation strategy for catastrophic chemical accidents which affect both plant workers and people in the surrounding community."[17] EPA and OSHA coordinate programs to protect employees and those who live near industrial sites, conduct joint inspections and training, and exchange information on violations. EPA and OSHA issued a Memorandum of Understanding that provides instructions and guidelines for cooperative enforcement efforts, mutual cross-training programs, information/data sharing, and other jointly agreed-on activities.[18]

The close working relationship between EPA and OSHA has grown as a result of CAA §112(r),[19] which mandates that EPA develop regulations to prevent accidental releases and their impacts outside a facility. EPA issued proposed rules on October 20, 1993.[20] After much controversy and litigation, EPA issued a supplemental notice of proposed rulemaking on April 15, 1996.[21] EPA published final regulations on June 20, 1996, effective August 19, 1996, requiring companies to develop Risk Management Programs (RMPs) to prevent accidental releases of chemicals.[22] There is considerable overlap between OSHA and final EPA regulations, although there are some important differences. In general, OSHA focuses more on on-site safety while EPA focuses on off-site potential hazards to the public, particularly on larger quantity releases that have the potential for off-site impacts.[23]

There are many issues and complexities for companies seeking to comply with EPA's risk management rule. There is even technical disagreement about the use of the word "risk."[24] An even greater controversy surrounds the exposure scenario requirements. An RMP must have a hazard assessment, including estimates of potential release, downwind effects, and potential exposure to populations. A five-year release history must be developed that includes actual hazardous events and durations of covered releases. A worst-case scenario must also be projected. The proposed 1993 rule required a totally unrealistic assumption: instantaneous loss of the entire inventory of a regulated substance without the benefit of either active or passive mitigation systems. The final rule requires a somewhat more realistic assumption: loss of the entire inventory of a regulated substance over a 10-minute period with the benefit of only a passive mitigation system. Many technical personnel including my own staff at Ato still view this scenario as unrealistic.[25] The final rule, however, allows for "alternate release scenarios" for each covered substance on the site.

Despite these concerns, Ato developed a process to comply with EPA's risk management rule.[26] Even before adoption of the rule, corporate management moved to an integrated risk model in three principal areas: safety engineering, risk engineering, and environmental issues. The company's safety programs are concerned with reducing injury and illness as well as process factors that could affect worker safety. Risk engineering minimizes risk to plant workers, people in the surrounding area, and the environment. Integrating risk and safety engineering in this way makes environmental issues part of the plan for handling everything from routine to worst-case issues.

In November 1994, we formed a steering committee composed of representatives from our process technology group, the corporate HES Department, and plant environmental people. The steering committee was designed to plan and direct a pilot operation, gather information and assess the operation, and develop plans to move the pilot program from idea to implementation. In December 1994, several key members of the steering committee visited the risk management planning offices of our French parent company, Elf Atochem Worldwide, to evaluate a proprietary risk management modeling system we developed in conjunction with European consultants.[27]

The steering committee began work after EPA issued its supplemental notice of proposed rulemaking in March 1995. In its first official action, the committee developed a pilot-phase methodology. We chose a consulting firm, developed a corporate workbook for RMP implementation, and selected pilot sites. Our consultant then proposed a three-phase program, outlined in Figure 4-3, to bring our RMP from plan to reality.

Figure 4-3
Sample Three-Phase RMP Implementation Program

Phase One: Hazard Assessment
- Air dispersion modeling software evaluation
- Risk scenario model comparison and selection
- Scenario selection and modeling
- Line of sight survey (conducted in house)

Phase Two: Existing Program Upgrade (Review and Modification of Pilot Sites' Existing Programs to Ensure EPA Compliance)
- Prevention program (including Process Safety Management/ Hazard and Operability)
- Reviews, safety precautions, maintenance, monitoring, and employee training
- Accident history
- Emergency response (including informing the public and local agencies, emergency preparedness, health care, and employee training)
  - Risk communication

Phase Three: RMP Development
- Development of an RMP for pilot plants
- Development of a corporate workbook for other facilities

After completing Phase One (hazard assessment) and beginning work on Phase Two (existing program upgrade), we settled on an RMP compliance proposal. We then initiated the pilot program at our Wichita, Kansas, facility. We selected a hazard assessment scenario, established a protocol for release modeling evaluation, and developed the first release model results for the Wichita plant.

Wichita was a natural candidate for the pilot site. On the risk side, the plant uses as raw materials several chemicals classified as "hazardous," although its principal products are not hazardous. Also, our Wichita facility is co-located and fully integrated with a Vulcan Chemicals facility. Vulcan had recently conducted an extensive evaluation of risk factors of its facility and developed a close working relationship with community leaders on safety and environmental issues. The data from its five-year program were made available to us and provided solid background for our own work. A particular benefit to our work was Vulcan's program to upgrade hazardous waste disposal at the Wichita plant and to increase community awareness and cooperation through a stepped-up "Community Involvement Group" effort.[28]

After preparing a draft RMP for the Wichita facility, it was registered with EPA and submitted to the State Emergency Response Commission in Kansas, to the Local Emergency Planning Committee in Wichita, and to other agencies with regulatory oversight, such as OSHA.

We saw the RMP rule and risk management in general as an on-site responsibility at each Ato plant and as part of doing business in the chemical industry. With the completion of Phase One of our program at Wichita and another pilot at our Carrollton, Kentucky, facility, we had as many questions as answers on how to get to full implementation, both at these pilot facilities and across the country. It took time to find answers before we were ready to implement our RMP fully.

Because EPA and OSHA are working together, so must their industrial counterparts in company environment and safety departments. Although many companies complete Hazard and Operability Reviews—detailed reviews of the process for failure modes—they probably require expansion. Such reviews, together with the means of reducing the hazards identified, need to be prioritized for existing facilities on the basis of potential exposure, from both property or production loss (risk engineering) and potential safety and environmental risks to workers and the surrounding community. The scope of these reviews should probably be expanded and should normally be conducted on a plant level by a team from operations, maintenance, and engineering with overview by safety, risk engineering, and environmental personnel.

Another means of ensuring integration is to examine existing job descriptions. In general, it is useful to keep job descriptions updated to ensure that they are consistent with the present objectives of your organization. (See Chapter 5, The Planning Document—Short-Range and Long-Range Planning and Goals.) It is also useful for educating your human resources department, which probably does not fully appreciate the rapid changes in this area and the effect on finding and appropriately compensating competent personnel. The exercise of reviewing job descriptions, particularly if done as a team effort, is an excellent vehicle for allowing your staff to appreciate fully the scope of each other's work, as well as the necessary overlaps. This is illustrated by Table 4-1, which lists examples from my time at Occidental. When overlaps are recognized, the ensuing discussion helps eliminate turf problems and encourages teamwork.

Table 4-1
Sample Job Descriptions

POSITION TITLE	POSITION SUMMARY	OVERLAPPING ELEMENTS
Vice President, Health, Environment, and Safety	■ Provides corporate-wide strategic direction for the protection of health, safety, the environment, and company assets and their impact on the preservation and enhancement of shareholder value.	■ Develops corporate policies and implementation procedures necessary to protect human health and the environment and to comply with applicable laws, rules, and regulations for OPC and its Industry Groups/Direct Reporting Divisions (IG/DRDs).
Director, Environmental Affairs and Technical Support	■ Provides corporate-wide strategic direction for the protection of human health and the environment, ensures the development of environmental management systems that provide for compliance with corporate policy and all applicable regulations, contributes to the effective management of environmental risks and liabilities, and preserves and enhances shareholder value.	■ Establishes management system(s) for evaluating and ensuring implementation of OPC policies and procedures in coordination with the other functional directors of Health, Environment, Safety, and Process Risk Management (HESPRM).
		■ Assesses IG/DRD compliance with applicable OPC policies and procedures and communicates findings to IG/DRD management, OPC management, and the Environmental, Health, and Safety Committee of the Board of Directors (ECOB) as appropriate.
		■ Supports issues identification and OPC position development and strategy for involvement in legislative and regulatory issues relating to the environment, assists in the areas of human health and safety, and provides technical, legislative, and regulatory advocacy and support to IG/DRD on environmental matters as requested by the Director, External Affairs and Compliance Support.
		■ Assures integration of environmental programs with business strategies within OPC and the IG/DRD.

POSITION TITLE	POSITION SUMMARY	OVERLAPPING ELEMENTS
Director, Safety, Environmental Health, and Assessment Programs	■ Provides corporate-wide strategic direction for the protection of health and safety, regulates compliance in the health and safety field, preserves and enhances shareholder value, and serves as the corporation's focal point for HESPRM assessment programs.	■ Develops corporate policies and implementing procedures related to the protection of health and safety and HESPRM assessment programs for OPC, its industry groups, and IG/DRDs. ■ Oversees implementation of OPC policies and procedures related to health and safety and HESPRM assessment programs. ■ Assesses IG/DRD compliance with applicable OPC policies and procedures and regulatory requirements and communicates findings to OPC, IG/DRD management, and ECOB, as appropriate. ■ Provides corporate-wide technical and regulatory direction for HESPRM assessment efforts, health and safety programs, and organizational development. ■ Assesses integration of health and safety programs and business strategies within OPC and IG/DRD.
Director, Process Risk Management	■ Provides corporate-wide strategic direction for process risk management.	■ Develops OPC policies that provide (1) protection from catastrophic losses arising from episodic events, (2) plant reliability and process integrity, and (3) the data necessary to integrate appropriate risk factors into business decisions. ■ Assesses IG/DRD compliance with OPC's policies and procedures and regulatory requirements and provides results to OPC and IG/DRD management and to the ECOB, as appropriate. ■ Integrates OPC's process risk management programs with the health, environment, and safety programs and assists with the administration of those programs. ■ Assures integration of process risk management programs with OPC & IG business strategy.
Director, External Affairs and Compliance Support	■ Provides strategic direction for OPC HESPRM legislative and regulatory programs and provides an external perspective on OPC and IG HESPRM programs and policies.	■ Identifies possible impact of HESPRM legislation and regulations on OPC and IG/DRD business strategies in coordination with directors of functional HESPRM areas.

Staffing and Turf Wars

One of the greatest obstacles to implementation of successful and cost-effective environmental programs is "turf." Even with the strongest management support, a program simply cannot succeed unless turf issues are minimized. I will discuss turf and staffing issues extensively because of their significance.

Occidental was fortunate in avoiding turf and staffing problems from the beginning. It is a company without a history of overstaffing or staff wars. When Dr. Hammer took over the company in 1957, its net worth was only $100,000. Throughout Occidental's expansion over the years, corporate headquarters functioned as the equivalent of a holding company with a very small staff. The divisions had substantial leeway, with limited reporting to corporate headquarters, and were encouraged to keep staff size down.

Occidental now includes a number of "industry groups"—individual subsidiaries or groups of subsidiaries in a particular line of business, such as chemical production or oil and gas operations. Although independent in many ways, Occidental's industry groups function, for environmental management purposes, as if they were divisions of the company. (For the sake of simplicity, this book uses the term "division" to include both actual divisions and industry groups.)

As discussed earlier, Occidental increased its emphasis on good environmental management in 1978. Because the divisions had been operating semiautonomously in the environmental area with effective staffs, the mandate for improved environmental management did not mean the growth of a massive corporate staff. Instead, growth consisted of the addition of one professional at headquarters. Corporate staff looked toward ensuring that there were capable environmental professionals in the divisions where the basic work was being—and should be—done. The role of corporate staff is to assist rather than replace or direct the efforts of division staff. The result is that jealousies and turf wars are rarely problems. Indeed, the corporate staff clearly is not large enough to take over for the divisions even if it wanted to. Instead, the corporate staff focuses on ensuring that the divisions and facilities have tools and personnel capable of doing the job.

Turf issues have also been minimal at Ato. As a division, we established a very competent and extensive staff. We also established our own policies and procedures. Corporate procedures provide corporate staff with authority to review and comment on appointments of senior divisional EHS personnel. If divisions have competent people, the corporate role is easier. Moreover, the corporate role at both Occidental and Ato (I am referring here to my role as Senior Vice President) of approving appointments helps ensure divisional environmental professionals a direct, functional line of communication with corporate staff that will help them obtain necessary resources. Under this arrangement, divisional managements know that the Board of Directors and corporate management place a high priority on good environmental management.

Divisional managements tend to have a deep distrust of corporate bureaucrats, whom they often view as interfering with their business and, even worse, not understanding it. This reaction is well justified in far too many cases. Many corporations have been—and a few even today remain—overstaffed, and staff members have to justify their existence by at least showing that they are doing something. Many companies have pared back corporate controls and allow divisions greater management freedom. This, in turn, generates an almost revenge mentality—a strong desire to get back at corporate, which may have made divisional life miserable—by ignoring corporate staff whenever possible. Cost pressure to reduce corporate and divisional staffs also blurs the lines of environmental responsibility.

One way to minimize turf wars is to ensure that corporate staff are sensitive to divisional needs. The "iron fist" approach of dealing with operating management or divisional environmental staffs simply does not work. All organizations have learned to resist pressures from the top. The dismal experiences of new federal agency administrators who try to change policies and means of control from the top down, rather than by gaining the confidence of the civil service, are good examples of the impossibility of achieving change without cooperation and trust. Professionals must work collectively at both corporate and divisional levels to develop strong programs.

Communication between corporate and divisional staffs is also critical. At Ato and Occidental, corporate staff maintained continuing dialogues with divisional managements (at Ato, the Group Presidents) to ensure that those managements understand that they are not being undercut. Corporate staff also have a mandate that allows full discussion with interested individuals in the divisions without interference from a rigid chain of command.

Hostility between corporate and divisional staff is one problem; inefficient staff management at both levels is another. Obviously, bloated staffs in either corporate or divisional headquarters are to be avoided. Even with reduced staffs, however, old tendencies die hard, and there is still too much management by committee. Committee meetings may be smaller because there are fewer people to attend, but it would be far better to grant broader authority and encourage risk-taking than to tie up scarce resources in needless paperwork and meetings.

How can these problems be avoided in environmental management? Peter Drucker and other management experts maintain that the key to management today is managing information.[29] Information management does not necessarily require large staffs. But many companies, even those with large staffs, still do not have mechanisms to ensure that significant information is received at corporate headquarters and made immediately available to decisionmakers. This is particularly ironic given the extensive computerized databases that are available for other company operations. The unavailability of significant information is exacerbated by many companies' efforts to decentralize and by the loss of institutional memory due to downsizing. Although decentralization and downsizing are useful in reducing decisionmaking time and encouraging entrepreneurship, care must be taken that they do not deprive corporate or divisional headquarters of vital information.

The corporation in today's regulatory and litigious climate must learn of potentially significant issues at the earliest possible time to avoid major problems. The underlying assumption for effective environmental management must be that what you don't know *will* hurt you. Obtaining and effectively using the necessary information can be accomplished with minimal staff, provided that barriers to obtaining significant data are reduced or eliminated. Occidental accomplished this by operating as a decentralized organization with a centralized information base. Ato is implementing a sophisticated data management system. (Information management is discussed in detail in Chapter 5.)

Perhaps the most significant factor allowing a small staff to function effectively is smallness itself—the absence of overstaffing throughout the entire corporation. Management experts today consider the concepts of "simple form, lean staff" and a "bias for action" to be key attributes of successful management. These concepts argue for combining thin staffing with short lines of decisionmaking. At Ato and Occidental, for example, comments on new procedures and approaches to regulations and legislation can be produced quickly, simply because very few people are required to make such decisions.

To reduce staff and make better use of resources, some companies are looking to the use of "shared services." The core of a safety or environment program can in fact be shared across a number of organizations.[30] This is a practice we used at Ato with an HES service organization in the HES department. We made it simpler for the facilities by having model plant environment and safety programs, polices, and procedures available through intranet, minimizing calls to corporate personnel. Sharing services eliminates redundancies across multiple divisions and provides for better transfer of best practices. Yet, an operational group's loss of control means that the service organization has to be measured carefully both in terms of its cost and its quality performance measures, aligning to business needs. This requires "[a]n agreed upon methodology between the client and the service provider as to how they are going to benchmark, how they will know that costs are out of line . . . ."[31]

"Outsourcing," the shift of work from internal staff to external contractors, is another major shift occurring in some corporations. Environmental management is not and should not be immune from the examination of non-core functions to see if they are candidates for outsourcing. If the EHS staff has grown too large and bureaucratic, some form of shake-up may be necessary.

> On the positive side, outsourcing makes short notice human resources and expanded expertise available. By outsourcing, organizations can staff for the basic workload and readily acquire additional experienced human resources on an as needed basis. Organizations can also augment in-house expertise with contractors. In many cases, this allows the organization to gain access to world class expertise and capability which they could not afford to maintain internally. With this type of on-demand access, organizations can assess state of the art programs and take advantage of technical advances while keeping down their headcount.[32]

The "world class expertise" promised may be far less experienced, however, and if a good program is in place, it may lose some of its value in the transition. Unlike some functions, environmental management is not discretionary. How it is performed, as discussed throughout this book, depends considerably on the individual corporate culture. A danger is that it can be viewed as a fad; without appropriate controls to ensure that the environmental management function and compliance are maintained, possible short-term gains will soon dissolve in management time to rectify mistakes and deal with agencies.[33] Contracting in this area, like other use of contractors, needs to be managed and without the in-house staff and skills to manage these efforts, the value will soon be lost. Institutional memory and relationships within an organization also provide significant efficiencies that can soon be lost with outsourcing. A major reason for having a competent in-house staff is that liability and compliance risk is managed internally.

One study found that "[s]everal organizations doubted that contractors could 'dependably' manage compliance programs."[34]

> Companies that had outsourced compliance elements experienced mixed success. They found that outsourcing resulted in:
>
> • staff resources being diverted from technical work to contract administration;
>
> • contractor performance being lower than expected of in-house staff;

- system adjustments to develop a method of accountability for the contractors; and

- a lower level of compliance.[35]

In short, there may be good reasons for outsourcing specific limited functions (or simply an organization's obsession with headcount may make outsourcing an organization imperative), but these decisions should be carefully studied, and probably piloted, before extensive change.

Another means of minimizing turf wars is to integrate key staff functions. Battles among staff groups can be just as counterproductive as fights between divisional and corporate staff. As discussed more fully below, the line between environment and safety is becoming increasingly vague. These two functions should report to the same manager to minimize potential problems. Because the medical function and industrial hygiene are also closely tied to environment and safety, it makes sense to have the same line of reporting for these two functions as well. The line between safety and risk engineering is even harder to identify. The risk engineering group is normally concerned about fires and explosions to the extent that they affect property losses. But fires and explosions obviously risk personnel safety as well. The answer is to assure that both functions have the same reporting structure to maximize their value and eliminate any gray areas. Of course, many of these issues, such as sudden releases, also have environmental implications. As noted previously, many organizations are reaching the same conclusions with respect to the reporting line for the security function.

Both Ato and Occidental have found that it makes sense to have the legislative and regulatory function on the same reporting line with respect to environment, health, and safety, although Occidental has changed reporting relationships. This does not mean that the reporting structure should include the traditional lobbyists in your Washington, D.C., office. Although they may report to environment and safety managers, individuals with technical and legal skills who have credibility with key regulatory and legislative officials because of their specific knowledge and drafting expertise, should at times become involved in lobbying efforts. (Governmental relations issues are discussed in more detail in Chapter 5.)

A more difficult question is the integration of the legal function. (Interaction with lawyers is discussed in more detail in Chapter 9.) In my own case, as both a practicing lawyer and a manager, the integration of the function was relatively easy, particularly because I reported to an Executive Vice President who was also Occidental's Senior General Counsel and Secretary. The environmental counsel reported to me on a strong, dotted-line relationship and there was no real friction between us because we had associated with each other professionally for several years before. At Ato, I worked closely with the General Counsel, and the environmental legal staff had a strong dotted-line relationship to me; we worked together as colleagues in a "seamless web." In most companies, the danger of reporting through the legal department is that there is a tendency to view environmental functions as legal, rather than operational. We were very careful at Occidental to make my department separate from the Legal Department.

As the environmental area has become more legally oriented, and more experienced lawyers have moved into senior environmental positions, the issue of distinguishing between legal and management positions has become more of a concern. If the legal department has a turf mentality, it may feel threatened by a lawyer in charge of the environmental function. Consequently, that individual sometimes needs to tread lightly with his or her legal skill when dealing with the legal department.

Recruiting Environmental Professionals

You may be the best general manager and be prepared to adopt the best system of management controls, but without adequate staff you simply will not be able to accomplish your mission. There are several excellent sources for competent personnel. Before you can take advantage of them, however, you may have to argue with your employee relations department, which may not fully understand how important it is to hire staff who can operate independently in the environmental area. Too many companies still employ technicians rather than managers, and employee relations departments can usually point to "comparable" staff in other companies. They may not recognize that "comparability" is not what you need, particularly if the allegedly comparable organization has a very large staff and each individual has limited responsibility. My response to the comparability argument is that I would rather have one swan than two turkeys working for me, and as a manager, I would rather manage programs than a large staff. If you can hire first-rate people who can function independently, you will be able to perform your tasks in the most cost-effective manner. Writing the job description to indicate that the recruit must be able to function independently and deal with a wide variety of people both inside and outside the company will help touch the magic bases with the employee relations department.

Assuming that, using your management and sales skills, you have had job descriptions and compensation schedules approved that will allow you to recruit first-rate people, you next face the assumption that you should, if possible, recruit from within the organization. With extensive downsizing in many companies, the pressure to hire in-house can be intense. If you are fortunate enough to have capable people within your company whom you can place in your environmental organization, this clearly may be the best source of talent. It always takes substantial time for a new person to understand the corporate culture and to learn whom to call and whom not to call to initiate action. If you are able to find a person who combines knowledge of the organization with sensitivity to environmental issues and the social policy behind legislation and regulations, together with the sales ability that any successful staff person must have, you will be fortunate. In one of Occidental's divisions, for example, several senior environmental managers had both technical skills and in some cases broad sales experience in the company before assuming their present positions, as did my Vice President for Remediation (now my successor) and Director of HES Plant Services at Ato.

In environmental management, people skills may be even more important than technical understanding. A person need not be a professional environmental manager to function in an environmental position, although the best manager usually combines broad understanding of the corporation with professional environmental skills. An operating manager who can speak the language of other operating managers can also be helpful in implementing and selling a program. But the former operating manager needs to step back and think conceptually to engage in more than a fire-fighting operation. This is particularly important in long-range planning and budgeting, where immediate payout for expenditures may not be readily apparent.

Unfortunately, too many corporations use hiring from within as an excuse to find slots for managers who have outlived their usefulness in some other department, particularly if there is extensive downsizing. These corporations are not giving the EHS functions proper priority, usually having these functions reporting too low in the organization to get attention. The way around this practice of "placing rejects" is to have particular individuals in mind and readily available to fill positions.

If you are recruiting from outside and have spent your entire career in a corporation, your first inclination will be to look for managers within other corporations. You should also look to trade associations as another good source of employees. Trade association work can help build contacts and establish networks. It also allows you to identify competent people in other companies or on the trade association staff whom you may be able to recruit for your operations.

Government agencies are also an excellent source of potential employees. Many people with strong technical and legal skills begin their careers in government agencies because they recognize that the level of responsibility and challenge given to junior personnel in government usually far exceeds what is available in industrial settings. Moreover, many people committed to an environmental ethic assume that government is the only place to work. A person who has had broad responsibility in a government agency and has a strong environmental commitment can be an ideal candidate for an environmental position in industry. Obviously, the bureaucrat who is uncomfortable with decisionmaking and who shows no signs of creativity is not an ideal candidate. We have all seen, however, the bright engineer or lawyer who finds holes in our arguments or who, when we are right, is willing to take a position supporting us. The tough but bright and rational regulator can make the transition to industry successfully and make a major contribution.

I recall about 25 years ago hiring a young lawyer out of the Justice Department, which, like EPA, is an excellent source of talent. He had recently enjoyed a major victory against an industry by developing a strong technical knowledge of that industry and then creating legal arguments to bolster his position. The decision against the industry came down shortly before he gave notice and came to work for me. About a week later, I had him sit in for me on a trade association meeting that included representatives of that industry. Their initial reaction at seeing this individual was sheer horror, until they realized that he had beaten them fair and square and without ideological malice. They also recognized that the same scientific and legal talent that had been victorious for the government could be useful in the industry setting.

The first challenge in recruiting a government employee is to show him or her that a person can be strongly committed to an environmental ethic in an industrial setting.[36] Indeed, a good environmental manager develops a compliance program that is far stronger than any a regulatory agency could develop, simply because he or she knows what can be done and how to motivate the personnel responsible for completing the job. A good environmental manager is also aware of agency sensitivities and develops programs that will minimize regulatory exposure.

If you plan to hire government employees or any other environmental professionals, it is important to recognize that you must be serious about your program. Environmental professionals are committed to resolving problems once they are discovered. If your company does not recognize the legal and moral implications of dealing with issues—and dealing with them credibly—you will have a hard time attracting environmental professionals, whether from other companies or from the government.

Finally, you should not rule out recruiting individuals who have worked for national citizens groups, such as the Natural Resources Defense Council, the Environmental Defense Fund, or the Sierra Club. Individuals in these organizations have obtained broad experience that is transferable to industry. Many of the points made above regarding government employees also apply to public interest group employees.

Conclusion

The basis for a strong environmental management program begins with the people responsible for its development and implementation. Focusing on organizational structure, integrating functions, staffing appropriately, minimizing turf battles, and recruiting are necessary steps toward any successful program. And today, the program must also be developed and implemented as a *business* program.

Notes to Chapter 4

1. In May 1981, Occidental's Board of Directors adopted a resolution authorizing implementation of a variety of recommendations concerning environmental issues. These included reaffirmation of the corporate policy to make required disclosures of environmental matters in a full and timely manner and establishment of an Environmental Committee of the Board of Directors to oversee corporate programs and reports. The recommendations arose from the settlement of a July 1980 SEC order, which, in turn, arose from Occidental's efforts to acquire the Mead Corporation in 1978.

Under the order, Occidental agreed to designate a director, an environmental official, and an independent consulting firm to prepare a report that would "recommend procedures to the full Board of Directors to ensure that Occidental will be in a position to disclose, in accordance with the federal securities laws on a complete, timely and accurate basis, all required information relating to environmental matters." *See* In the Matter of Occidental Petroleum Corporation, Exchange Act Release No. 16950 (July 2, 1980).

Other recommendations included preparation of an internal book on laws, obligations, and liabilities; preparation of a collection of federal and state laws and regulations applicable to each facility; revision of corporate policies and procedures, including separation of environmental policies from other policies; preparation by the divisions of division-specific policies and procedures; annual review of procedures; establishment of dual-path reporting (e.g., to the Health, Environment and Safety Department and to the Legal Department); development of a computerized database; preparation of an annual report; submission of reports on capital and operating costs; and establishment of training programs.

2. Ato has an environmental compliance hotline, which is run through the legal department, and also requires statements of accountability from its employees. (See Appendix F.)

3. Occidental procedures define "unascertainable" matters as "relevant and unresolved legal, factual, or technological questions or problems which render remedial actions, costs, or actual or contemplated claims or proceedings uncertain." Examples would be possible uncertainties arising from new regulations or new interpretations of existing regulations.

4. Pub. L. No. 107-204, 116 Stat. 745 (2002).

5. *See infra* discussion in Chapter 6.

6. 15 U.S.C. §2607(e), ELR Stat. TSCA §8(e).

7. For a detailed explanation of the environmental implications of the destruction of the World Trade Center, see Michael B. Gerrard, *Environmental Law Implications of the World Trade Center Disaster*, 13 Envtl. L. in N.Y., Jan. 2002, at 1.

8. *Whitman Pushes for Expanded EPA Terrorism Response Authority*, Envtl. Pol'y Alert, Dec. 26, 2001, at 34.

9. *House Democrats Raise Security Concerns Over GOP Reg Review*, ENVTL. POL'Y ALERT, Dec. 1, 2001, at 33.

10. OCCUPATIONAL SAFETY & HEALTH ADMINISTRATION, U.S. DEP'T OF LABOR, THE PHILLIPS 66 COMPANY HOUSTON CHEMICAL COMPLEX EXPLOSION AND FIRE 18 (Apr. 1990) [hereinafter OSHA REPORT].

11. 42 U.S.C. §§11001-11050, ELR STAT. EPCRA §§301-330.

12. OSHA REPORT, *supra* note 10, at 18.

13. *Id.* at 19.

14. *Id.* at 23.

15. 57 Fed. Reg. 6356 (Feb. 24, 1992) (codified as amended at 29 C.F.R. pt. 1910 (1996)). For a detailed discussion of the then proposed regulations at 55 Fed. Reg. 29150 (July 17, 1990) and their relationship to the 1990 CAA Amendments, see Frank Friedman, *The Overlap Between the Clean Air Act and Proposed OSHA Process Hazard Management Regulations*, HAZARDOUS WASTE & TOXIC TORTS L. & STRATEGY, Jan. 1991, at 1.

16. 57 Fed. Reg. at 6356 (preamble).

17. U.S. Dep't of Labor, Press Release No. 90-207, Apr. 26, 1990, at 3.

18. U.S. Dep't of Labor, Press Release No. 90-622, Nov. 28, 1990.

19. 42 U.S.C. §7412(r), ELR STAT. CAA §112(r).

20. 58 Fed. Reg. 54190 (Oct. 20, 1993).

21. 61 Fed. Reg. 16598 (Apr. 15, 1996).

22. *Id.* at 31668 (June 20, 1996).

23. For example, the EPA rule covers 50 fewer chemicals, specifies flammable materials individually, and has many higher threshold chemicals. John Plakosh, Manager, Risk Process Safety at Ato, made a side-by-side comparison of the EPA and OSHA chemical lists. His analysis indicated that 25 substances have higher threshold quantities (TQs). Those chemicals, except for one, have TQs greater than 10,000 pounds, and 39 chemicals on EPA's list have TQs greater than the OSHA process safety list, usually by a factor of 10. Also, it could be argued that the EPA listing of ammonia solutions with concentrations greater than 20 percent is more stringent than OSHA's concentration threshold of 44 percent. Only methyl chloride has a lower TQ than the OSHA list. These higher TQs indicate the difference in inventory levels needed to cause off-site consequences rather than the local plant effects of lower threshold substances.

The final EPA risk management program list includes 139 substances: 77 acutely toxic substances, 63 flammable gases and volatile liquids, and Vision 1.1 high explosives. Modifications have been proposed to the rule affecting explosives, flammables in gasoline and naturally occurring hydrocarbon mixtures, and other flammable mixtures, as well as the definition of stationary source with respect to transportation, storage incidental to transportation, and naturally occurring hydro-carbon reservoirs. *Id.* at 16598.

24. Marc Rothschild of Ato's process safety department argues that "risk" is the combination of consequence and likelihood. Risk takes into account many parameters, such as failure rate data, wind direction, atmospheric stability data, population distribution, location and strength of ignition sources, dispersion analysis, and receptor sensitivity. The outputs of a risk analysis are individual risk contours, societal risk curves, and fatal accident rates. This information is used to evaluate the existing risk against available standards and to suggest cost-effective measures to mitigate the risk. EPA's "*Risk* Management Plans" are misnamed as they address only consequence and not likelihood.

25. Marc Rothschild identifies several problems with this scenario. The worst-case analysis requirement allowing a 10-minute duration for gas releases is not less onerous than the originally proposed instantaneous release assumption. It may not be intuitive, but a 10-minute release is usually *worse* than an instantaneous release. The short explanation is that a 10-minute release is relatively long and thin, whereas an instantaneous release would be shorter and fatter with a correspondingly lesser impact range. For pressurized gases (e.g., propane, ammonia), the 10-minute duration is likely to be impossible to achieve in a real event. If released in a contained area (such as in a diked area at a tank farm), a fraction of the material will flash, cooling the remaining material to a liquid at its boiling point (44ÉF for propane, 28ÉF for ammonia), which would then evaporate over time. The heat required for evaporation mostly comes from the air. Given the night-time conditions of "F" stability and EPA's mandatory 1.5 meter/second (3.4 mph) wind speed, the resulting evaporation rate would be low. A test analysis for ammonia indicates that it would take several hours to completely evaporate, *not* 10 minutes.

In addition, the toxic endpoints are inappropriate. EPA (appropriately) selected toxic materials based on their acute hazard potential, yet chose toxic endpoints representing only moderately harmful, not acutely hazardous concentrations. The RMP toxic endpoints represent Emergency Response Planning Guideline ERPG-2 levels, which are the maximum concentrations at which nearly all individuals could be exposed for 60 minutes without developing irreversible or other serious health effects. This is hardly a health threshold of concern for the worst case, a one in 10,000 year event. A more realistic threshold would be ERPG-3 (fatality threshold upon 60-minute exposure). The distance to an ERPG-2 threshold is on the order of two to four times farther than to an ERPG-3 threshold.

The temperature assumptions are also unrealistic. EPA RMP requirements specify that the hottest temperature in the past three years is to be used for the modeling (which obviously occurs only during the day). It also specifies that "F" stability is to be used. "F" stability occurs only on clear nights when the earth is radiating heat. Therefore, these two requirements cannot ever coexist.

The vapor cloud explosion assumption is also unrealistic. The RMP requires an assumption that all flammable vapors can result in a vapor cloud explosion. In reality, only releases in a partially to totally confined area (such as in a process area) can result in such an explosion. Releases from tank farms and other remote areas cannot result in a vapor cloud explosion.

26. The following discussion of Ato's risk management program is adapted from Frank B. Friedman, *Risk Management Program Awards Good Planning,* CHEMICAL PROCESSING, Feb. 1996, at 34-37 (adapted with permission).

27. Developing proprietary packages is the rule in Europe, but it is the exception in the United States where certification by regulatory agencies makes in-house systems impractical. Regulations are different enough in France that we felt we could move to implementation more quickly with one of the modeling packages already on the market in the United States. Also, the more popular systems in use in the United States have been subject to extensive peer review and are viewed as more reliable by the regulatory agencies.

28. The Vulcan effort is the subject of an extensive case study conducted by members of the Center for Environmental Communication at Rutgers University and the Department of Environmental Sciences and Engineering at the University of North Carolina, Chapel Hill.

29. Peter Drucker is a renowned economist, management consultant, and expert in the field of corporate management. *See generally* PETER DRUCKER, TECHNOLOGY, MANAGEMENT & SOCIETY (1970); PETER DRUCKER, MANAGING FOR RESULTS: ECONOMIC TASKS AND RISK-TAKING DECISIONS (1964); PETER DRUCKER, THE PRACTICE OF MANAGEMENT (1954).

30. *Shared Service Edges Into EHS, Paring Staff, Upping Effectiveness,* 6 ENV'T, HEALTH & SAFETY MGMT., Sept. 25, 1995, at 3 (citing Kyle Datta, Booz-Allen & Hamilton).

31. *Id.*

32. Mark C. Posson, *The Risks and Benefits of Outsourcing Environmental Management,* 3 CORP. ENVTL. STRATEGY, Mar. 1996, at 5-6.

33. *See Reengineering Environment, Health and Safety,* CHEMICAL WK., June 5, 1996, at 32.

34. Posson, *supra* note 32, at 6.

35. *Id.*

36. For a general discussion, see Frank Friedman, *'60s Activism and '80s Realities—We've Come a Long Way,* ENVT. F., July 1983, at 8.

Chapter 5:
Implementing a Strong Environmental Management Program

In addition to management commitment, good staffing, and a workable organizational structure, corporations need to put into place a strong environmental program. The basic objectives of a good program are listed in Figure 5-1.

Figure 5-1
Objectives of a Strong Environmental
Management Program

• Strong management commitment to and involvement in a company's EHS management programs, and accountability for non-compliance with laws, regulations, and corporate policies is strictly enforced;

• Designing the organizational structure, whether centralized or decentralized, for effective program implementation, including appropriate policies, directives, and other action-assurance mechanisms;

• Developing a consistent and transparent process, which is an important element of maintaining reputation and reputation turnaround strategies;

• Integrating the environmental function with the safety and risk engineering (process risk) functions;

• Committing EHS staffs to maintaining a high level of professional expertise encompassing a range of essential disciplines and backgrounds;

• Seamlessly integrating the EHS management system with company general management system;

• Regular, timely, and uniform reporting from the operating line through senior management to the board of directors;

• Prompt identification and resolution of environmental issues;

• Establishment of preventive programs and procedures; and
• Identification of developing issues or trends.

To meet these objectives, a program should have the elements listed in Figure 5-2.

Figure 5-2
Elements of a Strong Environmental Management Program

- Strong corporate environmental policies and directives/ procedures;
- A high-quality reporting system, including a computerized, centralized information system (whether in a centralized or a decentralized management system);
- An internal planning document and timetable;
- A capital expenditure review system;
- A legislative and regulatory action program;
- Training and education programs; and
- A facility assessment program.[1]

This chapter discusses in detail each of these elements, except for the facility assessment program. Because facility assessments are so critical to environmental management, they are discussed at length in the following chapter.

In these cost-conscious times, it has been my experience that successful programs well integrated in the company's businesses can save a corporation substantial sums, while keeping both corporate and divisional staff size to a minimum. As discussed in the previous chapter, keeping staff to an absolute minimum is essential. To do so, it is necessary to review job functions and program needs continually, consolidating functions and eliminating unnecessary positions. In addition, development of broad-based directives/procedures and guidelines that can be monitored on an exception basis, rather than on day-to-day performance, allows corporate personnel to concentrate more effectively on long-range planning, program development, and compliance. A computerized database and the general use of computer-based techniques allow for effective and efficient use of data, facilitate understanding of issues, and free the staff to concentrate on broader issues.

Having an effective EMS will also avoid having a compliance-oriented system mandated by EPA or the DOJ as part of a settlement in an enforcement action. My experience in this area is that these government-imposed systems do not achieve the kind of integration and cost effectiveness that is the value of EMSs in the business context, despite the professed goal of the Compliance-Focused Environmental Management System (CFEMS)[2] "to integrate into a facility's daily operations an EMS that results in the company achieving and maintaining compliance over time...." "Once the EMS is developed, EPA's role is to ensure that the EMS is implemented according to the terms of the settlement agreement."[3]

In a survey taken of industry representatives involved with such mandated EMSs[4] it was found that it was difficult to determine "whether the EMS requirements correlate with an increase in environmental performance,"[5] although "[m]ost industry representatives credited the EMS with increased monitoring, recordkeeping, and reporting of environmental issues. Improvements in compliance with environmental laws and regulations were specifically noted." "All industry representatives reported that their respective EMS resulted in increased self discovery of environmental problems as well as increased awareness of environmental issues." It was also felt that "more incentives are needed to encourage EMS generally."[6]

Environmental Policies and Corporate Responsibility

In setting the stage for implementation of environmental programs, it is imperative to establish the company philosophy by promulgating an environmental policy.

Once corporate policy is set, it must then be translated into directives/procedures and guidelines for implementation. At the corporate level, as discussed subsequently, I prefer the use of the term "directive" rather than "procedure" to describe more general governance requirements, as opposed to more specific corporate procedures designed to provide operational guidance or facility-specific procedures designed by a division or the facility itself for a specific facility. Most companies use the term "procedures" for both. The Occidental corporate group has developed specific requirements for divisional environmental organizations throughout the corporation. Policies, directives/procedures, and guidelines each perform different functions and it is important to keep the three concepts separate. Policies should be broad-based, outlining the key aspects of an environmental program and establishing the company's commitment to that program. Means of implementing policies should be described separately in procedures and guidelines. Directives/procedures should be mandatory methods of implementing policies. Guidelines should be written when implementation of a policy does not lend itself to specific procedures or when a procedure itself needs additional explanation.

Generally, I prefer directives/procedures to guidelines because procedures are tighter. As a company's program matures, it may be practical and preferable to substitute procedures for guidelines. Occidental and Ato have replaced almost all of their guidelines with directives/procedures. For example, while Occidental has a procedure for review of property acquisitions and sales, the specific areas to consider vary with the scope of the transaction. Thus, an extensive guideline indicating specific areas to consider is more appropriate than a procedure requiring review of all areas of concern.

The divisions then need to develop and document appropriate programs to ensure that all current and proposed facilities, equipment, products, and procedures comply with corporate policy. They should also ensure that any prompt action required is taken, develop and document reporting procedures, and develop and document a timetable for implementing the programs.

In some companies, directives/procedures and guidelines may approach the form of a code with detailed instructions on each aspect of these areas. Detailed instructions and programs for providing awareness and training are common. At Ato, the approach is instead to focus on management *systems* indicating to the facilities what programs and system elements need to be in place. The Health, Environment, and Safety Policy (reprinted in Appendix D) specifically requires design and implementation of a variety of management systems. It is not micromanaged with exhaustive procedures. Ato does have procedures, but they are in a directive format. The goal is for the facilities to have *systems* and *programs* in place. HES provides corporate assistance and makes available through an intranet system, examples of programs and systems that are already in place in many of the facilities and are working effectively. This form of peer review is very effective, and Ato also uses management system audits (discussed in Chapter 6, Corporate Program Review) to ensure that facilities are on track.

Formulating an Environmental Policy

Most major corporations today have environmental policies. Some policies are relatively short with basic commitments, but incorporating by reference other documents that establish more specific requirements, making them in effect part of the "Policy." Others are longer with the commitments (such as those described below) specifically part of the Policy. These policies can be vague and meaningless, or they can be the cornerstones of strong environmental programs. If a policy includes, as it should, a commitment to make the expenditures necessary to implement it, it sends an appropriate message throughout the company. If it states, as does one company's policy, that "where physically and economically feasible" the company will "eliminate or minimize the undesirable consequences of its activity," and that the company "will surpass applicable standards in instances when it is in the [C]ompany's interests to do so," it can send a negative signal that the company's commitment is limited.

If you are developing or reviewing a corporate environmental policy, you should review principles such as those of the International Chamber of Commerce (see Chapter 3), the chemical industry's Responsible Care® guidelines (see Chapter 3), the Coalition for Environmentally Responsible Economies Project (CERES) Principles, and the Sustainability Reporting Guidelines developed by the Global Reporting Initiative (GRI) for the United Nations Environmental Program (see Chapter 3).[7] The CERES Principles, published by a coalition of environmental, church, and environmentally concerned investment organizations, "encourage companies 'to make a public accounting of the planet's ecological problems—and to pledge to do better.'"[8] They deal with the following issues:

- protection of the biosphere;
- sustainable use of natural resources;
- reduction and disposal of wastes;
- energy conservation;
- risk reduction;
- safe products and services;
- environmental restoration;
- informing the public;
- management commitment; and
- audits and reports.

The full text of these principles can be found at the end of this chapter.[9]

While many companies hesitate to adopt the CERES Principles in their entirety,[10] the CERES Principles have now been endorsed or adopted by more than 70 companies, including American Airlines, Coca-Cola, General Motors, Consolidated Edison, and Sunoco.[11]

Whatever source is used to develop or refine an environmental policy, modern or progressive environmental programs should be designed to protect the environment and achieve regulatory compliance while minimizing corporate exposure to long- and short-term capital requirements and operating expenses. To do so, the policy should contain several key elements.

There should first be a statement concerning the fundamental basis for the policy that reflects the corporation's desire to be responsible. Thus, Occidental's corporate environmental policy states, in part:

> Life and health are precious and must be safeguarded. If we are to sustain worldwide development, we must accept the world's natural resources are finite and are to be conserved and protected. Environmental protection is good for the community and is good business. Therefore, the protection of human health and the environment is one of Occidental's highest priorities.

As discussed earlier, Ato's policy stated as one of its "guiding principles" that "[w]e will endeavor to conduct our activities in a manner which protects the well-being of our employees, the public, and the environment and promotes environmentally sustainable manufacturing which meets the needs of the present without compromising the ability of future generations to meet their own needs (sustainable development)."[12]

An environmental policy should commit the company to compliance with the law. The policy should state that the company will conduct all operations, including sale and distribution of products and services, in compliance with applicable environmental laws, regulations, and standards. This commitment must be specific and without loopholes. The program should also adopt appropriate standards to protect people and the environment in cases in which laws and regulations are inadequate or do not exist. This approach should include international operations and provide for a standard of protection of health and the environment functionally equivalent to that which the company requires at its parent U.S. or EU locations. (See also Chapter 3, Environmental Management in the International Context.) It is crucial for today's corporations to commit to using modern control methods, procedures, and processes that are technically sound, economically feasible, and that minimize waste generation and releases. This commitment can also save money in the long run because pollution control equipment that is optional now may be mandatory in the future. Retrofitting pollution control equipment is generally more expensive and less cost effective; it is easier to design the equipment as part of a project than to shoehorn later changes in, or better still, not generate the pollutant at all.

An environmental policy should also provide the basis for an internal compliance system. Ato's statement of core values (Appendix F) makes it clear that the responsibility is at the highest levels: "Group Presidents . . . are directly accountable to the President and Vice President to whom they report." Internal compliance systems are neutral. They should remain constant regardless of changing political attitudes. The bottom line is that they make economic sense. Under a good internal compliance system, if it makes economic sense to have stricter environmental and health standards than the law requires, those standards will be in place. Conversely, legal standards will be challenged (although not as part of the compliance system) if they do not make economic sense and there are legal bases for challenge. Whatever the standards, the internal compliance effort should provide for an assessment program to ensure that each operating facility knows and is meeting its corporate and legal obligations.

The policy needs to set the stage for ensuring that the organization is positioned for compliance. David Willette, formerly Vice President, Operations Compliance, at Occidental's chemical subsidiary, OxyChem Division, defines the conditions for compliance listed in Figure 5-3.

Figure 5-3
Conditions for Compliance With Environmental Laws

- The organization and facilities must be *capable* of compliance.
- Compliance must be a natural endpoint of the way in which work is performed.
- Resources must be focused by priority.
- Measurement systems must be focused on precursor events.
- The capital budget must be adequate to meet needs.

Ensuring compliance therefore calls for a strategy that uses a "total incident" concept to capture and track *any* unwanted event or condition, focus on root cause issues, and use findings to target resources.

The policy should include the assumption that there is also a commitment to providing adequate funds to carry out a strong environmental program. Ato's policy states that "[s]enior management review of the company's health, environmental, and safety performance [will be] conducted and documented on a routine basis. Such reviews will address the allocation of human and financial resources necessary to maintain and uphold the guiding principles."[13] Providing stable funding is not always easy, particularly in troubled economic times, and if this commitment is not included in the policy, it can be ignored. Funding limitations put a strain on managers, both line and staff, and programs of excellence may be difficult to achieve. At a minimum, however, compliance with laws and regulations must be maintained. Responsible corporations pursue this goal even during recessions. Commitment to a strong corporate environmental program will build credibility with the government, making it willing to listen to suggestions. A company is then in a good position to assist in development of equitable and effective environmental rules and regulations.

Management Systems

There is considerable misunderstanding of what is an environmental management system. In critique of an article that claimed that a study of the chemical industry's Responsible Care program concluded that the use of an EMS does not predictably lead to better environmental performance,[14] Richard Wells, President of the Lexington Group, noted that "Responsible Care is a code of practice" while an

> EMS is a formal systematic *process* for making decisions expected to yield consistent, predicable results. It is institutional-

ized through its integration in the culture of the organization. . . . It must look at the totality of the organization's interactions with the environment and have a process in place to prioritize and focus on those that are most important to the organization. . . . It must contain a continual feedback and learning loop." He also notes the problems of so-called "compliance-oriented" EMS, which "diminishes a key value of an EMS, the requirement that the organization look within itself and determine its own values and commitments.[15]

The Policy, Statement of Core Values, and Corporate Directives—The Critical Corporate Documents—Systems, Programs, and Commitments

The policy and statement of core values (Appendices D and F) are designed to catalyze the changes that (1) recognize a broad-based environment, health, and safety management system; (2) provide assurances of compliance with law, regulations, and government programs while limiting corporate involvement in a decentralized organization; and (3) establish accountability and acceptable modes of corporate governance throughout the organization. The objective is that each unit will have systems in place and programs designed to meet fundamental corporate requirements. Each business unit is generally free to develop systems and programs to meet these requirements in its own way. The critical corporate documents are (1) an Environmental, Health, and Safety Policy (which meets corporate governance, regulatory needs and establishes accountability within the business units); (2) a statement of Core Environmental, Health, and Safety Responsibilities of Employees and Contractors; and (3) Corporate Directives, which will be designed to establish the minimum requirements for each business unit, such as an audit program, in order to meet the required elements contained in the Environmental, Health, and Safety Policy.

In other words, the policy is the equivalent of a constitution. The Core Values, which each employee and employee of contractors is required to sign an acknowledgment that they have read and understood, explains the basic responsibilities of managers, employees, and employees of contractors under this constitution. The Directives are the laws. Each business unit writes its own regulations (procedures) to comply with the constitution and laws.

The proposed policy included in Appendix D:

(1) Includes language that meets regulatory needs such as the Department of Justice Policy on Criminal Prosecutions Sentencing Guidelines, EPA Audit Policy, OSHA standards, and other agencies such as the Minerals Management Service

(MMS) understandings of appropriate policies;

(2) Clearly establishes accountability at the business units. As part of that accountability, certain "required elements" of a management system, which are auditable, are described in the Policy. As noted previously, the business units are free to develop their own procedures as long as they are consistent with the Policy; and

(3) The Policy also makes clear that "compliance" is not just compliance with law, but also compliance with company policy, directives, and standards.

Similarly, the statement of core values should be distributed in pamphlet form throughout the entire company to all employees, contractors, and employees of contractors. The sample document (Appendix F) states specifically that it "describes the core environment, health, and safety (EHS) responsibilities that apply to all employees and contractors in conducting their day-to-day activities while working at the company's facilities and operations." It also communicates the company's commitment and describes in general the relevant policies, directives standards, and procedures in order that every manager, employee, and employee of contractors has at least been provided with a basic overview of the importance of EHS and what are each person's commitments and responsibilities.

Corporate directives tell management who does what and how often. These documents do not, however, instruct the organization regarding how to perform tasks. The directives explain what the corporation has in mind in the broad language of the policy. In essence, they establish accountability throughout the organization for developing and implementing systems and programs which meet the "required elements" contained in the policy, which are in turn based on the three guiding principles, also contained in that policy—protection, performance, and compliance.

The environmental policy should require each division to develop a self-monitoring environmental assessment program to ensure compliance. (I prefer the term "assessment" to the term "audit" because, unlike a financial audit, there are fewer specific standards to audit against. For the sake of simplicity, however, this book uses the terms "assessment" and "audit" interchangeably.) A broad-based assessment program guidance document helps divisions establish the program and specifies a protocol for implementing it. The assessment program ensures routine, daily compliance and provides an overview of day-to-day operations. Assessments also help in environmental strategic planning, identifying areas where compliance costs can be reduced or risk avoided, environmental training of assessment team members, and developing greater environmental awareness throughout the corporation. (The assessment program and guidance document are discussed in detail in Chapter 6.)

As assessments generate specific follow-up recommendations, the policy should provide for a tracking system to allow both the division and the corporate group to ensure that each division carries out those recommendations. Ato uses a computerized database to track the recommendations.

The environmental policy should also establish programs of self-monitoring and reporting through multiple organizational channels. Although any large company, because of its size and diversity, will never be absolutely positive that it is always in compliance, such certainty is a goal worth pursuing. Thus, policy commitments to train employees to identify issues of environmental concern, emphasize individual responsibilities, and teach actions to be taken to protect the environment are critical. These commitments help emphasize line management responsibilities. Line responsibility for employee training is equally important in the safety area. Perhaps one reason that health, environment, and safety often are combined in a single corporate department is that similar management techniques are used to deal with these issues. Ato has emphasized this by having a combined health, environment, and safety policy.

The policy should encourage process innovations and fundamental research, including development of means to reduce waste generation and discharges of contaminants into the environment. Here, too, sound environmental policy and economics can coincide. There is economic justification to reduce waste as disposal and compliance costs increase. The situation is perhaps most like energy conservation. Many years ago, when oil cost $3.50 a barrel, the incentive to reduce energy costs was not terribly significant. But when oil reached a price of $18 to $20 per barrel—and at today's much higher costs for not only oil, but also natural gas—the economic incentive has greatly increased.

As noted previously, progressive environmental policies today should recognize broader social responsibility. Compliance is not enough—thus, the Ato policy's specific commitment to sustainable development taken directly from the Bruntland Commission definition to assure specific commitment.[16] Other language is now becoming increasingly in vogue and indicates an understanding of broader concerns. The term "civil society" is increasingly found in environmental policies and refers to the general public, specifically, nongovernmental, voluntary and nonprofit organizations, foundations, social enterprises, and stakeholders. Similarly, the term "environmental footprint" can be used to describe the extended environmental impact of the company and company-related activities at any time, including the amount of land and natural resources used. The term "triple bottom line" is often used to describe the broader concerns of a company. It is not only to make a profit but also to be environmentally conscious and socially responsible in the broader senses of the term. Finally, there is the concept of "transparency." This assumes that whatever a company does or however a company presents data, it should be readily understandable to civil society. Another way of internally describing the same impact is that an obligation or a requirement is "traceable," capable of being related directly or indirectly to a standard or requirement, through an unbroken chain of documentation without loss of meaning or intent. All of these terms do tie in to "sustainable development," which is subsequently described in detail.

Compliance Assurance Letter

A Compliance Assurance Letter is a very useful technique to ensure that each business unit is doing what it should in managing the EHS function. The head of a business unit is delegated substantial responsibility. The Compliance Assurance Letter, which the head of each business unit would be required to sign annually and submit directly to the General Counsel (with eventual submission to senior management and the Board, with a copy to the head of EHS), is a comprehensive document that provides a basis for ensuring a substantial portion of the accountability that must go with that responsibility. However, while the Compliance Assurance Letter needs to be coupled with other systems discussed in this book, it is by its nature one of the most critical tools for providing the necessary corporate assurances that management systems are functioning effectively.

Many companies have general compliance letters, but these letters to be effective should include details such as processes developed and implemented to further compliance with applicable EHS regulatory requirements and company policies; the status of audit findings; and investigation processes for all significant EHS incidents and the implementation of measures to prevent their occurrences. Here, again, the focus is systems in place. A business unit head would also want similar letters from those reporting to him/her in order to assure that appropriate due diligence has taken place. This approach is not very different from Sarbanes-Oxley, but is designed not only for compliance but to provide further assurances that systems are in place and working effectively. It is not only a compliance tool, but also an effective management tool.

The Compliance Assurance Letter also accomplishes the purpose of bringing forward to management and the Board those issues that may need immediate attention and allows management and the Board to understand what actions, including funding, may be necessary for correction and to provide appropriate capital through the budget process as may be necessary.

Corporate Responsibility in Context

Corporate environmental policies and corporate responsibility need to be placed in context. There may be misperceptions that frustrate companies with the best of intentions—and the best environmental programs.

Although a company may intend its environmental risk management program to demonstrate social responsibility, this goal may be elusive. The basis for generic assumptions as to social responsibility should be considered carefully. The strengths or weaknesses of the environmental program sometimes are irrelevant to specific incidents. For example, the breakup of the tanker, the *Exxon Valdez*, is perceived by many members of the public as traceable to Exxon's environmental program. The primary issue in that instance was not related to the environmental program, but to the competence of the tanker captain and other members of the crew. Ironically, when Exxon, while offering help to employees for alcohol or drug dependency, prohibited individuals with a history of alcohol or drug abuse from holding jobs where safety is critical (such as tanker captain), it was sued by the Equal Employment Opportunity Commission (EEOC) for discrimination under the 1990 Americans With Disabilities Act.[17] The U.S. Court of Appeals for the Fifth Circuit eventually overturned the EEOC decision.[18]

In addition, the public castigated Union Carbide for the tragic death of thousands of people in Bhopal, India, as a result of an accident in a chemical plant involving the release of an acutely toxic chemical. Union Carbide, however, claimed that there was strong evidence of sabotage by a disgruntled worker who took the valve off a tank and added water to contaminate product in the tank, not knowing that the chemical reaction would produce a toxic cloud.

Public perception is often disappointing for companies seeking to be environmentally responsible. Can only a company that manufactures ice cream be considered environmentally responsible, while companies with good loss prevention and loss control programs are not? I find it ironic that a chemical company, such as OxyChem, that recycled plastic containers used by a socially active ice cream company might not be deemed "environmentally responsible" as easily as the ice cream company would. Also, most would agree that regeneration of activated carbon, which is used in pollution control and purification processes, is an environmentally beneficial recycling process. Yet Ato, which had been in the business of regenerating spent activated carbon and reselling it to customers across the country, might not be deemed as "environmentally responsible" as an end user of the product, such as a public water supplier that provides treated drinking water or a beverage manufacturer that relies on activated carbon to improve the taste and appearance of its beverages. (Ato is also a leading supplier of environmentally friendly paint strippers used by most major airlines.)

In some cases, the wrong numbers may be used to demonstrate environmental protection or lack of protection. For example, in their efforts to measure program effectiveness, some environmental organizations have focused on the number of sites subject to remediation under federal and state cleanup statutes such as CERCLA.[19] Yet, the number of sites undergoing remedial action is not a reliable indication of today's management programs or social responsibility. Most of the sites subject to remediation resulted from practices that occurred at least 30 years ago. Also, today's contaminated sites are not accurate gauges of the social responsibility even of past practices, because companies are often held responsible under statutes with retroactive, strict liability provisions for practices that were legal, state of the art, or not viewed as damaging to the environment at the time.[20]

Environmental organizations also attempt to evaluate program effectiveness by quantifying the amount of so-called toxic materials released. This data is readily available for a variety of materials released by certain manufacturing operations that must be reported under §313 of EPCRA.[21] These gross numbers do not, however, tell you anything about the releases in relation to the effectiveness of process controls or the levels of production. These organizations chastised DuPont, for example, for its high release levels, but as the largest U.S. chemical company, it has the largest amount of total releases. Moreover, while some companies have been able to show significant reductions in releases in recent years, in some instances, the reductions were easy changes that should have been accomplished years ago. A company may not be able to show significant recent reductions if it has had a program in place for many years and made the easy reductions early on.

Some companies have also begun to publish "green reports," annual reports on the environment that are designed to show the public that the company is environmentally progressive. After browsing through the pretty pictures in many of these reports (which are, of course, printed on recycled paper), the reader quickly notices their limitations. Much of the information is already publicly available (such as the data on toxics required under EPCRA §313) or is subject to disclosure under the SEC rules if it is "material."[22] These green reports also list a variety of environmental accomplishments that, again, usually do not give any real basis for comparison. Many of the public-spirited gestures are, on closer inspection, not completely altruistic. For example, a company that needs authorization for a specific project will often make such gestures to obtain goodwill from the local public or permitting authority. Television and radio commercials attempting to show the caring nature of the company should also be examined objectively.

I do not mean to imply that companies should not publish green reports.

Publishing one can be very valuable to a consumer-based company simply because it will help sell the company's products. It may also be valuable for a company in an area such as waste management, which requires extensive and controversial permitting. In Ato's case, they published the first health, environment, and safety report in 1995 to highlight the significant improvements made in programs and to emphasize the importance of these programs. In Elf's case, the "report sets out to explain and communicate our efforts to integrate global environmental concerns into our industrial strategy."[23] The value for commodity companies with few public dealings is very limited, however, particularly because publishing extensive reports is very expensive, and the money could be better spent on specific efforts to improve environmental operations, although many of these reports are now published either primarily or solely on the company's website. Clearly, such a company should list some of its significant accomplishments and other important environmental issues and costs in its annual report or in a separate report. But evidence of a company's environmental responsibility and its loss-prevention and loss-control programs should not be weighed by the size of its green report, particularly until there are more generally accepted numerical indicators of performance. Of course, today with the availability of the Internet, few companies are "publishing" such reports in print in large number, but rather are making them available on the Internet and providing written copies only on request.[24] (See also the discussion in Chapter 3 of the Global Reporting Initiative.)

Care must also be taken in evaluating recommendations for socially responsible investments. The Investor Responsibility Research Center attempts to provide institutional investors with impartial information about the environmental performance of major U.S. corporations.[25] It is difficult, however, to compare one company to another. There are too many differences in product mixes, facility ages, and enforcement levels in different areas of the country to provide meaningful data. For a company that is involved in a variety of fields, it is further complicated and totally meaningless when the classification is incorrect.[26] Although the Center has substantially improved its data collection and rating-systems methodology, to understand a company's true level of performance, the organization and those who look at its ratings need to look more closely at the assumptions behind the underlying rating system or "impartial information" provided.

A Natural Capital Institute report critiques Social Responsibility Investing (SRI) for lack of standards and transparency on screening and holding of shareholder action. Paul Hawken, the founder of the institute, notes: "The term 'socially responsible investing' is so broad it is meaningless." "SRI mutual funds have no common standards, definitions, or codes of practices...."[27] A report written by the Institute critiques the global SRI industry for lacking transparency of how it screens its investments and which companies it holds specifically for shareowner action, among other things.[28] The Social Investment Forum (SIF), the SRI industry organization in the United States, admits that the SRI community is indeed inclusive of a broad diversity of values and investment styles. "'[Mr.] Hawken is correct that there are no rigid standards dictated for SRI funds to follow in the United States,' said Alisa Gravitz, vice president of SIF. 'SRI funds offer a wide range of options for investors in order to meet diverse ethical and investing criteria.'"[29]

Any type of ranking must be taken with a grain of salt. For example, the Hamburger Umwest Institute in Hamburg, Germany, working with the Council on Economic Priorities in New York and the Ecological Lifestyle Encouragement Center in Tokyo, published a list of the 50 largest chemical and pharmaceutical companies in relation to their environmental performance.[30] Many environmental professionals would take issue with their ranking of the worst performers, which included Merck and General Electric![31]

Some of the efforts to define social responsibility are a result of the frustration of many of these groups of what they see as a failure of government, particularly by the Bush Administration, to appropriately regulate. This "has led NGOs, to believe firmly that they must lead the effort to solve the problems that they (and increasingly the public) think the government and industry are incapable or unwilling to address."[32] These new regulators can be defined broadly to "include quasi-governmental organizations, trade associations, standard setting organizations, research organizations and EHS activist groups,"[33] which for different reasons may feel that regulations are not entirely satisfactory. Formerly a regulatory driven paradigm, NGOs have tried to fill in the gap where they perceive regulation did not exist. For example, many companies that have endorsed the CERES principles[34] "are finding themselves on the receiving end of activist shareholder resolutions supported by CERES."[35] In a discussion of a recent speech by former Vice President Gore, it was noted:

> The current American policy may prove bad for the energy industry, Mr. Gore told his gathered faithful. Pointing to Big Tobacco, he argued that Big Oil could go the same way. Oilmen may think CERES a fringe group. But its coalition includes such heavyweights as CalPERS, California's huge public-employees' pension fund, and represents over $3 trillion in invested capital. CERES members have already brought shareholder resolutions against various oil firms. They also have their sights set on big energy users and greenhouse-gas emitters across the board:

cement and construction, aluminium and steel, agri-business and more.[36]

"The decreasing trust in traditional institutions such as government, church and business was another factor for the rapid increase in the number of NGOs in the last two decades. Increasing awareness of the ongoing social inequality and continued environmental degradation across the world contributed significantly."[37] It has been suggested that the best means of dealing with these trends is to:

* Educate Business executives;
* Evaluate where you stand;
* Identify the new rulemakers that may affect your business;
* Formulate the slate of new metrics;
* Organization (what will work with the new paradigm); and
* Educate yourself.

The best means of measuring the effectiveness and social responsibility of programs in the environmental area (and the related areas of safety, process safety, and risk engineering) is to examine the scope of a company's entire management program. This is, of course, the purpose of this book: to provide a guide to what constitutes good environmental management practices.

Reporting—Management-by-Exception

One of the most critical elements in environmental management is regular, timely, and uniform reporting. In an effort to stay informed, however, a corporate department can overreach and require data on virtually everything, to the annoyance of division and field personnel. The massive amounts of data, which are often meaningless, result in superfluous "just in case" reports, which are easier to generate given today's information technology.[38] A better approach recognizes divisional sensitivities while ensuring that critical information is available to those who need it. The concept is that you do not need all information, but only information that is significant and concerns exceptions to the day-to-day routine. If you have that information, you can intervene when necessary. A specific reporting procedure implements this "management-by-exception" approach.

Occidental has institutionalized management-by-exception by requiring computerized reporting of "significant matters," "excursions," and "reportable incidents."

"Significant matters" are events or situations that have resulted or may result in:

(a) deviations from environmental standards or requirements affecting facilities or operations;

(b) adverse publicity or adverse community relations regarding a specific company action or operation;

(c) notices of violation or advisory actions by regulatory agencies regarding environmental control matters or permit compliance;

(d) legal actions either by or against a division;

(e) identified risks to the environment;

(f) interference with continued production or marketing of any product because of environmental considerations;

(g) substantial incremental expenditures or loss of business related to events or situations caused by environmental considerations;

(h) any problem for which the existing technical solution would impose a significant financial burden threatening the financial viability of the facility or operation; or

(i) any problem for which the staff cannot identify either remedial technology or cost of correction.

Any legal action under (c) or (d) and any item under (b), (e), or (i) above is considered significant without regard to potential costs and liabilities. An event or situation meeting any of the other criteria is considered significant if it may result in capital expenditures or potential costs exceeding $1 million. Different cut-off points may be appropriate for other corporations, depending on their size.

A significant matter arising from an accident or incident must be reported *immediately* to corporate headquarters, while any other significant matter must be reported as soon as possible during working hours. The corporate environmental department may then make recommendations to the division and can advise corporate management of the matter and the recommended action, if necessary.

"Excursion" is defined as:

any emission, discharge, or other release of material outside the parameters established in an agency-issued permit which limits the amount of such materials that can be discharged. This includes releases determined to be excursions based on measurements by official test procedures and reported to the agency. Excursions recorded by other means and which are not reported to the agency should be separately identified and reported.

Occidental did not make any distinction as to seriousness of excursions. The goal was to develop a state of mind that recognizes that excursions can be precursors to citations and should be avoided as part of normal operations, analogous to the safety practices of tracking "near" misses.

Some of the status information also includes "reportable incidents," which are defined as "any emission, discharge, or other release of material which is outside parameters established by any regulation or standard, other than a specific permit, which is reported to a government agency." This is a "leading" indicator of performance analogous to the use of "near misses" in the safety area. In the safety area, most safety professionals track "near misses," recognizing that the difference between a "near miss" and a serious incidence is often luck. Reducing the "near misses" in safety and determining the root cause of the incident is key to good safety performance. Similarly using the same management techniques on excursions significantly reduces the potential for violations. Some people view the term "near miss" as somewhat threatening and possibly discouraging reporting. Karen Murphy, Vice President of EHS at Ashland, suggests the term "good catch" as a more positive approach.[39] Reportable incidents do not include "items covered by spill or Superfund reports," these are reported as significant matters.

This system implements the requirement that all groups throughout the corporation use a common database to ensure consistency of information and records. It provides common data for the Environmental and Legal Departments. In addition, it provides follow-up and updating capabilities, with a complete history of any changes. The system results in complete and timely reporting of significant matters to corporate headquarters. It is extremely useful as a follow-up system for items such as action plans based on environmental assessments, and it allows easy identification of multiple-excursion areas and causes.

Another aid to good environmental management is preparation by the corporate staff of a monthly report for corporate management and the divisions. At Occidental, that report consisted of a summary letter on issues of interest; a fact sheet giving statistical information on excursions, citations, penalties paid, and assessments conducted; and detailed information on legislative/regulatory affairs. Thus, independent analyses of environmental issues are broadly and frequently circulated throughout the corporation. Those analyses help avoid surprises.

Ato prepares similar monthly reports, but is now also implementing a broad-based data collection and management system. The monthly reports contain information, some of which is significant to operating management, including, for example, the cost of outside consultants. Ato also tracks, for example, citations, reportable excursions, CERCLA reportable releases, and proposed and paid fines and penalties. On the safety side, Ato tracks, for example, total case incident rate, lost workday case incident rate, and lost workday severity rate. Government inspections are also tracked for the HES area.

Developing Information Systems

The preceding section discussed management of risk through a management-by-exception concept, which is designed to allow corporate and division staff immediate access to information on potential environmental problems. This section takes the concept of managing information a step further and discusses the computer as a management tool. As Peter Drucker has indicated, the revolutionary impacts of computerization have been more on operations rather than business decisions.[40] The section addresses the use of computerized management information systems (MISs). It also discusses ways to determine the necessary scope of environmental MISs (which are designed to facilitate management-by-exception of significant matters) and environmental database systems (which are designed to maintain detailed information on permits, effluent, waste, etc.). Finally, it suggests effective ways to "sell" both systems within your organization.

Computerized Management Information Systems

After you determine what information you need to avoid environmental surprises, you need to collect and interpret that information. A computerized MIS is extremely helpful here. Such a system should be the communication mode and database of most of the information needed to achieve environmental objectives. In particular, it should be capable of including the reportable items previously described and whatever other items you feel should be reported.

The purpose of an environmental MIS is to provide environmental professionals with a set of data-management tools to improve regulatory compliance, reduce risks and liabilities, and manage environmental costs. These tools together should constitute a comprehensive approach to managing key environmental issues, such as: material safety data sheets (MSDSs) for purchased and process materials; MSDSs for the company's products, intermediates, and wastes; commitment management (management-by-exception); standard operating procedures; site management and regulatory reporting for air emissions, hazardous and nonhazardous waste, water, and EPCRA compliance; site remediation; environmental aspects of process safety and emergency response; industrial hygiene; medical surveillance; and training.

An added benefit of an MIS of this type is improved productivity at the facility, business, and corporate levels. In fact, the MIS programs can be very valuable even if the software tools are provided only at the facility level. A corporate-wide system allows management at all levels to share in addressing a multitude of risks when necessary. Having common tools to manage and communicate actions during incidents and events will provide those who need to know access to appropriate information so they can coordinate action without multiple reporting. Consistent data and core software among all facilities will reduce the costs of acquisition, implementation, training, support, and maintenance.

Occidental developed its own computerized management system. This system, which is managed and monitored by the corporate Health, Environment and Safety Department, efficiently tracks all significant environmental incidents, reportable excursions from compliance requirements, and legal actions taken or pending. In addition, it can identify significant items for assessment teams, track action plans arising from environment and safety assessments, and provide statistical data for determination of trends and/or analysis of causes. The system also includes safety and process risk management.

Occidental's company-wide, on-line system resided in the company's mainframe computer. It allowed development of a record on any specific event, which can be retrieved only by the responsible facility, the division, and the corporate environmental and legal departments. The system can produce printed or on-line reports. Occidental developed a number of fixed format reports, but reports can also be tailored based on locations, types of issues, and/or specific date intervals. This way, the user gets just the information he or she needs, rather than being inundated with computer printout. For special cases, ad hoc reports can also be generated.

This system, like many client-based systems, has many benefits. First, as the official company tracking record on identified environmental issues, it ensures that all levels of the corporation have access to and operate with the same information base. Second, the system requires managers to identify key information clearly. Third, it requires establishment of a workplan for each issue, including a timetable for completion for each folio. In a nutshell, the whole concept of the system is to force action. As discussed in Chapter 6, the development of action plans together with a computerized follow-up system not only solves problems, it reduces legal exposure. Enhancements to the system have increased its utility in trend analysis. By coding events, proposed actions, and final resolution of action plans, people can now identify emerging trends in the types of problems they face and determine the most effective types of corrective action.

The system allows a small staff of corporate HES and process risk management professionals in Los Angeles and Washington, D.C., to develop and monitor programs, as well as ensure prompt and complete reporting of matters of significance to management. It has been of equal—if not greater—value to divisional professionals and is flexible enough to be applied in diverse industry groups such as chemical manufacturing; oil and gas exploration, production, and distribution; and coal and noncoal mining. At the facility level, the system has also substantially reduced the time spent generating paper and communicating by telephone. Indeed, the system has been readily accepted by the field largely because it is of value to the field; it is not simply a black box into which the field must enter data for corporate use.

Occidental's system is an EMS, *not* a database management system. It is not designed to maintain detailed information on permits, emissions, waste, and effluents. Particularly at the divisional or facility level, you may want such detailed information along with an EMS. A variety of commercially available systems capable of performing these database management tasks is now available.[41]

Ato has developed a system that is both an environmental management system and a database management system. It takes advantage of significant improvements in technology, both in hardware and software, and provides a reliable means to access, correlate, document, and integrate critical HES data into work processes on a real-time basis. It is significantly improving efficiency and accuracy while reducing overall costs of many work processes. It also meets government requirements to provide systems to ensure compliance and documentation of compliance.

A key feature of the system is commitment management. Ato has identified approximately 3,500 commitments resulting from permits, notices of violation, consent agreements, and consent orders. It must be able to manage these commitments and cannot afford to miss commitments for liability or risk management reasons. The commitment management portion of the system contains a calendar function that shows deadlines and other dates. Initially, corporate extracted and entered this data, both to ensure that it was done consistently and to avoid delays. Now a designated site individual will enter new information and updates. The system generates "exception" and "missed deadline" reports; these reports also provide explanations for changes in deadlines. Because of the legal significance of this information, changes can be made only with the approval of the HES department and the Legal Department. Reporting is automatic and, of course, Ato routinely audits system security.

Other information is tracked as well. The designated site individual tracks action items from corporate audits, internal investigations, and process hazard analyses, as well as injury/illness information for OSHA reporting. There may also be other site commitments that have nothing to do with legal requirements, such as site goals, which can be placed in the system, but need not be tracked by corporate or even subject to corporate scrutiny.

A similar approach has been taken to management of MSDSs. Corporate collected, sorted, indexed, and imaged the MSDSs and then prepared and shipped compact discs to each plant. The plants now provide new MSDSs to Corporate for processing each quarter. This has eliminated much duplication and assures that this material is accurate and timely. Ato is now utilizing software that will deal in the long term with outbound MSDSs, which it wants to correlate with the data management system for its customers. Like many chemical companies, Ato has a significant number of outbound MSDSs—approximately 4,100 each year, with a 15 percent increase each year and an update of 33 percent a year. While Ato does have systems in place to manage these MSDSs, there are presently six different systems. Because this creates a potential for problems, these six systems are now being integrated.

The tracking and documentation of Ato's training programs are becoming increasingly important. Some programs, particularly in the safety area, require up to 200 hours a year in initial training and 100 hours a year annually. Lack of documentation leads to easy violations and indeed inspectors in the HES area focus on documentation as these are the easiest violations to prove. Similarly, when employees change positions, their training requirements also change, and these changes and the training required need to be tracked. Ato's system not only tracks training requirements, but should also lead to review of course contents, including evaluations. Sites and individuals will learn of courses at other facilities, thus leading to improvement in the course-delivery system. In addition, Ato plans to make available appropriate course material through an intranet.

For modern management, companies must have the ability to monitor performance and analyze trends in a way that systems such as these help provide. To establish an MIS, each company must decide on a methodology that considers and addresses all policy, organization, work process, and technology issues to achieve the maximum payback possible. The review of the work process is the critical path. The software is secondary. The major value in these systems is the examination and reengineering of the work process, which avoids the "garbage in, garbage out" syndrome. At Ato, we found upon a review of one plant's systems that there were 13 steps between finding a problem and fixing it. The solution, obviously, was not automating the 13 steps, but rather fixing the broken system and eliminating most of the steps.

An important factor in making these systems work is giving the operations side of the business what it wants and needs. An MIS may not be viewed as that valuable to the plants, which may be concerned about such tracking and possible finger pointing. If, however, the value to the plants is significant, and it usually is, the fears of corporate knowledge and what will happen to the data diminish. Note that such systems are transparent; both the plants and, to the extent there is a need to know, corporate have access to the same data, without either one being aware of the other. (Some data, such as emission monitoring, are of little value to corporate.) In any event, I call this approach to data management the "Wizard of Oz" approach, namely, "[p]ay no attention to the man behind the curtain."

Developing and "Selling" Computerized Systems

If you acquire or develop an environmental management or database management system, you will want it to be technically advanced, proven, flexible, and appropriate to your level of computer literacy.[42] If the system will be broadly used, it is particularly important that it be user-friendly. Rather than developing systems from scratch, you are almost always better off purchasing commercially available products. Currently, there are several commercial systems emerging. The various groups involved, however—particularly some MIS groups and the confirmed computer hackers in your user group—are likely to lean toward building their own system because a commercial database often is not as advanced as they would like.

No commercial system will meet 100 percent of your specific needs, but the costs in money and time of designing your own system are usually prohibitive, and you will not have the advantage of professional experience, particularly in the never-ending debugging.[43] As a general rule, if an environmental database management system handles 85 percent of your needs, it pays to implement and then revise it. In view of the margins for error in designing your own system, if a commercial system suits at least 50 percent of your needs, you should still seriously consider buying and then upgrading it. The important thing is getting a system up and working rather than waiting for the perfect system. If a commercial system does not handle at least 50 percent of your needs, then you might want to consider building your own. Indeed, Occidental developed its own environmental management system because at that time there was no computerized system capable of performing the management tasks needed. Since then, times and computer software have changed.

You must have realistic expectations and allow ample margins of error in the assumptions you make in building a system. Everyone wants instant gratification, but it takes a significant commitment to design an effective application. As a rule of thumb, if the application takes longer than four months to design, it is probably too large and should be further broken down. Breaking down tasks is one way of limiting cost overruns. Cheops' Rule—namely, that nothing is ever built within time and budget—usually applies to building computer systems. The same rule applies to installing any commercial system, because there are almost always specific bugs unique to your operations that will take time and money to resolve.

In developing a system, the first step is to determine what you need: an environmental management system, a database management system, or both. At Occidental, for example, the corporate group has an environmental management system but has not needed an environmental database management system, although the divisions do have such systems. The corporate group has, however, developed a safety and health data management system, which it uses to track OSH Act reporting, among other things. The usual goal is to find or design a system that will satisfy all company needs for environmental information and documentation and, if possible, that will print out official forms. You may find it more desirable to have several systems than to wait for the so-called universal system that has yet to be designed.

In designing a system, you should recognize upfront that they do not last forever. Three to five years is the usual lifetime. The system must, therefore, be evolutionary in nature because all your informational and computer needs simply cannot be anticipated. Evolutionary flexibility is particularly important in view of the incredible changes in hardware and software that have occurred in the last few years. Occidental's MIS, for example, evolved over a seven-year period and is much more flexible and user-friendly than when it was first designed.

It is also important to determine whether you want the data centralized or decentralized. My experience is that combining mainframe or client server systems with field entry provides the benefits of both centralization and decentralization. If you want to share data, central control of the database is critical, along with a common data specification. Networking, particularly on a mainframe, works quite well. Recognize that both mainframe and nonmainframe systems are diverse. The possibilities include stand-alone systems at a single facility, multiple users at a single facility, or multiple users at multiple facilities. Any of those systems can be designed for exception reporting, as in the Occidental and Ato systems. PCs are an option and are almost universal. Security is an important issue with PC-based systems, and the importance of backing up data and maintaining consistency from transaction to transaction should never be ignored. Internet technology is also significant, but security is still an issue.

It is important to recognize that the quality of the information in your system depends on the input. John Coryell of DuPont has identified "Coryell's Corollary of Instant Data Gratification," which states, "[u]nless a data entry person gets some quick, positive feedback on the quality of the (just completed) data entry task, the data entry quality is likely to be disappointing." "When considering the available data management tools, the important issue to consider is what the professional EH&S manager actually needs or sees, and how data or information systems can help."[44] If the person entering the data assumes that it is going into a black box, cooperation will be limited. Unless it improves that person's quality of life—for example by providing useful data or cutting down on paperwork and phone calls—data will not get entered in a timely fashion. A rumbling dissatisfaction with the system will also develop. When you have people with different levels of computer literacy and understanding using a broad-based system, perceived problems with the system can easily be considered out of context and can destroy your work in selling that system.

In implementing a system, another key point is to look at existing sources of data. You will want to avoid entering data that are already being entered in another system. Entering data twice is simply inefficient, and the people doing it will not be very happy. You will need to determine where electronically entered data already exist in your organization and whether an electronic interface can be constructed. If you are going to sell a system, you clearly need to make maximum use of existing data.

Note also that when there are many potential users of a system, it is important to check whether existing computer capabilities can handle the traffic and whether overloading will slow down the practical use of the system, which can be frustrating to the data-entry person. In determining whether a system will work for you, it is important to know how many people will use the system and at what time of day.

Your biggest concern in deciding on a system is not the system itself, but its impact on the organization. The political problems in developing such systems can be more difficult than the technical problems. Knowledge is viewed as power, and when a new portion of the organization acquires data, there will be concern about what that group will do with the data. Fear of the use and misuse of data must be addressed. If it is a corporate versus divisional problem, the first rule is to make clear that there will be no "sandbagging" and that the primary goal of the system is to give the divisions a management tool. All that corporate will do is conduct limited oversight. The divisions must have confidence that when you obtain additional data, you will still give them the opportunity to fix a problem first, rather than running to upper management. Support for such a system needs to be developed, preferably from the bottom up. Top-down pressure will be actively resisted unless it is a command from top management. And even if commanded from top management, a system will not work without sufficient cooperation.

In pursuing the need for a safety and health system, Occidental's management worked first with the divisions, which at various meetings indicated what they were looking for to meet their own needs. Occidental then picked a system, with division input, that took care of most of the divisions' needs and at the same time satisfied corporate needs for oversight and guidance. Subsequently Occidental developed its own system, which not only included mainframe entry but also accepted data input using a customized PC data-entry tool. It was important to find a system that was very user-friendly, because the goal was not to add additional people for centralized entry, but to make the system valuable to the field and provide for field entry. At Ato, the continuing approach is field entry.

An interesting phenomenon will take place once these systems are instituted. Many people fear technology, particularly new technology. If the system is gradually implemented and not oversold, however, people will wonder what they did without it, particularly as the growing requirements of federal, state, and local reporting become increasingly overwhelming. Indeed, new uses for the system may be found. For example, the Risk Management and Security Departments at Occidental have also used a computerized management system based on the environmental system.

The Planning Document—Short-Range and Long-Range Planning and Goals

When I first joined Occidental in 1981, the task of understanding all the critical issues seemed overwhelming. This feeling is common to all of us who either come to environmental management as a new task or change jobs and take over the environmental function in a new company. To simplify the job and set priorities, I used a planning document to track the major issues and concerns within the company. The divisions subsequently found the concept advantageous and integrated their specific issues into the planning document. Thus, both corporate and division staff used the document for their own purposes. The corporate overview assisted in long-range planning and setting priorities without interfering in the tasks of the divisions.[45]

My planning document was a simple compilation of items considered important based on assessment findings; entries in the environmental management system; and issues emerging in the legislative or regulatory arena, the press, or the opinion of staff experts. It was not computerized, although the items could easily have been entered into the computerized environmental management system, if one had been available at that time.

The format included the objectives to be achieved, the approaches to be taken in achieving them, and the responsibilities and target dates for both the divisions and the corporate groups involved. No item under any heading was more than 25 words in length; most were 5 or 10. The document was updated and circulated for review and comment by the divisions approximately twice a year. Because it was included in reports to senior management and the Board of Directors, this clear statement of long-term issues and goals developed into a major lever forcing prompt action.

As the programs matured, this kind of detailed analysis became less significant. Though the planning document approach can be very helpful in simplifying and setting priorities, today there is a need to move toward more sophisticated approaches. When I joined Ato in 1994, a detailed planning program was already in place. Each industry group and facility at Ato routinely uses TQM to plan as they take control and establish accountability for their performance. (See Chapter 3, Total Quality Management). Corporate and the divisions at Occidental continue to be involved in planning, but both Ato and Occidental are looking more at the broader concepts of TQM: developing strategic goals, strategic plans, tactical plans, and following up on the broader issues raised in program reviews (see Chapter 6, Corporate Program Review). Occidental has substituted this approach for its original planning document.

In today's TQM environment, long-range planning should start with development of an overall corporate objective and a mission statement, followed by strategic objectives and methods of implementation. For example, Occidental (OPC) set as its corporate objective: "Continued support of management at all levels in achieving corporate goals and positioning [OPC] to seize and maintain competitive advantage in order to maximize shareholder value." The departmental mission is "to provide the corporation guidance and assurance in its efforts to enhance the quality of life for current and future generations through continuous improvement in the protection of human health and the environment and the safe conduct of all activities." Strategic objectives are:

> (1) Continuous improvement in the protection of company assets, human health, safety, and the environment,
>
> (2) Management of all activities consistent with OPC requirements (including verification of compliance with all governmental requirements), and
>
> (3) Identification and support opportunities for the integration of health, environment, safety, and process risk management (HESPRM) into OPC business planning and management process.

Methods to meet these objectives are:

(1) Support OPC senior management in communicating their ongoing commitment and expectations to protect human life, the environment and company assets to all levels of the corporation and the public,

(2) Identify and support opportunities for HESPRM to contribute to OPC business planning and management processes and programs,

(3) Provide direction for the integration of management within the HESPRM functions and activities, and

(4) Measure HESPRM contribution to the businesses of the corporation.

Figure 5-4[46] explains this process in TQM terms.

Figure 5-4
OPC HESPRM Management System

OPC HESPRM Management System

→ GOAL: Protect human health and the environment, provide a safe workplace for employees, and effectively manage allocation of resources (capital, human, etc.) to address HESPRM.

↓

→ OBJECTIVE: Ensure/verify continuous improvement in HESPRM, ensure/verify consistency with OPC HESPRM policies and procedures, and identify opportunities for HESPRM integration with business objectives/strategies.

↓

→ STRATEGY: EHS human resource development, systems evaluation/program reviews, consulting with industry groups (IGs) on an as needed basis, data trending/analysis, communication with OPC management, reporting to ECOB, EHS planning, and legislative/regulatory trending for compliance and planning.

↓

→ COMMUNICATION: Reporting to and meeting with ECOB, Administrators' meetings (heads of environment, safety, and risk engineering departments in the divisions), monthly reports to management, external affairs activities, etc.

↓

→ IMPLEMENTATION: Assessment participation, IG program reviews, IG project consulting, legislative/regulatory analysis, etc.

↓

→ MEASUREMENT: IG measurement data (as appropriate to attain objective), assessing compliance with legal requirements, costing information (e.g., contingent liabilities tracking), and other (value-added measures based on IG program effectiveness in managing OPC's risks and measures related to OPC management opportunities for HESPRM integration).

↓

FEEDBACK
←

Similar objectives have been adopted, or are in the process of being developed, at Ato. For example, Ato has described the mission of the HES management system in very simple terms: a system of control so that Ato manages the issues and they do not manage Ato. The subsets of the missions are consistent compliance (managed systems to ensure continuous control), improved long-term profitability, and sustainable protection (afforded by compliance, managed risk, and ethical considerations). The strategy consists of a strong partnership among HES, manufacturing, and business teams; a strong HES management system (a comprehensive, integrated, and flexible process that drives appropriate decisions and behavior); a focus on implementing system elements, not solely on compliance (if good systems are in place, compliance follows); and a focus on long-term profitability ("pay me now or pay me (a lot more) later," realizing that compliance may not always be good enough).

The planning program is a major element of both Occidental's and Ato's environmental programs because it contains the essence of the companies' long-term (five-year) and short-term (one-year) environmental strategies. Its primary objective is development of preventive programs and procedures based on issues and trends identified. Preventive strategy is especially important when minimizing liability is a goal. Many companies still have programs that simply react to regulations and problems as they arise. It is more effective, however, to take a proactive approach in which emerging issues are identified and programs are implemented to avoid or correct problems.

For companies using a more traditional planning process, the first step should be development of a planning document.[47] The document should begin with a long-range statement of objectives reflecting the environmental goals of the company (or division). These objectives are listed in Figure 5-5.

Figure 5-5
Objectives to Be Included in Long-Range Planning Documents

• Compliance with existing and yet-to-be-promulgated regulations;
• Maintenance of existing environmental programs;
• Resolution of issues that have technical, factual, or legal uncertainties;
• Performance of environmental activities that will deal with ethical issues and enhance the company's public image; and
• Identification of procedures needed to develop timely information for new products, facilities, and permits (for example, CAA prevention of significant deterioration data, NPDES application data, or TSCA premarket notification).

Figure 5-6
Additional Items to Include in Long-Range Planning Documents

- Specific objectives that apply to all divisions and facilities to be accomplished within a five-year time frame;
- A description of the method by which objectives will be monitored for completion;
- A description of the method for reporting progress toward satisfying these long-range strategic objectives; and
- A description of environmental research and development activities that will be conducted to solve environmental compliance problems or to further the state of the art in specific areas.[48]

Long-range planning helps you focus clearly on your program's requirements. Perhaps more significantly, it lets senior corporate and divisional management know that you are actually managing, not fighting fires. Long-range planning also places environmental management in the context of general management objectives. Also note the importance of individual plant action in meeting the long-range goals. Planning is not merely a function of corporate and division staff; facilities are specifically involved in determining how they will meet the goals. Defining the first year's goals and action plans generally seems easy. Identifying longer range programs and plans takes more thought.

Once a plan is in place, it is essential to monitor progress on its implementation. OxyChem developed an excellent spreadsheet formula that shows logic flow and serves as a follow-up system in implementing long-range plans. Its format is as follows.

- Column 1—Corporate goals.

- Column 2—Industry group or division objectives. These are the "evergreen" corporate goals adopted by and restated appropriately for the industry group or division.

- Column 3—Industry group or division results. These are strategic or conceptual statements describing the "how to" programs that will support the corporate goals over the next five years.

- Column 4—Industry group or division goals. These are tactical statements reflecting what must be accomplished this year to achieve the long-term results. They must be definitive and measurable.

- Column 5—Industry group or division action plans to accomplish the goals. These include action plans arising from assessments (including plans relating to plant compliance issues), plant goals (such as excursion goals), and individual performance measures and job responsibilities, as well as compliance-related programs to be implemented by corporate staff.

In summary, the exercise of long-range planning is extremely helpful in focusing programs beyond the present to meeting longer range goals and objectives that will not only strengthen the EHS programs, but will strengthen the corporation itself.

Capital Expenditure Review

Capital expenditure review is another example of a proactive approach. Review of the environmental effects of all Occidental's Authorizations for Expenditure (AFEs) and Ato's Appropriation Requests (ARs) is a preventive measure aimed at ensuring compliance with corporate requirements, regulatory requirements, and minimizing liability. These requests cover expenditures for construction of new facilities, modification of existing facilities, and acquisition or sale of assets. The review policy thus helps not only to take care of identified issues, but to avoid future problems.

Both Occidental and Ato corporate policy requires the requester to conduct an HES review of any capital expenditure request requiring approval by the Board of Directors, or the Executive Committee in Ato's case. Occidental's policy has been expanded to include reviews of requests approvable at lower levels by divisional staff and Ato follows a similar approach. In both companies, corporate legal and technical staff also review the requests before they are presented to the Board or Executive Committee. These staffs have considerable experience and can either assess a project's HES considerations or know enough to discuss the project with the appropriate division people, requesting elaboration of the comments or modification of the project as appropriate. Ato's process requires very specific involvement by the HES personnel. The director for environmental engineering, who is in the HES department, is involved directly in the AR process and in the actual implementation, working directly with Ato's Central Engineering, Planning, and Process Engineering Department. Also, the AR has a place for the signature of the Vice President for HES, and a project does not go before the Executive Committee unless the Vice President approves the HES review.

Extensive checklists should be prepared for the AFE or the AR reviews, particularly regarding acquisitions. (A sample Occidental checklist is included in Appendix G of this book.) It is important to tailor these checklists to your specific needs. Not every request requires evaluation of all elements on the checklist. Indeed, even in a major acquisition, it is impossible to review all of these elements in detail. Rather, the checklist is designed to ensure that some specialized concern is not overlooked in a capital expenditure or property acquisition or sale.

The reason for requiring such review is that spending money, particularly on plant expansion or equipment changes, and selling assets can have environmental and legal consequences. The start of construction or any modification to or addition of equipment can trigger a variety of permit requirements. For example, air emissions from an existing process may be permitted or grandfathered, but a process modification can trigger a status review and create potential retrofitting expenditures. Another process change might generate a new waste stream. This could greatly exacerbate existing permitting problems, or an agency could require cleanup of existing wastes as a condition for permitting the new stream. Using the modification to resolve any earlier environmental problems and ensuring that the modification includes measures to protect the environment, such as proper diking and secondary containment, can help minimize these difficulties. If there is going to be new construction and a crew doing a substantial amount of work, it is usually cheaper to perform other retrofit work at that time. AR review helps focus attention on these issues.

Such a review is also a useful vehicle for pressing necessary expenditures to avoid future environmental problems. For example, an environmental assessment may recognize that a facility manager does not have authority to spend the funds necessary to make an environmental improvement, but may still find that improvement necessary. The facility manager can request the funds through the AFE or AR procedure, and submission of an AFE or an AR would be an action plan. Review and comment authority provides an excellent vehicle to support the expenditure. It also helps develop awareness among operating management of the EHS issues, which helps avoid problems.

Finally, the review of asset sales helps focus attention on permitting and exposure issues. For example, if you sell part of an existing plant but keep the portion that includes water pollution control facilities, you may face permitting problems if the purchaser starts discharging new effluent streams into those facilities. The buyer faces similar concerns if the seller changes its effluent streams. Of course, the biggest concern in selling assets is potential exposure resulting from previous waste disposal practices. Many states require notification from the seller if there are hazardous wastes or substances on site, and New Jersey requires cleanup of sites before sale. The AFE or the AR review helps focus attention on exposure issues, which are discussed in detail in Chapter 7.

Occidental has used the AFE review successfully in connection with major acquisitions, planned construction projects, and in catching major problems with relatively small projects. Similar results are now being achieved at Ato. For example, an industry group at Occidental that had little experience with hazardous waste problems submitted a proposal to purchase a piece of property. The property had earlier been the site of a Navy facility, a tank farm, and an asphalt production plant. Needless to say, following the AFE review, that purchase was not made.

The AFE or the AR review should not, however, be a major source of paperwork or result in the equivalent of massive environmental impact reports or EISs. Normally, the requester simply provides a statement that the HES implications of the project have been considered, or a brief statement laying out those implications and the actions to be taken; if there are significant HES issues, the discussion is more detailed. The real cross-check is in the programmed involvement of HES professionals in the process and decisionmaking. If the AFE or the AR review becomes the equivalent of the EIS process, it will lose its effectiveness and encourage sniping at divisional and corporate bureaucracies.

Legislative and Regulatory Affairs

The first problem in governmental relations is simply making sure that you identify and obtain all the information you need and channel that information to the proper places in your organization. I do not know of any organization, either decentralized or centralized, that is satisfied with how it handles governmental relations in this regard, particularly on the state and local levels. Merely keeping everyone up-to-date on key changes in federal legislation and regulation has in the past required a sizable staff, although today many companies are eliminating these tasks and forcing the use of on-line services. Many law firms publish newsletters as services to clients; if reviewed by in-house counsel to ensure accuracy, these can be effective substitutes for your own newsletters regarding general legislative and regulatory developments. Also, the availability of on-line publications and diverse material on the Internet allows broad dissemination of data without the intervention of corporate staff.

Most organizations, including Ato and Occidental, do not have the staff to write memos detailing the specific impact of these developments on facilities. Centralized or decentralized organizations with large corporate staffs at one time devoted more time to these matters. Today, few companies have large corporate staffs for these purposes. Continuous memos on these issues are really not necessary, if you establish a network of key lawyers and managers to track them. Sometimes specific consulting assistance on strategic issues is helpful. At Ato, the environmental services staff tried to summarize the more critical regulations, and tailors summaries to specific plant needs. This approach will succeed if field personnel trust that the specialists know what they are doing and are sufficiently experienced to spot issues that may cause problems for facilities or divisions. If the specialist identifies such an issue, it is assumed that he or she will contact the division or field expert to confirm the problem and start developing a solution.

It is even more difficult to obtain and process effectively information on government issues at the state and local levels than at the federal level. At the federal level, a limited staff in Washington, D.C., can at least keep track of important developments. Information gathering is less formalized at the state and local levels. Unless a company has a full-time staff person or consultant doing this job, it can miss important issues, although on-line services can be very helpful. Trade association newsletters and computerized services will allow you to keep track of some legislation and regulations, but there is still that sinking feeling that something important may be missed. This is a particular problem if communication between corporate and field management is inadequate. If a plant or facility attempts to follow legislation and regulations without a fair level of sophistication in both the political process and environmental law, it is quite likely to miss an issue. Conversely, if the local people are not following a state or local issue, the corporate group could miss the issue's significance to the plant. Open lines of communication are therefore critical to the network approach discussed above. Corporate specialists can only help divisions and plants if they understand their situations and concerns.

After obtaining the necessary information on governmental issues, your company must decide how to address them. The proper handling of legislative and regulatory issues has not been given enough attention. Many industry representatives trying to cope with these issues either handle them ineffectively or simply give up in frustration. These patterns can be changed if a company focuses not on defending its current practices, but on resolving problems and identifying probable future requirements early. Trained professionals can accomplish these goals. Unfortunately, although management of the EHS issues has generally been turned over to professionals, the same cannot be said of specialized advocacy concerning environmental legislation and regulations. Far too few companies effectively coordinate their Washington efforts with their environmental professionals to reconcile regulatory and legislative needs and realities.

In many companies, this failure is primarily a result of unnecessary and counterproductive turf wars between traditional governmental affairs offices and the new breed of technical and legal professionals. Traditional governmental affairs offices often feel threatened by these specialists, who are now becoming more and more active in the governmental affairs offices' territory: the arcane world of Washington. Governmental affairs offices are less concerned about dealings with regulatory agencies, recognizing that they do not have specialized expertise in this area. They are primarily concerned about the legislative arena, in which their expertise previously has been unquestioned.

This discussion is not a denigration of traditional lobbyists. In most Washington offices, they have been and can continue to be effective. In regulatory agencies and in Congress, however, experienced technical and legal staff now handle much of the work in the EHS area, including preparation of concept papers and drafting. This is also true of environmental organizations, which recognize the critical importance of government staffs and employ highly knowledgeable individuals in their efforts to match the skills of those staffs.

In contrast, few companies have specialized, professional, Washington-based environmental staffs with equally high qualifications. To be effective, industry representatives must be viewed as skilled professionals attempting to solve problems, rather than just advocates. Most industry representatives are not so viewed, which is a major factor in the success of the environmental organizations. Many industry representatives simply do not have the specialized skills or personal credibility to deal effectively with the skilled governmental and environmental group staffs. Even companies with highly qualified staffs may limit their flexibility to negotiate rapidly, effectively, and credibly. Moreover, most companies are not organized to respond immediately to instant drafting requests by legislative and regulatory agencies.

The new environmental specialists in industry can be effective in dealing with government staffs. Indeed, they normally deal exclusively with staff rather than directly with members of the House of Representatives or the Senate. Because of the complexity of this area, members of Congress are almost at the mercy of staff, with little time to understand all the ramifications of much of the new legislation being promulgated. It is therefore critical to convince the staff, which often is hostile to industrial interests, of the utility and social value of your position. If traditional lobbyists work together with specialists, personally introducing them to members of Congress or staff, both groups can be maximally effective.

The two groups have to work together, and they have to realize that "we will fight them on the beaches" is usually not a successful philosophy in dealing with the EHS legislation, although in today's polarized atmosphere, it is very difficult to make any changes to environmental law, regardless of the political perspective. There are many concepts that may not make much sense from a traditional industry perspective—or, for that matter, from a technical or logical perspective—but, right or wrong, they may be ideas whose time has come. The successful industry advocate today recognizes that the goal is usually to minimize impact, working in the interstices of such legislation, rather than fighting the statutes in toto. This approach will do the advocate's employer the most good.

It is not easy to obtain effective representation that produces imaginative, cost-effective, and environmentally acceptable solutions to environmental issues. But it does not require a large budget—merely close coordination of the environmental professionals, the traditional Washington staff, and divisional staffs, as well as trust and mutual recognition of skills. Even the best representation will not always be effective, but one beneficial change in a regulation or proposed statute can pay for a specialized staff. Of course with today's cutbacks, there simply may not be qualified people to handle these issues at either the corporate or Washington levels. Issues beyond the next quarter are difficult to quantify and are difficult to fund with restricted budgets.

Awareness of social and political values and possessing the legal and scientific skills are critical factors in producing consensus and viable solutions. Short lines of communication also allow for rapid turnaround, which is vital to productive work in this area. Because Ato is headquartered in Philadelphia, a short distance from Washington, it has been able to maintain close liaison with the Washington office without having environmental representatives in Washington. In addition, Ato's representative has strong substantive abilities, which makes coordination and communication very easy.

Anyone attempting to obtain legislative and regulatory changes must maintain good relations with government agencies. Some ethical questions have been raised about the revolving-door policy that allows people who leave a government agency to represent private parties before that agency. Obviously, there can be abuse. The primary advantage of an ex-regulator, however, is not some kind of arcane knowledge of government procedures or of specific government actions, but rather a recognition of how government works, along with basic credibility with government personnel. If you work with people for years and establish a reputation for competence and credibility, you need not lose that reputation because you now represent a different party.

You should be aware, however, that

> [t]here is a heavy burden on the former regulator now representing the private party. He [or she] cannot compromise credibility for the sake of a one-shot gain by the client. The environmental community is small, and that one-shot gain will quickly deteriorate to a long-term loss. Quick decisions pro or con on issues and willingness to work with an individual rapidly evaporate, and

the opportunity to effectively represent the private client will quickly vanish. In essence, government agencies and environmental groups understand the difference between form and substance, and the corporate representative who is not suggesting reasonable positions cannot succeed.[49]

The same cautions apply to any environmental manager or lawyer attempting to build a long-term relationship with an agency.

The former regulator or public interest representative also has learned that neither regulatory agencies nor environmental groups are omniscient. Some regulatory schemes are poorly developed by inexperienced regulators, and some solutions are more costly than necessary. It is not a sin against the environment to consider costs among other priorities in achieving a goal. It is also important to work with agencies to improve their understanding of the application of new technologies. Technology forcing sometimes can go too far; simply because technology has worked on a bench scale does not mean it will work in practice. Industry tends to look for off-the-shelf technology, but sometimes agencies appear to push for technology that is off the wall. Usually, the best answer lies in between.

Finally, if you are frustrated at your lack of confidence in how your company handles the legislative and regulatory processes, remember that this frustration is endemic to environmental management. In times of limited resources, however, staffs simply will not be increased to the point where we all have a high level of confidence regarding governmental issues. These staffs were usually the first ones cut in earlier recessions, and management is not about to encourage restaffing. Such staffs are also difficult to justify in hard dollars. The generic issues that these staffs helped to control simply are not as well understood as challenges to the use or continued liability of a company's product, which immediately receive senior management support and resources. Thus, in this area of management, as in all others, the key is developing lines of communication between the field and headquarters. If this is done, decentralized and centralized organizations can implement effective programs. We must take our corporate cultures as we find them, but within those cultures, we can provide the necessary lines of communication. Budget limits need not pose insurmountable problems. Obviously, with an unlimited budget anyone should have an effective program. Few managers have that luxury, nor is it necessary. It is hoped that this book will help you design not only effective, but cost-effective programs.

Training and Education Programs

A strong environmental management program depends on continuing awareness of the status of and trends in environmental management and technology as developed by regulatory agencies, policymakers, scientists, and engineers.[50] This awareness is achieved through a continuing program of education and training that addresses the various needs of hourly employees, supervisors, environmental specialists, assessment team members, division managers, community residents, and local officials. The scope and detail of these programs varies with the corporate culture. Some companies use elaborate films; others bring people together for long training programs. Others, without using complicated systems, develop an ethic that makes training easier. Many of the best programs are modeled on or combined with safety awareness programs, which have a longer history of implementation and acceptance.

In general, to ensure that people maintain a high level of environmental awareness, training and education programs should cover the items listed in Figure 5-7.

Figure 5-7
Topics for Environmental Training and Education Programs

- Environmental awareness and compliance policies;
- Supervisory responsibilities;
- Corporate liabilities;
- Environmental technology updates;
- Working with regulatory agencies;
- Community support needs;
- Emergency response plans; and
- Impacts of new legislation and regulations.

A specialized training program should be directed to members of individual facility assessment teams (see Chapter 6, The Facility Assessment Team). The membership of these teams is likely to vary, especially in larger companies with many divisions or facilities subject to the assessment process; multiple teams may be necessary. This training should emphasize how to conduct the assessment in an effective and timely manner. The team also must possess the requisite knowledge of environmental regulations, facility operations, and division plans.

If a corporate staff is small, it is more difficult to establish strong training and awareness programs, but if there is cooperation and interest in the divisions, the corporate staff can do its job by ensuring that the divisions have good programs. Sometimes an organization with a small staff may need consultants to help implement such programs.

It should also be noted that some regulations specifically require training programs. As discussed above, any training undertaken must be fully documented to ensure regulatory compliance.

Conclusion

There is no comprehensive cookbook of environmental management programs. Although this chapter provides certain recipes, each recipe needs to be adapted and seasoned to taste, depending on the corporate culture involved. The skills of the "cook" are critical in that abilities to deal effectively with people, the HES issues, and corporate cultures are key to making these programs work.

Notes to Chapter 5

1. There are other ways to describe the key elements of a strong environmental management program. Arthur D. Little, a large consulting firm that does many environmental audits, views environmental management in three stages: problem solving, managing for compliance, and, the highest level, managing for assurance. The firm uses the following elements to describe a state-of-the-art environmental management program:

1. Clearly defined, broadly communicated policies and procedures;
2. An environmental, health, and safety program congruent with organizational structure;
3. Day-to-day management systems;
4. Formalized long-range planning program;
5. A formal risk management system;
6. Regulatory surveillance;
7. Management information systems;
8. Project and program reviews;
9. Issue-specific programs; and
10. Oversight and control.

ARTHUR D. LITTLE, INC., STATE OF THE ART ENVIRONMENTAL, HEALTH AND SAFETY PROGRAMS: HOW DO YOU COMPARE? (1990).

Other entities have developed their own formulations for evaluating environmental programs. Kenneth L. Manchen, *Rating Your Environmental Department*, POLLUTION ENGINEERING, Apr. 1990, at 81, contains a checklist for rating environmental management programs. Union Carbide developed its own formulation, focusing on five different levels. Level 1 is no program at all. Level 2 is reaction (damage control). Level 3 is compliance (laws and regulations). Level 4 is prevention (compliance plus). Level 5 is leadership, which includes showing management how good HES programs can add to a corporation's bottom line "through the development of new technology, customer-focused marketing and services and advertising." *Union Carbide: Moving Beyond Compliance*, ENVTL. MANAGER, June 1990, at 6. Level 4 "is where most of the environmentally leading edge companies are today. Such companies have extensive environmental training and audit programs and are often looking to reduce the level of waste they generate through comprehensive waste minimization programs. They anticipate problems with company standards that are often more stringent than those imposed by the government." *Id.*

2. Van E. Housman, *Environmental Management Systems in Federal Enforcement Settlements*, 34 ELR 10451 (May 2004).

3. *Id.*

4. *Id.* at 10453.

5. *Id.* at 10456.

6. *Id.*

7. The Social Investment Forum and its CERES Project developed these principles.

Originally known as the Valdez Principles, after the massive oil spill resulting from a tanker accident in Valdez, Alaska, they have since been revised and renamed the CERES Principles. The revised principles, adopted on April 28, 1992, are on file with the Coalition for Environmentally Responsible Economies, 711 Atlantic Ave., Boston MA 02111. The original principles were not signed by any major corporation. The corporate sector criticized them, particularly because they did not reflect today's sophisticated environmental management programs and they failed to articulate terms that would distinguish truly progressive companies from those that were still recalcitrant in protecting human health. *See* Frank Friedman, *Don't Sign the Valdez Principles*, ENVTL. F., Mar./Apr. 1990, at 32; Erik Meyers, *Business' New Ten Commandments*, ENVTL. F., Mar./Apr. 1990, at 33.

8. David R. Berz, *Keep Risk Reduction Decisions in the Board Room*, ENVTL. F., Mar./Apr. 1990, at 32.

9. The full text of the revised CERES Principles is as follows.

> *Introduction*—By adopting these Principles, we publicly affirm our belief that corporations have a responsibility for the environment, and must conduct all aspects of their business as responsible stewards of the environment by operating in a manner that protects the Earth. We believe that corporations must not compromise the ability of future generations to sustain themselves.
>
> We will update our practices continually in light of advances in technology and new understandings in health and environmental science. In collaboration with CERES, we will promote a dynamic process to ensure that the principles are interpreted in a way that accommodates changing technologies and environmental realities. We intend to make consistent, measurable progress in implementing these Principles and to apply them in all aspects of our operations throughout the world.
>
> 1. *Protection of the Biosphere*—We will reduce and make continual progress toward eliminating the release of any substance that may cause environmental damage to the air, water, or the earth or its inhabitants. We will safeguard all habitats affected by our operations and will protect open spaces and wilderness, while preserving biodiversity.
>
> 2. *Sustainable Use of Natural Resources*—We will make sustainable use of renewable natural resources such as water, soils and forests. We will conserve nonrenewable natural resources through efficient use and careful planning.
>
> 3. *Reduction and Disposal of Wastes*—We will reduce and where possible eliminate waste through source reduction and recycling. All waste will be handled and disposed of through safe and responsible methods.
>
> 4. *Energy Conservation*—We will conserve energy and improve the energy efficiency of our internal operations and of the goods and services we sell. We will make every effort to use environmentally safe and sustainable energy sources.

5. *Risk Reduction*—We will strive to minimize the environmental, health and safety risks to our employees and the communities in which we operate through safe technologies, facilities and operating procedures, and by being prepared for emergencies.

6. *Safe Products and Services*—We will reduce and where possible eliminate the use, manufacture, or sale of products and services that cause environmental damage or health or safety hazards. We will inform our customers of the environmental impacts of our products or services and try to correct unsafe use.

7. *Environmental Restoration*—We will promptly and responsibly correct conditions we have caused that endanger health, safety or the environment. To the extent feasible, we will redress injuries we have caused to persons or damage we have caused to the environment and will restore the environment.

8. *Informing the Public*—We will inform in a timely manner everyone who may be affected by conditions caused by our company that might endanger health, safety or the environment. We will regularly seek advice and counsel through dialogue with persons in communities near our facilities. We will not take any action against employees for reporting dangerous incidents or conditions to management or to appropriate authorities.

9. *Management's Commitment*—We will implement these Principles and sustain a process that ensures that the Board of Directors and Chief Executive Officer are fully informed about pertinent environmental issues and are fully responsible for environmental policy. In selecting our Board of Directors, we will consider demonstrated environmental commitment as a factor.

10. *Audits and Reports*—We will conduct an annual self-evaluation of our progress in implementing these Principles. We will support the timely creation of generally accepted environmental audit procedures. We will annually complete the CERES Report, which will be made available to the public.

Disclaimer—These Principles establish an environmental ethic with criteria by which investors and others can assess the environmental performance of companies. Companies that sign these Principles pledge to go voluntarily beyond the requirements of the law. These Principles are not intended to create new legal liabilities, expand existing rights or obligations, waive legal defenses, or otherwise affect the legal position of any signatory company, and are not intended to be used against a signatory in any legal proceeding for any purpose.

10. The CERES Principles require that companies annually complete an open-ended questionnaire, which is perhaps overly comprehensive in that it requires more data than industry people consider necessary.

11. *See* www.ceres.com for members, as well as in some cases, on-line reports.

12. Elf Atochem North America, Inc., Health, Environment, and Safety Policy 1 (issued Jan. 11, 1995, revised Apr. 25, 1997).

13. *Id.* at 2.

14. Richard P. Wells, *Misunderstandings on What EMSs Are*, Envtl. F., July/Aug. 2000, at 4.

15. *Id.*

16. World Comm'n on Env't and Dev., Our Common Future (1987).

17. David A. Price, *Kafka Wasn't Kidding*, Forbes, June 2, 1997, at 160.

18. *See* Wall St. J., Feb. 22, 2000, at 1.

19. 42 U.S.C. §§9601-9675, ELR Stat. CERCLA §§101-405.

20. In testimony relating to CERCLA liability for natural resources damages, Dick Stewart, former Assistant Attorney General, Environment and Natural Resources Division, DOJ, discussed the concept of retroactive liability.

> Proponents of retroactivity often respond by asserting that the benefi-ciaries of industrial development should pay for restoration. Often, the present owner who is being sued had nothing to do with the causes of the pollution. Retroactivity proponents fail to see the inherent inequity in this approach and assert that corporate America is the generic bene-ficiary of development and should pay for restoration. This approach to assigning the responsibility for restoration ignores the fact that federal, state and local governments, including trustees, generally encouraged the industrialization and benefited from the collection of royalties, sev-erance taxes, property taxes, payroll and income taxes, sales taxes, etc. The local communities also benefited from increased employment and from the development of the nation's infrastructure which was spurred by industrial development. If the beneficiaries of industrial activity are to be retroactively liable, then the list of beneficiaries should not be limited to the current corporate owners of sites.

Richard B. Stewart, Testimony on behalf of the Coalition for NRD Reform Before the Senate Comm. on Environment and Public Works 15-16 (Apr. 24, 1996).

In United States v. Olin Corp., 927 F. Supp. 1502, 26 ELR 21303 (S.D. Ala. 1996), the court held that the United States could not apply CERCLA retroac-tively to waste disposal activities that took place before CERCLA's enactment in 1980. On March 25, 1997, this decision was reversed. 107 F.3d 1506, 27 ELR 20778 (11th Cir. 1997).

21. 42 U.S.C. §11023, ELR Stat. EPCRA §313.

22. The SEC's interpretative release of May 1989 concerning the disclosure re-quired in Management's Discussion and Analysis of Financial Condition and Re-sults of Operations in SEC filings is discussed in Chapter 6. *See also* James G. Ar-cher et al., *SEC Reporting of Environmental Liabilities*, 20 ELR 10105 (Mar. 1990); Rabinowitz & Murphy, *Environmental Disclosure: What the SEC Requires*,

ENVTL. FIN., Spring 1991, at 31. Professor Mitch Crusto advocates substituting "cumulative materiality" in corporate environmental disclosure as a substitute for "green reports, discussed in more detail in Chapter 6. Mitchell F. Crusto, *Endangered Green Reports: "Cumulative Materiality" in Corporate Environmental Disclosure After Sarbanes-Oxley*, 25 ELR 10666 (Oct. 2005).

23. ELF AQUITAINE, ENVIRONMENTAL REPORT 2 (1998).

24. For a guide on how to do web-based reports and the "seven deadly sins" in report design, see http://www.accglobla.com (last visited Apr. 20, 2002). This website was developed by the London-based organization Next Step Consulting and the Association of Chartered Certified Accounts. *See Experts Issue Guide to Best Practices for Web-Based Reports*, 12 BUS. & THE ENV'T 7 (Dec. 2001).

25. For more information, see http://www.irrc.org.

26. For example, the Investor Responsibility Research Center's (IRRC's) 1992 publication incorrectly classified Occidental as an "integrated domestic oil company." At that time, Occidental was a commodity chemical company, an oil and gas exploration and production company, a natural gas pipeline company, and a coal company (scheduled for divestiture). Thus, the company's operations—and consequently its performance—was not adequately reflected.

Another example of an inconsistent comparison was found in the area of mine safety and the data presentation in the 1992 IRRC report regarding Mine Safety and Health Act penalties. Because the alleged citations listed under the Act are essentially all in coal mining operations, the correct comparison of Occidental's coal company would be against the coal industry's mining penalties. In comparing indices within the coal industry, the type of mining conducted, surface mining or underground mining, and the varying levels of agency enforcement in different parts of the country also affect these comparisons. Occidental was involved predominantly in underground mining, which traditionally has received greater agency scrutiny. The IRRC provided Occidental with a Mine Safety and Health Act penalty index of 35.3 (three-year average) for the coal industry. The Occidental penalty index for the same averaged time period was 34.3, demonstrating that Occidental's performance was better than the industry average. The IRRC's data, without correction, showed Occidental as substantially worse than the other "integrated domestic oil compan[ies]."

27. William Baue, *Paul Hawken Critiques Socially Responsible Investment: Is He On Target or Off Base?*, Nov. 4, 2004, *available at* http://www.socialfunds.com/news/article.cgi/article1564.html (last visited Sept. 14, 2005).

28. *Id.*

29. *Id.*

30. *New Ranking of Best and Worst Environmental Performers*, CHEMICAL WK., Apr. 24, 1996, at 14.

31. OxyChem strongly disputed the ranking. *See OxyChem Fights for a Clean Name*, CHEMICAL WK., May 29, 1996, at 47.

32. Richard MacLean & Brijesh Nanakumari, *The New Rule Makers: The Para-*

digm Shift in Environmental, Health, Safety, and Social Responsibility "Regulations" Now Underway, Corp. Envtl. Strategies, Sept. 2004, at 2-183 to 2-185.

33. *Id.* at 2-184 to 2-185.

34. *See supra* section entitled *Formulating an Environmental Policy.*

35. MacLean & Nanakumari, *supra* note 32, at 2-183.

36. *Feeling the Heat: Business and Climate Change*, The Economist, May 12, 2005.

37. MacLean & Nanakumari, *supra* note 32, at 2-190.

38. *See* Robert M. Rubin, *Organizing for Simplicity: The Role of Information Technology, in* Proceedings of the 5th Jerusalem Conference on Information Technology (JCIT) 589 (Oct. 22-25, 1990).

39. Interview with Karen Murphy, Vice President of EHS at Ashland.

40. Peter F. Drucker, *The Next Information Revolution*, Forbes ASAP, Aug. 24, 1998, at 47.

41. For example, International Business Communications in Southborough, Massachusetts, has held a variety of conferences on the latest software and has published extensive conference materials. However, software availability is constantly improving. New systems using newly available software should be closely examined and may give you "off the shelf" what you need.

42. For a guide on available environmental software, see Scott M. Johnson, *Guide to Environmental Software Products*, EM (Air and Waste Management Association) 1997. This reference is useful for an approach, but availability and useful upgrades change frequently. What was available in 1997 and what is available today has changed significantly.

43. Thomas M. Skove, *Software Systems for EHS Management*, 16 Nat. Resources & Env't 308 (Summer 2001).

44. The following discussion is derived in part from Frank B. Friedman & David A. Giannotti, *Environmental Self-Assessment, in* Law of Environmental Protection §7.05 (Sheldon M. Novick et al. eds., 1994).

45. For a good general description of the pitfalls and promises of a data management system, see Richard MacLean, *Information Technology Systems—Some Cost Millions—Are They Worth It?*, Managers Notebook, Jan./Feb. 2005, 12, *available at* http://www.eponline.com (last visited Sept. 14, 2005).

46. Prepared by Catharine DeLacy, former Vice President, Health, Environment and Safety, Occidental Petroleum Corporation.

47. Another means of determining a long-range strategy is to ask the following questions.

   • What are the most important two or three things you want to get done for the company?

- How are goals set in the company?
- How does the company communicate its goals?
- How does the company manage the regulatory dynamic and rate of change?
- What mechanisms are used to institutionalize the company's environmental position?
- Are there some basic concepts you manage by?
- How does the company decide which programs to initiate?
- Do you have a well-defined environmental strategy?

Sara McGee, *Creating an Environmental Department*, ENVTL. MANAGER, Nov. 1992, at 3-4.

48. Some companies have developed good objectives and ambitious goals. Procter & Gamble has developed the following clear and concise objectives for its environmental program:

- cost avoidance through superior performance,
- robust environmental and safety management systems,
- 100-percent deployment,
- trained people in place,
- superior performance as measured by an annual audit,
- compliance,
- statistically in control and capable systems,
- deployment of a multimedia pollution prevention system,
- business driven [looking for savings], and
- includes energy and all releases.

Personal Interview with George Carpenter, Director, Environment, Energy & Safety Systems, Procter & Gamble (1994).

In 1996, Dow set the following ambitious goals for the year 2005:

REDUCE . . .

- Injuries and illnesses/2,000,000 work hours - 90 percent
- Leaks and spill incidents - 90 percent
- Transportation incidents/per 10,000 shipments - 90 percent
- Process safety incidents - 90 percent
- Motor vehicle incidents/1,000 miles - 50 percent
- Incidents with Dow products at consumer facilities
- Priority compound - 75 percent
- Chemical emissions - 50 percent
- Waste and wastewater generated per pound of production - 50 percent
- Energy use per pound of production - 20 percent

Dow Details Aggressive 2005 EHS Goals, CHEMICAL WK., July 24, 1996.

49. Frank B. Friedman, *'60s Activism and '80s Realities—We've Come a Long Way*, ENVTL. F., July 1983, at 8, 11.

50. The following discussion on training and education programs is derived in part from Friedman & Giannotti, *supra* note 44, §7.05.

Chapter 6:
Environmental Auditing and Environmental Management

Responsible environmental management recognizes that what you don't know *will* hurt you. Environmental auditing is an important, although limited, means of helping to identify problems so that they can be addressed.[1]

An environmental auditing or assessment program is an objective, systematic, periodic, and documented review of practices and operations that may affect the environment. (I prefer the term assessment, although for the sake of simplicity, this book uses the two terms interchangeably.) Such a program is an integral part of a general management system, assisting a company in organizing and managing effective environmental programs. An environmental assessment program also provides benefits for financial planning, SEC reporting, personnel development, public and employee relations, expansion planning, legislative and regulatory strategy development, and evaluation of acquisitions and divestitures.

To be an effective management tool, auditing must be examined in the context of responsible management. As discussed in the preceding chapters, management goals are as follows:

• Development and implementation of corporate-wide policies, systems, programs, and guidelines providing independent assurances that the corporation is properly addressing environmental concerns.

• Implementation of a system for promptly identifying problems and advising management of those problems and the steps being taken to solve them.

• Maintenance of a system for independently determining the environmental compliance status of all facilities and subsidiaries and for ensuring that any required actions are taken. The purpose of auditing and other management programs is to ensure that the corporation is responding quickly and effectively to issues and concerns.

• Development and implementation of mechanisms for identifying emerging environmental issues as well as for coordinating planning for responses to issues involving more than one division.

• Minimization of the liability exposure of the corporation, its officers, and its employees.

An auditing program should be designed to further these goals. The basic criteria for judging the quality of a program are "top management support; an audit manager or team independent of production responsibilities; a structured program with written audit procedures; a system for reporting audit findings to senior management; and a corrective action program."[2] Such a program, when managed at the corporate level, helps ensure that effective systems for managing environmental risk and liabilities actually are in place, understood, and followed.

Although environmental auditing has received considerable attention,[3] it is only one aspect of environmental management. Auditing can provide only limited control and awareness of potential issues. An audit is merely a snapshot of existing controls at a facility. Any focus on auditing alone, without other strong systems, programs, and procedures, is misplaced.

Moreover, there is much controversy about environmental auditing, both in the United States and abroad. However, there is increasing pressure, particularly with the advent of Sarbanes-Oxley, to consider more specific and detailed standards as to scope and purpose. As the financial audit has progressed and become more detailed, should not the same concepts be applied to the environmental audit? The "standards" for environmental auditing developed by the Board of Environmental, Health & Safety Auditor Certifications (BEAC) in 1999[4] are presently under review.[5] Environmental auditing is not like financial auditing, which is conducted under formal procedures pursuant to rules and standards that allow comparisons and judgments of compliance.[6] There is disagreement about the degree to which audits should be structured and what their nature and scope should be. There is much debate about whether insiders or outsiders should conduct the audit, what qualifications auditors should have, and whether auditors should be certified. Disclosure of audit results and verification are also at issue.

The remainder of this chapter discusses the benefits and risks of environmental auditing, the significant elements that an environmental assessment program should have, and general information about areas of controversy in state, national, and international auditing policy.

Benefits and Risks of Environmental Auditing Programs

Environmental auditing or assessment programs offer significant legal and corporate benefits for both large and small companies. Careful evaluation of the environmental components of a business helps to ensure compliance with both environmental and securities laws. Assessment programs, along with other environmental management programs, reduce the risk of liability exposure. If environmental problems are addressed promptly, the overall environmental programs are more cost effective and will reduce long-term liability and environmental costs. There are also unquantifiable, but important benefits, such as improved employee development and public relations.

Despite these benefits, companies hesitate to institute auditing programs for fear that audits may uncover problems. Companies further fear that the problems will be disclosed, which may expose them to bad publicity or bring about or worsen their posture in government enforcement actions, citizen suits, or toxic tort litigation. Yet, as discussed below, the benefits of environmental assessments far outweigh the risks, and there are ways that the risks can be managed and minimized.

Legal and Corporate Benefits of Auditing

There is an array of benefits for companies that adopt a strong environmental assessment program.[7] They are listed below.

☐ *Ensuring Compliance.* A strong environmental assessment program is a key method of ensuring compliance with environmental laws and regulations, as well as company policies and programs. In view of the range of possible adverse consequences for violating environmental laws and regulations, it is critical to develop a method for ensuring compliance, or at least for determining whether potential noncompliance problems exist that need to be addressed.

The assessment itself is an important mechanism for determining the status of compliance. It focuses on early identification of actual or potential compliance problems and helps ensure that management is aware of the status of operations. The environmental program must be action-oriented to ensure that any problems discovered are eliminated and that no "smoking guns" remain unattended. Problems should be resolved in ways that reduce the risk of inadvertent violations and agency enforcement actions.

☐ *Avoiding Civil and Criminal Liability.* Virtually all of the environmental statutes provide sanctions for noncompliance. These can include civil penalties, criminal fines and imprisonment, injunctions, citizen suits, other actions, and permit or registration suspensions or revocations. There is continuing concern as to exposure to criminal prosecution, particularly as EPA has built up staff in this area (see Chapter 2, Criminal Liability—A Key Concern for the Environmental Manager). In addition to the criminal sanctions in the federal environmental statutes, a number of provisions in the U.S.

Criminal Code may impose criminal liability in environmental situations.[8]

Both corporations and their employees are subject to civil and criminal liability under the environmental laws. The environmental laws apply to "persons." Legally, "persons" include both corporations and individuals acting for corporations, including directors, officers, managers, and all employees. Moreover, an employee's knowing act may subject both the employee and the corporation to criminal fines. An individual who did not actually participate in an act may also be held criminally liable if that individual approved of the conduct, or negligently or knowingly failed to prevent the violation. Thus, there have been instances in which the government has argued that a corporate officer can be held vicariously liable for the conduct of subordinate employees. Purposeful failure to investigate or "deliberate ignorance" has been interpreted as knowledge for purposes of criminal liability.[9] A major benefit of an environmental assessment system is "that the corporation will be less apt to be prosecuted criminally and less apt to be subjected to punitive damages when sued by private parties."[10] (For a more detailed discussion of these and other criminal law issues, see Chapter 2, Criminal Liability—A Key Concern for the Environmental Manager.)

☐ *Ensuring Accurate Certifications.* An assessment may provide the basis for certification by a company official of the accuracy and completeness of a permit application.[11] This is a significant benefit because it is important that these certifications be accurate. Some of the environmental statutes requiring permits, such as RCRA and the FWPCA, provide criminal penalties for making false statements on permit applications.[12] Provisions in the U.S. Criminal Code can also apply.[13]

☐ *Ensuring Accurate SEC Disclosures.* Indirect enforcement of environmental laws and regulations through SEC actions is potentially more powerful than direct EPA enforcement. The securities and exchange laws and regulations require disclosure of environmental problems. (See Appendix K, ASTM *Standard Guide for Disclosure of Environmental Liabilities.*) Environmental assessments help ensure that publicly held companies submit timely and accurate reports. A finding by the SEC that a company has failed to disclose environmentally related matters, thereby deceiving investors, could jeopardize a company's ability to raise capital through new stock offerings or debt instruments. It could also cause the SEC to initiate costly and time-consuming administrative proceedings, which can give rise to shareholders' class actions and derivative suits.

The SEC requires reporting of environmentally related matters that include:

* two-year estimates of capital expenditures for environmental

compliance, or estimates for a longer period if they have been developed and failure to disclose them would be misleading;

• particular types of environmental proceedings, as described below; and

• under certain circumstances, as described below, company policies or approaches concerning environmental compliance.

Environmental proceedings that must be reported include all administrative or judicial proceedings that arise or are known to be contemplated under any federal, state, or local provisions regulating discharge of materials into the environment that fall into any of three categories. First, any private or governmental proceeding that is material to the business or financial condition of the corporation must be reported (see also detailed discussion of materiality under Sarbanes-Oxley).[14] Second, any private or governmental proceeding for damages, potential monetary sanctions, capital expenditures, deferred charges, or charges to income is reportable if the amount involved (exclusive of interest and costs) exceeds 10 percent of the current assets of the corporation.[15] Third, any governmental proceeding must be reported if monetary sanctions (exclusive of interest and costs) will or reasonably are expected to exceed $100,000.[16] Stated another way, an environmental proceeding need not be reported if there is a reasonable belief that the proceeding will result in fines of less than $100,000 and is not otherwise material to the business or financial condition of the company. Note that EPA is warning violators that they may be required to file disclosures with the SEC to inform investors about EPA-initiated actions.[17] Note that in July 2004, the U.S. Government Accountability Office (GAO) expressed concern about the current state of environmental disclosure, noting inconsistencies in reporting among companies, even among those in the same industry group.[18]

It is important to remember that reportable environmentally related proceedings are not limited to those initiated by an agency or private individual. Reportable proceedings can include any action, including any rule challenge or request for administrative hearing, initiated by the corporation alone, by the corporation with another company, or by an industry trade association in which the corporation is a named party, if the action meets any of the reporting conditions.

If a company policy is likely to result in enforcement actions and fines, the company must disclose the policy and an estimate of the fines. Even when disclosure or comments concerning a company's environmental policy are not required, any voluntary statements must be accurate.

The SEC's May 1989 interpretative release concerning the disclosure required in Management's Discussion and Analysis of Financial Condition and Results of Operations in SEC filings further details the scope of disclosure.[19] This release indicates that "once management knows of a potentially material environmental problem, it must disclose it unless it can determine that the problem is not reasonably likely to cause a material effect, either because the event is not likely to happen or if it does happen, the effect is not likely to be material."[20] Thus, in preparing SEC filings, data developed during routine assessments and assessments made for acquisition and sale of properties become important. Moreover, "[i]ndividuals preparing SEC filings should also be aware that outside consultants as well as inside departments often prepare cost estimates during due diligence reviews for acquisitions and refinancing."[21] Note also that in preparing documentation of the determinations required under the SEC interpretive release,

> management should be aware that documents prepared during in-house or outside investigations of environmental problems may not be privileged. Even if certain documents are privileged, the facts they contain may ultimately be discovered. Registrants should be careful not to make admissions of liability in documents prepared to facilitate decision-making regarding SEC filings.[22]

The SEC has clarified its views as to ascertaining "unascertainables" in its Staff Accounting Bulletin No. 92.[23] That bulletin notes that paragraph 8 ("Accounting for Contingencies") of the *Statement of Financial Accounting Standards No. 5*, commonly known as SFAS 5, states that "an estimated loss from a loss contingency shall be accrued by a charge to income if it is probable that a liability has been incurred and *the amount of the loss can be reasonably estimated.*"[24] Determining what can "reasonably be estimated" is a difficult area and the SEC has indicated in this bulletin that an environmental liability should be evaluated independently from any potential claim for recovery. Thus, the SEC now requires that contingent liabilities be disclosed on the face of the balance sheet and separate from the amount of claims for recovery from insurance carriers or other third parties. Notes to a balance sheet must include "information necessary to an understanding of the material uncertainties affecting both the measurement of the liability and the realization of recoveries."[25]

The SEC gives some very general guidance with respect to quantifying the extent of environmental or product liability, methods of remedy, and amounts of related costs when such estimates "frequently prove to be different from the ultimate outcome."[26] The SEC's response is that the measurement of liability "should be based on currently available facts, existing technology, and presently enacted laws and regulations, and should take into consideration the likely effects of inflation and other societal and economic factors."[27] If management is able to determine that the amount falls into a range and there is no better estimate within the range, then the "registrant should recognize the minimum amount of the range."[28]

The basis for measuring environmental liability is very important and is worth quoting in detail:

> In measuring its environmental liability, a registrant should consider available evidence including the registrant's prior experience in remediation of contaminated sites, other companies' cleanup experience, and data released by the Environmental Protection Agency or other organizations. Information necessary to support a reasonable estimate or range of loss may be available prior to the performance of any detailed remediation study. Even in situations in which the registrant has not determined the specific strategy for remediation, estimates of the costs associated with the various alternative remediation strategies considered for a site may be available or reasonably estimable. While the range of costs associated with the alternatives may be broad, the minimum clean-up cost is unlikely to be zero.[29]

Sarbanes-Oxley

As many others have noted, the Sarbanes-Oxley Act of 2002 is primarily about disclosure, imposing enhanced responsibility for disclosures upon top corporate officials.[30] It puts increased pressure on corporate accountants and attorneys to push information "up the chain." It requires CEOs and CFOs to certify, among other things, that the company has adequate "disclosure controls and procedures." Sarbanes-Oxley also requires CEOs and CFOs to evaluate disclosure controls every 90 days and disclose to the company's auditors and to the board's audit committee all significant deficiencies and weaknesses in the design or operations of the controls.

These new obligations are placed on top of the 20-year-old SEC requirements regarding the disclosures of environmental liabilities. Three existing SEC regulations and one financial accounting standard require the disclosure of "material" environmental liabilities. However, the SEC has never expressly delineated the matters it considers "material" to the financial condition of a company, and Sarbanes-Oxley has not provided such a definition either. Rather, the SEC relies on case law holding that a fact is "material" if a reasonable investor would take it into account in making an investment decision.[31]

The U.S. Supreme court has twice ruled on the issue. In a 1976 case, it concluded that an omission would be material if there is a substantial likelihood it would be viewed by a reasonable investor "as having significantly altered the 'total mix' of information made available."[32] Similarly, in a 1988 case, the Court declined to establish a bright-line rule for materiality, finding that it "will depend at any given time upon a balancing of both the indicated probability that the event will occur and the anticipated magnitude of the event in light of the totality of the company activity."[33]

"Materiality" of an environmental liability may be affected by several factors. The size of the company may carry significant weight; the failure to process an environmental complaint would be viewed quite differently at a large company that processes 100 such complaints each year, than at a small company that typically processes only two. Other factors may include whether the matter involves a regulatory compliance issue, or whether the matter involves concealment of an unlawful act. As summarized by Caroline Hermann, formerly of the Environmental Law Institute:

> In general, information is material if there is a substantial likelihood that a reasonable investor would find the information important to make a well-informed business investment decision. Determinations of materiality require "delicate assessments of the inferences a reasonable shareholder would draw from a given set of facts and the significance of these inferences to him." Materiality, as defined, is murky at best. Attempts to quantify materiality have used a rule of thumb, for example, to disclose claims equaling $100,000 or more, or 10% of a company's assets in a current or pending legal proceeding. However, the SEC cautions against relying solely on such benchmarks because they have no basis in law or in accounting standards. Instead "evaluation of materiality requires a registrant and its auditors to consider *all* the relevant circumstances, and that there are numerous circumstances in which misstatements below 5% could well be material."[34]

Sarbanes-Oxley has made the process of determining whether environmental costs and liabilities are "material" a matter of potentially ruinous personal liability for the highest level of corporate officers. Under the provisions of the new law, anyone who certifies a periodic report that does not comport with all applicable requirements is subject to fines and imprisonment—up to a $1 million fine and 10 years of imprisonment for a "knowing" offense, and up to a $5 million fine and 20 years of imprisonment for a "willful" offense.

In addition, Sarbanes-Oxley contains two new criminal provisions that are not limited to SEC-related matters. A new whistleblower protection law provides for fines and prison sentences for retaliation against an informant who provides information relating to the possible commission of any federal offense. A second provision prescribes up to 20 years of imprisonment for destroying documents in order to obstruct a federal investigation, or even in anticipation of a federal legal proceeding. Importantly, this broad new provision allows individuals to be prosecuted even if no official proceeding had begun, as long as the government can prove that the person destroyed records in contemplation of some official proceeding in the future. Note the importance of conducting a careful review of a company's records management program, above and beyond the EMS, given that it creates the potential for criminal liability for the destruction of documents in the ordinary course of a company's business.

Sarbanes-Oxley has also spawned a new era of cooperation between the U.S. Environmental Protection Agency (EPA) and the SEC, as previously discussed. In July 2004, the GAO published a report[35] stating "that there is inconsistency in reporting among companies, even among those in the same industry group. The report is unclear about whether this inconsistency results from significantly different circumstances for individual companies or if companies are applying the disclosure requirements differently. Consequently investors cannot easily evaluate an organization's environmental risks."[36] The report does find that "[w]ithout more compelling evidence that environmental disclosure is inadequate, the need for changes, guidance or increased monitoring and enforcement is unclear."[37] However, the report also recommends that the SEC and EPA "improve coordination to ensure that the SEC takes better advantage of EPA data relevant to environmental disclosure. In light of this report, it is likely that environmental disclosures in SEC filings may face increased scrutiny—from the SEC, EPA, and the GAO—in the future."[38] EPA is now seeking to enhance the sharing of information about EPA enforcement actions against publicly traded companies with the SEC and the public.

The disclosure requirements and penalties of Sarbanes-Oxley, along with heightened government and shareholder attention to environmental liabilities, have prompted many companies to consider whether their EMS is providing an acceptable level of compliance and whether it is pushing information necessary for SEC filings up the corporate ladder. "No longer can companies subjectively determine whether an environmental matter materially affects earnings. Now, under Sarbanes-Oxley, companies must go beyond a mere baseline requirement, and consider material known trends as well as uncertainties for inclusion in annual and quarterly reports."[39]

Prof. Mitch Crusto discusses the issues of "materiality" in detail in a recent article.[40] He discusses a proposal presented by the American Society of Testing and Materials (ASTM) "which would require a cumulative assessment of the financial importance of all environmental liabilities for 'materiality,'"[41] and concludes that "while Sarbanes-Oxley does not expressly address corporate environmental disclosure, large economic entities, including publicly traded corporations and the federal government should adopt the ASTM CMS over voluntarily published green reports."[42] "[I]t would be another important means of promoting investor confidence and facilitating a full evaluation of the true cost of environmental compliance and remediation. In addition to private enterprises, CMS would also be a useful tool for the federal government to evaluate and mange its enormous environmental liabilities."[43]

Note that the issue of financial disclosure and materiality is further complicated by a recent interpretation by the Financial Accounting Standards Board (FASB). Its standard, FAS 143, which became effective in December 2003, "treats accounting for asset retirement obligations (AROs)."[44] "In a nutshell, FAS 143 requires companies to recognize the fair value of an ARO in the period in which it is incurred, if a reasonable estimate of fair value can be made. A company's property, plant, and equipment are all examples of long-lived assets that may be subject to so-called retirement obligations, which includes abandonment, recycling, and disposal."[45] Companies tried to avoid FAS 143 by arguing that FAS 143 "did not apply to 'conditional' asset retirement obligations (so-called CAROs), that is, obligations for which the timing or method of the retirement was dependant on a future event out of the company's control."[46] The response of the FASB was to issue "interpretation No. 47 (FIN 47) which will become effective for fiscal years ending after Dec. 15, 2005. FIN 47 makes it clear that liability recognition for CAROs includes a broad swath of environmental conditions, and that recognition is appropriate if the fair value of liability can reasonably be estimated."[47]

In short, managers can no longer be satisfied if their EMS provides only compliance controls. They must also be confident that the EMS will allow the company's top managers to certify that adequate "disclosure controls and procedures" are in place regarding potential and actual material environmental liabilities.

The trend is toward increasing disclosure of environmental liability. On June 30, 1995, the American Institute of Certified Public Accountants issued a draft statement of position titled "Environmental Remediation Liabilities" for public companies. Note that "[m]ost insurance carriers have recently modified their standard D&O policies to include a broad pollution exclusion that expressly *denies coverage for claims under securities law alleging inadequate environmental disclosure*".[48] The draft statement presumed an unfavorable outcome with respect to challenges to strict liability and took the auditor "through every aspect of an efficient audit" under CERCLA.[49] This approach does not recognize, as do environmental professionals, that CERCLA's "monolithic uniformity breaks down in the face of facts peculiar to the particular problem to be addressed."[50] On October 10, 1996, the Institute published its final statement of position (SOP 96-1) on environmental liabilities. This statement was approved by the Financial Accounting Standards Board and became effective for fiscal years beginning after December 1, 1996.[51] The statement indicates that "the 'reasonably estimable' criterion is met when a *range* of loss can be reasonably estimated"[52] and "expenses associated with a particular phase or component of the overall cleanup must be accrued at the time they become individually estimable."[53] This document should be examined closely.

In 2003 the SEC reiterated its 2001 advice "Cautionary Advice Regarding Disclosure About Critical Accounting Policies." "The advice reminded companies that SEC rules governing the Management Discussion & Analysis filing require disclosure about 'trends, event, or uncertainties' that could have a material impact on reported financial information. Environmental uncertainties are cited as an example."[54] "The SEC review of Fortune 500 disclosures [in 2003] found specifically that environmental exposures and liabilities were frequently deficient."[55]

> Companies should ensure that their environmental management staff identifies potentially material environmental exposures and develops objective quantitative estimates of potentially material environmental exposures and objective quantitative estimates of potential financial impacts under reasonable alternative scenarios. Companies should include senior environmental affairs managers in the development and review of disclosure statements. The audit function should ensure that systems are in place to produce adequate information regarding known material environmental exposures and that such information is delivered to senior management and properly disclosed.[56]

This tightening interpretation of what financial information must be disclosed greatly increases the potential liability exposure for failure to disclose or properly accrue. Legal involvement is critical as these issues are examined.

☐ *Business Planning.* Environmental considerations can play a significant role in a company's business planning, including financial planning; planning for new product lines, new business lines, and modifications or expansions of current operations; and risk management. An environmental assessment program provides both corrective and preventive assistance by identifying potential problem areas and new restrictions that may require immediate or long-term capital or operating expenditures.

New products may be subject to current or proposed regulations that may affect production costs and marketing ability. For example, a new chemical may be subject to an order under TSCA §5(e) that limits its use or requires very extensive safety restrictions on its manufacture or processing.[57] A good environmental assessment program would identify these constraints, which would have to be factored into the company's economic considerations.

Environmental considerations are also important factors in acquisitions and divestitures. By helping to identify and evaluate environmental contingencies, an assessment can provide information on which assets should be sold and on whether to buy all or part of another company. (Chapter 7 discusses acquisition review in detail.)

Modification or expansion of an existing operation can also trigger significant environmental issues. For example, a new facility, whether in an attainment or a nonattainment area, may require extensive preconstruction review under the CAA.[58] Locating a facility on or near a former waste disposal site may result in expensive and long-term remedial measures. A good environmental assessment program will detect these potential problems. As noted previously, Occidental keeps track of much of this information through its computerized management system, and Ato has implemented a corporate-based data management system.

As liability insurance becomes increasingly important and difficult to obtain, an environmental assessment program can facilitate risk management decisions regarding the amounts and types of insurance coverage needed. For example, RCRA requires "financial assurance" from owners or operators of hazardous waste treatment, storage, or disposal facilities to cover closure and post-closure care, as well as liabilities arising from accidents. The assessment program can help provide the information necessary to secure these financial assurances through insurance, bonds, or other methods acceptable to the agencies.[59]

☐ *Employee Development.* Assessments can raise employee consciousness about the importance of compliance and the risks of noncompliance. Increased awareness can improve environmental performance. Employees' performance in ensuring and maintaining compliance can also be assessed and used as a factor in evaluations for salary increases and promotions. A clearly identified and implemented environmental program can also help employee morale and recruitment.

☐ *Public Relations.* An assessment program can provide the basis for positive public relations when no problems exist or when problems are found but are promptly and effectively corrected. Indeed, the very existence of an assessment program can be a public relations advantage. A company will also be able to respond promptly to the media in an emergency arising from an environmental incident because the assessment program will provide readily available information. Although a public relations effort does not it-self solve any environmental problem, it can help improve a bad image re-sulting from an actual or perceived poor environmental compliance record. A bad image can result in unwanted media attention, tie up management time responding to inquiries, and adversely affect sales and stock values.

☐ *Management of Legislative and Regulatory Affairs.* The knowledge that environmental assessments provide about a company's operations, includ-ing problems and compliance status, can be of great help in evaluating the impact of new environmental laws and regulations. This can enable the company to comment effectively on or even to challenge the constant stream of laws and regulations proposed and enacted.

Public Disclosure and Audit Privilege Legislation

The greatest barrier discouraging some companies from conducting audits and implementing other management programs is the fear of disclosure of significant problems. They fear that it will be impossible to protect negative findings from the public or enforcement agencies.

Indeed, disclosure of auditing results may occur, either inadvertently or because it is required by law. Many environmental laws have self-reporting requirements and, as discussed above, securities laws also impose disclo-sure requirements. Moreover, to take advantage of the penalty-reduction in-centives in EPA's final auditing policy discussed later in this chapter, com-panies must quickly disclose violations identified during audits.[60]

Data and information collected for management or other purposes may in fact be used in an enforcement proceeding, or even in more than one pro-ceeding. For example, EPA and the SEC have a cooperative agreement that allows the SEC access to EPA data, in essence to audit the adequacy of the data that companies disclose to the SEC.[61] Under the agreement, the SEC has offered to perform "full disclosures" of any corporation for EPA, and EPA allows the SEC access to various EPA files.[62] EPA has agreed to pro-vide the SEC with six categories of information on a quarterly basis. The types of information are listed in Figure 6-1.

Figure 6-1
Information Provided to the SEC by EPA

(1) Names of parties receiving Superfund notice letters, identifying them as potentially liable for the cost of a Superfund cleanup (source: Superfund enforcement tracking system);

(2) List of all filed (but not concluded) RCRA and CERCLA cases (source: Consolidated Enforcement Docket);

(3) List of all recently concluded civil cases under federal environmental laws (source: Consolidated Enforcement Docket);

(4) List of all filed criminal cases under federal environmental laws (source: Criminal Enforcement Docket);

(5) List of all facilities barred from government contractors under the Clean Air Act and the [FWPCA]; and

(6) List of all RCRA facilities subject to cleanup requirements (source: Corrective Action Reporting System).[63]

In exchange, the SEC stated it would "consider targeting Environmental Disclosures" for its enforcement efforts, according to an EPA source.[64]

Even so, in my judgment, legal exposure is the biggest red herring discouraging some companies from implementing audit systems and other management programs that document problems. While initial auditing programs and other information-based management programs should be developed cautiously, the benefits of review in reducing present and future liabilities far outweigh potential legal risks. My experience indicates that significant legal problems rarely arise in assessments, partly because assessments deal with many areas that the law already requires to be reported to agencies, such as permit excursions. Legal problems that do arise can be handled easily if counsel ensures that the assessment team understands its responsibilities, particularly how to deal with areas in litigation, how to write and what to include in reports, and what procedures to follow when potential violations exist.[65] However, anecdotal reports of EPA attempting to discover audits are growing, and this may cause more companies to consider doing audits under attorney-client privilege.

Far from increasing legal exposure, assessment programs can decrease that exposure. As previously discussed, hiding from problems by not making inquiry does not help. Corporate officers can be held vicariously liable for the conduct of subordinate employees, and purposeful failure to investigate or deliberate ignorance has been interpreted to be knowledge for purposes of criminal liability.[66] Assessment programs are one way to acquire the information you need to avoid this liability.

Although a smoking gun is every attorney's (and client's) nightmare, basically smoking guns are problems only if undiscovered or uncorrected. You still have legal concerns after discovery and correction, but dealing with the issue is usually the best way to minimize potential—particularly criminal—liability and is unlikely to increase that liability. Of course, this means that the decision to implement a program that may disclose problems must also be a decision to do something about those problems.[67]

There are also some ways, although not fail-safe ones, to seek to protect audits from disclosure. It is possible—and certainly advisable in the early stages of a program when the scope of issues are unknown—to seek protection through the use of attorney-client privilege.[68] Also, some courts have recognized a limited self-evaluation privilege as a matter of federal common law.[69] To employ a privilege, it is necessary to take all appropriate steps to create and retain the privilege. Claims of privilege for environmental audits have been upheld,[70] but it may be an uphill battle.[71]

In seeking to maintain a privilege for environmental assessments, special consideration must be given to the role of in-house counsel. One author has noted that

> [a]s a practical matter, because in-house counsel are frequently called upon to provide business as well as legal advice with respect to matters under investigation, it may be difficult for in-house counsel to establish and maintain the privilege. This problem is exacerbated when information obtained in the internal investigation is shared by in-house counsel with auditors, accountants, underwriters and corporate officials not involved in the defense of the case. Waiver of the privilege is likely in these situations. Moreover, the government is both more alert to the potential for waiver where in-house counsel is handling the internal investigation, and more disposed to press the issue.

This point is underscored by the following statement of the Director of the Division of Enforcement of the Securities and Exchange Commission at the time of the 1982 Annual Meeting of the ABA Corporation, Banking and Business Law Section:

> The Commission staff will be inquisitive when examining whether the privilege or the work product protections have been correctly established and maintained by house counsel. This curiosity does not reflect disrespect for the important role of house counsel; rather it is a recognition of

the practical difficulties that are inherent in their attempts to establish and to preserve privileged communications and work product materials.

Where a waiver has occurred, counsel could well be sought by the government as a witness in the case. Notes, memoranda and other attorney work product would be subject to production in such circumstances.[72]

Note, that in some instances, prosecutors are arguing that "cooperation" in a criminal case, requires waiver of attorney-client privilege.[73]

Because of the legal uncertainty surrounding the invocation of privileges—and the concern that companies would not conduct audits if they could not protect the results—some states have enacted laws specifically providing for an "environmental audit privilege" or "self-evaluation privilege,"[74] and many states are considering such laws. In addition, federal legislation was introduced that would create an evidentiary privilege for environmental audits.[75] EPA is strongly opposed to federal and state audit privilege legislation.[76] It reserves its right to bring independent actions against regulated entities in states with privilege laws. (For further discussion, see the EPA and Environmental Audits section later in this chapter).[77] Indeed, EPA Headquarters and several regions have weighed removing delegated authority for their air programs from certain states on the grounds that these states lack sufficient enforcement authority.[78] EPA has since decided to approve state air programs in states with such legislation on an interim basis.[79]

Despite its tough stance on audit privilege legislation, EPA has had a long-standing policy to refrain from routinely requesting voluntary audit reports.[80] If, however, EPA has independent evidence of a violation, it may seek any information, including audit reports, relevant to identifying violations or determining liability or the extent of harm or to otherwise support an enforcement action.[81] Under EPA's 1986 auditing policy, EPA indicated that it would seek a report "where [it] determines it is needed to accomplish a statutory mission, or where the Government deems it to be material to a criminal investigation."[82] The Agency noted that it expected "such requests to be limited, most likely focused on particular information needs rather than the entire report, and usually made where the information needed cannot be obtained from monitoring, reporting or other data otherwise available . . . ."[83]

Examples of when audits would be requested include:

- if called for by a consent decree or other settlement agreement;

- if a company places its management practices at issue by raising them as a defense; and

- if state of mind or intent is a relevant element of inquiry, as in a criminal investigation.[84]

Note that EPA's policy does not reduce the protection afforded by the attorney-client or other privilege, if audits and reports are conducted and prepared so as to be subject to that protection.[85]

The bottom line is that EPA may obtain copies of audits, and if it does, it will use them. Although EPA asserted in 1995 that its review of its criminal docket "did not reveal a single criminal prosecution for violations discovered as a result of an audit self-disclosed to the government,"[86] in some recent cases, EPA has used self-disclosed audit reports to expand and support criminal enforcement actions. Gerry Block, former Chief of the Environmental Crimes Section of the DOJ's Environment and Natural Resources Division, has stated:

> [T]hough EPA appears to shun the use of "mere" anecdotal evidence that prosecutors and investigators use internal audits as leverage to obtain plea bargains or civil settlements on the government's terms, such evidence exists in significant enough amounts that EPA cannot merely brush it aside as fiction. From my own experience, as both prosecutor and defense counsel, I can attest to several instances where the seized audit report played a pivotal role in a criminal investigation. The experience of having a prosecutor, who is hell-bent on making a criminal case, go over an internal audit line by line with the company's audit team and line management before the grand jury is not a pleasant one, and not calculated to advance the notion that a wide-open auditing program is beneficial. Therefore, while EPA may be able to fairly claim that it rarely, if ever, uses a disclosure based on an environmental audit to actually prosecute a company, such a claim says nothing about the seizure of audits and the use of them during criminal investigations. Nor does it say anything about good faith disclosures that lead directly to hefty civil settlements and that, as a result, equally deter some from voluntary auditing and disclosure and in penalizing those who are trying to do things right.[87]

Industry thus remains concerned that audit reports will be used against them.[88] Of course, as noted previously,[89] prosecutors are arguing that cooperation in a criminal case includes waiver of attorney-client privilege.

Since environmental assessments may in fact be disclosed, it is critical to make sure that auditors are properly trained, both in the technical aspects of conducting the audits and in report writing, to avoid unnecessary problems caused by unartful drafting. It is even more important that any violations or threats discovered are promptly addressed and steps are taken to prevent their future occurrence.

Designing an Effective Auditing Program

Once a decision has been made to proceed with an assessment or auditing program, the program must be carefully designed. There is no "one size fits all" approach to environmental auditing. No single program can apply to all companies or even to diverse businesses within one company. Many law firms and consulting firms are now suggesting a structured approach that incorporates exhaustive facility reviews, using extensive checklists and records inspections.[90] While such reviews are clearly necessary, particularly at the initiation of a program or in other exceptional cases, many of us believe that auditing should reflect a more management-oriented approach.[91]

Overall, auditing programs should be broadly designed to further corporate and environmental goals. If programs are merely compliance-oriented, companies will miss opportunities to improve efficiency, reduce risk, improve safety, and minimize the creation of wastes. They will also fail to detect areas for management improvement or provide for more effective use of resources. To avoid these pitfalls, auditing programs should include both corporate program reviews and assessments of individual facilities. Companies with such programs will be better positioned for the future.

Elements of an Effective Program

An effective environmental auditing program must be designed as a "seamless web" to address and integrate management and regulatory concerns. At Ato, this "web," which is set forth in company requirements, includes "Responsible Care®" (the code of the American Chemistry Council members), Ato's own policies and procedures, the components necessary to avoid *criminal* prosecution under DOJ policy (see Appendix C), the sentencing guidelines for organizations convicted of environmental crimes,[92] the EPA environmental auditing policies (see Appendices B and H), and other good management practices.

An appendix to EPA's first auditing policy statement identifies seven elements most likely to result in an effective program. These are listed in Figure 6-2.

Figure 6-2
Elements of an Effective Environmental Auditing Program

> • Explicit top management support for environmental auditing and commitment to follow up on audit findings;
> • An environmental auditing function independent of audited activities;
> • Adequate team staffing and auditor training;
> • Explicit audit program objectives, scope, resources, and frequency;
> • A process that collects, analyzes, interprets, and documents information and is sufficient, reliable, relevant, and useful to achieve audit objectives;
> • A process that includes specific procedures to prepare prompt, candid, clear, and appropriate written reports on audit findings, corrective actions, and implementation schedules; and
> • A process that includes quality control procedures to assure accuracy and thoroughness.[93]

EPA's second auditing policy statement supplements these basic principles with a further definition of "due diligence."[94] These principles can be used to design a good program. (See also this chapter, International Environmental Auditing Policy, and Chapter 3, Environmental Leadership Program.)

The auditing or assessment program should be described in a document. (An auditing program or procedure may be part of the entire environmental program. Although this may be convenient, it is not necessary as long as the assessment program is documented and easily accessible.) Events, such as changes in personnel or their responsibilities, changes in regulations, and acquisition of facilities require modifications to procedures. The assessment program should be kept current to maintain its effectiveness, create awareness of the current environmental status of all operations, and reduce the potential for undesirable surprises. At Occidental, the corporate department has produced an assessment program procedure that it updates with additional guidance memoranda. Each division must maintain its own assessment program. Division assessments must meet at least the minimum criteria specified in the corporate document as updated.

The auditing program document should contain, at a minimum, a description of the company, the company's environmental policies and organization, and an environmental categorization of facilities. (This may also be a collection of related documents, if this works effectively. For simplicity in this discussion, I use the term "auditing program document.") It should also address internal reporting, recordkeeping, and unascertainable issues. The basic program elements and program assessment documents should be consistent throughout all divisions (even if procedures differ), and definitions and terms should be used uniformly in assessments and compliance activities. Ato has many detailed protocols with appropriate references.

☐ *Description of the Company.* The assessment program document should begin with an overview of the company's major characteristics. This description should be detailed enough to provide a clear picture of the company's overall organization, products, and business areas. For a company with only one or two facilities, this could be a facility description. The purpose of this section is to provide an overview of the whole company, by division if appropriate, from a headquarters perspective. It is not a facility-by-facility accounting. Like the rest of the document, this section is designed for basic information and use by the environmental assessor. It should not be so detailed as to preclude easy use.

The description should include:

- location and description of corporate and divisional headquarters;

- major products or business areas;

- major departments or divisions;

- number and location of facilities; and

- a table listing each facility by name, principal business area or product, and person responsible for the facility.

☐ *Environmental Policy and Organization.* The auditing program guidance document should also include an environmental organizational chart showing the reporting and responsibility relationships of all key environmental staff, including the relationship of the senior environmental person to the line organization. (A sample organizational chart is included in Appendix E of this book.) Position descriptions setting forth the functions of key environmental staff should accompany the chart. These should be updated regularly.

☐ *Environmental Categorization of Facilities.* The auditing program document should have a procedure for the company and its divisions to categorize facilities with respect to potential environmental impact. Key factors and evaluation criteria may include:

- geography (domestic and foreign locations);

- function (for example, major processing facilities, warehouses, and waste disposal facilities);

- operating status (including present, past, and future sites);

- ownership (whether the company owns or only operates the facility);

- age and general condition of the facility;

- pollutant excursion incident history;

- type and quantity of material processed, stored, and disposed;

- past operations or practices;

- proximity to environmentally sensitive areas;

- sensitive local or community factors; and

- presence of environmental staff at the site.

A classification system can then be developed that ranks the facilities according to their potential for creating negative environmental impacts.

☐ *Internal Procedures for Reporting Environmental Matters.* The environmental assessment procedure document should include the company's internal policies and procedures for reporting significant environmental issues, regulatory activities, and legal actions. Each division should also establish internal policies and procedures that facilitate compliance with company requirements and ensure timely notification of division management of significant matters. The Ato and Occidental procedures previously discussed (Chapter 5, Reporting—Management-by-Exception) provide for compliance and timely notification.

The policies and procedures for reporting significant environmental matters should be consistent with other company reporting requirements. The procedures should provide for multipath reporting to the environmental and legal departments as well as to the finance department, which must account for capital, operating, and maintenance expenditures for environmental projects. The reporting system for "significant matters" should flow, using the computerized management system, from the facility level to the division level and then up to company headquarters or, as at Ato and Occidental, through the division and corporate headquarters simultaneously.

This type of reporting procedure promotes prompt and complete reporting with appropriate review at all levels of the company and provides reassurance that all legal and environmental departments are using the same database. It also gives management the opportunity to seek legal review at the earliest possible opportunity. This can help the attorney use attorney-client and work-product privileges effectively in investigating possible noncompliance issues. All levels of company management should receive appropriate guidelines on how to request legal advice and how to handle information to ensure the creation of, and maximum protection by, a privilege. (See earlier discussion of privileges, Public Disclosure and Audit Privilege Legislation.)

☐ *Internal Procedures for Recordkeeping.* The environmental assessment program document should set forth internal procedures for recordkeeping. Permits, monitoring reports, corporate policy statements, and other related records are key documents in an effective environmental management program. Well-organized maintenance and ready accessibility of these documents facilitate day-to-day environmental management and help ensure that the needs of the company and the requirements of various statutes and regulations are met. Each division should develop internal procedures for establishing and maintaining effective and efficient recordkeeping systems. These systems should be tailored to division needs and operations, but also set minimum standards for facility files in the following five areas.

   1. Types of Records to Be Maintained. Environmental record files should contain all documents essential to managing the facility's environmental program, including:

      • copies of laws, regulations, permits, corporate policy statements, and other guidelines applicable to the business of the facility or division;

      • copies of important correspondence related to the environmental management program;

      • records of monitoring and inspection activities;

      • local, state, and federal laws and regulations affecting the facility;

      • permits in effect and applications pending;

      • regulatory agency contacts;

- facility layout and process descriptions;

- air emission records, information on waterborne effluents and outfalls, water monitoring data, descriptions of solid wastes and their disposal methods, and waste monitoring data (including manifests);

- past practice descriptions, water supply descriptions, spill control plans, emergency response plans, and disaster plans;

- pertinent correspondence and company/division policies and procedures; and

- routine and nonroutine reports to government agencies.

If this material is readily available electronically, hard copies can be limited, subject to regulatory requirements. Additional documentation may be included as the division deems necessary.

2. Central Facility Environmental File. Records should be kept in a central file at each facility. This standard procedure makes it easier to verify the presence or absence of a record. It also ensures that all essential records are readily identifiable and quickly retrievable. When it is not practical to keep some records in the central file (laboratory books and records, for example) or if there is a large volume of older records that are archived for eventual disposal, a reference folder can be kept in the central file indicating the location of other files. Note that not all of these records need to be maintained in divisional or corporate headquarters, but they should all be accessible. As discussed in Chapter 5, computerized database management and environmental management systems can help keep records easily accessible to divisional and corporate management. Environmental files should be organized consistently throughout the division, although file organization need not be identical at all facilities.

3. Outdated Records. In general, records should be kept at least as long as required by law, regulation, permit, or corporate policy (whichever is longest). On the other hand, obsolete records and other documents should not be allowed to clutter the environmental file. A division should establish a computerized procedure for identifying appropriate retention times for generic classes of documents and for determining specific disposition schedules for individual records. All records removed from the

active environmental file because they are no longer current or needed should be reviewed for appropriate disposition (archives, retention, return to originator, or destruction).

There is no pat recommendation for disposition decisions. Most people keep too much paper in their files. I limit this excess by following an arbitrary rule of refusing to buy new file cabinets without significant justification. This forces continual review of files in addition to the reductions required by file-retention procedures. It also accelerates removal of the usual clutter of duplicate documents and out-of-date articles, notes, etc., that are no longer beneficial and that complicate the search for meaningful material. If material has not been used in three years, it is probably not worth keeping unless legally required. An assessment should be kept at least until the next assessment is conducted and the documentation on an action plan is completed. I recommend a policy of requiring action plans to be completed within one year.

4. Custodianship and Review. Because environmental records are important to every facility's continued operation and to avoiding corporate liability, it is prudent to assign responsibility for their safekeeping to a member of the environmental management staff or a qualified records manager. An individual other than the custodian should review the records file periodically to ensure adherence to established policies and standards.

5. Access and Availability. Integrity of the environmental records file is important to ensure that all essential records are intact and readily available for reference as needed. The company and all divisions should also promulgate policies on controlling access to environmental records and the release of information.

Individual environmental staff members may need working files containing copies of relevant documents housed in the central file. The same standards regarding access, release of information, and records disposition must be applied to working files as are applied to central files, and the environmental file custodian should have a record of all environmental working files.

All of the above standards generally refer to written records. To the extent feasible, they should also apply to electronic records. However, I do not know of anyone who has yet developed a good program to deal with electronic records, including records on obsolete software, purging e-mails, etc. This is a particularly worrisome area for both managers and lawyers, particularly with software available that can recreate eliminated files, drafts, and other documents. Note that any issues with respect to destruction of documents, e-mails, etc. should be checked with counsel. The sensitivity of organizations has increased dramatically (or should have increased dramatically) since the massive publication of the Enron/Arthur Anderson issues with respect to document and electronic document destruction.

☐ *Unascertainable Issues.* The assessment program document should identify and address "unascertainable issues." An unascertainable issue or problem is one whose nature and extent are uncertain because of insufficient factual, technological, or legal data. On occasion, a number of unascertainable issues, or issues with unascertainable aspects, may be identified at a company's facilities.

Unascertainable issues commonly fall into the following general categories:

- Problems of unknown dimension. For example, monitoring wells may detect potentially toxic materials below a facility, but the extent and severity of any risk to health or the environment, as well as the technological options and costs for treatment, may be unknown.

- Environmental issues for which no adequate, present-day remedial technology is known.

- Environmental laws or regulations whose implementation is unclear, existing regulations that are presently in litigation, or regulations under consideration that are not as yet approved or promulgated.

- Environmental issues that will require detailed engineering studies to develop solutions and ascertain ultimate compliance costs.

Including unascertainable issues in an assessment program shows that the company knows the issues it faces. The objective in addressing existing unascertainables, as well as those revealed by future assessments, is to identify those issues clearly and to plan their resolution. Ato's Executive Committee and Occidental's Environmental, Health, and Safety Committee of the Board of Directors are continually updated as to the status of unascertainable issues.

Corporate Program Review

Overall, the assessment program should provide for both a systemic review and assessments of individual facilities. Periodically, it is important to focus on the broad-range, integrated health, environment, safety, and risk engineering (HESRE) management issues that drive the quality of HESRE performance. In large corporations, the staff in HESRE programs tends to be compartmentalized; that is, specific functional units may be responsible for individual functional areas. Yet, the individual units may not recognize overlaps and the need for adequate coordination and communication. Moreover, many environmental programs are facility-specific and do not address the broader issues that are part of total quality management. Basic program management issues can go unnoticed, and yet important issues must be addressed as early as possible to reduce costs, as well as deal with potential liability issues relating to Sarbanes-Oxley.[95]

To minimize this problem, a "corporate program review" can be initiated that will highlight the weaknesses of compartmentalized or facility-specific reviews. The importance of such a review has greatly increased since the September 11, 2001, tragedies. For example, the concept of "foreseeability," both from a liability and a "worst-case" analysis has changed. Many EHS departments now have the security function as part of their portfolio. The program review needs to be broad enough to deal with the safety/security issues of terrorism, both conventional and nonconventional. The duty of care, related to the legal issue of "forseeability," indicates that a company should deal with these issues as part of the program review and assure that there is an appropriate disaster and emergency management plan and review the adequacy of those plans. The issues include continuity of business along with protection of people and assets from chemical, biological, or other weapons. The act of taking actions to protect assets and people, or the failure to take appropriate action, raise a variety of legal issues that are beyond the scope of this book, but clearly require the assistance of counsel. The goals of a program review are to (1) determine if the company or division's HESRE programs are consistent with corporate policies, procedures, standards, and guidelines, (2) evaluate these programs relative to their stated intent, (3) assess whether they are well integrated, and (4) capitalize on identified improvements. Such a review should be program-oriented and include recognition of risk reduction and safety-related issues such as process hazard reviews and waste minimization programs. In addition, program reviews should examine the interrelationships of such programs and the effective use of resources. Specifically, they should examine organization, planning, guidance, communication, documentation, monitoring, measurement of accomplishments, and management systems in place to ensure effective coverage of overlapping areas of the disciplines involved. In short, periodic program reviews can assist in identifying specific program element deficiencies, implementation inconsistencies, and inconsistent management criteria and execution.

It is important to keep the review as unbiased as possible. The critical point is not what occurred in the past or what is occurring now, but to determine if appropriate and necessary management systems are in place and functioning; if adequate resources are provided to ensure the systems' continuation and effectiveness; and if appropriate measures are executed to measure the quality of program performance, including the means to meet future challenges. Additionally, reviews may need to extend beyond HESRE components and include ongoing business management systems. Integration of HESRE into business decisionmaking may be critical for continued success of the program.

Periodic review of the adequacy of HESRE program implementation is perhaps the most important step to ensure that corporations have adequate loss-prevention and loss-control programs. Such reviews can aid in identifying the root causes of problems, including common management deficiencies that decrease the effectiveness of efforts to comply with policies, directives, procedures, and guidelines. The results may help managers identify issues relating to quality control and quality assurance mechanisms that need to be addressed in individual corporate programs. Moreover, identifying program deficiencies, if they are immediately corrected, does not usually generate the legal problems related to facility audits because of self-reporting requirements. Most significantly, identifying the program deficiencies will help cure specific problems that are occurring at facilities primarily *because of* program deficiencies.

In short, a broad and integrated valuation of HESRE programs as implemented can provide senior management valuable information that can positively affect the corporation's future performance and profitability.

Besides being an excellent management tool, program reviews also help provide an important additional safeguard in the United States. The July 1, 1991, DOJ policy on criminal prosecutions for environmental crimes addresses compliance programs. To secure any form of DOJ consideration to limit the use of information developed in environmental audits and other voluntary compliance efforts in criminal prosecutions, the audit and compliance program must be comprehensive.[96] Note also that there is recent case law in a nonenvironmental context holding a board of directors not liable for damages resulting from payments made to governmental and private parties resulting from violations of regulations. The company had a compliance system "reasonably designed to provide to senior management and to the board itself timely, accurate information sufficient to allow management and the board, each within its scope, to reach informal judgments concerning both the corporation's compliance with law and its business performance."[97] Program reviews will help ensure that HESRE programs are comprehensive, as well as deal with potential issues under Sarbanes-Oxley and assure that there is a compliance "culture, as mandated by the Federal Sentencing Guidelines."[98]

The first step in a corporate program review is a "desk-top" review of existing documents to assess HESRE "accountability" and quality assurance/quality control issues. This review involves examination of policies, standards, procedures, guidelines, directives, principles, and assessment reports. These documents can provide a framework for the review as well as an understanding of the management and operating infrastructure for divisions and the location of HESRE functions. Such a review may also lead to identification of problems to resolve with the policies and procedures themselves.

To evaluate HESRE accountability, the desk-top review should include an assessment of roles, organization, staffing, and resource allocation. This includes an examination of HESRE function descriptions, job descriptions, and the assignment of responsibility/accountability for these functions throughout all levels of the corporation. It is also necessary to review staffing, funding, and resource allocation to assess the actual commitment to HESRE programs.

Likewise, the desk-top review should include evaluation of program quality control/quality assurance issues. This review should not be limited to headquarters; similar reviews should take place at all levels of management, including the facility level. Documents reviewed should include descriptions of programs, charges to the groups involved, management support, assessment commitment programs, copies of third-party assessments, action plan reviews, follow up and documentation of quality control/quality assurance measures and activities built into HESRE programs.

To assess how HESRE programs are *really* functioning, it is necessary to interview key people at all levels throughout the corporation, including individual facilities. The program review needs to go beyond traditional assessment reviews to ensure that there is more to an organization's efforts than a book of procedures. Only interviews and visits will provide a true understanding of how the management systems work and how staff view and fulfill their responsibilities with respect to environment, health, and safety. In this way, trends in HESRE performance and implementation that may not have been obvious may emerge.

Both the desk-top and in-person assessment must evaluate implementation, organization, planning, guidance, communication, supervision, monitoring, documentation, measurement of accomplishments, and enforcement of company policies. It should also address whether there are management systems in place and functioning that ensure effective coverage of the overlapping areas of the several disciplines involved. There is a tendency in business to place all HESRE accountability at the plant level. Clearly, the plant manager should have primary responsibility for ensuring compliance with law and regulations and company policy, but those in senior management and in appropriate staff functions should share that responsibility. Therefore, provision of adequate funding and resources is a critical element to review. A program review can also assess how company and division cultures can play a critical role in understanding how commitment of resources to HESRE issues is accomplished.

The program review should also carefully consider operations, maintenance, and capital issues. In times of lower profits, there can be a tendency to change operating practices and reduce preventive maintenance more than is appropriate. If specifically looked for, these trends can show up in a program review, particularly after a variety of interviews and facility visits. The capital expenditure process should also be closely reviewed. The written process may show that capital will always be found for compliance; there can, however, be underlying problems. Perhaps determinations are made not to seek capital for compliance expenditures until too late in a given situation or decisions are made at an inappropriate level within an organization, or such requests, particularly when made late in the budget process, may not be viewed favorably by the higher levels of management and will be deferred. Here, again, the issue of management accountability is important. The decisions concerning HESRE issues should not be left solely to facility managers. All levels of management are accountable and should be held responsible for their part in making HESRE decisions.

All HESRE areas should go beyond the traditional modes of doing business and should be reviewed in a manner integral with all other management functions. If these reviews are thorough, management and operational problems can be identified and remedied at the appropriate levels of management. It has also been suggested that a "business risk" component be added to both compliance and program reviews to address big-picture issues. Intel, for example, has supplemented its audit protocols by specifically directing management attention to those environmental issues that have the most significant potential to disrupt business operations. Those issues might (or might not) be identified along the way during a compliance or management systems review, but the process of specifically identifying and analyzing the issues that have the greatest potential business risk for a facility is an attention-getter that drives home the relevance of the audit process to top managers.[99]

Facility Assessments

A key component of the environmental assessment program is the assessment of individual facilities. Site assessments determine the status of com-

pliance with federal, state, and local regulations and with company policies
and programs on a facility-by-facility basis. For comprehensive and cost-
effective assessment of individual facilities, a team of people should be assigned to conduct the audit. Over time, many staff members may be part of
assessment teams. Given the constantly changing makeup of the teams, procedures must be in place to ensure that assessments are conducted consistently and properly.

☐ *The Facility Assessment Team.* Assessments of individual facilities
should be carried out by an environmental assessment team, operating with
the full support and authority of management. The team performs the assessment and prepares the report that is the basis for measuring progress toward environmental objectives and for initiating action plans. The team is
the heart of the operations phase of the corporate and divisional environmental assessment program. Therefore, the leadership, composition, and
mix of skills and experience within the team deserve special attention.

The size and makeup of an assessment team depends on the size of the facility, the complexity of the environmental issues, and the period of time
since the last assessment. The team must have broad knowledge of applicable environmental regulations, policies, and company operations, as well as
an understanding of the individual facility's operation, and must be independent of the facility being reviewed.

There are several ways to ensure independence. Some companies have a
large number of people who do nothing but audits and who report either to
an auditing department or to the legal department. This structure is not necessary to achieve independence. Moreover, it isolates the audit, impeding
its best use as a management tool for operational improvement. The more
removed the audit is from the division and the more indirect the auditors'
perceived understanding of the operation, the more difficult it becomes to
implement the audit recommendations. The desired independence can be
achieved by using a team from the division's environmental department,
which is separate from operational control. If divisional personnel do the assessment, it is important to have a separate procedure to ensure independence and action. The procedure used at Occidental provides for review of
these audits by an independent corporate group. This ensures that significant issues surface and that appropriate action is taken. At Ato, a corporate
group did the audits and the reports and programs were directly reviewed by
the Director, HES Policies and Programs, and by me, along with regular
meetings. (For a further discussion of independence, see Controversies As
to What Is "Independent" Review later in this chapter.)

It is helpful to vary at least one member of the team at each assessment.
Continuity and understanding of the operation are important, but a fresh

point of view is also beneficial.

Although there may be times when an outside contractor or lawyer should control an audit, auditing should not be viewed as a full employment program for either group. Indeed, relatively small corporations can easily handle these programs effectively in-house with proper initial guidance.

Attorneys should direct and control assessments in specific, limited instances, including occasions when enforcement action or litigation has begun or is reasonably contemplated, or a government agency has asked for information. Some companies prefer to have an attorney manage their entire assessment program. The program described below, however, can be run by non-attorneys or run by attorneys, and allows for attorney control under special circumstances. In most instances, environmental assessment should be a management tool that is not under legal supervision. An attorney should nevertheless be available to advise each team. It is important in all cases that the attorney participate by ensuring that the team understands its responsibilities, including

- its charter and obligations;

- its operating procedures;

- definitions of such basic terms as "violation," "excursion," and "compliance";

- how to deal with areas that are already the subject of litigation;

- how to write reports and what items to include in them; and

- procedures to follow when potential violations exist.

In addition, the attorney should review the team's preliminary reports before they are issued in final form to be sure that items that are or should be subject to attorney-client or work-product privileges are adequately protected. The attorney should also be sure that a follow-up system is in place that will alert him or her if issues arise that require an attorney's expertise and assistance.

Some companies, particularly those that have determined that attempting to conduct assessments under attorney-client privilege may not be worth the effort, are not sure as to the future scope of attorney involvement. There may also be suspicion from environmental management that the attorneys may want to micromanage the assessment. Similarly, the attorneys may assume that every action by the environmental staff will result in potentially significant legal problems.

A good way of diffusing potential conflict and, at the same time, minimizing the concerns of both organizations is to have the attorneys actually participate in some representative assessments. (See also Chapter 9, Dealing With Lawyers, Engineers, Business Managers, and Consultants.) It is useful for the attorneys to actually see facilities in operation and understand what is in fact being assessed. The interaction in the informal setting and informal dress that climbing around a facility or traipsing around the "back forty" requires helps build confidence and understanding. It also allows the lawyers to become more responsive to the client's needs and allows the client to do its job free of unnecessary restrictions from the lawyers.

☐ *Conducting the Assessment.* The basic operational steps outlined below standardize the conduct of assessments.

☐ *Notification of the Facility.* The facility should be notified of the impending visit. There is usually little to be gained by surprise visits. The timing of the advance notice can vary, but a sufficient interval must be provided to allow the facility to prepare, to collect data, and to ensure staff availability. For large facilities, a pre-visit questionnaire may be used to prepare the site environmental manager and the assessment team for the visit. The questionnaire helps keep disruptions to a minimum by requesting in advance that the facility identify major environmental issues, make certain files available, and schedule key personnel for interviews. Care should be taken, however, that the facility does not view the assessment as a checklist exercise and that it recognizes that the review will be operationally oriented.

☐ *Review of Background Material.* The assessment team should review pertinent information on the facility, including the response to the pre-visit questionnaire, if used, and the results of any previous assessments. These reviews should be done with an eye toward identifying potentially significant issues. In the absence of a completed pre-visit questionnaire or past assessment, the team could review the following categories of information to become familiar with site operations:

- facility identification;

- environmental contacts at the facility;

- a topographical map or line drawing of the plant and its environs, including all buildings and structures and their uses, all vents and waste-collection points, intake and discharge structures, any existing monitoring facilities, nearby water bodies, nearby wetlands and springs, and all drinking water wells on the property and in the vicinity;

- existing federal, state, or local environmental permits issued to the facility and pending applications for such permits;

- compliance schedules, consent orders, judgments, waivers, or variances related to compliance with any environmental law;

- facility operations subject to citation, fine, or civil or criminal suit for violation of environmental requirements; and

- regulated substances used at the facility and locations of storage, processing, and disposal of each substance.

☐ *Team Meetings.* The assessment team should meet to discuss the background data received and to identify key areas to be highlighted during the site visit. The team should then meet with the division and facility management staff deemed appropriate by the site's environmental manager. The agenda should include an overview of the assessment concept; a brief description of the site's operations; and an overview of the facility's organization, major environmental concerns, training program, public relations, and anticipated regulatory requirements.

☐ *Conducting Interviews and Reviewing Files.* During the tour of the facility, the team should observe and evaluate general operating practices, interview site operators, and inspect records. The team should follow corporate or divisional guidelines on assessment protocol and methodology. Protocol requires that the visit be conducted in a constructive, nonadversarial fashion because of its sensitive nature. As in other areas, a nonadversarial approach is generally far more effective in obtaining action. If nothing else, it will usually draw out more information. The facility's management should view the assessment as a vehicle for bolstering requests for needed funding, not as a fault-finding expedition. If it views the assessment positively, more information will be volunteered and the operational nature of the review will be improved.

Divisions should have discretion to develop assessment methodology based on their various operations. Different approaches may be appropriate, including:

- Asking a comprehensive list of "yes or no" questions centered on the requirements of the regulations, leaving the team little flexibility. This approach is usually too restrictive and limits the possibility of operational improvements, which is one of the greatest advantages of assessments.

• Posing a series of more general questions to determine the general status of the facility.

• Listing areas for review and leaving the questions and response format up to the team. This approach usually works best if you have an experienced response team.

Appendix I contains a sample questionnaire for use in conducting an internal environmental and safety audit.

☐ *Development of On-Site and Off-Site Reports*. The team should discuss its observations while conducting the assessment, but should meet on-site afterwards to develop its findings before presenting any preliminary results. This session should result in a consensus on the potential weak points of the facility's program. Again, to be effective, an assessment should not just focus on compliance but should also be an operational review. The team should transcribe its findings as an on-site report. The team should use this on-site report, with preliminary conclusions, to brief the facility's management before the team leaves. The on-site report then serves as a working paper for the team in preparing the final report.

The team should complete the off-site, or final, report within one or two weeks after the audit, and the facility's manager should have an opportunity to comment on the final report. Today's use of lap-top computers allows almost the entire assessment report to be completed on site and action plans can be agreed on without extensive exchange of drafts and reviews. This speeds up the process and minimizes second-guessing. Of course, with most drafts now kept on someone's personal computer, removing outdated records has become a source of major frustration for the environmental manager and a goldmine for enforcement officials.

☐ *Frequency of Site Assessments*. Massive reviews are appropriate at the initiation of a program to ascertain facilities' basic problems and in other exceptional cases. Otherwise, many companies, such as Occidental, focus their audits on systems and on major flaws, although in response to detailed regulatory requirements and an enhanced appreciation of the importance of compliance, these audits are becoming increasingly detailed. Once facilities understand their basic environmental mission, the facility audit is merely a cross-check to determine that the systems are performing adequately. This allows auditing on a less frequent, focused, and, in my judgment, more cost-effective basis.[100]

Ato is moving in the same direction. Today, software is available that allows facilities to "self-assess." The software essentially uses the equivalent of a "fault tree," where answers to questions trigger further questions. This is particularly helpful in ensuring that issues are not missed in today's incredibly complex regulatory environment. In turn, as those tools are used, it allows the audit team to focus more on programs and provide compliance checks through, among other methods, review of the use of the self-assessment program.

Once facilities have been categorized according to their relative environmental significance in the auditing program document (See Environmental Categorization of Facilities, above), a plan must be developed that specifies how often site visits should be conducted. This will vary depending on the number of facilities, their categorization, and the resources available to conduct site visits. Each company or division should develop a plan suiting its own particular requirements.

For example, facilities categorized as posing few or no environmental problems still need to be reviewed periodically, perhaps once every three years, or whenever a significant change occurs in a process, the condition, or the status of the facility. Facilities categorized as having low potential for environmental problems could be assessed at least once every two years, or whenever a significant change occurs. On the other hand, facilities that have potentially serious environmental problems that could present significant liabilities if they are not reviewed more frequently could be assessed every 12 to 18 months. Facilities with the greatest potential for environmental liability could be assessed once every year. This last category rarely applies. A facility might fall into this highest-risk category because of the nature of its processes, operating conditions, or wastes, because of the perceptions of regulatory authorities or the general public, or because of a lack of programs and controls. (Note that even a small facility can still be significant in terms of exposure.) Also, each of these frequency suggestions can be extended, depending on the scope of the environmental programs (such as self-assessments) and safeguards in place.

Ensuring the Integrity of Auditing Programs

There are many proposals worldwide to help ensure that environmental audits are properly conducted. (See also International Environmental Auditing Policy discussed later in this chapter.) To achieve the best possible results from the assessment program, careful consideration must be given to the affiliations and qualifications of the people who conduct the audit. A key—and hotly disputed—issue is whether an audit should be conducted by outsiders or whether corporate personnel can be sufficiently "independent" to conduct the review. There is also a controversy as to whether auditors, either in-house or outside, should be certified. Several groups have proposed certification procedures and standards for the conduct of environmental audits. There are also proposals for standardization and verification of audit results.

Controversies As to What "Independent" Review Is[101]

A continuing and growing conflict exists between corporate personnel charged with environmental auditing responsibilities and outside consultants. There is also a potential conflict between in-house and outside counsel.

There is a perception among the public and some legislators that an environmental audit cannot be "independent" unless performed by an outsider. Many suspect that this perception is encouraged by outside consultants and lawyers. Similarly, many law firms are touting their expertise in performing full-scale auditing of a company's environmental compliance. There are times when both outside consultants and lawyers are necessary, particularly where in-house staffs are not sophisticated or may have been compromised, or where there is "a realistically high potential of uncovering significant irregularities."[102] But this is an area for potential abuse.

An example of the bias toward outside auditors is the Office of Technology Assessment's suggestion that a program be established for certifying public environmental auditors

> who could attest to the quality of site and cleanup data and reports. . . . Responsible party studies and cleanups would have to use certified public environmental auditors. Governmental agencies and groups receiving EPA Technical Assistance Grants would also be required to use certified public environmental auditors to the extent that the work was conducted by nongovernmental contractors for onsite investigation and engineering activities. The basis for certification would be meeting a set of criteria established by EPA after discussions with a number of organizations representing professional engineers, consulting engineers, hazardous waste professionals, and EPA's Science Advisory Board.[103]

Good environmental audits are not mere checklists; they are operational reviews. As long as there is a commitment to address problems that surface, program reviews and facility assessments can—and should—in most instances be done by qualified in-house people who are "independent" of production responsibilities, with limited outside assistance as may be required. An in-house individual familiar with the operations and considered credible by the facility being audited can determine far more about what is right or wrong with a facility than can an outsider. The bottom line is not to find mislabeled drums, for example, but to determine why the program allowed for mislabeling in the first place.

Careful delineation of roles and responsibilities throughout the corporation can help provide appropriate independence, as well as essential follow up on audit findings. As discussed in Chapter 4, Occidental has a dual system of reporting to an Executive Vice President and to an Environmental, Health, and Safety Committee consisting of two outside directors who are on the Executive Committee of the Board of Directors. The Occidental corporate department produced and updates an assessment procedure for implementation by the divisions. Environmental assessments are reviewed by staff not associated with manufacturing operations and are critiqued by the corporate group.[104] The corporate department also observes select on-site reviews, reviews site schedules, and ensures that recommended follow-up systems are in place and working. On occasion, Occidental's corporate personnel visit facilities for informal reviews apart from the normal assessment process. Problems have been observed on some of those visits and corrective actions initiated. Further, an independent view of operations by experienced personnel has frequently identified program or procedural modifications that can make compliance more economical. These procedures provide a degree of independence without which a system cannot function.

At Ato, I reported directly to the President and was a member of the Executive Committee. Consequently, I had a duty to ensure that audits were conducted properly and issues were addressed. Note also, as discussed subsequently, that we required that the Manufacturing Directors (the bosses of the plant managers) monitor the completion of action plans to ensure management accountability.

Certification of Auditors

There has been continued discussion, particularly highlighted by the developing ISO standards, as to whether individuals engaged in environmental auditing should be certified and even greater controversy as to the scope of such certification and what specific requirements it would entail.[105] Several groups support certification of environmental auditors. For example, the brochure of the American Institute of Environmental Property Auditing states that the Institute looks forward to certification because at present there are "no standards or criteria for the knowledge and expertise to be possessed by property transfer auditors." The Environmental Auditing Roundtable and the Institute of Internal Auditors have formed a joint venture called the Board of Environmental Auditor Certifications. This group has developed detailed standards,[106] which are available at www.beac.org. Specific tests and qualification requirements are required for certification status,[107] and an individual who has met these requirements is entitled to utilize the title of Certified Professional Environmental Auditor (CPEA).[108]

Proposals for certification have been joined by proposals for codes of conduct for environmental auditors in the United States and elsewhere. The Board of Certified Safety Professionals has developed a code of professional conduct, and the Institute of Internal Auditors has developed a similar code. Portions of these codes are reproduced at the end of this chapter,[109] and the Code of Ethics & Standards of Conduct is reproduced in Appendix J.

An alternative approach is to use a system of voluntary registration rather then certification. California has taken the view that if companies are to engage in environmental auditing, they should have qualified people available. The state reasons that many smaller companies do not have the expertise to determine who is qualified to conduct an environmental assessment. Registration of environmental assessors and publication of their qualifications provide a basis for that determination. Rather than creating a "consultants' full employment act" by making the use of registered assessors mandatory, the state provided for "voluntary registration of environmental assessors."[110]

To become a registered environmental assessor, an applicant must show through "academic training, occupational experience, and reputation" that he or she is "qualified to objectively conduct one or more aspects of an environmental assessment." The law recognizes that these qualifications can be found in members of a number of professions, such as "specialists trained as analytical chemists, professional engineers, epidemiologists, hydrologists, attorneys with expertise in hazardous substance law, physicians, industrial hygienists, toxicologists, and environmental program managers."[111] If an applicant demonstrates the appropriate length and type of experience and provides three or more references "who as employers or clients can attest to the accuracy of the evidence provided by the applicant, to the applicant's professional character, or both,"[112] the state will register the applicant. The state plans to publish a directory of registered environmental assessors. All of Occidental's corporate environment and safety staff, including myself, were registered environmental assessors in California.

California has basically taken a sensible approach to this issue.[113] It has recognized a core of professionals whom companies are free to use or not, but has not gotten in the way of the functional use of assessments. The concern of many environmental professionals has been *mandatory* use of so-called registered or certified assessors as the only assurance of "independent" review. There are clearly ways to ensure independence without requiring the unnecessary expense of hiring an outside contractor who may not be attuned to the best means of solving a problem within a corporate culture, who can create unnecessary legal expense, and who can interfere with good management practices. Many professionals are concerned that such mandatory use might stop assessment programs in their tracks. If outside contractors will increase companies' costs substantially and cannot really be integrated into the management use of audits, regulation will kill the practice it is trying to protect. EPA and California have specifically recognized this by avoiding mandatory registration, audits, or standards. (See EPA and Environmental Audits later in this chapter.)

In many ways, calls for certification or registration are analogous to efforts to create a specialty certification for environmental lawyers. The American Bar Association's Section of Environment, Energy, and Resources, which has a membership including many of the most experienced lawyers in the field, has opposed such certification. The field is simply too diverse to lend itself to easy characterization. Another analogy comes to mind: Supreme Court Justice Stewart's famous quip that he could not define obscenity, "but I know it when I see it."[114] Perhaps a listing of individuals holding themselves out as professionals, together with accessibility to credentials, references, and experience, is the only easy way. In environmental law, many individuals are obsessed with specific regulations or narrow areas of statutes. Some of us old-timers used to feel that we were environmental lawyers with at least a passing familiarity with the whole spectrum of environmental law. But even as the field becomes more complex, there is still the basic judgment factor. We may not know the specific answer, but experience tells us that there is a potential problem, and that either we should explore it or we should call in an expert.

Similarly, an environmental auditor need not be expert in every area, but he or she should have experience and judgment enough to recognize a potential groundwater problem, for example, without being a hydrologist. Environmental auditing courses being developed on many campuses can assist in the basics, but they cannot teach judgment. There is a need for more training courses, particularly in the fundamentals of the technical bases for environmental auditing. This expertise can be gained, providing the individual has a solid professional base. If not, environmental auditing becomes a rote exercise.

Moreover, a cost-effective and efficient environmental program requires a team of people, not all of whom need be environmental specialists. Some companies use internal financial auditors to perform some environmental audit functions, and this is likely to grow. Although the early environmental audits have progressed from limited checklists to program reviews, there is still a need for basic documentation checking. I submit that it is a waste of experienced environmental personnel to spend substantial amounts of time on record reviews, particularly with the use of data management systems that can easily be assessed and verified. I have found that using the financial auditors for detailed checks during their visits to facilities (which are not as frequent as the environmental audits) has been extremely helpful. They are very thorough and require extensive documentation as part of their normal auditing process. With some limited training and access to environmental professionals for specific questions, they can perform these review functions adequately. If they have questions, environmental professionals are available to answer them. Occidental has prepared an extensive control questionnaire and complementary audit program for their use in their reviews (reproduced as Appendix I of this book) to ensure that

- all company policies and procedures regarding environmental and safety issues are adhered to;

- proper documentation exists for areas of concern noted in the most recent assessments, any other identified issues have been addressed, and corrective action has been properly taken;

- documentation of all applicable regulations, training, and required reporting is maintained;

- compliance with all permit and regulatory requirements is properly and adequately documented in the environmental and safety records, and files are maintained in an organized fashion; and

- all work-related injuries and illnesses are recorded.

If environmental auditing is to mature and become more respectable, we must ensure that we are not perceived as the equivalent of junior financial auditors, but rather as experienced professionals with broad environmental skills, which are an integral part of environmental management. Increased use of internal financial auditors will free us to look at more important issues.

The future of environmental auditing rests on the ability to recognize the broader issues and to implement long-term programs such as waste minimization, particularly as with a multimedia approach, rather than with narrow expertise and the use of checklists. There is real concern that environmental auditing and environmental law should not become so specialized that the larger picture is lost. Environmental auditing must be part of the decisionmaking process if it is to be used effectively. This is the joy and the intellectual challenge of the work.

Standards for Environmental Auditing

The CERES Principles (discussed in Chapter 5, Environmental Policies and Corporate Responsibility) state that those adopting the principles "will support the timely creation of generally accepted environmental audit procedures."[115] Many organizations in the United States and abroad are seeking to develop standards for environmental auditing programs. To date, no single organization or entity has developed widely accepted standards. There continues to be much disagreement about whether auditing should be standardized and, if so, what the standards should be.

In the United States, two organizations have developed standards for environmental assessments. The Environmental Auditing Roundtable has prepared Standards for Performance of Environmental, Health, and Safety Audits, which are included in Appendix J of this book. The Environmental Committee of the American Society for Testing & Materials (ASTM) has approved a set of standards applicable to the innocent landowner defense.[116] It has been suggested that

> [a]lthough the EPA has not endorsed the ASTM site assessment standards as being per se sufficient purchase inquiry to invoke CERCLA's innocent-purchaser defense, the ASTM standards nevertheless give some uniform guidance to prospective purchasers and environmental consultants concerning the performance of a Phase I Environmental Site Assessment. Over time, the standards may provide a basis for a nationwide consensus to form around what constitutes "all appropriate inquiry."[117]

There are also many international efforts to develop standards for environmental assessments. GEMI (discussed in Chapter 3, Worldwide Management Initiatives to Promote Excellence) has released a standard assessment tool for worldwide distribution.[118] The tool translates the International Chamber of Commerce's Business Charter for Sustainable Development into "digestible corporate activities needed to attain the goals."[119] In addition, in conjunction with the Environmental Auditing Forum, the Environmental Auditing Roundtable, and the Institute for Environmental Auditing, the Canadian Standards Association and NSF International are developing and co-publishing voluntary North American documents in the fields of environmental management systems and environmental auditing. The International Organization for Standardization (ISO) also has a draft standard, ISO 14010. Note that there are other efforts, particularly in Europe, to find standardization. These are discussed at the end of this chapter.

Verification and Corrective Action

There are a variety of techniques to ensure that the value created by an assessment program is not lost. Corporate review and top-level management attention help ensure that internal environmental management procedures are followed and potential problems uncovered before they surface in regulatory agencies or the media. At Occidental, the Environmental, Health, and Safety Committee of the Board; the Executive Vice President and Senior General Counsel and Secretary (who is also a director); and the Executive Vice President and Senior Operating Officer review environmental assessments and the corporate group's critiques. Ato developed a similar scope of review, as well as management accountability for completion of action plans.

A high level of review is a great advantage. Far too often, a company assumes that it has resolved many of its problems simply by having an assessment program. The assessments may, however, be circulated only to lower middle-level management, and no recommendations are made and/or no actions are taken. Of course, the moment a facility has major enforcement problems, its assessment report will surface (many times even if attempts are made to protect it legally), and the company will have major difficulties explaining why no responsible manager took action to correct the deficiencies or why action was postponed. This is *not* a hypothetical situation. Experienced environmental lawyers and managers can cite too many examples of otherwise responsible companies that simply did not provide the management controls to ensure follow up on their assessments. These companies would find this lack of follow up inexcusable in a financial or operational context.

Ato, where I was both a Senior Vice President who reported directly to the President and a member of the Executive Committee, has established a dual track. While I was responsible for management of the compliance program, each group president was directly responsible for compliance. This includes the requirement that the manufacturing director, who reports to the group president, follow the audit action start and report specifically on action plans that are not timely completed. In addition, the Executive Committee devotes one meeting per quarter to environment and safety issues, and Ato has established a hotline for employees to report instances of noncompliance without fear of retribution. (A copy of Ato's Core Health, Environment, and Safety Responsibilities of Employees and Contractors is reproduced in Appendix F.)

At the national and international level, there has been much interest in development of self-evaluation and verification systems to help ensure environmental compliance. (See International Environmental Auditing Policy discussed later in this chapter.) There has been considerable publicity about evaluation programs, such as those envisioned in the CERES Principles (see Chapter 3, Worldwide Management Initiatives to Promote Excellence, and Chapter 5, Environmental Policies and Corporate Responsibilities). Many of these efforts are at least partially the result of environmental critics' claims that there are no hard numbers to evaluate a company's programs.

All of these efforts have the same fundamental failings discussed regarding the GEMI efforts, namely the difficulty in maintaining meaningful data for *outside* audiences or comparison of product lines or companies with each other. Whatever numbers are generated will be subject to criticism.

There will be no way to assure the critics of the uniformity and validity of the data. Moreover, some programs are important to some companies and others are not. This distinction will undoubtedly be lost on industry critics, particularly those who are more concerned about a company's products than its management systems. Even comparing different divisions with separate product lines is difficult. I suggest that if this is the rationale for adopting such a program, it is naive and a waste of money.

The foregoing is not meant to be a criticism of the GEMI efforts. I am simply concerned that "international standards" will become "one size fits all" requirements that will limit creativity and growth in environmental programs. If such standards are not adopted completely, a company might be concerned that its program is actually incomplete or is perceived by the public as incomplete. Yet, there is considerable internal value in self-assessment programs to assist in continuous improvement before or after a program review. They should not be used as a measure for comparing the status of one division against another, but as a means to measure progress toward program goals in each division. Stated simply, you should not be hung up on numbers. As discussed subsequently, the GEMI efforts and some of the European efforts should be looked at as useful guides for developing your own company's index of areas for evaluation.

National and International Environmental Auditing Policy

Environmental auditing, originally designed as a management tool, is now drawing governmental attention at the state, national, and international level. This section briefly describes how states, EPA, and various international entities are addressing issues in environmental auditing.

State Roles in Environmental Auditing

Many states have passed legislation concerning environmental auditing.[120] During 1995, nine states (Arkansas, Idaho, Kansas, Minnesota, Mississippi, Texas, Utah, Virginia, and Wyoming) enacted environmental audit-related legislation.[121] Additional states, including Michigan[122] and South Carolina,[123] implemented programs in 1996. Three states (North Carolina, Oklahoma, and Washington) implemented audit incentives as executive policy.[124] As of the end of 1997, there were 24 states with audit legislation and 11 with audit policies.[125] Iowa, Nebraska, and Wyoming enacted laws in 1998.[126] It is anticipated that more states will adopt either legislation or policy in this area.

EPA has taken a dim view of many state environmental auditing laws, contending that they "often conflict with federal delegating requirements and, consequently, present issues that have to be addressed in the context of program approvals, modifications and withdrawals."[127] While it is beyond the scope of this book to go into detail on this controversy,[128] the issue as alleged by EPA that "state laws that immunize serious violations fail to protect the environmental and public health adequately and discourage companies from making the investment in pollution control necessary to prevent such violators,"[129] can also be seen as a visible manifestation of the growing conflict (and frustration on both sides) between federal and state enforcement. There is also the danger that a company, in attempting to utilize a state audit statute, could be caught in a federal/state conflict.

It would be wise for companies to track these developments in the states where their facilities are located. As discussed above, individual states may impose certification requirements or standards and may also address privilege and disclosure issues.

EPA and OSHA Environmental and Safety Audits

As discussed earlier, EPA has published three formal policy statements on environmental auditing. EPA's Environmental Auditing Policy Statement, published on July 9, 1986,[130] and reproduced in Appendix B, sets forth general Agency policy on environmental auditing. On December 22, 1995, EPA published a "final" policy statement titled "Incentives for Self-Policing: Discovery, Disclosure, Correction and Prevention of Violations and a revised "final policy" on April 11, 2000."[131] The final statement and the revised final policy (reproduced in Appendix H) add incentives to encourage regulated entities to discover voluntarily, disclose, correct, and prevent violations of federal environmental laws.

In general, it is EPA policy to encourage regulated entities to use environmental auditing to help achieve and maintain compliance with environmental laws and regulations, as well as to help identify and correct unregulated environmental hazards. The 1986 policy statement specifically

- encourages regulated entities to develop, implement, and upgrade environmental auditing programs;

- discusses when EPA may request audit reports;

- explains how EPA's inspection and enforcement activities may respond to regulated entities' efforts to assure compliance through auditing;

- endorses environmental auditing at federal facilities;

- encourages state and local environmental auditing initiatives; and

- outlines elements of effective audit programs.

EPA cautions, however, that "the existence of an auditing program does not create any defense to, or otherwise limit, the responsibility of any regulated entity to comply with applicable regulatory requirements."[132] Also, audits do not replace regulatory agency inspections or activities required by law (such as emissions monitoring). In encouraging audits, EPA has specifically stated that it will not interfere with or dictate environmental management practices and that it wants auditing to remain voluntary (unless called for on a case-by-case basis in a consent decree or other settlement).[133]

In an important change in EPA position, the final policy and the revised final policy offered incentives, primarily in the form of penalty reductions, to encourage corporations and public agencies to conduct voluntary environmental compliance audits and to correct and to report any violations they discover as a result.[134] EPA issued the policy as guidance, not as a binding rulemaking. The Agency asserted, however, that EPA personnel will be expected to follow the policy in settlement agreements and that EPA "will take steps to assure national consistency."[135] As of September 1997, more than 500 facilities operated by more than 211 companies disclosed violations under the EPA policy.[136] For fiscal year 1998, "at least 200 companies disclosed violations at 950 facilities."[137] "As of October 1, 1995, approximately 670 organizations had disclosed actual or potential violations at more than 2,700 facilities."[138] The figures for fiscal year 2001 show 364 companies and 2,190 facilities taking advantage of the policy. The large increase in facilities (from 437 for fiscal year 1999) is attributed by EPA to "largely, in part, to the Agency's continuing efforts to encourage corporations with multiple faculties to conduct corporate-wide audits and develop corporate compliance systems." A large number of facilities continue to take advantage of the policy with 1096, 927, 614, and 1529 respectively for the fiscal years 2001, 2002, 2003, and 2004.[139] EPA has reached corporatewide agreements with the telecommunications and iron and steel sectors.[140] In general, the process does have value (Ato has successfully used it at one of its subsidiaries), but as discussed below, it needs to be used very carefully and under the right circumstances.

To benefit from the incentives contained in the April 11, 2000 policy, a company must meet most or all of the following nine conditions: (1) it must "discover" the violation either through an "environmental audit" or "compliance management system" that reflects "due diligence" in preventing, detecting, and correcting violations; (2) discovery and reporting must be "voluntary"; (3) discovery must be followed by prompt, written disclosure within 21 days of discovery or any shorter period required by law; (4) the company must discover and report the violation before commencement of any government investigation, citizen suit, third-party complaint, or "imminent discovery of the violation by a regulatory agency"; (5) the company must correct the violation within 60 days of discovery or notify EPA that remediation will take longer; (6) the company must agree to take steps to prevent recurrence of the violation including improving its audit system; (7) the company must not have had the same or a closely related violation within the past three years (time running from receiving notice of the violation) at the same facility or have a companywide pattern of similar violations at the parent level over the past five years (which in effect gives no credit for significant upgrades or improvements in companywide environmental management systems and compliance during the past few years); (8) the violation must not have violated a judicial or administrative order or consent agreement or resulted in or threatened an imminent and substantial endangerment; and (9) the company must cooperate with EPA by providing access to employees and documents. If a company meets *all* of the above conditions, EPA will not seek gravity-based penalties. If a company meets all but the first condition, EPA will reduce the gravity-based penalty by 75 percent. EPA has retained discretion, however, to recover any economic benefit of the noncompliance to preserve a "level playing field."[141]

The final policy states that EPA will not recommend to the DOJ that criminal charges be brought against any company, provided: (1) it meets all nine conditions; (2) there is no evidence of "a prevalent management philosophy or practice that concealed or condoned environmental violations," and (3) high-level managers were not consciously involved in or willfully blind to the violations. The policy also expressly reserves EPA's power to prosecute responsible individual managers and officers.

From industry's standpoint the final 1995 EPA policy left many areas of concern. First, the disclosure requirement was a major issue. The policy indicated that a company must "fully disclose[ ] a specific violation within 10 days (or such shorter period provided by law) after it has *discovered* that the violation has occurred or *may have occurred* in writing to EPA."[142] The catch 22 is determining both what is "discovered" or "may have occurred." Determining when the deadline begins, particularly when there is a need to do some preliminary investigating, is tricky. Reporting too early and setting the regulatory engine in motion is not advisable, but reporting too late may preclude use of the policy. EPA had indicated that it "may" accept late disclosures, but this provides "little comfort."[143] It is possible that "EPA will insist on disclosure within 10 days where the uncertainty has to do with interpreting regulatory requirements (a realm within which 'definitive determinations' often are made by regulatory authorities), while greater delays will be tolerated where the uncertainty has to do with factual circumstances requiring investigation by the entity."[144]

The pattern-of-violations aspect of the EPA policy is also an important concern. At first, EPA was considering targeting companies as "national violators," if EPA records indicate that the companies are having similar problems in different facilities in several states.[145] This could have been an "apples and oranges" situation, depending on how the violations are defined. Are they "recordkeeping" or "permit" issues, or are the violations more narrowly defined? In one matter before the EPA Board of Appeals, EPA has taken the position that a continuing violation not previously discovered by a corporation was a "repeat" violation and therefore not subject to the policy.[146] EPA has since scrapped the name "national violators" due to concern that the original title might unfairly stigmatize certain companies, but it will still target "multi-state companies which repeatedly violate environmental statutes."[147]

Another significant ambiguity in the policy is the exclusion for violations that "may have presented an imminent and substantial endangerment to human health or the environment."[148] The "imminent and substantial endangerment" language appears in many federal environmental statutory provisions, and judicial decisions interpreting those provisions have been interpreted broadly. An "endangerment" need not be actual harm, but merely threatened or potential harm, and the risk of harm need not be quantified.[149] Moreover, the term "imminent" does not mean an emergency or even immediacy; the threat "may not eventuate or be fully manifest for a period of many years."[150] Commentator James Stewart notes that

> [s]uch broad and liberal interpretations of the imminent and substantial endangerment language may have some justification under RCRA or other substantive environmental provisions. The use of such language in the Final Environmental Audit Policy, however, gives EPA almost unfettered discretion to classify a violation as one that may have presented an imminent and substantial endangerment so as to be outside of the protections of the Policy. This ambiguity and broad discretion adds to the uncertainty of whether any particular violation discovered in an environmental audit and self-reported to EPA will fall within the Final Environmental Audit Policy's protection.[151]

A major improvement in the policy is the willingness to accept "due diligence" as a basis for mitigation. In its 1995 policy, EPA stated in detail its criteria for due diligence. Because of the importance of these measures and because *all* of these measures must be complied with to obtain a 75 percent reduction of the gravity element of the total penalty, what constitutes "due diligence" is worth quoting in its entirety. The full definition is reproduced in Figure 6-3.

Figure 6-3
Definition of Due Diligence in EPA's Final Auditing
Policy Statement

"Due Diligence" encompasses the regulated entity's systematic efforts, appropriate to the size and nature of its business, to prevent, detect and correct violations through all of the following:

(a) Compliance policies, standards, and procedures that identify how employees and agents are to meet the requirements of laws, regulations, permits, and other sources of authority for environmental requirements;

(b) Assignment of overall responsibility for overseeing compliance with policies, standards, and procedures, and assignment of specific responsibility for assuring compliance at each facility or operation;

(c) Mechanisms for systematically assuring that compliance policies, standards and procedures are being carried out, including monitoring and auditing systems reasonably designed to detect and correct violations, periodic evaluation of the overall performance of the compliance management system, and a means for employees or agents to report violations of environmental requirements without fear of retaliation;

(d) Efforts to communicate effectively the regulated entity's standards and procedures to all employees and other agents;

(e) Appropriate incentives to managers and employees to perform in accordance with the compliance policies, standards and procedures, including consistent enforcement through appropriate disciplinary mechanisms; and

(f) Procedures for the prompt and appropriate correction of any violations, and any necessary modifications to the regulated entity's program to prevent future violations.[152]

The management program elements and systems identified in EPA's definition of due diligence are discussed throughout this book. However, in its April 11, 2000 final policy, while repeating these criteria, it did substitute the term "compliance management system" for "due diligence" while stating that there was "no substantive difference." The policy "clearly indicates that the compliance management system must reflect the regulated entity's due diligence in preventing, detecting, and correcting violations."[153]

Before EPA formally sanctioned environmental auditing programs, the benefits of programs were demonstrated in many businesses. (The benefits are detailed at the beginning of this chapter.) EPA's policies do not change these benefits. They do, however, place a federal imprimatur on environmental auditing, recognize the benefits and uses of this environmental management tool, and offer a penalty-reduction incentive that may be extremely valuable in certain instances.

On May 17, 1999, EPA issued proposed revisions to the audit policy.[154] The proposed revisions extend the period for reporting from 10 days to 21 days after a discovery by an "employee."[155] An interesting question is whether this should be after disclosure to a responsible manager. EPA rejected that view in its revised final policy.[156] EPA will also consider expanding this deadline to allow for additional facilities to be audited.

EPA also indicated that full cooperation does not require a waiver of all legal rights, but it is hard in reading the proposed policy to find which rights are not waived. EPA still retains its exclusion for multi-violators (regardless of when previous violations occurred) and violations that may cause imminent and substantial hazards. An additional preclusion is if a company is subject to an EPA multi-facility review, regardless of whether the company knows or does not know about the review, although this is somewhat modified in the revised final policy.[157]

The Occupational Safety and Health Administration (OSHA) now has its own policy on voluntary employer self-audits, providing that the Agency will not routinely request self-audit reports at the initiation of an inspection and use self-audit reports as a means of identifying hazards upon which to focus during an inspection.[158] It is not perceived that OSHA, unlike EPA, is enforcement-driven. OSHA has prepared a checklist of the generally recognized basic core elements of a safety program as part of its application for participation in its Voluntary Protection Programs (VPP). The VPP is designed to recognize and promote effective safety and health management. Many companies with strong safety programs have facilities in the program or strive to have facilities in the program. Membership in the VPP also limits OSHA inspections. Those facilities that meet all requirements are granted "Star" status and those at the "Merit" level have demonstrated the potential and willingness to achieve Star program status, and are implementing planned steps to fully meet all Star program requirements. Figure 6-4 describes the core elements of a safety and health program.

Figure 6-4
Core Elements of a Safety and Health Program as Defined by OSHA for Its VPP Program Management Leadership and Employee Involvement

• A managerial commitment to worker safety and health protection
• Top management personal involvement
• Safety and health concerns integrated into your overall planning cycle
• Safety and health protection managed in the same way as your productivity and quality are managed
• A written safety and health program appropriate for the size of your site and your industry that addresses all the elements in this checklist
• A results-oriented safety and health policy
• Clearly assigned safety and health responsibilities with documentation of accountability from top management to line supervisors
• Adequate authority given to carry out assigned responsibilities
• Necessary resources to meet responsibilities
• Quality of protection for all contract employees equal to that provided for your own employees
• Employee involvement in activities that have a major effect on your safety and health program
• Annual safety and health program evaluations with written narrative reports, recommendations for program changes, action plans and verification procedures

Worksite Analysis
• A method such as comprehensive safety and industrial hygiene surveys to identify existing or potential hazards in your workplace
• A pre-use analysis procedure for new processes, materials, or equipment to determine potential hazards
• Routine hazard analysis procedures such as JHAs, JSAs, BJAs, PHAs that result in improved work practices and/or training for employees
• A written hazard reporting system enabling employees to pass on their observations or concerns to management without fear of reprisal

• Accident investigations with written documentation
• Method of documenting all identified hazards until they are controlled or eliminated
• Analysis of trends in injury/illness experience and in hazards found, to identify patterns of problems and to implement program adjustments

Hazard Prevention and Control
• Access to certified safety and health professionals
• Engineering and administrative controls adequate for the hazards at the worksite
• Written safety rules and practices that are understood and followed by all employees
• A consistent disciplinary system applied to all employees (including supervisors and managers) who disregard the rules
• Written rules for use and maintenance of personal protective equipment
• Written plans to cover emergency situations
• Hazard correction tracking procedure
• Onsite or nearby medical and emergency services
• First aid and CPR-trained personnel available onsite during all shifts
• Use of occupational health professionals in hazard analysis as appropriate
• Documented ongoing monitoring and maintenance of workplace equipment

Safety and Health Training
• Manager, supervisor, and employee training with emphasis on safety and health responsibilities
• Training in the use and maintenance of personal protective equipment
• Emergency preparedness drills, including annual evacuations
• Documentation of all training received, including assessment procedures

International Environmental Auditing Policy

As in the United States, there has been much interest abroad in environmental auditing.[159] U.S. companies, particularly those with international operations, track developments in international policy on auditing quite closely. Ideally, there should be no distinction between environmental assessments of domestic and international operations. (See Chapter 3, Environmental Management in the International Context.)

Several European organizations are developing auditing standards and certification procedures. There are national organizations, such as the British Standards Institute (BSI), and an umbrella group, the ISO. Under the terms of the treaty establishing the European Economic Community, environmental standards must be developed and implemented. Many member countries would prefer that the European Union (EU) adopt ISO standards, rather than standards that may already exist in some countries in the Union. Much of the European effort on environmental auditing arises because, unlike U.S. laws, most European laws do not provide for self-monitoring and, therefore, the various enforcement agencies are struggling to obtain data.[160] Although compliance is voluntary, European auditing standards and certification requirements may have a profound impact on environmental auditing programs in the United States.

☐ *BSI Environmental Management System Principles.* Many companies in pursuit of "quality" have adopted the management system principles contained in ISO 9000, developed by the BSI as the European and internationally recognized quality system. Certification as being in conformance with ISO 9000 improves export possibilities, because many foreign companies either prefer or require that suppliers be certified as complying with ISO 9000.

The BSI prepared a comprehensive system for environmental management that went into effect on March 16, 1992 (BS7790).[161] Under §4.11, the system calls for "environmental management reviews."

> The organization's management shall, at appropriate intervals, review the environmental management system adopted to satisfy the requirements of this standard, to ensure its continuing suitability and effectiveness. The results of such reviews shall be published if the organization has a commitment to do so.

> Management reviews shall include assessment of the results of environmental management audits (see 4.10).

This is equivalent to the program review discussed earlier in this chapter.

Annex A of the standard contains a "Guide to Environmental Management System Requirements." The Annex states:

> The environmental management system should be designed so that emphasis is placed on the prevention of adverse environmental effects, rather than on detection and amelioration after occurrence. It should
>
> (a) identify and assess the environmental effects arising from the organization's existing or proposed activities, products or services;
>
> (b) identify and assess the environmental effects arising from incidents, accidents and potential emergency situations;
>
> (c) identify the relevant regulatory requirements;
>
> (d) enable priorities to be identified and pertinent environmental objectives and targets to be set;
>
> (e) facilitate planning, control, monitoring, auditing and review activities to ensure both that the policy is complied with, and that it remains relevant; and
>
> (f) be capable of evolution to suit changing circumstances.

Again, these are consistent with the systems and approaches described throughout this book.

The EU essentially adopted BS7790 as part of its eco-audit and management scheme discussed below.[162]

☐ *European Union Eco-Audit Regulation.* The EU Eco-Audit (EMAS) Regulation was adopted in March 1993.[163] There are strong pressures in the EU to adopt it as a part of "quality" standards.

Under Annex I, Section D, the Regulation sets forth the requirements for "good management practices."

> 1. A sense of responsibility for the environment amongst employees at all levels, shall be fostered.
>
> 2. The environmental impact of all new activities, products and processes shall be assessed in advance.
>
> 3. The impact of current activities on the local environment shall be assessed and monitored, and any significant impact of these activities on the environment in general, shall be examined.

4. Measures necessary to prevent or eliminate pollution, and where this is not feasible, to reduce pollutant emissions and waste generation to the minimum and to conserve resources shall be taken, taking account of possible clean technologies.

5. Measures necessary to prevent accidental emissions of materials or energy shall be taken.

6. Monitoring procedures shall be established and applied, to check compliance with the environmental policy and, where these procedures require measurement and testing, to establish and update records of the results.

7. Procedures and action to be pursued in the event of detection of non-compliance with its environmental policy, objectives or targets, shall be established and updated.

8. Cooperation with the public authorities shall be ensured to establish and update contingency procedures to minimize the impact of any accidental discharges to the environment that nevertheless occur.

9. Information necessary to understand the environmental impact of the company's activities shall be provided to the public, and an open dialogue with the public should be pursued.

10. Appropriate advice shall be provided to customers on the relevant environmental aspects of the handling, use and disposal of the products made by the company.

11. Provisions shall be taken to ensure that contractors working at the site on the company's behalf apply environmental standards equivalent to the company's own.[164]

The EMAS Regulation also requires the employment of "an accredited environmental verifier"[165] who "must be independent of the site's auditor"[166] and who is required to check:

a. whether the environmental policy has been established and if it meets the requirements of Article 3 and with the relevant requirements in Annex I;

b. whether an environmental management system and programme are in place and operational at the site and whether they comply with the relevant requirements in Annex I;

c. whether the environmental review and audit are carried out in accordance with the relevant requirements in Annex I and II; [and]

d. whether the data and information in the environmental statement are reliable and whether the statement adequately covers all the significant environmental issues of relevance to the site.[167]

The function of the accredited environmental verifier is to certify:

—compliance with all the requirements of [the EMAS] Regulation, particularly concerning the environmental policy, and programme, the environmental review, the functioning of the environmental management system, the environmental audit process and the environmental statements; [and]

—the reliability of the data and information in the environmental statement and whether the statement adequately covers all the significant environmental issues of relevance to the site.

The verifier will:

in particular, investigate in a sound professional manner, the technical validity of the environmental review or audit or other procedures carried out by the company, without unnecessarily duplicating those procedures.

Further:

the verifier will operate on the basis of a written agreement with the company which defines the scope of the work, enables the verifier to operate in an independent professional manner and commits the company to providing the necessary cooperation.

The verification will involve examination of documentation, a visit to the site including, in particular interviews with personnel, preparation of a report to the company management and solution of the issues raised by the report.

The documentation to be examined in advance of the site visit will include basic information about the site and activities there, the environmental policy and programme, the description of the environmental management system in operation at the site, details of the previous environmental review or audit carried out, the report on that review or audit and on any corrective action taken afterwards, and the draft environmental statement.

. . . . The verifier's report to the company management will specify:

a) in general, cases of non-compliance with the provisions of [the EMAS] Regulation, and in particular;

b) technical defects in the environmental review, or audit method, or environmental management system, or any other relevant process;

c) points of disagreement with the draft environmental statement, together with details of the amendments or additions that should be made to the environmental statement.[168]

The required use of "independent" verifiers and other EMAS provisions raise significant concerns about public disclosure of information obtained through audits. Public availability may be counterproductive and might limit audits to identifying only the most obvious issues, rather than providing the detailed reviews and issue identification that are extremely helpful in program implementation. There is an effort "to protect the confidentiality of information developed during the audit process by providing that external auditors and verifiers must 'not divulge, without authorization from the company management any information or data obtained in the course of their auditing or verification activities.'"[169] Yet, Article 5, Section 3(b), of the EMAS Regulation itself requires an environmental statement that discloses "significant environmental issues." Moreover, Article 5, Section 3(c), requires disclosure of "a summary of the figures on pollutant emissions, waste generation, consumption of raw materials, energy and water, noise, and other significant environmental aspects." The disclosure required by this "emissions register" is significantly broader than the EPCRA TRI.[170]

There is thus a major difference between the EMAS Regulation and EPA policy concerning disclosure of audits in the United States. While EPA auditing policy gives at least some deference to privacy concerns, the European Union takes the opposite approach. This difference arises because of both the lack of self-reporting requirements in European law and the EU's relatively limited enforcement options.[171] The European Commission lacks legal authority to bring *direct* enforcement actions against violators. It must instead litigate in the International Court of Justice to compel member states to enforce environmental requirements.[172] The EMAS Regulation is weighted toward the use of public disclosure to set the stage for pressure by nongovernmental organizations and the public rather than direct enforcement.[173]

☐ *The ISO 14000 Series*.[174] The U.N. Business Council for Sustainable Development requested that the ISO undertake a broad environmental standardization effort in preparation for the 1992 U.N. Conference on Environment and Development in Brazil. This led to establishment of the Strategic Advisory Group on the Environment (SAGE) in September 1991. SAGE's charter specified that SAGE was to:

1. Assess the needs for future international standardization to promote worldwide application of the key elements of sustainable industrial development, including, but not limited to consumer information and eco-labeling; the use and transport of resources, in particular raw materials and energy; and environmental effects during production, distribution, use of products, disposal and recycling;

2. Recommend an overall ISO/IEC [International Electrotechnical Committee] strategic plan for environmental performance and/or management standardization; including primary objectives, proposed new work items, timing needs and guidance for the inclusion of environmental considerations in product standards and test methods within the existing ISO/IEC technical committee system; and

3. Report its recommendations to the ISO and IEC Councils.

Since then, the ISO formed a Technical Committee to develop standards.[175] The Technical Committee would receive, but not be bound by, the work of SAGE. The Committee held its first meeting in June 1993. It has 30 member countries and eight observers and is divided into six subcommittees and one working group. These cover environmental management systems, environmental auditing, environmental labeling, environmental performance evaluation, life-cycle analysis, terms and definitions, and environmental aspects in product standards.[176]

There are now several ISO codes in different stages of development. They are: ISO 14000 (Environmental Management General Guidelines), ISO 14001 (EMS Specifications), ISO 14010 (Environmental Auditing), ISO 14020 (Environmental Labeling), ISO 14030 (Environmental Performance Evaluation), and ISO 14040 (Life-Cycle Analysis).[177] ISO 19011/12 is the procedure for auditing EMS. The new standard, ISO 19011, is designed to offer "guidelines for quality and /or EMS auditing."[178] It "actually cancels and replaces a variety of older standards Including ISO 14011 and

ISO 14012.[179] According to ISO BS EN ISO 19011: 2002 therefore offers guidelines for quality and/or EMS auditing. It is intended that by using this new standard, organizations can save time, effort and money by:

- Avoiding confusion over the objectives of the environmental or quality audit programme.

- Securing agreement of the goals for individual audits within an audit programme.

- Reducing duplication of effort when conducting combined environmental/quality audits.

- Ensuring audit reports follow the best format and contain all the relevant information.

- Evaluating the competence of members of an audit team against appropriate criteria.

Whatever the reason for the audit, however (e.g., certification, internal review, contract compliance, etc.) it is intended that organizations can move efficiently through the process by applying the guidelines.

☐ *Four Resources.* Within one single standard there are now four critical decision/support resources for the efficient planning, conduct and evaluation of quality and/or environmental audits:

- A clear explanation of the principles of management systems auditing.

- Guidance on the management of audit programmes.

- Guidance on the conduct of internal or external audits.

- Advice on the competence and evaluation of auditors.

At the core of the standard is a set of principles that will help anyone connected with an audit to perform effectively. And because it focuses primarily on the underlying processes of audit management, it can also be adapted for use when auditing any management system.[180]

ISO 14001 is the foundation of the ISO 14000 series. Adopted in mid-1996, ISO 14001 is the environmental management system standard. It requires organizations to conduct their environmental affairs within a structured management system integrated with overall management activity. It is designed to help ensure that organizations meet their environmental obligations and improve their environmental performance on an ongoing basis.[181]

Joe Cascio, Chairman of the U.S. Technical Advisory Group for ISO 14000, describes the system in the following way.

> ISO 14001 provides companies with a framework for achieving better environmental management. It outlines an environmental management system designed to address all facets of an organization's operations, products and services. The requirement in ISO 14001 to build and operate an environmental management system focuses the organization's efforts to establish reliable, affordable, and consistent approaches to environmental protection that engage all employees in the enterprise. The environmental protection system becomes part of the total management system, receiving the same attention as maintenance and production functions. Reliability is achieved through continual awareness and competence of all employees, rather than from extraordinary or isolated efforts of specialist.[182]

The elements of the ISO 14001 management standard are similar to those described throughout this book. These include understanding legal requirements and other initiatives including those that are "voluntary"; setting and documenting quantifiable environmental targets and objectives; a program for meeting objectives and targets (an environmental management program); providing adequate resources, roles, and responsibilities within that system; documented procedures to control operations with identified significant environmental aspects; procedures for identifying and responding to accidents and emergencies; broad training requirements (beyond those legally required in the United States); procedures for internal communication; communication of relevant environmental procedures to suppliers and contractors; documentation of each element of the management system; and a document control system to ensure that documents are maintained, accessible, current, and periodically reviewed.[183]

ISO 14001 has been revised effective November 2004.

Among those changes are:

• The scope of the EMS needs to be defined, "including what activities, operations, services and products are included within it. This needs to be documented possibly in the environmental policy." The EMS must be evaluated and documented showing how it fulfils the requirements of ISO 14001.

• Clarifying that the continual improvement process is "recurring."

- An organization's environmental policy has to be consistent with the scope of the EMS and its scope can not be wider than the actual scope of the EMS. "This allows interested parties asking for the environmental policy to gain information about the scope of the EMS and to learn what is and what is not covered in the organization's management system."

- The Policy must also be:

- Developed by top management.

- Covers the scope of the EMS and does not imply a wider scope.

- Covers all activity, products and services within the scope of the EMS

- Reflects other environmental requirements the organization may have subscribed to.

- Is distributed by everyone working for, or on behalf of, the organization, such as sub-contractors, contractors, temporary staff, and remote workers.

- The EMS must reflect its environmental "legal" requirements and other environmental requirements.

- Competence evaluation covers all persons working for, or on behalf of the organization, such as sub-contractors, contractors, temporary staff and remote workers, and that significant impact also covers potential impacts.[184]

There will be an 18-month transition period during which EMS certified as conforming to the original 1996 version of the ISO 14001 standard will be required to confirm with the newly revised ISO 14001:2004 standard. May 15, 2006 is the deadline.[185]

Although not an auditing standard, ISO 14001 addresses many features of an auditing program. There must be procedures for regularly monitoring and measuring the key characteristics of operations as they may affect the environment, along with tracking performance against objectives and targets and compliance with the law. Corrective action procedures must be established, including responsibility for investigating nonconformance and initiating corrective and preventive action. There must also be regular, *comprehensive* audits of the environmental management. Top management must periodically review the system to ensure its continuing adequacy and effectiveness along with reviewing any changes to the policy objectives and elements.[186] A primary goal of ISO 14001 is "continuous improvement," and these checks are part of this effort.

One area that is very helpful in improving awareness is identifying environmental aspects and impacts. Most facilities are not fully aware of their environmental aspects and impacts and this effort usually leads to mitigations and controls not previously considered. I have seen this particularly in reviews for EPA's National Environmental Performance Track programs.

Although elements such as these are part of any good environmental management system, many are skeptical about the benefits of ISO 14001. Environmental groups are concerned that the ISO standard fails to establish benchmarks for actual environmental performance.[187] These groups doubt that ISO 14001 "will actually influence either the company's compliance with its local environmental regulations or its willingness or capacity to prevent pollution."[188] Certainly, the standard by itself will not guarantee better environmental performance.

Industry, on the other hand, is skeptical for different reasons. Many of us are concerned about unnecessary paperwork and details that may be counterproductive, given today's sophisticated computerized systems. If the documentation of these computerized systems is not sufficient, some of their value may be lost. Moreover, there is fear that increased documentation requirements lead to grist for the mill of governmental agencies, corporate "gadflies," and toxic tort plaintiffs, among others.[189] "Corporate legal departments are likely to flash huge caution signs when asked for their views as to whether companies should embark on a formal certification process."[190]

Many people in industry also fear that government agencies may push ISO 14001 even further. Various governmental entities are looking to ISO 14001 as a means to enhance their environmental programs or reduce their inspection efforts. There has been some discussion of applying ISO 14001 to government contracts.[191] Also, EPA is looking at third-party verification through its ELP and XL projects (see Chapter 3). The Agency's Office of Water has announced "its intention to provide financial support, through a competitive grant process, for states that encourage and support the use of voluntary environmental management systems . . . , using the ISO 14001 International Standard as a baseline for facilities under state water programs. . . ."[192] That study concluded that "[f]ormal environmental management systems (EMS) can improve the environmental performance of government units and businesses as well as their operating and management efficiencies and system compliance.[193] EPA Region I has developed a "3PC" initiative, under which "participating companies [would] be expected to develop environmental management systems appropriate to their operations, modeled largely after the developing ISO 14000 standards."[194]

This initiative calls for an "ISO 14000-plus" program that would include an environmental management system plus performance standards, compliance audit guidelines, and procedures for correcting noncompliance. EPA National Performance Track program utilizes ISO 14001 as its base. This fuels industry concerns that a management-driven program may soon become compliance driven, and that ISO 14001 would be the "trailing edge" rather than the "leading edge."[195]

In this era of governmental downsizing, governments hope that companies with a program equivalent to ISO 14001 would likely be in substantial regulatory compliance. Pennsylvania has looked at ISO 14001 compliance as a means for mitigating its inspections, although the State has appeared to recognize the limitations of ISO 14001 as a compliance tool. In addition, EPA's Office of Water has considered "reductions in permit monitoring and reporting requirements for facilities that demonstrate superior performance and have a third-party registered environmental management system."[196] Concern remains, however, that a company could be in compliance with ISO 14001 and still have regulatory noncompliance and weaknesses in internal accountability. That same office, in comments to possible revisions of ISO 14001, suggested adding "full compliance" or moving to full compliance as part of the review.

Overview of ISO 14001 and Determinations to Certify or Not Certify—Political and Strategic Issues

U.S. industries are still, as a whole, skeptical of the value of ISO 14001 certification, but *not* of the value of environmental management systems (EMS). Most still take the position that unless there is a strong business justification for implementation, there is limited if any value from obtaining ISO 14001 certification in improving management, obtaining favors from government agencies, or being granted "credit" with the public. If strong environmental management systems are in place and they are "functionally equivalent" to ISO 14001, this is sufficient.[197]

Moreover, from a strategic standpoint, the same companies feel that rather than spend the time and money on ISO 14001 certifications, they should assure that their environmental management systems are strategically based. They should be focused on emerging issues such as global warming that may have significant, indeed perhaps profound, impacts, on future profitability.

While I deal with the issue of distinctions between the U.S. and EU regulatory regimes throughout this book, and other commentators—such as Chris Bell, Turner Smith, and William Thomas—have made similar points, it is useful for purposes of understanding the differences in pressures to certify to note some of the historical differences between the regulatory regimes. As a generalization, virtually all European regulatory systems are technically, not legally, driven. The regulations and statutes are nowhere near as detailed as in the United States. Nor are there the punitive aspects of enforcement that are the hallmark of U.S. environmental law. Technical people, not lawyers, normally resolve issues. Citizen suits are limited.

Another critical factor is the lack of transparency in most European regimes. Detailed data is easily available to both the public and competitors in the United States, but not in Europe. A good example of this difference is the differences between EMAS Regulation and EPA policy concerning disclosure of audits in the United States. Parenthetically, EMAS revisions are moving ahead to include ISO 14001 as part of EMS requirements. In essence, the distinctions between ISO 14001 and the EMAS Regulation are rapidly disappearing. Indeed, the "EMS component of EMAS can now be satisfied by implementation of ISO 14001 and the text of the ISO standard is included as an appendix to the EMAS 2 Regulation. EMAS 2 goes a step further than ISO 14001 in requiring initial reviews and disclosure statement regarding environmental performance."[198] However, EMAS requires independent verification that the EMS is delivering continuous environmental performance improvements and legal compliance as well as disclosure to the public. ISO 14001 is seen in Europe as a more inward-looking management tool, "a characteristic seen as a drawback for its use in public policy circles."[199] This is a view generally shared by U.S. regulators.

The EPA auditing policy places some limits on disclosure, recognizing that the U.S. enforcement regime creates legal consequences for disclosure. The EU takes the opposite approach. This difference arises because of both the lack of self-reporting requirements in European law and the EU's relatively limited enforcement options. The European Commission (EC) lacks legal authority to bring direct enforcement actions against violators. The EMAS Regulations are weighted toward the use of public disclosure to set the stage for pressure by NGOs and the public rather than direct enforcement. Thus, formal certified management systems in Europe, both ISO 14001 and EMAS, will continue to be more popular with regulators than in the United States.

Regulators in the United States have their doubts that ISO 14001 supports compliance. Certainly, the standard by itself will not guarantee better environmental performance. Perhaps the best example frequently cited is a Firestone/Bridgestone plant, which was the subject of intense litigation for allegedly manufacturing faulty tires, which is both ISO 9000 and ISO 14001 certified. Another comment that I have heard with respect to ISO 9000 is that "we still make a lousy product, but we do it consistently!"

A recent study by the Science and Technology Policy Research Unit of the University of Sussex, performed on behalf of the EC, gives credence to the skeptics. "An analysis of information from 280 European companies at 430 production sites turns up no statistically significant relationship between better environmental performance and certification either to ISO 14001 or the EU's ecomanagement and audit scheme [EMAS]."[200]

A recent study by the National Academy of Public Administration on ISO 14001, *Learning From Innovation in Environmental Protection*[201] is helpful in showing the value of ISO 14001 certification in certain cases. The study noted that, based on the amount of toxic substances released each year, below average performers in the United States are more likely to adopt ISO 14001 than their industry peers. The authors of the study conclude that many if not most of the U.S. facilities that have adopted ISO 14001 have done it to improve their practices because they lacked an effective environmental management standard. The other probable reason for certification is that these plants are larger, may be more subject to public scrutiny, and have managers who believe that formal registration will enhance their reputation.[202]

As noted earlier, ISO 14001 registration alone is not viewed very positively, either by environmental organizations or by government agencies, in the United States. Various organizations—including EPA, the Multi-State Working Group, and the Environmental Law Institute—are examining data derived from a baseline report conducted regarding 50 U.S. facilities. Those facilities are participating in a program that examines a three-year period prior to the institution of environmental management programs in 1998. The analysis may help to determine the effect of such programs and give some objective determination of value.[203]

Even those extolling the virtues of ISO 14001 certification recognize its weaknesses. As one commentator noted:

> This is not to say that ISO 14001 is a failsafe against regulatory violations; indeed there have been many cases whereby violations have occurred within registered companies. For example, Brazil's Petrobras, the largest petroleum company in South America, has experienced numerous oil spills and has been fined more than $100 million since its first facility was registered to ISO 14001 in January 1998. Despite these noncompliances, Petrobras retains its ISO 14001 registration status. In contrast, Ebara Corporation, one of Japan's largest electronic machinery manufacturers, voluntarily withdrew its ISO 14001 certificate in April 2000, after discovering a dioxin leak into rainwater drains that have been undetected for seven years. According to The ISO Survey, no ISO I4001 certificates have ever been withdrawn due to a failed recertification audit. This raises the question of credi-

bility of ISO 14001 and related registration practices, a debate that has been underway for some time.[204]

Many of us in the United States have been suspicious of some of the ISO 14001 certifications obtained in some other countries. While certification standards are supposed to be consistent throughout the world, the quality of audits and certification boards does vary, in some cases probably significantly.

Finally, in an extensive article on environmental management that I wrote with Richard MacLean (see Chapter 12, Green Arthritis) we noted:

> Much of business management's attention of late has been focused on certification to the ISO 14001 environmental management system standard. Certification can create the illusion that all must be well because the process is in place. But the standard only requires that a process must be in place, not that the performance improves as a result of the process. Consequently, business management's attention may shift from creating ever-higher performance goals to ensuring the completion of a procedure.[205] Although the data to date seems quite inconclusive.[206]

Additionally, the ISO implementation process can make it quite difficult to stay above the detail and develop an EMS with a strategic environmental direction. It is a good starting tool, but it is not the endpoint or substitute for a strategic environmental program. Indeed, if the entire goal is to get ISO-certified, the EMS implementation focus may shift to certification, regardless of performance.

Industry has viewed ISO 14001 as a management tool and has been concerned that agencies and environmental groups may want to turn it into a compliance mechanism—some form of an ISO 14001-plus as part of compliance decrees, etc. From a management standpoint, many environmental professionals feel that there have been enormous strides in industry in making environmental management systems part of the general business system, integrating it as part of the business and changing cultures. The regulatory agencies and environmental groups seem to view this as something that stands alone, which is contrary to the goals of industry environmental professionals.

Chris Bell, representing industry, has stated:

> ISO 14001 requires that top management establish, document, communicate and implement a policy that includes a commitment to compliance. Implementing the policy means that the EMS, taken as a whole, demonstrates that the organization is

making a systematic effort to identify and comply with its legal obligations. Noncompliance that rises to the level of a systematic problem is evidence that the commitment is not being met. To the extent that non-compliance is discovered, it should be addressed through the organization's corrective action procedures. The organization does not have to be in "full" compliance. Nor must the EMS be designed to attempt to identify every single instance of noncompliance. Not every instance of non-compliance is necessarily evidence of a systemic problem or even a significant environmental problem.[207]

Although ISO 14001 has been in effect for a relatively short time, there are various efforts to change it. Concern has been expressed that it is important to maintain consistency between ISO 9000 (quality standard) and ISO 14001 (management standard). This has not been a particular concern in the United States. However, EPA and some of the environmental public interest organizations are concerned that ISO 14001 does not provide compliance assurance.

Another issue is that EPA, in looking at "pollution prevention, wants to see its own definition in ISO 14001, which looks at elimination and gives a secondary role to recycling, etc.

A key issue now facing many companies is whether to become "certified" as in compliance rather than simply adopting ISO 14001 as an internal system.[208] While some kind of strong environmental management system is essential, it may not be necessary to meet an international standard. Moreover, obtaining value from ISO 14001 may not require formal certification. Yet, formal certification could be desirable for companies with big export markets, particularly when national governments are major customers[209] or for those with large markets in the motor vehicle industry, which is moving in the direction of requiring supplier ISO 14001 certification.

The American National Standards Institute (ANSI) and the Register Accreditation Board (RAB) have now formed a joint board, ANSI/RAB, that is qualifying various groups to act as ISO 14000 certifiers. This board definitely has credibility and acts as the U.S. accreditation body. If the certification is to build credibility, there is the concern as to equivalence of certification in the United States, Europe, and Asia. Moreover, if the means of certification are open to questions or regulators add an additional gloss of requirements, it may be extremely burdensome. Of course, if the certification process is too easy then it will not have credibility with either the public or the environmentalists. The agencies' credibility will also be on the line if they claim you met an international standard, but the public knows that companies are able to shop around to find a certifier who is in turn paid to certify your program.

Particularly for companies with strong programs, there is near unanimity in taking a wait-and-see approach, at least with respect to certification. Many companies, including Ato, are performing "gap" analyses, looking at their existing policies, procedures, and programs to determine where there are gaps from an ISO 14001 standpoint. It is difficult to analyze a company's web of initiatives and integrated programs and the results are very company-specific. It is now estimated that there are 6,000 in the United States, 80,000 worldwide.[210] The confusion as to the number may involve some duplicate registrations among organizations and facilities. It is also quite possible that the increase in certifications is primarily related to pressure from the automotive industry upon suppliers to certify their facilities. Ford, in particular, has put pressure on businesses with which it deals, and General Motors, Daimler Chrysler, and Toyota are following. The electronics industry is facing similar pressure, particularly in Europe and Asia. Some U.S. companies have commented privately that these certifications would not have happened in the United States but for European pressure, since their programs were in good shape and in most instances there was no significant business value to be found in the United States from certifying. Other U.S.-based operations of foreign-owned companies, which may be certified in European and other worldwide operations, are only certifying operations in the United States that need do so for business reasons, e.g., suppliers to the auto industry.

Companies weighing the pros and cons of compliance are also concerned about costs. One author found that "[i]nternal assessments comparing existing systems with 14001 indicate that the cost of revamping to meet ISO requirements will range from $100,000 to $200,000 per facility—and with no perceivable value to either the company or the environment in doing so."[211] She further notes:

> At best, certification indicates a level of commitment to systematic management and continuous improvement of environmental performance. There are other ways to measure supplier commitment and performance that do not require going to the expense involved with ISO, and companies are reluctant to impose unnecessary burdens on their supply base.[212]

While her conclusions may be disputed, costs can be high both in costs of consultants and value of time, particularly if a facility is not ISO 9000 certified and is not accustomed to this approach.

The American Chemistry Council (ACC) is moving forward with an effort that would allow third-party registration to both the ISO 14001 and Responsible Care®. A technical specification has been combined. The Responsible Care® 14001 certification process combines ISO 14001 and Responsible Care® and allows participating organizations to gain accredited certificates for both ISO 14001 Environmental Management Systems and Responsible Care® 14001 Management Systems in a single audit. RC 14001 was developed in cooperation with the Registrar Accreditation Board (RAB) and members of the auditing/registrar community. As part of this effort, ACC is looking at a mandatory certification/review process of some kind. From Ato's standpoint, it is developing excellent environmental management systems that will meet its requirements and be seamless. While it is moving to meet the spirit of ISO 14000 and probably going beyond it, Ato has some questions as to the value of all the paperwork. Its decision on certification will be based on business reasons (e.g., supplier demands, which after a slow start are beginning to materialize in, for example, the motor vehicle and electronics industries) and a viable certification process. Several Ato facilities are now certified.

ISO 14000 cannot be ignored. Like it or not, the ISO 14000 series will be a major part of environmental management in the next 10 years. If suppliers and customers pressure companies to be certified under ISO 14000, just as they now request that companies be certified under ISO 9000, companies will be forced to comply. Also, pressure for certification may well continue to come from regulatory agencies who see certification as a sign that a company has in place good environmental management practices.[213] However, unless there is a specific business case for either a facility or companywide certification strategy, it is likely that the "functional equivalence" policy will continue to be the option of choice. The fact that the auto industry, beginning with Ford Motor Company, has required certification has been a major factor in business decisions to pursue certification.

It may be easier to go forward with ISO 14001 certification if the company or facility is already certified under the ISO 9000 quality process. But if there is perceived to be no or limited business value in obtaining ISO 9000 certification, than there will certainly be even less value in ISO 14001 certification. ISO 9000 is also not without its critics. As noted previously, I have heard individuals within companies commenting about ISO 9000 to the effect that "we still make a lousy product, but we do it consistently." In reviewing the need for ISO 14001 certification, it is important to recognize the importance not only of consistency in a management system, but of assurances that the system is performance-oriented and strategically oriented. Indeed, Ford, which probably more than any other U.S. company, as a result of its requirement for ISO 14001 certification from its suppliers, has encouraged ISO 14001 certification to move forward, has now tied its efforts to an integrated quality and environmental management system.[214] "Ford recognized that the implementation of the FES [Ford Environmental System] was generally viewed by corporate and manufacturing facility personnel as bureaucratic and confusing. Worse, the implementation process was not clearly related to the Ford Enterprise Model, which incorporates the company's vision, mission, and values."[215] Ford also recognized that its "reputation as a company that focuses on environmental issues is largely measured by its products, such as vehicle air emissions, rather than the environmental performance of its manufacturing activities."[216] By combining the quality and environmental systems, Ford has "successfully eliminated the company's existing ISO 9001 [manuals] and the creation of long narrative document manuals that describe the interaction of the ISO 14001 standard and the FES."[217] Ford's integrated process "was developed, in part, as a way to eliminate ISO terminology in the rollout of the FES to the company's non-manufacturing facilities."[218]

Conclusion

Environmental auditing is rapidly evolving. Having begun as a basic management tool, it is becoming both more detailed as it checks compliance and broader as it examines management systems. It is now subject to various efforts to standardize procedures, including—with the advent of ISO 14000—de facto international standards. On one hand, regulators encourage auditing by giving credit to companies that have strong auditing programs in considering whether to prosecute them for violations they discover. At the same time, regulators discourage auditing by using audits as prosecution tools. State and federal legislative efforts used to encourage auditing by protecting the audits from agencies and plaintiff lawyers have been met by protests that the audit process could then be used to immunize criminal conduct. As in so many areas of environmental management, nothing is static in this area, except the importance of having tools that will assure compliance and achieve corporate goals.

Notes to Chapter 6

1. A section of the following discussion is adapted by permission of Clark Boardman Company, Ltd., from Frank B. Friedman & David A. Giannotti, *Environmental Self-Assessment, in* LAW OF ENVIRONMENTAL PROTECTION §7.05 (Sheldon M. Novick et al. eds., 2000).

2. Blumenfeld & Haddad, *Beyond the Battleground: A (Non) Regulatory Perspective on Environmental Auditing* (EPA Draft 1983), *reprinted in* ENVIRONMENTAL AUDITING HANDBOOK: A GUIDE TO CORPORATE AND ENVIRONMENTAL RISK MANAGEMENT (L. Harrison ed., 1984).

3. For a comprehensive analysis of auditing and environmental management, including citations to numerous articles, see WILLIAM L. THOMAS ET AL., CRAFTING SUPERIOR ENVIRONMENTAL ENFORCEMENT SOLUTIONS (Environmental Law Inst. 2000).

4. *See* Board of Environmental, Health & Safety Auditor Certifications (BEAC), *Standards for the Professional Practice of Environmental, Health and Safety Aduiting* 3, Dec. 1, 1999, *at* http://www.beac.org/ (last visited Sept. 14, 2005) ("[BEAC] was established as a joint venture of the Institute of Internal Auditors (IIA) and the Environmental Auditing Roundtable (EAR) to provide certification programs for the professional practice of environmental, health and safety" (EH&S auditing)).

5. The auditor is one of the reviewers.

6. Frank B. Friedman, *Organizing and Managing Effective Corporate Environmental Protection Programs*, ENVTL. F., May 1984, at 40; Kent, *Internal Environmental Review Programs—Pitfalls and Benefits*, J. WATER POLLUTION CONTROL FED'N, Mar. 1985, at 1.

7. For specific examples of the potential benefits of environmental audits, see BENEFITS OF ENVIRONMENTAL AUDITING: CASE EXAMPLES (1984), prepared for EPA and available from EPA's Office of Enforcement and Compliance Assurance.

8. *See, e.g.*, 18 U.S.C. §§2 (aiders and abettors), 3 (accessory after the fact), 4 (concealment of knowledge of a felony), 371 (conspiracy), 1001 (false statements), 1341 (frauds and swindles), 1505 (obstruction of agency proceedings).

9. 42 U.S.C. §6928(f), ELR STAT. RCRA §3008(f) (setting forth special rules for establishing criminal liability for a knowing endangerment violation).

10. Kent, *supra* note 6, at 193.

11. *See id.*

12. 42 U.S.C. §6928(d)-(f), ELR STAT. RCRA §3008(d)-(f); 33 U.S.C. §1319(c), ELR STAT. FWPCA §309(c).

13. *See, e.g.*, United States v. Johnson & Towers, Inc., 741 F.2d 662, 14 ELR 20634 (3d Cir. 1984), *cert. denied*, 469 U.S. 1208 (1985); 43 U.S.C. §6928(f), ELR STAT. RCRA §3008(f). *See also* United States v. Hopkins, 53 F.3d 533, 25 ELR 21178

(2d Cir. 1995), *cert. denied*, 116 S. Ct. 773 (1996); United States v. Weitzenhoff, 35 F.3d 1275, 24 ELR 21504 (9th Cir. 1994), *cert. denied*, 115 S. Ct. 939 (1995).

14. 17 C.F.R. §229.103(5)(A) (1996). A material proceeding is one to which a reasonable investor is substantially likely to attach importance in determining whether to purchase any security of the corporation. *Id.* §230.405.

15. *Id.* §229.103(5)(B).

16. *Id.* §229.103(5)(C).

17. *See* http://www.epa.gov.oeca/ore/sec.pdf (last visited Apr. 20, 2002). For material on disclosure and its implications on competitive intelligence, as well as a good table regarding what are disclosures, see Richard MacLean, *Formulating an Integrated Disclosure Strategy*, ENVTL. PROTECTION, Jan. 2002, at 36. Note that *Staff Accounting Bulletin No. 99: Materiality* raises questions on the so-called rule of thumb of a 5% deviation in a registrant's financial statement, indicating that a deviation even within that range can be material. According to the bulletin, "the magnitude of a misstatement is only the beginning of an analysis of materiality; it cannot be used as a substitute for a full analysis of all relevant considerations." Materiality "concerns the significance of an item to users of a registrant's financial statements." The bulletin further notes that a matter is "material if there is a substantial likelihood that a reasonable person would consider it important." The SEC then cites FASB as indicating:

> The omission of an item in a financial report is material if, in the light of surrounding circumstances, the magnitude of the item is such that it is probable that the judgment of a reasonable person relying upon the report would have been changed or influenced by the correction of the item.

SEC, STAFF ACCOUNTING BULLETIN NO. 99: MATERIALITY, Aug. 12, 1999, *available at* http://www.sec.gov/interps/account/sab99.htm (last visited Nov. 17, 2005). The SEC notes that the formulation by the accounting literature is in substance identical to the formulation used by the courts in interpreting the federal securities laws. The SEC advises that the courts look at the "total mix"—the size in numerical or percentage terms of the misstatement, as well as the factual context in which the user of financial statements would view the financial estimating. In other words, qualitative and quantitative factors are considered. FASB advises that "[t]there are numerous circumstances in which a misstatement below 5% could be material." Note that EPA itself has issued an "Enforcement Alert," U.S. EPA, SECURITIES AND EXCHANGE COMMISSION'S ENVIRONMENTAL DISCLOSURE REQUIREMENTS (2001), *available at* http://www.epa.gov/oeca/ore/enfalert/ (last visited Apr. 20, 2002) reminding everyone of SEC requirements and the fact that it is developing a centralized webpage which "will include information on recently concluded EPA enforcement actions that may be subject to SEC disclosure requirements" and a link to SEC's system "that enable users to access annual (10K) and quarterly (10-Q) disclosure statements, and other forms electronically."

18. *See* U.S. GAO, ENVIRONMENTAL DISCLOSURE: SEC SHOULD EXPLORE

Ways to Improve Tracking and Transparency of Information (2004) (GAO-04-808). *See also supra* notes 8-13 and accompanying text.

19. 54 Fed. Reg. 22427 (May 24, 1989). For a detailed discussion of this release and SEC reporting in general, see James G. Archer et al., *SEC Reporting of Environmental Liabilities*, 20 ELR 10105 (Mar. 1990).

20. 54 Fed. Reg. at 22427.

21. Archer et al., *supra* note 19, at 10107.

22. *Id.* at 10108.

23. Text accompanying notes 19-24 is taken from Frank B. Friedman, *Accounting for Unascertainables*, CORP. ENVTL. STRATEGY, Oct. 1993, at 59, 60-61 (reprinted with permission from the publisher). *See also* Lisa J. Sotto, *Companies That Fail to Make Adequate Disclosure of Potential Liabilities Have Become the Objects of Increased SEC Scrutiny,* NAT'L L.J., Dec. 4, 1995, at B5.

24. SEC, STAFF ACCOUNTING BULLETIN NO. 92, June 8, 1993, at 6.

25. *Id.*

26. *Id.* at 8.

27. *Id.*

28. *Id.*

29. *Id.* at 9. For a detailed discussion on disclosure, see Joseph J. Armao & Brian J. Griffith, *The SEC's Increasing Emphasis on Disclosing Environmental Liabilities*, 11 NAT. RESOURCES & ENV'T 31 (1997).

30. *See* Steven Solow, *Environmental Management Systems: Not Just for Environmental Compliance Anymore*, EXEC. COUNSEL MAG., Oct. 2004, at 39. A substantial portion of the following on Sarbanes-Oxley is primarily excerpted from that article with permission of the author. *See also* Caroline B.C. Hermann, *Corporate Environmental Disclosure Requirements,* 35 ELR 10308 (May 2005) and JEFFREY GRACER & LAWRENCE SCHNAPF, SPECIAL COMMITTEE ON ENVIRONMENTAL DISCLOSURE 2004 ANNUAL REPORT—THE YEAR IN REVIEW 2004, ABA SECTION OF ENVIRONMENT, ENERGY, AND RESOURCES LAW (2005).

31. *See supra* note 24.

32. TSC Indus., Inc. v. Northway, Inc., 426 U.S. 438, 449 (1978).

33. Basic, Inc. v. Levinson, 485 U.S. 224 (1988).

34. Hermann, *supra* note 30 (internal citations omitted) (emphasis in original).

35. *See* GAO, *supra* note 18.

36. *The Sarbanes-Oxley Act: What Else Will This Change for Environmental Staff,* MANAGING ENVTL. PERFORMANCE, Oct. 2004, 3. *See also* GRACER & SCHNAPF, *supra* note 30.

37. GRACER & SCHNAPF, *supra* note 30.

38. SIDLEY & AUSTIN, GAO REPORTS CALL FOR SEC AND EPA COOPERATION ON ENVIRONMENTAL DISCLOSURE, ENVIRONMENTAL ADVISORY (2004).

39. Hermann, *supra* note 30.

40. Michael F. Crusto, *Endangered Green Reports: "Cumulative Materiality" in Corporate Environmental Disclosure After Sarbanes-Oxley*, 35 ELR 10666 (Oct. 2005).

41. *Id. See also id.* at 10674-75.

42. *Id.*

43. *Id.* at 10678.

44. Jeffrey A. Smith, *New Standards for Financial Reporting of Environmental Liability: Introduction and Overview*, ABA SPECIAL COMM. ON ENVTL. DISCLOSURE NEWSL., Oct. 2005, at 2-3. That newsletter conains a variety of other articles that deal in detail with conditional asset retirement obligations.

45. *Id.* at 4.

46. *Id.*

47. *Id.*

48. Tom McMahon, *Forget Past: Disclosure Is Inevitable Wave of Future*, ENVTL. F., Sept./Oct. 2004, at 22 (emphasis in original).

49. Thomas M. Skove, *Proposed Accounting Guidance for Environmental Remediation Liabilities*, 26 Env't Rep. (BNA) 1980-81 (Feb. 9, 1996).

50. *Id.*

51. For a detailed description, see *Recent Developments in Accounting Rules Concerning Environmental Cleanup Liabilities, in* ENVIRONMENTAL PRACTICE BRIEFING, SHEARMAN & STERLING CLIENT PUBLICATION (1997).

52. *Id.* at 2.

53. *Id.*

54. McMahon, *supra* note 48.

55. Robert Repetto, *Are Companies Coming Clean?*, ENVTL. F., Sept./Oct. 2004, at 27.

56. *Id.*

57. 15 U.S.C. §2604(e), ELR STAT. TSCA §5(e).

58. 42 U.S.C. §§7401-7671q, ELR STAT. CAA §§101-618.

59. *See* discussion *supra* Chapter 2.

60. *See* Incentives for Self-Policing: Discovery, Disclosure, Correction, and Prevention of Violations, 65 Fed. Reg. 19618 (Apr. 11, 2000), ADMIN. MAT. 35763. This policy statement is reproduced in Appendix H.

61. Harrelson, *EPA Agrees to Information Exchange With SEC*, INSIDE EPA

SUPERFUND REPORT, Mar. 28, 1990, at 2; *see also* Benham, *SEC, EPA Team Go After Polluters*, INVESTOR'S DAILY, May 29, 1990, at 1; *Companies Tackle Environmental Disclosures*, INVESTOR'S DAILY, May 30, 1990, at 1.

62. Harrelson, *supra* note 61, at 2.

63. *Id.*

64. *See* discussion of Sarbanes-Oxley, *supra* Chapter 2.

65. *See* David A. Giannotti, *Advising the Corporate Client on Environmental Compliance*, ABA CORP. COMPLIANCE INST., July 9-10, 1983; *see also* Michael M. Gibson & Paul D. Fahrenthold, *New Perspectives on Corporate Risk and Ways to Reduce It*, ENVTL. F., Mar. 1983, at 35, 37-44.

66. The *Restatement (Second) of Torts* adopts the view that "[c]ompliance with a legislative enactment or an administrative regulation does not prevent a finding of negligence where a reasonable man would take additional precautions." RESTATEMENT (SECOND) OF TORTS §288C (1978). While the restatement does not necessarily reflect the position of many states, it does indicate potential additional exposure.

67. *See also Environmental Audits: Not for the Halfhearted*, ENVTL. MANAGER, July 1990, at 3; Raymond Kane, *Environmental Auditing: A Sound Risk if Done Right*, HAZARDOUS WASTE & TOXIC TORTS L. & STRATEGY, May 1990, at 1.

68. It is beyond the scope of this book to discuss the attorney-client privilege in detail. Briefly, the privilege is designed to protect confidential communications between an attorney and a client from forced disclosure, thus allowing a client to confide in an attorney, secure in the knowledge that no information will be disclosed. The privilege does not include everything arising from the existence of an attorney-client relationship. It is an exception to rules requiring full disclosure and therefore will be construed narrowly. The privilege applies to communications relating to facts of which the attorney was informed for the primary purpose of securing either an opinion on law or legal services or assistance in some legal proceeding.

> Communications between corporate counsel and the company's employees for the purpose of obtaining information relevant to legal matters as to which counsel must advise the company are subject to the company's attorney-client privilege. Upjohn Co. v. United States, 449 U.S. 383 (1981). This principle applies to former as well as current employees of the company. In re Coordinated Pretrial Proceedings in Petroleum Products Antitrust Litigation, 658 F.2d 1355 (9th Cir. 1981), *cert. denied*, 455 U.S. 990 (1982). Communications between employees and in-house counsel stand on the same legal footing as those between employees and outside counsel. In re LTV Securities Litigation, 89 F.R.D. 595, 601 (N.D. Tex. 1989).

Bennett et al., *The Role of Internal Investigations in Defending Against Charges of Corporate Misconduct, in* CRIMINAL ENFORCEMENT OF ENVIRONMENTAL LAWS 132 (ALI/ABA 1990). *See* Richard F. Ziegler, *Care on as to What Is a "Common*

Interest," Using Attorney-Client Privilege Litigation—Privileged Information, NAT'L L.J., Aug. 21, 2000, at A16.

69. *See, e.g.,* Reichhold Chems., Inc. v. Textro, 157 F.R.D. 522, 25 ELR 20307 (N.D. Fla. 1994).

70. *See* John S. Guttman, *Environmental Reviews Can Be Kept Confidential,* NAT'L L.J., June 20, 1994, at C12. *See also* United States v. Elf Atochem N. Am., No. H-93-604M, slip. op. (S.D. Tex. Aug. 8, 1994) (upholding attorney-client and work-product privileges with respect to documents seized by EPA); Olen Properties Corp. v. Sheldahl, 1994 U.S. Dist. LEXIS 7125, 24 ELR 20936 (C.D. Cal. Apr. 12, 1994) (attorney-client privilege applies to an environmental audit prepared by a consultant used as the basis of legal advice); Continental Ill. Nat'l Bank & Trust Co. v. Indemnity Ins. Co., No. 87 C-8439 (N.D. Ill. Oct. 30, 1989) (protecting a document that was prepared in response to a request for legal advice). For an excellent discussion of attorney-client privilege in the context of environmental audits, see COUNCIL FOR IMPROVED ENVIRONMENTAL AUDITS, CIEA WHITE PAPER SUPPORTING A QUALIFIED SELF-EVALUATION PRIVILEGE FOR INTERNAL ENVIRONMENTAL AUDITS (1995).

71. *See* WEISS, ISSUES OF CONFIDENTIALITY AND DISCLOSURE IN ENVIRONMENTAL AUDITING (EPA Office of Standards and Regulations, Regulatory Reform Staffs, Nov. 1983) and Frost & Siegel, *Environmental Audits: How to Protect Them From Disclosure,* 5 Toxics L. Rep. (BNA) 1211 (1991).

It is very difficult to establish the attorney-client privilege in an environmental assessment context. *See, e.g.,* United States v. Chevron U.S.A., Inc., No. 88-6681, 1989 U.S. Dist. LEXIS 12267 (E.D. Pa. Oct. 16, 1989), *cited in Courts Require Disclosure of Environmental Audits,* ENVTL. MANAGER, Mar. 1993, at 8 (holding that an audit must be disclosed even though an attorney was present because it was not shown that the attorney was present in his capacity as an attorney rather than simply as a business advisor).

In an extensive article detailing the criminal implications of environmental law, Daniel Riesel clearly spells out his view on the limitations of attorney-client privilege, concluding that "[o]nly where counsel conducts an audit to assist him in the defense of a specific case would it appear that the audit is safe from disclosure pursuant to a subpoena duces tecum." Daniel Riesel, *Criminal Prosecution and the Regulation of the Environment,* 1991 ALI/ABA COURSE OF STUDY — ENVTL. L. 375, 379, 421-23. Prosecutors argue that the attorney-client privilege is narrowly construed. Riesel further notes that

> [s]ince the doctrine only applies to legal advice and not to underlying facts, it is contended by the government that the doctrine does not apply to the data on which audits are based or to the fact that management was aware of such data. Thus, the government argues that the privilege should not be considered an umbrella to cover all the information that an attorney acquires in the course of his representation. If the audit was prepared by or for management and is simply transmitted to counsel, it is clear that the doctrine does not apply. Moreover, to the extent that the au-

dit identifies ongoing violations, the audit arguably is evidence of an on-going crime and thus loses any protection that it might otherwise have.

Id. at 422-23 (citations omitted).

72. Bennett et al., *supra* note 68, at 132 (citing John Doe Corp. v. United States, 675 F.2d 482 (2d Cir. 1982)). In Georgia Pac. Corp. v. GAF Roofing Mfg. Corp., No. 93 Civ. 5125 (RPP), slip op. (S.D.N.Y. June 25, 1996), the district court refused to allow attorney-client privilege with respect to an in-house environmental counsel's recommendations to his management as to (a) how environmental provisions could or should be changed, (b) how the changes would affect the transaction, and (c) whether he made a recommendation to management that they consider other options for the indemnification provisions in the agreement. The court held that this advice was in essence business advice in connection with negotiation rather than strictly legal advice. The court's conclusion was that the counsel was acting as "a negotiator on behalf of management" and "was acting in his business capacity." Georgia Pac. Corp., No. 93 Civ. 5125 (RPP), slip op. at 9. It was also relevant to the court that his advice was in the context of a business transaction and not in litigation.

73. *See supra* text page 24.

74. ARK. CODE ANN. §8-1-301; IDAHO CODE §33-530 (1995); MINN. STAT. §116.02; MISS. CODE ANN. §49-2-51; TEX. HEALTH & SAFETY CODE ANN. §361-601 (West 1995); UTAH CODE ANN. §19-7-101; WYO. STAT. §35-11-1105-06.

According to Gerry Block, the audit privilege many industry representatives desire mirrors those available in Colorado, Indiana, Kentucky, and Oregon, which generally contain the following provisions:

- An "audit" includes the primary report, memos analyzing portions of the report, and implementation plans that result from the report.

- These materials are not discoverable or admissible in evidence in civil or criminal proceedings, unless a court determines, during an *in camera* proceeding, that

> (1) the company has asserted the privilege for a fraudulent purpose;
>
> (2) the materials are not subject to the privilege; or
>
> (3) the company did not respond properly to any noncompliance identified by the audit.

- These materials are discoverable and admissible in evidence if:

> (1) the company has waived its privilege;
>
> (2) the materials were required by law anyway;
>
> (3) the materials were based upon observation, sampling, or monitoring of any regulatory agency; or

> (4) the materials were obtained from a source independent of
> the environmental audit.

> • In a criminal proceeding, the privilege is qualified, and audit mate-
> rial is available to a prosecutor who shows compelling need for the in-
> formation because the information is not otherwise available or cannot
> be obtained without unreasonable cost or delay.

Joseph G. Block, Testimony at EPA Public Meeting on Auditing Policy 10-11 (July 28, 1994) [hereinafter Block Testimony]. This testimony was made at a two-day public meeting on auditing in Washington, D.C. The comments at this meeting and all comments and correspondence submitted to EPA from outside parties are available to the public and contained in EPA's Auditing Policy Docket.

75. House bill H.R. 1047, 141 Cong. Rec. H12223 (daily ed. Feb. 24, 1995), introduced by Rep. Joel Hefley (R-Colo.), would have created an evidentiary privilege for "good-faith" voluntary audits. The privilege would not apply under several circumstances: (1) if the privilege is *expressly* waived; (2) if the audit report indicates violation of a federal law, and compliance efforts are not initiated "within a reasonable time"; (3) if there are "compelling circumstances"; (4) if the privilege is issued for a fraudulent purpose; or (5) if the audit report was prepared to avoid disclosure of information otherwise required by an investigation or an administrative or judicial proceeding. This bill would also have created a rebuttable presumption of immunity from civil and criminal penalties arising from voluntary disclosures of violations made pursuant to a voluntary environmental audit. Special Committee on Corporate Counsel, *1995 Annual Report, in* ABA Section of Natural Resources, Energy and Environmental Law, 1995 The Year in Review 377, 378 (contributed by Gary Rovner and edited by Pamela A. Lacey, with assistance from Frank B. Friedman, Charlotte H. Copperthite, and Paul W. Herring).

Senate bill S. 582, 141 Cong. Rec. S4262-73 (daily ed. Mar. 21, 1995), introduced by Sen. Mark Hatfield (R-Or.), had several similar provisions and would have achieved many of the same results.

The Senate bill

> would create an evidentiary privilege for any voluntarily produced environmental self-audit. The privilege would be unavailable in instances of fraud, where the privilege holder expressly waives the privilege, or where the audit indicates noncompliance and the violation is not remedied within a reasonable time after discovery. Unlike H.R 1047, however, the Senate bill would not circumvent the privilege where "compelling circumstances" are present. This ambiguous exception in the House bill threatens to swallow the privilege.

Id.

76. *See* 60 Fed. Reg. at 66710 and 65 Fed. Reg. at 19623-24.

77. *See State Audit Privilege Laws Must Uphold Minimum Federal Standards, EPA Official Says*, 27 Env't Rep. (BNA) 1043 (Sept. 13, 1996).

78. *EPA Weighs Blocking Air Permit Delegation to States With Audit Laws,* ENVTL. POL'Y ALERT, Mar. 27, 1996, at 16; *State Privilege-Immunity Laws for Audits Could Hurt Program Delegation, Official Says,* 26 Env't Rep. (BNA) 2253 (Mar. 29, 1996).

79. *EPA to Okay Interim Permit Programs Despite Audit Privilege Laws,* ENVTL. POL'Y ALERT, Apr. 10, 1996, at 15.

80. This policy was established in EPA's first policy on environmental auditing. Environmental Auditing Policy Statement, 51 Fed. Reg. 25004, 25007 (July 9, 1986) (reproduced in Appendix B). It was reaffirmed in EPA's 1995 final policy statement, 60 Fed. Reg. at 66708 and in its revised final policy, 65 Fed. Reg. at 19620 (reproduced in Appendix H).

81. 60 Fed. Reg. at 66711 and 65 Fed. Reg. at 19620.

82. 51 Fed. Reg. at 25007.

83. *Id.* Note also the Joint Explanatory Statement of the Committee of Conference on the CAA Amendments of 1990:

> Nothing in subsection 113(c) is intended to discourage owners or operators of sources subject to this Act from conducting self-evaluations or self-audits and acting to correct any problems identified. On the contrary, the environmental benefits from such review and prompt corrective action are substantial and section 113 should be read to encourage self-evaluation and self-audits.
>
> Owners and operators of sources are in the best position to identify deficiencies and correct them, and should be encouraged to adopt procedures where internal compliance audits are performed and management is informed. Such internal audits will improve the owners' and operators' ability to identify and correct problems before, rather than after, government inspections and other enforcement actions are needed.
>
> The criminal penalties available under subsection 113(c) should not be applied in a situation where a person, acting in good faith, promptly reports the results of an audit and promptly acts to correct any deviation. Knowledge gained by an individual solely in conducting an audit or while attempting to correct any deficiencies identified in the audit or the audit report itself should not ordinarily form the basis of the intent which results in criminal penalties.

H.R. REP. NO. 952, 101st Cong. 348 (1990).

This federal forbearance may not extend to citizen group litigation or litigation between potentially responsible parties in Superfund or related litigation. Under Superfund, potentially responsible parties include: (1) the owner and operator of a vessel or facility; (2) any person who owned or operated any facility at the time of disposal of any hazardous substance; (3) transporters of hazardous substances; and (4) generators of hazardous substances. 42 U.S.C. §9607(a)(1)-(4); ELR STAT. CERCLA §107(a)(1)-(4).

84. 51 Fed. Reg. at 25007.

85. *But see supra* note 48.

86. 60 Fed. Reg. at 66708.

87. Block Testimony, *supra* note 74, at 10-11.

88. *Final EPA Policy on Voluntary Audits Draws Praise, Criticism From Attorneys*, 20 Chem. Reg. Rep. (BNA) 1251 (Jan. 26, 1996).

89. *See supra* text page 24.

90. Olin Chemical Corporation, for example, followed this approach.

91. *See generally* Friedman, *supra* note 6; Kent, *supra* note 6.

92. 58 Fed. Reg. at 65764.

93. 51 Fed. Reg. at 25008-09.

94. 60 Fed. Reg. at 66710-11.

95. *See supra* text page 24.

96. This policy is discussed in Chapter 2, Criminal Liability—A Key Concern for the Environmental Manager, and reproduced in Appendix C.

97. In re Caremark Int'l, Inc. Derivative Litig., No. 13670, 1996 WL 549894 (Del. Ch. Sept. 25, 1996). The court referred not only to auditing, but to factors closely resembling the compliance factors in the sentencing guidelines. *Id.* at *10.

98. *See supra* text page 267.

99. David J. Hayes, *The Business Risk Audit*, ENVTL. F., Nov./Dec. 1996, at 19.

100. *See Next Wave of Environmental Auditing Focuses on Systems and Root Causes*, 4 ENV'T, HEALTH & SAFETY MGMT., May 20, 1996, at 4. It should be noted, however, that some auditing proposals or guidelines contemplate auditing on an annual basis for all facilities. For example, the CERES Principles discussed in Chapter 5 imply that all facilities would need to be audited annually. This would divert needed resources to low-risk facilities at the expense of more productive audits at potentially high-risk facilities.

101. The following is adapted from Frank Friedman, *Environmental Auditing in the 1990s*, 1 ENVTL. AUDITOR 229 (1990); Frank Friedman, *Don't Sign the Valdez Principles*, ENVTL. F., Mar./Apr. 1990, at 32.

102. Daniel Riesel, *Criminal Prosecution and the Regulation of the Environment*, 1993 ALI/ABA COURSE OF STUDY—ENVTL. L. 565. Such audits "should have significant lawyer participation in the design, supervision and actual conduct of the audit." *Id.* In this instance, legal protection is particularly important and it is argued that "the employment of outside counsel takes the audit out of the scope of an ordinary business endeavor and transforms it into the gathering of facts to support the rendering of legal advice." *Id.* at 564.

103. OFFICE OF TECHNOLOGY ASSESSMENT, COMING CLEAN—SUPERFUND PROBLEMS CAN BE SOLVED, Option 25 (1989).

104. Because Ato is a chemical company only, all of our audits are done by corporate staff. The audit teams may, however, include environmental professionals from other facilities. The director of Health, Environment, and Safety Audits reported to me.

105. This is an area of major concern internationally. The certification process detailed in the ISO 14000 series is very murky. For a discussion of ISO 14000, see *supra*The ISO 14000 Series.

106. Information on this effort can be found at http://www.beac.org.

107. *Id.*

108. *Id.*

109. Board of Certified Safety Professionals, Code of Professional Conduct:

Purpose

This Code sets forth the principles and standards of professional conduct to be observed by holders of documents of certification conferred by the Board of Certified Safety Professionals.

Principles

Certificants shall, in their professional activities, sustain and advance the integrity, honor and prestige of the Safety Profession by:

1. Using their knowledge and skill for the enhancement of the safety and health of people and the protection of property and the environment.

2. Being honest and impartial, and serving the public, employees, employers and clients with fidelity.

3. Striving to increase their own competence and the prestige of the safety profession.

4. Avoiding circumstances where compromise of professional conduct or conflict of interest may arise.

Standards

Certificants shall:

1. Hold paramount the safety and health of people and the protection of property and the environment in performance of professional duties and exercise their obligation to advise employers, clients or appropriate authorities of danger to people, property or the environment.

2. Perform professional services and assignments only in areas of their competence.

3. Issue public statements only in an objective and truthful manner.

4. Act in professional matters for employers or clients as faithful agents or trustees.

5. Build their professional reputation on merit of service.

6. Strive for continuous self-development while participating in their chosen professional safety discipline.

Institute of Internal Auditors, Standards for the Professional Practice of Internal Auditing:

1. Assessors must be independent of the facilities and organizations they are assessing and be objective in performing the assessment.

2. Assessments shall be performed with proficiency and due professional care.

3. Assessments shall be conducted by personnel who have the relevant professional experience, technical knowledge and skills in the disciplines needed to perform the assessment.

4. The scope of the assessment shall encompass the examination and evaluation of the appropriateness, adequacy and effectiveness of the organization's management system and the quality of performance in carrying out assigned responsibilities.

5. Assessment work shall include planning of the assessment, examining and evaluating information, communicating results and following up to ascertain that appropriate action is taken on reported assessment findings.

6. Assessment programs shall include quality assurance elements for the evaluation of the conduct of assessments.

110. CAL. HEALTH & SAFETY CODE §§25570-25570.4 (Deering 1996), as implemented in CAL. ADMIN. CODE §§19030-19032.

111. *Id.*

112. *Id.*

113. Unfortunately, some proposed legislation could give life to the environmental manager's worst nightmare. New Jersey proposed a program to examine and certify environmental auditors and to require industrial establishments to be audited annually by a certified auditor. Delaware considered requiring companies and those that are held out as auditors to pass tests and certain certification proceedings.

114. Jacobellis v. Ohio, 378 U.S. 184, 197 (1964).

115. *See* CERES Principles, *supra* Chapter 5, not 4.

116. *ASTM Environmental Committee OK's Innocent Landowner Standard*, INSIDE EPA SUPERFUND REP., Nov. 18, 1992, at 27. ASTM is now close to adopting a more general environmental auditing standard.

117. Keith M. Casto, *International Environmental Auditing and Site Assessment*, 1 OCCUPATIONAL & ENVTL. HEALTH 158, 184 (1995). This article contains a detailed analysis of these standards. *Id.* at 185-95.

118. Available from GEMI, One Thomas Cir., NW, 10th Fl., Washington DC 20005 (202) 296-7449, http://www.gemi.org.

119. ENV'T TODAY, July 20, 1992, at 3.

120. *See, e.g.,* OR. REV. STAT. §468,963 (1993); COLO. REV. STAT. 13-25-126.5 (1995).

121. *See* Skove, *supra* note 49.

122. *See* MICH. COMP. LAWS §§324.01-.90106 (adding part 148).

123. *See* 1996 S.C. ACTS 384.

124. The North Carolina Department of Environmental Health and Natural Resources issued its policy on September 1, 1995, and Oklahoma's Department of Environmental Quality issued its policy on January 23, 1995. The Washington State Department of Ecology's policy became effective December 20, 1994.

125. See detailed list in ENVIRONMENTAL AUDIT TASK FORCE, ABA NAT. RESOURCES, ENERGY, AND ENVTL. L. SEC., ANNUAL REPORT 198 (1997) [hereinafter ENVIRONMENTAL AUDIT TASK FORCE].

126. ABA SPECIAL COMM. ON ENVTL. AUDITS NEWSL., Mar. 1999, at 2-3.

127. EPA, Memo on Addressing State Audit, Immunity Laws and Legislation (Nov. 10, 1997), *cited in* ENVIRONMENTAL AUDIT TASK FORCE, *supra* note 125. *See also* Nancy K. Stoner & Wendy J. Miller, *National Conference of State Legislatures Study Finds That State Environmental Audit Laws Have No Impact on Company Self-Auditing and Disclosure of Violations*, 29 ELR 10265 (May 1999).

128. For a detailed analysis, see ENVIRONMENTAL AUDIT TASK FORCE, *supra* note 125.

129. *Id.*

130. 51 Fed. Reg. at 25004.

131. 60 Fed. Reg. at 66706 and 65 Fed. Reg. at 19617. For a discussion of the wisdom of whether to disclose or not to disclose violations under this policy, see Channing J. Martin, *Voluntary Disclosure of Environmental Violations: Is Mea Culpa a Good Idea or a Bad Move?*, 32 ELR 10692 (June 2002).

132. 51 Fed. Reg. at 25004.

133. EPA states that it will not mandate auditing, but the Agency may require auditing as part of a settlement. EPA notes that it is developing guidance for structuring appropriate environmental audit provisions for use in settlement negotiations and consent decrees. *Id.* at 25007. According to the policy, auditing is most likely to be mandated when a pattern of violations can be attributed to the absence of or poor results from an environmental management system or when the type or nature of violations indicates that similar problems may exist or occur. *Id.*

134. The following discussion of the EPA Final Disclosure and Audit Policy is adapted in part from Special Committee on Corporate Counsel, *supra* note 75, at 377-78. Copyright © 1996 by the American Bar Association. All Rights Reserved. Reprinted by permission.

135. 60 Fed. Reg. at 66710.

136. ENVIRONMENTAL AUDIT TASK FORCE, *supra* note 125, at 200.

137. EPA, ENFORCEMENT AND COMPLIANCE ASSURANCE FY98 ACCOMPLISH-MENTS REPORT 4 (June 1999) http://www.epa.gov/oeca/fy98accomp.pdf.

138. 65 Fed. Reg. at 19619.

139. *See* U.S. EPA, *FY 2004 End of Year Enforcement & Compliance Assurance Results* (Nov. 15, 2004), *available at* http://www.epa.gov/compliance/resources/reports/endofyear/eoy2004/fyo4results.pdf (last visited Sept. 14, 2005).

140. *See* http://es.epa.gov/oeca/main/2001eoy/2001numbers.html (last visited Apr. 20, 2002).

141. 60 Fed. Reg. at 66707 and 65 Fed. Reg. at 19617; Special Committee on Corporate Counsel, *supra* note 75, at 377-78.

142. 60 Fed. Reg. at 66711 (emphasis added).

143. *See Final EPA Policy on Voluntary Audits Draws Praise, Criticism From Attorneys*, 20 Chem. Reg. Rep. (BNA) 1251 (Jan. 26, 1996).

144. James T. Banks, *EPA's New Enforcement Policy: At Last, a Reliable Roadmap to Civil Penalty Mitigation for Self-Disclosed Violations*, 26 ELR 10227, 10234 (May 1996). This article does an excellent job of describing and analyzing the policy in detail.

145. *EPA Enforcement Office Targets Companies With Recurring Violations*, ENVTL. POL'Y ALERT, Jan. 31, 1996, at 39.

146. In re Harmon Electronics, RCRA No. 94-4 (EPA Envtl. Appeals Bd. May 1, 1996) (discussed in *EAB Hears Arguments in Audit Policy Case; Company Argues Actions Merit Penalty Decrease*, 27 Env't Rep. (BNA) 232-33 (May 10, 1996)).

147. *EPA Scraps Title of Inflammatory "National Violators" Enforcement Initiative,* INSIDE EPA, Oct. 11, 1996, at 1.

148. 60 Fed. Reg. at 66712.

149. *See, e.g.,* James Stewart, *Environmental Audits and Voluntary Disclosure Issues*, 25th Annual Conference, ABA SEC. NAT. RESOURCES, ENERGY & ENVTL. L., Keystone, Colo., Mar. 21-24, 1996, at tab 4 (citing United States v. Conservation Chem. Co., 619 F. Supp. 162, 192-193 (W.D. Mo. 1985).

150. *Id.* (quoting *Conservation Chem. Co.*, 619 F. Supp. at 194).

151. *Id.*

152. 60 Fed. Reg. at 66710-11.

153. 65 Fed. Reg. at 19621.

154. Evaluation of "Incentives for Self-Policing: Discovery, Disclosure, Correction and Prevention of Violations" Policy Statement, 64 Fed. Reg. 26745 (1999) (revisions proposed May 17, 1999).

155. *Id.* at 26752.

156. 65 Fed. Reg. at 19617.

157. *Id.* at 19622.

158. 65 Fed. Reg. 46498 (July 28, 2000).

159. For a general discussion and description of the various international proposals, see Ridgway M. Hall Jr. & Kristine A. Tockman, *International Corporate Environmental Compliance and Auditing Programs*, 25 ELR 10395 (Aug. 1995). *See also* Jennifer Nash & John Ehrenfeld, *Going Green*, Env't, Jan./Feb. 1996, at 16.

160. *See generally* Gerardo & Wasserman, Closing Remarks, *in Proceedings of the Second International Conference on Environmental Enforcement*, Hungary, Sept. 22-23, 1992.

161. The British Standard is available from the British Standards Institute, Two Park St., London, UK W1A 2BS.

162. *BS 7790 Moves Closer to Official Acceptance by EU; ISO 14000 With "Bridge" Not Far Behind*, Envtl. Sys. Update, Feb. 1995, at 1.

163. For a detailed analysis of the regulation, see Rod Hunter & Koen Muylle, European Community Deskbook, 2nd Edition (1999) [hereinafter EC Deskbook].

164. Council Regulation 1836/93 of June 1993 allowing voluntary participation by companies in the industrial sector in a Community eco-management and audit scheme, O.J. L 168/1 (July 10, 1993), Annex I (available in EC Deskbook, *supra* note 163, at 158).

165. There have been proposals to address the qualifications of those who will serve as verifiers. *See* Baillie & Wilkinson, Accreditation of Environmental Verifiers in the Framework of the Proposed Eco-Audit Scheme (Institute for European Environmental Policy, 1992).

166. EC Deskbook, *supra* note 163, at 154.

167. *Id.*

168. *Id.* at 165-66.

169. Keith M. Casto, *International Environmental Auditing and Site Assessment*, 1 Occupational & Envtl. Health, Apr./June 1995, at 179.

170. 42 U.S.C. §11012, ELR Stat. EPCRA §312.

171. Casto, *supra* note 137.

172. *Id.*

173. *See id.*

174. For a detailed analysis of the entire ISO 14000 program, see JOSEPH CASCIO, THE ISO 14000 HANDBOOK (1996) (published by CEEM Information Services).

175. Some of the SAGE work groups began to develop drafts of standards. The American National Standards Institute, representing the United States in this matter, viewed this as beyond the scope of SAGE's mandate and protested. *Global EHS Standards Setting Gets Political*, ENV'T, HEALTH & SAFETY MGMT., Oct. 12, 1992, at 2.

176. *Chemical Companies See Beneficial Results From ISO 9000 Registration*, CHEMICAL ENGINEERING NEWS, Apr. 25, 1994, at 10, 18-20.

177. *See* 20 Chem. Reg. Rep. (BNA) 1397 (Mar. 8, 1996).

178. *See* http://www.ISO14000.com (last visited Sept. 14, 2005).

179. *Id.*

180. *Id.*

181. Christopher L. Bell, *ISO 14001: Application of International Environmental Management System Standards in the United States*, 25 ELR 10678, 10680 (Dec. 1995). *See also ISO 14001: Potential Impacts on Environmental Practices of U.S. Companies, in* SHEARMAN & STERLING CLIENT PUBLICATIONS (First Quarter 1996).

182. Joe Cascio, *They Will Be Used for Good Reason, in ISO 14001: Performance Through Systems*, ENVTL. F., Nov./Dec. 1995, at 36, 38.

183. Bell, *supra* note 181, at 10681. For a detailed analysis and guide to implementing ISO 14001, see NICHOLAS P. CHEREMISINOFF & AVROM BENDAVID-VAL, GREEN PROFITS—THE MANAGER'S HANDBOOK FOR ISO 14001 AND POLLUTION PREVENTION (2001).

184. *See* Anne Marie Warris, Briefing note on the revision of ISO 14001:1996 to ISO DIS 14001:2003, prepared for Lloyd's Registry Quality Assurance, *available at* http://www.iso14000.com (last visited Sept. 14, 2005). *See also* M. JOEL BOLSTEIN, INNOVATION, MANAGEMENT SYSTEMS AND TRADING, 2004 ANNUAL REPORT, THE YEAR IN REVIEW 2004, ABA SECTION OF ENVIRONMENT, ENERGY, AND RESOURCES LAW (2005), at 366-367.

185. *See* BUS. AND THE ENV'T, Feb. 2005.

186. *See* Bell, *supra* note 181.

187. Gareth Porter, *Little Effect on Environmental Performance in ISO 14001: Performance Through Systems?*, ENVTL. F., Nov./Dec. 1995, at 36, 43 [hereinafter *ISO 14001*].

188. *Id.* These groups doubt that ISO 14001 will actually influence either the company's willingness or capacity to prevent pollution. *See* MANAGING A BETTER ENVIRONMENT: OPPORTUNITIES AND OBSTACLES FOR ISO 14001 IN PUBLIC POLICY AND COMMERCE (Pacific Inst. 2000); *Study Says 14001 Lags as a Vehicle for Public Policy*, ISO 14000 UPDATE, Apr. 2000, at 1.

189. David J. Freeman, *Standards Will Be Used—With Qualifications*, in *ISO 14001*, *supra* note 187, at 41.

190. *Id.*

191. Laurent Hourcle & Frederick J. Lees, *Applicability of ISO 14000 Standards to Government Contracts*, 27 ELR 10071 (Feb. 1997).

192. 62 Fed. Reg. 3036 (Jan. 21, 1997).

193. *See* Third Public Report—Drivers, Designs and Consequences of Environmental Management Systems, Mar. 12, 2001, *available at* http://ndems.crs.unc/edu/documents/consortium/exec.sum.pdf.

194. Ira Feldman, *Escape From Command and Control in ISO 14001*, *supra* note 187, at 39.

195. *Should We or Shouldn't We? An ADL 14001 Checklist*, 4 Env't, Health & Safety Mgmt., Apr. 8, 1996, at 3-4 [hereinafter *Should We or Shouldn't We?*].

196. Bell, *supra* note 181, at 10683.

197. For a detailed look at certification programs including ISO 14001, Responsible Care, and the American Forest and Paper Association's Sustainable Forestry Initiative, see Errol E. Meidinger, *Environmental Certification Programs and U.S. Environmental Law: Closer Than You May Think*, 31 ELR 10162 (Feb. 2001).

198. Ira Feldman & Douglas Weinfield, *EMS Roundup: Understanding the Emergence of Environmental Management Systems*, Trends, Jan./Feb. 2002, at 1.

199. *EMAS Languishes Ahead of Revision Due in the Fall*, ISO 14001 Update, June 2000, at 1.

200. *No Link Between Management Systems and Performance*, ISO 14001 Update, Jan. 2001, at 1.

201. *See* http://www.napawash.org/napa/epafile02.pdf (last visited Apr. 20, 2002).

202. *ISO 14001-Registered Facilities Are Profiled in the U.S.*, ISO 14001 Update, Aug. 2000, at 3.

203. *Baseline Report Completed for U.S. Facilities in Test Program*, ISO 14001 Update, June 2000, at 3.

204. Lorna J. Midgelow, *ISO 14001: A Status Review*, Envtl. Mgmt., Dec. 2001, at 16, 17-18.

205. Richard MacLean & Frank Friedman, *Green Arthritis*, Envtl. F., Nov./Dec. 2000, at 36, 47.

206. *Id.*

207. Christopher Bell, *How Does an ISO 14001 EMS Manage Compliance? U.S. Delegate Examines Legal Requirements of ISO 14001*, Int'l Envtl. Sys. Update (CEEM Inc., Reston, Va.), Mar. 1999, at 15.

208. *Should We or Shouldn't We?*, *supra* note 195, at 3-4. *See also* John S. Wilson

& RONALD A.N. MCLEAN, ISO 14001: IS IT FOR YOU? 27 (A.D. Little, First Quarter 1996); Carey A. Matthews, *The ISO 14001 Environmental Management Standard: An Innovative Approach to Environmental Protection*, 2 ENVTL. LAW. 817 (June 1996).

209. *Should We or Shouldn't We?*, *supra* note 195.

210. Communication from Joseph Cascio, former head of U.S. TAG (Mar. 25, 2005). *See also ISO 14001 Certification Numbers Up Worldwide*, BUS. & ENV'T, Nov. 2005, at 13. For the availability of the latest numbers see the ISO website on the Internet at http://www.iso.org.

211.Polly T. Strife, *Questioning ISO's Benefits for Leaders*, ENVTL. F., Jan./Feb. 1996, at 9.

212. *Id.*

213. *See* Carol Ehrle, *The Green Passport: If You Liked ISO 9000, You'll Love What's Coming Next*, RESOURCES, Jan. 1995, at 3. There are still questions as to many of the standards. *See Standards Under Development*, FOCUS ON 14000, Feb. 4, 1997, at 10-11.

214. John Connor & Robert W. Niemi, *ISO 14001 at Ford: Certification and Beyond*, ENVTL. MGMT., Dec. 2001, at 24.

215. *Id.* at 26.

216. *Id.*

217. *Id.* at 27.

218. *Id.* at 26.

Chapter 7:
Review of Acquisitions

Mergers and acquisitions have always been a critical issue for environmental managers. The growth in this area in recent years has been phenomenal. Some have stated that it reminds them of the mythical rapacious corporation entitled "Engulf and Devour"in Mel Brooks' film *Silent Movie*. This chapter deals primarily with some of the liability exposure issues in such combinations, but mergers and acquisitions test all of the management skills discussed in this book, including common sense. If you are told, for example, that a facility doesn't have groundwater problems, yet has been using solvents for the past 70 years, you should be inquisitive. If there is a lack of good management systems and clear lines of reporting, there are strong possibilities of liability exposure. There may be significant environmental issues, which perhaps even the company is not aware of. The dynamics of the deal and the credibility of the people may be just as important as the traditional "due diligence."

There are many pressures on the deal. Merger and acquisition proposals have a high failure rate. Even fewer are additive to shareholder value. "Only 17% of the major deals made during 1996-1998 increased shareholder value. In fact a study by KPMG International showed that 53% of 700 deals actually reduced shareholder value."[1] Do these failures show up immediately or on someone else's watch? Does the time span for the deal allow for intense review and can strong consultants, either inside or outside, limit the lack of intense review? Have consultants or in-house staff come in with too low a number because they don't want to kill a deal? Conversely, have inside people been too conservative in their numbers? Is there any real answer to "the Chairman or the CEO wants the deal?" If it is an international deal, how do you overcome cultural barriers? There is either an irrational fear of American laws or total disbelief in many cases. Environmental management systems will allow improved understanding of risk, but many companies are so decentralized that major risk decisions are made at too low a

349

level. These are just a few of the factors that go beyond the issues of "due diligence." Another is the "Green Arthritis" syndrome, which is discussed in Chapter 12, which assumes that today environmental progress has become ossified and environmental managers are afraid to take chances.

Another area that is usually not fully considered in the merger and acquisition area is the people. Sometimes the environmental manager does not have control over personnel decisions. Many times, however, the challenge is in merging divergent cultures. New blood often is very useful in your own organization—breaking up the mind set that we have always done it this way, and we will continue to do it this way. At the earliest possible time I have always met with my counterparts in the organization being acquired to work on a smooth transition and build allies. This is very critical for a smooth and seamless transition. The people are a resource along with the customers and facilities. This value is not often recognized since much of the justification of mergers is cost reduction and synergy which means staff reductions. Sometimes these decisions are made "by the numbers" rather than through a close look at needs and business objectives. As noted by Dick MacLean: "Don't assume that the deal makers understand the nuances of EHS. They may view EHS as just another service function and apply this logic to the restructurings. If anything, this is encouraged by the management consultant brought in to work out the details."[2]

The following discussion, which focuses on the technical and legal aspects of reviewing mergers and acquisitions, is not all-inclusive. It should, however, along with other material referenced, make you aware of the primary issues of concern. If you are inexperienced, get help. If you are experienced, don't assume that you have seen it all.

As stated previously, reviewing acquisitions is one of the most important responsibilities of today's environmental managers and environmental counsel. Sellers, purchasers, and lenders must be aware of potential environmental liability arising from these transactions. Both managers and lawyers put their jobs on the line in estimating the environmental exposure of acquisitions.

For example, the scope of liability for past disposal actions is extremely broad, and the current owner of a facility from which there is a release or threat of release is strictly liable without regard to causation.[3] The determination of "owner" or "operator" is also extremely broad, in some cases vitiating traditional concepts of corporate liability. There is no clear definition of these terms under either CERCLA[4] or RCRA.[5] One federal court of appeals decision held that a corporate officer could not be found liable under CERCLA unless the plaintiff could show, using the traditional corporate veil protection, that the named individuals were the alter ego for the corporation.[6] This ruling came even though EPA had filed an *amicus curiae* brief urging a contrary determination. Some courts, however, have adopted the Agency's position.[7]

Although CERCLA exempts secured creditors from owner/operator liability, financial institutions must be wary in their transactions because this exemption is limited.[8] Thus, lenders who foreclose on property do so at their own peril.[9] If a bank forecloses on a property, it could be considered in a "contractual relationship, existing directly or indirectly with the defendant" under CERCLA §107(b)(3).[10] The lender who forecloses may become an "owner or operator" subject to CERCLA liability.[11]

In *United States v. Fleet Factors Corp.*,[12] the Eleventh Circuit ruled that a secured creditor is liable under CERCLA if its involvement with the management of the facility is sufficiently broad to support the inference that it could affect hazardous waste disposal decisions. The court held that "a secured creditor may incur CERCLA liability by participating in the financial management of a facility to a degree indicating a capacity to influence the corporation's treatment of hazardous wastes."[13]

On April 29, 1992, EPA published a rule attempting to limit the *Fleet Factors* decision as to the range of activities that a secured party may undertake without being considered an owner or operator for purposes of CERCLA liability.[14] EPA's lender liability rule did not consider the pre-foreclosure policing and workout activities listed in Figure 7-1 to be "management."

Figure 7-1
Pre-Foreclosure Policing and Workout Activities Not Considered to Be "Management" Under EPA's Lender Liability Rule

- Requiring the borrower to clean up the facility prior to or during the life of the loan;
- Requiring compliance with applicable federal, state, and local environmental rules and regulations during the life of the loan;
- Securing or exercising authority to monitor or inspect the property, borrower's business or financial condition, or both; and
- Other requirements by which the lender is adequately able to police the loan, provided that the exercise by the lender of such other loan policing activities is not considered evidence of management participation under the "general test."[15]

The rule defined the workout activities listed in Figure 7-2 as not being considered participation in "management."

Figure 7-2
Workout Activities Not Considered to Be Participation in
"Management" Under EPA's Lender Liability Rule

- Restructuring or renegotiating the terms of the security interest;
- Requiring payment of additional rent or interest;
- Exercising forbearance;
- Requiring or exercising rights pursuant to an assignment of accounts;
- Requiring or exercising rights pursuant to an escrow agreement pertaining to amounts owing to an obligor;
- Providing specific or general financial or other advice, suggestions, counseling, or guidance; and
- Exercising any right or remedy the lender is entitled to by law or under any warranties, covenants, conditions, representations, or promises from the borrower.[16]

The lender liability rule remained subject to much uncertainty. In 1994, the D.C. Circuit in *Kelley v. U.S. Environmental Protection Agency* vacated EPA's lender liability rule, holding that EPA lacked congressional authority to interpret liability issues under CERCLA.[17] As a result, lenders are no longer "shielded from being held liable for engaging in workout or foreclosure activities. . . . The D.C. Circuit's vacatur of EPA's lender liability rule . . . has thrown the issue of what it means to hold a security interest 'without participating in management' back into confusion."[18] On December 11, 1995, EPA issued a policy memorandum regarding the enforcement of CERCLA against lenders and government entities that acquire property involuntarily.[19] EPA announced its decision to apply as guidance the lender liability rule promulgated in 1992[20] and vacated by the D.C. Circuit in 1994. On September 30, 1996, as part of banking reform legislation, CERCLA was revised to provide additional protection for lenders. The Asset Conservation, Lender Liability, and Deposit Insurance Protection Act of 1996 amended CERCLA to exclude lenders from the definition of "owner or operator" "so long as the lender does not 'participate in the management' of the property prior to foreclosure."[21]

Review of acquisitions is also important to the extent that once acquired, contaminated property may be difficult to unload. For example, in a bankruptcy proceeding, the trustee cannot use §544(a) of the Bankruptcy Code to abandon a hazardous waste site in contravention of a state statute or regulation that is reasonably designed to protect public health and safety from identified hazards.[22] Moreover, 49 states have enacted statutes authorizing them to require cleanup of sites contaminated with hazardous waste, and these requirements must be reviewed before selling or purchasing contaminated property.[23]

Scope and Structure of Review

It is beyond the scope of this book to discuss in detail all of the elements of a site review. The checklist included as Appendix G will give you some indication of how to define the scope of such a review. In addition, several critical items warrant particular consideration.[24]

Before acquiring any property or facilities, or any company that owns property or facilities, it is critical to conduct physical assessments of all sites where present or past operations could conceivably have caused environmental contamination. If you are acquiring a company, you should assess each facility it owns; each facility it leases or operates; and, if possible, each facility it has owned, leased, or operated in the past. These assessments are essential to identify potential liabilities under CERCLA, RCRA, and other federal and state laws. It is also useful to examine past and present tolling operations.

The assessment process should start as early in the acquisition process as possible to ensure completeness. You obviously have to consider the sensitivities of the seller in pressing for time, but because you will rarely have the opportunity to perform on-site testing, you will need ample time for document search and inspection. There is no hard-and-fast rule on how much time is necessary; it depends on the nature of the transaction and the type of asset being purchased. If you are purchasing a facility that you suspect may have groundwater problems, you will want more time than if you are purchasing a piece of property that from time immemorial has been rural farmland (unless you suspect pesticide contamination). If the seller is a "deep pocket" and is prepared to indemnify you broadly from liability, the review can be more limited than if the seller has limited assets and the property has been used for industrial purposes since the beginning of the Industrial Revolution.

Although it is important to check permitting and other issues regarding air emissions and effluent discharges, the leveraging impacts will usually come from past waste disposal and potential groundwater contamination. If time and personnel constraints limit your ability to conduct physical site reviews, sites with potential liability exposure should have first priority.

It is particularly important to determine whether the site was included in the survey completed by former Rep. Bob Eckhardt during the Superfund debate, which required major chemical companies to list their disposal of potentially hazardous waste. It is also important to check with state and federal agencies to determine whether the site is listed, or is being considered for listing, as a site requiring cleanup.

Even if a site is not listed, you should ascertain whether it is covered by any of the various federal and state laws that require cleanup expenditures or otherwise affect the value of the property. For example, the 1984 amendments to RCRA provide that all RCRA permits, including those issued for storage units and for postclosure care, must require "corrective action for all releases of hazardous waste or constituents from any solid waste management unit at [the] . . . facility . . . regardless of the time at which waste was placed in such unit."[25] EPA has interpreted these provisions as establishing authority under RCRA to clean up virtually any contamination at a plant site. Further, EPA contends that its RCRA "interim status" authority extends to releases from solid as well as hazardous waste sites and that it can therefore issue cleanup orders even when an owner or operator closes a facility under interim status.

Moreover, in some states, particularly New Jersey, acquisition of a site where industrial activities have previously taken place triggers a variety of state actions.[26] State laws can also significantly affect property valuation. In California, for example, a site's value can change if the site is classified as a "hazardous waste property" or as a "border zone property" that is within 2,000 feet of "significant disposal of hazardous waste."[27]

Physical site assessments should be performed by experts, preferably both legal and technical. Experience and expertise are needed to judge whether a facility requires physical assessment and, if so, how that assessment should be conducted and what should be examined. Experience is particularly useful in reviewing documentation and interviewing; indeed, there is no substitute for experience in determining what has been intentionally or unintentionally omitted from a statement. If you use outside counsel for site assessments, it is advisable to use environmental counsel rather than real estate counsel.

In Ato's case, corporate staff usually conduct site visits when reviewing acquisitions of capital assets that include land or manufacturing facilities. It only occasionally uses consultants to assist in field evaluations. When purchasing facilities or whole operating companies, many companies give the potential acquisition a copy of its checklist before the "due diligence" meetings on environmental matters.

If you use outside counsel or consultants for site reviews, you should question them closely. Outside representatives sometimes tend to low ball exposure estimates for fear of killing deals. Similarly, in making your own estimates, you may be concerned about being the deal killer. The best way to handle this concern is to make your estimates based on best-, median-, and worst-case assumptions, documenting the bases for your positions. Any work in this area should be done through and at the request of the legal department to minimize public access to the analyses. Care must be taken to request "legal" advice rather than "business" advice from the legal department to protect this material.[28]

Whether or not you use outside representatives, it is *your* obligation either as a manager or as counsel to ensure that estimates are realistic. Your role is to make the best estimate possible. It is then up to the business managers to look at this exposure and determine whether it is out of line in relation to the rest of the deal. Avoiding realistic estimates of exposure does service to no one. You should also avoid making overly pessimistic estimates to protect yourself on a long-range basis. This kind of approach is not helpful to management, and your credibility is at stake.

Many international companies have purchased U.S. facilities without a sufficient understanding of the economic and political implications of U.S. laws and potential liability exposure. As with domestic purchasers, documentation of the basis for your opinion and/or the need for in-depth review is important for international acquisitions, especially if there is a tendency to downplay the leveraging impact of environmental issues.

Information Reviewed

Certain information should be obtained from the company or facility management before the actual visit. This includes general identifying information, such as facility name and location; a description of the principal operations; copies of all relevant environmental policies, procedures, and guidelines; and a list of all specific federal, state, and local environmental regulations, standards, and guidelines applicable to the facility's operations.

Actual site assessments should begin with reviews of all relevant records and permits. Although preliminary site assessments may be made early in the investigation, a final site assessment should not be undertaken until after completion of the document review. Environmental personnel should also be questioned closely on the scope of the documentation and about their personal knowledge. The files will often show judgments that are not necessarily the "official" views of the company or facility being acquired, and this information will be very helpful in making more realistic estimates of exposure. General limitations placed on file reviews should be viewed with suspicion.

If practical and appropriate, an assessment should also include sampling and analysis of groundwater, soil, physical structures, surface waters and sediment, ambient air, or specifically permitted emission sources. Companies are often reluctant to allow sampling for fear of legal exposure. If undertaken, however, sampling and analysis should not begin until the review of records and permits has been completed. These documents are essential aids in locating possibly contaminated areas on the property, and the location of these areas is a major factor in planning and executing the sampling and analysis program.

The following sections discuss some of the most important categories of information that should be reviewed prior to an acquisition: licenses and permits, regulatory history and current status, prior ownership and operations, potential off-site liabilities, and insurance coverage.[29]

Licenses and Permits

As previously stated, it is important to review and evaluate the licenses and permits required for or possessed by facilities, as well as any pending applications for environmental permits or licenses. The review must consider not only existing requirements, but impending or potential requirements as well. It should include federal and state permits (for example, permits required by RCRA or the FWPCA), state permits by rule (for example, permits involving underground injection wells, underground storage tanks, or pretreatment standards), and state or local permits required by the CAA.

In addition to identifying which permits exist or are required, you should consider whether their limitations are achievable and acceptable. Will permit limits allow expansions or modifications of operations and, if so, will more stringent parameters be imposed? What federal, state, or local hurdles exist? Can the permits be transferred or must the new owner or operator apply for new ones? Will grandfathering be lost by a change in ownership? What public notice, comment, and hearing procedures would apply? Are new permit programs likely to apply soon? Are "interim program permits" likely to become more stringent or costly in the future or to lapse altogether?

Regulatory History and Current Status

It is important to determine a facility's history of compliance with regulatory requirements. You should review the facility's management files, concentrating on the items listed in Figure 7-3.

Figure 7-3
Items to Focus on When Reviewing a Facility's History of
Compliance With Regulatory Requirements

- Any permit violations, with or without fines or penalties;
- Excursions above applicable parameters (for example, in monthly discharge monitoring reports);
- Discharges at or near the limit of daily maximums, monthly averages, or other restrictions;
- Good management practices (for example, is the facility well managed and run when compared to Department of Transportation, Mine Safety and Health Administration, or OSHA standards?[30] Or is it just fortunate that it has not been inspected?);
- Required programs (for example, are RCRA groundwater monitoring programs, OSH Act hazard communication programs, and Spill Prevention Control and Countermeasure Plans in place and well designed?);
- Orders, citations, notices of violation, or similar administrative actions;
- Civil or criminal actions filed against the company with respect to any facility not in compliance with regulations, standards, or permits;
- Threatened or contemplated enforcement actions;
- Compliance schedules, consent orders, judgments, waivers, or variances related to compliance with any environmental program; and
- Fines or penalties levied or paid for any of the above matters.

As a rule of thumb, this review should cover the facility's activities for at least the previous five years.

Information on the last federal, state, and local agency inspections that covered environmental matters should be reviewed, including the dates, the contents of any reports, the nature of any actions required of the company, and the current status of any such actions.

All applicable recordkeeping and reporting requirements should also be reviewed and compared to actual practice at the facility. The review should include the relevant documents listed above and all information on the current status of the facility's recordkeeping and reporting. Again, individual interviews should be encouraged because they sometimes supply leads that may not be found in the records. You should also consider the adequacy of the facility's records. If the records are questionable, how many other records and resulting problems exist that have not been identified?

You should also contact all regulatory authorities that have jurisdiction over the facility. Note that local regulations may be broad in scope and may be enforced by agencies that normally have limited jurisdiction, such as local fire departments. Although it is advisable to obtain as much information as possible from the relevant agencies, you will find that many sellers are sensitive about these inquiries. Sometimes the inquiries can trigger dormant controversies concerning compliance or accelerate agency action to resolve pending permitting issues. If the seller has told the agency that its funds are insufficient, the agency may attempt to get involved in the deal to ensure that its interests are protected.

In general, how do applicable regulatory authorities regard the facility? As a problem or as a good citizen? If as a problem, will the authorities be pleased to see new ownership? Or is the activity or operation per se unwelcome in that area? Will a new owner receive a clean slate? Finally, you should learn of any potential additional enforcement actions that could leverage the transaction.

Is the facility the object of attention from local citizen or environmental groups? If so, is it favorable or unfavorable? Have there been any citizen or employee complaints concerning environmental activities at the facility? (As a rule of thumb, you should investigate any such complaints made within the last 10 years.) What is their current status? Are movements afoot to close the facility or restrict its operations? Does the facility generate air or water emissions that expose the local population to potential health risks? If so, is there evidence that local public opinion is sensitive to the issue? In general, what is the facility's standing in its community?

The above discussion is not all-inclusive. The checklist in Appendix G suggests many other areas and types of data that can be included in the compliance history and current status review.

Prior Ownership and Operations

If the facility is or ever was used for operations that could have caused environmental contamination, it is important to reconstruct the past history of the site, including the chain of title. The history should determine what operations were performed at the site during each period, who performed those operations, and whether those parties owned, leased, or merely operated the site. This survey should seek both evidence of contamination and the identities of responsible companies. The companies may still exist, and could share responsibility for remedying the contamination. This can be particularly important in view of the growing trend toward requiring cleanup.[31]

The strict construction of the following language exempting an "innocent purchaser" from liability under CERCLA § 107(b) does little to alleviate prospective purchasers' concerns about cleanup responsibility.

> To establish that the defendant had no reason to know [of hazardous waste disposal on the property] . . . the defendant must have undertaken, at the time of acquisition, all appropriate inquiry into the previous ownership and uses of the property consistent with good commercial or customary practice in an effort to minimize liability. For purposes of the preceding sentence the court shall take into account any specialized knowledge or experience on the part of the defendant, the relationship of the purchase price to the value of the property if uncontaminated, commonly known or reasonably ascertainable information about the property, the obviousness of the presence or likely presence of contamination at the property, and the ability to detect such contamination by appropriate inspection.[32]

The statutory language dealing with "appropriate inquiry into the previous ownership and uses of the property consistent with good commercial or customary practice" creates a difficult burden on a landowner attempting to qualify for the innocent-purchaser exemption.[33] Given today's widespread recognition of the need to do environmental reviews of property acquisitions, will there be many—if any—cases where a buyer can qualify as an innocent purchaser without performing such an assessment? Roger Marzulla, a former DOJ Assistant Attorney General, analogized the DOJ's view on the scope of the exemption to Diogenes looking for an honest man: if you didn't find the alleged contamination, you didn't look hard enough, and if you did find it, then you are not subject to the exemption.

Often, however, very little of the evidence that you would like to have is available. You simply will not—and cannot—have engineering certainty in these transactions. At best, even with extensive site reviews, you are dealing with order-of-magnitude numbers. Your best insurance is to have either strong in-house staff or good consultants who know the general kind of business or site that you are buying and who can give you a range of exposure estimates. You may have a sketchy record of the businesses on the site at the turn of the century, for example, but just knowing the nature of those businesses tells you a lot about the kind of chemicals that were probably used. Coupled with general knowledge of disposal practices at that time, this information will give a range of exposure estimates. It has been my experience working with a staff that has a broad range of operating and environmental experience that once we know what is being produced and what was previously produced on a site, there is usually not much difference in the estimated ranges of exposure before and after complete site review.

Potential Off-Site Liabilities

Off-site liability is usually the area where environmental costs leverage transactions. Under RCRA and CERCLA, a facility (or its corporate or individual owner) may have liability at every site where its wastes were ever disposed. Thus, it is essential to compile as complete a list as possible of all the wastes ever generated at a site and of all the sites to which those wastes were shipped. Moreover, some nonwaste products, such as recyclable materials, electrical transformers, and certain pesticide manufacturing equipment, can lead to off-site RCRA or CERCLA liability. You should also look for records of these types of items and track them to their destinations. The historical review discussed previously can suggest possible off-site liabilities that may not yet have been discovered.

Sources of pertinent information include the facility's customer lists, billing files, shipping files, hazardous waste manifests, and federal and state hazardous waste manifest files obtained through the Freedom of Information Act[34] or its state equivalents. Customer lists and, more importantly, lists of "recyclers" and waste disposal sites should be reviewed carefully. Present or future Superfund sites may appear. Here, again, it is vital that you make your own judgment as to the scope of Superfund liability. Companies or facilities being acquired tend to low ball exposure estimates, so your judgment is critical.

Insurance Coverage

All of the company's or facility's past insurance policies should be compiled. If possible, any previous owner's insurance coverage should also be identified. Insurance coverage information is very important as possible mitigation for potential site contamination, toxic-tort, and off-site Superfund liabilities.

Unfortunately, most companies have very poor files on past insurance policies. Although the insurance companies, agents, and brokers should be consulted, their records may not be any better, and their potential liability may make them unwilling to cooperate. State and federal government files can help you identify required insurance coverages. Sometimes local attorneys or court files can provide clues to the identity of insurance companies providing past coverage.

Insurance policies that have been located should be analyzed for coverage, exclusions, limits, and terms ("claims made" versus "occurrence," for example). As much of a historical overview as possible should be constructed. As discussed below, insurance coverage can be an important risk-mitigation measure. Note as discussed previously,[35] there are a variety of insurance policies and products available that may also mitigate potential exposure.

Possible Risk-Mitigation Mechanisms

Depending on the particular circumstances of each case, including the nature of the potential liability, a number of mechanisms can be employed to reduce risks to some extent, or at least to spread them over more parties.

Structure of the Transaction

The way an acquisition is consummated can, in some cases, be tailored to reduce risks. For example, it may be possible to purchase only a company's physical assets. From an environmental risk standpoint, an asset purchase frequently is less risky than a stock purchase or a merger. In some states, however, a company that purchases another's assets and carries on its business is considered to have assumed its liabilities, just as with a stock purchase. In such instances, purchase of some, but not all, assets of a company may be less risky. Individual state laws must be consulted on this and related issues.

A variety of subsidiaries and related corporate structures can also reduce risk in some cases. For instance, "A" Corporation could spin off a division as "B" Corporation, a wholly owned subsidiary, for the purpose of acquiring "C" Corporation or a specific asset of "C" Corporation. These creative arrangements have pros and cons from both business and liability standpoints, and those factors should be considered in detail.

Contract Provisions

Contract clauses such as warranties, indemnifications, and specific allocations of future liabilities resulting from past activities or preexisting contamination should always be considered and, if appropriate, used in any acquisition or sale. Assuming they can be bargained for (and this is a major assumption), these contract clauses can provide 100-percent coverage against risks—but with two critical provisos. First, these types of contractual arrangements never bind the government and are unlikely to affect the rights of private third parties who may be injured. At most, these clauses give the party sued by the government or a private plaintiff an action over and against the other contracting party. Second, these clauses are only as good as the financial soundness of the other party. An ironclad, 100-percent indemnification by a defunct or insolvent company is worthless.

The following minimum provisions should be included among the representations and warranties.

• All required federal, state, and local permits directly concerning, or related to, environmental protection and regulation of the property have been secured and are current.

• The seller is now, and has been, in full compliance with such environmental permits, and any other requirements under any federal, state, or local law, regulation, or ordinance.[36]

• There are no pending actions against the seller under any environmental law, regulation, or ordinance, and the seller has not received notice in any form of such action or of a possible action.

• There are no past or current releases of hazardous substances on, over, at, from, into, or onto any facility at the property, as those terms are understood under CERCLA.

• The seller is not aware of any environmental condition, situation, or incident on, at, or concerning the property that possibly could give rise to an action or to liability under any law, rule, ordinance, or common-law theory.

Note that obtaining these representations may be difficult because a seller is bound to object to some of the warranties as questionable and/or overly broad.

Except when it is clear that the seller (or buyer, as the case may be) is judgment-proof, an effort should always be made to address environmental conditions and to apportion liability in the purchase agreement. The contract should also reference certain baseline conditions and the parties should develop an allocation scheme to deal with existing conditions. Sometimes such schemes are based on sliding scales over certain time periods (e.g., 5 or 10 years) and can also include caps on liability. Allocations can be difficult when in future proceedings, the seller claims that it is the buyer's operations that have caused the condition giving rise to indemnity claims. The line between past and present operations is not always clear, particularly if the same chemical processes are used.

Every acquisition should be accompanied by written representations by the seller and his or her attorneys and accountants concerning the condition of the property, the compliance status of the facility, and existing or threatened environmental litigation. These representations will form the basis of any necessary future discussions or negotiations about environmental liabilities. In extreme cases, the representations may also serve as a basis for voiding the transaction for fraud or misrepresentation.

All of these representations and warranties should survive closing, should consider possible statute-of-limitations concerns, and should be tied to an indemnification clause, with all resulting liability to seller. Note that the term "liability" should be defined. Sellers usually assume that liability applies only in a specific adjudication. It is likely, however, that a seller will demand that there be a specific time limit on any representations and warranties and will also limit that indemnification to existing laws and regulations. It is particularly important if you are a seller to limit any representation specifically to existing laws and regulations to avoid any future misunderstandings.

Prior Agreements With Regulatory Authorities

There may be cases in which, for business reasons, it is desirable to purchase a facility that is in some degree of difficulty with a regulatory authority. For example, the facility may be threatened with permit revocation or may be hopelessly behind schedule under a consent order. In such a case, an effort should be made before purchase to obtain agreements from the appropriate authorities that a new schedule will be set, that is, that the purchaser will have a fresh start with an achievable schedule. Similarly, if a site is already contaminated, an agreement could be sought outlining a cleanup plan that would satisfy the authorities.[37]

A regulatory authority may be flexible in these matters because the alternative often is that the seller goes out of business, leaving the government to deal with a contaminated site and eliminating a source of employment that is important to the locality. Even if no agreement can be reached, advance discussions with regulatory authorities are invaluable for letting the would-be buyer know what burdens it is assuming or that it will have a cooperative approach.[38]

Insurance Coverage

Finally, insurance can provide significant protection both against on- and off-site cleanup and toxic-tort liability. The purchasing company should have appropriate coverage with adequate limits. The acquired company's own insurance coverage, however, is almost equally as significant because occurrence-based policies can provide coverage for present or future liabilities when the occurrence (for example, an act of disposal or a manufacturing operation that caused site contamination or slowly developing personal injuries) happened years earlier under previous ownership. Past policies are especially important today because insurance is usually difficult to acquire, very expensive, and sold on a "claims-made" basis. Note that today there are some new insurance mechanisms that are available. They are combined with remediation guarantees that will take over liability for a guaranteed price. These options should also be explored.

Conclusion

In recent years buyers and sellers have become much more sophisticated in recognizing the importance of environmental issues in virtually every form of real estate transaction. In some cases, parties have taken the position that any form of potential contamination or permit issue will terminate the transaction. This is an extreme position. These issues are business risks. Acquisition review and contract negotiation are means of quantifying the risk. The final business decision should be made on the basis of knowing the scope of the risk and evaluating it as part of the overall decision.

Notes to Chapter 7

1. Richard MacLean, *Doing the Deal—Part 1: The High Stakes in Business Transactions*, ENVTL. MGMT., Sept. 2000, at 18. "Three out of every four deals fail to achieve either their strategic, financial, or operational objectives. So in essence, before you even begin, the odds are stacked against you." *Id.* (quoting David Greenspan, Executive Vice-president of management advisors Clemente, Greenspan & Co.).

2. Richard MacLean, *Merger Mania Math*, ENVTL. PROTECTION MAG., May 2005, at 12.

3. New York v. Shore Realty Corp., 759 F.2d 1032, 15 ELR 20358 (2d Cir. 1985) (holding that CERCLA imposes strict liability on the current owner of a facility from which there is a release or threat of release, regardless of causation); Missouri v. Independent Petrochemical Corp., 610 F. Supp. 4, 15 ELR 20161 (E.D. Mo. 1985) (liability for third-party disposal); *see also Second Circuit Ruling Spells Out Superfund Land Owners' Liabilities,* ENVTL. F., Sept. 1985, at 15; Alfred R. Light, *United States of America v. Thomas Jefferson IV et al.,* ENVTL. F., Sept. 1985, at 17 (presenting a very clever satire on the broad scope of liability allegedly arising from a "disposal" action by Thomas Jefferson).

4. 42 U.S.C. §§9601-9675, ELR STAT. CERCLA §§101-405.

5. *Id.* §§6901-6992k, ELR STAT. RCRA §§1001-11012.

6. Joslyn Mfg. Co. v. T.L. James & Co., 696 F. Supp. 222, 19 ELR 20518 (W.D. La. 1988), *aff'd*, 893 F.2d 80, 20 ELR 20382 (5th Cir. 1990). For a discussion of this case and a contrary determination of a district court, Kelley v. ARCO Indus. Corp., 723 F. Supp. 1214, 20 ELR 20264 (W.D. Mich. 1989), see JENNER & BLOCK L. NEWS, Winter 1990, at 9. *See also* Murhy & Samson, *Corporate Responsibility for Environmental Damages,* WHITE & CASE INSIGHTS, Apr. 1990, at 23; Dan Riesel, *Environmental Concerns of Real Estate and Business Transactions,* 1990 A.L.I./A.B.A. COURSE OF STUDY—ENVTL. L. 423, 440.

7. *See, e.g.,* United States v. Kayser-Roth Corp., 910 F.2d 24, 27, 20 ELR 21462, 21463 (1st Cir. 1990), *cert. denied,* 498 U.S. 1804 (1991).

8. CERCLA excludes from the definition of "owner or operator" any "person, who, without participating in the management of a . . . facility hold indicia of ownership primarily to protect his security interest in the . . . facility." 42 U.S.C. §9601(20)(A)(iii), ELR STAT. CERCLA §101(20)(A)(iii). The definition has been limited, however, to providing "financial assistance and general, and even isolated instances of specific, management advice to . . . debtors without risking CERCLA liability if the secured creditor does not participate in the day to day management of the business or facility either before or after the business ceases operation." United States v. Fleet Factors Corp., 724 F. Supp. 955, 19 ELR 20529 (S.D. Ga. 1988), *aff'd,* 901 F.2d 1550, 20 ELR 20832 (11th Cir. 1990), *cert. denied,* 498 U.S. 1046 (1991). This case is discussed in detail in Riesel, *supra* note 4, at 442-44.

9. For an excellent discussion of lender liability, see Edward B. Sears & Laurie P.

Sears, *Lender Liability Under CERCLA: Uncertain Times for Lenders*, 24 ELR 10320 (June 1994).

10. *See* United States v. Maryland Bank & Trust Co., 632 F. Supp. 573, 581, 16 ELR 20557, 20560 (D. Md. 1986) (third-party defense to CERCLA liability may apply to hold liable bank that held title to hazardous substances disposal facility after foreclosure sale).

11. *See* United States v. Mirabile, No. 84-2280, 15 ELR 20994 (E.D. Pa. Sept. 4, 1985).

12. 901 F.2d 1550, 20 ELR 20832 (11th Cir. 1990).

13. *Id.* at 1557-59, 20 ELR at 20835-36. *See also* Philip R. Sellinger & Avery S. Chapman, *EPA's Proposed Rule on Lender Liability Under CERCLA: No Panacea for the Financial Services Industry*, 21 ELR 10618, 10619 (Oct. 1991). On remand, the district court held that application of the participation-in-management test depends, in part, on whether the defendant met the standard of a reasonable, similarly situated secured creditor. The court found the lender at issue to be liable. *Fleet Factors*, 821 F. Supp. at 707, 23 ELR at 20961.

14. Lender Liability Under CERCLA, 57 Fed. Reg. 18344 (Apr. 29, 1992).

15. *Id.* at 18383.

16. *Id.*

17. Kelley v. U.S. Environmental Protection Agency, 15 F.3d 1100, 24 ELR 20511, *reh'g denied*, 25 F.3d 1088 (D.C. Cir. 1994), *cert. denied sub nom.* American Bankers Ass'n v. Kelley, 63 U.S.L.W. 3538 (U.S. Jan. 17, 1995).

18. Sears & Sears, *supra* note 7, 24 ELR at 10330, 10331.

19. 60 Fed. Reg. 63517 (Dec. 11, 1995).

20. 57 Fed. Reg. at 18344.

21. 42 U.S.C.A. §9601 (Supp. 1997); *Congress Amends Superfund to Provide Additional Liability Protection for Lenders and Fiduciaries*, CHADBORNE & PARKE MEMORANDUM (Oct. 1996). For a detailed analysis, see Baxter Dunaway & Andrew C. Cooper, *Environmental Law, In the Recently Passed Appropriations Bill, Congress Clarified When Lenders and Fiduciaries Are Liable Under CERCLA for Cleanup of Property Held as Collateral*, NAT'L L.J., Nov. 11, 1996, at B6-B7, and Maureen F. Leary, *Assessing Environmental Liability of Lenders and Fiduciaries Under the Asset Conservation Act*, 9 ENVTL. L. IN N.Y. 1 (1998).

22. Midlantic Nat'l Bank v. New Jersey Dep't of Envtl. Protection, 474 U.S. 494, 16 ELR 20278 (1986). For a more detailed discussion, see Riesel, *supra* note 4, at 442-44.

23. New York and New Jersey have illustrative statutory schemes, which are generally based on a strict liability concept. *See* Riesel, *supra* note 4, at 454-55. For an extensive list of specific statutes and statutory terms, see *id.* at 454-57.

24. For some issues on joint ventures, see PAUL PIZZI & JOHN TURLEY, A NEW

Approach to Managing EHS Risks During Joint Ventures 2 (Pilko & Associates, Houston, Texas, Pilko Grey Paper, 1998).

25. 42 U.S.C. §6924(u), ELR Stat. RCRA §3004(u). Regulations promulgated under RCRA also require hazardous waste disposal operations to be noted on deeds. See 40 C.F.R. §264.119 (1996).

26. New Jersey's Environmental Cleanup Responsibility Act requires state action when any of an extensive list of industrial commercial activities has occurred. N.J. Stat. Ann. §§13:1K-6 to -28 (West 1991 & Supp. 1996). This statute was renamed the "Industrial Site Recovery Act" when amended in 1993. See 1993 N.J. Laws 139, amending N.J. Stat. Ann. §13K-1 et seq. The New Jersey Spill Compensation and Control Act establishes a "super-priority" lien on all property in the state for costs of government cleanup. N.J. Stat. Ann. §§58:10-23.11 to -.11z (West 1992 & Supp. 1996).

27. See Cal. Health & Safety Code §§25220-25241 (Deering 1996). A variance is needed for a wide variety of land uses. Id. §25232.

28. Georgia Pac. Corp. v. GAF Roofing Mfg. Corp., No. 93 Civ. 5125 (RPP), 1996 WL 29392 (S.D.N.Y. Jan. 25, 1996). For more information, see also Chapter 6, Public Disclosure and Audit Privilege Legislation.

29. The following discussion is derived in part from Frank B. Friedman & David A. Giannotti, Environmental Self-Assessment, in Law of Environmental Protection §7.05 (Sheldon M. Novick et al. eds., 1994). Adapted by permission of Clark Boardman Callaghan from Law of Environmental Protection (Sheldon M. Novick et al. eds., 2005). All use rights reserved by Clark Boardman Callaghan, 375 Hudson St., New York NY 10014.

30. 29 U.S.C. §§651-678.

31. See supra note 24 and accompanying text.

32. 42 U.S.C. §9601(35)(B), ELR Stat. CERCLA §101(35)(B). See also id. §9607(b), ELR Stat. CERCLA §107(b).

33. See Riesel, supra note 4, at 440-43, for a detailed analysis of the legislative history, the case law, and the difficulty of qualifying for the innocent purchaser exemption.

34. 5 U.S.C. §§552-552a, available in ELR Stat. Admin. Proc.

35. See discussion supra Chapter 2.

36. This provision is of increasing importance as many environmental requirements, such as reporting requirements, are not necessarily reflected in permits. Also note that obtaining such a broad representation may be difficult, and it is more likely that the seller will agree to warrant only "material" permits or compliance, with a schedule attached. The schedule or the contract itself will define the controlling standard of materiality. The schedule may also reference any other baseline condition and will usually include all permits necessary for operation and/or to be transferred. Moreover, in view of the increasing complexity of the area, it is quite

possible that a seller may balk at any warranty as against any "other requirement of law." It is likely that seller will qualify this "to the best of seller's knowledge." Many counsel in this area consider that the schedule is the most important document in negotiations, as it is the culmination of environmental due diligence review.

37. *See* De Minimis Landowner Settlements, Prospective Purchaser Settlements, 54 Fed. Reg. 34235 (Aug. 18, 1989).

38. *See* discussion *supra* Chapter 2.

Chapter 8:
Waste Minimization

Many companies are now exploring multimedia waste minimization. This concept defines waste very broadly to include all materials released into the environment, on or off site. In essence, it means reducing the amounts of air emissions, effluent, and hazardous and nonhazardous wastes generated. If nothing else, a waste minimization program recognizes the growing legal pressure to control remaining sources of pollution. It is easier and probably cheaper to develop your own reduction program than to wait for regulation. Reductions can come from source reduction, recycling, and other beneficial uses of materials. It also employs the use of life cycle analysis to determine if product or raw material substitution is appropriate as well as other examples discussed in Chapter 3 (Environmental Management in the 21st Century).

Waste minimization is not a new concept. At least since RCRA was amended in 1984 to require generators to certify that they have minimized their hazardous waste generation, many companies have made efforts to generate less solid and hazardous waste. These minimization programs, however, generally have not included reductions in air emissions or effluent discharges into water, even when the companies have been making those reductions as required by other statutes (such as the CAA, which creates constant pressure to reduce emissions of both conventional and toxic air pollutants). The passage of EPCRA[1] in 1986 inspired a change in this attitude. EPCRA put industry on notice that releases at levels once unquestioned are subject to public and legislative scrutiny and possible control. This chapter focuses on how to broaden minimization programs to encompass emissions and effluent as well as solid and hazardous wastes.

Solid Waste Reduction: A Case Study

In April 1991, McDonald's Corporation and the Environmental Defense Fund released an innovative report addressing the recommendations made by the organizations' joint task force on waste reduction. Recognizing that the fundamental nature of the business of McDonald's is "to serve hot, fresh food to a large group of customers efficiently in a limited period of time,"[2] the task force's overall objective was to reduce the environmental impact of McDonald's operations. Evaluation criteria included: (1) consistency with EPA's waste management hierarchy (reduce, reuse, recycle, and inciner-ate/dispose) with recognition that "changes aimed specifically at reducing solid waste may have other environmental impacts"; (2) magnitude of environmental impacts, both quantitatively and in terms of the "public's perception of such impacts"; (3) public health and safety, including recognition that "no option should be implemented that risks the health and safety of its employees, customers or the communities in which McDonald's operates" and that "public health concerns are driven by accurate information and not simply public perceptions"; (4) practicality, including customer attitudes; and (5) economic costs and benefits, including customer attitudes.[3] These efforts produced a corporate waste reduction policy and comprehensive waste reduction action plan.

The task force noted a major problem, namely that "[p]ackaging materials used by take-out and drive-thru customers (50-70% of the business, de-pending on a restaurant's location) cannot easily be collected by in-store re-cycling programs initiated by McDonald's. For those items, source-reduc-tion steps and design changes that allow packaging to fit into evolving community recycling programs will deliver the greatest environmental benefits."[4] In addition, "[t]he task force concluded that there is no single method for minimizing solid waste at McDonald's. Rather, there are a num-ber of specific solutions that, collectively employed, will achieve signifi-cant waste reductions."[5]

Waste minimization and recycling decisions are not simple and must be ex-amined on a case-by-case basis. (See also Chapter 3, Environmental Manage-ment in the 21st Century.) For example, there is a misconception that the deci-sion by McDonald's to replace polystyrene foam clamshells with a "paper" wrap was a "paper versus plastic" decision. The new packaging material was a three-layered sandwich wrap, which consisted of a layer of tissue inside, a sheet of polyethylene in the middle, and a sheet of paper on the outside. Thus, the company's decision to phase out polystyrene packaging and substitute pa-per-based wraps *cannot* be evaluated as a generic paper-versus-plastic issue. Instead, the merits of alternative materials emerge only after closely examin-ing the packages involved. The nature of the materials, as well as mode of production, current rate of recycling, etc., dramatically affect their relative environmental consequences and must be carefully taken into account in comparing the materials. In this case, the potential for recycling problems in collection, processing, and marketing were critical factors.[6]

EPCRA and Emissions Reductions

Even before EPCRA, many companies recognized the importance of knowing their emissions levels and voluntarily required their facilities to report releases internally. Some states also required reporting. Sometimes these efforts led to good news/bad news situations. Companies that had started reporting before EPCRA had time to prepare for the effects of their reports and, in some cases, to reduce their releases. But the reporting programs they had invested in were not always consistent with EPCRA. Moreover, it was sometimes a problem for companies to show that their programs were consistent with EPCRA's requirements if the bases for previous reporting were not well documented.

EPCRA contains several related programs for disseminating information on industrial use and release of toxic and hazardous substances.[7] EPCRA §313 requires many manufacturing facilities to report routine releases of "toxic chemicals" annually.[8] Section 312 requires most commercial and industrial facilities to report on inventories of "hazardous chemicals" possessed in excess of listed threshold quantities.[9]

When EPCRA became effective, many companies were primarily concerned about how to accomplish the basic tasks of obtaining information and presenting it in a meaningful manner. They were also concerned about how to determine correctly and consistently the amounts they had to report under §313. These determinations still present major difficulties. At industry's urging, Congress refrained from requiring actual measurement of releases, instead allowing companies either to measure releases or to estimate them based on a number of assumptions. Most companies have chosen to estimate and have spent considerable time teaching their personnel the necessary techniques. Estimation of releases is far from an exact science, and different techniques can yield different results. The relevant EPA guidance document tends to lead to overestimation.[10] If a company is primarily concerned with reducing its potential legal exposure for violations of EPCRA's reporting requirements, it can make its estimates "conservative" (that is, high).[11] If the company is more concerned that reporting higher amounts may lead to public concern or to legal exposure under other statutes, it can estimate the lowest defensible values.

Section 313 releases are routine and, before EPCRA, were simply accepted and controlled generically as smoke, particulates, or organics. These releases are now labeled "toxic," even though concentrations beyond plant fence lines may never approach levels that would actually cause adverse health effects.[12] Some companies, however, have been shocked at the size of the figures they have reported under EPCRA, particularly those on fugitive emissions,[13] which are especially difficult to estimate accurately and can be enormous. A calculated release rate of less than 2.5 pounds per hour (such as from equipment leaks) for 24 hours a day will total 10 tons a year. Even with a tiny leak rate, the total estimated emissions from a plant with thousands of flanges, pumps, and valves would be huge.

EPCRA reporting has resulted in increased public concern and regulatory activity regarding toxic releases. From a public relations standpoint alone, release figures need to be reduced; they look immense to the general public. Moreover, certain legislators wasted no time in highlighting them. For example, in March 1989,[14] Rep. Henry Waxman (D-Cal.) made public preliminary EPA estimates that U.S. industry releases 2.4 billion pounds of §313 "toxic pollutants" into the nation's air each year.[15] The chemical industry was cited as the largest emitter, releasing an estimated 886.5 million pounds per year. These numbers greatly increased pressures to amend the CAA to reduce emissions of so-called hazardous air pollutants. Indeed, environmentalists' use of §313 reports and the attendant publicity made enactment of new air toxic controls a foregone conclusion. The Environmental Defense Fund placed virtually any reporting entities' numbers on the web together with a ranking in the state and/or nationally in terms of specific pollutants or gross numbers. This has also increased pressure to reduce the numbers, not to mention environmental justice claims as to the impact on minority and low income groups of being exposed to such pollution.

EPCRA also increases the pressure on, and opportunity for, state and local governments to reduce releases, particularly air emissions. Many state and local agencies have sought to establish accurate inventories of hazardous or toxic air pollutants for development of regulatory programs. Now that EPCRA has given them the inventories, the agencies require emitters to establish strategies and timetables for reducing the pollutants, sometimes significantly. The agencies have approached the problem not in terms of reducing specific toxic or hazardous air pollutants, but in terms of particulate matter with a diameter of 10 microns or less (PM_{10}) and volatile organic precursors to ozone, the indicator pollutant for smog. Indeed, the reduction in ozone precursors required to attain the ozone standard under CAA §108[16] will probably be greater than any reduction resulting from additional regulation of the precursors for their own sakes. The potentially large amounts of fugitive emissions identified under EPCRA are tempting targets for regulatory agencies anxious to further reduce ozone precursors in nonattainment areas.

Voluntary Emissions Reductions

It is imperative that all companies examine their EPCRA figures and develop reduction strategies, ideally as components of overall waste minimization programs.[17] This is true for two reasons. First, as discussed above, changes in federal, state, and local regulation of air emissions are likely to require such reductions. Second, EPCRA offers opportunities for companies to improve their environmental programs. The statute provides incentives to track emissions and to develop good computerized tracking and reporting systems. Both these functions are key to good environmental programs.

Indeed, many corporate environmental departments—particularly before inventory requirements of the CAA Amendments of 1990 went into effect (which is probably the most valuable section in this complex and in many cases flawed legislation)—actually welcomed EPCRA as a way to obtain the emissions inventories that their facilities had been slow to develop. In addition, companies can—and should—use reporting to trigger waste reduction and potential cost savings.[18] By analogy, many progressive companies have achieved substantial hazardous waste reductions as a result of both regulatory and internal concentration on the costs of disposal and product loss in the form of leaks and other waste.[19]

New uses or markets have been found for materials that once were wastes. The situation today, as data from the EPCRA reports become widely available, is analogous to the situation after submission of some of the early RCRA reports. Large amounts of hazardous waste were publicized, and agencies and the public pressed industry to reduce them. In response, industry examined its practices and found many opportunities for waste reduction and cost savings, either in the traditional sense or in the "pay me now or pay me later" sense. It was cheaper to reduce wastes quickly than to wait for additional regulation. Similarly, economics combined with post-EPCRA regulatory pressure should create opportunities for substantial emissions reductions and potential cost savings. The cost savings may be less in the air pollution area, and all new regulatory programs create new expenses, but intelligent companies can turn EPCRA's requirements into at least limited targets of opportunity.

Voluntary emissions reductions can have substantial benefits in terms of public relations, liability, and costs. Well-publicized voluntary reductions will reduce public pressure against "industrial polluters." Moreover, if a company voluntarily reduces fugitive ozone-precursor emissions before regulations require those reductions, it may be able to reduce the cost of control programs. It can do this either by offsetting the reductions against emissions from future new sources or modifications or by selling them to other companies through its state's emissions banking system. Most importantly, if industry does not reduce emissions voluntarily, it can expect to face tighter regulation and increased costs.

Voluntary emissions reduction also has risks. First, the future of emissions banks is in question. Existing air programs allow sources to bank emission credits from shutdowns or reductions achieved beyond those required by law. As state agencies struggle to reduce ozone precursors, they will be tempted to "expropriate" banked credits to get federal reduction credits or to control industrial growth in particular areas.[20] Emissions banks have no deposit insurance; depositors may not recover the costs of their expropriated credits, particularly if they cannot show "vested rights." Second, voluntary reductions may not fully satisfy the federal requirements that are almost sure to come, so additional reductions may prove necessary. Because it is cheaper to add controls to a loosely controlled source than to a tightly controlled one, companies have actually been penalized for early reductions of emissions under the CAA.[21] It is therefore very important to keep detailed records sufficient to demonstrate unequivocally both the absolute and percentage reductions your voluntary controls achieve.

Advanced Waste Minimization Programs

Voluntarily reducing your emissions is the first step in establishing a post-EPCRA waste minimization program. The second step is tracking wastes from materials' acquisition to product and waste disposition. This tracking, sometimes called "product stewardship," is virtually a materials balance. Although difficult, it should at least be a goal.[22]

The third step is establishing a waste inventory that distinguishes wastes routinely produced during operations from those produced by nonrecurring events. Your program should focus on reducing recurring waste streams. It is not possible to minimize existing wastes resulting from nonrecurring events. For example, cleanups mandated by either RCRA or CERCLA for past situations usually require specific technologies or disposal methods. Such cleanups may preclude certain forms of disposal that might qualify as waste minimization. Therefore, because you will base reduction plans on your yearly waste total, it is deceptive to add nonrecurring wastes to that total without specific identification. The inventory should also differentiate hazardous from nonhazardous wastes, although both should be reduced.

In developing a waste minimization program, it is advisable to set indices of performance, long-range goals, and specific yearly numerical goals. Perhaps the best index of performance is a ratio of waste generated to product produced. This gives you an easily measurable goal that recognizes rises and falls in production.

Long-range goals should include: maximum reduction of manufacturing, mining, and processing discharges to all media; no emission, discharge, or disposal of any hazardous waste without treatment that minimizes or removes the hazard(s) to the extent feasible; and regular review of all processes or operations to ensure minimization of potential employee or community exposure. Your company should develop prioritization criteria, review a certain number of processes each year, and review all processes by a specific date.

Annual quantitative goals should implement the maximum-reduction and no-emission objectives and should specify reductions in wastes generated; wastes treated, destroyed, or disposed of on site; and wastes treated, destroyed, or disposed of off site. As discussed in Chapter 5, it is preferable for divisions to set these goals so that they have a proprietary interest in meeting them.

The ideal minimization program reduces the amount of waste generated. Waste that is not generated does not pose disposal problems or trigger additional air or water permit conditions. In addition, source reduction is the only type of waste minimization credited by regulatory agencies and the congressional Office of Technology Assessment. The Office of Technology Assessment defines waste minimization as "in-plant processes that reduce, avoid or eliminate" waste generation.[23] The Pollution Prevention Act of 1990[24] provides:

> The term "source reduction" does not include any practice which alters the physical, chemical, or biological characteristics or the volume of a hazardous substance, pollutant, or contaminant through a process or activity which itself is not integral to and necessary for the production of a product or the providing of a service.[25]

Source reduction is not, however, always technologically or economically feasible. In such cases, the second-best goal is to ensure that the waste generated does not pose a potential hazard to health or the environment.

Moreover, in many companies, it may be difficult to justify increased maintenance and capital requests in the areas of waste minimization, effluent or discharge reduction, and process hazard reduction, all in keeping with the expansion of general environmental, health, and safety requirements, without specific regulations requiring such measures. In other companies, there may be authorizations for expenditures approved that have little or no economic justification, but are based on environmental, health, and safety concerns. But this may not be widely known at lower levels of the company. It is important that the EHS staffs assure division personnel that they should not hide behind the "our management won't give us the money" excuse. Recognizing the normal, healthy conflict between environmental, health, and safety concerns and financial needs, it is important that these issues surface and are critically reviewed high enough in the organization to minimize the concerns noted above.[26]

An additional caveat should be considered in developing a pollution prevention program.[27] The existing federal regulatory structure may create strong disincentives to such a program. For example, proposed EPA permit regulations under the CAA Amendments of 1990 provide that a facility change of its feedstock from "toxic" chemical A to another listed chemical B, even if *less* toxic, may constitute a modification and could subject an entire facility to new source maximum available control technology requirements and permitting delays. Moreover, the new thresholds for preconstruction review are so low (in some cases 10 tons per year—or less than the 3 pounds an hour in *potentially* increased emissions) that virtually any change at a facility may trigger new source review and lengthy permitting requirements.[28] Some of this was reversed by new regulations which are still, as of the date of publication of this book, subject to intense litigation.

In addition, if new materials or controls alter the amount or nature of waste generated, RCRA requirements such as permits and reporting may be triggered, along with associated liabilities. Should a company use a recycling or recovery system such as a distillation column to minimize or eliminate the need for off-site disposal, that unit and/or material may be subject to RCRA Part B hazardous waste permitting, corrective action, and other requirements, such as air and water permitting. Recovery or removal of a toxic constituent from wastewater before discharge may constitute hazardous waste treatment under RCRA and thereby trigger RCRA Part B permitting. Air permitting may also be triggered by this change.

Finally, FWPCA implications cannot be ignored. Any process change or modification that alters the constituent profile of a water discharge will require a modification of the NPDES permit.[29] The Act has an "anti-backsliding" provision,[30] which prohibits any changes in an NPDES permit that would allow an increase in the discharge limits of individual pollutants. For example, if a means that is found to reduce the amount of pollutant X increases the amount of pollutant Y, that change would be difficult to make. Reductions in effluents or their toxic constituents may therefore become a cap. If a facility opts to reduce emissions by scrubbing, the necessary tanks for treatment and storage may trigger water permits, air permits, and RCRA permits, depending on the nature of the material, the definition of source, and the water treatment train.

Conclusion

3M has a successful waste minimization program entitled "Pollution Prevention Pays" (3P). Dow Chemical Co. calls its program "Waste Reduction Always Pays" (WRAP). The concept of "pays" gets management attention, but it is equally important to recognize that regulatory pressures will eventually require such reductions. Whether minimization programs are voluntary or mandatory, however, they can "improve productivity, increase product yields, decrease treatment costs and conserve energy while reducing potential liability costs."[31]

Notes to Chapter 8

1. 42 U.S.C. §§11001-11050, ELR Stat. EPCRA §§301-330 (enacted as Title III of the Superfund Amendments and Reauthorization Act of 1986 and often referred to as "SARA Title III").

2. McDonald's Corporation/Environmental Defense Fund, Waste Reduction Task Force, Final Report, Apr. 1991, at 9.

3. *Id.* at 9-10.

4. *Id.* at iii.

5. *Id.*

6. *Id.* at xii.

7. *See generally* Frank Friedman & Ernie Rosenberg, *Opportunities Under Community Right-To-Know Reporting,* Toxic Torts & Hazardous Waste Newsl., Aug. 1989, at 1. The assistance of Ernie Rosenberg, formerly Director of External Affairs and Compliance, Health, Environment, and Safety, Occidental Petroleum Corporation, and now President, Soap and Detergent Association, on the section relating to EPCRA is gratefully acknowledged.

8. 42 U.S.C. §11023, ELR Stat. EPCRA §313. This section only applies to facilities in Standard Industrial Classification Codes 20-39 with 10 or more employees.

9. *Id.* §11022, ELR Stat. EPCRA §312. This requirement applies to facilities covered by OSHA's Hazard Communication Standard, 29 C.F.R. §1910 (1996), which now includes virtually all commercial and industrial facilities. *See also* Mary Beth Arnett, *Risky Business: OSHA's Hazard Communication Standard, EPA's Toxics Release Inventory, and Environmental Safety,* 22 ELR 10440 (July 1992).

10. U.S. EPA, Estimating Releases and Waste Treatment Efficiencies for the Toxic Chemical Release Inventory Form (EPA 560/4-88-002, Dec. 1987).

11. Inflated initial reports also make it easier to show "decreases" in future years.

12. In contrast, other provisions of EPCRA, such as those addressing emergency plans and material safety data sheets, deal with lower probability events that facilities and companies have direct stakes in avoiding entirely because the financial exposure would be so great.

13. Fugitive emissions are emissions that result from equipment leaks, rather than from point sources such as stacks and vents.

14. This release was timed for maximum effect on members of Congress, who were home for the Easter recess.

15. On April 12, 1989, EPA issued corrected figures. It estimated releases of 2.7 billion pounds of toxic chemicals to air and 9.7 billion pounds to water. Ninety-five percent of these releases, however, were of sodium sulfate, a relatively innocuous byproduct of water pollution control. EPA delisted sodium sulfate because it is not particularly toxic.

16. 42 U.S.C. §7408, ELR Stat. CAA §108. These ozone-precursor controls will be required in over 100 urban areas that do not meet the ozone and PM_{10} standards. In an effort to address pollutant transport, legislative efforts continue to try to extend the controls to some areas that do meet the standards.

17. If your existing auditing program is not sufficient, it is advisable to consider a specific review of air quality issues. It has been suggested that "(t)he resulting snapshot often indicates important safety, engineering practice, and compliance issues and highlights areas where the company could improve its regulatory, legal or economic status and avoid or reduce liability." Van Wormer, *Air Quality Auditing: A Strategy for the 90s*, ENSR NEWSL. (ENSR), Nov. 2, 1990, at 1.

18. For example, 3M realized total savings of $530 million through 1991. B. SMART, BEYOND COMPLIANCE—A NEW INDUSTRY VIEW OF THE ENVIRONMENT 14 (1992). See *id.* at 11-36 for a description of a variety of company waste and source reduction programs.

19. For example, 3M Company estimates that between 1975 and April 1989, its program "Pollution Prevention Pays" (3P) achieved savings of $482 million worldwide ($408 million from U.S. operations and $74 million from international operations). *3M's Aim: Slash Emissions 90% by 2000*, ENVTL. MANAGER, June 1990, at 1. Solid waste (hazardous and nonhazardous) pollutants were reduced by more than 535,000 tons. *Id.* A longer term goal (90-percent reduction from a 1987 baseline) will require extensive research and development to redesign products and processes. *Id.*

20. The South Coast Air Quality Management District has already proposed to do this in southern California.

21. Frank Friedman & Ernie Rosenberg, *The Managers' Dilemma—Is There Any Good Advice in Preparing for Compliance With the Clean Air Act of 1990*, 22d Annual Conference, A.B.A. Sec. Nat. Resources, Energy & Envtl. L., Mar. 11-14, 1993, at 337-38.

22. For a description of the Dow Chemical Co. program, see Dombrowski, *Product Stewardship Offers a Safe and Profitable Future*, 139 SAFETY & HEALTH 62 (National Safety Council, May 1989).

23. *Waste Minimization*, UCLA HAZARDOUS SUBSTANCES CONTROL BULL. (University of California at Los Angeles, Los Angeles, Cal.), Spring 1989.

24. 42 U.S.C. §§13101-13109 (1994).

25. *Id.* §13102(5)(B).

26. One possible solution to this problem is to have all environmental, health, and safety projects that may have questionable economic justification reviewed by the appropriate division HESRE staff. That this channel is available should be publicized at the process development, engineering, and facility levels. Examples of items that might be included in special justifications include:

• time value of operating capital not invested in inventories;

- the value of extending the life of natural resources as well as the value of reduced byproduct (produced water, refuse or slime, and gypsum) disposal costs in the extractive industries when improved recovery is effected;

- the value of allowable banking or sale of emission reduction rights in nonattainment areas;

- reduction in monitoring and permitting costs for pits and underground tanks removed from service;

- reduction in disposal costs through waste minimization; and

- reduction in costs by avoiding foreseeable regulatory procedural compliance requirements.

Although some of these may be included in justifications, others cannot because they are considered "soft dollars." Others may not be quantifiable, but will be applicable in complying with pollution reduction and risk-minimization requirements. Intangible benefits include minimizing the possibility of enforcement actions or third-party claims, and expediting permit approvals by demonstrating corporate sincerity.

27. I am indebted to Ernie Rosenberg, formerly Director of External Affairs and Compliance, Health, Environment, and Safety, Occidental Petroleum Corporation, and now President, Soap and Detergent Association, for the following analysis.

28. EPA has filed numerous enforcement actions against utilities and other industries.Some of these actions have been settled or are on appeal.

29. 33 U.S.C. §1342, ELR STAT. FWPCA §402.

30. *Id.* §1342(o), ELR STAT. FWPCA §402(o).

31. Dombrowski, *supra* note 22, at 63.

Chapter 9:
Dealing With Lawyers, Engineers, Business Managers, and Consultants

As an environmental manager, you will deal with three main types of specialists: lawyers, engineers, and consultants. Your primary clients will be business managers. Members of these groups can be either very helpful or counterproductive. In some instances you will have authority to hire in-house people or specialists to handle specific situations. (See Chapter 4, Recruiting Environmental Professionals, for a discussion of techniques for hiring competent staff.) At other times you may be stuck with people that you did not hire and would not hire if given a choice. This chapter gives some suggestions for dealing with each group.

Dealing With Lawyers

Environmental managers must learn to work closely with lawyers if they are to have successful programs. Some managers may view this as analogous to learning to work closely with porcupines. For those environmental managers who are lucky or are able to work with lawyers, or both, in-house or outside counsel can be valuable allies in developing a program. If environmental managers are unlucky or are unable to work with lawyers because of either inability to understand the importance of legal issues or a simple clash of cultures, counsel can be a major pain in the neck.

The first step in establishing a productive relationship with your environmental counsel is picking the right counsel. To the extent you control the selection decision, you should consider several factors. First, environmental law is a recognized professional specialty. Modern federal environmental laws and regulations have been in place now for more than 30 years and have generated a complex body of administrative and judicial authority. Thus, one criterion for selecting an environmental lawyer should be the lawyer's experience in handling environmental matters, including specific areas such as air, water, hazardous waste, and Superfund. This is not to say that one of the legal department's general practitioners would be an unsuitable choice, but as in environmental management, experience helps considerably. In addition, effective environmental counsel recognize that environmental law is not limited to protection of health and the environment, but extends to implementation of wide-ranging social policies in areas of major public concern. Finally, to the extent possible, you should avoid counsel who respond to every potential risk by just saying no.

Whether you choose your environmental counsel with great care or have the choice made for you, it helps to be lucky. The skill and personality of the lawyer can make a major difference in the success of your program. Despite your best efforts, you are likely to face problems in dealing with counsel at some point in your career. The following discussion provides tips on handling two common types of "problem" lawyers.

The first type is the lawyer who says no to everything. For the conservative—or perhaps lazy—lawyer, it is always easier to say no than to develop a creative solution to a complex problem. Saying no eliminates all obvious risk. Some lawyers use this rationale to advise against doing environmental assessments, for example. As discussed in Chapter 6, there is no question that these assessments do present legal risks. But the creative lawyer, like the creative manager, recognizes that the risks of not finding problems can be much greater. The difference is that failure to discover a problem until too late cannot be directly pinned on the overly cautious lawyer.

Fortunately, we are now seeing fewer "Dr. Nos" in environmental legal practice. They are still too often found, however, particularly in companies that have not faced environmental crises. Companies that have faced such crises recognize that they are better off dealing with problems before they become major.

Before you conclude that your lawyer is overcautious about environmental assessments, remember that the decision to conduct such assessments must include dealing with any issues that are discovered. Both the lawyer and the manager must be certain that senior management recognizes this. In these instances, the cautious lawyer is being *properly* cautious, not overly cautious.

The second type of problem lawyer—who, fortunately, is fast approaching or has already passed retirement age—is the lawyer with a strong, traditional litigation background who attempts to read environmental laws and regulations narrowly. This lawyer thinks Superfund cases call for extensive motion practice, not realizing that in most instances, the only realistic approach is negotiation. He or she also sees a potential constitutional challenge in every statute or regulation. Many of these more traditional lawyers have had limited experience with administrative law, particularly the broad interpretations characteristic of environmental law. Environmental law differs from some older fields in that the narrow approach will usually get you nowhere.

A lawyer in either of these categories can be a major impediment to your program. If you encounter a "Dr. No," your natural response may be simply to insist that he or she recognize that you are the client and that it is his or her job to tell you "No, but . . ." rather than merely "No." This forces your lawyer to justify his or her position, including the lack of alternatives. Similarly, if your lawyer is a "strict constructionist," you may be tempted simply to demand that he or she accept the very different realities of environmental practice. As discussed below, this emotional, combative approach may work in extreme cases. Under ordinary circumstances, however, it can be counterproductive, just as it would be in dealing with any other problem staffer. There are usually better ways to deal with these attorneys and the views they represent.

Contradictory as it may sound, one major way to deal with the problem lawyer is to increase his or her participation in your program. For example, if the lawyer is concerned about environmental assessments, have him or her write the guidelines governing those assessments, participate in the assessments themselves, and/or review assessment team reports. (See also Chapter 6, The Facility Assessment Team.) To gain the support of a conservative legal department, you may also find it helpful—or even necessary—to place your assessment program under the attorney-client relationship, even though this may delay action on identified issues. Using the attorney-client privilege is particularly prudent if the assessments are likely to raise numerous legal issues. (For a more detailed discussion of the attorney-client privilege, see Chapter 6, Public Disclosure and Audit Privilege Legislation.)

Another way to increase attorney participation—and, hopefully, cooperation in your program—is to ask for and listen to legal advice when appropriate. The environmental manager needs legal advice in many areas, and needs to know when to request it. Lawyers usually welcome these requests. They recognize that preventive law is the best means of avoiding exposure, and they like to know that their clients recognize this as well. Asking for advice can, therefore, help cement a relationship with a lawyer. By regularly requesting advice, you can assure the lawyer that you want your program to comply with the law. More importantly, you can subtly convey the message that you want to use the lawyer on a regular basis, but not if the lawyer will only take the easy way out by saying no rather than trying to be creative.

Sometimes a perceived problem with a lawyer is simply a failure of communication. The answer here is engaging in more dialogue and finding creative solutions by working together. For example, a lawyer's apparent conservatism may rankle a manager who is anxious to proceed with a program. Simply asking the lawyer for the basis of his or her opinion (and I do not mean in a long, formal memo) can make a major difference in communication. If a "Dr. No" has to justify his or her opinion, he or she may be more willing to develop a solution. Conversely, if the manager understands the lawyer's rationale, the manager may come to agree that caution is appropriate.

When I was a lawyer at ARCO giving advice to clients (before I moved to positions of implementing my own advice, which I expect many managers view as the ultimate revenge on a lawyer), one of my best clients had the reputation of being impossible for lawyers. What I found, however, was that this client had never been given common sense reasons for legal opinions. When I gave him those reasons, the client, who was very bright, frequently raised additional factors that neither of us had considered. Together, in informal dialogue, we could usually find ways to obtain the desired results. In the few instances when the legal answer simply had to be "no," the client understood the reasoning and accepted the decision.

This anecdote illustrates two important points. First, the key is maintaining dialogue that enables the lawyer to understand the business, and the businessperson to understand the law. Neither side can hold back its respective facts and rationales. It is particularly important for the manager to make sure the lawyer knows and understands all the facts. Many managers—and, unfortunately, some lawyers—do not recognize that most law is not a matter of principle but a matter of applying facts to principles. If both the lawyer and the manager fully understand the facts, both can adequately perform their jobs. There is nothing more frustrating to a lawyer than preparing an extensive legal opinion and then finding out that he or she was given the wrong set of facts. Second, the manager must recognize that he or she is dealing with laws and regulations and that understanding the interpretation and application of legal requirements is the specific expertise of lawyers.

Education is another technique for curing "Dr. Nos" and "strict constructionists." Many of these lawyers improve after attending a few seminars or appropriate trade association committee meetings. For example, a wide variety of trade associations and private groups have been giving seminars on the importance of and the means of structuring environmental assessments. There are also numerous programs on environmental law and practice. Suggest to the lawyer that he or she attend an appropriate program. If he or she is reluctant, it might be appropriate to suggest to his or her boss that you feel such a program would benefit the lawyer to assist in advising you. Similarly, the lawyer may also benefit from trade association work with peers who are experienced in environmental law. There is nothing better than practical experience and peer review to change outmoded behavior patterns.

If, after trying the suggestions above, you are still stuck with an ineffective counsel, more drastic measures may be necessary. One option is to make sure that the record shows that decisions not to take action, or to take actions with which you do not agree, were made on counsel's advice. You should make clear to the lawyer your plans to do this. The lawyer should then realize that he or she cannot take the easy way out because he or she will be responsible for that advice as well. Similarly, if the lawyer's advice is simply not timely, it is helpful to document the request for the advice and the timing of the reply. Documentation will help if it is necessary to go to the lawyer's superiors for relief. Care must be taken, however, that this documentation does not itself create legal problems.

Although, as I cautioned earlier, you should not overuse the tactic of simply demanding good legal advice, this alternative may be appropriate in extreme situations. General counsel recognize the importance of happy clients and are willing to act if there is a personality clash, or if it is clear that inadequate advice is being given. Your general counsel is more likely to take your complaint seriously if you have a history of recognizing the need for legal advice and appropriately requesting that advice, and if your boss backs you.

An attempt to replace a lawyer demands much the same approach as an attempt to replace any other staffer whose performance is inadequate. As mentioned above, before you take this serious step, it is important to document the problems. Unless you have a good track record with the legal department, the effective burden of proof will probably be on you, because most general counsels have heard too many managers complain that a lawyer refused to support a scheme that seemed illogical or was clearly illegal. As discussed previously, facts make the law, and your argument to the general counsel must be bolstered by facts, not generalities.

To return to the positive side: if you have good, creative environmental counsel who are sensitive to environmental program needs, you are fortunate. Competent counsel can be extremely helpful in the health, environment, and safety area which, as a result of many applicable complex statutes and regulations, requires significant legal involvement. Indeed, there is a substantial number of lawyers in senior management positions in this area. In an ideal world this would not be the case. Solutions should focus on technical responses, not legal constraints. A whole generation of environmental law is not going to be repealed, however; the legal constraints are simply facts of life, and legal training helps managers deal with them.

While obeying these legal constraints, most lawyers in management positions nevertheless attempt to focus on technical solutions rather than legal solutions—and if they do not, they should. The lawyer-manager's development of technical solutions benefits from his or her recognition of legal constraints. For example, it is a lot easier to eliminate a waste stream, if possible, than to obtain a permit for it or to worry about the long-term impacts of its disposal. A lawyer who does not understand technology may, however, tend to focus solely on the legal responses that he or she does understand. Therefore, the legally trained manager needs strong technical support.

Conversely, the technically trained manager needs strong legal support. Legal exposure is simply too great a risk to ignore. Your title may be manager, director, or vice president, but if you ignore the law, you risk acquiring the additional title of "designated inmate." Whatever the senior manager's training, the technical and legal sides must function as a team if the operation is to be successful. One purpose of this book is to give both the manager and the lawyer an understanding of the basic tools of environmental management so that they can complete an effective environmental program and remain within legal constraints.

A word is in order regarding ways to use counsel in dealing with other departments or divisions. You will run into situations where, for example, as a corporate staffer, you suggest a program to a division and the response is, "We suggested that earlier, but Legal said we couldn't do it." This kind of comment should not be taken at face value. It is usually helpful for you and your counsel to meet with the division manager who claims he or she cannot do something because of legal advice, along with the person giving that advice. I have seen many occasions, both as a lawyer and as a manager, where the advice was not understood in the proper context.

Conversely, managers can often use legal advice to justify potentially unpopular programs. All managers are concerned about potential liability, and it is easy to "blame Legal" for a program. The smart lawyer will often encourage that approach, just as the corporate group may encourage a divisional manager who does not want to take heat for a program to "blame Corporate" for it.

Dealing With Engineers and Business Managers

In the previous section we had a few kind (and a few not so kind) words for the lawyers. This section deals with the best means of using the expertise of—and, when necessary, educating—engineers, as well as those business managers or senior managers who share the prejudices common among engineers. Unfortunately, many of us have had the pleasure of working for business managers who, out of frustration at their inability to understand the environmental management process, demanded long memoranda from us to justify everything we were doing or planning that did not fit into traditional business management. This section also includes some hints for dealing with this breed.

The unreconstructed lawyer, discussed in the previous section, who attempts to practice environmental law from a strict constructionist viewpoint and who, like the proverbial Bourbon kings, forgets nothing and learns nothing, has his or her counterpart in the engineering and business area. This engineer is usually technically competent, but environmentally insensitive. He or she might be an older engineer who remembers the days when environmental engineering consisted of not much more than a pipe to the nearest body of water. Today, with very limited controversy, although recognizing that this is not good environmental engineering, he or she is very dubious about the need for certain environmental controls. This engineer firmly believes that many environmental laws and regulations are unnecessary and lack sound scientific foundation. This engineer will, therefore, resist any changes unless he or she is convinced that the law absolutely requires them, and even then will try to do the bare minimum that the law requires. This individual may very well be right that many of the laws and regulations have serious technical flaws or are motivated strictly by politics, but this is irrelevant. As a manager, you must educate your staff to accept "regulatory truth" rather than "scientific truth," and to make whatever technical changes are necessary either to comply with or legally avoid a regulation, rather than quibbling over whether compliance is necessary from a technical standpoint. Lawyers may find this approach more congenial than engineers.

Another individual who can make your life difficult is the business manager or senior manager who resists changes both because, like the engineer discussed above, he or she believes they are scientifically unnecessary, and because he or she wants to hold down short-term costs. Such managers or engineers are even harder to deal with if they demand "engineering certainty" to back up any suggestion for change. They are particularly skeptical about the importance of emission and effluent inventories and the economics of solving problems cost effectively now, rather than waiting for additional—and more costly—regulation. The concept of "pay me now or pay me later" is not sufficiently concrete for these individuals, particularly if they have to pay the costs now rather than having someone else pay the costs later.

A third problem category includes engineers and business managers who assume that all government employees are idiots or ideologues attempting to ruin industry, or are just plain arrogant. Although these views are extreme and counterproductive, there are unfortunately enough examples of technical idiocy, ideology, and arrogance to keep these prejudices alive.

There is a story, perhaps apocryphal, about an early regional administrator of EPA who became involved in a negotiation over the effluent quality requirements to be included in an NPDES permit. The negotiations turned to pH and the industrial applicants indicated that they would be willing to attain a pH of 7. The regional administrator, a lawyer without technical training, responded angrily, "What do you mean, 7? We want the pH at 1!" Fortunately, there are fewer of these technical idiots around today.[1]

Most government employees are competent and try to be objective, especially if you give them a basis for doing so. But whatever the government employee's competence level or ideological preference, having a combative engineer as your technical expert may irreversibly damage your cause. This is especially likely if the government employee is equally arrogant or is making up for lack of experience with bravado. As mentioned above regarding lawyers, you win agency proceedings on facts, not on law. It is, therefore, important to produce technical experts who can persuade the agency of the facts supporting your positions. Even the majority of government employees who try to be objective will in many instances be deeply suspicious of your motivations and your credibility. You do not want the technical persons who represent your company reinforcing the employee's prejudices against industry, thus making it more difficult for you to deal with that agency in the future. (Although staff turnover can be heavy, agencies have long institutional memories.)

Another reason to keep such people out of negotiations is that they may be more susceptible to a common tactic analogous to the "country lawyer" ploy. Many of the more intelligent young government technical and legal staff will take advantage of their youth and act more inexperienced and naive than they actually are. Industry representatives who rush in on seeing their stereotypes confirmed soon find themselves bested in the negotiation. Many of us former regulators recall fondly the success of this ploy and are thus conscious of it when we represent industrial clients.

Note that I am not suggesting that the only technical person who can handle an agency negotiation is some outside expert with a long résumé. The most effective "expert" is usually the operational engineer with a "local accent" who can explain the situation in practical terms, stick to his or her area of expertise, and ignore the regulatory "dance." Nor am I suggesting that only the young engineers can represent industry effectively. Older engineers who have strong operational experience, but are not condescending, can be very impressive and looked at as role models. This is particularly true if they understand the agency point of view and can offer practical solutions that benefit both sides.

Assuming technical competence, how do we make the engineer or manager who falls into one of the three problem categories environmentally conscious and politically aware? If the person is basically intelligent, a dose of reality should help. Activity with peers in a trade association committee, as well as specific courses in environmental law, can help the engineer just as they can help the lawyer. Exposure to engineers with government experience can be very useful. Moreover, such activities are particularly useful in Washington to acquaint the individual with the legislative and regulatory process.

Dialogue within your organization is another method of educating engineers and managers. It is at times very frustrating—particularly when seeking technical specialists' advice on legislation—to hear requests for basic amendments to laws or regulations that have been in effect for years and are politically sacrosanct. In-house discussion on legislation and regulation can help familiarize technical staffs with the parameters of legislative and regulatory change. Communication among the technical, legal, and government relations staffs is critical here. This does not mean a variety of memoranda back and forth but frank, one-on-one discussions ensuring that everyone understands various points of view and political realities, feels that they have all the facts, and feels that their points of view have been considered.

Another helpful technique, particularly if you have good government contacts and credibility, is to arrange nonconfrontational opportunities for your engineers and managers to talk to government staff. You might set up an informal social meeting with your friends from government, letting them know in advance that you are trying to educate a member of your staff or a business manager. If the problem is that someone higher up in management does not understand the process, it may be useful to arrange meetings among management, government, and environmental group staff so that management can see that government employees and environmentalists not only are human beings, but may also understand your operations better than management realizes. To avoid further polarization and unnecessary role playing, these meetings should always be out of the context of specific issues of concern to the company. I have found this technique to be very helpful with senior managers who, in a nonadversarial setting, have come away with a new appreciation of government and environmentalist concerns. Following such dialogues, these internal bottlenecks can become your best supporters.

Incidentally, you should use the reverse of this approach if a negotiation reaches an impasse because of an unfortunate run-in with a stereotypically arrogant, ideological, or uninformed agency employee. Allowing a senior manager to tag along may help bolster your position within the corporation by showing that manager the difficulties you are experiencing based on the agency's refusal to understand "logic" as perceived within your company or industry.

Some engineers, like some lawyers, simply will never have the proper approaches to environmental engineering or dealing with their agency counterparts. In those instances, the only solution is to move heaven and earth to keep them out of your department—or to get them out if they are already in it. (See Chapter 4, Recruiting Environmental Professionals, for a discussion of some hiring techniques designed to avoid the unfortunate necessity of firing or transferring someone for their inability to do the job.)

Dealing With Consultants

Many of us have heard the consultant defined as an individual who borrows your watch and then charges you for telling you the time. This definition has received wide circulation because in many cases it is correct. To avoid getting into this situation, you must know when to use, how to choose, and how to manage consultants. Parenthetically, I have been giving the advice suggested in this section for many years, long before I became a consultant. The sensitivity to this issue, however, has been very helpful in my practice.

Use of consultants is most productive when they provide specific expertise that is not available in-house and that is necessary for a specific, limited
purpose. For example, consultants may be useful in preparing or evaluating
training programs. Use of consultants with specific technical expertise in
preparing EISs can also be cost effective, as can consultants used as a
sounding board for strategic advice. Consultants are under increasing business pressure. Many companies are negotiating national contracts, demanding and setting reduced prices and charges for overhead. Many environmental consultants look at themselves as specialized, but companies today are
increasingly looking at them as the equivalent of commodities. Quality is
assured; price is now the key factor.

Some companies have outside consultants perform environmental audits. I
generally do not recommend this because consultants lack inside credibility
and understanding of operations. Moreover, it is important to have the operational personnel themselves feel responsible for environmental awareness
and compliance. If used at all, consultants should generally be part of a team.
An outside consulting firm may be useful, however, in performing an initial
assessment if you feel that it is the only way to bring to management's attention the need for assessments. There are also times when a third party can provide an unbiased review of an existing audit program as a "fresh pair of eyes."
A good consultant with expertise in diverse areas may bring different, constructive approaches to the table. This may be particularly helpful if you are
attempting to upgrade your management or audit program and need to verify
to yourself or justify to senior management that the upgrade is necessary.

Finally, consultants, like outside lawyers, are frequently used simply because in-house people are unwilling to take the heat for an unpopular decision or because management is not satisfied unless a recommendation has
the imprimatur of an outside expert. Reliance on consultants may be part of
the corporate culture. Even if you resent this and know that you could do the
job just as well, you will be stuck with using consultants.

The decision to use consultants does not, however, terminate your management responsibilities. Your next task is to select the right consultant.
Few consulting firms—and few law firms—will resist claiming expertise
on a specific subject if you ask them about it. It is your job as a manager to
ascertain that this expertise really exists.

Referrals from other companies can be helpful. Bar associations may
also be good sources for determining the value of environmental consultants.[2] As in hiring any contractor, an in-person interview is imperative. You
need to ask tough questions such as, "How much will the work cost? Will
the price include preparation of written materials and a presentation, if necessary, to public agencies?" In addition, you should question the consultant
about prior experience with public agencies and individuals within the

agencies with whom he or she has had contact.[3] I have often found that the best and most cost-effective consultants are individuals with broad expertise operating on their own. Their overhead is limited and "what you see is what you get." Indeed, now as a private business consultant, I have followed my own advice for a business model, occasionally teaming with larger firms or other individuals if additional expertise is needed.

"Another important factor to consider, applicable in many situations, is what I call 'knowing how the game is played.' By this I mean experience with the regulatory process and personnel in the given jurisdiction where the work is to be done. This includes credibility with the regulators."[4] A further suggestion is that the potential client develop a request for the proposal (RFP) in order to help clarify what is desired of the consultant. "For complex projects, developing a concise scope may well be the most difficult part of the selection process."[5] However, I have found as a consultant that some of the larger consulting firms are so accustomed to RFPs that they have difficulty in trying to work with a client if the RFP is not clear. I have obtained business when a large consulting firm was pressing the client for a clear RFP, and when there is no RFP and in instances in which the client was unsure of what he or she wanted. I viewed my role as making it clear to the client that I understood his/her difficulty and that I would work with him or her to craft the appropriate solution. The RFP is a tool, not a box.

Managers may have had either excellent or poor experiences with consulting firms depending on the specific personnel used. An individual with a degree in environmental science and not much else will not be able to give cost-effective suggestions for dealing with issues, and/or may make recommendations that do not fit operational reality. Thus, in hiring consultants, just as in hiring outside counsel, it is important to insist not only that the firm have a good reputation for expertise in the area you are addressing, but that it use specific individuals who justify that reputation. Moreover, use of those individuals should be specified in the agreement with the consulting firm. Finally, if outside consultants are required for environmental assessments, acquisitions, or sales, it is imperative that some of the individuals on the job have operational experience. If nothing else, this will establish credibility with in-house operational personnel.

Once the consulting firm is hired, it should not receive carte blanche. *Your obligation is to manage that consultant.* If you define the scope of work explicitly and manage the consultant properly, a good consultant can provide what you want at the appropriate cost. Unless you remain in close coordination and set adequate guidelines, a consultant will study everything in-depth or prepare fancy reports that you do not need. In addition, unless you keep a close watch, use of consultants tends to create problems characteristic of the particular type of job the consultant is doing.

For example, consultants specializing in EISs are usually scientists rather than engineers and are usually very concerned about their scientific credibility. Of course, this credibility is key to a successful project, and it is necessary to have on your staff people who understand its importance. In seeking to prove that he or she has not "sold out" to industry, however, a consultant may overcompensate and reach conclusions unfavorable to you. And these conclusions may not be fully thought out. Questioning the consultant closely on the conclusions may reveal inherent weaknesses, but the individual's ego or suspicion that industry is trying to limit his or her objectivity may get in the way of reason. The best way to avoid unsatisfactory conclusions is to avoid having the consultant draw conclusions at all. The scientist should stick to science; he or she is not the decisionmaker. Similarly, environmental assessments should stick to facts, rather than reaching legal conclusions such as, "This is a violation of federal hazardous waste laws." Once the consultants have given them the information they need, other members of your organization are responsible for drawing the proper conclusions.

Two other problems commonly arise when consultants conduct environmental assessments. First, some consultants low ball future environmental costs for fear of being deal killers. Conversely, consultants may make overly broad recommendations, particularly if their firm is looking for long-term business or provides additional engineering or design services. Many consultants are "technology happy" and will propose effective, but gold-plated solutions to your problems. This tendency also appears in areas such as fire protection. Operating personnel frequently harbor the deep suspicion that a consultant will not feel fire protection is adequate unless it involves a steel beam cast in concrete and buried in a lake. In-house staffs often can find ways to provide equivalent protection at lesser cost.

A final consideration in dealing with consultants is confidentiality. If you hire a consultant to do a specific audit where you suspect legal problems, or to evaluate the environmental impacts of an acquisition, you may wish to protect the material the consultant obtains or generates. You can do this by structuring the agreement properly through your counsel and ensuring that the consultant follows the provisions designed to protect confidentiality. A nondisclosure agreement to prevent unauthorized disclosure of client information or consultant work product is advisable. Another means of protection is to have attorneys retain the consultant and to have the consultant bill the attorneys. The agreement may also need to state expressly that the consultant is being retained to provide advice in anticipation of litigation. The data gathered and any other written material should be the property of the attorneys, and its dissemination should be restricted. Like other material with legal implications, any written or oral reports from the consultant should be transmitted to the attorney, data should be segregated and marked as confidential communications, and sensitive material should be distributed only to those with a need to know.[6] Be aware, however, that there is no sure way of protecting environmental studies from disclosure.

In summary, the discussion in this chapter illustrates that all consultants are not merely out to tell you the time from your own watch. Consultants can be valuable resources if you know how to choose and manage them properly. Indeed, by leveraging consultants' expertise, you can greatly increase the effectiveness of your environmental management/compliance program, as well as providing strategic advice.

The Changing Roles of Environmental Professionals

The increasing demand for cost-effective environmental management is changing the nature, scope, and amount of work for both in-house and outside environmental professionals. (See also Chapter 4.)

Strong environmental programs that reduce legal exposure may significantly cut environmental costs—and environmental work, particularly for outside professionals. More small and medium-sized companies are developing environmental management programs, if audit privilege legislation becomes commonplace. With strong programs, there is management commitment to making necessary changes, environmental protection is integrated into the company's operations, and responsibility for compliance is widespread. Compliance and environmental awareness become a routine part of doing business.

To control the costs of implementing these programs, companies are now seeking to enhance in-house capabilities, better manage the roles of lawyers and other professionals, and reduce the amounts paid to outside lawyers and consultants.

Companies are taking steps to curb legal costs by improving and using their own in-house staff. Larger corporations are employing better trained, qualified, and compensated in-house attorneys. Environmental law is now less of a mystery. Companies are obtaining training for their lawyers, and many practitioners are available locally, including those with extensive EPA or state experience. And companies are ensuring that requests for outside counsel go first through the legal department. Of course, if in-house counsel are merely acting as conduits to outside counsel, they are in danger of being outsourced if outside counsel can do the work more efficiently and cheaply. Query: who manages "outside" legal work in that situation?

Ato has moved a considerable amount of outside consultant work for the plants to in-house staff. A plant cannot use an outside consultant for environmental work without the approval of the Manufacturing Director, who is the boss of the Plant Manager. The Manufacturing Director consults with the Health, Environment, and Safety Department before making decisions on consultants. The HES Department has a support staff to assist the plants. The staff will spend time at the plants and will actually do the work. But they must be timely and cost-effective. If outside consultants can do the work more cheaply and efficiently, the work will go to them. If not, the work can and should be done inside.

There are also efforts to better manage the role of lawyers. Most environmental "legal" work, such as interpretation of sophisticated technical regulations, can be done by qualified environmental professionals. The qualifications, training, and judgment of these professionals must be such that they recognize when they are in over their heads and need the help of lawyers. This reduces the need for both in-house and outside lawyers and provides for a more satisfying, productive, and cost-effective use of lawyers as part of the overall environmental team. Good management ensures that engineers are not doing the work of technicians and lawyers are not doing the work of engineers. As in every other area in a corporation, the focus is now on cost-effective management, and lawyers and legal work can also be managed (although the task has sometimes been analogized to herding cats).

Even when work is sent to outside professionals, there are efforts to reduce costs. The nature of the work sent to outside lawyers has changed. As the environmental competence of in-house lawyers has increased, companies place greater confidence in their work. Fewer clients will pay for compliance advice. Long legal memoranda are rarely requested. Companies can instead use the "bullet" rather than the "shotgun" approach to the use of outside counsel. They may seek very specialized advice, many times through a quick (and minimally billable) telephone call with a senior partner. Companies are also pressuring firms to reduce their fees. Consultants are under increasing business pressure. Companies such as Ato are negotiating national contracts, demanding and setting reduced prices and charges for overhead. Many environmental consultants look at themselves as specialized, but companies today are increasingly looking at them as the equivalent of commodities with price as the key factor.

Environmental law itself is maturing. As it does, the nature and amount of work for environmental professionals is stabilizing and in some cases decreasing. Congress and the states may still enact new environmental legislation, but it is likely that the high (or low—depending on your political views) watermark of the CAA Amendments of 1990 is past. Most environmental lawyers earn their fees by practicing at the outer limits of the law. There will always be outer limits to test, but the number and severity of these challenges are likely to diminish. Much of environmental law is now "local." As more Superfund sites are cleaned up and stronger laws reduce the creation of new sites, the number of CERCLA cases—and the work for lawyers and consultants—will also decline. As more environmental management systems are in place, as state audit privilege legislation becomes increasingly common, or as more companies take advantage of the EPA auditing policy, there can and should be less litigation over violations, but better rates of compliance. In short, there may be less work for environmental lawyers and consultants.

Environmental lawyers and consultants are not on the endangered species list, but the environment may not be as exciting or a growth area for new lawyers and environmental professionals. Some companies will not have gotten their act together or will experience management failures. Some companies in an excess of restructuring zeal have lost considerable institutional memory and expertise. Ironically, outside counsel and consultants are now performing these tasks, particularly when the system has broken down. It is likely that in many of these cases, management may need to rethink some of its restructuring assumptions and take a closer look at *total* costs, not just headcount, and also look more closely at longer term costs. (For a more detailed discussion of this topic, see Chapter 3, Environmental Management and Downsizing.)

There will also be government overreaching and agencies seeking to reach their quota of enforcement actions. There will likewise be a significant number of legitimate enforcement actions. Moreover, very significant institutional changes are underway. EPA is demonstrating a willingness to be flexible and making other administrative changes that would have been unheard of a few years ago, although there are many growing pains (see Chapter 3, The Challenge of Regulatory Reform). Similar trends are occurring in many states. In both legislatures and environmental agencies, the focus is on more flexibility and cost effectiveness, but in many cases implementation is slow and cautious. Although this focus provides opportunities for creative and valuable work by environmental lawyers and other professionals, still there are more lawyers chasing less work. Perhaps legal counseling and training are paying off and there is recognition that the law is a tool for compliance and not an end in itself. This may be bad for some lawyers and consultants, but is this bad for the nation?

Notes to Chapter 9

1. Environmental issues can indeed become very ideologically polarized. This polarization is particularly common in the issues surrounding risk assessment or the scope of cleanup at Superfund sites. Moreover, even seemingly minor events not directly related to particular sites can fuel suspicions about the ideological agendas of government employees. For example, in a speech to EPA employees, Dr. Barry Commoner delivered what the *New York Times* called "a fairly savage critique of their efforts to protect the nation's health from pollution. . . . He even dared use, in proposing a solution for the nation's pollution problems, what he called 'the S-word: socialism.'" Dr. Commoner further stated that we must end "'the taboo against social intervention in the production system'" and that "[r]emedying the nation's 'environmental failure' would 'require the courage to challenge the taboo against even questioning the present dominance of private interest over the public interest.'" At the end of his speech, "he received thunderous applause from the audience he had so unsparingly criticized." The *Times* further quoted an EPA staffer, identified by name and as "a frequent critic of the agency's policies," as saying that the Agency staff "agreed with 80 to 90 percent of what he said." Philip Shabecoff, *EPA Critic Enters the Lion's Den and Is Showered by Wild Applause*, N.Y. TIMES, Jan. 15, 1988, at B6. Needless to say, although this is an extreme case and not, in my view, representative of the views of most EPA staff, such reports seem to support the belief of some engineers and managers that agency staffs are irrevocably biased against industry, and perhaps even against capitalism.

2. For example, the Los Angeles County Bar Association's Environmental Law Section has a referral/match-up program for lawyers and consultants. Dennis, *How to Select and Use an Environmental Consultant*, 4 PRAC. REAL EST. LAW. 83, 88 (1988).

3. *Id.*

4. Michael McNally, *Choosing an Environmental Consultant—Lessons Learned*, TRENDS, Mar./Apr. 2001, at 11, 20.

5. *Id.*

6. *See id.* at 88-89.

Chapter 10:
Dealing With Federal and State Agencies, Citizen Groups, the Press, and the Public

T he purpose of this chapter is not to guide the corporate manager or legal practitioner through the maze of environmental laws and regulations, but to give helpful hints on dealing with the issues and people involved. The chapter does, however, discuss some legal issues, including those regarding the scope of review of agency decisions.[1]

The Regulators

Although federal and state decisions are often intertwined, it is important to distinguish between federal and state regulators.

Federal Regulators

The federal regulators, specifically EPA employees, are divided among the Washington, D.C., headquarters and 10 regions. On its face, EPA is a decentralized organization, but major policy issues require decisions from Washington.

The centralized-decentralized dichotomy breaks down on an issue-specific basis. For example, in the hazardous waste area, each region seems to have its own view of policy, and headquarters has found it almost impossible to ensure uniformity.[2] Each region is jealous of its turf, and often views headquarters as out-of-step with the real world and difficult to work with to obtain decisions. Headquarters returns the compliment, generally viewing the regions as not being totally aware of the Agency's mission and not always cognizant of the implications of its decisions. If these characterizations sound familiar to those of you attempting to deal with business organizational stresses, you probably now realize that one key to dealing with the Agency is recognition that in many respects its internal stresses are no different from those of any large organization. Of course, as a government agency, it is more vulnerable to congressional pressure. It is also slower to make decisions because it lacks incentives (other than statutory deadlines) for timely decisionmaking.

To deal successfully with EPA, or any other large government agency, it is critical to analyze the organizational structure and find out what moves the agency along. To obtain a favorable decision, it is also critical to determine what EPA will gain from such a decision, as well as what political and legal heat the decision will generate.[3] Your role as an advocate will be to craft a solution for the Agency that will fulfill its purposes and minimize the heat. The solution probably will not include everything your management desires, but this is also true of the outcome of litigation.[4]

If you are involved in an Agency rulemaking, you must bear in mind that EPA holds almost all the cards.

> [A] private party should recognize the character of the proceeding into which he is entering. The major federal environmental statutes (e.g., the Clean Air Act, Clean Water Act, Resource Conservation and Recovery Act) are goal-oriented. EPA has been given broad authority under each to deal with risk to public health or welfare from pollution of the air, water, or lands of the United States; however, specific guidance from Congress on how EPA is to interpret and implement these broad statutory mandates is generally sparse.
>
> Also, the rule-making procedures that implement these statutes do not follow the rules of "fair play" of a judicial proceeding. These are legislative rule makings where none of the judicial rules apply. In effect, EPA itself is witness, prosecutor, judge, and jury. Even the elemental features of reasonably accurate transcripts of proceedings and access to the record upon which the rule making is based are sometimes (as a practical matter) not available.[5]

You should also know that most EPA staffers, particularly the lawyers, are competent, committed to environmental protection, and inherently skeptical about industry. There has been a strong Agency bias against hiring personnel with industry experience, so very few EPA staffers have ever worked in industry. Many very capable lawyers come to the Agency because they strongly believe in environmental protection and because they feel that they will have excellent job opportunities on leaving the Agency. The legal staff at EPA (and at the DOJ's Environment and Natural Resources Division, which often represents EPA in litigation[6]) is of a very high quality, although many staffers are young and inexperienced. Although most EPA technical personnel are also competent, they have not necessarily had the same sense of mission and/or future career opportunity. This changed, particularly with the growth in opportunities for technical personnel experienced in hazardous waste. For a while, these opportunities led to rapid turnover, although this is now slowing down. Opportunities in both the legal and technical areas have diminished and reduced turnover may make a difference in Agency competence. However, a large number of people are expected to retire in the next few years.

In short, if you represent an applicant for a permit or an alleged violator of a regulation, you will usually face skilled but inexperienced staffers who are inherently skeptical about the merits of your position. You must overcome their skepticism. In most cases, this means you must engage in intelligent, good-faith negotiating. Patience in explaining your position and waiting for a decision must be the rule. It is usually not advantageous to come on strong with the regulator. Threats of political pressure, going over his or her head, or other attempts to throw your weight around normally will not help your client. Even the least experienced regulator has heard it all before, and all you will do is reinforce his or her derogatory image of industry.

There are times, however, when it is advisable to suggest to the staffer that you discuss the issue together with his or her boss so that you can both have the benefit of the boss' wisdom. Again, this advice may sound familiar in terms of working within a business system. It illustrates the importance of working with an agency's decisionmaking process much as you would work with the decisionmaking process of any other organization. Similarly, attempts to "go right to the top" to obtain a decision—without doing the necessary spadework beforehand—are not advisable. Your ability to achieve this kind of access may impress your management, but it usually will not obtain the desired decision. Going over a staffer's head without his or her knowledge, except in the most extreme cases, will only antagonize the staffer and make it harder to achieve the appropriate decision for your client. Agency managers are accustomed to this kind of maneuvering and will normally back their staff, unless there is a significant error in policy or judgment. Moreover, unless there are policy issues involved that must be decided immediately, the higher level official will want a briefing from his or her staff before making a decision. The usual time to go to the top is when lower level staff agree with you and you need a quick decision on the issue. With the staffer on your side, the decision will be quicker, and usually a favorable one.

If a region is not handling an issue satisfactorily, the temptation is to try to bypass it and go directly to Washington. This is analogous to appealing to headquarters because of unsatisfactory dealings with a district in the business sector. Obviously, the region will not look favorably on this approach, and you must use it cautiously. EPA Headquarters personnel are well aware of regional sensitivities, including the importance of protecting turf, and they will rarely overrule the region. Trying to get Washington involved in a strictly local controversy is usually a waste of time and will antagonize the decisionmakers in the region. Merely trying to determine whether there is a central policy that deals with your issue, or to obtain a general counsel's opinion,[7] is safer.

Even if there is an official policy, the region will not necessarily follow it. Many of us who practice in this area have experienced the frustration of referring to a memo from Washington on a subject, only to be told that the region will make its own decision. A memo that has been published in the *Federal Register* is more likely to be followed, although these memos are sometimes disregarded as well.[8] Therefore, you cannot assume that official guidance from Washington will force the regions to work constructively with you.

You may find it useful to hire a former regulator to assist you in dealing with EPA. You should not assume, however, that such a person will automatically be able to obtain the right decision within a reasonable time. The ability to understand how the Agency thinks and who pushes what buttons is quite helpful, but this advocate has his or her limits. Former regulators derive their competence and credibility from strong relationships with their former colleagues. In short, successful advocates in the environmental area will not, and should not, jeopardize their credibility for the sake of victory on a specific issue. This means that if your position is unsound, simply hiring a former insider will not solve your problem.[9]

In working with EPA, remember that the Agency is not monolithic. In some cases, EPA's technical staff or program managers may be more sympathetic to your position than its lawyers or enforcement staff are. Although it is dangerous to try to play off one group against another and you cannot rely on deals that have not been approved by the lawyers, it can be helpful to focus on working with technical personnel to develop a reasonable position that they can support. You should not, however, try to deal with program managers in the absence of counsel, unless the contacts have been strictly manager-to-manager without involvement by your counsel or EPA counsel. EPA attorneys are very sensitive about this, especially if you are a lawyer or if you are involved in actual litigation.[10] Although direct communication with "EPA program managers below the level where final decisions are made" is not unethical, because they are not "parties,"[11] EPA attorneys feel that this is going behind their back. "[F]ew actions will earn the distrust of government litigation counsel more surely than attempts to negotiate with program managers while excluding their counsel."[12]

There are also times when EPA program managers themselves mistrust their lawyers (or lawyers in general), and it can be helpful for you to meet with the program manager, accompanied by counsel on both sides. At that point, if you can encourage a dialogue between the two managers, while keeping both counsel as quiet as possible, settlement becomes more likely. Agency counsel, like private counsel, get caught up in the chase of litigation and tend to forget the objective. Getting the principals together under these circumstances can be extremely helpful, unless you have had little experience with Agency personnel and have little patience with the necessary (or unnecessary) bureaucratic constraints. The frustration level can be quite high, especially for those trained in technical disciplines.

Finally, you should be aware that negotiations can be particularly difficult when EPA contractors are involved. EPA often picks contractors based primarily on the lowest bid. Many of us have found that issues in complex litigation are resolved when the Agency finally spends the money to hire the most qualified contractor, rather than the cheapest. The competence and credibility of EPA's outside technical personnel are therefore critical.

Notwithstanding the desire of lawyers to be lawyers, the most important point to remember in dealing with EPA is that *most issues with the Agency are won, not on the law, but on technical arguments within the Agency.* "[Y]ou would be better advised to accept EPA's legal interpretations and to base your arguments for change on factual and policy grounds."[13] Your counsel's primary job should be to ensure that the best arguments are presented in as noncombative a manner as possible.

The role of good technical and policy experts cannot be overemphasized. Small businesses do not have these people in house, and few large companies have technical people with the patience and people ability to deal with their federal counterparts, who are usually young and inexperienced. Arrogant or patronizing industry representatives will jeopardize your case. If your in-house staffers do not have the necessary expertise and the proper attitudes, you may have to use outside specialists in EPA negotiations. Sometimes, however, small businesspeople or in-house people can be more successful than outside experts. If these people are sincere and credible, they can make their points even if they are not familiar with Agency jargon. The Agency's technical people will respond to sincerity and openness. Counsel's job will be to ensure that the proper record is made and to step back as far as possible. If the issue becomes a spitting match between lawyers, you are being done a disservice.

When considering litigation, it is important to recognize that the Agency's burden of proof in upholding its decision is usually easy to meet.[14] Conversely, if your internal advocacy with the Agency has been successful, a challenge to an Agency decision in your favor is also unlikely to prevail.

Where an Agency policy eases compliance with pollution control legislation, the challengers to that policy have the burden of proving that the policy is clearly precluded. The Court will not conduct a searching review in order to determine whether the Agency considered all of the environmental consequences of its actions and whether the purposes of the legislation have all been met. Thus, the Court will uphold an Agency action that eases strict mandates, except where the particular action is precluded by unambiguous statutory language or where the Agency failed to compile any record.[15]

Because courts are likely to uphold statutory interpretations, your best strategy for overturning an Agency determination in court is trying to distinguish your case on factual or policy grounds rather than making a head-on attack on the law.[16]

I am not suggesting that you should never threaten litigation. But if the Agency perceives that threats to its authority or position are not being made in good faith, both sides will find their positions cast in concrete. Conversely, if EPA perceives that a company will settle anything rather than litigate, the company's ability to negotiate reasonable settlements will quickly evaporate. If EPA perceives that the company will settle when there is a reasonable opportunity to settle, but will take a strong position when it firmly believes it is right, the company's credibility and, in turn, its settlement posture, will improve. When EPA realizes that threats to litigate are real and that the company has a good track record in winning, there are more opportunities to resolve matters reasonably.[17]

In recent years, advocacy before agencies and congressional staff has become even more complicated. This type of advocacy was not covered by previous lobbying laws, but may be covered by the Lobbying Disclosure Act of 1995,[18] which requires the registration of almost any organization (including a tax-exempt organization) or an individual retained by a client or employed to "lobby" members of Congress, congressional staff, certain White House or federal agency officials, and even certain members of the uniformed services. The term "lobbying contact" under the Act includes not only legislative contacts, but also many contacts with agency officials related to federal regulations, programs, policies, contracts, grants, and permits. The definition of "lobbying activities" is not restricted to direct contacts. It can also include "the preparation of planning activities, research and background papers" intended to assist the lobbying activity of others. Clearly, it is important to consult counsel on this evolving and confusing area.

State and Local Regulators

Many of the difficulties discussed above in working with EPA to develop optimum solutions are compounded when you must also work with state and local agencies. Almost every one of the major federal environmental statutes "establishes a framework for a federal-state 'partnership.'"[19] But the partnerships are troubled.

> The utopia envisioned by Congress in which the state and federal governments work together combining broad technical and scientific knowledge with intimate acquaintance with local conditions rarely works out in practice. Instead, the highly complex environmental statutes with their overlapping responsibilities, particularly in enforcement, give rise to a constant tension between federal and state agencies that runs all the way from differing interpretations of the same regulatory language to differing views on the seriousness of a particular regulatory violation.[20]

State and local agencies are important players on the environmental scene. As a representative of the regulated community, you need to be familiar with the characteristics of those agencies and with the consequences of the flaws in the federal-state partnership model. Most state and local agencies have limited resources. Federal statutes have increased the burden on states by requiring them to implement federal regulations, but federal funding has not been significantly increased and state funds have been limited. These are generally referred to as "unfunded mandates." Most state salary levels are substantially below federal levels, which makes it difficult for states to recruit and retain competent and experienced attorneys and technical staff. Despite their lower salaries, senior management officials in many states seem to be more career-oriented than EPA officials. Because of long tenure, they also have more practical experience.

State and local agencies are in some ways easier to deal with than EPA. First, perhaps because they do not have time for bureaucratic niceties, these agencies are generally much less formal than EPA in dealing with applicants or alleged violators, and higher level personnel who can make decisions are readily accessible. Lower level officials are also much more likely to be willing to bring matters to higher level personnel, who are more accustomed than their federal counterparts to making decisions. Furthermore, having a manager or technical specialist explain your company's situation, as suggested above regarding EPA, may be even more helpful here, where a "local accent" or shared acquaintances may increase credibility.

State and local officials are much more susceptible to political pressures than EPA. If a political situation gets too hot, the federal government can simply walk away from a local powder keg, as long as it does not have broader implications. State and local officials cannot do this. Moreover, ambitious local and state officials have been known to exaggerate the political pressures on agencies to further the officials' own political careers. If a state attorney general or a local city attorney wants to make an issue of your project or problem, finding a practical solution can be extremely difficult. It becomes even more complicated when "the head of the environmental agency and the attorney general come from different political parties and follow different agendas."[21]

Political pressure against your project can become intense if a citizen group claims significant local health problems. When an agency is under intense political pressure to address a perceived public emergency, you can seek to appeal to its rules and policies. This may have some effect, but often in such circumstances "the political powers in the government will sow the wind and the private defendant will reap the whirlwind."[22]

Political pressure can ensure that no matter what you do, either technically or legally, the matter will be decided by litigation to avoid political heat. Like EPA, state and local agencies frequently find that when an issue is politically hot, "inaction provokes fewer penalties than action and it is safe to spend or sue but dangerous to negotiate."[23]

The political sensitivities of state and local agencies can sometimes work to your advantage. State and local officials may respond to political pressures exerted on your own or your client's behalf. But great care must be used in exercising such pressure. Without fully understanding the law, some state and local governments are very receptive to the arguments of industrial clients to keep jobs in the community. You therefore risk the "Lord, protect me from my friends" syndrome of obtaining a favorable decision that is not legally supportable or subject to questioning by EPA and possible federal "overfiling." Your counsel can be very helpful in keeping you from being misled by such assurances.

On the federal level, political pressure will rarely help your client obtain the right decision, and indeed is usually counterproductive. Because federal authorities are generally more mission-oriented and less susceptible to political pressures, their broad authority over programs delegated to states also makes a political strategy at the state or local level very risky. You should use such a strategy only if the settlement or solution you propose is clearly within the law and within "policy." As a general rule, government agencies have an "inherent instinct for rules and policies."[24] In the field of environmental problem-solving and litigation,

> it is important to set the arguments within the terms of the policies, since those are the terms in which the government attorneys

are thinking. It is generally more advantageous to justify a desired result in terms of congruence with a policy than to suggest that the policy does not fit the facts and that disinterested analysis of the facts should prevail.[25]

If there are no policies directly on point, you should try to find an analogous policy.[26] It is also important to recognize that if a settlement is significant, or if a rulemaking is involved, it will in one way or another be subject to public comment.[27] Inconsistencies with policy or federal law will be brought out, and a loosely crafted resolution will not stand up.

Dealings with state and local agencies are further complicated by frequent turf fights with federal officials. It is important to check whether the federal government disagrees with state and local officials over policy or regulatory interpretation. Such disagreements frequently arise, for example, regarding implementation of the CAA through approved state implementation plans.[28] States and localities are required to write regulations meeting federal standards. A regulation that does not meet those standards will not obtain federal approval, but may nevertheless remain on the books of the state or locality. Thus, a state or local regulation may allow a proposed operation that does not have federal approval. If this situation occurs in an area that has not attained the air quality required under the CAA (a "nonattainment" area), the federal government may prohibit the project even if state and local officials have approved it. Your "friends" may have helped you win the battle, but you will have lost the war.[29]

Overlapping agency jurisdiction can be particularly critical in settlement negotiations.

> [I]t is especially important to establish and understand the authority of the attorneys on the other side of the table in an environmental suit. The private litigant should anticipate that, if settlement is reached with only part of the governmental structure, another office will look for the opportunity to add some icing to the settlement cake in order to justify and maintain its position within the government.[30]

This does not mean, however, that settlements can be negotiated with all agencies together. "The nature of the state-federal relationship often breeds rivalries and antagonisms that make common negotiation or settlement difficult and perhaps impossible. The different governments run on different timetables and have different frameworks for the review of settlements that often make coordination difficult."[31]

If you face this situation, "there will be times when settlement with one government and litigation against the other may be the most advisable course; for instance, if a reasonable settlement is available with the party with the strongest legal claim and no compromise is possible with the other."[32] Most compromises (especially in the hazardous waste area) must be approved by a court through some form of consent decree. Ideally, an experienced judge will be in a good position to place pressure on the nonsettling agency. As a practical matter, that agency has the burden of showing why it has not acted "reasonably" in trying to resolve a difficult matter. But if there is a perception of a sweetheart deal with the settling agency, this strategy can backfire, increasing the political pressure on the nonsettling agency to hang tough.

In summary, it is much more difficult to generalize about state and local agencies, or even about agencies with the same mission in different states, than about EPA and the DOJ, which have certain generic characteristics. State and local agencies' turf fights with federal agencies complicate the situation further. Some of the common-sense suggestions above may make interaction with these agencies a little easier.

Citizen Groups

As with federal, state, and local regulatory agencies, it is important to recognize what motivates citizen groups. Different groups may have different motivations, and their levels of competence and sophistication also vary substantially.

National organizations such as the Natural Resources Defense Council, the Sierra Club Legal Defense Fund (now Earth Justice), and the Environmental Defense Fund (now Environmental Defense) are well funded and employ extremely capable and generally experienced counsel. Their technical staffs are also usually quite competent, but have their own ideological biases. These groups engage in litigation on broad, national issues.[33] They will often back up local organizations if the issues have broader significance. The national organizations are also quite expert at mobilizing grass-roots support for their positions. Because agency staff are concerned about public criticism, the ability to influence public opinion is a valuable asset for these citizen groups.

The national organizations' litigation track record is also quite good, perhaps partly because they pick and choose their cases. Thus, if a national group has joined a local organization against your project, you know there is a problem. Although these groups still need to make the necessary record that will help them on appeal, that may not be an insurmountable difficulty.[34]

Local citizen groups vary much more than the national groups. Existing or proposed industrial projects frequently spur local involvement. If an EIS is required under NEPA because the federal government is involved at some decision point, public involvement is specifically required.[35] The state versions of NEPA also require public involvement. (See Chapter 11 for specific issues and concerns with respect to the EIS.) Similarly, if the project potentially affects an economically disadvantaged community or minority group, public involvement may be mandated. (See Chapter 2, Social Concerns: Environmental Justice and the Redevelopment of Industrial Areas.)

There are a variety of strategies for handling public involvement in both NEPA and non-NEPA matters.[36] In general,

> [l]ocal opposition (as well as that of national groups if the project appears to be precedent-setting or of specific interest) should be defused as quickly and as early as possible. Usually, the initial concern stems not from an ideological commitment to stop a project, but rather from economic or personal (subjective) values, such as a fear that the project will lower real estate or home values. There is a rule of reason, of course, for determining when this discussion should begin. If it begins too early, the local population understandably gets agitated because adequate data is not yet available. Conversely, if the process starts too late, the local population may feel the project is a *fait accompli*; they might then conclude that the only answer is to "pass the hat" and start litigation, and/or increase the involvement of state and local politicians seeking easy political mileage by being "pro-green." Rather, the time to make sure the populace and local groups are aware of the project is when [you have] a solid data base so that the various questions and legitimate concerns of the groups can be answered.[37]

Do not conclude from this that early involvement of local and national groups will necessarily prevent litigation, particularly if the project appears to be precedent-setting or of specific local interest. Such involvement has, however, an excellent chance of at least narrowing the issues and reducing the time required for a final decision on the permit. A final decision is made not when the permitting agency issues a permit, but when the final opportunity for appeal in the court system is exhausted.

Opportunities for settlement of these issues vary. Attorneys for citizen groups—particularly national groups—may be willing to compromise, but they must also answer to their clients. A businessperson may feel strongly about an issue on ideological grounds, but may be persuaded to give in because of the ultimate economic impact. The statutes, regulations, and agency staff, however, all reflect or have inherent biases against broad consideration of economic values. Citizen group clients who have brought or are preparing to bring suit on the basis of strong ideological positions are similarly unmotivated by economics. Therefore, potential settlements often must be formulated in terms of providing the greatest benefit to the environment.

Some argue that mediation, conciliation, or settlement can expedite a project.[38] These processes work best, however, within a very narrow structure, and then only if there is no major ideological dispute involving fundamental principles of concern to various environmental groups.[39]

Public Relations

Dealings with the public are absolutely critical to environmental management. The previous section mentioned the importance of meeting with the public early in the project context. Chapter 5 noted that many companies consider public relations[40] issues "significant matters" that must be reported in their environmental management systems. Chapter 6 discussed the public relations benefits of environmental assessments.

Although most companies have separate public relations departments, the environmental manager must also understand the importance of this area of expertise. Most of us do not consider ourselves experts in dealing with the press and the public, in developing campaigns that will persuade the public, or in managing disasters. But because public relations is a constant in our jobs, we need sufficient expertise to be able to give advice in all of the above areas in coordination with our public relations departments. Many companies, including Ato, provide training on dealing with the media. This is vital for environmental professionals. A detailed analysis of public relations techniques and detailed case studies on public relations triumphs or disasters are beyond the scope of this book, but the following sections explain some key rules for environmental managers.

Dealing With the Press

Company positions must be clearly enunciated and presented uniformly to all media at all times. There is nothing worse than different people in an organization saying slightly different things on the same issue. On an evolving issue, the company position might change, and continuity must be maintained.

It is also particularly important that the company develop its position with input from the various staff disciplines involved, including environmental, legal, and public relations. Should any one of these groups become overbearing, there can be serious repercussions. For example, if the legal department is not flexible and creative, the company may give the press too few facts and lose credibility.

Some company public relations departments are very careful to limit press contacts to specific spokespeople. This position is not usually a move to protect turf, but is based on a legitimate concern that unless you know the press mentality and the rules under which the press operates, it is very easy to have a public relations disaster.

Perhaps the greatest danger in dealing with the press is a false assumption that you are speaking "off the record." The number of people burned by this false assumption is countless. If you have developed a long-term relationship with a reporter who has a reputation for integrity, your background briefing or off-the-record comment may indeed be off the record. You can develop such a relationship by being a technical source for the reporter, not necessarily regarding specific matters involving your company. Most reporters who cover environmental issues do not have environmental experience or technical expertise. Their natural inclination is to be cynical about industry and assume the worst. Unless, by serving as a resource for technical data, you have educated a reporter, reduced the reporter's cynicism, and developed a long-term relationship with him or her, you must assume that anything you say to that reporter is on the record.

Despite the risks of dealing directly with the press, limiting press contacts strictly to your public relations department is not necessarily the most effective means of getting your story across. In many companies, a call from the press brings the standard answer of "I'll get back to you." Corporate bureaucracy prevents the call from being returned immediately, and then the reporter is past his or her deadline. The reporter will not only be unable to include your comments, he or she may also conclude that you have something to hide, particularly if the eventual contact is a public relations person who cannot answer the reporter's specific questions.

Indeed, the public relations department would prefer that your spokesperson be an operating or staff person who has specific expertise and understands relations with the press. If the public relations department's spokesperson is an expert in your field—which is rarely the case—he or she can be effective. In addition, many public relations departments run programs to train management to deal with the press. Such programs probably should be expanded. Technical and legal specialists should become more involved in public relations, just as they have become more involved in Washington advocacy. Ideally, a reporter will talk to the technical expert and the public relations expert together; this gives the reporter the best opportunity to understand your position clearly.

A company should have a policy on dealing with the press. Even in the absence of a policy, it is vital to check with a public relations expert about the credentials of the reporter requesting information. I learned the importance of such a check the hard way over 30 years ago. I was interviewed for a future radio program. What I did not know was that to make his points, the reporter planned to edit the interview and insert questions that he had not asked me. The "fixed" questions were asked to someone else whom the reporter favored. When the program aired, it sounded like a face-to-face debate. I was also unaware that this reporter had a reputation for playing this kind of game. I have done other radio debates since, but always live. The danger of having your statements taken out of context by editing is greater than you may think. Indeed, I have seen the raw and edited tapes of a well-known television investigative reporting program that has pulled similar stunts.

It is also important to be certain that what you say cannot be taken out of context even without reportorial dirty tricks. Reporters are looking for catchy statements and sometimes leave out qualifiers. When I first began to work for industry in 1970, I made a statement that could have been taken out of context with disastrous results. As a member of an unusual breed at that time—an environmental lawyer working for a corporation—I was on a New York City Bar Association panel entitled "Young Lawyers and the Legal Revolution." I made a comment that received extensive coverage in the *New York Times*. I first stated: "There are too many Neanderthals in corporations that have nearly wrecked the corporate system." If that comment had been reported without my qualifier, "but a surprising number of corporate executives have consciences," my career in the industrial sector might have been very short-lived. Instead, my company was delighted with the publicity, which also bolstered the general counsel's arguments to management that in the new fields with broad social policy considerations—particularly environmental law and civil rights law—it was important to hire lawyers who normally would not have considered corporate legal departments as a place of employment. I realized, however, that I had been lucky to escape trouble, and learned a valuable lesson on being very careful about statements with qualifiers.

Dealing With the Public

Credibility is critical to good public relations. You may have a public relations fiasco, such as the Ashland Oil tank disaster in which a large tank ruptured and spilled oil into a nearby Pennsylvania river, but there are opportunities for salvage. Often you can maintain credibility by promptly acknowledging your responsibilities and taking corrective action. Ashland, for example, moved very rapidly, recognizing that its legal defenses were minimal. It faced up to its responsibilities immediately and the chief executive made a variety of public statements that were well received. Another example, in a different context, of a good effort to turn around a disaster was Johnson & Johnson's response in the Tylenol™ poisoning case. In this product tampering case, a situation totally beyond its control, the company recognized how critical it was to regain consumer confidence, and spent a huge amount in recalling the product and redesigning its packaging.

Conversely, Exxon's response to the *Valdez* oil tanker spill in Alaska can be perceived as a classic miscalculation.[41] In the event of a perceived environmental or safety incident, the public expects the company's senior executives to be actively and openly involved in mitigation. The public also expects an apology. The company does not have to admit liability, but it must indicate that it cares. Nothing could undo the Bhopal tragedy, but the chairman of Union Carbide went immediately to India at some considerable personal risk. Exxon's failure to send its chairman immediately to Valdez, Alaska, and the resulting public perception that it did not care, has been viewed as having made a bad situation worse. One crisis management expert stated, "[a]s phony as it sounds, sending the chairman to the scene would have shown genuine concern for what happened there."[42] Apparently Exxon's chairman agreed, stating that "although his instinct had been to head to Alaska, he was persuaded not to by a consensus of his fellow Exxon executives."[43]

In the hazardous waste context, credibility can be extremely difficult to achieve. This was particularly true in the early days, just before Superfund, when there was strong political pressure to develop a groundswell for a Superfund law. The public and most politicians and reporters fail to recognize the distinction between trace amounts and harmful quantities of hazardous pollutants, or between situations in which exposure is unlikely and those in which there is an immediate pathway of exposure. If you attempt to deal with these issues head on, you probably will be accused of being callous.

A citizen group can make outrageous statements without any technical backup, and can release so-called health studies that may be full of holes.[44] If you attempt to refute these statements and studies with technical arguments, normally your audience's eyes will glaze over. Even if they listen, they probably will not believe you. After all, you are the polluter as opposed to the victimized citizen. Even if the health studies are eventually discredited, the "exposed" citizens will not believe that the studies are invalid and will probably sue. Any population naturally includes cases of cancer and birth defects. And companies' activities can sometimes cause health problems. The public (and some juries) immediately assume, however, that your activities are responsible for these conditions. Your only response to a situation in which public fear greatly exceeds the actual risk—commonly known as "chemophobia"—is long-term, low-key, and nonthreatening programs that attempt gradual education.

To prevent chemophobia from developing in the first place, you must maintain your image in the local community through grass-roots efforts. Employees should be encouraged to participate in local organizations so that they become known as individuals and not industry ogres. Arranging an "open house" at your local facility can also be helpful. The public normally assumes that a factory or plant is a horrendous place. If you have a well-run and well-kept facility, these visits may improve your local image. It is particularly useful to have the actual operators explain the processes. Usually, their pride in their work and in the facility will come through to the visitors. The chemical industry's Responsible Care® program encourages this kind of community involvement.

Where the issue is siting, concern for real estate values will awaken formerly latent environmental instincts. If they feel, rightly or wrongly, that your siting decision will reduce the value of their housing, members of even the most conservative and pro-business communities will turn out in droves, pass a large hat, and give you major difficulties. (See also Chapter 2, Social Concerns: Environmental Justice and the Redevelopment of Industrial Areas, for a discussion of brownfields issues.) You may have all the facts in the world indicating that your project will not harm the environment, but you still have to dispel concern about real estate values.

It is also important from a business standpoint for senior managers in industries viewed by the public as polluters to recognize that whether or not they are right, neither they nor their companies will be loved. This is particularly troublesome to senior managers who have devoted their lives to a company and, thus, want the company to be liked. This is an unrealistic expectation. At best, the public may look upon you as a responsible company within a polluting industry. Even achieving this level of acceptance is particularly difficult if your industry is considered a polluter and does not generate many jobs. Unfortunately, some senior managers have become virtually obsessed with attacks on their companies and spend an inordinate amount of time trying to change positions taken by public groups that simply are beyond the persuasive power of the senior managers or anyone else, to the detriment of their primary job of managing a company or a specific operation. Senior executives simply have to recognize that some forces are beyond their control.

Managers should also remember that, over time, most disasters—especially if they are handled properly, not only from an environmental management perspective, but from a public relations standpoint—become generic, and the involvement of the particular company becomes obscure.

Notes to Chapter 10

1. For a general discussion of environmental law, see LAW OF ENVIRONMENTAL PROTECTION (Sheldon M. Novick et al. eds., 2004); A PRACTICAL GUIDE TO ENVIRONMENTAL LAW (David Sive & Frank B. Friedman eds., 1987). The first two sections of this chapter are drawn from Frank B. Friedman, *Dealing With Federal and State Agencies and Citizen Groups, in* A PRACTICAL GUIDE TO ENVIRONMENTAL LAW (David Sive & Frank B. Friedman eds., 1987). Adapted by permission of the publisher, the Amer. L. Inst.-Amer. Bar Ass'n Committee on Continuing Professional Education.

2. *See generally* FREDERICK R. ANDERSON, NEGOTIATION AND INFORMAL AGENCY ACTION: THE CASE OF SUPERFUND (report to Administrative Conference of the United States, May 25, 1984).

3. *See generally* Alan W. Eckert, *Representing Private Clients in EPA Rule Making,* NAT. RESOURCES & ENV'T, Winter 1985, at 27.

4. *See* Angus Macbeth, *Settling With the Government,* NAT. RESOURCES & ENV'T, Winter 1985, at 9, 12. "Like private litigation, successful resolution of disputes with the government depends on understanding what the other side wants and why it wants it, so that creative lawyers can find the common ground that will make settlement possible." *Id.* at 12.

5. Arland T. Stein, *EPA Administrative Rule Making: A View From the Outside,* NAT. RESOURCES & ENV'T, Winter 1985, at 33.

6. F. Henry Habicht II, *Settling a Case With the Land and Natural Resources Division,* NAT. RESOURCES & ENV'T, Winter 1985, at 5.

> The [Environment and Natural Resources] Division represents the United States, its agencies, and its officials in matters relating to environmental protection and management of public land resources, including the acquisition of land for public use. In addition to the Environmental Protection Agency (EPA) and the Department of the Interior, the Division's most frequent clients include the departments of Agriculture, Commerce, Defense, Energy, and Transportation, as well as the General Services Administration.
>
> In its affirmative litigation as plaintiff, the Division represents agencies that are suing either to enforce a statute involving environmental protection or resource management or to acquire property through the power of eminent domain. *Id.*

7. These opinions are published by EPA and can be obtained by calling the EPA library at (202) 260-5919 with your specific request, or through on-line access to http://www.eli.org. They are also generally available on the EPA website.

8. For example, the former Superfund settlement policy established a general rule that the federal government would not settle for less than 80 percent of cleanup costs, but also provided for exceptions to this rule. Regional Agency personnel interpreted the exceptions very narrowly, and high-level personnel knew this. Never-

theless, Washington would rarely overrule the regions. Moreover, with the intense political pressure for hazardous waste site cleanup, the regions simply had no incentive to negotiate.

9. Frank B. Friedman, *'60s Activism and '80s Realities—We've Come a Long Way,* ENVTL. F., July 1983, at 8, 11. *See also* Eckert, *supra* note 3, at 32.

> You or your client will never live down a reputation for supplying false or unreliable information. There is a small but elite "bar" well known to EPA. These lawyers represent their clients vigorously, but treat agency staff, counsel, and managers with courtesy and respect. They are scrupulously fair in their dealings with EPA counsel; they can be counted on to keep their word. Their comments and pleadings are reliably accurate and well written. They are cooperative in administrative arrangements such as extensions of time, printing of the record, and scheduling of oral argument. They present their arguments forcefully, but without threats or insults. They persuade their clients to adopt reasonable positions likely to be acceptable to EPA before negotiations commence. It is plain that these lawyers are far more likely to help their clients get the relief they seek than those who approach the task of representation with less balance and finesse.

Id.

10. Eckert, *supra* note 3, at 32.

11. *Id.* (citing D.C. Bar Legal Ethics Comm., Op. 80 (Dec. 18, 1979)).

12. *Id.*

13. *Id.* at 30.

14. Thomas J. Stukane, *EPA's Bubble Policy After* Chevron v. NRDC*: Who Is to Guard the Guards Themselves?,* 17 NAT. RESOURCES LAW. 647 (1985). "The case reports are strewn with the wreckage of attempts to reverse EPA interpretations on fundamental questions of interpretation of Agency-administered statutes." Eckert, *supra* note 3, at 30.

15. Stukane, *supra* note 14, at 675 (footnotes omitted).

16. Eckert, *supra* note 3, at 30.

17. *See* Macbeth, *supra* note 4, at 12; *see also* Frank B. Friedman, *Corporate Environmental Programs and Litigation: The Role of Lawyer-Managers in Environmental Management,* 45 PUB. ADMIN. REV. 766 (1985).

18. Pub L. No. 104-65, 109 Stat. 691 (1995).

19. Macbeth, *supra* note 4, at 9.

20. *Id.*

21. *Id.* at 10.

22. *Id.* at 12.

23. ANDERSON, *supra* note 2, at 46.

24. Macbeth, *supra* note 4, at 11.

25. *Id.*

26. *Id.*

27. *Id.* DOJ regulations provide for public comment on all proposed settlements in pollution abatement cases. *Id.*

28. *See* 42 U.S.C. §7410, ELR STAT. CAA §110.

29. For example, there has been a controversy between the federal government and the South Coast Air Quality Management District over the banking of emissions as a result of shut-downs and other means of reducing emissions under the CAA. The federal government will approve banking of some emission reductions but not others. The District will accept some banking that the federal government will not, and it will not accept some banking that the federal government will accept. A permit applicant is in the position of having to comply with both sets of regulations, regardless of any assurances by the District that compliance with its regulations is all that is necessary.

30. *Id.* at 10.

31. *Id.*

32. *Id.*

33. Citizen groups have been involved in most major litigation in the air, water, and hazardous waste areas. *See* JEFFREY G. MILLER, CITIZEN SUITS: PRIVATE ENFORCEMENT OF FEDERAL POLLUTION CONTROL LAWS (1986); Dan Reisel, *Citizen Suits in Environmental Litigation, in* A PRACTICAL GUIDE TO ENVIRONMENTAL LAW 301 (David Sive & Frank B. Friedman eds., 1987).

34. Stukane, *supra* note 14, at 675 n.139 (citing Motor Vehicle Mfrs. Ass'n of the United States v. State Farm Mut. Auto. Ins. Co., 463 U.S. 29, 13 ELR 20672 (1983) (agency's decision to repeal rule designed to promote safety must be supported by the record)).

35. 40 C.F.R. §1501.7 (1993).

36. *See generally* Frank B. Friedman, *NEPA—An Industry Perspective,* ENVTL. F., Jan. 1985, at 39, 43.

37. *Id.* at 43.

38. The Conservation Foundation, among others, is acting as a mediator in several disputes. EPA is using negotiated rulemaking.

39. Friedman, *supra* note 36, at 43.

40. Many companies use the term "community relations," rather than "public relations," to describe dealing with the public because the term "public" relations connotes "press" relations.

41. Sherman, *Smart Ways to Handle the Press,* FORTUNE, June 19, 1989, at 69. *See also* Ross Sandler, *Courting Public Opinion,* ENVTL. F., Mar./Apr. 1992, at 10.

42. Sandler, *supra* note 41, at 14.

43. *Id.* at 14-15.

44. The report prepared for Congress by a study group under CERCLA §301 notes:

> The popular concern over the consequences of exposure to hazardous wastes has also resulted in overreaction. The "ghost dump" of Frayser, Tennessee, is one example where a highly charged atmosphere resulted in emotional meetings, Congressional hearings and talk of evacuating the area, even though no actual dump site existed. See *The Dump That Wasn't There,* 215 SCIENCE 645 (Feb. 5, 1982). There is an ongoing dispute, too, over the Love Canal scare, frequently referred to during the passage of CERCLA, and the quality of the May 1980 study of alleged chromosome defects among the residents of houses near the site. *See* Havender, *Assessing and Controlling Risk, in* BARDACH AND KAGEN, SOCIAL REGULATION: STRATEGIES FOR REFORM 21, 47 (1982); Levine, LOVE CANAL: SCIENCE, POLITICS AND PEOPLE (1982); *Psycho-Social Impact of Toxic Waste Dumps,* 127 CONG. REC. E5894 (Dec. 16, 1981) (Rep. John LaFalce); Kolata, *Love Canal: False Alarm Caused by Botched Study,* 208 SCIENCE 1239 (June 13, 1980); Holden, *Love Canal Residents Under Stress,* 208 SCIENCE 1242 (June 13, 1980).

SUPERFUND SECTION 301(e) STUDY GROUP, INJURIES AND DAMAGES FROM HAZARDOUS WASTES—ANALYSIS AND IMPROVEMENT OF LEGAL REMEDIES, A REPORT TO CONGRESS IN COMPLIANCE WITH SECTION 301(e) OF THE COMPREHENSIVE ENVIRONMENTAL RESPONSE, COMPENSATION, AND LIABILITY ACT OF 1980 (P.L. 96-510), Serial No. 97-12, §I n.5, printed for the use of the Senate Committee on Environment and Public Works, 97th Cong., 2d Sess. (Sept. 1982).

Chapter 11:
The Environmental Impact
Statement Process

It is beyond the scope of this book to describe specific permitting processes or to discuss NEPA[1] or state "NEPAs"[2] in detail. This chapter gives some basic suggestions on handling the EIS process. I have worked with NEPA since its early days, advising the oil and gas and mining industries on the basics and practical realities of implementing the statute,[3] and on a variety of litigation and projects involving NEPA and those industries.

For those of you who are new to this area, NEPA was the first statute of the environmental "revolution" and was designed to ensure that projects' environmental impacts would be fully considered. The key section of NEPA is §102(2)(C), which requires an EIS for "major Federal actions significantly affecting the quality of the human environment."[4] This language is fairly simple, but has spawned extensive litigation over specific fact patterns. In my wildest imagination, I never would have dreamed that there would still be substantial litigation more than 30 years after NEPA was promulgated. Such actions include most federal permitting activities, exclusive of EPA permits. An EIS must address the following:

(i) the environmental impact of the proposed action,

(ii) any adverse environmental effects which cannot be avoided should the proposal be implemented,

(iii) alternatives to the proposed action,

(iv) the relationship between local short-term uses of man's environment and the maintenance and enhancement of long-term productivity, and

(v) any irreversible and irretrievable commitments of resources which would be involved in the proposed action should it be implemented.[5]

States have promulgated similar laws, usually using the term "environmental impact report" (EIR) instead.[6]

The law itself is simple, but the politics of completing an adequate EIS are complicated and need to be addressed in detail. EIS preparation involves all the issues and skills discussed in previous chapters. It is particularly important to ensure that a project will not be stopped by an injunction because of "irreparable harm that would result absent such an injunction."[7] Environmental groups have to show more than just that an impact statement is inadequate to obtain an injunction, and the courts have become increasingly reluctant to "second-guess the scientists, experts, economists, and planners who make the environmental [impact] statement."[8] This does not mean that inadequate EISs will not be successfully challenged.

It is important to meet the criteria for an adequate EIS. As one court has stated:

> [I]n our opinion an EIS is in compliance with NEPA when its form, content, and preparation substantially (1) provide decision-makers with an environmental disclosure sufficiently detailed to aid in the substantive decision whether to proceed with the project in the light of its environmental consequences, and (2) make available to the public, information of the proposed project's environmental impact and encourage public participation in the development of that information.[9]

It is clear that trying to fight or undermine the EIS process will not generally work. Industry representatives have therefore recognized that their most important function in the EIS process is to ensure that adequate studies are completed for use in the statement. This approach reduces the risks of delay and additional expense in the litigation process.

It is particularly important to ensure that agency shortcuts in the name of "policy" do not actually delay projects substantially. Both government and industry attorneys have learned to advise their clients of the danger of encouraging projects that will not withstand environmental scrutiny. Consequently, this chapter will discuss how you and your counsel can ensure the adequacy of the EISs.

Substantial agreement on what needed to be done to comply was reached early in NEPA's history. The original NEPA regulations have been basically unchanged since they were first promulgated on November 19, 1978.[10] On June 9, 1978, the then-General Counsel of the Council on Environmental Quality (CEQ), Nick Yost, inserted language in the preamble to the proposed regulations noting that there was agreement between the American Petroleum Institute (which I represented) and the Sierra Club (represented by its then-President Bill Futrell (subsequently President of the Environmental Law Institute)) as to the issues and potential solutions:

> There was extraordinary consensus among the diverse witnesses. All, without exception, expressed the view that NEPA benefited the public. Equally widely shared was the view that the process had become needlessly cumbersome and should be trimmed down. Witness after witness said that the length and detail of [EIS] made it extremely difficult to distinguish the important from the trivial. The degree of unanimity about the good and bad points of the NEPA process was such that at one point an official spokesman for the oil industry rose to say that he adopted in its entirely the presentation of the President of the Sierra Club.[11]

The times were different and three young lawyers who knew and respected each other could in essence reach agreement that would stand the test of time. A very significant factor in the long-term effective implementation of that statute has been the continuity of senior counsel for both the CEQ and DOJ—Dinah Bear at CEQ and Bill Cohen at DOJ.

Some of us recognized early on that NEPA is a procedural statute and as long as there is full disclosure, the impact statement process should work. Thus, I have advocated that the "weight" of evidence is guided by the "Manhattan telephone book approach" to the weight—the more data, the more protection. This is contrary to the original intention of the Act, which assumed short statements of a few pages, but it does work as the best defense.

Similarly, as noted above, sometimes government efforts to shortcut come under the category of "Lord protect me from my friends." Many years ago, I was disturbed that an agency was shortcutting in developing an EIS for a project of concern to my employer. An attorney representing the Natural Resources Defense Council had similar concerns, but for different reasons. We went in together to the agency, shocking the agency, which at that time had not seen that kind of cooperation between industry and public interest groups, but we succeeded in obtaining a solid EIS that also withstood litigation.

Over the years, many of us in industry have also found value in the process, although sometimes frustrated by its length and complexity. Understanding the broader implications of a project is helpful in planning. Determining what are the public concerns early on help permitting and as noted earlier, most of us in industry appreciate the fundamental philosophy that the federal government should not go forward with major action unless it understands the environmental implications.

The basis for these anecdotes is to illustrate that for the large project, where extensive permits may be required, which in turn take time, many of us representing industry are accustomed to the realities of the process. Again, the rationale that there needs to be a mechanism that assures that the federal government is accountable for significant actions which "may significantly affect the quality of the human environment," makes sense. That said, any regulatory structure, system, or policy should be reexamined over the years. The public database today and the easy availability of that data are far greater than it was when NEPA was promulgated. The experience of the agencies on various issues has also improved and in many instances the EIS process has become repetitive and rote. If there are ways of achieving functional equivalence of environmental awareness without writing massive tomes to avoid litigation, perhaps these methods should be considered so long as the basic policy behind the statute remains in place. It is not a sin against the environment to develop generic approaches if they would work. This is the rationale behind CEQ's efforts to reexamine the process:

> On May 20, 2002, Council on Environmental Quality (CEQ) established a (NEPA) Task Force to review the current NEPA implementing practices and procedures in the following areas: technology and information management; interagency and intergovernmental collaboration including joint-lead processes; programmatic analyses and subsequent tiered documents; and adaptive management. In addition, the NEPA Task Force will look at other NEPA implementation issues such as the level of detail included in agencies' procedures and documentation for promulgating categorical exclusions; the structure and documentation of environmental assessments; and implementation practices that would benefit other agencies. [12]

CEQ envisioned that "the information gained and disseminated by the NEPA Task Force will help federal agencies update their practices and procedures and better integrate NEPA into federal agency decision making." [13]

Many of the comments received called for more generic statements, less reconsideration and a revision of regulations to reflect changing case law. For example, the Western Urban Water Coalition[14] noted that it "favors the use of comprehensive NEPA analyses that will serve as the basis for long-term planning. Reopening completed NEPA procedures on such project is undesirable. CEQ should develop procedures that provide for comprehensive NEPA reviews that do not require reconsideration absent major new developments and continuing agency involvement that establishes decision-making duties on an ongoing basis." That organization also noted that its members "favor coordinated NEPA processes that allow all requisite federal and state actions to be covered in a single NEPA review. The NEPA guidance should put a premium on comprehensive review procedures that, in a single procedure, involve all required agencies in the most efficient manner possible."[15]

Cost was also an issues and costs could be reduced

> through guidance that specifies, among other issues: how inter-agency teams will function and establish binding timeframes; how to tier off of previous NEPA compliance; how to incorporate applicants into the process; and how to ensure that other procedures that cover the same action (e.g., consolidation under the Endangered Species Act and Fish and Wildlife Coordination Act) are coordinated with the NEPA review.[16]

Another solution advocated was more programmatic review and an all-inclusive process that brings in the public and governmental agencies early on in the process to avoid later creating "a situation where stakeholders are in a position to claim they lacked access to the process and are positioned to raise procedural objections at a later data."[17]

All of these comments are in my view appropriate, but implementation of change will be difficult, not because these criticisms do not make sense, but the concern of all parties that "the devil is in the details."

My concern, however, is not with change per se or revaluating a statute or policy, but what change and reevaluation may mean in today's polarized atmosphere. The willingness to work together, the bipartisanship which was the basis for the early federal air and water legislation, does not exist today and probably will not change for the foreseeable future. Thus, if efforts to change a policy or program that have worked and have considerable case law behind it, will in turn result in extensive litigation and uncertainty, that doesn't help industrial projects. The unfortunate reality, particularly relating to forestry and the public lands, is that the polarization is so great that even if a change or approach does makes sense, it will be characterized as the worst sin known to humankind.

The real issues are more fundamental than NEPA. They relate to how public lands and forests will be managed and resources developed. Perhaps I have reached the stage in life where I long for the "good old days" where people and groups might differ, but they approached the issues with civility. These issues need to be resolved within their underlying regulatory regimes and public policies, but this is virtually impossible with intense distrust and partisan bickering. We now know and understand the NEPA process. It is time-consuming and projects can be delayed by litigation, but at least there is usually light at the end of the tunnel. Unless changes are made carefully, within existing case law, uncertainty will breed additional delay, which is not in industry's interest. These changes may simply not be worth the effort. Legislative change is unlikely unless there are significant shifts in the present balances in Congress. Thus, any changes made in policy and regulation, as a result of CEQ's efforts will be probably fought fiercely and be subject to litigation.

In September 2003, the CEQ issued its report.[18] "The CEQ held several regional roundtable workshops to discuss the taskforce recommendations in 2003 and 2004, but has not yet announced specific proposals."[19]

> Although not directly related to the NEPA Task Force Report, the Department of Interior (DOI) substantially revised its NEPA procedures and policies consistent with the report's recommendations. These revisions emphasize "consensus based management" and "community based training" to enhance public participation and "adaptive management" using monitoring and enforcement programs to track mitigation measures.[20]

With that background, the following describes the various aspects of the NEPA process.

The Lead Agency

Many projects are subject to the jurisdiction of more than one federal or state agency. Any of the agencies could prepare the EIS, but one agency will act as the "lead agency" to assume supervisory responsibility for preparation of the statement.[21] The competence of this agency and the speed with which it will undertake to prepare the EIS are important to the applicant. In addition, jealousies often develop among the agencies, and it is important to determine the attitudes of the agencies toward each other as early as possible.

It is also essential to establish what people will be available and whether the federal lead agency can work together with the state lead agency. Selection of the federal and state lead agencies must be coordinated, particularly in a state such as California where the state EIR will be prepared at the same time as the federal EIS. It may be possible to use part or all of the federal EIS as part of the state EIR, so the two statements will be consistent.

In a controversial project involving several agencies, selection of the lead agency may take from three to six months. "Any Federal agency, or any State or local agency or private person substantially affected by the absence of lead agency designation, may make a written request to the potential lead agencies that a lead agency be designated."[22] The CEQ has federal responsibility for supervising the EIS process and can be helpful in mediating conflicts.[23] An agency should not be selected because it is known for its speed, as opposed to its competence, in developing EISs. An agency notorious for shortcuts that will help an applicant expedite the EIS process is not necessarily the best lead agency, because shortcuts can lead to delays in the review process and probable litigation.

In conjunction with selection of the lead agency, the applicant should prepare a full outline of what it believes the EIS should include. Its own legal analysis will be extremely helpful in avoiding agency shortcuts. A suggested outline of the areas that need to be covered can also help expedite the process, because it gives an agency at least a working draft at an early time. This is particularly useful if the staff is inexperienced or unfamiliar with the project.

Assembling a Task Force

Federal and state agencies normally do not have the personnel readily available to devote substantial time to a complicated project. Considerable effort may be necessary in Washington, D.C., or in the project's home state to ensure the assignment of competent personnel. Agencies are reluctant to remove staff from their normal duties for long periods even if a project has some form of national priority. Consequently, it may take three months just to assemble the necessary task force to work on the EIS.

An applicant may feel greatly frustrated when, after doing a substantial amount of environmental work, it finds that the task force assigned to the project has had limited or no previous experience in the EIS process. Months may be necessary merely to understand what is involved in the project and to develop the necessary writing techniques. Thus, the applicant's early assembly of data in a usable form is quite important.

Preparation of an Environmental Impact Analysis

Unless extensive data are readily available and the agency is very experienced in the area, the applicant should prepare a complete environmental impact analysis for use by the agency or agencies involved. This can be very expensive, but cutting the time required for preparing the EIS can save money, particularly if you and/or your financing institution are anxious to begin the project.

Accurate Data

First-rate data may dispel some of the opposition, or at least cause the opposition to consider the possible outcome seriously before it decides to litigate. Many times I have teased my friends in the environmental community that they will have a hard time finding competent experts to challenge a project because we have already hired the best. It is important to use credible consultants in developing the environmental analysis. If the consultants have solid reputations in the scientific community, the agency may determine that only limited cross-checks are necessary to ensure a perception that the agency, rather than the applicant, has completed the EIS. Thus, complete duplication of the applicant's work and analysis will be avoided.

It is particularly helpful to get the advice of local environmental groups, who may be opposed to a project, as to the scope of the available studies and additional studies that they feel are necessary. An early meeting with them can correct many misconceptions before their positions harden and they raise funds to attempt to stop the project. Their input can also be extremely helpful in planning the project. Although early contact may not eliminate litigation, it can narrow the issues that will be litigated. Patience and control of temper are critical to avoid early and irrevocable polarization.

Time Factors

It is also important to recognize that one or more years of baseline data may be necessary to determine the environmental impacts of a complicated project. The agency needs to know the air quality, water quality, and biological bases for that period. Alternative sites for the project and the impacts on these sites must also be considered. Agencies may have extensive information and, on rare occasions, additional studies may not be necessary, but usually the schedule for the project must include time for obtaining data.

Moreover, some agencies, such as the Nuclear Regulatory Commission, require an applicant to prepare an EIR before the agency begins drafting the EIS. It can take a full year to prepare an EIR. Agencies that do not require an EIR before beginning the EIS can have some of the baseline analysis and data prepared as the EIS is being drafted.

Preparation of a Draft EIS

If no additional studies are necessary and the project has some priority within the agency, nine months to a year should be enough time to complete an adequate draft EIS. During the preparation period, discussions should be held with the agencies that would normally review the statement to determine what areas they consider critical. All agencies concerned with the project should be involved at the earliest possible time. Prior contact can expedite the formal review of the draft EIS and limit potential negative comments. Courts will consider as significant negative comments by environmental agencies such as EPA.

Agencies should be encouraged to seek the advice of the applicant, environmental groups, and other interested agencies in preparing the EIS. The agency that ignores them may complete a very poor draft statement. If all groups are essentially satisfied with the scope of the EIS and its consideration of the issues, litigation and costly additional delays may be eliminated.

Too often the agencies simply will not have the expertise of the applicant, who may have devoted years to analysis and study before making a major financial decision to build the project. Both the agency and the applicant should designate liaison personnel to ensure that materials are received and continuous contact is maintained.

The CEQ's regulations do not provide specific timetables for comment because of the feeling that they would be too "inflexible."[24] The regulations do, however, provide for a minimum of 45 days for interested agencies to review a draft EIS.[25] This period, as well as a two- to three-week period for printing the EIS, should be considered in arranging a time schedule.

Public Hearings

Although most federal agencies do not require them on a draft EIS, public hearings are usually held if the project is sizable or controversial. Early guidelines adopted by the CEQ before the regulations were promulgated require at least 15 days' notice, but if the project is controversial, an additional 15 to 30 days are usually provided prior to the hearing.[26]

The applicant should thoroughly review the draft EIS and be prepared to criticize it at the hearing.

The hearing is a good time to indicate where the agency has overstated the environmental impacts of the project. The applicant may also see understated impacts, and it is good practice in ensuring the adequacy of the EIS and improving the applicant's credibility to indicate potentially understated impacts at the public hearing. Because it is virtually impossible to hide the negative environmental impacts of a project, it is to the applicant's advantage to reveal them and reap the benefits of credibility and EIS soundness. NEPA is essentially a full-disclosure law.

Written Comments

Written comments are considered part of the EIS,[27] and are also extremely important in ensuring its adequacy. Agencies must respond to them.[28] Thus, if areas in the EIS are weak or need expansion or revision, the applicant should prepare extensive written comments and thus force the agency to do the necessary work to complete an adequate EIS. Note that EISs have never been rejected for being too voluminous and that sometimes the "weight of the evidence" in reviewing an EIS is literally measured in pounds.

If there are extensive written comments and hearings, the agency should not be encouraged to expedite completion of the final statement until the applicant is certain that the agency can adequately respond to the comments. Usually, it takes about three months to respond properly to both oral and written comments.

Outside Consultants

The EIS process is time-consuming and expensive. Use of outside consultants by applicants and, to a certain degree, by the agencies themselves (usually at the applicant's expense), is favored. As long as the agency and not the applicant prepares the EIS, these consultants are legally acceptable.[29]

An outside consultant experienced in preparing impact statements can shorten the process by three to six months. Even if the time is not shortened, at least the final product will have a better chance of being satisfactory. Nevertheless, some agencies will continually second-guess consultants and nullify their value.

Both the agency and the applicant should be certain that the consultant has a good idea of the scope of the project and the areas that an adequate EIS must include. Thus, the proposal should indicate the scope of the consultant's work. He or she must be given room to make independent decisions, but time schedules should be set and the scope of the necessary studies should be predetermined, allowing flexibility to revise provisions as problems are discovered.

Public Involvement

As discussed in Chapter 10 (see section on Citizen Groups), the EIS scoping process specifically requires public involvement.[30] It is preferable to arrange meetings with potentially opposing parties before the formal scoping process to keep such opposition from coalescing. You should also be ready to provide information necessary to address matters of local concern.[31]

Conclusion

In EIS preparation, as in almost all areas of interface with environmental regulators, the most significant job of the manager and the attorney is handling the administrative process before litigation is initiated. It is critical to use environmental counsel early on as a means of preventing litigation. Too often, attorneys are not included in the earliest stages of EIS planning and preparation, but are brought in only when litigation has become imminent and it is too late to make the necessary record. NEPA cases are won or lost on records. The most important record is the intangible one of working early on with *all* parties, including potential opposition, to avoid litigation or at least to ensure that issues are narrowed and that your position is backed up by a sound, voluminous EIS that will be difficult to challenge.

The best example I know (as mentioned previously in this chapter) to demonstrate the importance of this advice occurred in the early 1970s. I was engaged in some frustrating attempts to convince an agency to broaden both the scope and the depth of a proposed EIS. My concern was primarily based on what appeared to be substantial vulnerability to a citizen suit. At the same time, a colleague of mine with a national environmental organization was equally frustrated by the agency's recalcitrance. I suggested, and he agreed, that we both meet with senior agency officials to express our concerns. This unusual request provoked the action we were both seeking, and the EIS was greatly improved. No lawsuit was filed at that time, although another citizen group unsuccessfully challenged the EIS in another context several years later.

Notes to Chapter 11

1. 42 U.S.C. §§4321-4370d, ELR Stat. NEPA §2 et seq. *See* Sive & Cohen, *NEPA Practice, in A Practical Guide to Environmental Law* 169 (David Sive & Frank B. Friedman, eds. 1987). Much of this chapter appeared in an earlier form in Frank B. Friedman, *The Environmental Impact Statement Process*, 22 Prac. Law. 47 (1976). Adapted by permission of the publisher, the American Law Institute-American Bar Association Committee on Continuing Professional Education. The original version was reprinted in *George C. Coggins & Charles F. Wilkinson, Federal Public Land and Resources Law* (2d ed. 1987).

2. Practice varies from state to state. For an example of the complexity of state NEPAs, see S. Duggan et al., Guide to the California Environmental Quality Act (CEQA) (1987).

3. Friedman, *Recent NEPA Effects on Industrial Development*, 9 Nat. Resources L. 479 (1976) and *Operational Impact of NEPA and Related Environmental Laws, Regulations and Orders on Mineral Operations*, 19 Rocky Mtn. Mineral L. Inst. 47 (1974).

4. 42 U.S.C. §4332(2)(C), ELR Stat. NEPA §102(2)(C).

5. *Id.*

6. *See, e.g.,* California Environmental Quality Act, Cal. Pub. Res. Code §21000 et seq.

7. Kleppe v. Sierra Club, 427 U.S. 390, 6 ELR 20532 (1976).

8. National Helium Corp. v. Morton, 486 F.2d 995, 1006, 4 ELR 20041 (10th Cir. 1973) (Breitenstein, J., concurring), *cert. denied*, 416 U.S. 993 (1974).

9. Trout Unlimited v. Morton, 509 F.2d 1276, 1283, 5 ELR 20151 (9th Cir. 1974).

10. 43 Fed. Reg. 55978 et seq.

11. *Id.* at 25231 (June 9, 1978).

12. *See* http://ceq.eh.doe.gov/nepa/nepanet.htm.

13. *Id.*

14. Comments submitted September 23, 2002, CQ 474.

15. *Id.*

16. *Id.*

17. *Id.*

18. The Nepa Task Force, CEQ, Report to the Council on Environmental Quaility—Modernizing NEPA Implementation (2003), available at http://ceq.eh.doe.gov/ntf/20030929memo.pdf (last visited Sept. 14, 2005).

19. Norman Carlin, Environmental Impact Assessment 2004 Annual Report—The Year in Review 2004, ABA Section of Environment, Energy, and Resources Law 356 (2005).

20. *Id.* at 356-57.

21. 40 C.F.R. §1501.5 (1996).

22. *Id.* §1501.5(d).

23. The status of the CEQ was once in flux. President Clinton proposed abolishing the agency in 1993 and its staff and funding were subsequently reduced. In September 1994, however, yielding to congressional pressure to keep the CEQ alive, President Clinton nominated a new chairperson. Its role has increased during the Bush Administration.

24. *Id.* §1501.8.

25. *Id.* §1506.10(c).

26. NEPA; Implementation Procedures, Appendix I & Appendix II, 38 Fed. Reg. 20550 (Aug. 1, 1973) (CEQ guidelines).

27. National Helium Corp. v. Morton, 486 F.2d 995, 1001, 4 ELR 20041 (10th Cir. 1973), *cert. denied*, 416 U.S. 993 (1974).

28. 40 C.F.R. §1503.4.

29. *See* 38 Fed. Reg. at 20550. The rationale for allowing consultants to prepare EISs is discussed in Natural Resources Defense Council v. Callaway, 524 F.2d 79, 87, 5 ELR 20640 (2d Cir. 1975):

> The evil sought to be avoided . . . is the preparation of the EIS by a party, usually a state agency, with an individual "axe to grind," i.e., an interest in seeing the project accepted and completed in a specific manner as proposed. Authorship by such a biased party might prevent the fair and impartial evaluation of a project envisioned by NEPA. Here no problem of self-interest on the part of the author exists. As the Navy's hiree, the independent consultant has no interest but the Navy's to serve and is fully responsible to the Navy for any shortcomings in the EIS. Therefore, we see no difference for NEPA purposes between this procedure and preparation of the EIS by Navy personnel. In both cases the preparers are guided exclusively by the interests of the Navy and the dictates of the NEPA process.

Id.

30. 40 C.F.R. §1501.7.

31. *See* Frank B. Friedman, *NEPA—An Industry Perspective*, ENVTL. F., Jan. 1985, at 39, 43.

Chapter 12:
Green Arthritis

This book has discussed some very positive changes in environmental management and also some very negative challenges. In November 2000, my colleague Dick MacLean and I published an article in the *Environmental Forum* entitled *Green Arthritis*,[1] where we essentially summarized the negatives. In that article, we stated that "[e]nvironmental progress has become ossified, as the major actors replay the battles of the past: environmentalists persist in seeing old problems as continuing crises. Regulators still triumphantly announce new enforcement actions. And industry touts sustainable development while continuing mostly to seek simple compliance."[2] We anticipated a firestorm of protest against these conclusions, having insulted virtually the entire environmental community. Instead, both privately and publicly we heard from numerous sources in all the affected constituencies that our thesis was correct.[3] While it is always pleasant to have your positions validated, we were hoping that perhaps we were wrong. Unfortunately, the reaction to the September 11, 2001, tragedy by many companies has been further cutbacks and government is more concerned with terrorism and other security issues, not the environment.[4] Perhaps the future will allow all of us to be more optimistic. In any event, the following describes the green arthritis syndrome and some possible cures. This book and the suggested solutions contained in it hopefully provide potential cures or at least palliatives for green arthritis. Many if not most of the points contained in this chapter have been made in one form or another in this book, but it is useful to put them together to understand this syndrome. Many of you are now living with that syndrome or will soon be exposed to it.

We Have Come a Long Way, but Is It Far Enough?

If the environmental movement in the United States were a person, she would be world famous and proud of her spectacular achievements that have influenced and guided the world. But the Grand Old Lady is growing old prematurely. She is not moving as fast as she once did. There are new upstarts in Europe that seem to be drawing all the attention. Her friends that were with her from the start in industry, governments, and NGOs whisper that they are frustrated with the lack of progress and the loss of leadership that she once held.

Of course, she might respond that things are different now and without the crises that were constant in her younger years, she doesn't need to be as spry. Many would shake their heads and say this is just an excuse. They are worried that her unwillingness to lead comes at the worst possible time, when significant global concerns loom over the horizon. Is her arthritic condition curable?

Perhaps, but it will require a combination of leadership and courage at every level. The lack of leadership is mostly by the government, including at the presidential level, but the U.S. Congress and business also bear responsibility, as do the environmental groups. Without clear direction and in the absence of a crisis du jour there is a lack of commitment by all. People may talk about the importance of the environment, but they lack this ethic when it comes to their daily lives, particularly if it may cause them any inconvenience.

This criticism is strong (it will look to many that this is the Don Rickles approach and I have insulted everyone!) but I think it is valid. In essence, the premise is that the main players—government, the environmental groups/citizens and business—are mired in the mindset that developed in the beginnings of the federal efforts on environmental issues in the 1970s and are unable to deal effectively with today's issues and potential solutions. Terry Davies, a Senior Fellow with Resources for the Future and a former senior EPA official, noted:

> Much of the current control system is not working. No one can understand or make sense of the laws and regulation, cooperation is required from too many actors and the whole structure is Kafkaesque. . . . Both the environmental and business communities have hunkered down to defend the status quo. . . . The one ray of hope may be the States, who continue to perform their time-honored role of "laboratories of democracy."[5]

The following contains some suggestions for EPA and the environmental community, but the focus of the following is primarily on industry. A six-step approach has been put forward that begins with an evaluation of the possible competitive threats and opportunities, moves on to an evaluation of internal resources, and concludes with the creation of a supporting climate for innovation. This book contains extensive material on how to move companies forward and this chapter is primarily centered on why some of these fundamentally different approaches are needed.

Early Symptoms

You do not need a doctorate in political science to recognize that managing the flow of information is a major factor in controlling political, social, and economic outcomes. Over the past 30 years the spread of democracy and communications tools such as the Internet have allowed an unprecedented flow of information on the environment. What one sees today is a bewildering array of messages spanning the gamut from enormous progress to a planet self-destructing. Marla Cone in a *Los Angeles Times* article describes the situation this way: "Sure the Cuyahoga River is no longer on fire, but the planet is still a mess. The challenge of the future is to confront the increasingly complex threats to our air and food and water and children."[6] There is no doubt that real progress has been made. Steven Rauch, in the *National Journal* cites the substantial reductions in all the major air pollutants since 1970, despite the population growing by one-third and vehicle-miles and gross domestic product doubling:

> Sulfur dioxides and carbon monoxide are down by two-thirds, nitrogen oxides by almost 40 percent, ozone by 30 percent; lead is effectively banished. In the cities, unhealthy-air days are down by more than half, just since 1988. Releases of toxic materials into the environment have declined 42 percent since then; soil erosion falls by almost 40 million tons a year. . . .[7]

Yet a recent poll by Environmental Defense found that 57% of adults surveyed said that U.S. environmental conditions are worse today than 30 years ago and 67% agreed "despite the Clean Air Act and Clean Water Act, air and water pollution seem to continue to get worse."[8] This perception was even more pronounced in younger people, obviously not old enough to remember what the past was really like.

If it is confusing to the public, how have regulatory agencies responded to focus our resources most effectively to deal with the remaining issues? Not very well. Even *defenders* of the current systems admit that the current system is inflexible, shortsighted, and inefficient. As Dan Fiorino, an EPA division director stated: "Much has been made of the 'reinvention' of environmental regulation in the 1990s. However, nearly all recent efforts to reinvent environmental regulation in the United States have come to little more than a tinkering with specific elements of a highly complex system."[9]

Is There Motivation for Change at EPA?

Unfortunately, a major barrier to reexamining the nation's approach to these issues is the lack of political advantage in pressing the public to deal with the remaining problems. Yes, there are still too many people who have significant breathing problems and there are many rivers that have not reached the "fishable" and "swimmable" goals of the Clean Water Act. But, these issues are nowhere near the "crisis" levels that led to our current federal environmental laws. Why continue to expend an inordinate amount of precious political capital on these issues?

A complicating factor is that many of the remaining issues are societal issues without clearly identified offenders. For example, it is recognized by environmental professionals that the primary remaining water quality problems are related to nonpoint sources. Yet, most of the water enforcement efforts are still devoted to point sources, a less politically flammable target. Does "no crisis, no deep pockets, no photo-op" equate to "no problem"?

Could this failure to develop measures consistent with the new realities be self-interest? Most regulators, despite protestations to the contrary, continue to be suspicious of management systems as a vehicle for environmental compliance. Many EPA staffers have spent their entire careers in the Agency and are ready for retirement. They grew up with the traditional means of controlling pollution. After more than 30 years of federal environmental law, there has to be significant progress, but you won't find it in the words of many federal regulators. As noted previously, the remarks of Eric Schaeffer (formerly Director, Office of Regulatory Enforcement) at an American Bar Association meeting are typical of enforcement personnel: "EPA's docket is full of cases involving prominent companies that have sophisticated management systems and terrific codes of behavior written into their corporate policies and posted on their walls."[10] From EPA's standpoint, there are still too many significant violations and there continues to be a strong need to monitor state regulatory systems. Is there some effort here to justify jobs and appropriations? Enforcement on the federal level was separated from policy as an administrative reform during the Clinton Administration. Is enforcement (as opposed to compliance) becoming an end instead of a means of implementing policy?

While there may be some state programs that are not adequately implementing federal programs or enforcing the law, does this justify all of the resources in the extensive regional offices of the EPA? Clearly, such offices were necessary in the early days of federal environmental law, when strong state programs were few and far between. Is this necessary today, or should some of these people be delegated to the states? As noted by Christopher

Tolue, the Washington representative for the Environmental Council of States (ECOS):

> During the 30 years since the birth of the current environmental system, one factor has changed considerably—the willingness and capacity of States to provide environmental service. About 74% of all major federal environmental programs that can be delegated to States for day-to-day management have been delegated. In fact, in 1993 only about 40% of these programs had been delegated.... From 1986 to 1996, state spending on the environment increased by 140%.[11]

To be fair to EPA, it is difficult to change paradigms when partisan politics demand simple numbers to describe progress to their constituents. It is easier to count legal actions than to measure environmental quality. Robbie Roberts, former Executive Director of the ECOS, best characterized the issue of numbers: "[D]rawing conclusions about the state of the environment from the number of enforcement actions was like estimating how many high school students understood Shakespeare by counting the number that had been expelled from English Class."[12]

EPA is attempting to devise performance-based measures to replace traditional "beans." But as George Hawkins, an EPA attorney working on then-Vice President Al Gore's national performance review noted:

> Debate about the effectiveness of different types of actions is hampered by the difficulty in measuring the consequences of such actions in environmental terms. Until these measures are understood, it will be too easy to judge EPA by counting enforcement actions taken and harder to justify other problem-solving actions that are designed to eliminate the causes of environmental harm.[13]

EPA is also trying to develop a performance track that rewards environmental leaders. But as Elliott Laws, then-Executive Director of Outlook Policy Forum noted: "[O]ur [current] regulatory system, which is based on our traditional 'ethic' of environmental protection, is not designed to promote or support [a performance track] system. It is questionable whether . . . the system can even allow it."[14] EPA is now looking at a comprehensive rulemaking to provide real incentives for companies to participate. No doubt this will not only be very controversial, but also very risky for the regulators. If somehow, someway, somebody beats the system, that regulator will face the wrath of the politicians. There is little incentive for making changes that could be perceived as weakening regulations or gutting enforcement.

EPA may be faulted for a lack of leadership in this area, but ample fault can also be found in Congress and at the presidential level. Government, and particularly Congress and the president, respond to crisis and without a crisis, real or perceived, there is little incentive for change or leadership. This is particularly the case if efforts to make changes will be met with political firestorms. The EPA budget is also considered as part of an appropriation process that includes many other agencies and rarely gets the kind of attention it should. There are too many constituencies supporting the status quo to look closely at priorities, analogous to the defense budget process that makes it extremely difficult to close unneeded bases and use the money where it will be of more value. As noted by Michael Lyons:

> Environmental agencies may appear to be ineffective, but they are being asked to do the impossible. They are caught between uncompromising interest groups that voice unreasonable demands; a policy technocracy that inconclusively debates risks and standards; and a Congress that establishes unrealistic goals, mindlessly proliferates mandates, and yet reserves most of its budget for higher political priorities such as entitlements.[15]

What's in It for the Environmental Groups?

For environmental groups, there is little motivation to trust the agencies or businesses. They see little value in saving a company time and money or, in many cases, even acknowledging that it is doing a good job. After all, these same groups may have to attack these same companies one day. Indeed, the public's perception of a health crisis or lax government enforcement helps justify the need for these groups and stimulates needed funding. Organizational viability for much of the environmental community is based on fundraising, and it is more difficult to raise funds without a crisis, real or perceived.

More and more environmental activism is grassroots, with strong national and international networks driven by the Internet. The fragmentation problem also significantly impacts on policy outcomes. As further noted by Lyons:

> Increasingly splintered, the environmental movement has a diffuse agenda that invites policy fragmentation. The movement presses endlessly for new programs, but the programs do not amount to results.
>
> To establish greater control over policy outcomes, environ-

mentalists must recognize the fragmentation problem and establish greater discipline within their own ranks. They need to build internal consensus over policy priorities. They must resist the allure of promises that Congress makes but never intends to keep. They must not equate political or administrative proceedings that superficially give them input with policy that genuinely furthers their objectives. They must try to introduce greater coherence and realism into their expectations, striving for laws that give the agencies at least a fighting chance to serve the broader interests of the nation.[16]

While many of the national groups are trying to focus on longer term issues, they are also facing accusation of "sell-outs" by local activists. This perception is aided and abetted by the environmental justice advocates who have made permitting and siting a civil rights issue.

For many of these groups, the perception of the evil corporation or state has become a reality. This is not to deny that there should be concerns about the impact of highly contaminated areas on health. Certainly, it was easier to site higher polluting operations in low economic areas, which were dominated by people of color. However, the perception that the environment is worse, and that people will not be protected by either the state or the corporation, encourages automatic rejection of industrial development.

This has the perverse impact of encouraging companies to move to greenfield areas where there are at least procedural safeguards that allow the permitting process to continue even in the face of local opposition. Of course, this also removes the potential jobs that might have been created in the lower income area. As discussed previously (see Chapter 2, Social Concerns: Environmental Justice and the Redevelopment of Industrial Areas) the issue of legal remedies for perceived environmental justice concerns is rapidly changing.

In a recent controversial article, provocatively titled the "Death of Environmentalism, Global Warming Politics in a Post Environmental World,"[17] Michael Schellenberger and Ted Nordhaus, in the context of global warming argue that "in their public campaigns, not one of America's environmental leaders is articulating a vision of the future commensurate with the magnitude of the crisis."[18] Shellenberger and Nordhaus believe that

[b]y failing to question their most basic assumptions about the problem and the solution, environmental leaders are like generals fighting the last war—in particular the war they fought and won for basic environmental protections more than 30 years ago. It was then that the community's political strategy became

defined around using science to define the problem as "environmental" and crafting technical policy proposals as solutions.[19]

They believe that in the context of what Europe is doing in the global
warming area that "[e]nvironmentalists are learning all the wrong lessons
from Europe. We closely scrutinize the *policies* without giving much
thought to the *politics* that made the policies possible."[20] Their proposed solution is that "[w]hat the environmental movement needs more than anything else right now is to take a collective step back to rethink everything.
We will never be able to turn things around as long as we understand our
failures as essentially tactical, and make proposals that are essentially technical." A "more powerful movement depends on letting go of old identities,
categories and assumptions, so that we can be truly open to embracing a
better model."[21] In summary, "[f]rom their point of view if environmentalism is not dead, it is in dire need of resuscitation with a strong dose of vision,
spiced with a focus on longer-term strategy, and having the goal of appeal to
a broader constituency. In short, politics matter."[22]

A New Shade of Green

The in-your-face pollution issues of the past could be solved by a regulatory
system requiring emission control devices on process equipment and
cleanup standards for contaminated sites. The new generation of issues cannot be addressed with these same remedies. How well will the environmental groups adapt to these new realities? Beating up the usual suspects may
raise funds, but does it really solve problems that are more intricately woven
into our societal fabric?

The World Trade Organization (WTO) protest was about fundamental
concerns about how nations (or their surrogates) govern and trade in a
global market and the direct and indirect impact on the environment without
input and equal participation by those impacted by the group's actions. It's
not just taking issue with a leaking landfill, a smelly harbor, or a dead sea
turtle. Fundamental cracks in the system can't be addressed with simplistic
solutions like packaging your products in recycled paper. Most significantly, system issues can impact everyone along the supply chain.

The WTO protests were a start, but the jury is still out on whether environmental organizations will form a cohesive front to tackle fundamental
societal issues or resort to the safer route of crisis and criminal de jour. As
Robert F. Kennedy Jr. noted:

> [T]here are times, of course when companies deserve bashing.
> But platitudes will not save the world's remaining rain forests.
> We need a more sophisticated approach, one that will allow us

to negotiate with those corporations willing to commit themselves to the highest environmental standards. The problem, after all, is not caused by U.S. corporations, but by government decisions driven by a complex cycle of debt, poverty and growing population.[23]

Insightful words, but difficult to take forward. For example, the Sierra Club experienced its members' wrath when it tried to tackle population growth and immigration. Is their retreat from these issues and the unspoken failure of these groups to drive an environmental ethic (regulate business, but don't interfere with our lifestyles) just another sign of green arthritis?

The Business Environmental View—Looking Backward

Viewed by the metrics that business executives track, things have never been better. Compliance has improved, and emissions are down. Most companies are, however, operating with an eye on the past, flush from the success of meeting the regulatory challenges of the 1970s and 1980s. Like the person who has fallen off a 30-story building and, after 15 floors, looks up and concludes everything is just fine.

The new global environmental dynamic remains an enigma to business. Businesses continue to deal with the environmental issues that may impact the next quarter (i.e., between floors 15 and 16) while they talk of sustainable development. For industry executives, maintaining the status quo is the preferred "strategy." Environmental issues are almost always framed in the context of regulatory compliance and public relations—a cost sink. Take action—it costs money with no return on investment. If the compliance record is improving, emissions are down, and the public is calm, why change?

The environmental managers who are charged with the responsibility of keeping things under control are stretched and stressed. Business managers today better understand the resources needed to meet regulatory issues. Beginning in the mid-1990s the "hands off" treatment of environmental programs came to an abrupt end. Over the past ten years, environmental departments have been subjected to the same brutal scrutiny and cost-cutting as any other department. Proactive programs such as pollution prevention have reaped the low hanging fruit and have become maintenance efforts. Programs have matured to the point that many can be outsourced entirely or grouped into internal "shared service" departments competing with external service providers.

The movement to consolidate or outsource all staff services comes at a time when environmental activities are often viewed narrowly as legal and public relations functions. Just what is the strategic value difference between the accounts payable group and the environmental services department, anyway? To some business managers, very little. For environmental concerns, attitudes and perceptions matter. Indeed, they can drive the effort, for better or worse. For example, the formal policy of "compliance" appears in some companies to have been replaced with an unwritten policy of "no major noncompliances"—a subtle yet significant shift.

Environmental department managers in industry usually remain on the perimeter—behind a Green Wall, as Robert Shelton calls it (see Chapter 3). They are viewed as the problem-fixers, not the strategists; the regulatory cops, not the visionaries. Environmental managers, and particularly middle managers, are understandably worried. They are specialists in a relatively small niche that is not growing any larger for the first time in nearly two decades. Labeled as service providers, it is difficult to compete head-to-head with candidates in other professions seeking mainstream management positions.

The impact on environmental professionals has been subtle, not even noticeable to many business managers. What we have seen is a growing reluctance on the part of environmental managers to push forward bold new ideas at a time when industry is facing more profound challenges than it did 30 years ago. Green arthritis is rampant. "Don't rock the boat!" has replaced: "Save the planet!" as the mantra of environmental professionals. "I need to get only three more years in until retirement" has replaced: "We need to change our decisionmaking processes." Budgetary strangulation and personal worry have narrowed the focus to compliance, public relations, and incremental improvement. The environmental manager is driven into a maintenance/service mentality.

The bottom line is that the environmental management processes used by many companies today are inadequate to examine emerging issues that may have a profound impact on their long-term profitability. Just as the agencies and environmental groups continue to focus on the old paradigm of the crisis du jour and punishing the culprits, companies are looking at a narrow view of compliance, outdated indicators, and public relations.

But Enough of This Negativity!

It is recognized that the preceding messages come across as uninhibited organization-bashing. Yes, it can be described as decidedly unbalanced, unfair, inadequately supported, and would never hold up in court! The positive things that organizations have done would take volumes to describe. But, this is the proverbial 2x4 in the face, not the gentle wake-up call.

What many of us sense and what is attempted to be conveyed to you, the reader, is that there is a complex mix of organizational and personal agendas in play today that taken in total lead to environmental incrementalism at nearly every level in the United States. Everything is relative, and what is alarming is the gap between what could be accomplished and what is actually being done today. No one is at fault; we are all at fault. It is time to deal with it openly.

Any student of emerging global issues recognizes that the environmental problems are more significant than the narrow concerns such as urban sprawl that dominate the public's attention. Environmentalists claim that the sustainability of life on earth is at stake. They may or may not be correct. But what we can say with certainty is that the indicators point to a transition to something very, very different. If the issues we are facing were a continuation of the past concerns, incrementalism may be an acceptable solution.

Global issues such as diminishing fish populations, persistent organic pollutants, and groundwater levels are very long term and very difficult to resolve. As someone once said: "There is no reset button on Mother Nature." We had better be right about what we are doing today. There is, however, no sense of urgency for tackling volatile issues with lengthy gestation periods, especially for political leaders of a population that is doing quite well, thank you. It is all too easy to deflect and direct accountability for problems dispersed globally.

The consequences of this past decade of stalled progress in the United States are only just now beginning to manifest themselves—not as a new environmental crisis on channel 5 news at eleven, but as a very subtle loss of leadership. As Paul Hagen noted: "*The United States is slowly ceding leadership on important international* environmental issues to other nations. In the process, our ecological and economic interests are increasingly at risk."[24] Nothing to get the public excited, but the long-term consequences are more important to the average citizen than Love Canal. The key, operative words are *leadership* and *economic interests*.

In these confused times, where is the leadership? Where are the new ideas and creativity coming from? Not in the United States. For example, in a recent research program by the Competitive Environment on sustainable development metrics, the key players that are shaping the landscape were identified. The vast majority are European- or Canadian-based organizations.[25] Senior environmental professionals who have lived with these issues over the past 30 years express a similar view: the United States is not where the action is. As Leslie Carothers, former Vice President, United Technologies Corporation and now President of ELI, stated: "Today the most aggressive—even provocative—proposals are sprouting from Brussels and member states of the European Union."[26] The humor is there—Brussels sprouts—but the implications to U.S. industry are not very amusing.

The Democrats have claimed to be the environmental-friendly party, but what did they deliver from 1992-2000 relative to what this country is capable of achieving? Environmentalists grew disenchanted early in the Clinton

Administration after their expectations for major new initiatives never materialized. Blame it on the Republicans for undermining progress? Possibly, but much of the progress to date was a result of initiatives under Republican administrations. I find it interesting that the Republicans focused on leadership as a central theme in the 2000 election, and less so in the 2004 election, but early significant political missteps in the environmental area by the Bush Administration and concentration on international issues leave a sizeable gap between talk and action.

The lack of environmental leadership is about as subtle as diminishing water table levels and raises about the same level of interest in the general public. But both have far reaching consequences to that average citizen, because of the second key point, economic interests. Recently, there have been individuals who have started to clearly articulate the implications of these emerging global issues. For example, Paul Hawken, Amory and L. Hunter Lovins, Carl Frankel, and John Elkington share a common vision that future markets will be heavily influenced, if not driven, by a "triple bottom line" that adds environmental equality and social justice to the familiar economic bottom line. Learning to spot emerging trends along these three axes will define the successful corporations—the ones that achieve sustainability.

The 21st century environmentalists argue that companies overlooking or misreading these trends in social responsibility and/or public perception, at a minimum, miss competitive business opportunities. They may also face financial and public relations difficulties such as those experienced by a string of companies such as Nike, Texaco, Exxon, Shell, General Electric, Freeport McMoRan, and Monsanto, to name only a few.

Moving Forward

I do not pretend to have the answer to the national leadership question. That is something that ultimately the voters, the president, and Congress will need to sort out. Nor do I claim to have the solution for the green arthritis that seems to have infected so many of this nation's institutions. I do have, however, a fairly good understanding of the internal dynamics inside businesses from my varied career working with business executives. This is a proposed six-step cure for business green arthritis.

First, Get a Medical Check-Up

Probably the greatest challenge is to convince business executives that their companies may have the disease. While most major companies will contend that they have a long-term strategy, which focuses on changing markets (consumer demographics), raw material (availability and price trends), technology (innovations in computer technology, etc.), and other socioeconomic trends (e.g., e-commerce and communication), environmental issues are usually not considered significant. Management often views these issues in the narrow context of regulatory compliance and public relations, rather than in the context of the impact on the company's products and strategies.

Management can fall into the trap of assuming that their business is immune to these issues. In the past they could look at the regulations and test the soil at the fence line and felt confident. But, the environment is a very powerful source of emotional metaphors. Perceptions have the power to radically shape entire markets overnight, as Monsanto and Novartis are currently finding out with bioengineered food.

Today Greenpeace learns there is polyvinyl chloride in Barbie and puts pressure on Mattel, Inc., which turns her into vegetable-based plastic. What!? You say, a *toy* company? But of course and predictable! But only if you look a step down the supply chain and consider vinyl chloride monomer and plasticizer. How many steps, beyond their own, are companies examining today? And more significantly, how are they evaluating each? The short answers are not many and not very well. The challenge is to make the management processes robust. One way to detect if things are stalled in past thinking patterns is to take the green arthritis test (see Figure 12-1).

Figure 12-1. Testing for Green Arthritis

Use the following list to determine if your organization may be suffering from green arthritis. An affirmative response to several of the following questions does not necessarily indicate green arthritis is present. If, however, a dozen or more are answered in the affirmative, you may need "medical intervention" to cure the "disease."

Strategy and Vision
- Does the EHS vision statement read more like a value statement?
- Is there no clear vision of where the company's EHS effort is headed?
- Do strategic plans look more like project lists rather than a roadmap to attain the desired future state?
- Is there a disconnect between the vision and reality? For example, "environmental excellence" or some other cliché is used to describe the vision, but the programs and activities are more in keeping with compliance and industry norms.
- Is there excess focus on process completion (e.g., the number of audits completed) rather than more meaningful metrics?

Communication
- Are status reports and other executive board of director (BOD) com-

munications edited repeatedly as they flow up through the organization? Do the final bear little resemblance to the urgency or candidness of the original?

• Is there a reluctance to stand out from the pack? For example, certain programs are innovative and creative, but management does not want to share/publicize these for fear of being identified as "a leader," even though these programs would not represent a loss in competitive advantage.

• Are status reports to the chief executive officer (CEO) or BOD presented by someone other than EHS management? Does a non-EHS executive in the chain of command handle these critical communications?

• Is there a perceived "fire wall" surrounding upper management protecting them from negative news and opinions contrary to mainstream thinking?

• Do the staff members feel bullied and intimidated from challenging the views of upper EHS management?

Decisionmaking

• Is excessive energy focused on working the internal and external bureaucracies rather than on promoting creativity and more competitive approaches to environmental protection?

• Are innovative ideas cut in the earliest stages because it is assumed that upper management will not approve these new programs

• Is excessive time spent in program or planning meetings that seem to go nowhere; decisions to move forward occur slowly, almost painfully?

• When options are presented, are the boldest and potentially the most rewarding action plans consistently rejected in favor of safer alternatives?

• If the company is recognized for its business success as an industry leader, are the actual (i.e., as judged by independent reviewers) environmental efforts out of sync with this top-tier position?

• Is there reluctance to use experienced independent advisors to review and possibly challenge the current vision, goals, policies, programs, and so on?

• Is compatibility with existing business management practices given a disproportionate weight in deciding which programs to recommend?

• Are consultants selected that consistently support and reinforce existing approaches?

Organization

• Are staffs on constant edge over rumored or announced cutbacks, reorganizations, mergers, acquisitions, etc.?

• Are resource levels allowing only fire fighting at minimal compliance?

• Is there friction among organizations over the staff resource distribution?

• Do these battles appear to be driven by power and control, rather than concern for the most effective placement of resources?

• Are senior EHS managers who are assigned additional, core business-related responsibilities reluctant to use their increased influence in the organization to promote EHS advances? Indeed, do they seem to only grow more cautions and conservative?

Second, Develop a Broader View of Corporate Responsibility

A transition to a triple bottom line will not be easy. Shifting public and ethical values are challenges politicians struggle with, and they are especially difficult for business leaders who historically viewed their responsibility ending at the fence line delineated by regulatory constraints. Business managers are held accountable for the continuing viability of the business they run and must deal with the world as it is, not as they wish it. Irrespective of the guilty party question, global environmental issues will have dramatic influence on future markets.

Companies becoming more dependent on a global supply chain and international markets face a new environmental paradigm. Social responsibility issues, such as labor conditions, of which environmental protection is one component, can and will have had a profound effect on earnings for companies. Do you wait for Congress and EPA to sort it out? For U.S.-based multinationals, what difference do U.S. environmental regulations make in a *global* economy?

People want companies to be more transparent, invite greater participation, and assume greater responsibility for their products from cradle to new cradle (i.e., recycled material brought back into the process). The time frame dictated by Wall Street is not the only reality.

Companies must consider future events in the context of decades, if not generations. They cannot and *should not* turn to regulatory solutions, since traditional approaches such as end-of-the-pipe controls are inefficient. The future solutions lie with the products and processes themselves. Easier said than done, however. How can a strategic environmental management strategy that speaks of the possibility of an unknown economic gain sometime in the future successfully challenge the current business trinity of (1) a high probability of (2) a significant economic gain (3) by Friday? The promise and the rewards are there, though it will take the innovators and leaders to make the first courageous steps.

Third, Understand Your Own Environment

Take careful inventory of your past and current EHS issues. Map out your future on these issues as they relate directly and *especially* indirectly to your strategic business plan. Surprisingly, these basic steps are where companies fail more often than not. They think they have these items well under control. This is especially challenging for lawyers who may view control in the framework of legal compliance.

What companies usually have under control are the procedural, regulatory compliance, and public relations aspects of their business, not the strategic ones. The performance metrics that CEOs and BODs review are most often related to targets that do not give insight into what will really matter on the horizon five or more years out.

For example, much of business management's attention of late has been focused on ISO 14001 certification, in part because of its product market implications. Certification can create the illusion that all must be well because the process is in place. The standard does not require, however, performance improvement baselines or goals, just that a process is created to facilitate this action. Consequently, business management's attention may shift from stretch performance goals to ensuring the completion of a procedure.

Additionally, the ISO implementation process can make it quite difficult to stay above the detail and develop an environmental management system (EMS) with a strategic environmental direction. It is a good starting tool, but it is not the endpoint or a substitute for a strategic environmental program. Indeed, if the entire goal is to get ISO certified, the EMS implementation focus may shift to certification, regardless of actual performance.

The bottom line is that the environmental management processes used by many companies today are inadequate to examine emerging issues that may have a profound impact on their long-term profitability. John Elkington calls a rigorous self-examination a "sustainability audit." To adequately perform a review of this depth a company risks taking a hard assessment of current practices that may raise some potentially unpleasant news. Maybe things are not really under control. The key question becomes: "Is it better to know and then take necessary action, or to not know at all?"

Fourth, Change Your Perspective—This Is Enlightened Self-Interest, and Should Not Be Viewed by You or Your Company as Tree Hugging

Companies focus on quarterly profits. But they also examine the issues over the horizon in laying out their business strategy. Environmental issues can be the killer issue or the defining competitive advantage. The sustainable corporation is all about enlightened self-interest in emerging markets. It is not some new business fad but a strategic look at emerging trends.

Major business trends can proceed at unpredictable rates, just as the public's reaction to environmental metaphors. What is certain is that the CEOs that take the first steps take the greatest risks . . . and stand to gain the greatest rewards. Just as Jack Welch was labeled as "Neutron Jack" for business practices that became commonplace a decade later, General Electric stands today as one of the world's largest, most respected corporations.

CEOs and other business executives have driven many of the stretch efforts by companies over the past decade. If people claim that environmental concepts are "ingrained" in their companies, with rare exceptions they are referring to environmental operational and compliance aspects, not the strategic aspects associated with sustainability. For industry in general the track record in environmental leadership to date has been mixed, at best. Real competitive advantage in the future will come from action, not empty public relations rhetoric today.

Fifth, Make Sure That You Have the Right Resources

Companies have frequently relied on management consultants to examine the effectiveness of their environmental departments, often in conjunction with companywide reengineering efforts. A number of these have failed miserably. The most common error is the application of standard ratios of staff size to some common industry metric. For service departments with repetitive, defined tasks such as payroll, this approach makes sense. For EHS departments, such ratios can be a recipe for disaster. (See Chapter 6, Corporate Program Review, and Chapter 3, Environmental Management and Downsizing.)

Executive management and BODs will need to take extra effort to ensure that their leadership is not only in tune with their thinking, but that they have the skills necessary to meet their objectives. Even if the primary goal is compliance, their leadership must have the skills to identify and bring to management's attention competitive threats and possible opportunities.

Senior environmental managers are subject to the same weaknesses and shortcomings of other senior business managers, including turf protection, reluctance to change, risk avoidance, and primacy of personal objectives over company. Executive management can, however, see through the smoke screen that may hide problems related to the running of a business. They have, after all, worked their way up through the organization and know how to properly run the company. Business executives can spot a performance stumble, a lost commitment, or a misdirected plan a mile away, but not necessarily when it comes to environmental issues. In many instances, company senior management is dominated by people with financial backgrounds, rather than manufacturing or operations, and can be almost totally divorced from the practical realities of environmental management and issues.

In some respects, the maturing of the profession has brought on an arrogance that exists within any profession. "We know what we are doing." My own experience has been that environmental professionals are increasingly more reluctant to test new ideas and less willing to accept criticism from their peers. It becomes difficult to differentiate this attitude with the deep-seated worry over not rocking the boat and their own self-preservation. Regardless of root cause, the net effect may be a potential to miss competitive advantage; pick safe, proven programs, not necessarily new ones that may be more efficient.

Sixth, Create the Right Climate for Innovation

Being a change agent at the cutting edge today requires encouragement, trust building, and an open sharing of views. Put bluntly, you may need to prod your staff out of hiding. Your marching orders need to be consistent and in keeping with your intended objectives. If the dominant message coming from above is compliance at minimal cost, you cannot expect to receive much more. Even more problematic is the directive of environmental excellence while committing to resources barely able to sustain compliance. Success requires three components:

First, the inspiration for future leadership will come from the top down, not from the bottom up. Progressive CEOs and BODs will take advantage of potential competitive opportunities brought on by the emergence of global environmental issues. They know that environmental issues do not end with compliance, but start there. The CEO's involvement in building supportive networks for the senior environmental managers to pursue these opportunities is essential for accomplishing this objective.

Second, filtration must be eliminated up *and down* the organization. Filtration up the line is a universal issue with all business issues. For social responsibility issues including EHS, filtration can result in criminal charges and punitive damages—a public relations nightmare. CEOs and BODs must take extraordinary precautions to ensure that they are getting the full facts, not the "happy-face spin." There has been considerable consciousness-raising as a result of Enron, etc. and the resulting increased demands of the Sarbanes-Oxley legislation to understand what is happening in an organization. The classic danger sign is when the BOD is being updated on environmental issues by the highest person in the management chain who is *not* the environmental manager.

We have found that the filtration also extends down the organization for environmental directives. The CEO or BOD may want "environmental excellence," but that message gets reinterpreted down the management chain until at the manufacturing site it comes out as basic compliance at lowest cost. Whether the filtration is up or down, it is management's responsibility to institute the due diligence systems to ensure that it does not happen and it understands its risks. It is a fundamental question of business ethics.

Third, executive management must be willing to listen to the critics waving the warning signs. If none seem to be out there, they need to find them, both inside and outside the company. You can be assured that they are there, if you look. This is not a public relations exercise, but an effort to identify the fundamental competitive threats and opportunities for the company. Multinationals will move toward tools such as external advisory committees to challenge their internal resources and strategies.

Fourth, industry needs to be honest with itself and with the public. The public should be given the facts, both good and bad. Attempts to put a positive spin on environmental issues—dubbed "greenwash"—have backfired time and time again. The demand for full disclosure and increased public participation will only accelerate. CEOs and BODs should encourage and expand these efforts to build public trust. But "signing on" to new initiatives and reaping the public relations benefits should be only the first steps.

Conclusion

The first step in curing any disease is to face that there may actually be a problem. Claiming that everything is getting better at an ever-accelerating pace may win accolades in some quarters, just as shouting that the end of the planet is near may raise funds. These messages are voiced daily in journals and magazines. What has not been articulated is the undercurrent of frustration that scores of my senior colleagues express in private daily.

This frustration on the part of our colleagues and ourselves is not a growing negativism or cynicism, but anguish over the enormous opportunities that this country is letting slip by. So much more could be done, resources spent more productively, and opportunities pursued for the benefit of all Americans, not to mention the improvement of environmental conditions worldwide. Referring back to the metaphor, the Grand Old Lady has tremendous potential, but she is doomed to the role of observer as the upstarts lead the world on a fundamentally different track from the one she lead in the 1970s. Is there a simple, quick fix—a magic pill—to solve the problem? I think not. The cure will be very painful and will require courage by us all.

I will be shocked if you agree with everything said in this brutally frank assessment. No doubt that most readers will be able to pick apart various aspects of this analysis. But even if you agree with only a fraction of what has been put forward, that should give you pause to consider what you are doing to cure the Grand Old Lady.

Notes to Chapter 12

1. Richard MacLean & Frank Friedman, *Green Arthritis*, ENVTL. F., Nov./Dec. 2000, at 36. This chapter is primarily adapted from that article.

2. *Id.* at 36.

3. *See* Bob Smet, *Kudos for Blaming Everyone Equally*, ENVTL. F., Mar./Apr. 2001, at 4.

4. Richard MacLean, *Countdown to Zero*, ENVTL. PROTECTION, Oct. 2001, at 57.

5. Terry Davies, *Tinkering Is Not Enough*, ECOSTATES, Summer 2000, at 12.

6. Marla Cone, *Environmental Science*, L.A. TIMES (MAGAZINE), July 25, 1999, at 32.

7. Jonathan Rauch, *Social Studies: America Celebrates Earth Day 1970—for the 31st Time*, NAT'L J., Apr. 29, 2000, n.p.

8. *Id.*

9. Daniel Fiorino, *Rethinking Environmental Regulation: Perspectives on Law and Governance*, 23 HARV. ENVTL. L. REV. 442, 442 (1999).

10. Eric V. Schaeffer, *Enforcement in the Next Millennium—21st Century Approaches to Noncompliance*, A.B.A. SECTION ON ENVIRONMENT, ENERGY & RESOURCES, 29th Annual Conference (Mar. 9-12, 2000).

11. Christopher Tolue, *A View From the Hill: High Hopes*, ECOSTATES, Summer 2000, at 9, 11.

12. Robert Roberts, Address at the 27th National Spring Conference on the Environment sponsored by the American Bar Association Standing Committee on Environmental Law, Potomac, Md. (June 13, 1998).

13. George S. Hawkins, *Compliance and Enforcement Changes in Congress and EPA*, 11 NAT. RESOURCES & ENV'T 42 (1997).

14. Elliott P. Laws, *Need Statutory Authority for Reform*, ENVTL. F., Nov./Dec. 1999, at 51.

15. Michael Lyons, *Congressional Self-Interest, Bureaucratic Self-Interest, and U.S. Environmental Policy Implementation*, 30 ELR 10786, 10792 (Sept. 2000).

16. *Id.*

17. *See* http://thebreakthrough.org/images/Death_of_Envirnmentalism.pdf. This was originally released at an October 2004 meeting of the Environmental Grantmakers Association and reprinted in Grist, an environmental law news website (www.grist.org) on January 31, 2005. *See* Environmentalism, NAT. RESOURCES & ENV'T, Spring 2005, at 70.

18. *Id.* at 6.

19. *Id.* at 7.

20. *Id.*

21. *Id.*

22. *Id.*

23. Robert F. Kennedy Jr., *Amazon Sabotage*, WASH. POST, Aug. 24, 1992, at A17.

24. Paul E. Hagen, *The Green Diplomacy Gap*, ENVTL. F., July/Aug. 2000, at 28 (emphasis added).

25. Personal Interview with Richard MacLean, President, Competitive Environment.

26. Leslie Carothers, *Issues Sprout From Brussels, Europe*, ENVTL. F., May/June 2000, at 12.

Chapter 13:
Conclusion

This book summarizes many of the environmental management lessons that I and others have learned over the years. Some of its suggestions, such as those on dealing with regulators, are unique to the environmental area. Many others, such as those on interactions between staff and line management, simply apply good, general management techniques in the environmental context. Basicly, good management is vital in the environmental area, if only because environmental costs are so high. (For a discussion of costs, see Chapter 3, The Cost of Environmental Protection.)

The greatest change in the environmental management area is movement away from a primary emphasis on technical or legal regulatory issues to more emphasis on pure management and integration of the HES function and risk management in general into operations, maintenance, and general business practices. Indeed, one of the most valuable efforts of the staff at Ato was a review of the entire HES function in its plants. It worked jointly with the process technology group to determine appropriate staffing (engineering, technical, and hourly), organizational structure, HES operations, maintenance, etc. It also reviewed the effect of potential process changes and automation on overall costs and staffing. Staffing costs are not free goods, and there are many process changes that become cost effective when the full cost of staff time is considered.

Many environmental management techniques come down to getting the most out of the people in your organization. An EMS, like any other management system, must ensure that each individual's performance is recognized so that good work receives credit and bad work cannot be blamed on committees. Effective environmental management also requires an interdisciplinary approach. No one discipline has all the solutions, and turf problems must be resolved to allow the organization to make full use of engineers, lawyers, consultants, and other professionals. The ability to work with people is a critical ingredient of successful environmental management.

This book makes many recommendations that do not cost much and that can save significant amounts. Minimization of turf problems, for example, creates major opportunities for cost savings. Even the recommendations that require significant up-front investments can pay for themselves in the long run by making management more cost effective. For example, computerized data management systems cost money, but by enabling you to detect problems early and handle information efficiently, they can save far more.

An effective environmental management department can be a profit center. When I was with Occidental, its operating management paid our department the ultimate compliment. A consulting firm had inquired as to whether Occidental would be interested in using some of the department's time to work as outside consultants. A senior operations executive responded that hour for hour, the amount the department saved the company by working in-house substantially exceeded the amount it would bring in by working outside. Ato has built a very strong in-house staff, both technically and legally, that has dramatically reduced outside costs and, more importantly, reduced the exposures that result in these costs.

Reduction of costs—especially transaction costs—is one main theme of this book. As discussed in Chapter 3, pollution control is frequently cheaper outside the United States because less must be spent on studies, consultants, lawyers, paperwork, and resulting delays. Reducing these transaction costs in the United States would clearly be in the public interest. This interest is often ignored, which is frustrating for the environmental manager. High transaction costs result partly from the history of environmental regulation and partly from widespread paralysis in decisionmaking. Regulatory agencies are frequently paralyzed by the intense and conflicting demands they face, and companies may be paralyzed if decisionmaking moves slowly upward through numerous organizational levels. It is indeed unfortunate that so much time and money are devoted to transactional issues rather than to the environmental protection we all desire. Conversely, the issue of "Green Arthritis," which needs to be addressed by industry, government, and the NGO community, is a serious concern.

A detailed analysis of the impediments to potential ways to reduce environmental transaction costs, such as market-based techniques (e.g., emission trading to limit sulfur dioxide and reduce acid rain under the CAA Amendments of 1990) instead of command-and-control regulation, is beyond the scope of this book. Such analysis is sorely needed. Indeed, additional work is needed on environmental management in general. The existing literature is growing, but is still surprisingly sparse. I hope that this book will continue to help inspire further work in this important field.

Appendix A:
Environment, Health, and Safety Acronyms

Environment, Health, and Safety (EHS) Acronyms
(Chemical Manufacturers Association)

AAC:	Acceptable Ambient Concentration
AAL:	Acceptable Ambient Limit
ABS:	Acrylonitrile-Butadiene-Styrene
ACGIH:	American Conference of Governmental Industrial Hygienists
ACL:	Alternate Concentration Limit
ADI:	Allowable Daily Intake
ADL:	Acceptable Daily Intake
AIHA:	American Industrial Hygiene Association
AIHC:	American Industrial Health Council
AIRS:	Aerometric Information Retrieval System
ALAPCO:	Association of Local Air Pollution Control Officials
AMSA:	Association of Metropolitan Sewerage Agencies
ANPR or	
ANPRM:	Advance Notice of Proposed Rulemaking
ANSI:	American National Standards Institute, Inc.
APA:	Administrative Procedure Act
API:	American Petroleum Institute
APME:	Association of Plastics Manufacturers in Europe
AST:	Above Ground Storage Tank
ASTSWMO:	Association of State and Territorial Solid Waste Management Officials
ARAR:	Applicable or Relevant and Appropriate Requirement (Under SARA)
ASIWPCA:	Association of State and Interstate Water Pollution Control Administrators
ASTHO:	Association of State and Territorial Health Officers
ATSDR:	Agency for Toxic Substances and Disease Registry
AWMA:	Air and Waste Management Association (formerly Air Pollution Control Association)
BACT:	Best Available Control Technology—the standard for pollution control technology which must be met by major new or modified pollution emission sources in areas with above-standard air quality.
BAF:	Bioaccumulation Factor

BAT: Best Available Technology—degree of treatment to be applied to all toxic pollutants and nonconventional pollutants based generally upon control technology which has been demonstrated as technically and economically feasible but which may not yet have been applied in any facility.

BATEA: Best Available Technology Economically Achievable

BCC: Bioaccumulative Chemical of Concern—list of pollutants targeted by the Great Lakes Water Quality Initiative.

BCF: Bioconcentration Factor

BDAT: Best Demonstrated Available Technology (RCRA LDRs)

BDT: Best Demonstrated Technology

BEI: Biological Exposure Index

BID: Background Information Document

BIF: Boiler and Industrial Furnace (RCRA Regulations)

BMD: Benchmark Dose

BMP: Best Management Practice

BOD: Biological Oxygen Demand

BPJ: Best Professional Judgment—the decision of a qualified person, based on experience and training, concerning a scientific or engineering question.

BPT: Best Practical Technology—degree of treatment to be applied to all industrial wastes by July 1, 1977, based generally upon the average pollution control performance achieved by the best existing plants.

BTU or Btu: British Thermal Unit

CAA: Clean Air Act (1970)

CAAA: Clean Air Act Amendments (1977, 1978, 1990)

CAAAC: Clean Air Act Advisory Committee

CAER: Community Awareness and Emergency Response

CAG: Carcinogen Assessment Group (EPA)

CAIR: Comprehensive Assessment Information Rule

CAMU: Corrective Action Management Unit (RCRA)

CAPCOA: California Air Pollution Control Officers Association

CARB: California Air Resources Board

CAS: Chemical Abstract Service (CAS Numbers)

CASAC: Clean Air Scientific Advisory Committee (EPA advisory group)

CBEC:	Concentration Based Exemption Criteria (RCRA)
CCAI:	Coalition for Clean Air Implementation
CCC:	Chlorine Chemistry Council
CCPS:	Center for Chemical Process Safety (AIChE)
CDC:	Centers for Disease Control
CDE:	Control Device Evaluation
CEA:	Council of Economic Advisors
CEFIC:	The European Chemical Industry Council
CEPP:	Chemical Emergency Preparedness Program (EPA)
CENR:	Committee on Environment and Natural Resources
CERCLA:	Comprehensive Environmental Response, Compensation, and Liability Act (1980)
CFC:	Chlorofluorocarbon
CFR:	Code of Federal Regulations
CIBO:	Council of Industrial Boiler Owners
CIC:	Chemical Industry Council
CIIT:	Chemical Industry Institute of Toxicology
CMA:	Chemical Manufacturers Association
CO:	Carbon Monoxide
COD:	Chemical Oxygen Demand
CN:	Cyanide
CRTK:	Community Right-To-Know
CSGWPP:	Comprehensive State Ground Water Protection Program
CTG:	Control Techniques Guidelines—technology assessments prepared by EPA to provide guidance on the best controls available for use by categories of existing sources; used to establish RACT.
CTT:	Chronic Toxicity Test
CVM:	Contingent Valuation Method—controversial methodology for estimating "non-use" value in calculating natural resource damages assessments.
CWA:	Clean Water Act (1977, 1987)
DAF:	Dilution Attenuation Factor
"D" Wastes:	Wastes considered hazardous under RCRA by virtue of a characteristic: Flammability, Corrosivity, Reactivity, or Toxicity.
DEC:	Department of Environmental Conservation (NY)
DEM:	Department of Environmental Management (RI)

DEPE: Department of Environmental Protection and Energy (NJ)

DER: Department of Environmental Management (PA)

DNREC: Department of Environmental Resources and Environmental Control (DE)

DOC: Dissolved Organic Carbon

DOE: Department of Energy (U.S.); Department of Ecology (WA)

DOD: Department of Defense (U.S.)

DOI: Department of the Interior (U.S.)

DOHS: Department of Health Services (CA, AZ)

DOL: Department of Labor (U.S.)

DMR/QA: Discharge Monitoring Reports/Quality Assurance

DRE: Destruction and Removal Efficiency (incineration)

DSE: Domestic Sewage Exclusion

DSW: Definition of Solid Waste

EC: Effective Concentration; European Community

ECETOC: European Chemical Industry Ecology and Toxicology Centre

ECHO: Enhanced Characteristics Option (RCRA)

ED: Effective Dose

EDF: The Environmental Defense Fund

EDSTAC: EPA's Endocrine Disrupter Screening and Testing Advisory Committee

EHS: Extremely Hazardous Substance; Employee, Health, and Safety; or Environmental, Health, and Safety

EHSOC: CMA's Environment, Health, Safety, and Operations Committee

EIP: Economic Incentives Program under the Clean Air Act

EIS: Environmental Impact Statement—a logical analysis of the effects on the environment that will or may reasonably be expected to occur as a result of a proposed action.

EL: Exposure Level

ELP: Environmental Leadership Program (EPA)

EOP: End-of-Pipe-Treatment—those processes that treat a combined plant waste stream for pollutant removal prior to discharge.

EP: Extraction Procedure for determining toxicity characteristic

EPA:	Environmental Protection Agency (U.S.)
EPCRA:	Emergency Planning and Community Right-To-Know Act of 1986, also known as SARA Title III
ERC:	Emission Reduction Credit
ERP:	Early Reduction Program—implemented by EPA under Section 112(i)(5) of the CAA.
ERPG:	Emergency Response Planning Guidelines
ETC:	Environmental Technology Council (formerly Hazardous Waste Treatment Council)
ETPS:	Emissions Trading Policy Statement (EPA document)
"F" Wastes:	RCRA Hazardous wastes from nonspecific sources
FACA:	Federal Advisory Committee Act
FASE:	Foundation for Advancements in Science and Education
FCCSET:	Federal Coordinating Council for Science, Engineering, and Technology
FCM:	Food Chain Multiplier
FDA:	Food and Drug Administration (U.S.)
FGD:	Flue Gas Desulfurization—any pollution control process which treats stationary source combustion flue gas to remove sulfur oxides.
FIFRA:	Federal Insecticide, Fungicide, and Rodenticide Act (1970)
FLM:	Federal Land Manager
FOE:	Friends of the Earth
FOIA:	Freedom of Information Act
FR:	*Federal Register*
FRP:	Fiberglass Reinforced Plastic
FWPCA:	Federal Water Pollution Control Act of 1972—sets effluent control limits for all industries discharging into waters of the United States.
GACT:	Generally Available Control Technology—level of control for area sources of hazardous air pollutants.
GAO:	General Accounting Office
GATT:	General Agreement on Tariffs and Trade
GC/CD:	Gas Chromatograph/Conventional Detector
GC/MS:	Gas Chromatograph/Mass Spectrometer
GEMI:	Global Environmental Management Initiative
GEP:	Good Epidemiology Practices
GLI:	Great Lakes Water Quality Initiative—EPA Region V

	program to develop guidelines for uniform water quality standards in the Great Lakes Basin.
GLT$_x$RX:	Great Lakes Toxics Reduction Initiative
GLP:	Good Laboratory Practice
GLWQI:	Great Lakes Water Quality Initiative—also known as the Great Lakes Initiative (GLI).
GPC:	General Plan Configurations
GPRMC:	European Organization for Reinforced Plastics/Composites Materials
HAD:	Health Assessment Documents
HAP:	Hazardous Air Pollutant
HAZWOPER:	Hazardous Waste Operations and Emergency Response Regulations (OSHA 29 CFR 1910.120)
HBN:	Health Based Numbers
HC:	Hydrocarbons
HCS:	Hazard Communication Standard (OSHA)
HEAST:	Health Effects Assessment Summary Tables (EPA)
HHAG:	Health Hazards Assessments Group (EPA)
HI:	Hazard Index
HLV:	Hazard Limiting Value
HOC:	Halogenated Organic Compounds
HON:	Hazardous Organic NESHAP—MACT rule for Synthetic Organic Chemical Manufacturing Industry (SOCMI).
HRS:	Hazard Ranking System—scoring system that determines whether a site will be added to the national priority list (NPL).
HSWA:	Hazardous and Solid Waste Amendments—1984 Amendments to RCRA.
HWIR:	Hazardous Waste Identification Rule (RCRA)
HWTC:	The Hazardous Waste Treatment Council
IARC:	International Agency for Research on Cancer
ICAP:	Inductively Coupled Argon Plasma
ICCA:	International Council of Chemical Associations
IDLH:	Immediately Dangerous to Life or Health
IEHR:	Institute for Evaluating Health Risks—an independent nonprofit corporation in Washington, D.C. providing an evaluation of health risks.
IERL:	Industrial Environmental Research Laboratory (EPA)

IJC:	International Joint Commission between the U.S. and Canada
IPCS:	International Programme on Chemical Safety
IRIS:	Integrated Risk Information System
IRPTC:	International Registry of Potentially Toxic Chemicals
ISO:	International Standards Organization
"K" Wastes:	RCRA Hazardous Wastes from Specific Sources
LAER:	Lowest Achievable Emission Rate (air)
LC:	Lethal Concentration (air)
LD:	Lethal Dose (oral or dermal)
LDAR:	Leak Detection and Repair Procedures for Fugitive Emissions
LDR:	Land Disposal Restrictions (RCRA)
LEL:	Lower Explosive Limit
LEPC:	Local Emergency Planning Commission
LIDAR:	Light Detection and Ranging
LOAEL:	Lowest Observed Adverse Effect Level
LOEL:	Lowest Observed Effect Level
LUST:	Leaking Underground Storage Tank
MACT:	Maximum Achievable Control Technology (CAA)
MATC:	Maximum Allowable Toxicant Concentration
MAWP:	Maximum Allowable Working Pressure
MCL:	Maximum Containment Level
MCLG:	Maximum Containment Level Goal
MDL:	Method Detection Level
MED:	Minimum Effective Dose
MEI:	Maximum Exposed Individual
MISWD:	Municipal and Industrial Solid Waste Division (EPA)
MLE:	Maximum Likelihood Estimates
MRL:	Minimum Risk Level
MSDS:	Material Safety Data Sheet
MSHA:	Mining Safety and Health Administration (DOI)
MTD:	Maximum Tolerated Dose
MTR:	Minimum Technology Requirements [RCRA Sec. 3004(0)]
NA:	Nonattainment Area
NAAQS:	National Ambient Air Quality Standards

NACEPT:	National Advisory Committee on Environmental Policy and Technology
NACOSH:	National Advisory Committee on Occupational Safety and Health
NAM:	National Association of Manufacturers
NAPCTAC:	National Air Pollution Control Techniques Advisory Committee (EPA advisory group)
NAPAP:	National Acidic Precipitation Advisory Panel
NAS:	National Academy of Science
NCI:	National Cancer Institute
NCP:	National Contingency Plan
NCTR:	National Center for Toxicological Research
NDWAC:	National Drinking Water Advisory Council
NEAC:	National Environmental Justice Advisory Council
NEJAC:	National Environmental Justice Advisory Council
NELAC:	National Environmental Laboratory Accreditation Conference
NEPA:	National Environmental Policy Act
NESA:	National Emissions Standards Act (1967)
NESHAP:	National Emission Standard for Hazardous Air Pollutants
NIEHS:	National Institute of Environmental Health and Safety (NIH)
NIH:	National Institute of Health
NIOSH:	National Institute of Occupational Safety and Health
NOAA:	National Oceanic and Atmospheric Administration
NOAEL:	No Observable Adverse Effect Level
NODA:	Notice of Data Availability
NOEC:	No Observed Effect Concentration—also known as No Observed Effect Level (NOEL).
NO_x:	Abbreviation for nitrogen oxides or oxides of nitrogen
NPDES:	National Pollutant Discharge Elimination System—the national permitting system authorized under Section 402 of the FWPCA.
NPL:	National Priorities List—list of sites to be cleaned up under the federal Superfund program.
NPRM:	Notice of Proposed Rulemaking
NPS:	National Park Service
NRC:	National Research Council (affiliate of NAS)

NRDA:	Natural Resource Damages Assessment (CERCLA, OPA)
NRDC:	Natural Resources Defense Council
NSPS:	New Source Performance Standards (air)
NSR:	New Source Review under CAA
NSTC:	National Science and Technology Council
NTP:	National Toxicology Program (NIEHS)
OAQPS:	Office of Air Quality Planning and Standards (EPA)
OAR:	Office of Air and Radiation (EPA)
OCPSF:	Organic Chemicals, Plastics, and Synthetic Fibers Manufacturing Point Source Category
ODW:	Office of Drinking Water (EPA)
OECD:	Organization for Economic Cooperation and Development
OECD SIDs:	Screeing Information Data Set (within OECD)
OECM:	Office of Compliance Monitoring (EPA)
OEP:	Office of Environmental Policy (White House)
OERR:	Office of Emergency and Remedial Response (EPA)
OGC:	Office of General Counsel
OHEA:	Office of Health and Environmental Assessment (EPA)
OIRA:	Office of Information and Regulatory Affairs (OMB)
OMB:	Office of Management and Budget
OPA:	Oil Pollution Act of 1990—addresses response, liability, and penalties for oil and chemical spills to navigable water.
OPPE:	Office of Policy, Planning, and Evaluation (EPA)
OPPT:	Office of Pollution Prevention and Toxics (EPA)
OPS:	Organic Chemicals/Plastics and Synthetics Industrial Category
ORD:	Office of Research and Development (EPA)
OSHA:	Occupational Safety and Health Administration
OSTP:	Office of Science and Technology Policy (White House)
OSW:	Office of Solid Waste (EPA)
OSWER:	Office of Solid Waste and Emergency Response (EPA)
OTS:	Office of Pesticides and Toxic Substances (EPA)
OW:	Office of Water (EPA)
"P" Wastes:	Commercial Chemical Products Considered Acutely Hazardous Wastes Under RCRA if Discarded Off-Specification, or Spilled.
PAH:	Polynuclear Aromatic Hydrocarbon

PA/SI: Preliminary Assessment/Site Investigation

PAVE: Program for Assessing Volatile Emissions

PBT: Persistent and Bioaccumulative Toxics

PEL: Permissible Exposure Limit

PER: Process Emission Regulations

pH: A measure of the acidity of alkalinity of a material, liquid or solid.

PIC: Product of Incomplete Combustion; or Prior Informed Consent (International)

PIRG: Public Interest Research Group (U.S.)

PM: Particulate Matter

PMN: Premanufacture Notification

POM: Polycyclic Organic Matter

POSSEE: Plant Organizational Software System for Emissions from Equipment

POTWs: Publicly Owned Treatment Works

PPA: Pollution Prevention Act (1990)

ppb: parts per billion

PPC: Pollution Prevention Code in the Responsible Care® Initiative

PP: Pollution Prevention

ppm: parts per million

PQL: Practical Quantitation Limit

PRP: Potentially Responsible Parties (CERCLA)

Prop 65:   California's Safe Drinking Water and Toxic Enforcement Act

ppb: parts per billion

PSD: Prevention of Significant Deterioration

PSES: Pretreatment Standards for Existing Sources (CWA)

PSNS: Pretreatment Standards for New Sources (CWA)

QA: Quality Assessment

QC: Quality Control

QRA: Quantitative Risk Assessment/Analysis

RAC: Risk Assessment Council (EPA)

RACM: Reasonably Available Control Measure

RACT: Reasonably Available Control Technology

RAF: Risk Assessment Forum (EPA)

RAP:	Remedial Action Plan
RAS:	Risk Assessment Study
RC®:	Responsible Care®
RCRA:	Resource Conservation and Recovery Act (1976)
RD/RA:	Remedial Design/Remedial Action (EPA)
REG NEG:	Regulatory Negotiated Rulemaking
RFI:	Remedial Facility Investigation
RFP:	Reasonable Further Progress
RIA:	Regulatory Impact Analysis—analysis of the effects of a particular regulatory program on the regulated community and the economy.
RI/FS:	Remedial Investigation/Feasibility Study
RIS:	RCRA Implementation Study
RMCL:	Recommended Maximum Contaminant Levels
ROD:	Record of Decision
ROG:	Reactive Organic Gases
ROSE:	Remote Optical Sensing of Emissions
RQ:	Reportable Quanitities (Superfund)
RRI:	EPA's Regulatory Reform Intiative
RTECS:	Registry of Toxic Effects of Chemical Substances
SAB:	Science Advisory Board (EPA Advisory group)
SAGE:	Strategic Advisory Group on Environment (ISO)
SARA:	Superfund Amendments and Reauthorization Act (1986)
SARA III:	SARA (Community Right-To-Know Provisions)
SDWA:	Safe Drinking Water Act
SI:	Surface Impoundment
SIC:	Standard Industrial Classification
SIP:	State Implementation Plans
SNARL:	Suggested No Adverse Response Level
SNC:	Significant Non-Compliance
SNUR:	Significant New Use Regulation/Rule (TSCA)
SO_x:	Sulfur Oxides
SOCMA:	Synthetic Organic Chemical Manufacturers Association
SOCMI:	Synthetic Organic Chemicals Manufacturing Industry
SPI:	Society of the Plastics Industry
SS:	Suspended Solids
STAPPA:	State and Territorial Air Pollution Program Administrators

STEL:	Short-Term Exposure Limit (usually 15 minutes)
STORET:	Storage and Retrieval System—EPA data bank.
Superfund:	Popular term applied to (CERCLA) and the Reauthorization Act of 1986.
SWMU:	Solid Waste Management Unit (RCRA)
TACB:	Texas Air Control Board
TBC:	"To Be Considered" Requirement (Under NCP)
TC:	Toxicity Characteristic; Toxic Concentration
TCLP:	Toxicity Characteristic Leaching Procedure (RCRA)
TD:	Toxic Dose
TEG:	The Endocrine Group (group of trade associations)
THC:	Total Hydrocarbons
Third-Third:	Refers to the manner in which EPA divided rulemaking on LDRs under RCRA into three broad sections.
TITLE III:	SARA (Community Right-To-Know Act)
TLV:	Threshold Limit Value
TMDL:	Total Maximum Daily Loads
TPH:	Total Petroleum Hydrocharbons
TPQ:	Threshold Planning Quantity (SARA Title III)
TRE:	Toxicity Reduction Evaluation
TRI:	Toxics Release Inventory Under EPCRA
TSCA:	Toxic Substance Control Act (1976)
TSD:	Technical Support Document
TSDF:	Treatment, Storage and Disposal Facility (RCRA)
TSP:	Total Suspended Particulates
TSS:	Total Suspended Solids
TUR:	Toxic Use Reduction
TWA:	Time Weighted Average
"U" Wastes:	Commercial Chemical Products Considered Toxic Hazardous Wastes under RCRA when Discarded Off-Specification, or Spilled.
UCR:	Upper Confidence Range
UIC:	Underground Injection Control
US:	United States of America
USC:	United States Code
USDA:	U.S. Department of Agriculture
USGS:	U.S. Geological Survey

UST:	Underground Storage Tank
VOCs:	Volatile Organic Compounds (air)
VOL:	Volatile Organic Liquid
VPP:	Voluntary Protection Program (OSHA)
VSD:	Virtually Safety Dose
WEF:	Water Environment Federation (formerly Water Pollution Control Federation)
WEPCo:	Rulemaking pursuant to court decision involving the *Wisconsin Electric Power Co. v. Reilly*, 893 F.2d 901 (7th Cir. 1990); rule will address types of changes that trigger NSPS or NSR
WER:	Water Effects Ratio
WETT:	Whole Effluent Toxicity Testing
WHO:	World Health Organization
WQ2000:	Water Quality 2000
WQC:	Water Quality Criteria
WQS:	Water Quality Standard
WTO:	World Trade Organization
33/50:	An EPA project inviting all manufacturers to make reductions in 17 targeted chemicals.
3/3:	Refers to the last section of Third-Third under RCRA which has been the subject of considerable litigation.

Appendix B: Environmental Auditing Policy Statement

Environmental Protection Agency
Environmental Auditing Policy Statement
51 Fed. Reg. 25004 (July 9, 1986)

SUMMARY: It is EPA policy to encourage the use of environmental auditing by regulated entities to help achieve and maintain compliance with environmental laws and regulations, as well as to help identify and correct unregulated environmental hazards. EPA first published this policy as interim guidance on November 8, 1985 (50 FR 46504). Based on comments received regarding the interim guidance, the Agency is issuing today's final policy statement with only minor changes.

This final policy statement specifically:

• Encourages regulated entities to develop, implement and upgrade environmental auditing programs;

• Discusses when the Agency may or may not request audit reports;

• Explains how EPA's inspection and enforcement activities may respond to regulated entities' efforts to assure compliance through auditing;

• Endorses environmental auditing at federal facilities;

• Encourages state and local environmental auditing initiatives; and

• Outlines elements of effective audit programs.

Environmental auditing includes a variety of compliance assessment techniques which go beyond those legally required and are used to identify actual and potential environmental problems. Effective environmental auditing can lead to higher levels of overall compliance and reduced risk to human health and the environment. EPA endorses the practice of environmental auditing and supports its accelerated use by regulated entities to help meet the goals of federal, state and local environmental requirements. However, the existence of an auditing program does not create any defense to, or otherwise limit, the responsibility of any regulated entity to comply with applicable regulatory requirements.

States are encouraged to adopt these or similar and equally effective policies in order to advance the use of environmental auditing on a consistent, nationwide basis.

DATES: This final policy statement is effective July 9, 1986.

FOR FURTHER INFORMATION CONTACT:

Leonard Fleckenstein, Office of Policy, Planning and Evaluation, (202) 382–2726;

or

Cheryl Wasserman, Office of Enforcement and Compliance Monitoring, (202) 382-7550.

SUPPLEMENTARY INFORMATION:

ENVIRONMENTAL AUDITING POLICY STATEMENT

I. Preamble

On November 8, 1985 EPA published an Environmental Auditing Policy Statement, effective as interim guidance, and solicited written comments until January 7, 1986.

Thirteen commenters submitted written comments. Eight were from private industry. Two commenters represented industry trade associations. One federal agency, one consulting firm and one law firm also submitted comments.

Twelve commenters addressed EPA requests for audit reports. Three comments per subject were received regarding inspections, enforcement response and elements of effective environmental auditing. One commenter addressed audit provisions as remedies in enforcement actions, one addressed environmental auditing at federal facilities, and one addressed the relationship of the policy statement to state or local regulatory agencies. Comments generally supported both the concept of a policy statement and the interim guidance, but raised specific concerns with respect to particular language and policy issues in sections of the guidance.

General Comments

Three commenters found the interim guidance to be constructive, balanced and effective at encouraging more and better environmental auditing.

Another commenter, while considering the policy on the whole to be constructive, felt that new and identifiable auditing "incentives" should be offered by EPA. Based on earlier comments received from industry, EPA believes most companies would not support or participate in an "incentives-based" environmental auditing program with EPA. Moreover, general promises to forgo inspections or reduce enforcement responses in exchange for companies' adoption of environmental auditing programs—the "incentives" most frequently mentioned in this context—are fraught with legal and policy obstacles.

Several commenters expressed concern that states or localities might use the interim guidance to *require* auditing. The Agency disagrees that the policy statement opens the way for states and localities to require auditing. No EPA policy can grant states or localities any more (or less) authority than they already possess. EPA believes that the interim guidance effectively encourages *voluntary* auditing. In fact, Section II.B. of the policy states: "because audit quality depends to a large degree on genuine management commitment to the program and its objectives, auditing should remain a voluntary program."

Another commenter suggested that EPA should not expect an audit to identify all potential problem areas or conclude that a problem identified in an audit reflects normal operations and procedures. EPA agrees that an audit report should clearly reflect these realities and should be written to point out the audit's limitations. However, since EPA will not routinely request audit reports, the Agency does not believe these concerns raise issues which need to be addressed in the policy statement.

A second concern expressed by the same commenter was that EPA should

acknowledge that environmental audits are only part of a successful environmental management program and thus should not be expected to cover every environmental issue or solve all problems. EPA agrees and accordingly has amended the statement of purpose which appears at the end of this preamble.

Yet another commenter thought EPA should focus on environmental performance results (compliance or non-compliance), not on the processes or vehicles used to achieve those results. In general, EPA agrees with this statement and will continue to focus on environmental results. However, EPA also believes that such results can be improved through Agency efforts to identify and encourage effective environmental management practices, and will continue to encourage such practices in non-regulatory ways.

A final general comment recommended that EPA should sponsor seminars for small businesses on how to start auditing programs. EPA agrees that such seminars would be useful. However, since audit seminars already are available from several private sector organizations, EPA does not believe it should intervene in that market, with the possible exception of seminars for government agencies, especially federal agencies, for which EPA has a broad mandate under Executive Order 12088 to provide technical assistance for environmental compliance.

Requests for Reports

EPA received 12 comments regarding Agency requests for environmental audit reports, far more than on any other topic in the policy statement. One commenter felt that EPA struck an appropriate balance between respecting the need for self-evaluation with some measure of privacy, and allowing the Agency enough flexibility of inquiry to accomplish future statutory missions. However, most commenters expressed concern that the interim guidance did not go far enough to assuage corporate fears that EPA will use audit reports for environmental compliance "witch hunts." Several commenters suggested additional specific assurances regarding the circumstances under which EPA will request such reports.

One commenter recommended that EPA request audit reports only "when the Agency can show the information it needs to perform its statutory mission cannot be obtained from the monitoring, compliance or other data that is otherwise reportable and/or accessible to EPA, or where the Government deems an audit report material to a criminal investigation." EPA accepts this recommendation in part. The Agency believes it would not be in the best interest of human health and the environment to commit to making a "showing" of a compelling information need before ever requesting an audit report. While EPA may normally be willing to do so, the Agency cannot rule out in advance all circumstances in which such a showing may not be possible. However, it would be helpful to further clarify that a request for an audit report or a portion of a report normally will be made when needed information is not available by alternative means. Therefore, EPA has revised Section III.A., paragraph two and added the phrase: "and usually made where the information needed cannot be obtained from monitoring, reporting or other data otherwise available to the Agency."

Another commenter suggested that (except in the case of criminal investigations) EPA should limit requests for audit documents to specific questions. By including the phrase "or relevant portions of a report" in Section III.A., EPA meant to emphasize it would not request an entire audit document when only a relevant portion would suffice. Likewise, EPA fully intends not to request even a portion of a report if needed information or data can be otherwise obtained. To further clarify this point EPA has added the phrase, "most likely focused on particular information needs rather than the entire report," to the second sentence of paragraph two, Section III.A. Incorporating the two comments above, the first two sentences in paragraph two of final Section III.A. now read: "EPA's

authority to request an audit report, or relevant portions thereof, will be exercised on a case-by-case basis where the Agency determines it is needed to accomplish a statutory mission or the Government deems it to be material to a criminal investigation. EPA expects such requests to be limited, most likely focused on particular information needs rather than the entire report, and usually made where the information needed cannot be obtained from monitoring, reporting or other data otherwise available to the Agency."

Other commenters recommended that EPA not request audit reports under any circumstances, that requests be "restricted to only those legally required," that requests be limited to criminal investigations, or that requests be made only when EPA has reason to believe "that the audit programs or reports are being used to conceal evidence of environmental non-compliance or otherwise being used in bad faith." EPA appreciates concerns underlying all of these comments and has considered each carefully. However, the Agency believes that these recommendations do not strike the appropriate balance between retaining the flexibility to accomplish EPA's statutory missions in future, unforeseen circumstances, and acknowledging regulated entities' need to self-evaluate environmental performance with some measure of privacy. Indeed, based on prime informal comments, the small number of formal comments received, and the even smaller number of adverse comments, EPA believes the final policy statement should remain largely unchanged from the interim version.

Elements of Effective Environmental Auditing

Three commenters expressed concerns regarding the seven general elements EPA outlined in the Appendix to the interim guidance.

One commenter noted that were EPA to further expand or more fully detail such elements, programs not specifically fulfilling each element would then be judged inadequate. EPA agrees that presenting highly specific and prescriptive auditing elements could be counter-productive by not taking into account numerous factors which vary extensively from one organization to another, but which may still result in effective auditing programs. Accordingly, EPA does not plan to expand or more fully detail these auditing elements.

Another commenter asserted that states and localities should be cautioned not to consider EPA's auditing elements as mandatory steps. The Agency is fully aware of this concern and in the interim guidance noted its strong opinion that "regulatory agencies should not attempt to prescribe the precise form and structure of regulated entities' environmental management or auditing programs." While EPA cannot require state or local regulators to adopt this or similar policies, the Agency does strongly encourage them to do so, both in the interim and final policies.

A final commenter thought the Appendix too specifically prescribed what should and what should not be included in an auditing program. Other commenters, on the other hand, viewed the elements described as very general in nature. EPA agrees with these other commenters. The elements are in no way binding. Moreover, EPA believes that most mature, effective environmental auditing programs do incorporate each of these general elements in some form, and considers them useful yardsticks for those considering adopting or upgrading audit programs. For these reasons EPA has not revised the Appendix in today's final policy statement.

Other Comments

Other significant comments addressed EPA inspection priorities for, and enforcement responses to, organizations with environmental auditing programs.

One commenter, stressing that audit programs are *internal* management tools, took exception to the phrase in the second paragraph of section III.B.1. of the interim guidance which states that environmental audits can 'complement' regulatory oversight. By using the word 'complement' in this context, EPA does

not intend to imply that audit reports must be obtained by the Agency in order to supplement regulatory inspections. 'Complement' is used in a broad sense of being in addition to inspections and providing something (i.e., self-assessment) which otherwise would be lacking. To clarify this point EPA has added the phrase "by providing self-assessment to assure compliance" after "environmental audits may complement inspections" in this paragraph.

The same commenter also expressed concern that, as EPA sets inspection priorities, a company having an audit program could appear to be a 'poor performer' due to complete and accurate reporting when measured against a company which reports something less than required by law. EPA agrees that it is important to communicate this fact to Agency and state personnel, and will do so. However, the Agency does not believe a change in the policy statement is necessary.

A further comment suggested EPA should commit to take auditing programs into account when assessing all enforcement actions. However, in order to maintain enforcement flexibility under varied circumstances, the Agency cannot promise reduced enforcement responses to violations at all audited facilities when other factors may be overriding. Therefore the policy statement continues to state that EPA may exercise its decretion to consider auditing programs as evidence of honest and genuine efforts to assure compliance, which would then be taken into account in fashioning enforcement responses to violations.

A final commenter suggested the phrase "expeditiously correct environmental problems" not be used in the enforcement context since it implied EPA would use an entity's record of correcting nonregulated matters when evaluating regulatory violations. EPA did not intend for such an inference to be made. EPA intended the term "environmental problems" to refer to the underlying circumstances which eventually lead up to the violations. To clarify this point, EPA is revising the first two sentences of the paragraph to which this comment refers by changing "environmental problems" to "violations and underlying environmental problems" in the first sentence and to "underlying environmental problems" in the second sentence.

In a separate development EPA is preparing an update of its January 1984 *Federal Facilities Compliance Strategy*, which is referenced in section III. C. of the auditing policy. The Strategy should be completed and available on request from EPA's Office of Federal Activities later this year.

EPA thanks all commenters for responding to the November 8, 1985 publication. Today's notice is being issued to inform regulated entities and the public of EPA's final policy toward environmental auditing. This policy was developed to help (a) encourage regulated entities to institutionalize effective audit practices as one means of improving compliance and sound environmental management, and (b) guide internal EPA actions directly related to regulated entities' environmental auditing programs.

EPA will evaluate implementation of this final policy to ensure it meets the above goals and continues to encourage better environmental management, while strengthening the Agency's own efforts to monitor and enforce compliance with environmental requirements.

II. General EPA Policy on Environmental Auditing

A. Introduction

Environmental auditing is a systematic, documented, periodic and objective review by regulated entities [1] of facility operations and practices related to meeting environmental requirements. Audits can be designed to accomplish any or all of the following: verify compliance with environmental requirements; evaluate the effectiveness

of environmental management systems already in place; or assess risks from regulated and unregulated materials and practices.

Auditing serves as a quality assurance check to help improve the effectiveness of basic environmental management by verifying that management practices are in place, functioning and adequate. Environmental audits evaluate, and are not a substitute for, direct compliance activities such as obtaining permits, installing controls, monitoring compliance, reporting violations, and keeping records. Environmental auditing may verify but does not include activities required by law, regulation or permit (e.g., continuous emissions monitoring, composite correction plans at wastewater treatment plants, etc.). Audits do not in any way replace regulatory agency inspections. However, environmental audits can improve compliance by complementing conventional federal, state and local oversight.

The appendix to this policy statement outlines some basic elements of environmental auditing (e.g., auditor independence and top management support) for use by those considering implementation of effective auditing programs to help achieve and maintain compliance. Additional information on environmental auditing practices can be found in various published materials. [2]

Environmental auditing has developed for sound business reasons, particularly as a means of helping regulated entities manage pollution control affirmatively over time instead of reacting to crises. Auditing can result in improved facility environmental performance, help communicate effective solutions to common environmental problems, focus facility managers' attention on current and upcoming regulatory requirements, and generate protocols and checklists

---

[1] "Regulated entities" include private firms and public agencies with facilities subject to environmental regulation. Public agencies can include federal, state or local agencies as well as special-purpose organizations such as regional sewage commissions.

[2] See, e.g., "Current Practices in Environmental Auditing," EPA Report No. EPA–230–09–83–006, February 1984; "Annotated Bibliography on Environmental Auditing," Fifth Edition, September 1985, both available from: Regulatory Reform Staff, PM–223, EPA, 401 M Street SW, Washington, DC 20460.

which help facilities better manage themselves. Auditing also can result in better-integrated management of environmental hazards, since auditors frequently identify environmental liabilities which go beyond regulatory compliance. Companies, public entities and federal facilities have employed a variety of environmental auditing practices in recent years. Several hundred major firms in diverse industries now have environmental auditing programs, although they often are known by other names such as assessment, survey, surveillance, review or appraisal.

While auditing has demonstrated its usefulness to those with audit programs, many others still do not audit. Clarification of EPA's position regarding auditing may help encourage regulated entities to establish audit programs or upgrade systems already in place.

B. EPA Encourages the Use of Environmental Auditing

EPA encourages regulated entities to adopt sound environmental management practices to improve environmental performance. In particular, EPA encourages regulated entities subject to environmental regulations to institute environmental auditing programs to help ensure the adequacy of internal systems to achieve, maintain and monitor compliance. Implementation of environmental auditing programs can result in better identification, resolution and avoidance of environmental problems, as well as improvements to management practices. Audits can be conducted effectively by independent internal or third party auditors. Larger organizations generally have greater resources to devote to an internal audit team, while smaller entities might be more likely to use outside auditors.

Regulated entities are responsible for taking all necessary steps to ensure compliance with environmental requirements, whether or not they adopt audit programs. Although environmental laws do not require a regulated facility to have an auditing program, ultimate responsibility for the environmental

performance of the facility lies with top management, which therefore has a strong incentive to use reasonable means, such as environmental auditing, to secure reliable information of facility compliance status.

EPA does not intend to dictate or interfere with the environmental management practices of private or public organizations. Nor does EPA intend to mandate auditing (though in certain instances EPA may seek to include provisions for environmental auditing as part of settlement agreements, as noted below). Because environmental auditing systems have been widely adopted on a voluntary basis in the past, and because audit quality depends to a large degree upon genuine management commitment to the program and its objectives, auditing should remain a voluntary activity.

III. EPA Policy on Specific Environmental Auditing Issues

A. Agency Requests for Audit Reports

EPA has broad statutory authority to request relevant information on the environmental compliance status of regulated entities. However, EPA believes routine Agency requests for audit reports [3] could inhibit auditing in the long run, decreasing both the quantity and quality of audits conducted. Therefore, as a matter of policy, EPA will *not* routinely request environmental audit reports.

EPA's authority to request an audit report, or relevant portions thereof, will be exercised on a case-by-case basis where the Agency determines it is needed to accomplish a statutory mission, or where the Government deems it to be material to a criminal investigation. EPA expects such requests to be limited, most likely focused on particular information needs rather than the entire report, and usually

---

[3] An "environmental audit report" is a written report which candidly and thoroughly presents findings from a review, conducted as part of an environmental audit as described in section II.A., of facility environmental performance and practices. An audit report is not a substitute for compliance monitoring reports or other reports or records which may be required by EPA or other regulatory agencies.

made where the information needed cannot be obtained from monitoring, reporting or other data otherwise available to the Agency. Examples would likely include situations where: audits are conducted under consent decrees or other settlement agreements; a company has placed its management practices at issue by raising them as a defense; or state of mind or intent are a relevant element of inquiry, such as during a criminal investigation. This list is illustrative rather than exhaustive, since there doubtless will be other situations, not subject to prediction, in which audit reports rather than information may be required.

EPA acknowledges regulated entities' need to self-evaluate environmental performance with some measure of privacy and encourages such activity. However, audit reports may not shield monitoring, compliance, or other information that would otherwise be reportable and/or accessible to EPA, even if there is no explicit 'requirement' to generate that data.[4] Thus, this policy does not alter regulated entities' existing or future obligations to monitor, record or report information required under environmental statutes, regulations or permits, or to allow EPA access to that information. Nor does this policy alter EPA's authority to request and receive any relevant information—including that contained in audit reports—under various environmental statutes (e.g., Clean Water Act section 308, Clean Air Act sections 114 and 208) or in other administrative or judicial proceedings.

Regulated entities also should be aware that certain audit findings may by law have to be reported to government agencies. However, in addition to any such requirements, EPA encourages regulated entities to notify appropriate State or Federal officials of findings which suggest significant environmental or public health risks, even when not specifically required to do so.

[4] See, for example, "Duties to Report or Disclose Information on the Environmental Aspects of Business Activities," Environmental Law Institute report to EPA, final report, September 1985.

B. EPA Response to Environmental Auditing

1. General Policy

EPA will not promise to forgo inspections, reduce enforcement responses, or offer other such incentives in exchange for implementation of environmental auditing or other sound environmental management practices. Indeed, a credible enforcement program provides a strong incentive for regulated entities to audit.

Regulatory agencies have an obligation to assess source compliance status independently and cannot eliminate inspections for particular firms or classes of firms. Although environmental audits may complement inspections by providing self-assessment to assure compliance, they are in no way a substitute for regulatory oversight. Moreover, certain statutes (e.g. RCRA) and Agency policies establish minimum facility inspection frequencies to which EPA will adhere.

However, EPA will continue to address environmental problems on a priority basis and will consequently inspect facilities with poor environmental records and practices more frequently. Since effective environmental auditing helps management identify and promptly correct actual or potential problems, audited facilities' environmental performance should improve. Thus, while EPA inspections of self-audited facilities will continue, to the extent that compliance performance is considered in setting inspection priorities, facilities with a good compliance history may be subject to fewer inspections.

In fashioning enforcement responses to violations, EPA policy is to take into account, on a case-by-case basis, the honest and genuine efforts of regulated entities to avoid and promptly correct violations and underlying environmental problems. When regulated entities take reasonable precautions to avoid noncompliance, expeditiously correct underlying environmental problems discovered through audits or other means, and implement measures to prevent their recurrence, EPA may exercise its discretion to consider such actions as honest and genuine efforts to assure compliance. Such consideration applies particularly when a regulated entity promptly reports violations or compliance data which otherwise were not required to be recorded or reported to EPA.

2. Audit Provisions as Remedies in Enforcement Actions

EPA may propose environmental auditing provisions in consent decrees and in other settlement negotiations where auditing could provide a remedy for identified problems and reduce the likelihood of similar problems recurring in the future.[5] Environmental auditing provisions are most likely to be proposed in settlement negotiations where:

• A pattern of violations can be attributed, at least in part, to the absence or poor functioning of an environmental management system; or

• The type or nature of violations indicates a likelihood that similar noncompliance problems may exist or occur elsewhere in the facility or at other facilities operated by the regulated entity.

Through this consent decree approach and other means, EPA may consider how to encourage effective auditing by publicly owned sewage treatment works (POTWs). POTWs often have compliance problems related to operation and maintenance procedures which can be addressed effectively through the use of environmental auditing. Under its National Municipal Policy EPA already is requiring many POTWs to develop composite correction plans to identify and correct compliance problems.

C. Environmental Auditing at Federal Facilities

EPA encourages all federal agencies subject to environmental laws and regulations to institute environmental

auditing systems to help ensure the adequacy of internal systems to achieve, maintain and monitor compliance. Environmental auditing at federal facilities can be an effective supplement to EPA and state inspections. Such federal facility environmental audit programs should be structured to promptly identify environmental problems and expeditiously develop schedules for remedial action.

To the extent feasible, EPA will provide technical assistance to help federal agencies design and initiate audit programs. Where appropriate, EPA will enter into agreements with other agencies to clarify the respective roles, responsibilities and commitments of each agency in conducting and responding to federal facility environmental audits.

With respect to inspections of self-audited facilities (see section III.B.1 above) and requests for audit reports (see section III.A above), EPA generally will respond to environmental audits by federal facilities in the same manner as it does for other regulated entities, in keeping with the spirit and intent of Executive Order 12088 and the EPA *Federal Facilities Compliance Strategy* (January 1984, update forthcoming in late 1986). Federal agencies should, however, be aware that the Freedom of Information Act will govern any disclosure of audit reports or audit-generated information requested from federal agencies by the public.

When federal agencies discover significant violations through an environmental audit, EPA encourages them to submit the related audit findings and remedial action plans expeditiously to the applicable EPA regional office (and responsible state agencies, where appropriate) even when not specifically required to do so. EPA will review the audit findings and action plans and either provide written approval or negotiate a Federal Facilities Compliance Agreement. EPA will utilize the escalation procedures provided in Executive Order 12088 and the EPA *Federal Facilities Compliance Strategy* only when agreement between agencies cannot be reached. In any event, federal agencies are expected to report pollution

---

[5] EPA is developing guidance for use by Agency negotiators in structuring appropriate environmental audit provisions for consent decrees and other settlement negotiations.

abatement projects involving costs (necessary to correct problems discovered through the audit) to EPA in accordance with OMB Circular A-106. Upon request, and in appropriate circumstances, EPA will assist affected federal agencies through coordination of any public release of audit findings with approved action plans once agreement has been reached.

IV. Relationship to State or Local Regulatory Agencies

State and local regulatory agencies have independent jurisdiction over regulated entities. EPA encourages them to adopt these or similar policies, in order to advance the use of effective environmental auditing in a consistent manner.

EPA recognizes that some states have already undertaken environmental auditing initiatives which differ somewhat from this policy. Other states also may want to develop auditing policies which accommodate their particular needs or circumstances. Nothing in this policy statement is intended to preempt or preclude states from developing other approaches to environmental auditing. EPA encourages state and local authorities to consider the basic principles which guided the Agency in developing this policy:

• Regulated entities must continue to report or record compliance information required under existing statutes or regulations, regardless of whether such information is generated by an environmental audit or contained in an audit report. Required information cannot be withheld merely because it is generated by an audit rather than by some other means.

• Regulatory agencies cannot make promises to forgo or limit enforcement action against a particular facility or class of facilities in exchange for the use of environmental auditing systems. However, such agencies may use their discretion to adjust enforcement actions on a case-by-case basis in response to honest and genuine efforts by regulated entities to assure environmental compliance.

• When setting inspection priorities regulatory agencies should focus to the extent possible on compliance performance and environmental results.

• Regulatory agencies must continue to meet minimum program requirements (e.g., minimum inspection requirements, etc.).

• Regulatory agencies should not attempt to prescribe the precise form and structure of regulated entities' environmental management or auditing programs.

An effective state/federal partnership is needed to accomplish the mutual goal of achieving and maintaining high levels of compliance with environmental laws and regulations. The greater the consistency between state or local policies and this federal response to environmental auditing, the greater the degree to which sound auditing practices might be adopted and compliance levels improve.

Dated: June 28, 1986.

Lee M. Thomas,
Administrator.

Appendix—Elements of Effective Environmental Auditing Programs

Introduction: Environmental auditing is a systematic, documented, periodic and objective review by a regulated entity of facility operations and practices related to meeting environmental requirements.

Private sector environmental audits of facilities have been conducted for several years and have taken a variety of forms, in part to accommodate unique organizational structures and circumstances. Nevertheless, effective environmental audits appear to have certain discernible elements in common with other kinds of audits. Standards for internal audits have been documented extensively. The elements outlined below draw heavily on two of these documents: "Compendium of Audit Standards" (©1983, Walter Willborn, American Society for Quality Control) and "Standards for the Professional Practice of Internal Auditing" (©1981, The Institute of Internal Auditors, Inc.). They also reflect Agency analyses conducted over the last several years.

Performance-oriented auditing elements are outlined here to help accomplish several objectives. A general description of features of effective, mature audit programs can help those starting audit programs, especially federal agencies and smaller businesses. These elements also indicate the attributes of auditing EPA generally considers important to ensure program effectiveness. Regulatory agencies may use these elements in negotiating environmental auditing provisions for consent decrees. Finally, these elements can help guide states and localities considering auditing initiatives.

An effective environmental auditing system will likely include the following general elements:

I. *Explicit top management support for environmental auditing and commitment to follow-up on audit findings.* Management support may be demonstrated by a written policy articulating upper management support for the auditing program, and for compliance with all pertinent requirements, including corporate policies and permit requirements as well as federal, state and local statutes and regulations.

Management support for the auditing program also should be demonstrated by an explicit written commitment to follow-up on audit findings to correct identified problems and prevent their recurrence.

II. *An environmental auditing function independent of audited activities.* The status or organizational locus of environmental auditors should be sufficient to ensure objective and unobstructed inquiry, observation and testing. Auditor objectivity should not be impaired by personal relationships, financial or other conflicts of interest, interference with free inquiry or judgment, or fear of potential retribution.

III. *Adequate team staffing and auditor training.* Environmental auditors should possess or have ready access to the knowledge, skills, and disciplines needed to accomplish audit objectives. Each individual auditor should comply

with the company's professional standards of conduct. Auditors, whether full-time or part-time, should maintain their technical and analytical competence through continuing education and training.

IV. *Explicit audit program objectives, scope, resources and frequency.* At a minimum, audit objectives should include assessing compliance with applicable environmental laws and evaluating the adequacy of internal compliance policies, procedures and personnel training programs to ensure continued compliance.

Audits should be based on a process which provides auditors: all corporate policies, permits, and federal, state, and local regulations pertinent to the facility; and checklists or protocols addressing specific features that should be evaluated by auditors.

Explicit written audit procedures generally should be used for planning audits, establishing audit scope, examining and evaluating audit findings, communicating audit results, and following-up.

V. *A process which collects, analyzes, interprets and documents information sufficient to achieve audit objectives.* Information should be collected before and during an onsite visit regarding environmental compliance(*1*), environmental management effectiveness(*2*), and other matters (*3*) related to audit objectives and scope. This information should be sufficient, reliable, relevant and useful to provide a sound basis for audit findings and recommendations.

a. *Sufficient* information is factual, adequate and convincing so that a prudent, informed person would be likely to reach the same conclusions as the auditor.

b. *Reliable* information is the best attainable through use of appropriate audit techniques.

c. *Relevant* information supports audit findings and recommendations and is consistent with the objectives for the audit.

d. *Useful* information helps the organization meet its goals.

The audit process should include a

periodic review of the reliability and integrity of this information and the means used to identify, measure, classify and report it. Audit procedures, including the testing and sampling techniques employed, should be selected in advance, to the extent practical, and expanded or altered if circumstances warrant. The process of collecting, analyzing, interpreting, and documenting information should provide reasonable assurance that audit objectivity is maintained and audit goals are met.

VI. *A process which includes specific procedures to promptly prepare candid, clear and appropriate written reports on audit findings, corrective actions, and schedules for implementation.*
Procedures should be in place to ensure that such information is communicated to managers, including facility and corporate management, who can evaluate the information and ensure correction of identified problems. Procedures also should be in place for determining what internal findings are reportable to state or federal agencies.

VII. *A process which includes quality assurance procedures to assure the accuracy and thoroughness of environmental audits.* Quality assurance may be accomplished through supervision, independent internal reviews, external reviews, or a combination of these approaches.

Footnotes to Appendix

(*1*) A comprehensive assessment of compliance with federal environmental regulations requires an analysis of facility performance against numerous environmental statutes and implementing regulations. These statutes include:
Resource Conservation and Recovery Act
Federal Water Pollution Control Act
Clean Air Act
Hazardous Materials Transportation Act
Toxic Substances Control Act
Comprehensive Environmental Response, Compensation and Liability Act
Safe Drinking Water Act
Federal Insecticide, Fungicide and Rodenticide Act
Marine Protection, Research and Sanctuaries Act
Uranium Mill Tailings Radiation Control Act
In addition, state and local government are likely to have their own environmental laws.

Many states have been delegated authority to administer federal programs. Many local governments' building, fire, safety and health codes also have environmental requirements relevant to an audit evaluation.

(*2*) An environmental audit could go well beyond the type of compliance assessment normally conducted during regulatory inspections, for example, by evaluating policies and practices, regardless of whether they are part of the environmental system or the operating and maintenance procedures. Specifically, audits can evaluate the extent to which systems or procedures:

1. Develop organizational environmental policies which: a. implement regulatory requirements; b. provide management guidance for environmental hazards not specifically addressed in regulations;

2. Train and motivate facility personnel to work in an environmentally-acceptable manner and to understand and comply with government regulations and the entity's environmental policy;

3. Communicate relevant environmental developments expeditiously to facility and other personnel;

4. Communicate effectively with government and the public regarding serious environmental incidents;

5. Require third parties working for, with or on behalf of the organization to follow its environmental procedures;

6. Make proficient personnel available at all times to carry out environmental (especially emergency) procedures;

7. Incorporate environmental protection into written operating procedures;

8. Apply best management practices and operating procedures, including "good housekeeping" techniques;

9. Institute preventive and corrective maintenance systems to minimize actual and potential environmental harm;

10. Utilize best available process and control technologies;

11. Use most-effective sampling and monitoring techniques, test methods, recordkeeping systems or reporting protocols (beyond minimum legal requirements);

12. Evaluate causes behind any serious environmental incidents and establish procedures to avoid recurrence;

13. Exploit source reduction, recycle and reuse potential wherever practical; and

14. Substitute materials or processes to allow use of the least-hazardous substances feasible.

(*3*) Auditors could also assess environmental risks and uncertainties.

Appendix C:
Policy on Criminal Prosecutions for Environmental Violations

Factors in Decisions on Criminal Prosecutions for Environmental Violations in the Context of Significant Voluntary Compliance or Disclosure Efforts by the Violator
(Department of Justice July 1, 1991)

I. Introduction

It is the policy of the Department of Justice to encourage self-auditing, self-policing and voluntary disclosure of environmental violations by the regulated community by indicating that these activities are viewed as mitigating factors in the Department's exercise of criminal environmental enforcement discretion. This document is intended to describe the factors that the Department of Justice considers in deciding whether to bring a criminal prosecution for a violation of an environmental statute, so that such prosecutions do not create a disincentive to or undermine the goal of encouraging critical self-auditing, self-policing, and voluntary disclosure. It is designed to give federal prosecutors direction concerning the exercise of prosecutorial discretion in environmental criminal cases and to ensure that such discretion is exercised consistently nationwide. It is also intended to give the regulated community a sense of how the federal government exercises its criminal prosecutorial discretion with respect to such factors as the defendant's voluntary disclosure of violations, cooperation with the government in investigating the violations, use of environmental audits and other procedures to ensure compliance with all applicable environmental laws and regulations, and use of measures to remedy expeditiously and completely any violations and the harms caused thereby.

This guidance and the examples contained herein provide a framework for the determination of whether a particular case presents the type of circumstances in which lenience would be appropriate.

II. Factors to be Considered

Where the law and evidence would otherwise be sufficient for prosecution, the attorney for the Department should consider the factors contained herein, to the extent they are applicable, along with any other relevant factors, in determining whether and how to prosecute. It must be emphasized that these are examples of the types of factors which could be relevant. They do not constitute a definitive recipe or checklist of requirements. They merely illustrate some of the types of information which is relevant to our exercise of prosecutorial discretion.

It is unlikely that any one factor will be dispositive in any given case. All relevant factors are considered and given the weight deemed appropriate in the particular case. See *Federal Principles of Prosecution* (U.S. Dept. of Justice, 1980), Comment to Part A.2; Part B.3.

A. *Voluntary Disclosure*

The attorney for the Department should consider whether the person[1] made a voluntary, timely and complete disclosure of the matter under investigation. Consideration should be given to whether the person came forward promptly after discovering the noncompliance, and to the quantity and quality of information provided. Particular consideration should be given to whether the disclosure substantially aided the government's investigatory process, and whether it occurred before a law enforcement or regulatory authority (federal, state or local authority) had already obtained knowledge regarding noncompliance. A disclosure is

---

1. As used in this document, the terms "person" and "violator" are intended to refer to business and nonprofit entities as well as individuals.

not considered to be "voluntary" if that disclosure is already specifically required by law, regulation, or permit.[2]

B. Cooperation

The attorney for the Department should consider the degree and timeliness of cooperation by the person. Full and prompt cooperation is essential, whether in the context of a voluntary disclosure or after the government has independently learned of a violation. Consideration should be given to the violator's willingness to make all relevant information (including the complete results of any internal or external investigation and the names of all potential witnesses) available to government investigators and prosecutors. Consideration should also be a given to the extent and quality of the violator's assistance to the government's investigation.

C. Preventive Measures and Compliance Programs

The attorney for the Department should consider the existence and scope of any regularized, intensive, and comprehensive environmental compliance program; such a program may include an environmental compliance or management audit. Particular consideration should be given to whether the compliance or audit program includes sufficient measures to identify and prevent future noncompliance, and whether the program was adopted in good faith in a timely manner.

Compliance programs may vary but the following questions should be asked in evaluating any program: Was there a strong institutional policy to comply with all environmental requirements? Had safeguards beyond those required by existing law been developed and implemented to prevent noncompliance from occurring? Were there regular procedures, including internal or external compliance and management audits, to evaluate, detect, prevent and remedy circumstances like those that led to the noncompliance? Were there procedures and safeguards to ensure the integrity of any audit conducted? Did the audit evaluate all sources of pollution (*i.e.,* all media), including the possibility of cross-media transfers of pollutants? Were the auditor's recommendations implemented in a timely fashion? Were adequate resources committed to the auditing program and to implementing its recommendations? Was environmental compliance a standard by which employee and corporate departmental performance was judged?

D. Additional Factors Which May [Be] Relevant

1. Pervasiveness of Noncompliance

Pervasive noncompliance may indicate systemic or repeated participation in or condonation of criminal behavior. It may also indicate the lack of a meaningful compliance program. In evaluating this factor, the attorney for the Department should consider, among other things, the number and level of employees participating in the unlawful activities and the obviousness, seriousness, duration, history, and frequency of noncompliance.

2. Internal Disciplinary Action

Effective internal disciplinary action is crucial to any compliance program. The attorney for the Department should consider whether there was an effective system of discipline for employees who violated company environmental compliance policies. Did the disciplinary

---

2. For example, any person in charge of a vessel or of an on shore facility or an offshore facility is required to notify the appropriate agency of the United States Government of any discharge of oil or a hazardous substance into or upon *inter alia* the navigable waters of the United States. Section 311(b)(5) of the Clean Water Act, 33 U.S.C. 1321(b)(5), as amended by the Oil Pollution Act of 1990, Pub. L. 101-380, §4301(a), 104 Stat. 485, 533 (1990).

system establish an awareness in other employees that unlawful conduct would not be condoned?

3. Subsequent Compliance Efforts

The attorney for the Department should consider the extent of any efforts to remedy any ongoing noncompliance. The promptness and completeness of any action taken to remove the source of the noncompliance and to lessen the environmental harm resulting from the noncompliance should be considered. Considerable weight should be given to prompt, good-faith efforts to reach environmental compliance agreements with federal or state authorities, or both. Full compliance with such agreements should be a factor in any decision whether to prosecute.

III. Application of These Factors to Hypothetical Examples[3]

These examples are intended to assist federal prosecutors in their exercise of discretion in evaluating environmental cases. The situations facing prosecutors, of course, present a wide variety of fact patterns. Therefore, in a given case, some of the criteria may be satisfied while others may not. Moreover, satisfaction of various criteria may be a matter of degree. Consequently, the effect of a given mix of factors also is a matter of degree. In the ideal situation, if a company fully meets all of the criteria, the result may be a decision not to prosecute that company criminally. Even if satisfaction of the criteria is not complete, still the company may benefit in terms of degree of enforcement response by the government. The following hypothetical examples are intended to illustrate the operation of these guidelines.

Example 1:

This is the ideal case in terms of criteria satisfaction and consequent prosecution leniency.

1. Company A regularly conducts a comprehensive audit of its compliance with environmental requirements.

2. The audit uncovers information about employees' disposing of hazardous wastes by dumping them in an unpermitted location.

3. An internal company investigation confirms the audit information. (Depending upon the nature of the audit, this follow-up investigation may be unnecessary.)

4. Prior to the violations the company had a sound compliance program, which included clear policies, employees training, and a hotline for suspected violations.

5. As soon as the company confirms the violations, it discloses all pertinent information to the appropriate government agency; it undertakes compliance planning with that agency; and it carries out satisfactory remediation measures.

6. The company also undertakes to correct any false information previously submitted to the government in relation to the violations.

7. Internally the company disciplines the employees actually involved in the violations, including any supervisor who was lax in preventing or detecting the activity. Also, the company reviews its compliance program to determine how the violations slipped by and corrects the weaknesses found by that review.

8. The company discloses to the government the names of the employees actually responsible for the violations, and it cooperates with the government by providing documentation necessary to the investigation of those persons.

Under these circumstances Company A would stand a good chance of being favorably considered for prosecutorial leniency, to the extent of not being criminally prosecuted at all.

---

3. While this policy applies to both individuals and organizational violators, these examples focus particularly upon situations involving organizations.

The degree of any leniency, however, may turn upon other relevant factors not specifically dealt with in these guidelines.[4]

Example 2:

At the opposite end of the scale is Company Z, which meets few of the criteria. The likelihood of prosecutorial leniency, therefore, is remote. Company Z's circumstances may include any of the following:

1. Because an employee has threatened to report a violation to federal authorities, the company is afraid that investigators may begin looking at it. An audit is undertaken, but it focuses only upon the particular violation, ignoring the possibility that the violation may be indicative of widespread activities in the organization.

2. After completing the audit, Company Z reports the violations discovered to the government.

3. The company had a compliance program, but it was effectively no more than a collection of paper. No effort is made to disseminate its content, impress upon employees its significance, train employees in its application, or oversee its implementation.

4. Even after "discovery" of the violation the company makes no effort to strengthen its compliance procedures.

5. The company makes no effort to come to terms with regulators regarding its violations. It resists any remedial work and refuses to pay any monetary sanctions.

6. Because of the non-compliance, information submitted to regulators over the years has been materially inaccurate, painting a substantially false picture of the company's true compliance situation. The company fails to take any steps to correct that inaccuracy.

7. The company does not cooperate with prosecutors in identifying those employees (including managers) who actually were involved in the violation, and it resists disclosure of any documents relating either to the violations or to the responsible employees.

In these circumstances leniency is unlikely. The only positive action is the so-called audit, but that was so narrowly focused as to be of questionable value, and it was undertaken only to head off a possible criminal investigation. Otherwise, the company demonstrated no good faith either in terms of compliance efforts or in assisting the government in obtaining a full understanding of the violation and discovering its sources.

Nonetheless, these factors do not assure a criminal prosecution of Company Z. As with Company A, above, other circumstances may be present which affect the balance struck by prosecutors. For example, the effect of the violation (because of substance, duration, or amount) may be such that prosecutors would not consider it to be an appropriate criminal case. Administrative or civil proceedings may be considered a more appropriate response.

Other examples:

Between these extremes there is a range of possibilities. The presence, absence, or degree of any criterion may affect the prosecution's exercise of discretion. Below are some examples of such effects:

1. In a situation otherwise similar to that of Company A, above, Company B performs an audit that is very limited in scope and probably reflects no more than an effort to avoid prosecution. Despite that background, Company B is cooperative in terms of both bringing itself into compliance and providing information regarding the crime and its perpetrators. The result could be any of a number of outcomes, including prosecution of a lesser charge or a decision to prosecute the individuals rather than the company.

---

4. For example, if the company had a long history of noncompliance, the compliance audit was done only under pressure from regulators, and a timely audit would have ended the violations much sooner, those circumstances would be considered.

2. Again the situation is similar to Company A's, but Company C refuses to reveal any information regarding the individual violators. The likelihood of the government's prosecuting the company are [sic] substantially increased.

3. In another situation similar to Company A's, Company D chooses to "sit on" the audit and take corrective action without telling the government. The government learns of the situation months or years after the fact.

A complicating fact here is that environmental regulatory programs are self policing: they include a substantial number of reporting requirements. If reports which in fact presented false information are allowed to stand uncorrected, the reliability of this system is undermined. They also may lead to adverse and unfair impacts upon other members of the regulated community. For example, Company D failed to report discharges of X contaminant into a municipal sewer system, discharges that were terminated as a result of an audit. The sewer authority, though, knowing only that there have been excessive loadings of X, but not knowing that Company D was a source, tightens limitations upon all known sources of X. Thus, all of those sources incur additional treatment expenses, but Company D is unaffected. Had Company D revealed its audit results, the other companies would not have suffered unnecessary expenses.

In some situations, moreover, failure to report is a crime. *See, e.g.,* 33 U.S.C. §1321(b)(5) and 42 U.S.C. §9603(b). To illustrate the effect of this factor, consider Company E, which conducts a thorough audit and finds that hazardous wastes have been disposed of by dumping them on the ground. The company cleans up the area and tightens up its compliance program, but does not reveal the situation to regulators. Assuming that a reportable quantity of a hazardous substance was released, the company was under a legal obligation under 42 U.S.C. §9603(b) to report that release as soon as it had knowledge of it, thereby allowing regulators the opportunity to assure proper clean up. Company E's knowing failure to report the release upon learning of it is itself a felony.

In the cases of both Company D and Company E, consideration would be given by prosecutors for remedial efforts; hence prosecution of fewer or lesser charges might result. However, because Company D's silence adversely affected others who are entitled to fair regulatory treatment and because Company E deprived those legally responsible for evaluation cleanup needs of the ability to carry out their functions, the likelihood of their totally escaping criminal prosecution is significantly reduced.

4. Company F's situation is similar to that of Company B. However, with regard to the various violations shown by the audit, it concentrates upon correcting only the easier, less expensive, less significant among them. Its lackadaisical approach to correction does not make it a strong candidate for leniency.

5. Company G is similar to Company D in that it performs an audit and finds violations, but does not bring them to the government's attention. Those violations do not involve failures to comply with reporting requirements. The company undertakes a program of gradually correcting its violations. When the government learns of the situation, Company G still has not remedied its most significant violations, but claims that it certainly planned to get to them. Company G could receive some consideration for its efforts, but its failure to disclose and the slowness of its remedial work probably mean that it cannot expect a substantial degree of leniency.

6. Comprehensive audits are considered positive efforts toward good faith compliance. However, such audits are not indispensable to enforcement leniency. Company H's situation is essentially identical to that of Company A, except for the fact that it does not undertake a comprehensive audit. It does not have a formal audit program, but, as a part of its efforts to ensure compliance, does realize that it is committing an environmental violation. It thereafter takes steps otherwise identical to those of Company A in terms of compliance efforts and cooperation. Company H is also a likely candidate for leniency, including possibly no criminal prosecution.

In sum, mitigating efforts made by the regulated community will be recognized and evaluated. The greater the showing of good faith, the more likely it will be met with leniency. Conversely, the less good faith shown, the less likely that prosecutorial discretion will tend toward leniency.

IV. Nature of this Guidance

This guidance explains the current general practice of the Department in making criminal prosecutive and other decisions after giving consideration to the criteria described above, as well as any other criteria that are relevant to the exercise of criminal prosecutorial discretion in a particular case. This discussion is an expression of, and in no way departs from, the long tradition of exercising prosecutorial discretion. The decision to prosecute "generally rests entirely in [the prosecutor's] discretion." *Bordenkircher v. Hayes*, 434 U.S. 357, 364 (1978).[5] This discretion is especially firmly held by the criminal prosecutor.[6] The criteria set forth above are intended only as internal guidance to Department of Justice attorneys. They are not intended to, do not, and may not be relied upon to create a right or benefit, substantive or procedural, enforceable at law by a party to litigation with the United States, nor do they in any way limit the lawful litigative prerogatives, including civil enforcement actions, of the Department of Justice or the Environmental Protection Agency. They are provided to guide the effective use of limited enforcement resources, and do not derive from, find their basis in, nor constitute any legal requirement, whether constitutional, statutory, or otherwise, to forego or modify any enforcement action or the use of any evidentiary material. See *Principles of Federal Prosecution* (U.S. Dept. of Justice, 1980) p.4; *United States Attorneys' Manual* (U.S. Dept. of Justice, 1986) 1-1.000.

---

5. Although some statutes have occasionally been held to require civil enforcement actions, *see, e.g., Dunlop v. Bachowski*, 421 U.S. 560 (1975), those are unusual cases, and the general rule is that both civil and criminal enforcement is at the enforcement agency's discretion where not prescribed by law. *Heckler v. Chaney*, 470 U.S. 821, 830-35 (1985); *Cutler v. Hayes*, 818 F.2d 879, 893 (D.C. Cir. 1987) (decisions not to enforce are not reviewable unless the statute provides an "inflexible mandate").
6. *Newman v. United States*, 382 F.2d 479, 480 (D.C. Cir. 1967).

Appendix D:
Health, Environment,
and Safety Policy

elf atochem **ATO**	Subject: ELF ATOCHEM NORTH AMERICA, INC.	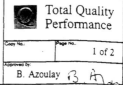 Total Quality Performance
Issue Date: January 11, 1995		Copy No.: / Page No.: 1 of 2
Revision Date: April 25, 1997		Approved by: B. Azoulay

HEALTH, ENVIRONMENT, AND SAFETY POLICY

Guiding Principles: Elf Atochem North America, Inc. is committed to the following three principles:

Compliance: We will manage our business activities to meet the requirements of all company policies, procedures and commitments as well as all applicable governmental laws and regulations.

Protection: We will endeavor to conduct our activities in a manner which protects the well-being of our employees, the public, and the environment and promotes environmentally sustainable manufacturing which meet the needs of the present without compromising the ability of future generations to meet their own needs (sustainable development).

Performance: We will strive to continuously improve all aspects of our health, environmental, and safety performance.

Every employee and agent of Elf Atochem North America, Inc. and its U.S. majority-owned subsidiaries is required to uphold these three principles.

Required Elements: Management systems designed to uphold these principles will be developed, implemented, and maintained. Such systems will reflect the following policy requirements:

- *Corporate Priority:* Compliance, protection, and performance are among the highest priorities in the conduct of our business activities.

- *Organizational Responsibility and Leadership:* Upholding the three guiding principles is a core responsibility of each employee of the company. Employees will be held accountable if they fail to uphold this responsibility. Managers have the additional responsibility of providing leadership in health, environmental, and safety areas by demonstrating Elf Atochem's commitment to these principles of compliance, protection, and performance through their actions.

- *Integration in Organizational Planning and Function:* Systems are designed, implemented, and documented to identify and evaluate health, environmental, and safety related risks so that health, environmental, and safety factors are appropriately addressed in the company's planning and operation.

- *Programs:* Programs are designed, implemented, and documented to direct company activities in a manner which fulfills the requirements of the three guiding principles. Systems to identify and evaluate health, environmental, and safety related work risks; provide a safe and healthful work place; manage change; identify and quantify all applicable emissions; provide for the prevention of pollution and other health, environmental, and safety related risks; establish realistic goals for health, environmental, and safety; and measure and track our health, environmental, and safety performance are designed and implemented in order to facilitate an ongoing process of planning, implementing, reviewing and strengthening those activities which affect our health, environmental and safety performance.

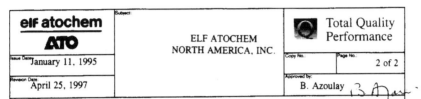

elf atochem **ATO**	Subject:	ELF ATOCHEM NORTH AMERICA, INC.	Total Quality Performance
Issue Date: January 11, 1995			Copy No.: / Page No.: 2 of 2
Revision Date: April 25, 1997			Approved by: B. Azoulay

HEALTH, ENVIRONMENT, AND SAFETY POLICY

- *Maintenance Systems:* Systems are designed, implemented, and documented so that our facilities and operations are maintained and change managed in a manner which fulfills the requirements of the three guiding principles. Preventive and predictive maintenance programs are included where appropriate.

- *Communication:* Communication and reporting systems are designed, implemented, and documented for the timely and accurate communication of health, environmental, and safety information between the company and our employees, our customers, the public, government agencies, and others, as appropriate.

- *Training:* Programs are designed, implemented, and documented so that employees, contractors, and visitors to our facilities receive health, environmental, and safety training commensurate with their job responsibilities or needs and the requirements of this Policy.

- *Employee Participation and Performance Review:* Meaningful employee involvement and participation are recognized as major contributing factors in the success of all our health, environmental and safety efforts. They are recognized as company values and encouraged and supported throughout the company. In addition, employee performance evaluations will include an assessment of how employees meet their responsibilities for compliance with health, environmental and safety laws and this Policy.

- *Assessments:* Company-owned facilities, toll manufacturers, and selected contractors are evaluated to verify health, environmental, and safety compliance or to identify potential risks to the company associated with those operations. Systems are designed, implemented, and documented to appropriately address issues identified during these assessments in a timely manner.

- *Health, Environmental, and Safety Oversight:* Senior management review of the company's health, environmental, and safety performance is conducted and documented on a routine basis. Such reviews will address the allocation of human and financial resources necessary to maintain and uphold the guiding principles.

- *Product Stewardship:* Programs are designed and implemented to incorporate health, environmental and safety considerations as appropriate in the development, production, sale, distribution, storage, handling and ultimate disposal of our products.

Form QD-1001   IF "ATO" IS NOT IN RED, DO NOT USE THIS

Appendix E:
Sample Health, Environment, and Safety Department Organizational Chart

Health, Environment & Safety
Elf Atochem North America, Inc.

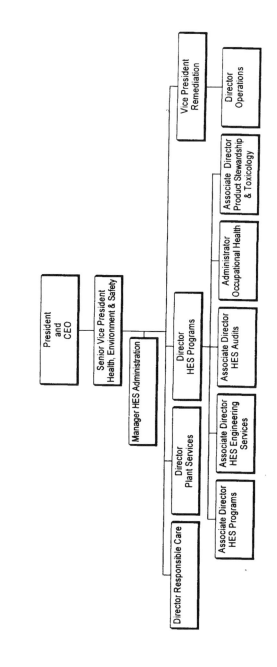

Appendix F:
Core Health, Environment, and Safety Responsibilities of Employees and Contractors

Elf Atochem North America, Inc.'s Health, Environment, and Safety Policy

Table of Contents

A. Purpose of This Pamphlet

This document describes the core health, environment, and safety (HES) responsibilities which apply to all employees and contractors in conducting their day-to-day activities while working at Elf Atochem North America, Inc.'s facilities or operations. In addition, this document is designed to communicate Elf Atochem's commitment to HES protection and performance as defined in Elf Atochem's Health, Environment, and Safety Policy and briefly describes the relevant Elf Atochem policies and procedures.

B. Scope of Elf Atochem's Health, Environment, and Safety Programs

Elf Atochem's HES programs include policies, procedures, standards, and guidance materials designed to fulfill Elf Atochem's commitment to health, environment, and safety and comply with applicable legal requirements and company standards. While some of these elements are described briefly in this document, it is important that you consult the individual policies, procedures, and other materials which form Elf Atochem's HES programs to fully understand Elf Atochem's commitment.

C. Elf Atochem's Health, Environment, and Safety Commitment

Elf Atochem is committed to conducting its operations in a safe, responsible manner, to minimizing emissions and wastes, and to reducing risks to health and the environment. Compliance with all applicable legal requirements is mandatory and is considered essential to upholding the company's commitment.

This commitment to HES compliance, protection, and performance starts at the top, with the CEO and the Executive Committee. As an example, on a routine basis, the Executive Committee dedicates time to a review of health, environment, and safety matters. Further, the Senior Vice President, Health, Environment, and Safety is a standing member of the Executive Committee. In addition, the success of our HES programs requires the commitment of our employees and contractors. Inherent in this commitment is the obligation of all Elf Atochem facilities and operations to evaluate their activities against applicable company and legal requirements and, in the spirit of continuous improvement, to develop and implement a plan to strengthen their activities, where needed.

D. Core Health, Environment, and Safety Responsibilities

1. Responsibilities of Elf Atochem Employees and Contractors

A wide variety of HES standards and other requirements apply to Elf Atochem's operations. Some are self-directed internal procedures while others are mandated by law. While this document does not attempt to list or explain every requirement applicable to every individual or job function, the document does list the core responsibilities which apply under broad circumstances and must be understood and followed by employees and contractors. These core HES responsibilities, and other applicable HES requirements, will be further defined through HES policies, procedures, and standards established by your supervisor, your group's HES professionals, or the corporate HES department.

The core health, environment, and safety responsibilities which apply to employees and contractors are to:

a. Understand your job responsibilities and your role in carrying out Elf Atochem's HES policies and procedures.

b. Conduct your day-to-day activities in a manner which complies with all applicable company and legal requirements and promotes safety and protection of human health and the environment.

c. Communicate information on HES issues or incidents to your supervisor and others in the company, as appropriate.

d. Be truthful, accurate, and complete in maintaining records, submitting documents, and making statements and reports to company personnel, government agencies, and others.

e. Cooperate with the company's HES audit teams and other HES personnel.

There are also many job-specific HES responsibilities which may apply when conducting your day-to-day jobs. If you are unsure about which specific HES requirements apply to you or if you are unsure about how to fulfill any of your responsibilities, contact your supervisor.

2. Additional Responsibilities of Management

In addition to the above, supervisors and other managers in the company must work with the HES professionals in their organization to fulfill the following additional responsibilities:

a. Identify the specific HES responsibilities which apply to your employees;

b. Ensure sufficient training is conducted so that employees may uphold their HES responsibilities;

c. Identify HES issues, if and when they occur, including being open to the concerns of employees;

d. Develop and implement action plans to resolve identified HES issues by taking those actions which may be necessary and consistent with Elf Atochem's HES commitment;

e. Communicate identified HES issues and their resolution to appropriate members of the organization, especially your employees;

f. Provide for adequate consideration of HES factors throughout the company's planning and operational activities;

g. Develop and implement programs designed to prevent the occurrence of HES issues and reduce short and long-term risks and costs to the company; and

h. Ensure checks and balances control and discourage behavior and activities which may undermine Elf Atochem's commitment to HES matters.

Group Presidents and the other senior staff managers reporting to the President and/or Executive Vice Presidents have full responsibility, and as members of the Executive Committee have authority, for all of the activities and functions necessary to implement the company's HES policies and procedures within their organizations. Each of these individuals is directly accountable for these responsibilities to the President and Executive Vice Presidents to whom they report.

The corporate HES department will provide direction, support, and guidance on HES matters to the company and will establish programs which reduce the company's short and long-term HES risks and costs. Through the development of HES policies and programs, the application of technical expertise, and through partnerships with the operating and staff groups, HES will assist the company in achieving its long-term goals.

E. Internal Reporting of Non-Compliance and Other Health, Environment, and Safety Issues

One of the core HES responsibilities of employees and contractors is to communicate information on HES issues or incidents to your supervisor and others within Elf Atochem, as appropriate. You should feel free to do this, through any of several different mechanisms, without fear of punishment or other retaliation.

For example, if you are aware of a potential compliance issue which you believe is not being appropriately addressed you should first report the issue directly to your supervisor.[1] If you reasonably believe that your supervisor has not taken appropriate action to address such issues, or if you fear punishment, retaliation or other discrimination for making such a report, you should either report the issue to other appropriate internal company personnel, or contact the Elf Atochem Compliance Hotline. Appropriate internal company personnel could include the facility HES manager, corporate HES staff, facility operations manager, or plant manager.

This hotline is answered 24 hours a day by employees of an independent telephone answering service called The Network. The telephone service will convey the information received to Elf Atochem's Office of General Counsel who will notify senior management. The company will initiate an investigation as appropriate.

Callers do not need to identify themselves when calling this hotline. The operator will request basic information from the caller, including a description of the issue and the location of the facility of concern. Callers may request a follow-up report from The Network (in which case the caller's identity will not be given to Elf Atochem) or callers may ask that they be identified to Elf Atochem for a direct follow-up report.

It is the express policy of Elf Atochem that no individual employee or contractor may be discharged, disciplined, or in any other way discriminated against by reason of the fact that they have made a report to the Elf Atochem Compliance Hotline or have otherwise cooperated in the investigation of a report to the hotline.

F. Employee and Contractor Training on These Core Health, Environment, and Safety Responsibilities

New Elf Atochem employees and contractors will receive and review a copy of this Core Health, Environment, and Safety Responsibilities document during their employee orientation and will sign an acknowledgement regarding their core responsibilities before starting work at an Elf Atochem facility or operation. Existing employees and contractors will also receive and review this document and sign an acknowledgement.

Additional copies of this document are available from the human resources manager or the HES manager at each facility, through the HES ATO Fax service and from the Office of the Senior Vice President of Health, Environment, and Safety, upon request.

---

1. Where such reports relate to an incident, for example, a reportable release, the report must be made in accordance with established incident reporting procedures.

G. Enforcement of Elf Atochem's Health, Environment, and Safety Program

It is the policy of Elf Atochem to include HES factors, including compliance with regulatory and company requirements, as an integral part of the performance evaluation of employees and contractors. Failure to adhere to applicable HES requirements may result in disciplinary measures including formal warning, suspension, or termination of employment. Where appropriate, contractors will be held liable for monetary damages associated with failure to abide by Elf Atochem's HES standards and contractors may be banned from consideration for future projects.

July 1, 1996

_____

Bernard D. Azoulay
President & Chief Executive Officer

_____

Frank B. Friedman
Senior Vice President
Health, Environment, and Safety

Elf Atochem North America, Inc.
Core Health, Environment, and Safety, Responsibilities
of Employees and Contractors

In accordance with the company's Health, Environment, and Safety Policy, Elf Atochem North America has established a variety of health, environment, and safety (HES), policies, procedures, and other requirements which apply at its facilities and operations. These requirements are designed to sustain compliance with applicable legal requirements and to promote the protection of health, safety, and the environment.

The document you have just received describes five of the most basic of these HES requirements. These five requirements are considered your "core" HES responsibilities. To uphold these responsibilities you must:

1. Understand your job responsibilities and your role in carrying out Elf Atochem's HES policies and procedures.

To uphold the company's HES policies you must first know what is expected of you. Supervisors have the responsibility of defining those expectations for their employees. If you are unsure about which specific HES requirements apply to you or if you are unsure about how to fulfill any of your responsibilities, contact your supervisor.

2. Conduct your day-to-day activities in a manner which complies with all applicable company and legal requirements and promotes the protection of health, safety, and the environment.

Once you understand your job responsibilities, you must carry them out in a manner which complies with all applicable company and legal requirements and promotes protection of human safety and health and the environment. As with all job responsibilities, failure to uphold your HES responsibilities may result in disciplinary action. Compliance with company and legal requirements is an essential responsibility for all of us.

3. Communicate information on HES issues or incidents to your supervisor and others in the company, as appropriate.

Contact Elf Atochem's Compliance Hotline, at [telephone number], if other means of communication within the company has not resolved the issue satisfactorily.

4. Be truthful, accurate, and complete in maintaining records, submitting documents, and making statements and reports to company personnel, government agencies, and others.

5. Cooperate with the company's Health, Environment, and Safety (HES) audit teams and other HES personnel.

While these are the core HES responsibilities which apply to all employees and contractors, there are also many job-specific HES requirements which may apply when conducting your day-to-day jobs. If you are unsure about how these core HES responsibilities apply to you or if you are unsure about any of the other HES requirements which may apply to your particular job, contact your Elf Atochem supervisor.

Please print and sign your name, below, indicating that you have read and understand the Core Health, Environment, and Safety Responsibilities document, including the Health, Environment, and Safety Policy. This applies to all employees and contractors working at Elf Atochem's facilities or operations.

_____   _____   _____

Printed Name   Signature   Date

Appendix G:
Checklist for
Acquisition Review

GUIDELINES FOR ACQUISITIONS

CONTENTS

GUIDELINES FOR ACQUISITIONS

o OPERATIONS

For all present and past facilities, including jointly-owned facilities operated by others, review

- Name of the facility.

- Address.

- General description of products and functions.

- Contact names, positions and phone numbers.

- Facility's environmental, health and safety organization and manpower.

- Whether the facility is still in operation.

- The facility's operating history including all prior uses by all prior owners and operators with respect to the a) raw materials used, and intermediates, products and wastes produced in the past, b) raw materials presently used, and intermediates, products and wastes presently produced. For materials in category b) above, Material Safety Data Sheets (MSDSs) should be obtained or reviewed for all raw materials used at the plant, and for all intermediate streams and products. Obtain all MSDSs or similar documents, or chemical analyses, that describe current wastes and waste streams. Cross references: Onsite Corrective Action, page 8; plans and drawings, page 20.

- 2 -

o <u>TOXIC SUBSTANCES CONTROL ACT (TSCA) COMPLIANCE</u>

   - Review available records concerning whether all components of
     current and planned commercial products, and current and
     planned isolated intermediates, are listed on the TSCA
     Inventory of commercial chemical substances. Review status of
     all Premanufacture Notifications (PMNs) that have been
     submitted. If any PMNs have been withdrawn prior to agency
     action, determine why. Determine whether any substance for
     which a PMN has been submitted is subject to a section 5(e)
     (Regulation Pending Development of Information) or 5(f)
     (Protection Against Unreasonable Risks) order.

   - Determine whether any chemical substance that is a component of
     a commercial product is subject to a Significant New Use Rule
     (SNUR).

   - Obtain a list of all chemicals manufactured, processed, used or
     distributed for which the company or another party has filed
     either a TSCA §8(e) substantial risk notice or a §8(d) health
     and safety data reporting notice, and obtain a summary of the
     information whicn has been submitted to the U. S. Environmental
     Protection Agency (EPA) pursuant to those reporting
     requirements.

   - Obtain the number(s) assigned to the §8(e) notice(s) by the
     EPA, and copies of that agency's analyses of the submitted
     information.

   - Review records of allegations of significant adverse health or
     environmental effects maintained pursuant to TSCA §8(c) to
     ascertain alleged effects and public concern with operations or
     with products and product lines.

- 3 -

- Review products and product components that are subject to testing under a Section 4 test rule, and products/product components that are likely candidates for future agency action under Section 4.
- Review all EPA TSCA inspection reports, and internal records of follow-up by the company and/or the Agency.
- List by location any known or suspected carcinogens, teratogens, other reproductive toxins, and mutagens manufactured, processed, used or distributed. List all carcinogens by the classifications used by the International Agency for Research on Cancer (IARC). This list is to be inclusive of chemical substances handled by formulation contractors. Cross reference: Industrial Hygiene, page 15.
- Review use and handling of PCBs, and procedures for helping ensure compliance with PCB requirements.

o EXCURSION LOGS AND ENVIRONMENTAL AUDITS/ASSESSMENTS
- List the types of events that excursion logs, call-in systems or similar systems that are designed to serve as a record of permit excursions, spills, etc. are intended to capture.
- Review and assess the latest annual or other summary of such events, and review and assess actions taken.
- Review all environmental audit or assessment reports pertaining to each currently operating facility including but not limited to owned, leased, and tolling facilities, and formulation contractors, and reports pertaining to follow-up activity.

- 4 -

- Determine if there is a system in place for identifying
  excursions from governmental, generally accepted, or internal
  workplace exposure limits. If such a system exists, determine
  the events that it is intended to capture, review and assess
  the latest annual or other summary of such events, and review
  and assess actions taken. Cross reference: Industrial
  Hygiene, Page 15.
- Review probable regulations that may impact excursion logs and
  environmental audits/assessments.
- Review internal estimates of costs to remedy any existing
  deficiencies in compliance, etc. as noted in excursion logs and
  in audits/assessments.
- Based on all of the above, estimate future capital costs and
  operating expenses to remedy existing deficiencies.

o PRODUCT SAFETY AND TESTING EXPENSES
- Review product safety and toxicology organization, staffing and
  support, including laboratory facilities that are owned, leased
  or otherwise dedicated to the company.
- List all current products, product components and intermediate
  streams and review the results of past product safety (i.e.
  toxicology) testing programs pertaining to those materials.
  Cross reference: Operations, page 1.
- List all ongoing toxicity testing whether on products, product
  components, or intermediate streams, including testing for
  chronic effects (carcinogenicity and reproductive effects), and
  the operations or products that may be impacted by the results

- 5 -

of such testing. Obtain status reports and preliminary results
when available. Include ongoing testing by trade associations,
the Chemical Industry Institute of Toxicology (CIIT), etc. that
may impact the company's operations or products.

- List all probable testing requirements by federal agencies
  during the next 5 years that may impact the company's
  operations or products.

- List all internal product safety testing recommendations and
  relevant recommendations within trade association, CIIT, etc.
  which have not yet been acted on by commencing such testing.

- Review internal estimates of and actual costs to the company of
  all toxicity testing currently in progress, and cost estimates
  for all testing which has been recommended but not yet
  commenced.

- Review toxicity testing budgets and actual costs for the past 5
  years for products, product components and intermediate
  streams, including testing that is carried on by trade
  associations, CIIT, etc. for which the company has financial
  responsibility.

- Based on the above information, make a forecast of toxicity
  testing expenses for the company for each of the next 5 years.

o SUPERFUND SITES AND NOTIFICATIONS

- Review §103(c) notifications under the Comprehensive
  Environmental Response, Compensation and Liability Act (CERCLA
  or "Superfund").

- Review Eckhardt list submissions regarding waste disposal.

- 6 -

- Review status of each site where company has been named a PRP
  with respect to Remedial Investigation (RI), Feasibility Study
  (FS), Record of Decision (ROD), steering committee organization
  and chairman/contact.

- Review status of each Superfund site where company has not been
  named a PRP, but where involvement is known or suspected, with
  respect to RI, FS, groundwater surveys, ROD, etc.).

- Review compliance with Superfund Amendment and Reauthorization
  Act (SARA) Title III requirements.

- Review consultants' reports and internal company reports on
  significant Superfund sites and significant problem areas to
  ascertain nature and magnitude of potential liability.

- Review volumes and types of wastes sent to each site by the
  company. Cross references: Eckhardt list submissions, page 5;
  §103(c) notifications, page 5.

- List sites for which toxicity (in addition to volumetric share)
  is being considered by the steering committee or other
  appropriate group in apportioning liability. Review status of
  negotiations on liability apportionment, and ascertain the
  volume and nature of wastes generated by the company and sent
  to those sites.

- Review internal estimates of percentile volumetric share and
  total cost share (including all future costs) to remediate each
  site.

- Review sources of wastes (i.e. identity of plants or other
  operations) that led to involvement at each site.

- 7 -

- Review all consultants' reports and internal company records concerning any alleged or potential groundwater contamination at present or past sites or facilities. Cross references: Onsite Corrective Action, page 8; plans and drawings page 20.
- Review all of the above with respect to the company's joint ventures, partnerships, etc.
- Review identity of disposal sites currently used by the company's facilities together with any audits or assessments of those sites. Cross reference: Eckhardt list submissions, page 5; $103(c) notifications, page 5; company's "list of approved disposal sites," page 20.
- Considering all of the above, estimate future costs to remediate each site for which the company has or will probably have financial responsibility under CERCLA, and company's share of those costs.

o INSURANCE CLAIMS
- Review all insurance claims, including the nature and amount of each claim, made by the company and pertaining to any environmental matter.

o NEW JERSEY ECRA STATUS AND EXPENSES (AND COMPLIANCE WITH SIMILAR REQUIREMENTS OF OTHER STATES)
- Review status of New Jersey facilities under ECRA.
- Review Site Evaluation Submissions and current status of sampling plans and remediation efforts.

- 8 -

- Review company's projected costs for ECRA compliance for each facility.

- Based on all available information, estimate future capital costs and operating expenses for ECRA compliance.

- Review all of the above for other applicable states that have requirements similar to New Jersey ECRA.

o LAND-BAN AND RETROFIT IMPACTS

- Review all facilities that require permitting under RCRA.

- Review required annual RCRA reports for offsite locations and amounts sent offsite each year. Cross reference: company's "list of approved disposal sites," page 20.

- Review records concerning financial responsibility requirements.

- List types and volumes of wastes (including wastewaters) generated at each site.

- List and characterize all onsite treatment, storage and disposal facilities, including but not limited to surface impoundments, waste piles, incinerators, waste treatment tanks, and deepwells. Cross reference: Deepwells, page 10; plans and drawings, page 20.

- Review the expected impact of RCRA retrofit rules on surface impoundments and landfills, including RCRA-exempt surface impoundments.

- Review the expected impacts of the land-ban decisions under RCRA for both onsite and offsite disposal.

- Review any variance requests made related to land ban or retrofit.

- 9 -

- Review internal projected costs for alternate disposal, treatment or retrofit.
- Based on all of the above information, estimate future capital costs and operating expenses associated with land ban and retrofit.

o <u>ONSITE CORRECTIVE ACTION</u>
- Review descriptions of present and past solid waste management units and treatment, storage or disposal facilities at each site. Cross reference: plans and drawings, page 20.
- Review Eckhardt list submissions regarding onsite disposal.
- Review plant history and lists of materials handled, and locations at which materials were or are handled, as they may relate to soil or groundwater contamination potential. Cross references: plant operating history, page 1; plans and drawings, page 20.
- Review hydrogeology characterization of present and past sites when available. Cross reference: plans and drawings, page 20; potential groundwater contamination, page 6.
- Review RCRA and non-RCRA groundwater monitoring and assessment data for each present and past site. Cross reference: potential groundwater contamination, page 6.
- Review data on soil contamination at each present and past site.
- Review internal estimates of costs for remediation of known and suspected soil or groundwater contamination problems.
- Based on the above information, estimate future capital costs and operating expenses associated with onsite corrective action.

- 10 -

o <u>STORAGE TANKS AND INCINERATORS</u>
  - Other than the situations covered under land-ban and retrofit requirements and onsite corrective actions (above), review any upgrading expected in order to meet the RCRA standards for incinerators and storage tanks, including ancillary equipment and piping.
  - Review present and past use and current inventory of storage tanks for petroleum and related materials and hazardous substances, and compare with probable upgrade rules. Include locations, types, and conditions of tanks and their present and past contents. Note whether tanks are aboveground, or partially or wholly underground. Cross reference: plans and drawings, page 20.
  - Review whether storage tanks are associated with known or suspected soil or groundwater contamination. Cross reference: Onsite Corrective Action, page 8; plans and drawings, page 20.
  - Review permits for upgrading of incinerators and storage tanks. Cross reference: Current Permits and Recent Compliance, page 12.
  - Review internal cost estimates associated with required or advisable upgrading of storage tanks and incinerators.
  - Based on the above information, estimate future capital costs and operating expenses associated with storage tanks and incinerators.

o <u>INVENTORIED WASTES FOR DISPOSAL</u>
  - Determine whether there are any hazardous or other wastes (drums, lab wastes etc.) in inventory for disposal, and the

- 11 -

chemical nature of such wastes. Prepare a listing of such wastes and estimate cost of disposal.

o DEEPWELLS
    - List all facilities which use deepwells for waste disposal.
    - Review the nature of each deepwell, and results of any tests for mechanical integrity.
    - Review the State and Regional regulatory environment, bans, actions and probable actions related to deepwells.
    - Review selected technologies, available cost estimates, established cost reserves and any existing capital forecasts associated with current deepwell disposal.
    - Determine past and present deepwell waste characteristics (flow, toxicity, etc.).
    - Estimate costs to withdraw from each well including any remediations, including capital costs and operating expenses necessary for alternate disposal.

o WASTEWATER TREATMENT AND COMPLIANCE
    - Characterize types and volumes of wastewater (direct and indirect discharges) for all pollutants including conventional pollutants, priority pollutants and pesticide pollutants.
    - Review wastewater toxicity and biomonitoring results for all discharges and assess the impact of any probable in-stream limits.
    - Review expected adverse impacts of direct discharges on water quality of receiving streams including any water quality

- 12 -

limited streams, and review waste load allocations either
presently imposed or projected.

- Review internal assessments of expected technologies and costs
  to comply with any guidelines, toxicity limits, pretreatment
  standards, water-quality forced limits, etc.

- Estimate future capital costs and operating expenses associated
  with meeting present and probable future requirements.

o AIR COMPLIANCE AND ISSUES

- Review data base on air emissions of pollutants that are
  subject to National Emissions Standards for Hazardous Air
  Pollutants (NESHAPs) regulations.

- Separately review any studies and/or submissions relating to
  any radionuclides.

- Review air quality attainment status at domestic manufacturing
  facilities, and review facility emissions expected to be
  impacted under the State Implementation Plans (SIPs).

- Determine whether there are any Class I areas that could be
  impacted by any facility, and the facility's regulatory status.

- Review Waxman list submissions.

- Review all studies and/or submissions conducted or made because
  of or in connection with Prevention of Significant
  Deterioration (PSD) requirements.

- Review monitoring systems and control equipment at each
  facility.

- Review current production rate information for consistency with
  permit applications and for emission inventory data.

- 13 -

- Review internal forecasts of costs to achieve probable abatement requirements, and the nature of the technology needed to achieve abatement.
- Estimate future capital costs and operating expenses associated with meetings present and probable future requirements.

o CURRENT PERMITS AND RECENT COMPLIANCE
- List all current environmental permits and their expiration dates. Include names of compliance officers and contacts.
- Assess the frequency and nature of reportable and non-reportable water discharge permit and Publicly Owned Treatment Works (POTW) ordinance violations and exceedances for the last 5 years. Cross reference: Excursion Logs and Environmental Audits/Assessments, page 3.
- Assess the frequency and nature of reportable and non-reportable air permit violations and exceedances for the last 5 years. Cross reference: Excursion Logs and Environmental Audits/Assessments, page 3.
- Assess the frequency and nature of Superfund (CERCLA)-reported releases for the last 5 years. Cross reference: Excursion Logs and Environmental Audits/Assessments, page 3.
- Review community complaint issues (whether or not included in the TSCA §8(c) file) and litigation with respect to emissions, odor, noise or other releases for the last 5 years. Cross reference: TSCA §8(c) file, page 2; past and present environmental and toxic tort litigation; page 20.

- 14 -

- Review RCRA, water, and air regulatory inspection findings, federal, state and local, and list any deficiencies and company or agency follow-up, during the last 5 years. Cross reference: Excursion Logs and Environmental Audits/Assessments, page 3.
- Determine if there is a system in place for assuring RCRA manifest closeout.
- Review internal estimates of costs to remedy significant compliance problems.
- Based on all of the above, estimate future capital costs and operating expenses to remedy significant compliance problems.

o COMPLIANCE ORDERS
- Review all Compliance Orders, Administrative Orders, Notices of Violation or any similar documents received during the last 5 years, and list separately those currently active. Review and assess internal cost estimates to bring the facility or facilities into compliance. Cross reference: Current Permits and Recent Compliance, page 12.

o 10-K AND 10-Q SUBMISSIONS
- Review the most recent submissions for environmental matters, as well as 10K and 10Q submissions for the past 5 years.

o OCCUPATIONAL HEALTH
- Review medical health organization, staffing, budget and responsibilities at the general office and at other locations.

- 15 -

- Review and assess existing medical surveillance programs for employees.
- Separately identify any special examinations or biological monitoring conducted on employees.
- Obtain a summary of all anecdotal medical information and case studies that may indicate a relationship between products, processes, or workplace conditions and human health.
- List all completed, ongoing and planned epidemiology studies of any type, e.g. cross-sectional studies, prospective or retrospective morbidity or mortality studies, etc., whether carried out internally, by consultants, or by government authorities such as the National Institute for Occupational Safety and Health (NIOSH). Note any follow-up action recommended or taken by any party.
- Based on the above, and on available toxicology information, assess potential future liabilities. Estimate future capital costs and operating expenses associated with minimizing relevant risks.

o INDUSTRIAL HYGIENE
- Review industrial hygiene organization, staffing and responsibilities at the general office and at each facility including analytical support.
- Identify chemical and physical agents to which employees are potentially exposed at each site. Cross reference: Operations, page 1.

- 16 -

- Using the above list of chemicals, identify chemical substances that are within the following categories: Known or suspect human carcinogens and other categories of carcinogens by IARC classification; teratogens or other reproductive toxins; mutagens; systemic toxins; OSHA or American Conference of Industrial Hygienists (ACGIH) listed chemicals; chemicals regulated under comprehensive OSHA health standards (29 CFR 1910.1001ff); chemicals with internal company exposure limits. Cross reference: TSCA Compliance, page 2.

- Review the personnel and area exposure monitoring data collected at each facility over the past 3 years on the chemical and physical agents noted above.

- Review the asbestos management program for each facility and assess the status of asbestos identification and of any abatement or removal projects either planned or underway.

- Review internal projected costs to complete any asbestos removal or abatement projects. Estimate future costs to achieve "asbestos-free" status at facilities.

- Identify any major ongoing or planned engineering projects to achieve reduction of workplace exposures to chemical or physical agents along with respective estimated costs.

- Review internal hearing conservation program for employees.

- Based on the above, estimate future capital costs and operating expenses to achieve goals.

o OSHA COMPLIANCE
   - Review results of OSHA inspections that have occurred during the past 5 years. Determine the types and severities of

- 17 -

citations received and status of their resolution, including
any outstanding items under contest. Note the circumstances
and resolution with OSHA of all employee deaths that were or
that were alleged to be work-related.

- Review the company's hazard communication program designed to
  comply with the federal OSHA Hazard Communication Regulation
  (OSHA HCR).

- Review the results of OSHA inspections specifically with
  respect to OSHA HCR compliance, and whether any violations
  involve failure to warn employees of chronic health risks, and
  the chemical substances involved in such failure to warn.

- Ascertain compliance with the OSHA comprehensive health
  standards (29 CFR 1910.1001ff). Cross reference: Industrial
  Hygiene, Page 15.

- Review any internal "written compliance programs" specific to
  chemical agents covered by the above comprehensive health
  standards, and describe efforts to reduce workplace exposures
  below the respective PELs. Cross reference: Industrial
  Hygiene, page 15.

o EMPLOYEE SAFETY

- Review the company's policies and guidelines pertaining to the
  safety of its employees.

- Using the OSHA 200 logs, and cross-referencing the TSCA §8(c)
  file, review the company's occupational injury and illness
  experiences at each facility for the last 5 years. Cross
  reference: Company's workers' compensation experience, page 20.

- 18 -

o PROCESS SAFETY

   - Review available process descriptions for major processes at
     each facility.

   - Review layout drawings for each site and assess spacing of
     process structures, control centers, auxiliary process
     equipment, tank farms, truck/rail docking stations, and office
     complexes. Cross reference: plans and drawings, page 20.

   - Review any studies conducted on potential process failures that
     could lead to major releases of hazardous materials.

   - Review the Emergency and Hazardous Chemical Inventory Form
     submitted pursuant to §312(a) of Title III of the Superfund
     Amendments and Reauthorization Act of 1986 (SARA) for each
     facility. Ascertain maximum quantities handled/stored at each
     site, manners of use, and general locations of such chemicals.

   - Review internal safety design standards pertaining to process
     interlock/trip systems, instrumentation, containment and
     emergency relief systems, emergency release control, and piping
     systems.

   - Review internal guidelines or standards pertaining to
     inspection and/or testing of critical safety devices (e.g.
     special alarms, process shut-downs, interlocks, and rupture
     relief).

   - Review the most recent safety audit reports covering processes
     in both domestic and foreign locations and assess status of
     major recommendations.

   - Determine occurrences of any major process-related adverse
     events (major fires, explosions, etc.) within the last 10 years

- 19 -

and review incident investigation reports produced internally or by external consultants or others such as insurance carriers.

- Review internal estimates of costs for both ongoing and planned projects to reduce the risks of potentially dangerous process events.

- Based on the above, estimate future capital expenditures and operating costs in the process safety area for both ongoing and planned projects.

o FIRE PROTECTION AND CONTROL

- Obtain a list of combustible and flammable liquids and solids handled in bulk at each manufacturing and formulation site. Ascertain maximum quantities handled or stored at each site and manner of storage.

- Review internal fire protection standards or codes pertaining to inerting and to explosion protection for atmospheric storage tanks, gas and oil-fired furnaces, and tank car and tank truck unloading.

- Assess the application of internal fire protection standards in locations handling combustible and flammable materials.

- Review site drawings showing installed fire protection systems, including water supply and distribution, and sprinkler and deluge control. Ascertain likely fire demand and adequacy of existing water supply at each facility. Cross reference: plans and drawings, page 20.

- Review the adequacy and technology of sprinkler systems and deluge protection.

- 20 -

- Review fire occurrences during the past 10 years, and the investigation reports covering major events resulting in significant property damage and/or process outage.
- Review fire protection surveys that have been conducted during the past 10 years either internally or by outside consultants, e.g., by insurance carriers. Ascertain status of major recommendations and company's projected cost to remedy deficient items.
- Based on the above, estimate future capital costs and operating expenses associated with fire protection and control.

o OTHER
- Obtain plans and drawings for all current and former plant sites showing locations of production and storage facilities, potential waste "problem areas," and waste discharges.
- Note plant locations in relation to Superfund sites.
- Review the company's list of approved disposal sites for wastes, and its list of approved recycling facilities.
- Review reserves for mine or other reclamation.
- Review copies of all consultants' reports pertaining to mining or other facilities.
- Note the states in which the company's facilities are located, and the nature of state environmental, safety or health laws and regulations that are more stringent than federal laws.
- Review how those more stringent requirements may affect the assessments made pursuant to these Guidelines for Acquisitions.

- 21 -

- Review permitting files for the sites for which permits are being sought to incinerate or to dispose of hazardous wastes. Cross reference: Storage Tanks and Incinerators, page 9, Onsite Corrective Action, page 8.

- Review status of past and present product liability litigation, and of past and present environmental and toxic tort litigation and relate such litigation to past and current plants, processes and waste disposal sites. Review nature of claims, amounts of damages and/or nature of other relief which is sought, and current status of litigation. Note whether litigation tends to focus on particular products, product lines, plants, processes or waste disposal sites.

- Review the company's workers' compensation experience for the last 5 years. Ascertain the status of outstanding employee claims and review the projected costs to close existing costs. Note whether claims tend to focus on particular plants or processes.

- Determine the nature of all occupational disease workers' compensation claims, and note their relationship to specific plants, processes, etc. Estimate future costs to close the existing cases, and estimate the extent of potential future liability from employees who have not yet filed claims. Note the potential for third party liability from spouses, etc.

- Review any Environmental Impact Statements (EISs) and Environmental Assessments (EAs), and any Clean Water Act §404 studies. For EISs and EAs that are required pursuant to the National Environmental Policy Act (NEPA), assess status, and note existence and status of any litigation.

- 22 -

- Review contract provisions regarding environment safety and
  health liabilities associated with jointly-owned facilities,
  whether those facilities are operated by the company being
  reviewed or operated by others.
- Review sales of facilities, subsidiaries, etc. for
  environmental indemnification responsibilities.

JRW/tls-1749H

Appendix H:
Incentives for Self-Policing: Discovery, Disclosure, Correction, and Prevention of Violations

Incentives for Self-Policing: Discovery, Disclosure, Correction and Prevention of Violations (EPA, April 11, 2000)

I. Explanation of Policy

A. Introduction

On December 22, 1995, EPA issued its final policy on "Incentives for Self-Policing: Discovery, Disclosure, Correction and Prevention of Violations" (60 FR 66706) (Audit Policy, or Policy). The purpose of the Policy is to enhance protection of human health and the environment by encouraging regulated entities to voluntarily discover, disclose, correct and prevent violations of Federal environmental law. Benefits available to entities that make disclosures under the terms of the Policy include reductions in the amount of civil penalties and a determination not to recommend criminal prosecution of disclosing entities.

Today, EPA issues revisions to the 1995 Audit Policy. The revised Policy reflects EPA's continuing commitment to encouraging voluntary self-policing while preserving fair and effective enforcement. It lengthens the prompt disclosure period to 21 days, clarifies that the independent discovery condition does not automatically preclude Audit Policy credit in the multi-facility context, and clarifies how the prompt disclosure and repeat violations conditions apply in the acquisitions context. The revised final Policy takes effect May 11, 2000.

B. Background and History

The Audit Policy provides incentives for regulated entities to detect, promptly disclose, and expeditiously correct violations of Federal environmental requirements. The Policy contains nine conditions, and entities that meet all of them are eligible for 100% mitigation of any gravity-based penalties that otherwise could be assessed. ("Gravity-based" refers to that portion of the penalty over and above the portion that represents the entity's economic gain from noncompliance, known as the "economic benefit.") Regulated entities that do not meet the first condition—systematic discovery of violations—but meet the other eight conditions are eligible for 75% mitigation of any gravity-based civil penalties. On the criminal side, EPA will generally elect not to recommend criminal prosecution by DOJ or any other prosecuting authority for a disclosing entity that meets at least conditions two through nine—regardless of whether it meets the systematic discovery requirement—as long as its self-policing, discovery and disclosure were conducted in good faith and the entity adopts a systematic approach to preventing recurrence of the violation.

The Policy includes important safeguards to deter violations and protect public health and the environment. For example, the Policy requires entities to act to prevent recurrence of violations and to remedy any environmental harm that may have occurred. Repeat violations, those that result in actual harm to the environment, and those that may present an imminent and substantial endangerment are not eligible for relief under this Policy. Companies will not be allowed to gain an economic advantage over their competitors by delaying their investment in compliance. And entities remain criminally liable for violations that result from conscious disregard of or willful blindness to their obligations under the law, and individuals remain liable for their criminal misconduct.

When EPA issued the 1995 Audit Policy, the Agency committed to evaluate the Policy after three years. The Agency initiated this evaluation in the spring of 1998 and published its preliminary results in the Federal Register on May 17, 1999 (64 FR 26745). The evaluation consisted of the following components:

· An internal survey of EPA staff who process disclosures and handle enforcement cases under the 1995 Audit Policy;
· A survey of regulated entities that used the 1995 Policy to disclose violations;
· A series of meetings and conference calls with representatives from industry, environmental organizations, and States;

· Focused stakeholder discussions on the Audit Policy at two public conferences co-sponsored by EPA's Office of Enforcement and Compliance Assurance (OECA) and the Vice President's National Partnership for Reinventing Government, entitled "Protecting Public Health and the Environment through Innovative Approaches to Compliance";

· A Federal Register notice on March 2, 1999, soliciting comments on how EPA can further protect and improve public health and the environment through new compliance and enforcement approaches (64 FR 10144); and

· An analysis of data on Audit Policy usage to date and discussions amongst EPA officials who handle Audit Policy disclosures.

The same May 17, 1999, Federal Register notice that published the evaluation's preliminary results also proposed revisions to the 1995 Policy and requested public comment. During the 60-day public comment period, the Agency received 29 comment letters, copies of which are available through the Enforcement and Compliance Docket and Information Center. (See contact information at the beginning of this notice.) Analysis of these comment letters together with additional data on Audit Policy usage has constituted the final stage of the Audit Policy evaluation. EPA has prepared a detailed response to the comments received; a copy of that document will also be available through the Docket and Information Center as well as on the Internet at www.epa.gov/oeca/ore/apolguid.html.

Overall, the Audit Policy evaluation revealed very positive results. The Policy has encouraged voluntary self-policing while preserving fair and effective enforcement. Thus, the revisions issued today do not signal any intention to shift course regarding the Agency's position on self-policing and voluntary disclosures but instead represent an attempt to fine-tune a Policy that is already working well.

Use of the Audit Policy has been widespread. As of October 1, 1999, approximately 670 organizations had disclosed actual or potential violations at more than 2,700 facilities. The number of disclosures has increased each of the four years the Policy has been in effect.

Results of the Audit Policy User's Survey revealed very high satisfaction rates among users, with 88% of respondents stating that they would use the Policy again and 84% stating that they would recommend the Policy to clients and/or their counterparts. No respondents stated an unwillingness to use the Policy again or to recommend its use to others.

The Audit Policy and related documents, including Agency interpretive guidance and general interest newsletters, are available on the Internet at www.epa.gov/oeca/ore/apolguid. Additional guidance for implementing the Policy in the context of criminal violations can be found at www.epa.gov/oeca/oceft/audpol2.html.

In addition to the Audit Policy, the Agency's revised Small Business Compliance Policy ("Small Business Policy") is also available for small entities that employ 100 or fewer individuals. The Small Business Policy provides penalty mitigation, subject to certain conditions, for small businesses that make a good faith effort to comply with environmental requirements by discovering, disclosing and correcting violations. EPA has revised the Small Business Policy at the same time it revised the Audit Policy. The revised Small Business Policy will be available on the Internet at www.epa.gov/oeca/smbusi.html.

C. Purpose

The revised Policy being announced today is designed to encourage greater compliance with Federal laws and regulations that protect human health and the environment. It promotes a higher standard of self-policing by waiving gravity-based penalties for violations that are promptly disclosed and corrected, and which were discovered systematically—that is, through voluntary audits or compliance management systems. To provide an incentive for entities to disclose and correct violations regardless of how they were detected, the Policy reduces gravity-based penalties by 75% for violations that are voluntarily discovered and promptly disclosed and corrected, even if not discovered systematically.

EPA's enforcement program provides a strong incentive for compliance by imposing stiff sanctions for noncompliance. Enforcement has contributed to the dramatic expansion of environmental auditing as measured in numerous recent surveys. For example, in a 1995 survey by Price Waterhouse LLP, more than 90% of corporate respondents who conduct audits identified one of the reasons for doing so as the desire to find and correct violations before government inspectors discover them. (A copy of the survey is contained in the Docket as document VIII-A-76.)

At the same time, because government resources are limited, universal compliance cannot be achieved without active efforts by the regulated community to police themselves. More than half of the respondents to the same 1995 Price Waterhouse survey said that they would expand environmental auditing in exchange for reduced penalties for violations discovered and corrected. While many companies already audit or have compliance management programs in place, EPA believes that the incentives offered in this Policy will improve the frequency and quality of these self-policing efforts.

D. Incentives for Self-Policing

Section C of the Audit Policy identifies the major incentives that EPA provides to encourage self-policing, self-disclosure, and prompt self-correction. For entities that meet the conditions of the Policy, the available incentives include waiving or reducing gravity-based civil penalties, declining to recommend criminal prosecution for regulated entities that self-police, and refraining from routine requests for audits. (As noted in Section C of the Policy, EPA has refrained from making routine requests for audit reports since issuance of its 1986 policy on environmental auditing.)

1. Eliminating Gravity-Based Penalties

In general, civil penalties that EPA assesses are comprised of two elements: the economic benefit component and the gravity-based component. The economic benefit component reflects the economic gain derived from a violator's illegal competitive advantage. Gravity-based penalties are that portion of the penalty over and above the economic benefit. They reflect the egregiousness of the violator's behavior and constitute the punitive portion of the penalty. For further discussion of these issues, see "Calculation of the Economic Benefit of Noncompliance in EPA's Civil Penalty Enforcement Cases," 64 FR 32948 (June 18, 1999) and "A Framework for Statute-Specific Approaches to Penalty Assessments," #GM-22 (1984), U.S. EPA General Enforcement Policy Compendium.

Under the Audit Policy, EPA will not seek gravity-based penalties for disclosing entities that meet all nine Policy conditions, including systematic discovery. ("Systematic discovery" means the detection of a potential violation through an environmental audit or a compliance management system that reflects the entity's due diligence in preventing, detecting and correcting violations.) EPA has elected to waive gravity-based penalties for violations discovered systematically, recognizing that environmental auditing and compliance management systems play a critical role in protecting human health and the environment by identifying, correcting and ultimately preventing violations.

However, EPA reserves the right to collect any economic benefit that may have been realized as a result of noncompliance, even where the entity meets all other Policy conditions. Where the Agency determines that the economic benefit is insignificant, the Agency also may waive this component of the penalty.

EPA's decision to retain its discretion to recover economic benefit is based on two reasons. First, facing the risk that the Agency will recoup economic benefit provides an incentive for regulated entities to comply on time. Taxpayers whose payments are late expect to pay interest or a penalty; the same principle should apply to corporations and other regulated entities that have delayed their investment in compliance. Second, collecting economic benefit is fair because it protects law-abiding companies from being undercut by their noncomplying competitors, thereby preserving a level playing field.

2. 75% Reduction of Gravity-Based Penalties

Gravity-based penalties will be reduced by 75% where the disclosing entity does not detect the violation through systematic discovery but otherwise meets all other Policy conditions. The Policy appropriately limits the complete waiver of gravity-based civil penalties to companies that conduct environmental auditing or have in place a compliance management system. However, to encourage disclosure and correction of violations even in the absence of systematic discovery, EPA will reduce gravity-based penalties by 75% for entities that meet conditions D(2) through D(9) of the Policy. EPA expects that a disclosure under this provision will encourage the entity to work with the Agency to resolve environmental problems and begin to develop an effective auditing program or compliance management system.

3. No Recommendations for Criminal Prosecution

In accordance with EPA's Investigative Discretion Memo dated January 12, 1994, EPA generally does not focus its criminal enforcement resources on entities that voluntarily discover, promptly disclose and expeditiously correct violations, unless there is potentially culpable behavior that merits criminal investigation. When a disclosure that meets the terms and conditions of this Policy results in a criminal investigation, EPA will generally not recommend criminal prosecution for the disclosing entity, although the Agency may recommend prosecution for culpable individuals and other entities. The 1994 Investigative Discretion Memo is available on the Internet at http://www.epa.gov/oeca/ore/ aed/comp/acomp/a11. html.

The "no recommendation for criminal prosecution" incentive is available for entities that meet conditions D(2) through D(9) of the Policy. Condition D(1) "systematic discovery" is not required to be eligible for this incentive, although the entity must be acting in good faith and must adopt a systematic approach to preventing recurring violations. Important limitations to the incentive apply. It will not be available, for example, where corporate officials are consciously involved in or willfully blind to violations, or conceal or condone noncompliance. Since the regulated entity must satisfy conditions D(2) through D(9) of the Policy, violations that cause serious harm or which may pose imminent and substantial endangerment to human health or the environment are not eligible. Finally, EPA reserves the right to recommend prosecution for the criminal conduct of any culpable individual or subsidiary organization.

While EPA may decide not to recommend criminal prosecution for disclosing entities, ultimate prosecutorial discretion resides with the U.S. Department of Justice, which will be guided by its own policy on voluntary disclosures ("Factors in Decisions on Criminal Prosecutions for Environmental Violations in the Context of Significant Voluntary Compliance or Disclosure Efforts by the Violator," July 1, 1991) and by its 1999 Guidance on Federal Prosecutions of Corporations. In addition, where a disclosing entity has met the conditions for avoiding a recommendation for criminal prosecution under this Policy, it will also be eligible for either 75% or 100% mitigation of gravity-based civil penalties, depending on whether the systematic discovery condition was met.

4. No Routine Requests for Audit Reports

EPA reaffirms its Policy, in effect since 1986, to refrain from routine requests for audit reports. That is, EPA has not and will not routinely request copies of audit reports to trigger enforcement investigations. Implementation of the 1995 Policy has produced no evidence that the Agency has deviated, or should deviate, from this Policy. In general, an audit that results in expeditious correction will reduce liability, not expand it. However, if the Agency has independent evidence of a violation, it may seek the information it needs to establish the extent and nature of the violation and the degree of culpability.

For discussion of the circumstances in which EPA might request an audit report to determine Policy eligibility, see the explanatory text on cooperation, section I.E.9.

E. Conditions

Section D describes the nine conditions that a regulated entity must meet in order for the Agency to decline to seek (or to reduce) gravity-based penalties under the Policy. As explained in section I.D.1 above, regulated entities that meet all nine conditions will not face gravity-based civil penalties. If the regulated entity meets all of the conditions except for D(1)—systematic discovery—EPA will reduce gravity-based penalties by 75%. In general, EPA will not recommend criminal prosecution for disclosing entities that meet at least conditions D(2) through D(9).

1. Systematic Discovery of the Violation Through an Environmental Audit or a Compliance Management System

Under Section D(1), the violation must have been discovered through either (a) an environmental audit, or (b) a compliance management system that reflects due diligence in preventing, detecting and correcting violations. Both "environmental audit" and "compliance management system" are defined in Section B of the Policy.

The revised Policy uses the term "compliance management system" instead of "due diligence," which was used in the 1995 Policy. This change in nomenclature is intended solely to conform the Policy language to terminology more commonly in use by industry and by regulators to refer to a systematic management plan or systematic efforts to achieve and maintain compliance. No substantive difference is intended by substituting the term "compliance management system" for "due diligence," as the Policy clearly indicates that the compliance management system must reflect the regulated entity's due diligence in preventing, detecting and correcting violations.

Compliance management programs that train and motivate employees to prevent, detect and correct violations on a daily basis are a valuable complement to periodic auditing. Where the violation is discovered through a compliance management system and not through an audit, the disclosing entity should be prepared to document how its program reflects the due diligence criteria defined in Section B of the Policy statement. These criteria, which are adapted from existing codes of practice—such as Chapter Eight of the U.S. Sentencing Guidelines for organizational defendants, effective since 1991—are flexible enough to accommodate different types and sizes of businesses and other regulated entities. The Agency recognizes that a variety of compliance management programs are feasible, and it will determine whether basic due diligence criteria have been met in deciding whether to grant Audit Policy credit.

As a condition of penalty mitigation, EPA may require that a description of the regulated entity's compliance management system be made publicly available. The Agency believes that the availability of such information will allow the public to judge the adequacy of compliance management systems, lead to enhanced compliance, and foster greater public trust in the integrity of compliance management systems.

2. Voluntary Discovery

Under Section D(2), the violation must have been identified voluntarily, and not through a monitoring, sampling, or auditing procedure that is required by statute, regulation, permit, judicial or administrative order, or consent agreement. The Policy provides three specific examples of discovery that would not be voluntary, and therefore would not be eligible for penalty mitigation: emissions violations detected through a required continuous emissions monitor, violations of NPDES discharge limits found through prescribed monitoring, and violations discovered through a compliance audit required to be performed by the terms of a consent order or settlement agreement. The exclusion does not apply to violations that are discovered pursuant to audits that are conducted as part of a comprehensive environmental management system (EMS) required under a settlement agreement. In general, EPA supports the implementation of EMSs that promote compliance, prevent pollution and improve overall environmental performance. Precluding the availability of the Audit Policy for discoveries made through a comprehensive EMS that has been implemented pursuant to a settlement agreement might discourage entities from agreeing to implement such a system.

In some instances, certain Clean Air Act violations discovered, disclosed and corrected by a company prior to issuance of a Title V permit are eligible for penalty mitigation under the Policy. For further guidance in this area, see "Reduced Penalties for Disclosures of Certain Clean Air Act Violations," Memorandum from Eric Schaeffer, Director of the EPA Office of Regulatory Enforcement, dated September 30, 1999. This document is available on the Internet at www.epa.gov/oeca/ore/apolguid.html.

The voluntary requirement applies to discovery only, not reporting. That is, any violation that is voluntarily discovered is generally eligible for Audit Policy credit, regardless of whether reporting of the violation was required after it was found.

3. Prompt Disclosure

Section D(3) requires that the entity disclose the violation in writing to EPA within 21 calendar days after discovery. If the 21st day after discovery falls on a weekend or Federal holiday, the disclosure period will be extended to the first business day following the 21st day after discovery. If a statute or regulation requires the entity to report the violation in fewer than 21 days, disclosure must be made within the time limit established by law. (For example, unpermitted releases of hazardous substances must be reported immediately under 42 U.S.C. 9603.) Disclosures under this Policy should be made to the appropriate EPA Regional office or, where multiple Regions are involved, to EPA Headquarters. The Agency will work closely with States as needed to ensure fair and efficient implementation of the Policy. For additional guidance on making disclosures, contact the Audit Policy National Coordinator at EPA Headquarters at 202-564-5123.

The 21-day disclosure period begins when the entity discovers that a violation has, or may have, occurred. The trigger for discovery is when any officer, director, employee or agent of the facility has an objectively reasonable basis for believing that a violation has, or may have, occurred. The "objectively reasonable basis" standard is measured against what a prudent person, having the same information as was available to the individual in question, would have believed. It is not measured against what the individual in question thought was reasonable at the time the situation was encountered. If an entity has some doubt as to the existence of a violation, the recommended course is for the entity to proceed with the disclosure and allow the regulatory authorities to make a definitive determination. Contract personnel who provide on-site services at the facility may be treated as employees or agents for purposes of the Policy.

If the 21-day period has not yet expired and an entity suspects that it will be unable to meet the deadline, the entity should contact the appropriate EPA office in advance to develop disclosure terms acceptable to EPA. For situations in which the 21-day period already has expired, the Agency may accept a late disclosure in the exceptional case, such as where there are complex circumstances, including where EPA determines the violation could not be identified and disclosed within 21 calendar days after discovery.

EPA also may extend the disclosure period when multiple facilities or acquisitions are involved.

In the multi-facility context, EPA will ordinarily extend the 21-day period to allow reasonable time for completion and review of multi-facility audits where: (a) EPA and the entity agree on the timing and scope of the audits prior to their commencement; and (b) the facilities to be audited are identified in advance. In the acquisitions context, EPA will consider extending the prompt disclosure period on a case-by-case basis. The 21-day disclosure period will begin on the date of discovery by the acquiring entity, but in no case will the period begin earlier than the date of acquisition.

In summary, Section D(3) recognizes that it is critical for EPA to receive timely reporting of violations in order to have clear notice of the violations and the opportunity to respond if necessary. Prompt disclosure is also evidence of the regulated entity's good faith in wanting to achieve or return to compliance as soon as possible. The integrity of Federal environmental law depends upon timely and accurate reporting. The public relies on timely and accurate reports from the regulated community, not only to measure compliance but to evaluate health or environmental risk and gauge progress in reducing pollutant loadings. EPA expects the Policy to encourage the kind of vigorous self-policing that will serve these objectives and does not intend that it justify delayed reporting. When violations of reporting requirements are voluntarily discovered, they must be promptly reported. When a failure to report results in imminent and substantial endangerment or serious harm to the environment, Audit Policy credit is precluded under condition D(8).

4. Discovery and Disclosure Independent of Government or Third Party Plaintiff

Under Section D(4), the entity must discover the violation independently. That is, the violation must be discovered and identified before EPA or another government agency likely would have identified the problem either through its own investigative work or from information received through a third party. This condition requires regulated entities to take the initiative to find violations on their own and disclose them promptly instead of waiting for an indication of a pending enforcement action or third-party complaint.

Section D(4)(a) lists the circumstances under which discovery and disclosure will not be considered independent. For example, a disclosure will not be independent where EPA is already investigating the facility in question. However, under subsection (a), where the entity does not know that EPA has commenced a civil investigation and proceeds in good faith to make a disclosure under the Audit Policy, EPA may, in its discretion, provide penalty mitigation under the Audit Policy. The subsection (a) exception applies only to civil investigations; it does not apply in the criminal context. Other examples of situations in which a discovery is not considered independent are where a citizens' group has provided notice of its intent to sue, where a third party has already filed a complaint, where a whistleblower has reported the potential violation to government authorities, or where discovery of the violation by the government was imminent.[1] Condition D(4)(c)—the filing of a complaint by a third party—covers formal judicial and administrative complaints as well as informal complaints, such as a letter from a citizens' group alerting EPA to a potential environmental violation.

Regulated entities that own or operate multiple facilities are subject to section D(4)(b) in addition to D(4)(a). EPA encourages multi-facility auditing and does not intend for the "independent discovery" condition to preclude availability of the Audit Policy when multiple facilities are involved. Thus, if a regulated entity owns or operates multiple facilities, the fact that one of its facilities is the subject of an investigation, inspection, information request or third-party complaint does not automatically preclude the Agency from granting Audit Policy credit for disclosures of violations self-discovered at the other facilities, assuming all other Audit Policy conditions are met. However, just as in the single-facility context, where a facility is already the subject of a government inspection, investigation or information request (including a broad information request that covers multiple facilities), it will generally not be eligible for Audit Policy credit. The Audit Policy is designed to encourage regulated entities to disclose violations before any of their facilities are under investigation, not after EPA discovers violations at one facility. Nevertheless, the Agency retains its full discretion

---

1. Where such reports relate to an environmental incident, for example, a reportable release, the report must be made in accordance with established incident reporting procedures.

under the Audit Policy to grant penalty waivers or reductions for good-faith disclosures made in the multi-facility context. EPA has worked closely with a number of entities that have received Audit Policy credit for multi-facility disclosures, and entities contemplating multi-facility auditing are encouraged to contact the Agency with any questions concerning Audit Policy availability.

5. Correction and Remediation

Under Section D(5), the entity must remedy any harm caused by the violation and expeditiously certify in writing to appropriate Federal, State, and local authorities that it has corrected the violation. Correction and remediation in this context include responding to spills and carrying out any removal or remedial actions required by law. The certification requirement enables EPA to ensure that the regulated entity will be publicly accountable for its commitments through binding written agreements, orders or consent decrees where necessary.

Under the Policy, the entity must correct the violation within 60 calendar days from the date of discovery, or as expeditiously as possible. EPA recognizes that some violations can and should be corrected immediately, while others may take longer than 60 days to correct. For example, more time may be required if capital expenditures are involved or if technological issues are a factor. If more than 60 days will be required, the disclosing entity must so notify the Agency in writing prior to the conclusion of the 60-day period. In all cases, the regulated entity will be expected to do its utmost to achieve or return to compliance as expeditiously as possible.

If correction of the violation depends upon issuance of a permit that has been applied for but not issued by Federal or State authorities, the Agency will, where appropriate, make reasonable efforts to secure timely review of the permit.

6. Prevent Recurrence

Under Section D(6), the regulated entity must agree to take steps to prevent a recurrence of the violation after it has been disclosed. Preventive steps may include, but are not limited to, improvements to the entity's environmental auditing efforts or compliance management system.

7. No Repeat Violations

Condition D(7) bars repeat offenders from receiving Audit Policy credit. Under the repeat violations exclusion, the same or a closely-related violation must not have occurred at the same facility within the past 3 years. The 3-year period begins to run when the government or a third party has given the violator notice of a specific violation, without regard to when the original violation cited in the notice actually occurred. Examples of notice include a complaint, consent order, notice of violation, receipt of an inspection report, citizen suit, or receipt of penalty mitigation through a compliance assistance or incentive project.

When the facility is part of a multi-facility organization, Audit Policy relief is not available if the same or a closely-related violation occurred as part of a pattern of violations at one or more of these facilities within the past 5 years. If a facility has been newly acquired, the existence of a violation prior to acquisition does not trigger the repeat violations exclusion.

The term "violation" includes any violation subject to a Federal, State or local civil judicial or administrative order, consent agreement, conviction or plea agreement. Recognizing that minor violations sometimes are settled without a formal action in court, the term also covers any act or omission for which the regulated entity has received a penalty reduction in the past. This condition covers situations in which the regulated entity has had clear notice of its noncompliance and an opportunity to correct the problem.

The repeat violation exclusion benefits both the public and law-abiding entities by ensuring that penalties are not waived for those entities that have previously been notified of violations and fail to prevent repeat violations. The 3-year and 5-year "bright lines" in the exclusion are designed to provide regulated entities with clear notice about when the Policy will be available.

8. Other Violations Excluded

Section D(8) provides that Policy benefits are not available for certain types of violations. Subsection D(8)(a) excludes violations that result in serious actual harm to the environment or which may have presented an imminent and substantial endangerment to public health or the environment. When events of such a consequential nature occur, violators are ineligible for penalty relief and other incentives under the Audit Policy. However, this condition does not bar an entity from qualifying for Audit Policy relief solely because the violation involves release of a pollutant to the environment, as such releases do not necessarily result in serious actual harm or an imminent and substantial endangerment. To date, EPA has not invoked the serious actual harm or the imminent and substantial endangerment clauses to deny Audit Policy credit for any disclosure.

Subsection D(8)(b) excludes violations of the specific terms of any order, consent agreement, or plea agreement. Once a consent agreement has been negotiated, there is little incentive to comply if there are no sanctions for violating its specific requirements. The exclusion in this section also applies to violations of the terms of any response, removal or remedial action covered by a written agreement.

9. Cooperation

Under Section D(9), the regulated entity must cooperate as required by EPA and provide the Agency with the information it needs to determine Policy applicability. The entity must not hide, destroy or tamper with possible evidence following discovery of potential environmental violations. In order for the Agency to apply the Policy fairly, it must have sufficient information to determine whether its conditions are satisfied in each individual case. In general, EPA requests audit reports to determine the applicability of this Policy only where the information contained in the audit report is not readily available elsewhere and where EPA decides that the information is necessary to determine whether the terms and conditions of the Policy have been met. In the rare instance where an EPA Regional office seeks to obtain an audit report because it is otherwise unable to determine whether Policy conditions have been met, the Regional office will notify the Office of Regulatory Enforcement at EPA headquarters.

Entities that disclose potential criminal violations may expect a more thorough review by the Agency. In criminal cases, entities will be expected to provide, at a minimum, the following: access to all requested documents; access to all employees of the disclosing entity; assistance in investigating the violation, any noncompliance problems related to the disclosure, and any environmental consequences related to the violations; access to all information relevant to the violations disclosed, including that portion of the environmental audit report or documentation from the compliance management system that revealed the violation; and access to the individuals who conducted the audit or review.

F. Opposition to Audit Privilege and Immunity

The Agency believes that the Audit Policy provides effective incentives for self-policing without impairing law enforcement, putting the environment at risk or hiding environmental compliance information from the public. Although EPA encourages environmental auditing, it must do so without compromising the integrity and enforceability of environmental laws. It is important to distinguish between EPA's Audit Policy and the audit privilege and immunity laws that exist in some States. The Agency remains firmly opposed to statutory and regulatory audit privileges and immunity. Privilege laws shield evidence of wrongdoing and prevent States from investigating even the most serious environmental violations. Immunity laws prevent States from obtaining penalties that are appropriate to the seriousness of the violation, as they are required to do under Federal law. Audit privilege and immunity laws are unnecessary, undermine law enforcement, impair protection of human health and the environment, and interfere with the public's right to know of potential and existing environmental hazards.

Statutory audit privilege and immunity run counter to encouraging the kind of openness that builds trust between regulators, the regulated community and the public. For example, privileged information on compliance contained in an audit report may include information on the cause of violations, the extent of environmental harm, and what is necessary to correct the violations and prevent their recurrence. Privileged information is unavailable to law enforcers and to members of the public who have suffered harm as a result of environmental violations. The Agency opposes statutory immunity because it diminishes law enforcement's ability to discourage wrongful behavior and interferes with a regulator's ability to punish individuals who disregard the law and place others in danger. The Agency believes that its Audit Policy provides adequate incentives for self-policing but without secrecy and without abdicating its discretion to act in cases of serious environmental violations.

Privilege, by definition, invites secrecy, instead of the openness needed to build public trust in industry's ability to self-police. American law reflects the high value that the public places on fair access to the facts. The Supreme Court, for example, has said of privileges that, " [w]hatever their origins, these exceptions to the demand for every man's evidence are not lightly created nor expansively construed, for they are in derogation of the search for truth." United States v. Nixon, 418 U.S. 683, 710 (1974). Federal courts have unanimously refused to recognize a privilege for environmental audits in the context of government investigations. See, e.g., United States v. Dexter Corp., 132 F.R.D. 8, 10 (D.Conn. 1990) (application of a privilege "would effectively impede [EPA's] ability to enforce the Clean Water Act, and would be contrary to stated public policy.") Cf. In re Grand Jury Proceedings, 861 F. Supp. 386 (D. Md. 1994) (company must comply with a subpoena under Food, Drug and Cosmetics Act for self-evaluative documents).

G. Effect on States

The revised final Policy reflects EPA's desire to provide fair and effective incentives for self-policing that have practical value to States. To that end, the Agency has consulted closely with State officials in developing this Policy. As a result, EPA believes its revised final Policy is grounded in commonsense principles that should prove useful in the development and implementation of State programs and policies.

EPA recognizes that States are partners in implementing the enforcement and compliance assurance program. When consistent with EPA's policies on protecting confidential and sensitive information, the Agency will share with State agencies information on disclosures of violations of Federally-authorized, approved or delegated programs. In addition, for States that have adopted their own audit policies in Federally-authorized, approved or delegated programs, EPA will generally defer to State penalty mitigation for self-disclosures as long as the State policy meets minimum requirements for Federal delegation. Whenever a State provides a penalty waiver or mitigation for a violation of a requirement contained in a Federally-authorized, approved or delegated program to an entity that discloses those violations in conformity with a State audit policy, the State should notify the EPA Region in which it is located. This notification will ensure that Federal and State enforcement responses are coordinated properly.

For further information about minimum delegation requirements and the effect of State audit privilege and immunity laws on enforcement authority, see "Statement of Principles: Effect of State Audit/ Immunity Privilege Laws on Enforcement Authority for Federal Programs," Memorandum from Steven A. Herman et al., dated February 14, 1997, to be posted on the Internet under www.epa.gov/oeca/oppa.

As always, States are encouraged to experiment with different approaches to assuring compliance as long as such approaches do not jeopardize public health or the environment, or make it profitable not to comply with Federal environmental requirements. The Agency remains opposed to State legislation that does not include these basic protections, and reserves its right to bring independent action against regulated entities for violations of Federal law that threaten human health or the environment, reflect criminal conduct or repeated non-compliance, or allow one company to profit at the expense of its law-abiding competitors.

H. Scope of Policy

EPA has developed this Policy to guide settlement actions. It is the Agency's practice to make public all compliance agreements reached under this Policy in order to provide the regulated community with fair notice of decisions and to provide affected communities and the public with information regarding Agency action. Some in the regulated community have suggested that the Agency should convert the Policy into a regulation because they feel doing so would ensure greater consistency and predictability. Following its three-year evaluation of the Policy, however, the Agency believes that there is ample evidence that the Policy has worked well and that there is no need for a formal rulemaking. Furthermore, as the Agency seeks to respond to lessons learned from its increasing experience handling self-disclosures, a policy is much easier to amend than a regulation. Nothing in today's release of the revised final Policy is intended to change the status of the Policy as guidance.

I. Implementation of Policy

1. Civil Violations

Pursuant to the Audit Policy, disclosures of civil environmental violations should be made to the EPA Region in which the entity or facility is located or, where the violations to be disclosed involve more than one EPA Region, to EPA Headquarters. The Regional or Headquarters' offices decide whether application of the Audit Policy in a specific case is appropriate. Obviously, once a matter has been referred for civil judicial prosecution, DOJ becomes involved as well. Where there is evidence of a potential criminal violation, the civil offices coordinate with criminal enforcement offices at EPA and DOJ.

To resolve issues of national significance and ensure that the Policy is applied fairly and consistently across EPA Regions and at Headquarters, the Agency in 1995 created the Audit Policy Quick Response Team (QRT). The QRT is comprised of representatives from the Regions, Headquarters, and DOJ. It meets on a regular basis to address issues of interpretation and to coordinate self-disclosure initiatives. In addition, in 1999 EPA established a National Coordinator position to handle Audit Policy issues and implementation. The National Coordinator chairs the QRT and, along with the Regional Audit Policy coordinators, serves as a point of contact on Audit Policy issues in the civil context.

2. Criminal Violations

Criminal disclosures are handled by the Voluntary Disclosure Board (VDB), which was established by EPA in 1997. The VDB ensures consistent application of the Audit Policy in the criminal context by centralizing Policy interpretation and application within the Agency.

Disclosures of potential criminal violations may be made directly to the VDB, to an EPA regional criminal investigation division or to DOJ. In all cases, the VDB coordinates with the investigative team and the appropriate prosecuting authority. During the course of the investigation, the VDB routinely monitors the progress of the investigation as necessary to ensure that sufficient facts have been established to determine whether to recommend that relief under the Policy be granted.

At the conclusion of the criminal investigation, the Board makes a recommendation to the Director of EPA's Office of Criminal Enforcement, Forensics, and Training, who serves as the Deciding Official. Upon receiving the Board's recommendation, the Deciding Official makes his or her final recommendation to the appropriate United States Attorney's Office and/or DOJ. The recommendation of the Deciding Official, however, is only that—a recommendation. The United States Attorney's Office and/or DOJ retain full authority to exercise prosecutorial discretion.

3. Release of Information to the Public
   Upon formal settlement, EPA places copies of settlements in the Audit Policy Docket. EPA also makes other documents related to self-disclosures publicly available, unless the disclosing entity claims them as Confidential Business Information (and that claim is validated by U.S. EPA), unless another exemption under the Freedom of Information Act is asserted and/or applies, or the Privacy Act or any other law would preclude such release. Presumptively releasable documents include compliance agreements reached under the Policy (see Section H) and descriptions of compliance management systems submitted under Section D(1).
   Any material claimed to be Confidential Business Information will be treated in accordance with EPA regulations at 40 CFR Part 2. In determining what documents to release, EPA is guided by the Memorandum from Assistant Administrator Steven A. Herman entitled "Confidentiality of Information Received Under Agency's Self-Disclosure Policy," available on the Internet at www.epa.gov/oeca/sahmemo.html.

II. Statement of Policy—Incentives for Self-Policing: Discovery, Disclosure, Correction and Prevention of Violations

A. Purpose
   This Policy is designed to enhance protection of human health and the environment by encouraging regulated entities to voluntarily discover, disclose, correct and prevent violations of Federal environmental requirements.

B. Definitions
   For purposes of this Policy, the following definitions apply: "Environmental Audit" is a systematic, documented, periodic and objective review by regulated entities of facility operations and practices related to meeting environmental requirements.
   "Compliance Management System" encompasses the regulated entity's documented systematic efforts, appropriate to the size and nature of its business, to prevent, detect and correct violations through all of the following:
   (a) Compliance policies, standards and procedures that identify how employees and agents are to meet the requirements of laws, regulations, permits, enforceable agreements and other sources of authority for environmental requirements;
   (b) Assignment of overall responsibility for overseeing compliance with policies, standards, and procedures, and assignment of specific responsibility for assuring compliance at each facility or operation;
   (c) Mechanisms for systematically assuring that compliance policies, standards and procedures are being carried out, including monitoring and auditing systems reasonably designed to detect and correct violations, periodic evaluation of the overall performance of the compliance management system, and a means for employees or agents to report violations of environmental requirements without fear of retaliation;
   (d) Efforts to communicate effectively the regulated entity's standards and procedures to all employees and other agents;
   (e) Appropriate incentives to managers and employees to perform in accordance with the compliance policies, standards and procedures, including consistent enforcement through appropriate disciplinary mechanisms; and
   (f) Procedures for the prompt and appropriate correction of any violations, and any necessary modifications to the regulated entity's compliance management system to prevent future violations.
   "Environmental audit report" means the documented analysis, conclusions, and recommendations resulting from an environmental audit, but does not include data obtained in, or testimonial evidence concerning, the environmental audit.

"Gravity-based penalties" are that portion of a penalty over and above the economic benefit, i.e., the punitive portion of the penalty, rather than that portion representing a defendant's economic gain from noncompliance.

"Regulated entity" means any entity, including a Federal, State or municipal agency or facility, regulated under Federal environmental laws.

C. Incentives for Self-Policing

1. No Gravity-Based Penalties

If a regulated entity establishes that it satisfies all of the conditions of Section D of this Policy, EPA will not seek gravity-based penalties for violations of Federal environmental requirements discovered and disclosed by the entity.

2. Reduction of Gravity-Based Penalties by 75%

If a regulated entity establishes that it satisfies all of the conditions of Section D of this Policy except for D(1)—systematic discovery—EPA will reduce by 75% gravity-based penalties for violations of Federal environmental requirements discovered and disclosed by the entity.

3. No Recommendation for Criminal Prosecution

(a) If a regulated entity establishes that it satisfies at least conditions D(2) through D(9) of this Policy, EPA will not recommend to the U.S. Department of Justice or other prosecuting authority that criminal charges be brought against the disclosing entity, as long as EPA determines that the violation is not part of a pattern or practice that demonstrates or involves:

(i) A prevalent management philosophy or practice that conceals or condones environmental violations; or

(ii) High-level corporate officials' or managers' conscious involvement in, or willful blindness to, violations of Federal environmental law;

(b) Whether or not EPA recommends the regulated entity for criminal prosecution under this section, the Agency may recommend for prosecution the criminal acts of individual managers or employees under existing policies guiding the exercise of enforcement discretion.

4. No Routine Request for Environmental Audit Reports

EPA will neither request nor use an environmental audit report to initiate a civil or criminal investigation of an entity. For example, EPA will not request an environmental audit report in routine inspections. If the Agency has independent reason to believe that a violation has occurred, however, EPA may seek any information relevant to identifying violations or determining liability or extent of harm.

D. Conditions

1. Systematic Discovery

The violation was discovered through:

(a) An environmental audit; or

(b) A compliance management system reflecting the regulated entity's due diligence in preventing, detecting, and correcting violations. The regulated entity must provide accurate and complete documentation to the Agency as to how its compliance management system meets the criteria for due diligence outlined in Section B and how the regulated entity discovered the violation through its compliance management system. EPA may require the regulated entity to make publicly available a description of its compliance management system.

2. Voluntary Discovery

The violation was discovered voluntarily and not through a legally mandated monitoring or sampling requirement prescribed by statute, regulation, permit, judicial or administrative order, or consent agreement. For example, the Policy does not apply to:

(a) Emissions violations detected through a continuous emissions monitor (or alternative monitor established in a permit) where any such monitoring is required;

(b) Violations of National Pollutant Discharge Elimination System (NPDES) discharge limits detected through required sampling or monitoring; or

(c) Violations discovered through a compliance audit required to be performed by the terms of a consent order or settlement agreement, unless the audit is a component of agreement terms to implement a comprehensive environmental management system.

3. Prompt Disclosure

The regulated entity fully discloses the specific violation in writing to EPA within 21 days (or within such shorter time as may be required by law) after the entity discovered that the violation has, or may have, occurred. The time at which the entity discovers that a violation has, or may have, occurred begins when any officer, director, employee or agent of the facility has an objectively reasonable basis for believing that a violation has, or may have, occurred.

4. Discovery and Disclosure Independent of Government or Third-Party Plaintiff

(a) The regulated entity discovers and discloses the potential violation to EPA prior to:

(i) The commencement of a Federal, State or local agency inspection or investigation, or the issuance by such agency of an information request to the regulated entity (where EPA determines that the facility did not know that it was under civil investigation, and EPA determines that the entity is otherwise acting in good faith, the Agency may exercise its discretion to reduce or waive civil penalties in accordance with this Policy);

(ii) Notice of a citizen suit;

(iii) The filing of a complaint by a third party;

(iv) The reporting of the violation to EPA (or other government agency) by a "whistleblower" employee, rather than by one authorized to speak on behalf of the regulated entity; or

(v) imminent discovery of the violation by a regulatory agency.

(b) For entities that own or operate multiple facilities, the fact that one facility is already the subject of an investigation, inspection, information request or third-party complaint does not preclude the Agency from exercising its discretion to make the Audit Policy available for violations self-discovered at other facilities owned or operated by the same regulated entity.

5. Correction and Remediation

The regulated entity corrects the violation within 60 calendar days from the date of discovery, certifies in writing that the violation has been corrected, and takes appropriate measures as determined by EPA to remedy any environmental or human harm due to the violation. EPA retains the authority to order an entity to correct a violation within a specific time period shorter than 60 days whenever correction in such shorter period of time is feasible and necessary to protect public health and the environment adequately. If more than 60 days will be needed to correct the violation, the regulated entity must so notify EPA in writing before the 60-day period has passed. Where appropriate, to satisfy conditions D(5) and D(6), EPA may require a regulated entity to enter into a publicly available written agreement, administrative consent order or judicial consent decree as a condition of obtaining relief under the Audit Policy, particularly where compliance or remedial measures are complex or a lengthy schedule for attaining and maintaining compliance or remediating harm is required.

	WORKPAPER REFERENCE	COMPLETED BY/DATE

SOLID AND HAZARDOUS WASTE MANAGEMENT

14. Review the list of solid and hazardous wastes and the amount being generated. (This information may be included in the environmental assessment reports, or applicable environmental reference manuals.)

   A. Is this information properly documented?
   B. Does the document action indicate whether this waste is disposed of on or off-site and by what means?

15. Document the procedures for off-site disposals of hazardous waste.

   A. How are these manifests controlled?
   B. How are "manifest exceptions" handled?
   C. Is the manifest record system properly maintained, and does it provide for adequate documentation of this activity?
   D. Does the plant perform a periodic review of vendor performance, and is this review properly documented?
   E. Determine if transporters not contracted by the waste disposal company are reviewed for EPA license prior to being used as a transporter of hazardous waste.

16. Review the inventory of drummed waste.

   A. Is it in accordance with applicable state and federal requirements?
   B. Determine how the drums are documented as to when hazardous waste is first placed in the drum?
   C. From review of this documentation, determine if any hazardous drummed waste has been held over 90 days.
   D. What controls are in place to ensure drummed waste is not held for over 90 days?
   E. Is all of this information adequately documented?

17. Review the last assessment and determine that the disposal sites are within the provisions of the Resource Conservation and Recovery Act (RCRA), and other federal, state, or local regulations.

18. Select a sample of hazardous waste manifests, and determine if shipping destinations are included in the list of authorized disposal sites.

19. Determine if facility disposes of hazardous waste (either generated on-site or received from off-site). Obtain information regarding the disposal methods, and review documentation that disposal methods meet regulatory requirements including necessary permits.

20. Determine if there are any documented locations that were used as waste disposal sites in the past.

   A. Determine if any groundwater tests have been performed.

   B. Determine if there is any evidence of ground water contamination.
   C. Determine if this information has been documented.

Revised: 4-1-91

6. Prevent Recurrence

The regulated entity agrees in writing to take steps to prevent a recurrence of the violation. Such steps may include improvements to its environmental auditing or compliance management system.

7. No Repeat Violations

The specific violation (or a closely related violation) has not occurred previously within the past three years at the same facility, and has not occurred within the past five years as part of a pattern at multiple facilities owned or operated by the same entity. For the purposes of this section, a violation is:

> (a) Any violation of Federal, State or local environmental law identified in a judicial or administrative order, consent agreement or order, complaint, or notice of violation, conviction or plea agreement; or
>
> (b) Any act or omission for which the regulated entity has previously received penalty mitigation from EPA or a State or local agency.

8. Other Violations Excluded

The violation is not one which (a) resulted in serious actual harm, or may have presented an imminent and substantial endangerment, to human health or the environment, or (b) violates the specific terms of any judicial or administrative order, or consent agreement.

9. Cooperation

The regulated entity cooperates as requested by EPA and provides such information as is necessary and requested by EPA to determine applicability of this Policy.

E. Economic Benefit

EPA retains its full discretion to recover any economic benefit gained as a result of noncompliance to preserve a "level playing field" in which violators do not gain a competitive advantage over regulated entities that do comply. EPA may forgive the entire penalty for violations that meet conditions D(1) through D(9) and, in the Agency's opinion, do not merit any penalty due to the insignificant amount of any economic benefit.

F. Effect on State Law, Regulation or Policy

EPA will work closely with States to encourage their adoption and implementation of policies that reflect the incentives and conditions outlined in this Policy. EPA remains firmly opposed to statutory environmental audit privileges that shield evidence of environmental violations and undermine the public's right to know, as well as to blanket immunities, particularly immunities for violations that reflect criminal conduct, present serious threats or actual harm to health and the environment, allow noncomplying companies to gain an economic advantage over their competitors, or reflect a repeated failure to comply with Federal law. EPA will work with States to address any provisions of State audit privilege or immunity laws that are inconsistent with this Policy and that may prevent a timely and appropriate response to significant environmental violations. The Agency reserves its right to take necessary actions to protect public health or the environment by enforcing against any violations of Federal law.

G. Applicability

(1) This Policy applies to settlement of claims for civil penalties for any violations under all of the Federal environmental statutes that EPA administers, and supersedes any inconsistent provisions in media-specific penalty or enforcement policies and EPA's 1995 Policy on "Incentives for Self-Policing: Discovery, Disclosure, Correction and Prevention of Violations."

(2) To the extent that existing EPA enforcement policies are not inconsistent, they will continue to apply in conjunction with this Policy. However, a regulated entity that has received penalty mitigation for satisfying specific conditions under this Policy may not receive additional penalty mitigation for satisfying the same or similar conditions under other poli-

cies for the same violation, nor will this Policy apply to any violation that has received penalty mitigation under other policies. Where an entity has failed to meet any of conditions D(2) through D(9) and is therefore not eligible for penalty relief under this Policy, it may still be eligible for penalty relief under other EPA media-specific enforcement policies in recognition of good faith efforts, even where, for example, the violation may have presented an imminent and substantial endangerment or resulted in serious actual harm.

(3) This Policy sets forth factors for consideration that will guide the Agency in the exercise of its enforcement discretion. It states the Agency's views as to the proper allocation of its enforcement resources. The Policy is not final agency action and is intended as guidance. This Policy is not intended, nor can it be relied upon, to create any rights enforceable by any party in litigation with the United States. As with the 1995 Audit Policy, EPA may decide to follow guidance provided in this document or to act at variance with it based on its analysis of the specific facts presented. This Policy may be revised without public notice to reflect changes in EPA's approach to providing incentives for self-policing by regulated entities, or to clarify and update text.

(4) This Policy should be used whenever applicable in settlement negotiations for both administrative and civil judicial enforcement actions. It is not intended for use in pleading, at hearing or at trial. The Policy may be applied at EPA's discretion to the settlement of administrative and judicial enforcement actions instituted prior to, but not yet resolved, as of the effective date of this Policy.

(5) For purposes of this Policy, violations discovered pursuant to an environmental audit or compliance management system may be considered voluntary even if required under an Agency "partnership" program in which the entity participates, such as regulatory flexibility pilot projects like Project XL. EPA will consider application of the Audit Policy to such partnership program projects on a project-by-project basis.

(6) EPA has issued interpretive guidance addressing several applicability issues pertaining to the Audit Policy. Entities considering whether to take advantage of the Audit Policy should review that guidance to see if it addresses any relevant questions. The guidance can be found on the Internet at www.epa.gov/oeca/ore/apolguid.html.

H. Public Accountability
EPA will make publicly available the terms and conditions of any compliance agreement reached under this Policy, including the nature of the violation, the remedy, and the schedule for returning to compliance.

I. Effective Date
This revised Policy is effective May 11, 2000.

Appendix I:
Sample Internal Environmental and Safety Audit Questionnaire

Objectives

- To determine that corporate, industry group, and/or plant procedures adequately address environmental and safety concerns.

- To determine that a recent environmental assessment has been performed and items identified have been addressed.

- To determine that all applicable regulations, training and required reporting is properly documented.

- To determine compliance with all permit and regulatory requirements is properly documented.

- To determine that all work related injuries and illnesses are recorded.

Questions	Yes	No	N/A

ENVIRONMENTAL

Organization and Facility Description

1. Does the entity or function being audited maintain copies of all applicable company environmental policies and procedures?

2. Do internal reporting requirements exist delineating a clear reporting structure within the local environmental organization?

3. Do these requirements clearly note which organizations are obligated to provide data and information to the environmental group?

4. Does a mechanism exist for reporting excursions, incidents, significant matters, etc. to the appropriate individuals and organizations in the company and to the applicable government agencies?

5. Do recordkeeping requirements exist to ensure adherence to permits, rules and regulations?

6. Do these recordkeeping requirements clearly define responsibility for safekeeping of these records? (These procedures should include provisions for maintaining permits, monitoring reports and other records.)

7. Are records kept in a central file or by a designated individual at each facility providing for good control and accessibility? If a central control is not in place, at a minimum, is a reference folder maintained that includes file and location references?

8. Is access to records adequately controlled, and are the records maintained in an orderly fashion?

9. Is the record filing system consistent for all environmental activities?

10. Has a recent environmental assessment been performed? What is the date of the last report prepared? _____ Obtain a copy.

11. Has the facility documented a summary of all environmental compliance requirements which apply to their plant or location? (This information may be found in the environmental assessment reports, applicable environmental reference manuals or operating permits.) Has documentation been updated within the last 12 months?

Revised: 1-1-91

1 of 8

Questions	Yes	No	N/A
12. Does the facility have copies or access to applicable federal, state and local regulations?			
13. Does the facility have or have access to a system (such as the environmental action system (EAS)) or a service that provides it with the following information:			
A. A listing of matters such as significant incidents or reportable excursions?			
B. Legal actions taken or pending?			
C. A listing of all environmental issues by a control or folio number?			
D. An action plan for resolution of each environmental issue with timetables and milestones?			
E. Compliance requirements applicable to items listed in (A) through (D)?			
F. Community Right-to-know program (required for all facilities)?			

Water Quality

14. Does a list of waste water discharge permits that are presently in force exist? (This information may be summarized in the environmental assessment reports or applicable environmental reference manuals.) If so, obtain a copy.

15. If the plant has waste or waste water ponds, are the required permits maintained? If so, obtain a copy.

16. Is the facility in compliance with water quality requirements during storm periods?

17. If the facility is not in compliance with water problems during storm periods, do they have a program for correction?

18. If the facility has any monitoring wells, are the required permits maintained? If so, obtain a copy.

19. If the facility has any injection wells, are current permits maintained for each of these wells?

Air Quality

20. Does a list of air emission permits presently in force exist? (This information may be found in the environmental assessment reports or applicable environmental reference manuals.) If so, obtain a copy.

21. Has a recent regulatory air inspection been performed? If so, when was the last inspection? _____ Obtain a copy.

22. Has there been any change in the operation since the last assessment, either a new process or significant change to an existing process that would have required new permits or changes in existing permits? Have these permits been secured? If not, have they been applied for?

23. Is an emission inventory maintained to help monitor emission levels?

Questions	Yes	No	N/A

24. Are these inventories periodically updated?

25. Are periodic emissions tests performed by company and/or air pollution control agency personnel?

Solid and Hazardous Waste Management

26. Does the facility maintain a list of solid and hazardous generated wastes? Is the amount generated shown? Obtain a copy.

27. Do manifests exist for each off-site shipment of hazardous waste?

28. Does the facility have a system to verify and maintain receipt of a copy of each manifest required to be returned by the off-site disposal operator?

29. Is an annual hazardous waste summary provided to the state.

30. Is a statement regarding the plants "waste reduction efforts" issued annually to the state? Obtain a copy.

31. Is an inventory of drummed waste maintained?

32. Is a listing of this drummed waste inventory maintained? Obtain a copy.

33. Are drums dated as to when hazardous waste is first placed in the drum?

34. Is there an industry group or division list or other form of record denoting authorized disposal sites?

35. If not, has the disposal site used by the plant been reviewed and approved, and has this information been adequately documented?

36. Does a list of hazardous wastes disposed of on-site exist? If so, obtain a copy.

Vinyl Chloride Monomer (VCM)

36. If the plant has any VCM related activities, is this information documented?

37. Is there a fugitive emission identification and control program? (This information may be found in applicable environmental reference manuals.)

38. Are the results of the fugitive emission identification and control program adequately documented?

Polychlorinated Biphenyls (PCBs)

39. Does this facility contain polychlorinated biphenyls (PCBs), PCB equipment. (e.g., transformers, capacitors, electromagnets, electric motors, hydraulic systems, heat transfer systems, compressors), or containers of PCBs or PCB mixtures? (This information may be found in the environmental assessment reports, or applicable environmental reference manuals.)

40. Are periodic inspections made of any PCB equipment that is in service? Are these inspections adequately documented?

Revised: 1-1-91

Questions	Yes	No	N/A

Asbestos

41. Has the facility conducted and documented a survey of asbestos located within the facility? If friable asbestos is present, is there a plan for encasement, removal, disposal or other appropriate action under applicable regulations? Obtain a copy of each document.

Spill Control and Emergency Plans

A Spill Prevention, Control, and Countermeasure (SPCC) Plan is a specific requirement of 40 Code of Federal Regulations (CFR), and pertains to the storage and use of oil, (including gasoline diesel, crude oil, fuel oil, and vegetable oil). The requirement is in addition to any other requirement (regulatory or company) for a spill contingency plan.

Questions	Yes	No	N/A

42. Does the facility have an SPCC plan updated within the last 3 years?

43. Has the facility been without any reported spills within the last six months?

44. Does the facility have any emergency response or other disaster control contingency plan?

45. Does this emergency response plan include a community hazard communication program, and does it cover fire, storm, bomb threat, gas releases, etc.?

General

46. If the facility transfers product via pipeline, is there an in-house pipeline inspection, surveillance and maintenance program?

47. Are environmental regulations and requirements communicated to on-site contractors in documented form?

48. Are all AFEs reviewed by environmental personnel at the appropriate levels to determine if the project may have an environmental effect and that the effect is provided for?

Safety

Organization and Facility Description

1. Does the facility have corporate and/or local safety policies and procedures (i.e., training, hazard communication, etc.)? Obtain a copy.

2. Has there been a recent safety assessment report issued? Obtain a copy.

General

3. Does the facility maintain a list and/or inventory of all chemicals (raw materials, intermediates, finished products)?

Revised: 1-1-91

<u>Questions</u>	Yes	No	N/A

4. Are material safety data sheets (MSDSs) available for all chemicals for which an MSDS is required?

    <u>Note:</u> The MSDSs are required under two different sets of regulations. The occupational Safety & Health Administration (OSHA) requires the MSDSs for compliance with its Hazard Communication Standard and the Environmental Protection Agency (EPA) requires the MSDSs as part of its Community Right-to-Know regulations.

5. Is the purchasing department aware of the requirement to obtain the MSDSs for purchased raw materials?

6. Are safety regulations and requirements communicated to on-site contractors in documented form?

7. Is there an industry group or facility drug and alcohol abuse policy meeting the OPC policy requirements?

8. Are outside consultants used in a cost-effective manner?

<u>Chemical Exposure</u>

For all chemicals in your facility for which there are OSHA Permissible Exposure Limits (PELs) or Threshold Limit Values (TLVs), employee exposure should be determined or estimated. A listing of these limits and values may be obtained from Corporate Industrial Hygiene. Sometimes, a careful review of the exposure potential will result in the conclusion that exposure is minimal or non-existent. In other cases, it will be necessary to actually sample to determine the extent of exposure. If exposure (without regard to the use of personal protective equipment) is above the action level (1/2 of the limit), then a program of routine sampling must be established, and an engineering solution investigated. Chemicals for which there are substance-specific standards (asbestos, formaldehyde, vinyl chloride, etc.) should be sampled routinely to generate sufficient data to allow exposure to be estimated with more confidence. (See Substance Specific Standards Section).

<u>Questions</u>	Yes	No	N/A

9. If as a result of sampling an overexposure is believed to exist, have the individual employees who were monitored been provided with proper personal protective equipment?

    A.   Is its use enforced?

10. Is there an action plan to engineer out the source of overexposure?

11. Is ventilation checked regularly and results documented?

12. Have representative exposure samples been taken for all chemicals with OSHA-PELs or American Conference of Governmental Hygienists-Threshold Limit Values (ACGIH-TLVs) at your facility?

13. Are samples taken on a scheduled basis?

14. Are they representative of an 8-hour TWA?

15. Are area Standard Threshold Exposure Level (STEL) and Ceiling samples taken?

16. Are employees notified of monitoring results?

17. Is there prompt follow-up on high exposures?

Revised: 1-1-91

Questions	Yes	No	N/A
18. Is there proper documentation of:			
A. Monitoring data?			
B. Sampling/Analytical procedures?			
C. Results?			

Substance Specific Standards

If your facility handles chemicals which have been specifically regulated by OSHA as listed below, the requirements of that standard(s) must be met.

Substance Specific Standards have been promulgated by OSHA for the following:
Refer to Specific Reg: 29 CFR 1910

Asbestos	Dimethylaminoazobenzene
Coal tar pitch volatiles	N-Nitrosodimethylamine
4-Nitrobiphenyl	Vinyl chloride
a-Naphthylamine	Inorganic arsenic
Methyl chloromethyl ether	Lead
3,3'-Dichlorobenzidine and salts	Coke oven emissions
bis-Chloromethylether	Cotton dust
b-Naphthylamine	1,2-Dibromo-3-chloropropane
Benzidine	Acrylonitrile
4-Aminodiphenyl	Benzene
Ethyleneimine	Formaldehyde
b-Propiolactone	Ethylene oxide
2-Acetylaminofluorene	

19. Have the specific requirements of these standards been addressed as to:

A. Sampling to measure action level?
B. PEL, ceiling and STEL concentration?
C. Change rooms and shower facilities?
D. Medical monitoring?
E. Medical removal from workplace exposure?
F. Recordkeeping and training?
G. Is there a written program where required?
H. Have regulated areas been established and demarcated as required?

Access to Exposure and Medical Records

OSHA regulations require that employees be informed **annually** that they have a right to see and/or obtain a copy of their exposure and medical records. Should an employee ask to see his/her data, we have fifteen days to comply. Requests for exposure data will likely be minimized if you discuss the results of any sampling with employees as they are obtained. The notification of right of access can be done by posting an appropriate announcement on the bulletin board, or by discussion during a safety or communications meeting. If you use the latter method, you must document that fact. Records are required by the standard to be preserved and maintained for the duration of employment, plus thirty years.

Questions	Yes	No	N/A
20. Are employees informed annually of their right to exposure data and medical records, both past and present?			
21. Are employees notified of their personal exposure data as collected?			
22. Can the facility meet the 15-day time frame to supply requested records?			

Revised: 1-1-91

Questions	Yes	No	N/A
23. Do the employees know of the existence, the location and availability of records?			
24. Do employees know the designated person who maintains these records?			
25. Do employees know of their right of access?			
26. Is a copy of the standards (OSHA 1910.20) readily available for employee examination?			

Noise - Hearing Conservation

There is no OSHA requirement for a written noise program. The regulation does require that it be determined whether employees are exposed at or above the "action level" of 85 dBA as an eight-hour time-weighted average (TWA). If they are, the affected employees must be given training, access to hearing protection and audiometric testing.
There should be an up-to-date noise survey on file to show the compliance officer. Noise surveys should be updated whenever new noise sources are added, or at least every two years. If indicated by the survey, dosimetry should be performed on employees in high noise environments.

Mine Safety & Health Act (MSHA) does have requirements concerning noise levels, depending on the operation. Questions 39 an 40 refer only to MSHA Regulations.

Questions	Yes	No	N/A
27. Has a sound level survey of the facility been performed to identify areas above 85 dBA within the past two years?			
28. Are areas above 90 dBA posted with signs?			
29. Are workers offered an annual audiometric exam?			
30. Has representative 8-hour dosimetry been conducted on those individuals identified by the sound level survey?			
31. Are employees given annual training?			
32. Does this training include effects of noise on the ear, and the principles of noise generation?			
33. Is a copy of the OSHA Noise Standard 1910.95 readily available for employees to examine?			
34. Is proper hearing protection provided for identified employees? Are employees trained in care and use?			
35. In areas over 90 dBA, is hearing protection usage enforced?			
36. Does the program include documentation of: A. Area and personal sampling? B. Audiometric testing? C. Annual training?			
37. Is the documentation readily available?			
38. Is special training given to employees who have experienced a standard threshold shift?			

Questions	Yes	No	N/A
39. Has a program been implemented to provide hearing protection under MSHA regulations?			
40. If a program has not been implemented, have noise surveys been performed in areas above 85 dBA in accordance with MSHA regulations?			

Interview with: _____ _____ _____
                        (Name)   (Title)   (Date)

Objectives

The general objective of this review is to provide assurance that all environmental and safety related activities are adequately documented where practical. Specific objectives of these reviews are listed below.

- To ensure that all OPC/Industry Group policies and procedures regarding environmental and safety issues are being adhered to.

- To ensure proper documentation exists for areas of concern noted in the most recent assessments and any other identified issues have been addressed and corrective action has been properly taken.

- To ensure that documentation of all applicable regulations, training, and required reporting is maintained.

- To ensure that compliance with all permit and regulatory requirements are properly and adequately documented in the environmental and safety records, and to ensure these files are maintained in an organized fashion.

- To ensure that all work related injuries and illness are recorded.

In satisfying the audit objectives, the auditor is encouraged to use the information included in the environmental and safety assessment reports, and applicable environmental and safety reference and standard operating procedure manuals located at the audit site. Information from these sources may help accomplish many of the following audit procedures.

	WORKPAPER REFERENCE	COMPLETED BY/DATE
Procedures		
ENVIRONMENTAL		
ORGANIZATION AND FACILITY DESCRIPTION		
1. Review all applicable company environmental policies and procedures.		
2. Review the most recent environmental assessment report issued, recognizing any confidentiality requirements, and determine that it contains a brief summary of all environmental activities, facilities, processes, and new construction. This information should include all facilities or processes that are related to, or could result in, air emissions, water effluents and outfalls, hazardous or solid waste etc. In short, this should include all activities which do or might have an environmental effect on land, air, or water. Review the environmental assessment to identify issues or activities not included on the related action plan and review action plan to determine if adequate follow-up had been performed and documented. Determine if the action plans were entered into the EAS system.		

Use the following points as a guide to determine the following:

A.   Physical location in the plant?
B.   Operating status of the units or processes?
C.   Age and general condition?
D.   Pollution excursion incident and citation histories?
E.   Type and quantity of material processed?
F.   Proximity to environmentally sensitive/high exposure areas?
G.   Sensitive local or community factors?
H.   Presence and structure of environmental staff?
I.   Identification of hazardous processing locations?

3.   Using the information obtained in Step 2, determine the scope of this review.   Select a sample (which should include some of the high risk facilities) to review in greater detail.

4.   Review the recordkeeping activity and determine the adequacy of controls, including entry of all excursions and other identified issues into the Environmental Action System (EAS).   Recordkeeping procedures will vary by location, however, where applicable the following points can be used to determine the adequacy and reasonableness of controls:

A.   For the sample selected in Step 3, determine if the records are reasonably complete. Although all of the following will not always apply, they offer some types of data which might be included in environmental records. (This data may be included in the environmental assessment reports or applicable environmental reference manuals.)

1)   Applicable laws and regulations (ref. Step 4).
2)   Permits in effect and pending applications for new permits (ref. Steps 4,8,9 and 11 thru 13).
3)   Timeliness of application(s) for permit renewal(s).
4)   Names and telephone numbers of individuals to contact at the regulatory agencies.
5)   Facility layout and process descriptions (ref. step 3).
6)   Monitoring data and/or estimation methods on air emissions (ref. Step 13).
7)   Monitoring data on water effluents, and outfalls and overall water quality (ref. Steps 8 thru 12).
8)   Required data on solid and/or hazardous waste, waste descriptions, storage and treatment, disposal methods, disposal locations, manifests (ref. Steps 15 thru 21).
9)   Listing of disposal sites used in the past.
10) Emergency response, disaster control, contingency, and other local community awareness and incident control plans (ref. Steps 27 thru 29).
11) Company/division policies and procedures (ref. Step 1).
12) Applicable reports to government agencies; routine and nonroutine (ref. Step 4).   (Routine such as National Pollution Discharge Elimination System (NPDES) reports and nonroutine such as spill reports.)

Revised: 4-1-91

5. Determine the following information has been recorded and documented in accordance with the OPC Health, Environment and Safety Procedure No. 2.11, "Reporting Environmental Matters":

   A. A listing of matters such as significant incidents or reportable excursions?
   B. Legal actions taken or pending?
   C. A listing of all environmental issues by a control or folio number?
   D. An action plan for resolution of each environmental issue, with timetables and milestones?
   E. Compliance requirements applicable to items listed in (a) through (d)?
   F. Community Right-to-know program (required for all facilities)?

WATER QUALITY

6. Determine if any excursions occurred in the last 12 months. Determine if resolution of these incidents were properly documented and recorded. Determine analytical quality control and assurance tests have been properly documented? Select a sample period and perform a comparison of the agency reports to the laboratory results.

   A. From a review of the environmental records, is it evident that all incidents falling outside of permit requirements were properly reported and documented? In these cases was corrective action taken and adequately documented?

7. Review the permits required for waste or waste water ponds. (This information may be included in the environmental assessment reports or applicable environmental reference manuals.)

   A. If so, determine if they require groundwater checks and periodic reporting of these results.
   B. Are ground water checks documented?
   C. Have any exceptions to permit requirements (if applicable) been properly documented and reported?

8. Review the last assessment action plan, and determine if any temporary noncompliance water problems during storm periods have been addressed.

9. Review the permits that are required for monitoring wells.

   A. What reporting requirements are placed on the plant? (This information may be included in the environmental assessment reports or applicable environmental reference manuals.)
   B. Is there documentation to indicate that the well design and operation is within the permit and regulatory agency requirements?
   C. Select a sample period and perform a comparison of the agency reports to the laboratory results.
   D. Have reported monitoring results (last 12 months) been documented and transmitted to the Industry Group HQ?
   E. Have all exceptions to agency requirements been properly reported and entered into the EAS?

Revised: 4-1-91

10. Review the current permit for each injection well. (This information may be documented in the environmental assessment report or applicable environmental reference manuals.)

    A. Do the permits or regulations require periodic testing and reporting?

    B. If so, select a sample of test results and compare the lab results to the agency reports.

    C. By review of the records, can we determine that all exceptions to permit requirements were properly reported and documented?

AIR QUALITY

11. Of the air emission permits presently in force, select a sample period and perform a comparison of the reports to the agency to the emission test results.

    A. Have all exceptions to the permit requirements been reported as required?

    B. Have steps been taken and documented to avoid these issues in the future?

12. Highlight any exceptions noted in the last regulatory air inspection performed. Determine if corrective action has been taken and if these efforts have been adequately documented and entered into EAS.

13. For facilities operating within a geographic area not meeting federal air quality standards (these issues are not restricted to nonattainment areas), perform the following:

    A. Review applicable air pollution control agency emission standards. Obtain an understanding of the permitting process (i.e., preparation of the construction application by company personnel and the granting of an authority to construct by the agency and document procedures followed. Determine if the facility has had a change in operation (i.e., new process or significant change to an existing process) since the last environmental assessment was performed. If so, how does this change affect the permits? Are new permits or changes to the existing permits required? Have these permits been secured or applied for? Review the permits and their applicable requirements.

    B. Select a sample of emission sources and test for proper authorization to construct from the agency.

    C. Review company procedures followed and controls in place to ensure that emission standards are not exceeded.

    D. For any fines or citations issued within the last year, determine that these have been adequately resolved and action taken to ensure the violation does not reoccur. Determine that information was entered into EAS.

VINYL CHLORIDE MONOMER (VCM)

21. Determine if the plant has any VCM related activities?

     A.   Obtain a list of all equipment in place that is used
          to alert personnel as to the levels of emissions in
          the workplace. Has this information been documented?
     B.   Determine if there is any documentation that shows
          what levels of emissions (fugitive or emergency
          venting/release) are acceptable. (This VCM related
          information may be found in the environmental assess-
          ment reports or applicable environmental reference
          and operating procedure manuals).

22. Determine if there has been any emergency venting/release
    incidents in the last three months?

     A.   What is the status of the incidents?
     B.   Was a notice of violation or penalty received?
     C.   Was the cause of the problem identified and
          rectified?
     D.   Was this activity properly documented?

23. Select a sample period and determine if there were any
    fugitive emission incidents.

     A.   Is there adequate documentation for each emission?
     B.   Were these incidents and their related effects prop-
          erly documented and reported in accordance with
          applicable requirements?
     C.   If periodic agency reports are required, perform a
          comparison of the emission levels in the agency
          reports and the on-site recorder levels.
     D.   Is there consistency in the information reported and
          the data actually recorded?

POLYCHLORINATED BIPHENYLS (PCBs)

24. For any electrical equipment containing dielectric fluid,
    has a positive determination been made that the equipment
    does or does not contain PCBs? Is the equipment labeled
    properly?

25. Determine if the facility performs and documents an annual
    inventory of equipment containing PCBs. Determine the
    retention period for annual PCB inventory records. Do the
    annual reports contain information such as the following:

     A.   Date and source of PCB articles, chemicals, and mix-
          tures received?
     B.   Date and type of article, chemicals, and mixtures
          removed from service?
     C.   Accounting of amount received, amount removed, and
          amount remaining at facility?
     D.   For amounts removed is there a complete record of
          disposition?

Revised: 4-1-91

26. For periodic inspections made of any PCB equipment that is in service, determine the following:

    A. Are the inspections documented?
    B. If any leaks or spills were found, was the appropriate corrective action taken and documented?
    C. Is there documentation of any contaminated soil disposal?
    D. Is adequate spill containment provided for in service PCB equipment?

27. Determine if the storage area appears to meet the regulatory requirements listed below and if appropriate documentation is maintained. The following are examples of items which should be considered in reviewing the storage areas:

    A. Roof to prevent rain water from reaching PCB items.
    B. Storage area properly labeled.
    C. Spill containment to contain twice the internal volume of the largest PCB containing article.
    D. Containment area should not have any drains, valves, expansion joints, sewer lines or other openings. Does the storage facility meet these requirements?
    E. All articles marked with the date they are placed in storage.
    F. All articles in storage checked for leaks at least every 30 days and records of checks maintained.
    G. Impervious (concrete) flooring with curbs.

28. Determine if a Food or Feed Risk Analysis has been conducted of PCB equipment and if all PCB transformers have been removed from Food or Feed conditions.

ASBESTOS

29. Has the plant conducted a survey to determine the presence and condition of any asbestos? (This information may be included in the environmental assessment reports or applicable environmental reference manuals.)

    A. Is there documentation to evidence that all insulation has been checked for asbestos content?
    B. Are all areas containing asbestos properly marked?
    C. Have all of these areas been adequately contained?
    D. Have all of these efforts been properly documented?

30. Determine if there is a procedure for notifying agencies prior to removal and disposal of asbestos containing materials and if proper handling and monitoring procedures are followed.

SPILL CONTROL AND EMERGENCY PLANS

A Spill Prevention, Control, and Countermeasure (SPCC) Plan is a specific requirement of 40 Code of Federal Regulations (CFR), and pertains to the storage and use of oil, (including gasoline, diesel, crude oil, fuel oil, and vegetable oil). The requirement is in addition to any other requirement (regulatory or company) for a spill contingency plan.

Revised: 4-1-91

31. Determine if an SPCC Plan is required for the facility based upon the amount of oil stored on site.

    A. Has the SPCC Plan been approved by a registered professional engineer?

    B. Has the SPCC Plan been updated at least every three years?

    C. Has the inspections required by the SPCC Plan been documented?

32. Determine if there have been any reported spills in the last six months. Determine if corrective actions have been taken and properly documented.

33. Determine if the facility operates a ship or barge dock.

    A. Does the spill control plan include the dock facilities?

    B. Do the environmental reference manual or the dock operating procedures address environmental concerns at the dock?

    C. Has this information been distributed to all affected personnel?

    D. Is the facility in compliance with U.S. Coast Guard regulations? (For example hydrostatic testing and recordkeeping of product transfer hoses).

34. For the emergency response or other disaster control contingency plan, determine the following:

    A. Has the emergency contingency plan been updated in the last 12 months?

    B. Has this plan been adequately communicated to the agencies required under SARA Section 3?

    C. What plans are there to update this program in accordance with the new right-to-know laws where applicable?

GENERAL

35. Determine if the in-house pipeline operations program addresses inspection, surveillance maintenance, and postings of line markers in accordance with Department of Transportation (DOT) regulations. Physically review portions of the pipeline (and related rights-of-way controlled by the facility), and ensure adequate markings have been placed and that the area is well maintained.

36. Determine that environmental or safety related areas have been marked with signs and markings in compliance with regulations, and if there is a plot plan or blueprint that identifies these areas. (Markings may include: boundaries, permit number, owner, and product name information. This information may be maintained by the safety department since in many cases this area is safety related.)

Revised: 4-1-91

	WORKPAPER REFERENCE	COMPLETED BY/DATE

37. Determine if there is a central file where complaints from neighbors or other interested parties are maintained.

    A.   Have there been any recent complaints?

    B.   Did any of these complaints relate to a discharge or exception to a permit allowance, and were these incidents properly documented and reported to the appropriate agencies where required?

    C.   Is this information properly documented?

    D.   When corrective action was taken was the correction documented?

38. Determine if the facility sponsors training programs for all personnel involved in environmental activities to ensure the personnel are aware of the most current regulation and compliance requirements.

    A.   Do these programs include information regarding the most current right-to-know regulations?

    B.   Is this training activity properly documented? (This training may be included in the routine new employee orientation, or periodic operations safety meetings, and may also be included in the applicable environmental reference manuals.)

39. Determine that contractors perform in compliance with applicable environmental regulations and how the facility ascertains they are in compliance.

40. Determine if there is any threatened or pending legal action against the company. Determine if this information has been communicated to the appropriate industry group and corporate personnel and entered into the EAS.

41. Select a sample of AFEs and ensure all AFEs are reviewed by environmental personnel at the appropriate levels to determine if the project may have an environmental effect and that the effect is provided for.

SAFETY

ORGANIZATION AND FACILITY DESCRIPTION

1. Review all applicable safety policies and procedures and obtain a summary of local safety programs (i.e. training, hazard communication, etc.).

2. Determine if local safety procedures address the following areas: (This information may be included in applicable safety manuals and/or standard operating procedure.)

    A.   Internal reporting requirements delineating a clear reporting structure within the local safety organization. Do they clearly note what organizations are obligated to provide data and information to the safety group?

    B.   A mechanism for reporting accidents, injuries and significant matters to appropriate individuals and organizations in the Industry Group and Corporation, and to the applicable government agency.

Revised: 4-1-91

C. Recordkeeping requirements to assure adherence to
    OSHA/MSHA recording and reporting requirements.

    1) Do they clearly define responsibility for cate-
    gorization of injuries/illnesses to determine
    which are recordable? Is there a review proce-
    dure on categorization?

    2) Is there a review procedure to assure that
    appropriate worker compensation claims are
    recorded in the OSHA/MSHA logs?

    3) Is there clearly defined responsibility for
    safekeeping of the records?

    4) Is there a defined procedure and file document-
    ing required safety and hazard communication
    training?

    5) Are five years of OSHA logs maintained on file?

D. Review OSHA guidelines for mercury level testing for
    workers exposed to mercury in the work environment,
    if applicable.

3. Review the most recent safety assessment report issued
    including the action plan and any other areas of concern
    noted in the assessment report.

A. Determine if the facility or industry group has docu-
    mented their follow-up on these items.

B. What is the follow-up system?

C. Are there adequate controls over documentation of
    these efforts?

4. Review the facility's hazard communications activities.
    This information should include identification of hazardous
    materials purchased, produced or shipped; an inventory of
    hazardous material stored, used or produced on site; exis-
    tence of material safety data sheets on these materials,
    their inclusion in training programs for both employees and
    on-site contractors. Determine if proper records are being
    maintained.

A. Select a sample of Material Safety Data Sheets
    (MSDSs) and ensure a MSDS is available for all chemi-
    cals for which a MSDS is required.

    Note: The MSDSs are required under two different sets
    of regulations. OSHA requires the MSDSs for compli-
    ance with its Hazard Communication Standard, and the
    EPA requires the MSDSs as a part of its Community
    Right-to-Know regulations.

B. Review shipping documents to determine compliance
    with DOT hazardous materials shipping regulations.

    1) Are proper DOT product descriptions, quantity
    or weight identified?

    2) Are approved containers being utilized?

    3) Is the facility in compliance with cargo tank
    and railcar requirements?

    4) Has the nature of the cargo and its hazards
    been communicated to the driver?

C. Is there a program for minimizing inventories of haz-
    ardous materials?

	WORKPAPER REFERENCE	COMPLETED BY/DATE

5. Determine if the facility has documented the applicable OSHA or MSHA regulations and any local and/or company safety requirements. (This information may be found in the safety assessment reports or applicable safety reference manuals.) Does the facility have copies of, or access to, applicable federal, state, and local regulations?

6. Recordkeeping procedures will vary by location, however, the following points can be used to determine compliance with applicable government regulation. This includes such items as:

   A. Are the records kept in a central file or by a designated individual at each facility providing for good control and accessibility to these records. If a central control is not in place, at a minimum is a reference folder maintained which includes file and location references?
   B. Is access to the records adequately controlled, and are the records maintained in an orderly fashion?
   C. Is the record filing system consistent for all safety activities?
   D. From the records identified in step b, select a sample and determine if the records are reasonably complete and that the OSHA logs include all reportable items as defined in the U.S. Department of Labor - Bureau of Labor Statistics <u>Definitions of Recordable Injuries,</u> and for the MSHA logs, the Directorate of Technical Support--Denver Technical and Health Center--Division of Mining. Information Systems <u>Informational Report for Notifying MSHA of Accidents, Injuries, Illnesses and Employment</u>.
   E. In order to assure conservative interpretation of the above guidelines, review the first aid logs to determine if there have been any cases of multiple visits by the same individual in a short period of time for treatment of the same or similar injuries or illness that may have not been reported on every occasion. Determine if this review has been documented.
   F. Review recordkeeping concerning chemical exposure and determine compliance with OSHA requirements.
   G. Test for compliance with 29 CFR Part 1904.5 to determine that:

      1) The annual summary of occupational injuries and illnesses was certified by the preparer as being true and correct.
      2) The annual summary was posted by February 1.

7. Review OSHA/MSHA noise conservation requirements and determine adherence to applicable regulations.

GENERAL

8. Select a sample of on-site contractors and determine if there is documentation of contractor's compliance with the OPC and/or industry group contractor safety policy. Determine if the contractor's safety program was reviewed prior to contract execution.

9. Select a sample of AFEs and ensure all AFEs are reviewed by safety personnel at the appropriate levels to determine if the project may have a safety effect and that the effect is provided for.

Revised: 4-1-91

	WORKPAPER REFERENCE	COMPLETED BY/DATE

10. Review the documentation of actions taken in response to Risk Engineering Report recommendations.

11. Determine if the facility or industry group has formal safety policies and procedures, and if they are documented and made available to all employees. To check implementation of the policies and procedures, perform a facility inspection, and make spot observations on the following points:

A. Is jewelry (rings, necklaces, ear rings etc.) being worn where it is forbidden?
B. Are workers using required eye protection, safety shoes and/or hard hats?
C. Are workers wearing loose clothing around machinery?
D. Where indicated, is breathing apparatus available and stored in easy access, in working condition and properly inspected? Determine if employees who use respirators have received a physician's certification in compliance with 29 CFR 1910.134.
E. Are workers given respiratory training where breathing apparatus is required? Is the training documented? Are respirators in proper working condition?
F. Are workers who use respirators required to be free of interfering facial hair?
G. Are "NO SMOKING" and other required safety signs clearly posted in designated areas?
H. Are fire alarm boxes, fire hose cabinets, and extinguisher areas clearly marked? Are these areas unobstructed? Is there a plot plan indicating the location of all fire fighting equipment in the plant? Has this plan been posted and adequately distributed to all employees? Determine if hydrostatic testing is performed and documented on fire extinguishers in compliance with 29 CFR 1910.157.
I. Are fire extinguishers inspected regularly? Select a sample of extinguishers and determine inspections are being properly documented.
J. Are safe containers available for the movement of small quantities of flammables?
K. Are there safe disposal facilities for hazardous or flammable residues?
L. Are antistatic electricity devices fitted where necessary?
M. Determine if employees are receiving annual audiograms in compliance with 29 CFR 1910.95.

12. Document and test required annual medical examinations:

A. Audiometric required by 29 CFR 1900.95, noise conservation program.
B. Lung capacity test required by 29 CFR 1900.134, respiratory surveillance.
C. Physicians clearance for operators to use respirators required by 29 CFR 1900.120.

ENVIRONMENTAL STATUTORY AND COMMON LAW

IN THE COMMERCIAL SETTING

I. INTRODUCTION

Hazardous materials are a fact of life. Their presence may pro-
foundly affect the value of land and expose all parties involved in real
estate transactions to significant liabilities. The transfer of real
property which contains, or which may contain, hazardous substances, or
operations which utilize such substances, can pose difficult problems for
the buyer and the seller as well as for those in the financial community.
In order to make informed business decisions, it is imperative that all
parties are aware of the nature and the scope of the problem.

Environmental risks in a transaction can arise in two ways:
responsibility for cleaning up contaminated property and responsibility
for compliers with environmental protection laws. In this portion of the
seminar we will outline basic environmental responsibilities. These
will, in turn, highlight the need to identify, and where possible remedy,
preexisting contamination in an effort to minimize the liability regardless of whether it arises under common law tort theories, statutory
cleanup provisions, or general environmental compliance statutes.

II. SPECIFIC FEDERAL STATUTES

Prior to the 1970's, environmental law basically consisted of common law tort principles (see Section V, infra) and a few limited federal
or state statutes. However, in response to increasing public awareness
Congress quickly produced a series of major statutes which established a
federally enforceable regulatory scheme covering most environmental media
- the National Environmental Policy Act (1969), the Clean Air Act (1970),
the Clean Water Act (1972), the Resource Conservation and Recovery Act
(1976), and the Toxic Substance Control Act (1978). This meteoric growth
in environmental legislation is graphically illustrated by Figure 1 which
identifies some eighty or so enactments affecting the environment. See,
also, Table 1.

With prospective controls well established, Congress in the 1980's began to look back at past practices and closed the loop with the enactment of the Comprehensive Environmental Response, Compensation and Liability Act of 1980 which quickly became known as "Superfund" (the Act is also known, as many environmental statutes are, by its acronym, CERCLA). The Emergency Planning and Community Right-to-Know Act (1986) added a new emphasis on public disclosure.

In this memorandum, only those major environmental laws most frequently encountered in real estate transactions are summarized. Where a single Congressional enactment contains several independent programs, each program is separately addressed. Like any other legal issue, the applicability and interpretation of each statute will depend to some extent on the location and use of the property as well as a number of other factors. Always seek the advise of qualified environmental legal counsel before determining your response.

TABLE 1. Federal Laws on Environmental Protection

RHAA	-	Rivers & Harbors Appropriations Act (Refuse Act) (1899)
OPA	-	Oil Pollution Act (1990)
OCSLA	-	Outer Continental Shelf Lands Act (1953)
NHPA	-	National Historic Preservation Act (1966)
WSRA	-	Wild & Scenic Rivers Act (1968)
NEPA	-	National Environmental Policy Act (1969)
CAA	-	Clean Air Act (1990)
OSHA	-	Occupational Safety & Health Act (1970)
FWPCA	-	Federal Water Pollution Control Act (1972)
MPRSA	-	Marine Protection Research & Sanctuaries Act (1972)
CZMA	-	Coastal Zone Management Act (1972)
NCA	-	Noise Control Act (1972)
FIFRA	-	Federal Insecticide, Fungicide & Rodenticide Act (1972)
MMPA	-	Marine Mammal Protection Act (1972)
MLAA	-	Mineral Leasing Act Amendments (1973)
ESA	-	Endangered Species Act (1973)
SDWA	-	Safe Drinking Water Act (1974)
HMTA	-	Hazardous Materials Transportation Act (1975)
TSCA	-	Toxic Substances Control Act (1976)
RCRA	-	Resource Conservation and Recovery Act (1976)
CWA	-	Clean Water Act (1977)
SMCRA	-	Surface Mining Control and Reclamation Act (1977)
UMTRCA	-	Uranium Mill Tailings Radiation Control Act (1978)
CERCLA	-	Comprehensive Environmental Response, Compensation, & Liability Act (1980)
SARA	-	Superfund Amendments and Reauthorization Act (1986)
EPCRA	-	Emergency Planning and Community Right-to-Known Act (1986)
AHERA	-	Asbestos Hazard Emergency Response Act (1986)
SPA	-	Shore Protection Act (1988)

A. Principal Federal Statutes

1. Comprehensive Environmental Response,
    Compensation and Liability Act - "Superfund"

Perhaps the most significant federal statute imposing liability for clean-up of contaminated soils and groundwater is the Comprehensive Environmental Response, Compensation and Liability Act of 1980 ("CERCLA") as amended in 1986 by the Superfund Amendments and Reauthorization Act ("SARA"). 42 U.S.C. Section 9601 et seq. Under CERCLA, where the United States Environmental Protection Agency ("EPA") determines there may be an imminent and substantial endangerment to the public health or the environment because of an actual release (or even the threat of a release) of a hazardous substance from a facility, it can either undertake response actions on its own or direct any one or more potentially responsible parties ("PRPs") to undertake certain response actions. Response actions can run the gamut from mere monitoring of the situation to simple removal and proper (re)disposal of the source materials to complete remediation and cleanup of all contaminated soils and groundwater.

Under CERCLA, both current and past owners or operators of a facility are among those that may be liable for the cost of response actions. The liability is strict (i.e., fault is not required) and can be joint and several (i.e., any one party can be required to bear 100 percent of the cost, where the resulting contamination is not easily divisible). The affirmative defenses are limited to the following: 1) an act of God, 2) an act of war, or 3) the act (or omission) of a third party having no direct or indirect contractual relationship with the PRP. Arguably only the latter, often called the third party defense, can be utilized.

CERCLA provides that a deed or other instrument transferring property is a "contract." Thus, environmental contamination of property by any predecessor in title can make the "third party defense" unavailable. However, CERCLA does provide somewhat of a "safe harbor" for the current owner who can show that at the time he acquired the property he had no knowledge or reason to know that the property was in fact contaminated. In order to be entitled to use the "innocent landowner defense," an owner must show that, at the time of purchase, he had undertaken the "appropriate inquiry" and "appropriate investigation" with respect to possible contamination. We will address the "innocent landowner" defense in greater detail in a forthcoming session.

Even where these initial studies do not reveal a problem, subsequent discovery of site contamination imposes a duty to notify any potential purchaser of the discovery. Failure to provide such information will result in the loss of the right to the "safe harbor," even though the seller was not responsible for the contamination and no longer holds title to the property. 43 U.S.C. 9601(f)(35).

Under CERCLA, EPA is authorized to recover costs from "responsible persons." The courts have recognized that personal liability may extend to directors, shareholders, officers, and employees of a corporation where they control or are actively involved in the conduct of corporate affairs. A secured lender may, as long as the lender does not participate in the management of the facility, escape liability. However, by foreclosing a security interest in property which becomes a "Superfund" site, the lender may be deemed an owner or operator liable for cleanup costs. The fact that the lender was not factually responsible for the contamination is legally irrelevant.

From a compliance audit standpoint, the most important requirements of CERCLA are those in Sections 102 requiring industrial and transportation facilities to report immediately to EPA's National Response Center releases of hazardous substances listed, as directed by CERCLA Section 102, if a release to the environment exceeds the "reportable quantity" for the substance specified in EPA's regulations. Release is broadly defined to include spills and discharges to soil, air, and water but excludes permitted and certain routine discharges and those confined to occupational exposures. Contemporaneous reporting to state and local environmental and emergency response agencies is often required.

2.   Resource Conservation and Recovery Act-Subtitle C

The Resource and Conservation and Recovery Act ("RCRA"), as amended by the Hazardous and Solid Waste Amendments of 1984 ("HSWA"). 42 U.S.C.

Section 6901 et seq., was the first federal legislation aimed solely at regulation of "hazardous wastes." RCRA created a "cradle-to-grave" regulatory system for controlling and tracking hazardous wastes from the time they are generated through their storage, treatment and disposal. Whenever a proposed acquisition involves an industrial operation along with real estate, the facility's compliance with environmental regulations will be at issue. For facilities producing hazardous wastes which the prospective purchaser plans to operate, it is imperative that any environmental property evaluation include the operation's current compliance status with RCRA's permit and manifesting systems. Thus, it has become critical to determine if you are looking at a facility which is, or has been, in some way connected with the generation, handling, storage or disposal of a RCRA hazardous waste.

The importance of waste characterization can not be over emphasized. RCRA (and EPA's implementing regulations) separates waste materials into two categories: "solid wastes" and "hazardous wastes." A solid waste includes practically any "discarded" (i.e., abandoned) material regardless of its physical form. A waste does not have to be a solid to qualify as a solid waste; it may be a solid, a liquid, a semi-solid (i.e., sludge), or even a containerized gas. See, 42 U.S.C. Section 6903(27), 40 C.F.R. Section 261.2.

Only a material determined to be a RCRA solid waste may also be a RCRA "hazardous waste." Any person producing a RCRA solid waste is legally obligated to determine if that waste is a RCRA hazardous waste. See, 40 C.F.R. Sections 261.3, 261.20. With certain exceptions, solid waste is also hazardous waste if it is "listed" on one of several regulatory lists or if it exhibits any of four identifying characteristics. EPA has established three lists: wastes from certain specific sources, 40 C.F.R. Section 261.32; certain enumerated wastes from nonspecific sources, 40 C.F.R. Section 261.31; and certain discarded commercial chemical products together with their containers and spill cleanup residue, 40 C.F.R. Section 261.33. A solid waste becomes classified as a "characteristic" hazardous waste, even if it is not included on one of these lists, if laboratory analysis indicates any one of four hazardous characteristics: ignitability, corrosivity, reactivity or extraction process toxicity ("EP Toxicity"). See, 40 C.F.R. Sections 261.3, 261.20. Almost any facility that produces a listed or characteristic hazardous waste is brought under one or more of EPA's rules for generation, storage, treatment or disposal of hazardous wastes.

Only where less than 100 kilograms (220 pounds) of hazardous waste is produced per month is the waste "generator" substantially exempt from full RCRA regulation; production of amounts between 100 kilograms and 1000 kilograms (2200 pounds) per month results in classification as a "small quantity generator" with the imposition of on-site storage restrictions together with substantial reporting and recordkeeping requirements. Included in this is the preparation and use of Uniform Hazardous Waste Manifests to document custody transfer of the waste to transporter(s) and ultimately the disposal site operator.   Generators subject to full regulation are allowed to accumulate hazardous wastes on-site for no longer than 90 days without obtaining a permit for operation of a RCRA storage facility.   Treatment or disposal of hazardous waste also requires a permit. See, generally, 40 C.F.R. Section 264.

Under RCRA, companies engaged in treatment, storage and disposal of hazardous wastes are required to have operating permits which impose strict requirements for closure and post-closure care, including the maintenance of financial responsibility assurances. For most industrial facilities, historical "releases" of hazardous wastes or hazardous constituents from on-site waste management have resulted in some degree of soil and/or groundwater contamination. Permits for these facilities are also subject to "corrective action" requirements dictating cleanups analogous to CERCLA remediation projects. 42 U.S.C. Section 6924(u).

A RCRA permit can be transferred to a new purchaser but only after it has first been modified, or revoked and reissued to name the new owner and "incorporate such other requirements as may be necessary." 40 C.F.R. Section 270.40. Although permit transfer can sometimes be accomplished with only a "minor modification" to the permit, if material alterations are to be made to the facility after purchase, the permit and its limiting conditions may be modified by the agency. 40 C.F.R. Section 270.41-42. The impact of increasingly stringent standards on planned facility alterations must be factored into any proposed acquisition plans.

One of the more significant changes to the original RCRA hazardous waste program came through implementation of the "land ban" under HSWA which generally prohibits the disposal of specified untreated wastes in any landfill. The first type of waste to come under the land disposal ban was bulk or noncontainerized liquid hazardous waste. Rules addressing additional types of listed hazardous wastes have now been issued. The land ban program required EPA to set waste treatment standards that must be met by the waste generator prior to any landfilling. Only if, after testing and certification, the waste meets the applicable treatment standard can the material be land disposed. See 40 C.F.R. Section 268, et seq.

While primarily providing the framework for controlling the treatment and disposal of hazardous wastes, RCRA Section 7003 also authorizes actions against persons contributing to an "imminent and substantial endangerment" to human health or the environment caused by the handling, storage, treatment, transportation or disposal of any hazardous or solid waste, to compel the cleanup of the site.

If the transaction involves property which proves to be contaminated by hazardous wastes, the parties potentially liable for cleanup will include a new owner. Once EPA has determined that an "imminent and substantial endangerment" exists, it may seek an injunction that restrains activities contributing to the contamination and require remedial activities to be undertaken. 42 U.S.C. Section 6973. An "innocent" purchaser can be called upon to remediate problems created by former owners.

3.   RCRA Subtitle D - Solid Wastes

Pursuant to Subtitle D of RCRA, 42 U.S.C. Section 6941-6949(a), regulation of nonhazardous solid wastes is primarily to be the responsibility of the states. Subtitle D does, however, establish a federal prohibition against the disposal of either solid or hazardous wastes in "open dumps." 42 U.S.C. Section 6944(b), 6945(a) and (c)(2). Thus, if the purchased property includes an on-site dump operating without a permit or in violation of permit standards, the new owner may be subjected to federal enforcement action, even if no hazardous wastes have been discarded at the site. This possibility simply highlights the need for careful assessment of the historical and current use of the entire tract prior to acquisition.

4.   RCRA Subtitle I - Underground Storage Tanks

Transactions involving real estate with underground storage tanks are obvious situations in which a company may face unexpected environmental liability. If the new owner is found to have caused a leak or to now own or lease a UST system which has leaked, the company may face unexpected environmental liability.

The HSWA amendments to RCRA added Subtitle I, 42 U.S.C. Section 6991, et seq., which called for a comprehensive federal regulatory program for underground storage tanks ("USTs"). This legislation filled a gap which existed between CERCLA and RCRA Subtitle C. Neither CERCLA nor RCRA Subtitle C were amenable to clean up of releases from USTs. Due to the express exclusion of petroleum, EPA lacked the necessary authority under CERCLA to effect cleanup from leaking USTs containing petroleum products. See 42 U.S.C. Section 9601(14) (the "petroleum exclusion"). Since the primary thrust of RCRA is the regulation of waste disposal practices, EPA would have had to classify the use of leaking underground product storage tanks as a waste disposal practice to have utilized RCRA.

Under the amendments to RCRA, compliance can now be enforced through administrative orders or through the courts. Section 9003(h) empowers EPA to require the owner or operator of a leaking UST to cleanup

petroleum releases while Section 9006 authorized EPA to issue administrative orders or initiate civil actions in federal district court to
enforce compliance with Subtitle I regulations.

In addition to emphasis on corrective actions and cleanup of
releases, Subtitle I establishes the framework for an extensive set of
regulations addressing registration, design, construction, installation,
and operational controls as well as proof of financial responsibility.
See, 40 C.F.R. Subpart 280. RCRA required owners to register all tanks
either in use after 1984 or abandoned since 1974 if they remained in the
ground unused. 42 U.S.C. Section 6991(a), 50 Fed.Reg. 46602. Existing
UST systems (i.e., those installed before December 1988) are required to
be upgraded to provide for corrosion protection and leak detection over
the next ten years. This retrofitting is scheduled on the basis of the
tank's age; older tanks are to be addressed by December, 1989. Devices
to prevent spills and overfills must also be retrofitted to existing
systems.

Even existing UST systems on the property which are to be taken out
of service (either temporarily or permanently) are subject to regulation.
The permanent closure requirements include a requirement to conduct an
evaluation of the subsurface around the tank. The discovery of any contamination within the excavation may trigger certain response and remediation obligations.

Any developer expecting to install a new UST system should consider
that the system will be required to meet all new registration, design,
installation and operational requirements at the time of installation.

5.   The Clean Air Act

The Clean Air Act ("CAA"), 42 U.S.C. Section 7401 et seq., establishes an air quality management system centered on air quality goals
(National Ambient Air Quality Standards or "NAAQS") for ubiquitous air
pollutants and imposes a number of requirements for the attainment and
maintenance of the NAAQS. States then develop their own control programs
to attain and maintain the various NAAQS. These programs are combined
into State Implementation Plans ("SIPs") which are reviewed and formally

approved by EPA and are enforceable by that agency as well as the state. The SIP must demonstrate attainment of the NAAQS, describe state emission control strategies, contain legally enforceable regulations including procedures for new source review, and outline the state program for air quality monitoring.

Any new "major" source of air pollution (or any major modification to an existing source) is required to employ stringent emission controls to meet "new source performance standards" ("NSPS") set by EPA, but generally enforced by the states. These standards reflect the emission limitation and emission reduction achievable by applying the best demonstrated technology of continuous emission reduction. Thus, any anticipated expansion or modification of facilities on the property must consider not only the adequacy of current air pollution control systems but the impact of imposition of NSPS requirements as a result of modifying the existing facilities.

The proposed installation of any new major source of air pollution, or major modifications to an existing source, must also demonstrate that their emissions will not adversely impact ambient air quality. In "attainment areas," i.e., those meeting the NAAQS, the Act's prevention of significant deterioration ("PSD") program, may require on-site ambient air quality studies that can entail collection and analysis of monitoring data for up to a year prior to obtaining the permit necessary to begin construction. PSD permit applicants may also be required to conduct computerized modeling to predict their proposed emission impacts on air quality.

Areas in which the existing ambient air quality is not within NAAQS, i.e., "nonattainment areas," are required to apply even more stringent new and modified new source review regulations. Any proposed major source must agree to emission controls that will meet the "lowest achievable emission rate," it may then be required to obtain sufficient "offsets" before a permit to construct can be issued; the total allowable emissions from other existing sources together with those anticipated from the new source must be less than the total emissions from currently

Revised: 1-1-91   ATTACHMENT A existing sources. A developer of property must consider whether he will be able to obtain the necessary offsets to allow the contemplated development in view of the ambient air quality in the area. In nonattainment areas, the ability to transfer air permits may prove to be an important economic aspect of real estate transactions.

In addition to standards for common air pollutants, i.e., particulate matter, sulfur dioxide, nitrogen oxides, carbon monoxide, and ozone, the act requires EPA to establish National Emission Standards for Hazardous Air Pollutants ("NESHAPs"). In 1971, EPA designated asbestos as such a hazardous air pollutant. 36 Fed.Reg. 5931; 40 C.F.R. Section 61.01(a). Property owners and developers must pay particular attention to the asbestos NESHAP since it regulates the renovation or demolition of any building or facility containing asbestos as well as the disposal of waste asbestos. 40 C.F.R. Section 61.140 et seq.

6.   The Clean Water Act

The Clean Water Act ("CWA"), 33 U.S.C. Section 1251, et seq., (a/k/a the Federal Water Pollution Control Act, "FWPCA") imposes a number of requirements that can affect owners of real property. Under the National Pollutant Discharge Elimination System ("NPDES") a permit is required for the discharge of any "pollutant" from a "point source" (e.g., any pipe, ditch, conduit, etc.) into any of the various types of "waters of the United States." NPDES permits specify both the nature and the quantity of discharge that is allowable and can be technology-based requiring the use of the "best available technology" ("BAT") or be based on the water quality of the receiving stream. With the imposition of water-quality based standards, the uses of property may be limited if located along a water quality limited (i.e, a polluted) stream or a stream with a highly protective designated use. See, 40 C.F.R. Sections 122-124 (NPDES implementing regulations).

Section 404 of the CWA is overseen by the United States Army Corps of Engineers and requires a property owner to obtain a permit prior to any construction activity in "waters of the United States" as well as any "wetland," (a quite broadly defined term). As part of the process of obtaining a permit for activity in a wetland, a person may be required to obtain other wetlands which will be preserved in "mitigation" of those which are to be developed.

CWA Section 311, 33 U.S.C. Section 1321, prohibits the discharge of oil in "harmful quantities" (i.e., any amount which causes a film or sheen on water). 40 C.F.R. Section 110.3. Spill response and cleanup duties belong to the product custodian without regard to the fault. The "person in charge" of the facility also has an affirmative duty to immediately report any discharge of "harmful quantities" of oil to the National Response Center ("NRC") or the EPA regional office. 40 C.F.R. Section 110.10. Section 311(j) requires land based facilities to comply with EPA implementing regulations which now include the preparation of Spill Prevention, Control and Countermeasure ("SPCC") Plans for all locations with above-ground oil storage capacity greater than 1,320 gallons (42,000 gallons for underground storage). 40 C.F.R. Section 112.1(d)(2).

Purchasers should determine the adequacy of the facility's SPCC Plan and its associated spill history. See C.F.R. Section 112.7 (guidelines for preparation and implementation of SPCC plans).

7.   The Toxic Substances Control Act

The Toxic Substances Act ("TSCA"), 15 U.S.C. Section 2601 et seq., requires the testing, premanufacturing notice and recordkeeping for chemical substances or mixtures that will be produced in substantial qualities if they could be anticipated to enter the environment in substantial quantities or if there may be substantial human exposure.

TSCA Section 6(e) is devoted to the control of and ultimate elimination of polychlorinated biphenyls ("PCBs"). EPA's implementing regulations impose strict requirements on the use, storage and disposal of PCBs. Although PCBs are no longer manufactured, they are still found in the insulating fluids of many existing pieces of electrical equipment such as transformers and capacitors. Most PCB-containing transformers and certain large capacitors located in restricted-access areas may be used for the remainder of their useful lives, subject to routine inspection and recordkeeping under EPA rules. However, their use in locations creating a risk to food or feed has been prohibited since 1985. Thus, the existence of PCB-containing equipment may restrict the use of property.

PCBs can also be a serious concern where its use in equipment has resulted in contamination of building or grounds from leaking fluids. Additional care must be exercised when this equipment is serviced, retired, sold, disposed of or even when dismantled for salvage.

8. The Emergency Planning and Community Right-To-Know Act - SARA Title III

When Congress reauthorized the Superfund statute in 1986, it included what has become known as Title III or the "Right-to Know" provisions. Included in Title III of SARA is the Emergency Planning and Community Right-To-Know Act ("EPCRA") enacted as free-standing law within SARA. 42 U.S.C. Section 11001, et seq. The Act represents Congress' response to public concern raised by the disaster in Bhopol, India where in late 1984, thousands were killed as a result of the release of a toxic gas from a chemical facility. Title III mandated the establishment of state and local emergency response organizations charged with developing emergency release response plans and imposes a series of notification and reporting requirements on a wide range of facilities regarding the presence and release of specific chemicals.

Title III imposes rigorous notification requirements for releases (spilling, leaking, escaping, discharging, etc.) of over 600 EPCRA "hazardous substances" in amounts greater than or equal to certain specified reportable quantities ("RQs"). See, 40 C.F.R. 302.1 et seq. Although the requirements are closely related to CERCLA's reporting requirements, they are not identical.

The "Community Right-to-Know" provisions of Title III are intended to increase public access to information in order to facilitate the development of local emergency response planning. Any facility which has more than the designated "threshold planning quantity" of any listed "extremely hazardous substance" on-site is required to periodically report that information to the appropriate emergency response commission. Any release that may result in off-site exposures requires immediate notification of state and federal authorities.

    B.   Secondary Federal Statutes

        1.   Safe Drinking Water Act

The Safe Drinking Water Act ("SDWA"), 42 U.S.C. Section 300(f), et seq., in addition to specifying a scheme for primary and secondary standards for acceptable levels of contaminants in public water supplies, provides for the protection of underground drinking water supplies through a federal-state program regulating the disposal of hazardous wastes via underground injection wells. Both new and existing wells are required to obtain permits to operate.

It is important to note, however, that public water systems include "non-community" systems such as hotels, motels, factories and other businesses that produce their own drinking water. 40 C.F.R. Section 141.2. A third class of public water systems, the "non-transient non-community" system serving at least twenty-five of the same persons over six months per year, may be faced with the imposition of federal primary drinking water regulations. See, 52 Fed.Reg. 25695 (1987). The national primary drinking water standards specify maximum contaminant levels ("MCLs") and treatment techniques as well as stringent monitoring requirements. Any purchaser seeking to acquire commercial property which includes its own system for supplying drinking water should be familiar with the pertinent regulatory requirements imposed on these systems.

The 1986 SDWA amendments prohibited the use of lead pipe, solder or flux when installing or repairing any public water system and required that under certain conditions notice be given the persons that might be affected by lead contamination of their drinking water. 42 U.S.C. Section 300g-6. Other amendments in late 1988 provide for the recall of water fountains (coolers) with certain leaded pipes or solder. Pub. L. No. 100-572 (1988). While this may not be a "deal breaker," it does deserve the attention of any prospective purchaser.

2.   National Environmental Policy Act

The National Environmental Policy Act ("NEPA"), 42 U.S.C. Section 4321, et seq., as one of the first major pieces of federal environmental legislation forms the basic national charter for protection of the environment. NEPA requires federal agencies to: prepare a detailed statement on the environmental impact ("EIS") for every proposed "major federal action significantly affecting the quality of the human environment;" and, describe appropriate alternatives to any recommended course of action concerning alternative uses of available resources.

The statute indicates that actions which are subject to federal control and responsibility, i.e., federal permits, licenses, loans, grants, leases and so forth, may require preparation of an EIS even though actual federal involvement in the activity is minimal. Thus, in certain cases, permits required by any of the number of previously discussed statutes can fall within the definition of a major federal action under NEPA. NRDC v. USEPA, 859 F.2d 156, 167 (DC Cir. 1988) (Issuance of a new source discharge permit constituted a major federal action for NFPA purposes): Where this is the case, the proposal will result in the agency preparing an EIS addressing not only the proposed action but any alternatives which might mitigate the adverse impacts as well. Most agencies require the permit applicant to prepare an environmental assessment which the agency will use to determine whether the agency issues a finding of no significant impact or proceeds to prepare an EIS.

3.   National Historic Preservation Act

The National Historical Preservation Act ("NHPA"), 16 U.S.C. Section 470 et seq., requires that federal agencies consider the impact of their decisions on historical and cultural resources. 40 C.F.R. Section 6.301. If the activity may cause irreparable loss or destruction of significant scientific, prehistoric, historic or archaeological data, the owner may be required to undertake data recovery or preservation activities. See, 48 Fed.Reg. 44716 (September 29, 1983) (National Park Service Technical standards and guidelines regarding archaeological preservation). Where an undertaking may affect a property with historical, architectural, or cultural values and is on, or eligible for listing on, the National Register of Historic Places, a determination of eligibility from the Department of the Interior must be requested under the procedures in 36 C.F.R. Part 63. 40 C.F.R. Section 6.301(b). A company may be required to undertake an investigation of property to satisfy these requirements where it seeks a federal permit, etc.

    4.   Rivers and Harbors Act

The Rivers and Harbors Appropriations Act of 1899 ("RHAA"), 33 U.S.C. Section 401, et seq., requires that any structure which may impede or impact a navigable waterway must be authorized by permit. Because of the definition of "navigable waterway", almost any development of property along any surface water must be evaluated in order to determine whether a permit will be necessary under RHAA.

    5.   Occupational Safety And Health Act

The Occupational Safety and Health Act ("OSHA"), 29 U.S.C. Section 651, et seq., regulates the exposure of persons to contaminants in the workplace. The Occupational Safety and Health Administration, a division of the United States Department of Labor, has a number of areas in which it exercises what may appear to be overlapping statutory duties with EPA. For instance, both agencies are concerned with a number of issues surrounding the use and handling of hazardous materials such as asbestos and pesticides.

With its adoption of hazard communication regulations, sometimes known as the "workers right-to-know" rules, every employer must assess the toxicity of chemicals it uses and provide appropriate training as well as material safety data sheets ("MSDS") to inform their workers of potential chemical risks. 29 C.F.R. Section 1200.

The adequacy of the facility's compliance program should be identified prior to closing so that the purchaser can evaluate the impact of these rules on continued operation or planned expansion (or redirection) of activities at the facility.

    6.   Federal Insecticide, Fungicide, and Rodenticide Act

The Federal Insecticide, Fungicide, and Rodenticide Act ("FIFRA"), 7 U.S.C. Section 136 et seq., first enacted in 1947 is a federal program for pesticides. The statute also imposes civil and criminal penalties for the sale or distribution of unregistered pesticides, for mislabeling of pesticides, and for the use of these products inconsistent with their labeling.

III. PRINCIPAL STATE LAWS

    A.   Oklahoma Statutes

    Although Oklahoma does not have a state counterpart to the federal CERCLA program, it does operate a number of the programs which parallel or in some cases administer many of the other federal programs. Therefore, State rules must not be overlooked when assessing the potential impact of environmental constraints on property transfers.

    1.   Oklahoma Controlled Industrial Waste Disposal Act

    The Oklahoma Controlled Industrial Waste Disposal Act ("CIWDA"), 63 O.S. Section 1-2001, et seq., is the state's counterpart to RCRA regulating hazardous wastes under the name of "controlled industrial waste." The State has been granted federal authority to operate its program in lieu of the federal hazardous waste program. 49 Fed.Reg. 50362 (December 27, 1984). Thus, Oklahoma, through the Oklahoma State Department of Health ("OSDH"), is responsible for carrying out most aspects of the RCRA program. OSDH has primary enforcement responsibility, although EPA Region VI retains some responsibility to conduct its own inspections and institute enforcement actions.

WHERE TO FIND SELECTED FEDERAL ENVIRONMENTAL REGULATIONS

ARMY CORPS OF ENGINEERS

Dam Permits	33 CFR Part 321
Definition of Navigable Waters of the United States	33 CFR Part 329
Enforcement, Supervision and Inspection	33 CFR Part 326
General Policies	33 CFR Part 320
Nationwide Permits	33 CFR Part 330
Permit Processing	33 CFR Part 325
Permits for Discharges of Dredged or Fill Material	33 CFR Part 323
Permits for Ocean Dumping of Dredged Material	33 CFR Part 324
Permits for Work Affecting Navigable Waters	33 CFR Part 322
Public Hearings	33 CFR Part 327

CLEAN AIR ACT

Air Quality Planning Areas	40 CFR Part 81
Ambient Air Monitoring Reference and Equivalent Methods	40 CFR Part 53
Ambient Air Quality Surveillance	40 CFR Part 58
Citizen Suit Notification	40 CFR Part 54
Clean Air Act Exemptions	40 CFR Part 69
Delayed Compliance Orders	40 CFR Part 65
Motor Vehicle and Aircraft Controls	40 CFR Parts 85-87
National Ambient Air Quality Standards (NAAQS)	40 CFR Part 50
National Emission Standards for Hazardous Air Pollutants	40 CFR Part 61
Noncompliance Penalties	40 CFR Parts 66-67
Performance Standards for New Stationary Sources	40 CFR Part 60
Regional Consistency	40 CFR Part 56
State Implementation Plan Requirements (SIP; PSD)	40 CFR Parts 51-52
Stratospheric Ozone Protection	40 CFR Part 82

CLEAN WATER ACT

Citizen Suit Notification	40 CFR Part 135
Discharge of Oil and SPCC Plans	40 CFR Parts 109-112
Effluent Limitation Guidelines and Performance Standards; Pretreatment Standards	40 CFR Parts 405-471
List of Conventional and Toxic Pollutants; pH Limits	40 CFR Part 401
NPDES Criteria and Standards	40 CFR Part 125
NPDES Permit Program	40 CFR Part 122
Permit Decisionmaking Procedures	40 CFR Part 124
Pretreatment Regulations	40 CFR Part 403
Procedures for Improving State Water Quality Standards	40 CFR Part 131
Secondary Treatment Regulations	40 CFR Part 133
State Certification of Activities Requiring a Federal License or Permit	40 CFR Part 121
State SPDES Permit Program Requirements	40 CFR Part 123
Test Procedure Guidelines for Pollutant Analysis	40 CFR Part 136
Water Quality Planning and Management	40 CFR Part 130

EMERGENCY PLANNING AND COMMUNITY RIGHT-TO-KNOW ACT

Emergency Planning Notification Procedures-Spill Reporting	40 CFR Parts 302 & 355
Hazardous Chemical Reporting (MSDS)	40 CFR Part 370
Toxic Chemical Release Reporting (Form R)	40 CFR Part 372
Trade Secrecy Claims and Disclosure to Health Professionals	40 CFR Part 350

ENVIROMENTAL IMPACT STATEMENTS, COASTAL ZONE MANAGEMENT ACT, AND ENDANGERED SPECIES ACT

Coastal Zone Management Act NOAA Regulations	15 CFR Parts 921-933
Environmental Impact Statements Council on Environmental Quality Regulations	40 CFR Parts 1500-1508
Joint Agency Endangered Species Regulations	50 CFR Parts 17:401-453

FREEDOM OF INFORMATION ACT

EPA Procedures	40 CFR Part 2

Revised: 1-1-91

ATTACHMENT B

OCEAN DUMPING

Ocean Dumping   40 CFR Parts 220-229

OCCUPATIONAL SAFETY AND HEALTH ADMINISTRATION

General   29 CFR Parts 1900-1928

Hazard Communication   29 CFR Part 1910.1200

Occupational Health and Safety Standards   29 CFR Part 1910

PESTICIDES

Agricultural Commodity Tolerances   40 CFR Part 180
  and Exemptions

Agricultural Worker Protection Standards   40 CFR Part 170

Animal Feed Tolerances   40 CFR Part 186

Certification of Pesticide Applicators   40 CFR Part 171

Certification of Usefulness   40 CFR Part 163

Emergency Use Exemptions   40 CFR Part 166

Enforcement   40 CFR Part 162

Experimental Use Permits   40 CFR Part 172

Food Tolerances   40 CFR Part 185

Good Laboratory Practice Standards   40 CFR Part 160

Hearings   40 CFR Part 164

Labeling Requirements   40 CFR Part 156

Packaging Requirements   40 CFR Part 157

Pesticide Acceptance; Disposal and   40 CFR Part 165
  Storage Procedures

Pesticide Registration and   40 CFR Part 152
  Classification Procedures

Policies and Interpretations   40 CFR Part 153

Procedures Governing the Rescission of   40 CFR Part 173
  State Primary Enforcement Responsibility
  for Pesticide Use Violations

Production and Distribution Books   40 CFR Part 169
  and Records

Registration Data Requirements   40 CFR Part 158

Registration of Pesticide-Producing   40 CFR Part 167
  Establishments; Reports and Labeling

Registration Standards	40 CFR Part 155
Special Review Procedures	40 CFR Part 154

RCRA HAZARDOUS WASTE MANAGEMENT REGULATIONS

Final Permit Standards for Treatment, Storage, and Disposal Facilities	40 CFR Part 264
General-Definitions and Delisting Procedures	40 CFR Part 260
Generator Standards	40 CFR Part 262
Identification and Listing of Hazardous Waste-Definition of Solid/Hazardous Waste; Recycling; Small Quantity Generators	40 CFR Part 261
Interim Status Standards for Treatment, Storage, and Disposal Facilities	40 CFR Part 265
Land Disposal Restrictions	40 CFR Part 268
Permit Issuance Procedures	40 CFR Part 270
Recyclable Material Standards; Used Oil/Waste Combustion; Batteries	40 CFR Part 266
State Programs	40 CFR Parts 271-272
Transporter Standards	40 CFR Part 263
Underground Storage Tanks	40 CFR Part 280

SAFE DRINKING WATER ACT

Drinking Water Standards (MCL and MCLG)	40 CFR Parts 141-143
National Secondary Drinking Water Regulations	40 CFR Part 143
Underground Injection Control Programs	40 CFR Parts 144-148

SUPERFUND

Citizen Rewards for Information on Superfund Criminal Violations	40 CFR Part 303
National Contingency Plan	40 CFR Part 300
National Priorities List	40 CFR Part 300, Appendix B
Natural Resource Damage Assessments (Department of Interior)	43 CFR Part 11
Reimbursement to Local Governments for Emergency Response to Hazardous Substance Releases	40 CFR Part 310
Spill Reporting-Reportable Quantities	40 CFR Parts 302 & 355

Revised: 1-1-91

ATTACHMENT B

TOXIC SUBTANCES CONTROL ACT

Allegations that Chemical Substances Cause Significant Adverse Reactions to Health or the Environment (TSCA & 8(c))	40 CFR Part 717
Asbestos	40 CFR Part 763
Chemical Imports and Exports	40 CFR Part 707
Chemical Information-Preliminary Assessment Information Report-Production, Use, Exposure (TSCA &8(a))	40 CFR Part 712
Data Reimbursement	40 CFR Part 791
Dibenzo-Para-Dioxins/Dibenzofurans	40 CFR Part 766
Fully Halogenated Chlorofluoroalkanes	40 CFR Part 762
General	40 CFR Parts 700-702
Good Laboratory Standards	40 CFR Part 792
Health and Safety Data Reporting (TSCA & 8(d))	40 CFR Part 716
Identification of Specific Substance and Mixture Testing Requirements	40 CFR Part 799
Inventory Reporting (TSCA & 8(b))	40 CFR Part 710
Metal Working Fluids	40 CFR Part 747
PCB Use	40 CFR Part 761
Premanufacture Notification Exemptions	40 CFR Part 723
Premanufacture Notification (TSCA &5)	40 CFR Part 720
Reporting and Recordkeeping	40 CFR Part 704
Section 6 Rulemaking Procedures	40 CFR Part 750
Significant New uses of Chemical Substances	40 CFR Part 721
Testing Consent Agreements and Test Rules	40 CFR Part 790
Testing Guidelines; Health, Chemical Fate, Environmental Effects	40 CFR Parts 795-798

WETLAND REGULATIONS

EPA

Section 401(b) Guidelines	40 CFR Part 230
Section 404 Program Definitions; Exempt Activities	40 CFR Part 232
Section 404(c) Veto Procedures	40 CFR Part 231
State 404 Programs	40 CFR Part 233

Appendix J:
Code of Ethics & Standards of Conduct

Code of Ethics & Standards of Conduct

Code of Ethics

PURPOSE: A distinguishing mark of a profession is acceptance by its members of responsibility to the interests of those it serves. Members of the Board of Environmental Auditor Certifications (BEAC) must maintain high standards of conduct to effectively discharge this responsibility.

APPLICABILITY: This Code of Ethics is applicable to all Members and Provisional Members. Membership in the BEAC is a voluntary action. Applicants may not misrepresent any credential in support of application. By acceptance, Members and Provisional Members assume an obligation of self-discipline above and beyond the requirements of laws and regulations.

The Standards of Conduct set forth in this Code of Ethics provide basic principles in the practice of environmental auditing. Members and Provisional Members should realize that their individual judgment is required in the application of these principles.

Members or Provisional Members who are judged by the Board of Directors of the BEAC to be in violation of the Standards of Conduct of the Code of Ethics shall be subject to forfeiture of their membership.

Standards of Conduct

MEMBERS AND PROVISIONAL MEMBERS shall exercise honesty, objectivity, and diligence in the performance of their duties and responsibilities. Members and Provisional Members shall exhibit loyalty in all matters pertaining to the affairs of their organizations or to whomever they may be rendering a service. However, Members and Provisional Members shall not intentionally and knowingly be a party to any illegal or improper activity related to environmental, health and safety laws or otherwise indicating a lack of personal integrity.

MEMBERS AND PROVISIONAL MEMBERS shall not engage in acts or activities which are discreditable to the profession of environmental auditing or to their organizations including, but not limited to acts or missions of a dishonest, deceitful or fraudulent nature.

MEMBERS AND PROVISIONAL MEMBERS shall refrain from entering into any activity that may be in conflict with the interest of their organizations or which would prejudice their ability to carry out objectively their duties and responsibilities.

MEMBERS AND PROVISIONAL MEMBERS shall not accept anything of value from anyone that would impair or be presumed to impair their professional judgment.

MEMBERS AND PROVISIONAL MEMBERS shall undertake only those services they can reasonably expect to complete with professional competence.

MEMBERS AND PROVISIONAL MEMBERS shall adopt suitable means to comply with professional audit standards as outlined in BEAC's *Standards for the Professional Practice of Environmental, Health and Safety Auditing.*

MEMBERS AND PROVISIONAL MEMBERS shall be prudent in the use of information acquired in the course of their duties. They shall not use confidential information for any personal gain nor in any manner that would be contrary to law.

MEMBERS AND PROVISIONAL MEMBERS, when reporting on the results of their work, shall reveal all material facts known to them which, if not revealed, could either distort reports of operations under review or conceal unlawful practices.

MEMBERS AND PROVISIONAL MEMBERS shall continually strive for improvement in their proficiency and skills and in the effectiveness and quality of their service.

MEMBERS AND PROVISIONAL MEMBERS shall cooperate fully with an inquiry in the event of any alleged breach of these Code of Ethics and Standards of Conduct.

MEMBERS AND PROVISIONAL MEMBERS shall not represent their acts or statements in such a way as to lead others to believe that they officially represent the BEAC, unless they are duly authorized to do so by the BEAC Board of Directors.

MEMBERS AND PROVISIONAL MEMBERS, in the practice of their profession, shall be ever mindful of the obligation to maintain the high standards of competence, morality, and dignity promulgated by the BEAC.

Appendix K: Standard Guide for Disclosure of Environmental Liabilities

Designation: E 2173 – 01

Standard Guide for
Disclosure of Environmental Liabilities[1]

This standard is issued under the fixed designation E 2173; the number immediately following the designation indicates the year of original adoption or, in the case of revision, the year of last revision. A number in parentheses indicates the year of last reapproval. A superscript epsilon (ε) indicates an editorial change since the last revision or reapproval.

1. Scope

1.1 *Purpose*—The purpose of this guide is to provide a series of options or instructions consistent with good commercial and customary practice in the United States for environmental liability disclosures accompanying audited and unaudited financial statements. This guide is intended to supplement and be consistent with Generally Accepted Accounting Principles (GAAP).[2]

1.2 *Objectives*—The objectives of this guide are to determine the conditions warranting disclosure and the content of appropriate disclosure.

2. Referenced Documents

2.1 *ASTM Standards:*
D 5746 Classification of Environmental Condition of Property Area Types for Defense Base Closure and Realignment Facilities[3]
E 1527 Practice for Environmental Site Assessments: Phase I Environmental Site Assessment Process[3]
E 1739 Guide for Risk Based Corrective Action Applied at Petroleum Release Sites[3]
E 2137 Guide for Estimating Monetary Costs and Liabilities for Environmental Matters[3]

2.2 *EPA Directives:[4]*
United States Environmental Protection Agency, OSWER Directive 9610.17: Use of Risk-Based Decision-Making in UST Corrective Action Programs

3. Terminology

3.1 *Definitions of Terms Specific to This Standard:*

3.1.1 *CERCLA*—Comprehensive Environmental Response, Compensation and Liability Act of 1980 (as amended, 42 USC Section 9601 *et seq.*).

3.1.2 *CERCLIS*—Comprehensive Environmental Response, Compensation and Liability Information System, the list of sites compiled by the EPA that the EPA has investigated or is currently investigating for potential hazardous substance contamination for possible inclusion on the National Priorities List.

3.1.3 *CFR*—Code of Federal Regulations.

3.1.4 *claim*—a demand for payment.

3.1.5 *environmental liabilities*—accrued liabilities and loss contingencies associated with conditions that present an unacceptable risk of harm to public health or the environment and that would be the subject of an enforcement action or other legal action.

3.1.6 *EPA*—United States Environmental Protection Agency.

3.1.7 *Federal Register, (FR)*—publication of the United States government published daily (except for federal holidays and weekends) containing all proposed and final regulations and some other activities of the federal government. When regulations become final, they are included in the Code of Federal Regulations (CFR), as well as published in the Federal Register.

3.1.8 *financial statements*—include, but are not limited to, statements associated with shareholder reporting, loans, mergers, acquisitions, or divestitures.

3.1.9 *materiality*—the significance of an item to users of a financial statement that considers all relevant and surrounding circumstances. A material item is one that its omission or misstatement is of such a magnitude in the surrounding circumstances that either the judgment of a reasonable person relying on the financial statement would have been changed or influenced by its inclusion or correction, or there is a substantial likelihood that the item, after assessing the inferences, and their significance, drawn from the given set of facts associated with the financial statement, would be viewed as significantly altering the information made available to the investor or shareholder. Relevant sources of information and references are included in Appendix X2.

3.1.10 *National Priorities List (NPL)*—a list compiled by the EPA pursuant to CERCLA 42 USC § 9605(a)(8)(B) of properties with the highest priority for cleanup pursuant to the EPA's Hazard Ranking System. See 40 CFR Part 300.

3.1.11 *Potentially Responsible Party (PRP)*—any individual, legal entity, or government—including owners, operators, transporters, or generators—potentially responsible for, or contributing to, conditions that present an unacceptable risk of

---

[1] This guide is under the jurisdiction of ASTM Committee E50 on Environmental Assessment and is the direct responsibility of Subcommittee E50.03 on Environmental Risk Management/Sustainable Development/Pollution Prevention.
Current edition approved Dec. 10, 2001. Published February 2002.
[2] This guide alone does not satisfy or include all disclosure requirements under GAAP, SEC, or any other agency or regulatory body. Appendix X1 provides some examples of where such requirements are contained.
[3] *Annual Book of ASTM Standards*, Vol 11.04.
[4] Available from the United States Environmental Protection Agency (U.S. EPA), Ariel Rios Building, 1200 Pennsylvania Ave., N.W., Washington, DC 20460.

E 2173

harm to human health or the environment and that would be the subject of an enforcement action or other legal action.

3.1.12 *RCRA*—Resource Conservation and Recovery Act (as amended, 42 USC § 6901 *et seq.*).

3.1.13 *reasonably possible*—the likelihood, or probability, associated with a given event occurring that lies in the range between remote and probable. The probability values assigned to remote and probable will depend on the industry, the aggregate number of sites, observations, and possible outcomes, and the uncertainty associated with estimating probabilities.

3.1.14 *release*—any spilling, leaking, pumping, pouring, emitting, emptying, discharging, injecting, escaping, leaching, dumping, or disposing into the environment.

3.1.15 *remedial or corrective action*—all environmental response activities to an environmental liability.

3.1.16 *reporting entity*—any business or public agency preparing a financial statement.

3.1.17 *site*—real property affected by an environmental liability.

4. Significance and Use

4.1 *Uses*—This guide is intended for use on a voluntary basis by a reporting entity that provides disclosure in their financial statements regarding environmental liabilities. The degree and type of disclosure depends on the scope and objective of the financial statements.

4.2 *Principles*:

4.2.1 The following principles are an integral part of this guide and are intended to be referred to in resolving any ambiguity or dispute regarding the interpretation of disclosures regarding environmental liabilities.

4.2.1.1 *Uncertainty Not Eliminated*—Although a reporting entity, as of the time when its financial statements are prepared, may hold a certain position with regard to the existence and extent of its environmental liabilities, there remains uncertainty with regard to the final resolution of factual, technological, regulatory, legislative, and judicial matters, which could affect its environmental liabilities.

4.2.1.2 *Disclosure Dependent on Circumstances*—Not every environmental liability warrants the same level of detail in its disclosure. Disclosure will be guided by the scope and objective of the financial statement, and accordingly, by the materiality of the environmental liability and the level of information available.

4.2.1.3 *Comparison with Subsequent Disclosures*—Subsequent disclosures that convey different information regarding the extent or magnitude of the reporting entity's exposures should not be construed as indicating the initial disclosures were inappropriate. Disclosures shall be evaluated on the reasonableness of judgments and inquiries made at the time and under the circumstances in which they were made. Subsequent disclosures should not be considered valid standards to judge the appropriateness of any prior disclosure based on hindsight, new information, use of developing analytical techniques, or other factors. However, information on trends may be of value to a user of financial statements.

4.2.1.4 *Not Exhaustive*—Appropriate disclosure does not necessarily mean an exhaustive disclosure of the reporting

entity's environmental liabilities. There is a point at which the cost of obtaining information or the time required to gather it outweighs the usefulness of the information and, in fact, may be a material detriment to the orderly preparation of financial statements and the ability of readers to understand the information contained therein. However, all relevant and reasonably ascertainable information should be used to determine the content of appropriate disclosure for environmental liabilities.

4.2.1.5 *Assessment of Risk*—As the reporting entity becomes aware of an environmental liability or an environmental compliance issue, the condition or issue should be evaluated to assess the actual or potential risk to human health and environment. This process may be dependent on the regulatory environment, an understanding of the specifics of the condition or issue, and potential future uses. For example, guidance on petroleum release sites is provided in Guide E 1739 and additional guidance is provided in EPA OSWER Directive 9610.17. The degree of risk suggests the appropriate response actions and should be a factor in the level of effort devoted to developing the cost and liability estimates associated with the environmental condition or the compliance issue.

5. Determining Whether a Disclosure is Warranted

5.1 *Circumstances Associated with Environmental Liabilities*:

5.1.1 Following are the major circumstances that might give rise to environmental liabilities:

5.1.1.1 Enforcement of environmental laws or regulations regarding investigation, clean-up, maintenance, and other costs. Such circumstance arises if the EPA, a state agency, or a local government has named the reporting entity a PRP on a site, or a reporting entity is required to perform corrective action under RCRA, or is required to remediate a contaminated property under any other environmental law.

5.1.1.2 Contractual assumptions of risk or risk transfer agreements. The most familiar forms of risk transfer agreements are insurance contracts, hold harmless agreements, indemnity agreements, and similar terms within contracts for the transfer of property.

5.1.1.3 Commencement of litigation or assertion of a claim or assessment by a party alleging legal liability on the part of the reporting entity.

5.1.1.4 Information is known by the reporting entity that indicates an environmental liability has been incurred.

5.2 *Sources of Information*—This guide identifies standard sources that should be reviewed by a reporting entity to properly determine if conditions warrant disclosure. Such sources may include but are not limited to:

5.2.1 Published List of PRP's,

5.2.2 Federal National Priorities List (NPL) site list,

5.2.3 CERCLIS list,

5.2.4 Published list of sites and identified responsible parties under state environmental laws,

5.2.5 Environmental suits involving the reporting entity,

5.2.6 Lists of leaking underground storage tanks (LUSTs),

5.2.7 Title searches of at least fifty years on known sites that were currently or previously owned or operated by the reporting entity,

2

Standard Guide for Disclosure

 E 2173

5.2.8 Known payments by the reporting entity for environmental claims and costs,

5.2.9 Environmental claims or demands involving the reporting entity, other than filed suits, and

5.2.10 Reporting entity's environmental records, for example, the results of site assessment or investigation reports, environmental audits, monitoring results.

6. Content of the Disclosure Accompanying Financial Statements

6.1 *Application*:

6.1.1 The content of the disclosures addressed by this guide are provided by management and are not meant to replace the disclosure requirements as prescribed or regulated through GAAP, SEC, or any other agency or regulatory body. This guide would apply to management's discussion and analysis accompanying financial statements as an example.

6.2 *Disclosures to be Made for Material Environmental Liabilities*:

6.2.1 Disclosure should be made when an entity believes its environmental liability for an individual circumstance or its environmental liability in the aggregate is material. These amounts include, but are not limited to, damages attributed to the entity's products or processes, cleanup of hazardous waste or substances, reclamation costs, fines, and litigation costs.

6.2.2 The following disclosures should be made by reporting entities for the material circumstance(s) in 6.2.1:

6.2.2.1 Statement regarding the judgment or assumptions used by the reporting entity regarding the likelihood of liability from any or all individual sites, actions, suits, cases, claims, requests for payment, notices or demands, and the potential materiality of that liability.

6.2.2.2 Statement regarding the number of sites for which the reporting entity has been named as a PRP and the number of claims, suits, actions, demands, requests for payment, notices, or cases that have been presented to the reporting entity for environmental liabilities.

6.2.2.3 The reporting entity's estimate of its environmental liabilities, a description of the approach used to estimate the

amounts, and the amounts accrued by the reporting entity for environmental liabilities.

(*1*) Environmental liabilities should be stated prior to reduction for amounts anticipated to be recovered from any third parties (for example, recoveries from insurance companies).

(*2*) The reporting entity should disclose the cost estimation methodology employed for accrued liabilities and a characterization of any material loss contingencies. Refer to Guide E 2137.

(*3*) In a situation where a reporting entity believes it has a material environmental liability but cannot quantify all or part of that liability, a written statement shall be included that describes the conditions or problems associated with estimating the liability.

6.2.2.4 The reporting entity's estimate of anticipated recoveries and a description of their approach to estimate the amount of anticipated recoveries from other parties by means of risk transfer agreement(s) that are associated with the estimated liabilities. The description should disclose any significant issues regarding the collectibility of recoveries.

6.2.2.5 A discussion of key external and internal environmental factors regarding the timing or amount of the liabilities, or recoveries. These factors include, but are not limited to, the following:

(*1*) Uncertainties with respect to joint and several liability that may affect the magnitude of the contingency, including disclosure of the aggregate expected cost to remediate particular sites that are individually material if the likelihood of contribution by other significant parties has not been established.

(*2*) The nature and terms of cost-sharing arrangements with other PRP's.

(*3*) The anticipated time frame over which the accrued or presently unrecognized amounts for environmental liability may be paid out.

7. Keywords

7.1 disclosure; environmental liability; financial statement; reporting entity

3

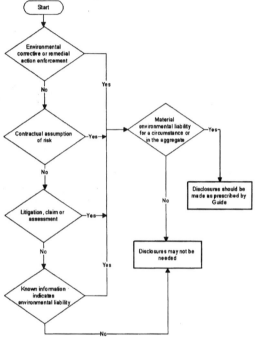

FIG. 1 Disclosure of Environmental Liabilities

APPENDIXES

(Nonmandatory Information)

X1. RELATED DOCUMENTS

Financial Accounting Standards Bulletin (FASB) Interpretation No. 14, "Reasonable Estimation of the Amount of a Loss and Interpretation of FASB-5."

FASB Statements/ FAS 5: Accounting For Contingencies, Issued March 1975.

Security and Exchange Commission (SEC) Staff Accounting Bulletin No. 92.

SEC Regulations S-K.

American Institute of Certified Public Accountants (AICPA) Statement of Position 96-1, Environmental Remediation Liabilities (Including Auditing Guidance), October 10, 1996.

SEC Staff Accounting Bulletin No. 99—Materiality, dated August 12, 1999.

ASTM D 5746 - 98 Classification of Environmental Condition of Property Area Types for Defense Base Closure and Realignment Facilities.[3]

X2. MATERIALITY REFERENCES

X2.1 The most recent authoritative literature on materiality is "SEC Staff Accounting Bulletin No. 99—Materiality," dated August 12, 1999. (See Appendix X1.) The "bulletin expresses the views of the staff that exclusive reliance on certain quantitative benchmarks to assess materiality in preparing financial statements and performing audits of those financial statements is inappropriate." Several other references are provided below regarding the definition of materiality.

X2.2 SEC Concept Release on Management's Discussion and Analysis of Financial Condition and Operations, April 24, 1987.

X2.3 TSC Industries Inc. versus Northway, Inc. 426 U.S. 438, 448 (1976). (Note: Concluded that an "omitted fact is material if there is a substantial likelihood that a reasonable shareholder would consider it important in deciding how to vote." To fulfill materiality requirement "there must be a substantial likelihood that the disclosure of the omitted fact would have been viewed by the reasonable investor as having significantly altered the 'total mix' of information available."

Materiality should not be so expansive as to result in shareholders being "bur[ied] in an avalanche of trivial information.")

X2.4 In re Caterpillar Inc., SEC Docket 147, March 31, 1992. (Indicates that material information is information "necessary [for the investor] to understand the registrant's financial statements.")

X2.5 SEC Regulation S-K, Item 103, Legal Proceedings 17 CFR 229.103. (Instruction 5 to Item 103 requires disclosure of environmental proceedings when such proceedings: *(1)* are material to the business or financial condition of the registrant; *(2)* involve primarily a claim for damages that exceeds ten percent of the current assets of the registrant and its subsidiaries on a consolidated basis; or *(3)* involve a governmental authority as a party and such proceedings result in monetary sanctions, unless the registrant reasonably believes that the proceeding will result in no monetary sanctions or in monetary sanctions, exclusive of interest and costs, of less than $100,000.)

Glossary

AFE:	Authorizations for Expenditure
AR:	Appropriation Request
ARCO:	Atlantic Richfield Company
ASTM:	American Society of Testing and Materials
Ato:	Elf Atochem North America, Inc.
BSI:	British Standards Institute
CAA:	Clean Air Act
CEQ:	Council on Environmental Quality
CERCLA:	Comprehensive Environmental Response, Compensation, and Liability Act
CERES:	Coalition for Environmentally Responsible Economies Project
CSI:	Common Sense Initiative
DOJ:	U.S. Department of Justice
ECOB:	Environment, Health, and Safety Committee of the Board of Directors, Occidental Petroleum Corporation
EHS:	environment, health, and safety
EIR:	Environmental Impact Report
EIS:	Environmental Impact Statement
ELI:	Environmental Law Institute
ELP:	Environmental Leadership Program

EMAS: European Union Eco-Audit Regulation

EMS: Environmental Management System

EPA: U.S. Environmental Protection Agency

EPCRA: Emergency Planning and Community Right-To-Know Act

ERPG: Emergency Response Planning Guideline

FCA: False Claims Act

FWPCA: Federal Water Pollution Control Act (also known as the Clean Water Act)

FY: fiscal year

GEF: Global Environment Facility

GEMI: Global Environmental Management Initiative

GM: General Motors Corporation

HES: health, environment, and safety

HESPRM: health, environment, safety, and process risk management

HESRE: health, environment, safety, and risk engineering

IG/DRD: Industry Groups/Direct Reporting Divisions

IRRC: Investor Responsibility Research Center

ISO: International Standards Organization

LCA: life-cycle analysis

MIS: management information system

MSDS: material safety data sheet

NEPA: National Environmental Policy Act

NPDES: national pollutant discharge elimination system

OPC: Occidental Petroleum Corporation

OSHA: Occupational Safety and Health Administration

OSH Act: Occupational Safety and Health Act

PC:	personal computer
PM$_{10}$:	particulate matter (with a diameter of 10 microns or less)
RCRA:	Resource Conservation and Recovery Act
RMP:	Risk Management Program
SAGE:	Strategic Advisory Group on the Environment
SEC:	Securities and Exchange Commission
TQ:	threshold quantity
TQM:	Total Quality Management
TRI:	Toxics Release Inventory
TSCA:	Toxic Substances Control Act
WRAP:	Waste Reduction Always Pays
XLEPA:	EXcellence and Leadership Program